Lecture Notes in Artificial Intelligence 10565

Subseries of Lecture Notes in Computer Science

More information about this series at http://www.springer.com/series/1244

Maosong Sun · Xiaojie Wang
Baobao Chang · Deyi Xiong (Eds.)

Chinese Computational Linguistics and Natural Language Processing Based on Naturally Annotated Big Data

16th China National Conference, CCL 2017
and 5th International Symposium, NLP-NABD 2017
Nanjing, China, October 13–15, 2017
Proceedings

Editors
Maosong Sun
Tsinghua University
Beijing
China

Baobao Chang
Peking University
Beijing
China

Xiaojie Wang
Beijing University of Posts
and Telecommunications
Beijing
China

Deyi Xiong
Soochow University
Suzhou
China

ISSN 0302-9743 ISSN 1611-3349 (electronic)
Lecture Notes in Artificial Intelligence
ISBN 978-3-319-69004-9 ISBN 978-3-319-69005-6 (eBook)
https://doi.org/10.1007/978-3-319-69005-6

Library of Congress Control Number: 2017956073

LNCS Sublibrary: SL7 – Artificial Intelligence

Printed on acid-free paper

This Springer imprint is published by Springer Nature
The registered company is Springer International Publishing AG
The registered company address is: Gewerbestrasse 11, 6330 Cham, Switzerland

Preface

Welcome to the proceedings of the 16th China National Conference on Computational Linguistics (16th CCL) and the 5th International Symposium on Natural Language Processing Based on Naturally Annotated Big Data (5th NLP-NABD). The conference and symposium were hosted by Nanjing Normal University located in Nanjing City, Jiangsu Province, China.

CCL is an annual conference (bi-annual before 2013) that started in 1991. It is the flagship conference of the Chinese Information Processing Society of China (CIPS), which is the largest NLP scholar and expert community in China. CCL is a premier nation-wide forum for disseminating new scholarly and technological work in computational linguistics, with a major emphasis on computer processing of the languages in China such as Mandarin, Tibetan, Mongolian, and Uyghur.

Affiliated with the 16th CCL, the 5th International Symposium on Natural Language Processing Based on Naturally Annotated Big Data (NLP-NABD) covered all the NLP topics, with particular focus on methodologies and techniques relating to naturally annotated big data. In contrast to manually annotated data such as treebanks that are constructed for specific NLP tasks, naturally annotated data come into existence through users' normal activities, such as writing, conversation, and interactions on the Web. Although the original purposes of these data typically were unrelated to NLP, they can nonetheless be purposefully exploited by computational linguists to acquire linguistic knowledge. For example, punctuation marks in Chinese text can help word boundaries identification, social tags in social media can provide signals for keyword extraction, and categories listed in Wikipedia can benefit text classification. The natural annotation can be explicit, as in the aforementioned examples, or implicit, as in Hearst patterns (e.g., "Beijing and other cities" implies "Beijing is a city"). This symposium focuses on numerous research challenges ranging from very-large-scale unsupervised/semi-supervised machine leaning (deep learning, for instance) of naturally annotated big data to integration of the learned resources and models with existing handcrafted "core" resources and "core" language computing models. NLP-NABD 2017 was supported by the National Key Basic Research Program of China (i.e., "973" Program) "Theory and Methods for Cyber-Physical-Human Space Oriented Web Chinese Information Processing" under grant no. 2014CB340500 and the Major Project of the National Social Science Foundation of China under grant no. 13&ZD190.

The Program Committee selected 108 papers (69 Chinese papers and 39 English papers) out of 272 submissions from China, Hong Kong (region), Singapore, and the USA for publication. The acceptance rate is 39.7%. The 39 English papers cover the following topics:

- Fundamental Theory and Methods of Computational Linguistics (6)
- Machine Translation (2)
- Knowledge Graph and Information Extraction (9)
- Language Resource and Evaluation (3)

- Information Retrieval and Question Answering (6)
- Text Classification and Summarization (4)
- Social Computing and Sentiment Analysis (1)
- NLP Applications (4)
- Minority Language Information Processing (4)

The final program for the 16th CCL and the 5th NLP-NABD was the result of a great deal of work by many dedicated colleagues. We want to thank, first of all, the authors who submitted their papers, and thus contributed to the creation of the high-quality program that allowed us to look forward to an exciting joint conference. We are deeply indebted to all the Program Committee members for providing high-quality and insightful reviews under a tight schedule. We are extremely grateful to the sponsors of the conference. Finally, we extend a special word of thanks to all the colleagues of the Organizing Committee and secretariat for their hard work in organizing the conference, and to Springer for their assistance in publishing the proceedings in due time.

We thank the Program and Organizing Committees for helping to make the conference successful, and we hope all the participants enjoyed a memorable visit to Nanjing, a historical and beautiful city in East China.

August 2017

Maosong Sun
Ting Liu
Guodong Zhou
Xiaojie Wang
Baobao Chang
Benjamin K. Tsou
Ming Li

Organization

General Chairs

Nanning Zheng	Xi'an Jiaotong University, China
Guangnan Ni	Institute of Computing Technology, Chinese Academy of Sciences, China

Program Committee

16th CCL Program Committee Chairs

Maosong Sun	Tsinghua University, China
Ting Liu	Harbin Institute of Technology, China
Guodong Zhou	Soochow University, China

16th CCL Program Committee Co-chairs

Xiaojie Wang	Beijing University of Posts and Telecommunications, China
Baobao Chang	Peking University, China

16th CCL and 5th NLP-NABD Program Committee Area Chairs

Linguistics and Cognitive Science

Shiyong Kang	Ludong University, China
Meichun Liu	City University of Hong Kong, SAR China

Fundamental Theory and Methods of Computational Linguistics

Houfeng Wang	Peking University, China
Mo Yu	IBM T.J. Watson, Research Center, USA

Information Retrieval and Question Answering

Min Zhang	Tsinghua University, China
Yongfeng Zhang	UMass Amherst, USA

Text Classification and Summarization

Tingting He	Central China Normal University, China
Changqin Quan	Kobe University, Japan

Knowledge Graph and Information Extraction

Kang Liu	Institute of Automation, Chinese Academy of Sciences, China
William Wang	UC Santa Barbara, USA

Machine Translation

Tong Xiao	Northeast University, China
Adria De Gispert	University of Cambridge, UK

Minority Language Information Processing

Aishan Wumaier	Xinjiang University, China
Haiyinhua	Inner Mongolia University, China

Language Resource and Evaluation

Sujian Li	Peking University, China
Qin Lu	The Hong Kong Polytechnic University, SAR China

Social Computing and Sentiment Analysis

Suge Wang	Shanxi University, China
Xiaodan Zhu	National Research Council of Canada

NLP Applications

Ruifeng Xu	Harbin Institute of Technology Shenzhen Graduate School, China
Yue Zhang	Singapore University of Technology and Design, Singapore

16th CCL Technical Committee Members

Rangjia Cai	Qinghai Normal University, China
Dongfeng Cai	Shenyang Aerospace University, China
Baobao Chang	Peking University, China
Xiaohe Chen	Nanjing Normal University, China
Xueqi Cheng	Institute of Computing Technology, CAS, China
Key-Sun Choi	KAIST, Korea
Li Deng	Microsoft Research, USA
Alexander Gelbukh	National Polytechnic Institute, Mexico
Josef van Genabith	Dublin City University, Ireland
Randy Goebel	University of Alberta, Canada
Tingting He	Central China Normal University, China
Isahara Hitoshi	Toyohashi University of Technology, Japan
Heyan Huang	Beijing Polytechnic University, China
Xuanjing Huang	Fudan University, China
Donghong Ji	Wuhan University, China
Turgen Ibrahim	Xinjiang University, China

Shiyong Kang	Ludong University, China
Sadao Kurohashi	Kyoto University, Japan
Kiong Lee	ISO TC37, Korea
Hang Li	Huawei, Hong Kong, SAR China
Ru Li	Shanxi University, China
Dekang Lin	NATURALI Inc., China
Qun Liu	Dublin City University, Ireland; Institute of Computing Technology, CAS, China
Shaoming Liu	Fuji Xerox, Japan
Ting Liu	Harbin Institute of Technology, China
Qin Lu	Polytechnic University of Hong Kong, SAR China
Wolfgang Menzel	University of Hamburg, Germany
Jian-Yun Nie	University of Montreal, Canada
Yanqiu Shao	Beijing Language and Culture University, China
Xiaodong Shi	Xiamen University, China
Rou Song	Beijing Language and Culture University, China
Jian Su	Institute for Infocomm Research, Singapore
Benjamin Ka Yin Tsou	City University of Hong Kong, SAR China
Haifeng Wang	Baidu, China
Fei Xia	University of Washington, USA
Feiyu Xu	DFKI, Germany
Nianwen Xue	Brandeis University, USA
Erhong Yang	Beijing Language and Culture University, China
Tianfang Yao	Shanghai Jiaotong University, China
Shiwen Yu	Peking University, China
Quan Zhang	Institute of Acoustics, CAS, China
Jun Zhao	Institute of Automation, CAS, China
Guodong Zhou	Soochow University, China
Ming Zhou	Microsoft Research Asia, China
Jingbo Zhu	Northeast University, China
Ping Xue	Research & Technology, the Boeing Company, USA

5th NLP-NABD Program Committee Chairs

Maosong Sun	Tsinghua University, China
Benjamin K. Tsou	City University of Hong Kong, SAR China
Ming Li	University of Waterloo, Canada

5th NLP-NABD Technical Committee Members

Key-Sun Choi	KAIST, Korea
Li Deng	Microsoft Research, USA
Alexander Gelbukh	National Polytechnic Institute, Mexico
Josef van Genabith	Dublin City University, Ireland
Randy Goebel	University of Alberta, Canada

Isahara Hitoshi	Toyohashi University of Technology, Japan
Xuanjing Huang	Fudan University, China
Donghong Ji	Wuhan University, China
Sadao Kurohashi	Kyoto University, Japan
Kiong Lee	ISO TC37, Korea
Hang Li	Huawei, Hong Kong, SAR China
Hongfei Lin	Dalian Polytechnic University, China
Qun Liu	Dublin City University, Ireland; Institute of Computing, CAS, China
Shaoming Liu	Fuji Xerox, Japan
Ting Liu	Harbin Institute of Technology, China
Yang Liu	Tsinghua University, China
Qin Lu	Polytechnic University of Hong Kong, SAR China
Wolfgang Menzel	University of Hamburg, Germany
Hwee Tou Ng	National University of Singapore, Singapore
Jian-Yun Nie	University of Montreal, Canada
Jian Su	Institute for Infocomm Research, Singapore
Zhifang Sui	Peking University, China
Le Sun	Institute of Software, CAS, China
Benjamin Ka Yin Tsou	City University of Hong Kong, SAR China
Fei Xia	University of Washington, USA
Feiyu Xu	DFKI, Germany
Nianwen Xue	Brandeis University, USA
Jun Zhao	Institute of Automation, CAS, China
Guodong Zhou	Soochow University, China
Ming Zhou	Microsoft Research Asia, China
Ping Xue	Research & Technology, the Boeing Company, USA

Local Organization Committee Chair

Weiguang Qu	Nanjing Normal University, China

Evaluation Chairs

Ting Liu	Harbin Institute of Technology, China
Shijin Wang	IFLYTEK CO., LTD., China

Publications Chairs

Erhong Yang	Beijing Language and Culture University, China
Deyi Xiong	Soochow University, China

Publicity Chairs

Min Peng	Wuhan University, China
Zhiyuan Liu	Tsinghua University, China

Tutorials Chairs

Yang Liu	Tsinghua University, China
Xu Sun	Peking University, China

Sponsorship Chairs

Wanxiang Che	Harbin Institute of Technology, China
Qi Zhang	Fudan University, China

System Demonstration Chairs

Xianpei Han	Institute of Software, Chinese Academy of Sciences, China
Xipeng Qiu	Fudan University, China

16th CCL and 5th NLP-NABD Organizers

Chinese Information Processing Society of China

Tsinghua University

Nanjing Normal University

Publishers

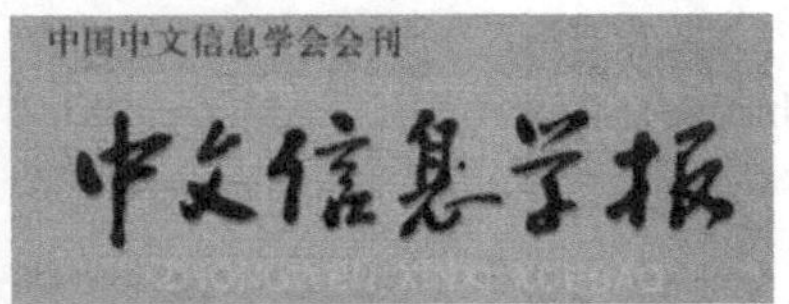

Journal of Chinese Information Processing

Science China

Lecture Notes in Artificial Intelligence
Springer

Journal of Tsinghua University
(Science and Technology)

Sponsoring Institutions

Platinum

Gold

Silver

Bronze

Evaluation Sponsoring Institutions

Contents

Text Classification and Summarization

Social Computing and Sentiment Analysis

NLP Applications

Fundamental Theory and Methods of Computational Linguistics

Arabic Collocation Extraction Based on Hybrid Methods

Alaa Mamdouh Akef, Yingying Wang, and Erhong Yang(✉)

School of Information Science, Beijing Language and Culture University, Beijing 100083, China
alaa_eldin_che@hotmail.com, yerhong@blcu.edu.cn

Abstract. Collocation Extraction plays an important role in machine translation, information retrieval, secondary language learning, etc., and has obtained significant achievements in other languages, e.g. English and Chinese. There are some studies for Arabic collocation extraction using POS annotation to extract Arabic collocation. We used a hybrid method that included POS patterns and syntactic dependency relations as linguistics information and statistical methods for extracting the collocation from Arabic corpus. The experiment results showed that using this hybrid method for extracting Arabic words can guarantee a higher precision rate, which heightens even more after dependency relations are added as linguistic rules for filtering, having achieved 85.11%. This method also achieved a higher precision rate rather than only resorting to syntactic dependency analysis as a collocation extraction method.

Keywords: Arabic collocation extraction · Dependency relation · Hybrid method

1 Introduction

Studies in collocation have been advancing steadily since Firth first proposed the concept, having obtained significant achievements. Lexical collocation is widely used in lexicography, language teaching, machine translation, information extraction, disambiguation, etc. However, definitions, theoretical frameworks and research methods employed by different researchers vary widely. Based on the definitions of collocation provided by earlier studies, we summarized some of its properties, and taking this as our scope, attempted to come up with a mixed strategy combining statistical methods and linguistic rules in order to extract word collocations in accordance with the above mentioned properties.

Lexical collocation is the phenomenon of using words in accompaniment, Firth proposed the concept based on the theory of "contextual-ism". Neo-Firthians advanced with more specific definitions for this concept. Halliday (1976, p. 75) defined collocation as "linear co-occurrence together with some measure of significant proximity", while Sinclair (1991, p. 170) came up with a more straightforward definition, stating that "collocation is the occurrence of two or more words within a short space of each other in a text". Theories from these Firthian schools emphasized the recurrence (co-occurrence) of collocation, but later other researchers also turned to its other

M. Sun et al. (Eds.): CCL 2017 and NLP-NABD 2017, LNAI 10565, pp. 3–12, 2017.
https://doi.org/10.1007/978-3-319-69005-6_1

properties. Benson (1990) also proposed a definition in the BBI Combinatory Dictionary of English, stating that "A collocation is an arbitrary and recurrent word combination", while Smadja (1993) considered collocations as "recurrent combinations of words that co-occur more often than expected by chance and that correspond to arbitrary word usages". Apart from stressing co-occurrence (recurrence), both of these definitions place importance on the "arbitrariness" of collocation. According to Beson (1990), collocation belongs to unexpected bound combination. In opposition to free combinations, collocations have at least one word for which combination with other words is subject to considerable restrictions, e.g. in Arabic, خلف (breast) in الناقة خلف (the breast of the she-camel) can only appear in collocation with خلف (she-camel), while الناقة (breast) cannot form a correct Arabic collocation with المرأة (cow) and البقرة (woman), etc.

In BBI, based on a structuralist framework, Benson (1989) divided English collocation into grammatical collocation and lexical collocation, further dividing these two into smaller categories, this emphasized that collocations are structured, with rules at the morphological, lexical, syntactic and/or semantic levels.

We took the three properties of word collocation mentioned above (recurrence, arbitrariness and structure) and used it as a foundation for the qualitative description and quantitative calculation of collocations, and designed a method for the automatic extraction of Arabic lexical collocations.

2 Related Work

Researchers have employed various collocation extraction methods based on different definitions and objectives. In earlier stages, lexical collocation research was mainly carried out in a purely linguistic field, with researchers making use of exhaustive exemplification and subjective judgment to manually collect lexical collocations, for which the English collocations in the Oxford English Dictionary (OED) are a very typical example. Smadja (1993) points out that the OED's accuracy rate doesn't surpass 4%. With the advent of computer technology, researchers started carrying out quantitative statistical analysis based on large scale data (corpora). Choueka et al. (1983) carried out one of the first such studies, extracting more than a thousand English common collocations from texts containing around 11,000,000 tokens from the New York Times. However, they only took into account collocations' property of recurrence, without putting much thought into its arbitrariness and structure. They also extracted only contiguous word combinations, without much regard for situations in which two words are separated, such as "make-decision".

Church et al. (1991) defined collocation as a set of interrelated word pairs, using the information theory concept of "mutual information" to evaluate the association strength of word collocation, experimenting with an AP Corpus of about 44,000,000 tokens. From then on, statistical methods started to be commonly employed for the extraction of lexical collocations. Pecina (2005) summarized 57 formulas for the calculation of the association strength of word collocation, but this kind of methodology can only act on the surface linguistic features of texts, as it only takes into account the recurrence and arbitrariness of collocations, so that "many of the word combinations that are extracted by these methodologies cannot be considered as the true collocations" (Saif 2011). E.g.

"doctor-nurse" and "doctor-hospital" aren't collocations. Linguistic methods are also commonly used for collocation extraction, being based on linguistic information such as morphological, syntactic or semantic information to generate the collocations (Attia 2006). This kind of method takes into account that collocations are structured, using linguistic rules to create structural restrictions for collocations, but aren't suitable for languages with high flexibility, such as Arabic.

Apart from the above, there are also hybrid methods, i.e. the combination of statistical information and linguistic knowledge, with the objective of avoiding the disadvantages of the two methods, which are not only used for extracting lexical collocations, but also for the creation of multi-word terminology (MWT) or expressions (MWE). For example, Frantzi et al. (2000) present a hybrid method, which uses part-of-speech tagging as linguistic rules for extracting candidates for multi-word terminology, and calculates the C-value to ensure that the extracted candidate is a real MWT. There are plenty of studies which employ hybrid methods to extract lexical collocations or MWT from Arabic corpora (Attia 2006; Bounhas and Slimani 2009).

3 Experimental Design for Arabic Collocation Extraction

We used a hybrid method combining statistical information with linguistic rules for the extraction of collocations from an Arabic corpus based on the three properties of collocation. In the previous research studies, there were a variety of definitions of collocation, each of which can't fully cover or be recognized by every collocation extraction method. It's hard to define collocation, while the concept of collocation is very broad and thus vague. So we just gave a definition of Arabic word collocation to fit the hybrid method that we used in this paper.

3.1 Definition of Collocation

As mentioned above, there are three properties of collocation, i.e. recurrence, arbitrariness and structure. On the basis of those properties, we define word collocation as combination of two words (bigram[1]) which must fulfill the three following conditions:

a. One word is frequently used within a short space of the other word (node word) in one context.

This condition ensures that bigram satisfies the recurrence property of word collocation, which is recognized on collocation research, and is also an essential prerequisite for being collocation. Only if the two words co-occur frequently and repeatedly, they may compose a collocation. On the contrary, the combination of words that occur by accident is absolutely impossible to be a collocation (when the corpus is large enough). As for how to estimate what frequency is enough to say "frequently", it should be higher than expected frequency calculated by statistical methods.

[1] It is worth mentioning that the present study is focused on word pairs, i.e. only lexical collocations containing two words are included. Situations in which the two words are separated are taken into account, but not situations with multiple words.

b. One word must get the usage restrictions of the other word.

This condition ensures that bigram satisfies the arbitrariness property of word collocation, which is hard to describe accurately but is easy to distinguish by native speakers. Some statistical methods can, to some extent, measure the degree of constraint, which is calculated only by using frequency, not the pragmatic meaning of the words and the combination.

c. A structural relationship must exist between the two words.

This condition ensures that bigram satisfies the structure property of word collocation. The structural relationships mentioned here consist of three types on three levels: particular part-of-speech combinations on the lexical level; dependency relationships on the syntactic level, e.g. modified relationship between adjective and noun or between adverb and verb; semantic relationships on the semantic level, e.g. relationship between agent and patient of one act.

To sum up, collocation is defined in this paper as a recurrent bound bigram that internally exists with some structural relationships. To extract collocations according to the definition, we conducted the following hybrid method.

3.2 Method for Arabic Collocation Extraction

The entire process consisted of data processing, candidate collocation extraction, candidate collocation ranking and manual tagging (Fig. 1).

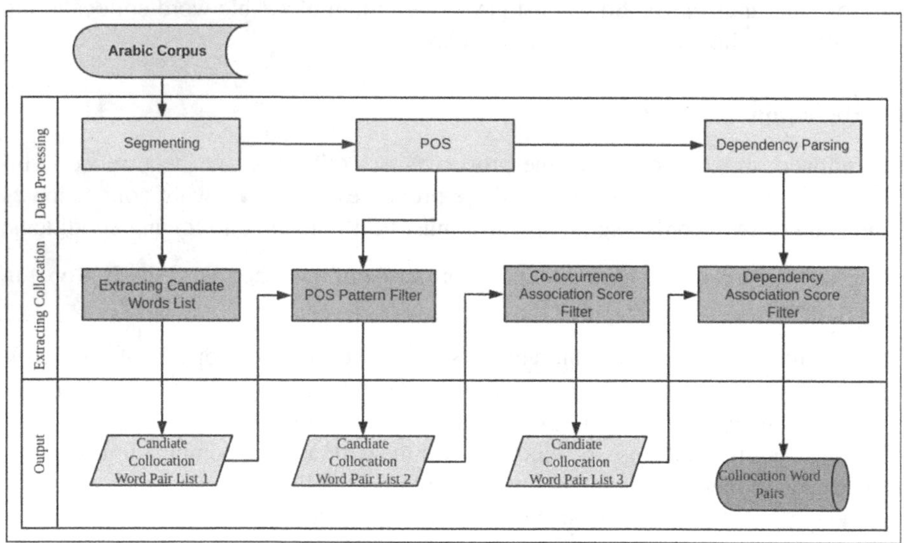

Fig. 1. Experimental flow chart

Data processing. We used the Arabic texts from the United Nations Corpus, comprised of 21,090 sentences and about 870,000 tokens. For data analysis and annotation, we used the Stanford Natural Language Processing Group's toolkit. Data processing included word segmentation, POS tagging and syntactic dependency parsing.

Arabic is a morphologically rich language. Thus, when processing Arabic texts, the first step is word segmentation, including the removal of affixes, in order to make the data conform better to automatic tagging and analysis format, e.g. the word يدعمها (to support something), after segmentation ها+يدعم. POS tagging and syntactic dependency parsing was done with the Stanford Parser, which uses an "augmented Bies" tag set. The LDC Arabic Treebanks also uses the same tag set, but it is augmented in comparison to the LDC English Treebanks' POS tag set, e.g. extra tags start with "DT", and appear for all parts of speech that can be preceded by the determiner "Al" (ال). Syntactic dependency relations as tagged by the Stanford Parser, are defined as grammatical binary relations held between a governor (also known as a regent or a head) and a dependent, including approximately 50 grammatical relations, such as "acomp", "agent", etc. However, when used for Arabic syntactic dependency parsing, it does not tag the specific types of relationship between word pairs. It only tags word pairs for dependency with "dep(w1, w2)". We extracted 621,964 dependency relations from more than 20,000 sentences.

This process is responsible for generating, filtering and ranking candidate collocations.

Candidate collocation extracting. This step is based on the data when POS tagging has already been completed. Every word was treated as a node word and every word pair composed between them and other words in their span were extracted as collocations. Each word pair has a POS tag, such as ((w1, p1), (w2, p2)), where w1 stands for node word, p1 stands for the POS of w1 inside the current sentence, w2 stands for the word in the span of w1 inside the current sentence (not including punctuation), while p2 is the actual POS for w2. A span of 10 was used, i.e. the 5 words preceding and succeeding the node word are all candidate words for collocation. Together with node words, they constitute initial candidate collocations. In 880,000 Arabic tokens, we obtained 3,475,526 initial candidate collocations.

After constituting initial candidate collocations, taking into account that collocations are structured, we used POS patterns as linguistic rules, thus creating structural restrictions for collocations. According to Saif (2011), Arabic collocations can be classified into six POS patterns: (1) Noun + Noun; (2) Noun + Adjective; (3) Verb + Noun; (4) Verb + Adverb; (5) Adjective + Adverb; and (6) Adjective + Noun, encompassing Noun, Verb, Adjective and Adverb, in total four parts of speech. However, in the tag set every part of speech also includes tags for time and aspect, gender, number, as well as other inflections (see to Table 1 for details). Afterwards, we applied the above mentioned POS patterns for filtering the initial candidate collocations, and continued treating word pairs conforming to the 6 POS patterns as candidate collocations, discarding the others. After filtering, there remained 704,077 candidate collocations.

Table 1. Arabic POS tag example.

POS	POS tag
Noun	DTNN, DTNNP, DTNNPS, DTNNS, NN, NNP, NNS, NOUN
Verb	VB, VBD, VBN, VBG, VBP, VN
Adjective	ADJ, JJ, JJR
Adverb	RB, RP

Candidate collocation ranking. For this step, we used statistical methods to calculate the association strength and dependency strength for collocations, and sorting the candidate collocations accordingly.

The calculation for word pair association strength relied on frequency of word occurrence and co-occurrence in the corpus, and for its representation we resorted to the score of Point Mutual Information (PMI), i.e. an improved Mutual Information calculation method, and also a statistical method recognized for reflecting the recurrent and arbitrary properties of collocations, and being widely employed in lexical collocation studies. Mutual Information is used to describe the relevance between two random variables in information theory. In language information processing, it is frequently used to measure correlation between two specific components, such as words, POS, sentences and texts. When employed for lexical collocation research, it can be used for calculating the degree of binding between word combinations. The formula is:

$$\mathrm{pmi}(w_1, w_2) = \log \frac{p(w_1, w_2)}{p(w_1)p(w_2)} \tag{1}$$

$p(w_1, w_2)$ refers to the frequency of the word pair (w_1, w_2) in the corpus. $p(w_1)$, $p(w_2)$ stands for the frequency of word occurrence of w_1 and w_2. The higher the frequency of co-occurrence of w_1 and w_2, the higher $p(w_1, w_2)$, and also the higher the $\mathrm{pmi}(w_1, w_2)$ score, showing that collocation (w_1, w_2) is more recurrent. As to arbitrariness, the higher the degree of binding for collocation (w_1, w_2), the lower the co-occurrence frequency between w1 or w2 and other words, and also the lower the value of $p(w_1)$ or $p(w_2)$. This means that when the value of $p(w_1, w_2)$ remains unaltered, the higher the $\mathrm{pmi}(w_1, w_2)$ score, which shows that collocation (w_1, w_2) is more arbitrary.

The calculation of dependency strength between word pairs relies on the frequency of dependency relation in the corpus. The dependency relations tagged in the Stanford Parser are grammatical relations, which means that dependency relations between word pairs still belong to linguistic information, constituting thus structural restrictions for collocations. In this paper, we used dependency relation as another linguistic rule (exception of the POS patterns) to extract Arabic collocation. Furthermore, the amount of binding relations that a word pair can have is susceptible to statistical treatment, so that we can utilize the formula mentioned above to calculate the Point Mutual Information score. We used the score to measure the degree of binding between word pairs, but the $p(w_1, w_2)$ in the formula refers to the frequency of dependency relation of (w_1, w_2) in the corpus, whilst $p(w_1)$, $p(w_2)$ still stand for the frequency of word occurrence of w_1 and w_2. The higher the dependency relation of w_1 and w_2, the higher the value of

$p(w_1, w_2)$, and also the higher the $pmi(w_1, w_2)$ score, meaning that collocation (w_1, w_2) is more structured.

This step can be further divided into two stages. First we calculated the association score (as) for all collocation candidates and sorted them from the highest to the lowest score. And then we traverse all $((w_1, p_1), (w_2, p_2))$ collocate candidates, and if (w_1, w_2) possessed a dependency relation in the corpus, then we proceeded to calculate their dependency score (ds), so that every word pair and the two scores composed a quadruple $AC((w_1, p_1), (w_2, p_2), as, ds))$. If (w_1, w_2) do not have a dependency relation in the corpus, then ds is null. After calculating the strength of dependency for all 621,964 word pairs and sorting them from the highest to the lowest score, the word pairs and strength of dependency constitute a tripe $DC(w_1, w_2, ds)$.

Manual Tagging. In order to evaluate the performance of the collocation extraction method suggested in the present paper, we extracted all collocation candidates for the Arabic word تنفيذ execute" (AC quadruples where all w_1 is تنفيذ or its variants[2]) and all dependency collocations (DC triples where all w_1 is تنفيذ or its variants), obtaining a total of 848 AC quadruples and 689 DC triples. However, only word pairs in 312 of the AC quadruples appear in these 689 DC triples. This happens because the span set in the methods for collocation candidates in quadruples is 10, while analysis of the scope of syntactical dependency analysis comprises the whole sentence. Thus, words outside of the span are not among the collocation candidates, but might have a dependency relation with node words. Afterwards, each word pair in AC quadruples and DC triples were passed on to a human annotator for manual tagging and true or false collocation.

4 Results and Analysis

The Tables 2 and 3 below present the proportional distribution of the results from the collocation candidates for تنفيذ, as well as their precision rate. "True collocations" refer to correct collocations selected manually, while "false collocations" refer to collocation errors filtered manually. "With Dependency relation" indicates that there exists one kind of dependency relation between word pairs, while "Without Dependency relation" indicates word pairs without dependency relation. So "With Dependency relation" indicates collocations selected by the hybrid method presented in this paper, "true collocation" and "With Dependency relation" stand for correct collocations selected using hybrid methods. As to precision rate, "Precision with dependency relation" in Table 2 represents the precision rate of the hybrid method which comprises POS patterns, statistical calculation and dependency relations. "Precision without dependency relation" represents the precision rate using POS patterns and statistical calculation, without dependency relations. "Precision with dependency relation only" in Table 3 represents the precision rate of the method only using dependency relations[3].

---

[2] One Arabic word could have more than one from in corpus because Arabic morphology is rich, so تنفيذ has 55 different variants.

[3] Bigrams sorted by their dependency score (ds), which actually is the Point Mutual Information Score.

Table 2. The numerical details about extracted collocations using the hybrid method.

			as > 0	as > 1	as > 2	as > 3	as > 4	as > 5	as > 6
Percent of candidate collocation		100	78.89	77.36	45.28	30.90	17.57	9.79	6.49
Percent of true collocations	With Dependency relation	23.11	19.93	19.69	12.85	8.25	4.72	2.00	1.53
Percent of false collocations		13.68	7.31	6.72	2.71	1.77	0.83	0.71	0.35
Percent of rue collocations	Without Dependency relation	17.10	15.92	15.80	11.32	8.14	4.25	2.83	1.53
Percent of false collocations		46.11	35.97	35.14	18.40	12.74	7.78	4.25	3.07
Precision with dependency relation		62.82	73.16	74.55	82.58	82.35	85.11	73.91	81.25
Precision without dependency relation		40.21	45.44	45.88	53.39	53.05	51.01	49.40	47.27

Table 3. The numerical details about extracted collocations using dependency relation.

		ds > 0	ds > 1	ds > 2	ds > 3	ds > 4	ds > 5	ds > 6	ds > 7
Percent of candidate collocation	100.0	92.29	83.00	70.71	56.57	40.43	29.29	17.86	11.29
Percent of true collocations	38.14	37.57	36.00	31.86	25.71	18.57	13.00	7.29	4.71
Percent of false collocations	61.86	54.71	47.00	38.86	30.86	21.86	16.29	10.57	6.57
Precision with dependency relation only	38.14	40.71	43.37	45.05	45.45	45.94	44.39	40.80	41.77

From the tables above, we can see that the precision of the hybrid method has been significantly improved compared to the precision of method without dependency relation and with dependency relation only. More concretely, we can find that in the set of candidate collocations (bigrams) extracted and filtered by POS patterns, PMI score and dependency relations, true collocations have much higher proportions than false collocations. But the result is completely opposite in the set of candidate collocations (bigrams) extracted without dependency relations, i.e. false collocations have much higher proportions than true collocations. This data illustrates that the potential is very great for one word collocation internally exists with some kind of dependency relation, but not all collocations do. Thus the results are enough to illustrate that it is reasonable to use dependency relation as a linguistic rule to restrict collocation extraction. However, when we only use dependency relation as a linguistic rule to extract collocations, just as the data showed in Table 3, false collocations also have much higher proportions than true collocations. This data illustrates that dependency relation is not sufficient enough, and that POS patterns are also necessary to restrict collocation extraction.

There is an example that illustrates the effect of dependency relation as a linguistic rule to filter the candidate collocations. The bigram رتبة, تنفيذي has a very high frequency in the Arabic corpus, ranking second, رتبة meaning "the level of". And when the two words co-occur in one sentence of the corpus, which mostly means "the level of the executive (organ or institution)", there is no dependency relation between the two words, so the bigram is filtered out. There are so many situations like this bigram that can be successfully filtered out, which can significantly improve the precision rate of the hybrid method of collocation extraction.

As mentioned above, not all collocations have an internal dependency relation and not all bigrams that have internal dependency relation are true collocations. Such as bigram قرر, تنفيذ, which means "decide to implement", تنفيذ (implementation) is the object of قرر (decide), there is a dependency relation between the word pair. But we can annotate the bigram as a "false collocation" without hesitation. These kinds of bigrams result in the error rate of the hybrid method. Beyond this, another reason for error rate can be the incorrect dependency result analyzed by the Stanford Parser. The hybrid method of this paper only uses dependency relation as one linguistic rule, without being entirely dependent on it, so the precision of the hybrid method is much higher than the method only using dependency relations.

To sum it all up, the hybrid method presented in this paper can significantly improve the precision of collocation extraction.

5 Conclusion

In this study, we have presented our method for collocation extraction from an Arabic corpus. This is a hybrid method that depends on both linguistic information and association measures. Linguistic information is comprised of two rules: POS patterns and dependency relations. Taking the Arabic word تنفيذ as an example, by using this method we were able to extract all the collocation candidates and collocation dependencies, as well as calculating its precision after manual tagging. This experiment's results show that by using this hybrid method for extracting Arabic words, it can guarantee a higher precision rate, which heightens even more after dependency relations are added as rules for filtering, achieving 85.11% accuracy, higher than by only resorting to syntactic dependency analysis as a collocation extraction method.

References

Attia, M.A.: Accommodating multiword expressions in an arabic LFG grammar. In: Salakoski, T., Ginter, F., Pyysalo, S., Pahikkala, T. (eds.) FinTAL 2006. LNCS, vol. 4139, pp. 87–98. Springer, Heidelberg (2006). doi:10.1007/11816508_11

Benson, M.: Collocations and general-purpose dictionaries. Int. J. Lexicogr. **3**(1), 23–34 (1990)

Benson, M.: The Structure of the Collocational Dictionary. Int. J. Lexicography, **2**(1) (1989)

Bounhas, I., Slimani, Y.: A hybrid approach for Arabic multi-word term extraction. In: International Conference on Natural Language Processing and Knowledge Engineering 2009, NLP-KE, vol. 30, pp. 1–8. IEEE (2009)

Church, K.W., Hanks, P., Hindle, D.: Using Statistics in Lexical Analysis. Lexical Acquisition (1991)

Choueka, Y., Klein, T., Neuwitz, E.: Automation Retrieval of Frequent Idiomatic and Collocational Expressions in a Large Corpus. J. Literary Linguist. Comput. **4** (1983)

Frantzi, K., Sophia, A., Hideki, M.: Automatic recognition of multi-word terms: the C-value/NC-value method. Int. J. Digital Libraries **3**, 115–130 (2000)

Halliday, M.A.K.: Lexical relations. System and Function in Language. Oxford University Press, Oxford (1976)

Pecina, P.: An extensive empirical study of collocation extraction methods. ACL 2005, Meeting of the Association for Computational Linguistics, pp. 13–18, University of Michigan, USA (2005)

Saif, A.M., Aziz, M.J.A.: An automatic collocation extraction from Arabic corpus. J. Comput. Sci. **7**(1), 6 (2011)

Sinclair, J.: Corpus, Concordance, Collocation. Oxford University Press, Oxford (1991)

Smadja, F.: Retrieving collocations from text: extract. Comput. Linguist. **19**(19), 143–177 (1993)

Employing Auto-annotated Data for Person Name Recognition in Judgment Documents

Limin Wang, Qian Yan, Shoushan Li(✉), and Guodong Zhou

Natural Language Processing Lab, School of Computer Science and Technology, Soochow University, Suzhou, China
{lmwang, qyan}@stu.suda.edu.cn, {lishoushan, gdzhou}@suda.edu.cn

Abstract. In the last decades, named entity recognition has been extensively studied with various supervised learning approaches depend on massive labeled data. In this paper, we focus on person name recognition in judgment documents. Owing to the lack of human-annotated data, we propose a joint learning approach, namely Aux-LSTM, to use a large scale of auto-annotated data to help human-annotated data (in a small size) for person name recognition. Specifically, our approach first develops an auxiliary Long Short-Term Memory (LSTM) representation by training the auto-annotated data and then leverages the auxiliary LSTM representation to boost the performance of classifier trained on the human-annotated data. Empirical studies demonstrate the effectiveness of our proposed approach to person name recognition in judgment documents with both human-annotated and auto-annotated data.

Keywords: Named entity recognition · Auto-annotated data · LSTM

1 Introduction

Named entity recognition (NER) is a natural language processing (NLP) task and plays a key role in many real applications, such as relation extraction [1], entity linking [2], and machine translation [3]. Named entity recognition was first presented as a subtask on MUC-6 [4], which aims to find organizations, persons, locations, temporal expressions and number expressions in text. The proportion of Chinese names in the entities is large, according to statistics, in the "People's Daily" in January 1998 corpus (2,305,896 words), specifically, the average per 100 words contains 1.192 unlisted words (excluding time words and quantifiers), of which 48.6% of the entities are Chinese names [5]. In addition to the complex semantics of Chinese, the Chinese name has a great arbitrariness, so the identification of the Chinese name is one of the main and difficult tasks in named entity recognition.

In the paper, we focus on the person name recognition in judgment documents. The ratio of person name in judgment documents is very big, including not only plaintiffs, defendants, entrusted agents, but also other unrelated names, such as outsider, eyewitness, jurors, clerk and so on. For instance, Fig. 1 shows an example of a judgment document where person names exist. However, in most scenarios, there is insufficient

M. Sun et al. (Eds.): CCL 2017 and NLP-NABD 2017, LNAI 10565, pp. 13–23, 2017.
https://doi.org/10.1007/978-3-319-69005-6_2

annotated corpus data for person name recognition in judgment document and to obtain such corpus data is extremely costly and time-consuming.

民事 裁定书
（2016）川
原告 <ENAMEX TYPE="PERSON">*阿衣子*</ENAMEX>
被告 <ENAMEX TYPE="PERSON">*艾现英*</ENAMEX>
……
陪审员<ENAMEX TYPE="PERSON">*胡士戎*</ENAMEX>
书记员<ENAMEX TYPE="PERSON"> *丁丁*</ENAMEX>
(English Translation:
Civil Judgment
(2016) Chuan
Plaintiff <ENAMEX TYPE="PERSON"> Yizi A</ENAMEX>
Defendant <ENAMEX TYPE="PERSON">Xianyin Ai</ENAMEX>
……
Jurors <ENAMEX TYPE="PERSON">Shirong Hu</ENAMEX>
Clerk <ENAMEX TYPE="PERSON">Ding Ding</ENAMEX>
)

Fig. 1. An example of a judgment document with the person names annotated in the text

Fortunately, we find that the judgment documents are well-structured in some parts. For example, in Fig. 1, we can see that in the front part, the word "原告 (Plaintiff)" often follows a person name. Therefore, to tackle the difficulty of obtaining human-annotated data, we try to auto-annotate much judgment documents with some heuristic rules. Due to the large scale of existing judgment documents, it is easy to obtain many auto-annotated sentences with person names and these sentences could be used as training data for person name recognition.

E1:
原 告 <ENAMEX TYPE="PERSON"> ***阿 衣 子*** *</ENAMEX> 诉 称, 被 告 <ENAMEX TYPE="PERSON">* ***艾现英*** *</ENAMEX> 和她的 邻居* ***高山*** *一起 曾经 带着 案外人****方亮*** *出现 在 其 出租屋 。……*

(**English Translation:**
Plaintiff <ENAMEX TYPE="PERSON"> Yizi A </ENAMEX> complained, defendant <ENAMEX TYPE="PERSON"> Xianyin Ai </ENAMEX>, along with her neighbor GaoShan, had brought outsider FangLiang appearing in her rental. ……
)

One straightforward approach to using auto-annotated data in person name recognition is to merge them into the human-annotated data and use the merging data to train a new model. However, due to the automatic annotation, the data is noisy. That is to say, there still exist some person names are not annotated. For example, in E1, there are four person names in the sentence, but we can only annotate two person names via the auto-annotating strategy.

In this paper, we propose a novel approach to person name recognition by using auto-annotated data in judgment documents with a joint learning model. Our approach uses a small amount of human-annotated samples, together with a large amount of auto-annotated sentences containing person names. Instead of simply merging the human-annotated and auto-annotated samples, we propose a joint learning model, namely Aux-LSTM, to combine the two different resources. Specifically, we first separate the twin person name classification task using the human-annotated data and the auto-annotated data into a main task and an auxiliary task. Then, our joint learning model based on neural network develops an auxiliary representation from the auxiliary task of a shared Long Short-Term Memory (LSTM) layer and then integrates the auxiliary representation into the main task for joint learning. Empirical studies demonstrate that the proposed joint learning approach performs much better than using the merging method.

The remainder of this paper is organized as follows. Section 2 gives a brief overviews of related work on name recognition. Section 3 introduces data collection and annotation. Section 4 presents some basic LSTM approaches and our joint learning approach to name recognition. Section 5 evaluates the proposed approach. Finally, Sect. 6 gives the conclusion and future work.

2 Related Work

Although the study of Chinese named entities is still in the immature stage compared with the English named entity recognition. But there is a lot of research on Chinese named recognition. Depending on the method used, these methods can be broadly divided into three categories: rule method, statistical method and a combination of rules and statistics.

The rule method mainly uses two kinds of information: the name classification and the restrictive component of the surname: that is, when mark the name with the obvious character in the analysis process, the recognition process of the name is started and the relevant component, which limits the position of the name before and after.

In the last decades, named entity recognition has been extensively studied with various supervised shallow learning approaches, such as Hidden Markow Models (HMM) [6], sequential perceptron model [7], and Conditional Random Fields (CRF) [8]. Meanwhile, named entity recognition has been performed in various styles of text, such as news [6], biomedical text [9], clinical notes [10], and tweets [11].

An important line of previous studies on named entity recognition is to improve the recognition performance by exploiting extra data resources. One major kind of such researches is to exploit unlabeled data with various semi-supervised learning approaches, such as bootstrapping [12, 13], word clusters [14], and Latent Semantic Association (LSA) [15]. Another major kind of such researches is to exploit parallel corpora to perform bilingual NER [16, 17].

Recently, deep learning approaches with neural networks have been more and more popular for NER. Hammerton [18] applies a single-direction LSTM network to perform NER with a combination word embedding learning approach. Collobert [19] employs convolutional neural networks (CNN) to perform NER with a sequence of word embeddings. Subsequently, recent studies perform NER with some other neural networks, such as BLSTM [20], LSTM-CNNs [21], and LSTM-CRF [22].

3 Data Collection and Annotation

3.1 Human-annotated Data

The data is built by ourselves and it is from a kind of law documents named judgments. Choosing this special kind of document as our experimental data is mainly due to the fact that judgments always have an invariant structure and several domain-specific regulations could be found therein, which makes it a good choice to test the effectiveness of our approach. We obtain the Chinese judgments from the government public website (i.e., http://wenshu.court.gov.cn/). The judgments are organized in various categories of laws and we pick the Contract Law. In the category, we manually annotate 100 judgment documents according the annotation guideline in OntoNotes 5.0 [23]. Two annotators are asked to annotate the data. Due to the clear annotation guideline, the annotation agreement on name recognition is very high, reaching 99.8%.

3.2 Auto-annotated Data

Note that a Chinese judgment always has an invariant structure where plaintiffs and defendants are explicitly described in two lines in the front part. It is easy to capture some entities from two textual patterns, for example, "原告 NAME1, (Plaintiff NAME1,)" and "被告 NAME2, (Defendant NAME2,)" where "NAME1" or "NAME2" denotes a person name if the length is less than 4. Therefore, we first match the name through the rules in the front part of judgment instruments. Second, we only selected the sentences containing the person name as the auto-annotated samples from the entire judgment documents. In this way, we could quickly obtain more than 10,000 auto-annotated judgment documents.

4 Methodology

4.1 LSTM Model for Name Recognition

In this subsection, we propose the LSTM classification model. Figure 2 shows the framework overview of the LSTM model for name recognition.

Formally, the input of the LSTM classification model is a character's representation x_i, which consists of character unigram and bigram embeddings for representing the current character, i.e.,

$$x_i = v_{c_{i-1}} \oplus v_{c_i} \oplus v_{c_{i+1}} \oplus \ldots \oplus v_{c_{i+1},c_{i+2}} \quad (1)$$

Where $v_{c_i} \in R^d$ is a d-dimensional real-valued vector for representing the character unigram c_i and $v_{c_i,c_{i+1}} \in R^d$ is a d-dimensional real-valued vector for representing the character bigram c_i, c_{i+1}.

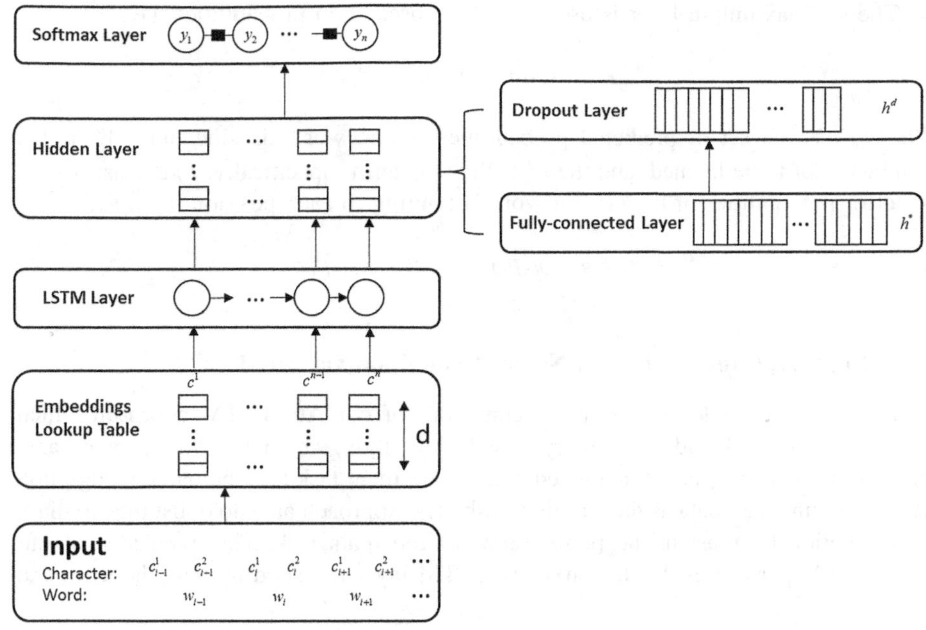

Fig. 2. The framework overview of the LSTM model for character-level NER

Through the LSTM unit, the input of a character is converted into a new representation h_i, i.e.,

$$h_i = LSTM(x_i) \tag{2}$$

Subsequently, the fully-connected layer accepts the output from the previous layer, weighting them and passing through a normally activation function as follows:

$$h_i^* = dense(h_i) = \phi(\theta^T h_i + b) \tag{3}$$

Where $\phi(x)$ is a non-linear activation function, employed "relu" in our model. h_i^* is the output from the fully-connected layer.

The dropout layer is applied to randomly omit feature detectors from network during training. It is used as hidden layer in our framework, i.e.,

$$h_i^d = h_i^* \cdot D(p^*) \tag{4}$$

Where D denotes the dropout operator, p^* denotes a tunable hyper parameter, and h_i^d denotes the output from the dropout layer.

The softmax output layer is used to get the prediction probabilities, i.e.,

$$P_i = softmax(W^d h_i^d + b^d) \tag{5}$$

Where P_i is the set of predicted probabilities of the word classification, W^d is the weight vector to be learned, and the b^d is the bias term. Specifically, P_i consists of the posterior probabilities of the current word belonging to each position tag, i.e.,

$$P_i = <p_{i,B-PER}, p_{i,I-PER}, p_{i,E-PER}, p_{i,O}> \tag{6}$$

4.2 Joint Learning for Person Name Recognition via Aux-LSTM

In the Fig. 3 delineates the overall architecture of our Aux-LSTM approach which contains a main task and an auxiliary task. In our study, we consider the person name recognition with the human-annotated data as the main task and the name recognition with auto-annotated data as the auxiliary task. The approach aims to enlist the auxiliary representation to assist in the performance of the main task. The main idea of our Aux-LSTM approach is that the auxiliary LSTM layer is shared by both the main and

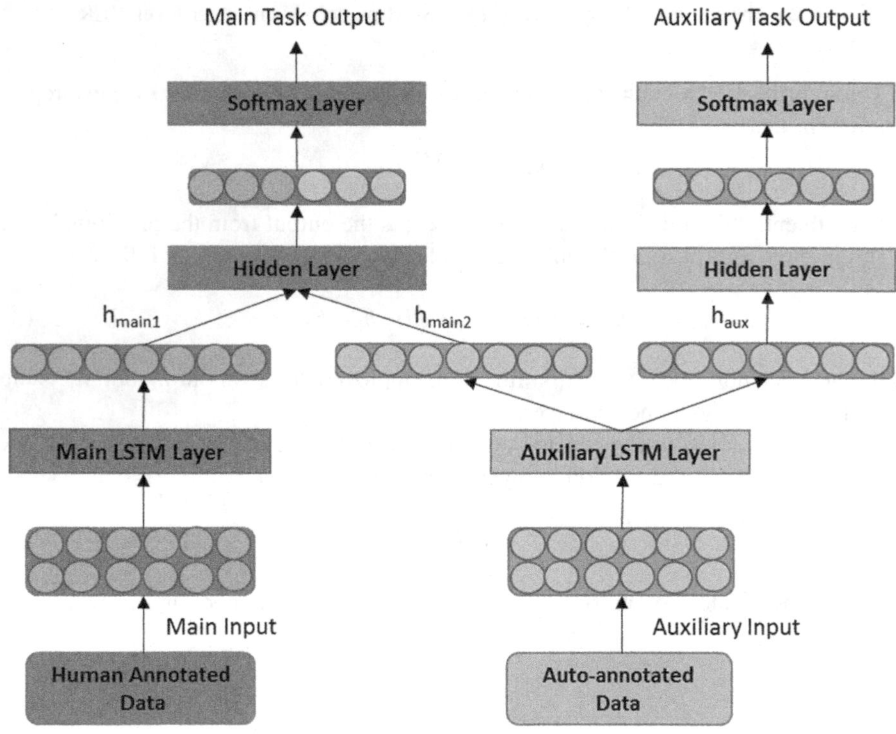

Fig. 3. Overall architecture of Aux-LSTM

auxiliary task so as to take advantage of information from both the annotated and auto-annotated data.

(1) **The Main Task:**

Formally, the representation of main task is generated from both the main LSTM layer and the auxiliary LSTM layer respectively:

$$h_{main1} = LSTM_{main}(T^{input}) \tag{7}$$

$$h_{main2} = LSTM_{aux}(T^{input}) \tag{8}$$

where h_{main1} represents the output of classification model via main LSTM layer and h_{main2} represents the output of classification model via auxiliary LSTM layer.

Then we concatenate the two representation as the input of the hidden layer in the main task:

$$h^d_{main} = dense_{main}(h_{main1} \oplus h_{main2}) \tag{9}$$

where h^d_{main} denotes the outputs of fully-connected layer in the main task, and $\oplus$ denotes the concatenate operator as a 'concat' mode.

(2) **The Auxiliary Task:**

The auxiliary classification representation is also generated by the auxiliary LSTM layer, which is a shared LSTM layer and is employed to bridge across the classification models. The shared LSTM layer encodes both the same input sequence with the same weights and the output h_{aux} is the representation for the classification model via shared LSTM model.

$$h_{aux} = LSTM_{aux}(T^{input}) \tag{10}$$

Then a fully-connected layer is utilized to obtain a feature vector for classification, which is the same as the hidden layer in the main task:

$$h^d_{aux} = dense_{aux}(h_{aux}) \tag{11}$$

Other layers such as softmax layer, as shown in Fig. 2, are the same as those which have been described in Sect. 4.1.

Finally, we define our joint cost function for Aux-LSTM as a weighted linear combination of the cost functions of both the main task and auxiliary task as follows:

$$loss_{Aux-LSTM} = \lambda(loss_{main}) + (1 - \lambda)(loss_{aux}) \tag{12}$$

In the above equation, λ is the weight parameter, $loss_{main}$ and $loss_{aux}$ is the loss function of main task and auxiliary task respectively. We take 'adadelta' as the optimizing algorithm. All the matrix and vector parameters in neural network are initialized with uniform samples in $\left[-\sqrt{6/(r+c)}, \sqrt{6/(r+c)}\right]$, where r and c are the numbers of rows and columns in the matrices [24].

5 Experimentation

In this section, we have systematically evaluated our approach to person name recognition together with both human annotated and the auto-annotated data.

5.1 Experimental Settings

Data Setting: The data collection has been introduced in Sect. 3.1. In the main task, we randomly select 20 articles of human-annotated data as training data and another 50 articles of human-annotated as the test data. In the auxiliary task, we randomly select the number of training samples corresponding to the number of 5 times, 10 times, 20 times, 30 times and 40 times as the training data and the test data is the same as that in the main task.

Features and Embedding: We use the current character and its surrounding characters (window size is 2), together with the character bigrams as features. We use word2vec (http://word2vec.googlecode.com/) to pre-train character embeddings using the two data sets.

Basic Classification Algorithms: (1) Conditional Random Fields (CRFs), one popular supervised shallow learning algorithms, is implemented with the CRF++-0.53[1] and all the parameters are set as defaults. (2) LSTM, as the basic classification algorithm in our approach, is implemented with the tool Keras[2]. Table 1 shows the final hyper-parameters of the LSTM algorithm.

Table 1. Parameter settings in LSTM

Parameter description	Value
Dimension of the LSTM layer output	128
Dimension of the full-connected layer output	64
Size of the batch	32
Dropout probability	0.5
Epochs of iteration	20

Hyper-parameters: The hyper-parameter values in the LSTM and Aux-LSTM model are tuned according to performances in the development data.

[1] https://www.crf.it/IT.

[2] https://github.com/fchollet/keras.

Evaluation Measurement: The performance is evaluated using the standard precision (P), recall (R) and F-score.

5.2 Experimental Results

In this subsection, we compare different approaches to person name recognition with both human-annotated and auto-annotated data. The implemented approaches are illustrated as follows:

- **CRF:** It is a shallow-learning model which has been widely employed in name recognition, and it simply merges the human-annotated data and the auto-annotated samples together as the whole training data.
- **LSTM:** It is deep learning model which has been widely employed in the natural language processing community, and the training data is the same as that in CRF.
- **Aux-LSTM:** This is our approach which develops an auxiliary representation for joint learning. In this model, we consider two tasks: one is the name recognition with the human-annotated data, and the other is the name recognition with the auto-annotated data. The approach aims to leverage the extra information to boost the performance of name recognition. The parameter λ is set to be 0.5.

Table 2 shows the number of characters, sentences and person names in auto-annotated documents with different sizes. From this table, we can see that, there are a great number of person names that could be automatically recognized in judgment documents. When 1000 documents are auto-annotated, there are totally 79411 recognized person names, which make the auto-annotated data a big-size training data for person name recognition.

Table 2. The number of character, sentence and person name in different auto-annotated data

Number of auto-annotated documents	Number of characters	Number of sentences	Number of person names
100	173370	7128	8970
200	317845	13690	17286
400	606795	26134	29810
600	895745	39703	47578
800	1184695	51502	62742
1000	1473645	64817	79411

Table 3 shows the performance of different approaches to person name recognition when different size of human-annotated and auto-annotated data are employed. Specifically, the first line named "0" means using only human-annotated data and the second line "100" means using both human-annotated data and 100 auto-annotated judgment documents. From this table, we can see that,

- When no auto-annotated data is used, the LSTM model performs much better than CRF, mainly due to its better performance on Recall.

Table 3. Performance comparison of different approaches to name recognition

	CRF			LSTM			Aux-LSTM		
	P	R	F	P	R	F	P	R	F
0	94.4	41.9	58.1	77.3	60.0	67.58	— —	— —	— —
100	96.1	74.5	83.9	94.2	82.9	88.2	92.7	84.5	**88.4**
200	97.3	80.3	88.0	94.1	86.2	90.0	95.9	90.5	**93.1**
400	97.6	82.8	89.6	96.3	86.3	91.0	95.3	91.7	**93.5**
600	98.2	85.0	91.1	96.4	85.5	90.6	94.0	90.4	**92.2**
800	98.1	86.7	92.0	96.3	87.0	91.4	96.6	94.2	**95.3**
1000	97.7	87.4	92.3	97.5	86.4	91.6	95.5	91.4	**93.4**

- When a small size of auto-annotated data is used, the LSTM model generally performs better than CRF in terms of F1 score. But when the size of auto-annotated data becomes larger, the LSTM model performs a bit worse than CRF in terms of F1 score. No matter the LSTM or CRF model is used, using the auto-annotated data always improves the person name recognition performances with a large margin.
- When the auto-annotated data is used, our approach, i.e., Aux-LSTM, performs best among the three approaches. Especially, when the size of the auto-annotated data becomes larger, our approach performs much better than LSTM. This is possibly because our approach is more robust for adding noisy training data.

6 Conclusion

In this paper, we propose a novel approach to person name recognition with both human-annotated and auto-annotated data in judgment documents. Our approach leverages a small amount of human-annotated samples, together with a large amount of auto-annotated sentences containing person names. Instead of simply merging the human-annotated and auto-annotated samples, we propose a joint learning model, namely Aux-LSTM, to combine the two different resources. Specifically, we employ an auxiliary LSTM layer to develop the auxiliary representation for the main task of person name recognition. Empirical studies show that using the auto-annotated data is very effective to improve the performances of person name recognition in judgment documents no matter what approaches are used. Furthermore, our Aux-LSTM approach consistently outperforms using the simple merging strategy with CRF or LSTM models.

In our future work, we would like to improve the performance of person name recognition by exploring the more features. Moreover, we would like to apply our approach to name entity recognition on other types of entities, such as organizations and locations in judgment documents.

Acknowledgments. This research work has been partially supported by three NSFC grants, No. 61375073, No. 61672366 and No. 61331011.

References

1. Bunescu, R.C., Mooney, R.J.: A shortest path dependency kernel for relation extraction. In: Proceedings of EMNLP, pp. 724–731 (2005)
2. Dredze, M., McNamee, P., Rao, D., Gerber, A., Finin, T.: Entity disambiguation for knowledge base population. In: Proceedings of COLING, pp. 277–285 (2010)
3. Babych, B., Hartley, A.: Improving machine translation quality with automatic named entity recognition. In: Proceedings of the 7th International EAMT Workshop, pp. 1–8 (2003)
4. Chinchor, N.: MUC7 Named Entity Task Definition (1997)
5. Ji, N.I., Kong, F., Zhu, Q., Peifeng, L.I.: Research on chinese name recognition base on trustworthiness. J. Chin. Inf. Process. **25**(3), 45–50 (2011)
6. Zhou, G., Su, J.: Named entity recognition using an Hmm-based chunk tagger. In: Proceedings of ACL, pp. 473–480 (2002)
7. Collins, M.: Discriminative training methods for hidden Markov models: theory and experiments with perceptron algorithms. In: Proceedings of EMNLP, pp. 1–8 (2002)
8. Finkel, J.R., Grenager, T. Manning, C.: Incorporating non-local information into information extraction systems by gibbs sampling. In: Proceedings of ACL, pp. 363–370 (2005)
9. Yoshida, K., Tsujii, J.: Reranking for biomedical named entity recognition. In: Proceedings of BioNLP, pp. 209–216 (2007)
10. Wang, Y.: Annotating and recognizing named entities in clinical notes. In: Proceedings of ACL-IJCNLP, pp. 18–26 (2009)
11. Liu, X., Zhang, S., Wei, F., Zhou, M.: Recognizing named entities in tweets. In: Proceedings of ACL, pp. 359–367 (2011)
12. Jiang, J., Zhai, C.: Instance weighting for domain adaptation in NLP. In: Proceedings of ACL, pp. 264–271 (2007)
13. Brooke, J., Baldwin, T., Hammond, A.: Bootstrapped text-level named entity recognition for literature. In: Proceedings of ACL, Short Paper, pp. 344–350 (2016)
14. Brown, P.F., deSouza, P.V., Mercer, R.L., Della Pietra, V.J., Lai, J.C.: Classbased n-gram models of natural language. Comput. Linguist. **18**, 467–479 (1992)
15. Guo, H., Zhu, H., Guo, Z., Zhang, X., Wu, X., Su, Z.: Domain adaptation with latent semantic association for named entity recognition. In: Proceedings of NAACL, pp. 281–289 (2009)
16. Burkett, D., Petrov, S., Blitzer, J., Klein, D.: Learning better monolingual models with unannotated bilingual text. In: Proceedings of CONLL, pp. 46–54 (2010)
17. Che, W., Wang, M., Manning, C.D., Liu, T.: Named entity recognition with bilingual constraints. In: Proceedings of NAACL, pp. 52–62 (2013)
18. Hammerton, J.: Named entity recognition with long short-term memory. In: Proceedings of CONLL, pp. 172–175 (2003)
19. Collobert, R., Weston, J., Bottou, L., Karlen, M., Kavukcuoglu, K., Kuksa, P.: Natural language processing (almost) from scratch. J. Mach. Learn. Res. **12**, 2493–2537 (2011)
20. Huang, Z., Xu, W., Yu, K.: Bidirectional LSTM-CRF models for sequence tagging. CORR, abs/1508.01991 (2015)
21. Chiu, J.P.C., Nichols, E.: Named entity recognition with bidirectional LSTM-CNNs. Trans. Assoc. Comput. Linguist. **4**, 357–370 (2016)
22. Lample, G., Ballesteros, M., Subramanian, S., Kawakami, K., Dyer, C.: Neural architectures for named entity recognition. In: Proceedings of NAACL-HLT, pp. 260–270 (2016)
23. Hovy, E.H., Marcus, M.P., Palmer, M., Ramshaw, L.A., Weischedel, R.M.: Ontonotes: the 90% solution. In: Proceedings of NAACL-HLT, pp. 57–60 (2006)
24. Glorot, X., Bengio, Y.: Understanding the difficulty of training deep feedforward neural networks. J. Mach. Learn. Res. **9**, 249–256 (2010)

Closed-Set Chinese Word Segmentation Based on Convolutional Neural Network Model

Zhipeng Xie(✉)

School of Computer Science, Fudan University, Shanghai, China
xiezp@fudan.edu.cn

Abstract. This paper proposes a neural model for closed-set Chinese word segmentation. The model follows the character-based approach which assigns a class label to each character, indicating its relative position within the word it belongs to. To do so, it first constructs shallow representations of characters by fusing unigram and bigram information in limited context window via an element-wise maximum operator, and then build up deep representations from wider contextual information with a deep convolutional network. Experimental results have shown that our method achieves better closed-set performance compared with several state-of-the-art systems.

Keywords: Chinese word segmentation · Deep learning · Convolutional neural networks

1 Introduction

Chinese word segmentation (or CWS in short) is an fundamental task in Chinese information processing. It has to be performed before downstream syntactic and semantic analysis of Chinese text that has no explicit word delimiters. A lot of statistical methods have been proposed to solve the CWS problem [1,12,14,15,18].

Recently, with the upsurge of deep learning, there is a trend of applying neural network models to NLP tasks, which adaptively learn important features from word/character embeddings [2,10] trained on large quantities of unlabelled text, and thus greatly reduce efforts of hand-crafted feature engineering [5].

Zheng et al. [19] made the first try to apply embedding-based neural model to Chinese word segmentation. They used unigram embeddings in local windows as input for a two-layer feedforward network to calculate tag scores for each character position. The final decision is made by a Viterbi-like decoder algorithm based on the predicted tag scores and the transition probabilities between tags, where the transition probabilities have explicitly modeled the strong dependencies between tags.

Mansur et al. [9] worked in a way similar to [19]. They proposed the feature-based neural network where features are represented as feature embeddings, and used character bigram embeddings as additional features to improve segmentation.

M. Sun et al. (Eds.): CCL 2017 and NLP-NABD 2017, LNAI 10565, pp. 24–36, 2017.
https://doi.org/10.1007/978-3-319-69005-6_3

Pei et al. [11] proposed a max-margin tensor neural network to explicitly model the interactions between history tags and context characters by exploiting tag embeddings and tensor-based transformation. It also adopts the window approach, which concatenates the embeddings of characters within the window. The concatenated vector is then fed into the next layer which performs linear transformation followed by an element-wise activation function such as tanh.

Ma and Hinrichs [8] proposed an embedding matching approach which models the matching between configurations and character-specific decisions. It makes decision by considering character-action combinations instead of atomic, character independent actions in [11].

The models described above build up shallow-presentations of characters from their fixed-size windows, which can be thought of as a single convolutional layer with limited receptive field. To solve this problem, Chen et al. [4] introduced the LSTM neural network to build feature representations for CWS, where the LSTM exploits input, output and forget gates to decide how to utilize and update the memory of previous information.

These character-based neural models described have achieved competitive word segmentation results. However, there still exist two main problems:

Firstly, the methods in [8,11,19] works with only a single convolutional layer (or equivalently, a feedforward layer on a fixed-size window), where the problem is that the information can not flow from one position to another. To facilitate the information flow, one choice is to represent history predictions (of previous character positions) as embeddings in tag scoring pha olyse, as done in [11] and [8], but this design decision is made at the cost of losing the ability of fully exploiting the current multi-core architecture. Another possibility is to model the complicated tag-tag interactions in the inference phase [4,19], which, however, complicates the algorithmic framework and also deprives the model of the ability of modeling the tag-character interactions.

The second problem is how to compose the feature embeddings from its context. Methods based on windows of fixed size is rigid and have only limited context size. The LSTM layer has a potentially unbounded dependency range within their receptive field, but this comes with a computational cost as each state needs to be computed sequentially in both training and testing phases.

The solution we propose here is to make use of a deep convolutional network, which has a large, but not unbounded, receptive field. The information (inclusive of tag-related information) at the lower level can flow to adjacent positions and get composed adaptively into higher-level representations. Such an implicit modeling of tag-tag and tag-character interactions is more flexible. Another advantage is that the convolutional model is easy to process all the characters of a sentence in parallel during both training and testing, leading to highly-efficient segmentation. We have tested BiLSTM model on the commonly-used PKU and MSR datasets, and the computational cost is about 10 times higher than the model with four convolutional layers.

Furthermore, different from existing CWS systems which often make use of external linguistic resources such as unsupervised text corpus (or the character embeddings pretrained on large text corpus) and dictionary, our model work in a closed-set scenario, which can make us focus on the method itself.

2 The Proposed Model

The architecture of our model is briefly illustrated in Fig. 1, which consists of three main component:

- *Shallow representation.* It first constructs a shallow representation for each character in the given sentence, by fusing the unigram and bigram information from its local context window.
- *Deep representation* It then adaptively constructs hierarchically deeper representations to combine the lower-level representations of each position, where information can flow between adjacent character representations. **Tag Scoring Module** It assigns tag scores to each character based on its deep representation.

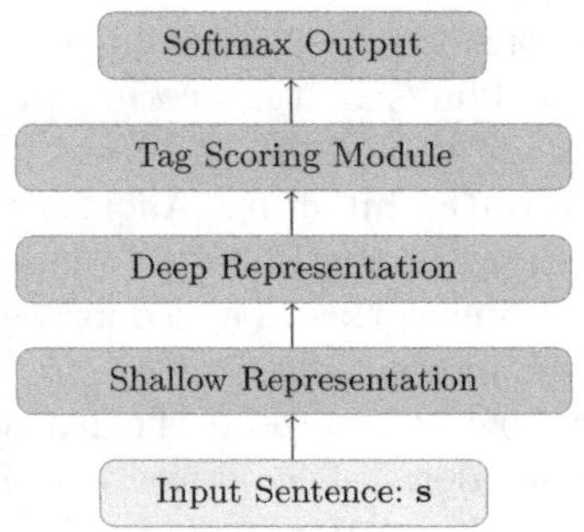

Fig. 1. The architecture for our model

Let $\mathbf{s} = c_1 \cdots c_{|\mathbf{s}|}$ denote the input Chinese sentence, where c_j is the j-th Chinese character in $\mathbf{s}$ and $|\mathbf{s}|$ is the length of the sentence. Each unigram (or character) in $\mathbf{s}$ can be simply represented as an embedding vector that is independent of its context. However, in Chinese word segmentation, the unigram embedding itself is usually not enough to determine the relative position of the character within the word it belongs to, because a specific character may appear at the beginning, in the middle or at the end of a word, depending on the particular context (or the surrounding characters).

2.1 Shallow Reprensentations

For each specific character c_j at position j in the input sentence $\mathbf{s}$, its shallow representation is a fixed-size vector which contains the important features fused from the unigrams and the bigrams within a small context window. In this paper, the small context window is of size 3 by default.

As shown in Fig. 2, the shallow representation $\mathbf{x}_j^{(0)}$ of a character c_j can be obtained by applying an elementwise max operator on its unigram shallow representation $\mathbf{x}_j^{(u)}$ and its bigram shallow representation $\mathbf{x}_j^{(b)}$, where $\mathbf{x}_j^{(u)}$ is the combination of three unigram embeddings of the characters c_{j-1}, c_j, and c_{j+1}, while $\mathbf{x}_j^{(b)}$ is the combination of two bigram embeddings of the bigram b_{j-1} and b_j. The details are described as follows.

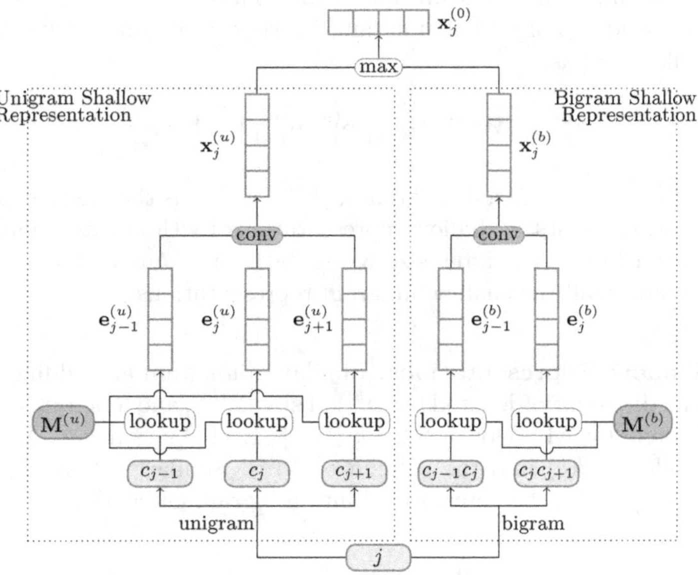

Fig. 2. Shallow representation for the character at position j

An input sentence $\mathbf{s}$ is normally represented as a sequence of unigrams $c_1 \cdots c_{|s|}$ where $|s|$ is the length of the sentence and c_i $(1 \leq i \leq |s|)$ is the i-th character in $\mathbf{s}$. A special character (\$ in this paper) can be used to denote the begin or the end of sentence, i.e. $c_0 = \$$ and $c_{|s|+1} = \$$. An alternative is to represent $\mathbf{s}$ as a sequence of bigrams $b_0 \cdots b_{|s|}$, where $b_i = c_i c_{i+1}$ $(0 \leq i \leq |s|)$ denotes the i-th bigram in $\mathbf{s}$. Here, the 0-th bigram $b_0 = \$c_1$ and the $|s|$-th bigram $b_{|s|} = c_{|s|}\$$. Please note that the sequence of unigrams and the sequence of bigrams are of different lengths.

Unigram Shallow Representations. Let $\Sigma^{(u)}$ denote the unigram dictionary of size $|\Sigma^{(u)}|$, and $\mathbf{M}^{(u)}$ denote the (character) unigram embedding matrix of size $d_u \times |\Sigma^{(u)}|$, where d_u is the dimensionality of unigram embeddings (300 by default). Each character $c \in \Sigma^{(u)}$ has an associated index $ind(c)$ into the column of the embedding matrix.

At position j of the sentence $\mathbf{s}$, the unigram embedding $\mathbf{e}_j^{(u)} \in \mathbb{R}^{d_u \times 1}$ of c_j can be obtained by applying a lookup-table operation on $\mathbf{M}^{(u)}$:

$$\mathbf{e}_j^{(u)} = \text{lookup}(\mathbf{M}^{(u)}, c_j) = \mathbf{M}^{(u)} \cdot e_{ind(c_j)}$$

where $e_{ind(c_j)}$ is the one-hot representation of the character c_j, i.e. a $|\Sigma^{(u)}|$-dimensional binary column vector that is zero for all elements except for the element at the index $ind(c_j)$.

The shallow unigram representation of the character c_j can be composed by fusing the embeddings of its left unigram, its right unigram and itself. Specifically, it is calculated as:

$$\mathbf{x}_j^{(u)} = \mathbf{W}^{(us)} \left[\mathbf{e}_{j-1}^{(u)} \; \mathbf{e}_j^{(u)} \; \mathbf{e}_{j+1}^{(u)} \right] + \mathbf{b}^{(us)}$$

where $\mathbf{W}^{(us)} \in \mathbb{R}^{d_s \times d_u \times 3}$ is a 3-way tensor, $\mathbf{b}^{(us)} \in \mathbb{R}^{d_s}$ is the bias vector, and d_s is the dimensionality of the shallow representations (with 300 as default value). A convolutional layer with filter size 3, stride 1 and same-padding is used to efficiently compute all the shallow unigram representations.

Bigram Shallow Representations. Similar to unigram embeddings, we also have a bigram dictionary (denoted by $\Sigma^{(b)}$) of size $|\Sigma^{(b)}|$, and a bigram embedding matrix (denoted by $\mathbf{M}^{(b)}$) of size $d_b \times |\Sigma^{(b)}|$. Each bigram $b \in \Sigma^{(b)}$ has an associated index $ind(b)$ into the column of $\mathbf{M}^{(b)}$. Similarly, each bigram $b_j = c_j c_{j+1}$ $(0 \leq j \leq |s|)$ can be transformed into a bigram embedding:

$$\mathbf{e}_j^{(b)} = \mathbf{M}^{(b)} \cdot e_{ind(b_j)}$$

At position j, the shallow bigram representation of the character c_j can be composed by fusing the embeddings of its left bigram $b_{j-1} = c_{j-1}c_j$ and its right bigram $b_j = c_j c_{j+1}$, which c_j belongs to. In particular, the shallow bigram representation is defined as follows:

$$\mathbf{x}_j^{(b)} = \mathbf{W}^{(bs)} \left[\mathbf{e}_{j-1}^{(b)} \; \mathbf{e}_j^{(b)} \right] + \mathbf{b}^{(bs)}$$

where $\mathbf{W}^{(bs)} \in \mathbb{R}^{d_s \times d_b \times 2}$ is a 3-way tensor, $\mathbf{b}^{(bs)} \in \mathbb{R}^{d_s}$ is the bias vector. To efficiently compute all the shallow bigram representations, a convolutional layer with filter size 2, stride 1 and valid-padding is used.

Feature Fusion via Elementwise Maximum Merging. Since our model have got unigram shallow representation and bigram shallow representation in parallel from the same input sentence to get, the next problem is how to fuse them into a single representation. One straightforward method is to concatenate them into a representation with double-sized dimensionality. However, it is observed that such a concatenation leads to the phenomenon of overfitting. Instead, we fuse the shallow unigram and bigram representations via elementwise maximum merging:

$$\mathbf{x}_j^{(0)} = max\left(\mathbf{x}_j^{(u)}, \mathbf{x}_j^{(b)}\right)$$

It is expected that such an elementwise maximum operator could yield to a high-quality shallow feature representation.

In our model, both the unigram embedding and the bigram embedding matrices are both initialized randomly and get updated during the training phase, which makes our model a closed-set segmentor that does not rely on any external data or knowledge resource. In addition, the dimensionalities of the unigram embeddings, bigram embeddings and shallow representations are all set to 300 by default.

2.2 Deep Representations

The shallow representations have modeled the contextual information of characters, but the contextual information is limited on a small context window of size 3. To incorporate wider contextual information into the representations, we make use of a deep module that consists of multiple stacked convolutional layers, as illustrated in Fig. 3. Let L to be the number of convolutional layers in the deep module ($L = 4$ by default).

Because the task at present is to perform character-based CWS, we have to preserve the temporal resolution throughout the module. Therefore, we make the following design choices:

- The filter size in each convolutional layer is set to a fixed integer S (by default, $S = 3$), with padding such that the temporal resolution is preserved;
- The stride is set to 1 in each convolutional layer (otherwise, the temporal resolution would be reduced);
- We do not use any down sampling (pooling layer) between adjacent convolutional blocks, because the functionality of pooling is to reduce the temporal dimensions.

Let L denote the number of convolutional layers in the deep module. The working mechanism of the l-th convolutional block ($1 \leq l \leq L$) is described below:

- A convolutional layer with F filters is performed by taking the dot-product between each filter (or kernel) matrix and each window of size S in the input

sequence $\mathbf{x}^{(l-1)}$, resulting in F scalar values for each position j in input sentence. By default, the value of F is set to 600 for all convolutional layers in this module.
- Next, a element-wise ReLU activation function is applied to make nonlinear transformation, so negative activations are discarded.

Stacking such L convolutional layers together results in a receptive field of $((S-1)\times L+1)$ positions of the original input sentence. The receptive field of the units in the deeper layers of a convolutional network is larger. Deep neural networks can adaptively learn how to best combine the lower-level representations of S positions into a higher-level representation in a hierarchically layer-by-layer manner.

One simplest way is to use the output $\mathbf{x}^{(L)}$ from the L-th layer as the final deep representation. But we adopt another way in this paper: the final deep representation is calculated as the elementwise summation of the outputs from all the L layers in the deep module:

$$\mathbf{r} = \sum_{l=1}^{L} \mathbf{x}^{(l)}$$

where the elementwise summation has some sense of short-cut connections. Please note that it is only a problem of design choice, and both of them have similar segmentation performance.

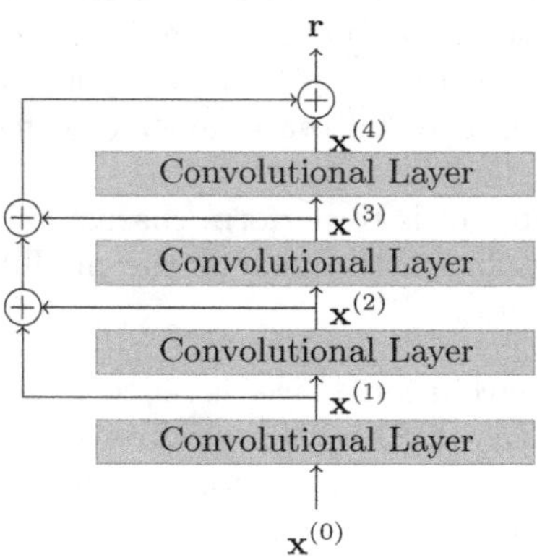

Fig. 3. A deep module of 4 convolutional layers

2.3 Tag Scores

After the final deep representations have been calculated, each character c_j $(1 \leq j \leq |\mathbf{s}|)$ is now represented as an F-dimensional vector $\mathbf{r}_j$. The next step is to transform the deep representation $\mathbf{r}_j$ into a K-dimensional vector of tag scores

$\mathbf{y}_j$, where the tag set adopted here is {'B', 'M', 'E', 'S'}, and hence $K = 4$. In the tag set, 'S' denotes a single character word, while 'B', 'M' and 'E' denotes the begin, middle and end of a multi-character word respectively.

To implement this transformation, our model uses a two-layer feed-forward neural network:

$$\mathbf{y}_j = f_2 \left(g \left(f_1 \left(\mathbf{r}_j \right) \right) \right)$$

where f_2 and f_1 are two affine transformations, and g is a element-wise ReLU activation.

Specifically, we have:

$$\mathbf{h}_j = \text{ReLU} \left(\mathbf{W}^{(s,1)} \cdot \mathbf{r}_j + \mathbf{b}^{(s,1)} \right)$$

and

$$\mathbf{y}_j = \mathbf{W}^{(s,2)} \cdot \mathbf{h}_j + \mathbf{b}^{(s,2)}$$

where $\mathbf{W}^{(s,1)}$ is a matrix of size $F \times F$, $\mathbf{b}^{(s,1)}$ is a vector of size F, $\mathbf{W}^{(s,2)}$ is a $F \times K$ matrix, and $\mathbf{b}^{(s,2)}$ is a vector of size K.

2.4 Dropout

Dropout is an effective technique to regularize neural networks by randomly drop units during training. It has achieved a great success when working with feed-forward networks [13], convolutional networks, or even recurrent neural networks [16].

In our model, dropout is applied to both the output of shallow representations and the input of the final layer in the deep representation module, which sets the values of units to zero with the same dropout rate (set to 0.6 as default value). We call it the technique $dropout_{normal}$, to distinguish from the following technique of $dropout_{block}$.

Besides the normal dropout technique, we also use another $dropout_{block}$ technique to make the model robust to unknown character unigrams or bigrams (OOVs). It drops unigrams and bigrams according to their frequencies in the training data. More specifically, the probability that a unigram c gets dropped is:

$$p_{blockdrop}(c) = \frac{M_u}{M_u + freq(c)}$$

and the probability to drop out a bigram b is

$$p_{blockdrop}(b) = \frac{M_b}{M_b + freq(b)}$$

where $freq(\cdot)$ denotes the frequency number of a unigram or bigram in the dataset, M_u and M_b are two positive numbers (set as 30 and 60 by default). Clearly, a unigram or bigram is more likely to be dropped out, if it appears less frequently in the training corpus.

2.5 Tag Prediction and Word Segmentation

Given the tag scores for a position j, the prediction $\hat{t}_j$ is the tag with the highest predicted tag score:

$$\hat{t}_j = \arg\max_k y_{j,k}$$

where $y_{j,k}$ is the predicted score of tag k at position j.

After all positions have their tags predicted, the sentence is segmented in a simple heuristic way: A character with tag 'B' or 'S' will start a new word, while a character with tag 'M' or 'E' will append itself to the previous word. As a result, the potential inconsistencies in predicted tags are resolved in a near-random manner. For example, the inconsistent adjacent predictions "BMB" will be implicitly changed to "BEB", "BBS" to "BES", etc.

2.6 Model Training

Given the training sentences and ground truth $\{\mathbf{s}_i, \mathbf{t}_i\}_{i=1}^N$, our goal is to learn the parameters that minimize the cross-entropy loss function:

$$\mathbf{L}(\Theta) = \frac{1}{\sum_{i=1}^N |\mathbf{s}_i|} \sum_{i=1}^{N} \sum_{j=1}^{|\mathbf{s}_i|} \log \frac{\exp y_{i,j,t_{i,j}}}{\sum_k \exp y_{i,j,k}}$$

where Θ is the set of all parameters, $t_{i,j}$ denotes the gold tag for the position j in sentence $\mathbf{s}_i$, $y_{i,j,k}$ denotes the score of tag k for the position j in $\mathbf{s}_i$.

Here, as a rule of thumb, we do not include a L2-regularization term in the loss function because dropout has been used to regularize our model.

We used Adam [7] to train our models with a learning rate of 0.0005, a first momentum coefficient $\beta_1 = 0.9$, and a second momentum coefficient $\beta_2 = 0.999$. Each model was trained for 50 epochs with minibatch size of 16 sentences.

3 Experiments

Datasets. To evaluate our model, we used two widely used benchmark datasets, PKU and MSR, provided by the Second SIGHAN International Chinese Word Segmentation Bakeoff[1] [6]. The segmentation results are evaluated by the *F-score*.

To make the comparison fair, we converted the Arabic numbers and English characters in the testing set of PKU corpus from half-width form to full-width form, because they are in full-width form in the training set. This conversion is commonly performed before segmentation in related research work. Except this conversion, we did not make any preprocessing on the datasets.

[1] http://sighan.cs.uchicago.edu/bakeoff2005/.

3.1 Results

Table 1 lists the closed-set results of our neural model, together with the best closed-set results in 2nd SIGHAN bakeoff (Best05) and several state-of-the-art neural models, on PKU and MSR datasets. It can be easily seen that our model has achieved the best performance among all the neural models in closed-set settings.

Table 2 summarizes the closed-set results of our model and the open-set results of several state-of-the-art neural CWS systems. It is astonishing that our model without using any pretrained embeddings has also achieved the best performance even when compared with the state-of-the-art neural systems that make use of various pretrained unigram, bigram or word embeddings.

Table 1. Comparison of closed-set F-score with other closed-set neural CWS systems

Models	PKU	MSR
Best05 (closed-set)	95.0	96.4
Zheng et al. [19] (closed-set)	92.4	93.3
Pei et al. [11] (closed-set)	93.5	94.4
Ma and Hinrichs [8] (closed-set)	95.1	96.6
Cai and Zhao [3] (closed set)	95.2	96.4
Our model (closed set)	**95.6**	**97.4**

Table 2. Comparison of closed-set F-score with other open-set neural CWS systems

Models	PKU	MSR
Zheng et al. [19] + *pretraining*	92.8	93.9
Pei et al. [11] + *pretraining*	94.0	94.9
Pei et al. [11] + *pretraining & bigram*	95.2	97.2
Cai and Zhao [3] + *pretraining*	95.5	96.5
Zhang et al. [17] (*with pretrained unigram, bigram and word embeddings*)	95.1	97.0
Our model (closed-set	**95.6**	**97.4**

In addition, when we replace the deep convolutional module with a BiLSTM module, it achieves similar F-score on both the datasets, but runs about 10 times slower on the same desktop with a Nvidia GTX1080Ti graphics card. Both of them are implemented with Tensorflow in Python.

3.2 Ablation Analysis

In our model, there are three main working techniques: bigram, deep module, and dropout. To investigate their contributions, we removed each of them from the model, the results are shown in Table 3. In addition, we also consider the contributions of the two distinct dropout techniques, $dropout_{normal}$ and $dropout_{block}$, respectively.

Table 3. Ablation analysis of our model on PKU dataset

Models	PKU
Our model	**95.6**
$-bigram$	95.4
$-deepmodule$	93.5
$-dropout_{normal}$	95.3
$-dropout_{block}$	94.5
−(both $dropout_{normal}$ and $dropout_{block}$)	94.3

It can be easily seen that all the main techniques have their own contribution to the performance of our model. Among all these techniques, the $dropout_{normal}$ and the *bigram* are relatively weak, while *deepmodule* and $dropout_{block}$ are more important. It can also be observed that $dropout_{block}$ has more contribution than $dropout_{normal}$, but they are complementary to each other.

4 Conclusion

In this paper, we propose a novel neural model for CWS, which is based on convolutional architecture. It uses an elementwise maximum operator to fuse the unigram and bigram features from a local context window into shallow representations, and then builds up deeper and deeper representations adaptively via a deep convolutional network. Experiments on two commonly-used datasets PKU and MSR have shown that our closed-set model has better performance, not only than several closed-set neural methods, but also than several open-set state-of-the-art neural models.

Our model is different from the existing neural ones in several aspects:

- The model makes use of deep convolutional network for CWS, where the receptive fields are sufficiently large for CWS, and the information at each position can flow to its adjacent positions bi-directionally. In comparision, existing methods that work on the basis of traditional window-based segmentation [8,11,19] have only limited receptive field.

- Recent approaches that make use of recurrent neural networks (typically, LSTM) have potentially infinite receptive field in building representations for characters in an input sentence. However, the sequential processing mechanism of recurrent neural networks makes it too costly to build hierarchical representations. Instead, the deep convolutional network is suitable for the exploitation of modern multi-core computation ability such as GPU.

Finally, as future work, it is possible to integrate external resources, such as pretrained unigram and bigram embeddings or domain lexicons, into our model, which is expected to achieve a better open-set segmentation performance.

Acknowledgments. This work is supported by National High-Tech R&D Program of China (863 Program) (No. 2015AA015404), and Science and Technology Commission of Shanghai Municipality (No. 14511106802). We are grateful to the anonymous reviewers for their valuable comments.

References

1. Andrew, G.: A hybrid markov/semi-Markov conditional random field for sequence segmentation. In: Proceedings of the 2006 Conference on Empirical Methods in Natural Language Processing, pp. 465–472 (2006)
2. Bengio, Y., Ducharme, R., Vincent, P., Jauvin, C.: A neural probabilistic language model. J. Mach. Learn. Res. **3**, 1137–1155 (2003)
3. Cai, D., Zhao, H.: Neural word segmentation learning for Chinese. In: Proceedings of the 54th Annual Meeting of the Association for Computational Linguistics, vol. 1, Long Papers, pp. 409–420. Association for Computational Linguistics, Berlin, Germany, August 2016
4. Chen, X., Qiu, X., Zhu, C., Liu, P., Huang, X.: Long short-term memory neural networks for Chinese word segmentation. In: Proceedings of the 2015 Conference on Empirical Methods in Natural Language Processing, pp. 1197–1206 (2015)
5. Collobert, R., Weston, J., Bottou, L., Karlen, M., Kavukcuoglu, K., Kuksa, P.: Natural language processing (almost) from scratch. J. Mach. Learn. Res. **12**, 2493–2537 (2011)
6. Emerson, T.: The second international Chinese word segmentation bakeoff. In: Proceedings of the Second SIGHAN Workshop on Chinese Language Processing, pp. 123–133 (2005)
7. Kingma, D., Ba, J.: Adam: A method for stochastic optimization. arXiv preprint arXiv:1412.6980 (2014)
8. Ma, J., Hinrichs, E.: Accurate linear-time Chinese word segmentation via embedding matching. In: Proceedings of the 53rd Annual Meeting of the Association for Computational Linguistics, pp. 1733–1743 (2015)
9. Mansur, M., Pei, W., Chang, B.: Feature-based neural language model and Chinese word segmentation. In: Proceedings of IJCNLP, pp. 1271–1277 (2013)
10. Mikolov, T., Sutskever, I., Chen, K., Corrado, G.S., Dean, J.: Distributed representations of words and phrases and their compositionality. In: Advances in Neural Information Processing Systems (NIPS), pp. 3111–3119 (2013)
11. Pei, W., Ge, T., Chang, B.: Max-margin tensor neural network for Chinese word segmentation. In: ACL, vol. 1, pp. 293–303 (2014)

12. Peng, F., Feng, F., McCallum, A.: Chinese segmentation and new word detection using conditional random fields. In: Proceedings of Coling, pp. 562–568 (2004)
13. Srivastava, N.: Improving neural networks with dropout. Ph.D. thesis, University of Toronto (2013)
14. Tseng, H., Chang, P., Andrew, G., Jurafsky, D., Manning, C.: A conditional random field word segmenter for SIGHAN bakeoff 2005. In: Proceedings of the Fourth SIGHAN Workshop on Chinese Language Processing, pp. 168–171 (2005)
15. Xue, N., Shen, L.: Chinese word segmentation as LMR tagging. In: Proceedings of the Second SIGHAN Workshop on Chinese Language Processing, vol. 17, pp. 176–179 (2003)
16. Zaremba, W., Sutskever, I., Vinyals, O.: Recurrent neural network regularization. arXiv preprint arXiv:1409.2329 (2014)
17. Zhang, M., Zhang, Y., Fu, G.: Transition-based neural word segmentation. In: Proceedings of the 54th Annual Meeting of the Association for Computational Linguistics, vol. 1, Long Papers, pp. 421–431. Association for Computational Linguistics, Berlin, Germany, August 2016
18. Zhang, Y., Clark, S.: Chinese segmentation with a word-based perceptron algorithm. In: Proceedings of the 45th Annual Meeting of the Association of Computational Linguistics, pp. 840–847 (2007)
19. Zheng, X., Chen, H., Xu, T.: Deep learning for Chinese word segmentation and POS tagging. In: Proceedings of the 2013 Conference on Empirical Methods in Natural Language Processing, pp. 647–657 (2013)

Improving Word Embeddings for Low Frequency Words by Pseudo Contexts

Fang Li(✉) and Xiaojie Wang

School of Computer, Beijing University of Posts and Telecommunications, Beijing, China
{golifang,xjwang}@bupt.edu.cn

Abstract. This paper investigates relations between word semantic density and word frequency. A distributed representations based word average similarity is defined as the measure of word semantic density. We find that the average similarities of low frequency words are always bigger than that of high frequency words, when the frequency approaches to 400 around, the average similarity tends to stable. The finding keeps correct with changes of the size of training corpus, dimension of distributed representations and number of negative samples in skip-gram model. It also keeps on 17 different languages. Basing on the finding, we propose a pseudo context skip-gram model, which makes use of context words of semantic nearest neighbors of target words. Experiment results show our model achieves significant performance improvements in both word similarity and analogy tasks.

Keywords: Word embedding · Low frequency word

1 Introduction

Representation of word meaning has long been a fundamental task in natural language processing. Traditional methods treat each word a symbol. Distributional representation [1,13,20] represented a word by its context vector, which is high-dimensional and sparse. Distributed representations (i.e. word embeddings) encode words as low-dimensional real-valued vectors. Lots of models, including Collobert and Weston embeddings (C&W) [6], HLBL [17], word2vec [15] and GloVe [18] etc., have been proposed for learning word embeddings. Word embeddings have been widely used in language modeling [2], NER [21], parsing [6] and some other natural language processing tasks.

Meanwhile, there was an extensive work on revealing the properties of distributed representations. [11] demonstrated that skip-gram negative sampling (SGNS) is an implicit weighted matrix factorization of the shifted point mutual information matrix. [12] pointed out that SGNS is an explicit matrix factorization of the words co-occurrence matrix.

Ideally, the vector space spanned by word embeddings is mainly driven by semantics of words [7]. And the frequency of a word should not be an important

M. Sun et al. (Eds.): CCL 2017 and NLP-NABD 2017, LNAI 10565, pp. 37–47, 2017.
https://doi.org/10.1007/978-3-319-69005-6_4

parameter. However, [19] found that word embeddings do contain frequency information, frequency is an important factor on word encoding. [21] evaluated Brown clusters based representations, C&W and HLBL word embeddings on NER task. Experiments showed that most of NER errors are made on words with low frequencies. Brown clusters based representations outperform other distributed representations on low frequency words.

Recently, some models have been proposed to improve embeddings for low frequency words. By exploiting the internal structures of Chinese words, [5] used Chinese characters as features for words with different frequencies. [3] made use of an alphabet based n-gram to improve the embeddings of low frequency words for morphologically rich languages. In generally, these models exploit features that can be shared among different words, thus low frequency word can be enhanced by these features.

However, there are still lots of questions remained for further exploring, such as what is the problem on embeddings of low frequency words? How low frequency hurt embeddings of words? Answers to these questions might provide a principled approach to improve the quality of embeddings for low frequency words.

This paper investigates some of the aforementioned questions. We start the investigation from word semantic density. A distributed representation based word average similarity is firstly defined as a measure for word semantic density. We then find an interesting phenomenon: low-frequency words always have bigger average similarities than those words with high frequency. Further experimental results show that there is a stable relation between average similarities and word frequency. The relation show stability under the different parameters of skip-gram model as well as different languages. Basing on the finding, we propose a pseudo context skip-gram model, which makes used of context words of semantic nearest neighbors of target words. Unlike the feature sharing approach [3,5], this strategy is not language dependent and can be applied in conjunction with other methods simultaneously. Experiment results show our model achieves significant performance improvements in both word similarity and analogy tasks.

2 The Empirical Relation

2.1 Semantic Nearest-Neighbors

Let C be a corpus of a language, D is the vocabulary of C, $D = \{w_1, ...w_i, ... w_{|D|}\}$. Let V_{w_i} be the distributed representation of word $w_i, i = 1, ..., |D|$. We denote the similarity between w_i and w_j as

$$sim(w_i, w_j) = cos\_sim(V_{w_i}, V_{w_j}) \tag{1}$$

where cos_sim denote cosine similarity.

A 154MB English corpus is used to train the skip-gram model[1] by word2vec[2] with its default parameter setting. The similarities between all words in D are then computed by Eq. (1). Table 1 gives top 10 nearest-neighbors of three words. The three words have different frequencies in the corpus. We can find that the similarities between top 10 nearest-neighbors and word "azeotrope" with frequency = 20 are bigger than those of word "invest" with frequency = 200, the similarities between top 10 nearest-neighbors and word "invest" are higher than those of word "manual" with frequency = 500. i.e., low frequency words are more similar to their nearest-neighbors than that of words with high frequency.

Table 1. Three words with their frequencies and top 10 nearest neighbors are shown. Those words are chosen by frequency from low, median and high. The similarity of each neighbor in top 10 nearest neighbors is also given.

Word	Frequency	Top 10 nearest-neighbors (similarity)
Azeotrope	20	D2O(0.888) eutectic(0.887) A1c(0.887) HDO(0.879) azeotropic(0.875) miscibility(0.873) COF(0.870) hydrophobicity(0.870) Saturation(0.870) SWNT(0.866)
Invest	200	recoup(0.783) investing(0.763) repay(0.747) privatize(0.743) invested(0.734) insure(0.720) allocate(0.719) innovate(0.717) exchequer(0.715) approvals(0.715)
Manual	500	bookkeeping(0.692) computerized(0.688) pantograph(0.666) Braille(0.664) manuals(0.664) typesetting(0.657) copying(0.643) QWERTY(0.635) automatic(0.627) Procedural(0.624)

Are these some special cases? Or is there a universal law behind? We further inspect it on all words in vocabulary.

2.2 Semantic Density

Let the semantic density of w_i be the average similarity between its word embedding and all other words in D, it is denoted by $avg\_sim(w_i)$ and calculated by Eq. (2).

$$avg\_sim(w_i) = \frac{1}{|D|} \sum_{w_j \in D} sim(w_i, w_j) \tag{2}$$

Let f_{w_i} be the frequency of word w_i, we then define the semantic density of the words with frequency $= K$. Given a frequency K, M words are uniformly sampled from the set of all words with frequency $= K$ (For simplification, M words instead of all words are sampled. We find $M = 50$ is enough in experiments). Let S_K denotes the set of these M words, $AvgS_K$ denotes average similarity of words with frequency $= K$, is then calculated by (3)

[1] CBOW has similar results. We therefore only give the results of skip-gram.
[2] https://code.google.com/archive/p/word2vec/.

$$AvgS_K = \frac{1}{M} \sum_{w_i \in S_K} avg\_sim(w_i) \quad (3)$$

$AvgS_K$ is computed for K range from 5 to 1000 in a 154 MB English corpus. Figure 1(a) is the curve of $AvgS_K$ about K. As depicted in the figure, when K increases, $AvgS_K$ declines, i.e., low frequency words have larger $AvgS_K$ than those with high frequency. low frequency words are closer to other words in average, they have bigger semantic density. More frequent words have lower $AvgS_K$ and lower semantic density. But when frequency reaches at 400 around, the curve tends to stable. i.e., words with big enough frequencies will have stable semantic density.

In order to inspect the change rate of the average similarity, we fit the K-$AvgS_K$ by a polynomial function, we find that a 5th order polynomial function $y = [-2.99, 8.63, -9.38, 4.75, -1.14, 3.88]^T[(10^{-3}x)^5, (10^{-3}x)^4, (10^{-3}x)^3, (10^{-3}x)^2, 10^{-3}x, 1(10^{-3}x)^5]$ fits the curve well, the polynomial function is also illustrated in Fig. 1(a). We then compute the gradient of the polynomial function. The gradient curve is presented in Fig. 1(b). These two figures demonstrate that as K increases, $AvgS_K$ decreases, but the rate of change continues to decline, when frequency is near about 400, the similarity reaches a stable value.

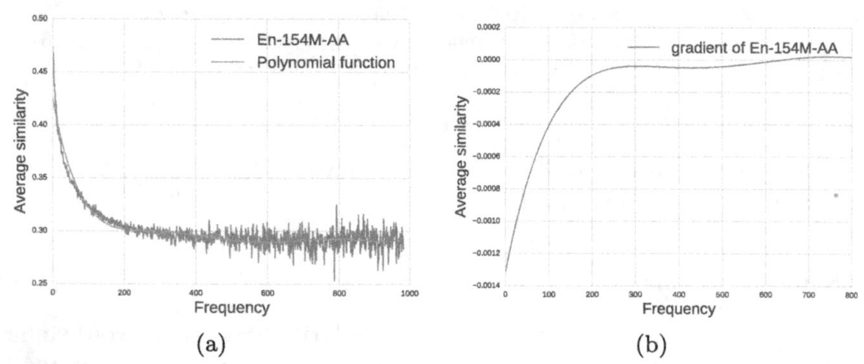

Fig. 1. The average similarity curve and its gradient curve are shown. Left: The average similarity curve on the 154 MB english corpus (En-154M-AA) and its polynomial fitting curve are shown. Right: The gradient of the polynomial fitting curve are given.

3 Invariance of the Relation

This section investigates the invariance of our proposed relation. We figure out if this relation holds for various settings for training word embeddings, including several important hyper-parameters in word embeddings learning model (skip-gram is considered in this paper) and languages. Details are described as follows.

- Dose this relation hold when trained on different but sufficiently large corpus size?
- Dose this relation hold with different dimensions?
- Dose this relation hold with different languages?
- Dose this relation hold with other hyper-parameters?

3.1 Corpus Size

Three Chinese corpora with the size of 300 MB, 5.6 GB and 8.4 GB are used for training word embeddings respectively. The K-$AvgS_K$ curves for different corpora are shown in Fig. 2(a). They have similar shapes but with different average similarity. Word embeddings trained on a large corpus has a lower average similarity than that on a small corpus, suggest that the word embeddings trained on a big corpus are more distinguishable than that on a small corpus. A word will become more distinguishable when it occurs more frequently. However, according to Zipf's law [24], even with a large corpus the low frequency words still exists. So do large semantic density of words. And the gradients of all curves tend to be zeroes when frequency nearly arrives at 400.

3.2 Dimension of Word Embeddings

Word embeddings with different dimensions from 100 to 1,000 (by step size of 100) are obtained. K-$AvgS_K$ curves for different dimensions are illustrated in Fig. 2(b). The legend "zh_100" means that the language is Chinese and the dimension is 100.

The figure shows that the shape of curves does not significantly change with the dimension. But embeddings with a larger dimension has lower average similarity and semantic density. That comply with the intuition that as the dimension grows, word embeddings become more sparse. As with other situations, the gradients of different curves also tends to zeroes when the frequency nearly approaches to 400.

3.3 Different Languages

So far, we have investigated the hypothesis on English and Chinese. How about other languages? We train word embeddings on seventeen languages. All corpora for different languages are available in wikipedia[3]. Two different English corpora (En and En_full) are used in this experiment.

The K-$AvgS_K$ curves for seventeen languages are presented in Fig. 2(c). The curves for all languages are similar. Specifically, they go down with the increasing of the frequency. And approach to stable values when the frequency equals 400 around. Different languages have different stable values. Among all those languages, Dutch has the biggest stable value, while French has the smallest one. The gradient of all K-$AvgS_K$ curves also tend to 0 when frequency is near

[3] https://dumps.wikimedia.org/backup-index.html.

400. From this figure, we draw the same conclusion as above that gradients of all $K\text{-}AvgS_K$ curves tend to be zeroes when the frequency is near 400. This implies that the relations between the frequency K and $AvgS_K$ hold. And 400 is the boundary of low frequency words and the other words for all seventeen languages.

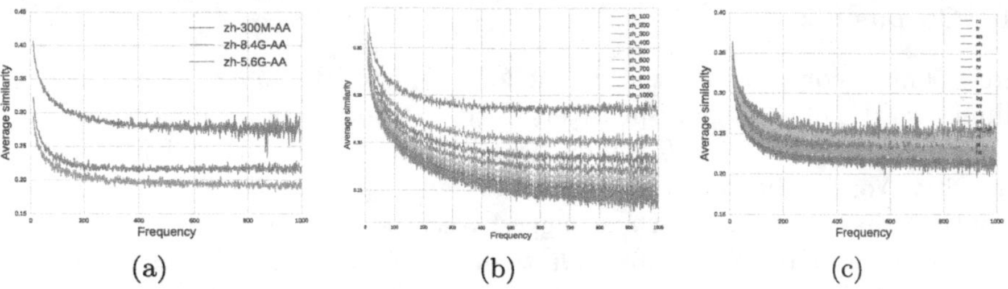

Fig. 2. Average similarities impacted by three factors, corpus size, embeddings dimension and languages are shown, respectively. (a) Average similarities with frequencies in three different sizes of corpora. (b) Average similarities with frequencies in different embeddings dimensions from 100 to 1,000 with the step size of 100. (c) Average similarities for seventeen languages are reported. and each language is represented by its ISO code.

3.4 General Discussion

Except for three parameters above, we have verified that the hypothesis is also invariant for other parameters, such as number of negative samples, rejection threshold of models. Due to the space limit we do not present here.

Our hypothesis, gives hints on how to improving word embeddings, especially for low frequency words. We will propose an efficient way in next section.

On the other hand, to explore reasons behind the linguistic phenomenon is also important. Polysemy might be a part explanation for the phenomenon. Since frequent words normally be more polysemous, therefore might have lower average similarities than those of low frequency words. Nevertheless, the phenomenon gives us more information. The invariance on different model parameters and different languages, decrease of $K\text{-}AvgSk$ curves stops when frequency beyond 400, all these cannot be simply explained by polysemy.

4 Pseudo-context Word Embedding

To improving word embeddings, we propose a strategy called "pseudo context" to get much more training data for low frequency words by making use of semantic nearest-neighbors of them. The strategy can be easily incorporated into various existing word embedding models. In this paper, we take skip-gram as an example to introduce the pseudo context based skip-gram (PCSG).

Let corpus $C = w_1, w_2, ..., w_N$ be a sequence of words. V is the vocabulary of all words in C. The objective function of skip-gram model is to maximize the log-likelihood of a center word w_n predicting its context word. The equation is shown in (4).

$$\mathcal{L} = \sum_{n=0}^{N} \sum_{c \in C_n} \log P(w_c|w_n) \tag{4}$$

where the context $C_n = n - L, ..., n - 1, ..., n + 1, ...n + L$ is the set of index of words within the sized L window of target word w_n. Evaluating the conditional probability $P(w_c|w_n)$ is computationally expensive, which involves the normalized probability of w_n predicting w_c over all other words in the vocabulary. Thus, skip-gram model employs negative sampling to approximate this probability. Its objective function is as follows,

$$\mathcal{L} = \sum_{n=0}^{N} \sum_{c \in C_n} l(w, c) \tag{5}$$

$$l(w, c) = \log \frac{1}{1 + e^{-V_c \cdot V_w}} + k \sum_{c' \sim P_D} \frac{1}{1 + e^{V_{c'} \cdot V_w}} \tag{6}$$

where V_w is the word vector of word w, and c is the word in the context of w. c' is a sample drawn form the distribution of negative words P_D. k is the number of negative samples, which is a trade-of between approximating accuracy and computational complexity.

In PCSG, different objective functions are used for high frequency words and low frequency words. A word is took as low frequency when its frequency is lower than a given threshold T. Objective function for high frequency words remain as in (5). For low frequency word w_m, a different object function is defined. We first construct a similar words set S_m for w_m. The set S_m consists of top N semantic nearest neighbor words of w_m. For any word w_s in this set, we take context words of it as context words of w_m as well. For a context word w_c of w_s, it may not be a true context word of w_m. However, since the two words w_s and w_m are similar, they tend to have similar context according to distributional hypothesis [10]. We call w_c as a **pseudo context** word of w_m. During the training, when w_m is updated, a word w_s from S_m is uniformly sampled, the objective is to maximize the probability of w_s predicting w_c. Equation (4) is therefore replaced by Eq. (7).

$$\mathcal{L} = \sum_{n=0}^{N} \sum_{c \in C_n, s \in S_n} \log P(w_c|w_n) + \log P(w_c|w_s) \tag{7}$$

Negative sampling method can also be applied. The corresponding objective function for low frequency word is (8).

$$\mathcal{L} = \sum_{n=0}^{N} \sum_{c \in C_n, s \in S_n} l(w,c) + l(s,c) \quad (8)$$

In which the two terms $l(w,c)$ and $l(s,c)$ are defined in Eq. (6).

5 Experiments

Implementation details. Our baselines are skip-gram (SG) model from word2vec program[4] and CWE+P model from CWE program[5]. Wikipedia corpus is used to train word vector for different languages. All the models are trained with 5 negative samples with rejection threshold 10^{-3} and keep words appearing at least 5 times. The dimension of word vectors is set to 100. By introducing pseudo context for low frequency words, our method increases the computational complexity by approximately 30% in English corpus. However, our implementation is well optimized, about 1.7 times faster than the word2vec implementation of skip-gram. Our code will be available online[6].

We compare the performance of different models on two word based tasks, word relatedness and analogy reasoning.

Table 2. Evaluation accuracies($\times$100) on analogy task. For semantic questions, we report the results on different sections and the total dataset.

	English							Chinese			
	Semantic						Syntactic	Semantic			
	Total	capital-common-countries	capital-world	currency	city-in-state	Family	Total	Total	capital-common-countries	city-in-state	Family
SG	38.29	64.29	41.75	2.94	15.38	72.22	54.25	67.98	70.33	76.57	48.48
PCSG	45.59	73.81	53.33	2.94	20.84	63.40	54.54	69.95	70.99	80.57	52.27
CWE	/	/	/	/	/	/	/	66.01	67.03	78.29	46.21
Δ	7.30	9.52	11.58	0	5.46	−8.82	0.29	1.96	0.66	2.28	3.79

Word analogy task. An analogy question is like "France is to Paris as Italy to X". In this example, the word X is predicted by finding a word whose vector has the highest cosine similarity with vector $V(France) - V(Italy) + V(Paris)$. Here "Rome" is the correct answer.

Two datasets, google analogy dataset [16] on English and the one from [5] on Chinese are used in our experiments. Analogy questions in English dataset are divided into semantic and syntactic questions. Semantic questions contain five sections. The example given above is from the "capital-common-countries" section of semantic question. An example of syntactic question is "free is to freely

[4] https://code.google.com/archive/p/word2vec/.
[5] https://github.com/Leonard-Xu/CWE.
[6] https://github.com/mklf/PCWE.

as usual is to X", where the answer is "usually". Chinese does not contain the same morphological information, so only semantic question is provided, which contains three sections.

Accuracies for sections and for the total dataset are reported in Table 2. In Chinese, besides SG model, CWE model [5] is also used for comparison. By training word and character embeddings together, CWE model also uses the information of Chinese characters. The results are reported in Table 2. We see that (1) PCSG substantially outperforms the other models on semantic questions in both English and Chinese datasets. (2) There is minor change on performances of syntactic questions. We infer the reason is that nearest neighbor words in S_n are semantically similar words of w_n, which have nearly no syntactic information. If syntactic information can be incorporated in the nearest neighbor word selection phase, for example, filtering out the subset of words with same prefix or suffix in S_n in morphologically rich languages, syntactic performance may also be improved. The detailed implementation is left for future work.

Table 3. Evaluation results on various datasets ($\rho \times 100$). For datasets RW, MEN and PKU500, the correlation coefficient only on low frequency (< 400) words are also measured.

	English					Chinese				German	
	WS353	RW		MEN		PKU500		C240	C297	ZG222	Gur350
		all	< 400	all	< 400	all	< 400				
SG	67.67	39.19	31.91	62.50	53.91	35.50	43.67	54.65	54.74	39.48	61.39
PCSG	69.36	42.59	36.40	65.22	57.33	36.86	48.31	56.85	57.03	44.80	62.71

Word relatedness task. This task contains a set of word pairs. The cosine distance of word vectors is computed to score the similarity between a pair of word. Then the spearman correlation coefficient ρ between scores by vector of words and human judgments are then obtained. A higher coefficient for word vectors means a better performance.

Several publicly available word similarity datasets in three languages are used. They consist of three English datasets, WordSim353 (WS353) [8], RareWords (RW) [14], MEN [4], three Chinese datasets PKU500 [22], CWE240(C240), CWE297(C297) [5] and two German datasets ZG222 [9], Gur350 [23]. Among those datasets, RW, MEN and PKU500 have 183, 732, 47 low frequency (frequency < 400) word pairs respectively. Whereas the other datasets contain less than 20 low frequency word pairs.

The spearman correlation coefficient ρ for different models and different datasets are shown in Table 3. For datasets RW, MEN and PKU500, the correlation coefficient only on low frequency words are also measured. We can find that (1) PCSG outperforms SG on all languages and datasets by a margin of 2%–5%. (2) More improvements are achieved for low frequency words on RW, MEN and PKU500. (3) The pseudo context strategy can be applied to different languages.

Evidently, introducing pseudo context helps to build better word vectors, especially for low frequency words. The results show word vectors trained by PCSG actually include more semantic information by making use of pseudo context.

6 Conclusion and Future Works

One of the goals of computational linguistics is to find interesting linguistic phenomena and reveal their natures in a computational way.

This paper finds some interesting linguistic phenomena based on distributed representations of words. A hypothesis on the relation between distributed representation based average similarities and the frequency of words is proposed. That is low frequency words have larger average similarities. As the frequency increases, the average similarity decreases. When the frequency reaches to 400 around, the average similarity becomes stable. Experimental results show that the relation holds on word embeddings trained by different sizes of corpora and parameter settings. Also, it holds on different languages as well.

Basing on those findings, we propose a pseudo context strategy for low-frequent words. By applying this strategy to skip-gram model, we achieve significant improvement on both word relatedness and analogy tasks, especially on low-frequent words.

Acknowledgments. This paper is supported by 111 Project (No. B08004)NSFC (No.61273365), Beijing Advanced Innovation Center for Imaging Technology, Engineering Research Center of Information Networks of MOE, and ZTE.

References

1. Baroni, M., Lenci, A.: Distributional memory: a general framework for corpus-based semantics. Comput. Linguist. **36**(4), 673–721 (2010)
2. Bengio, Y., Ducharme, R., Vincent, P., Jauvin, C.: A neural probabilistic language model. J. Mach. Learn. Res. **3**(Feb), 1137–1155 (2003)
3. Bojanowski, P., Grave, E., Joulin, A., Mikolov, T.: Enriching word vectors with subword information. arXiv preprint (2016). arXiv:1607.04606
4. Bruni, E., Boleda, G., Baroni, M., Tran, N.K.: Distributional semantics in technicolor. In: Proceedings of the 50th Annual Meeting of the Association for Computational Linguistics: Long Papers, vol. 1, pp. 136–145. Association for Computational Linguistics (2012)
5. Chen, X., Xu, L., Liu, Z., Sun, M., Luan, H.: Joint learning of character and word embeddings. In: Proceedings of IJCAI, pp. 1236–1242 (2015)
6. Collobert, R., Weston, J.: A unified architecture for natural language processing: deep neural networks with multitask learning. In: Proceedings of the 25th International Conference on Machine Learning, pp. 160–167. ACM (2008)
7. Faruqui, M., Tsvetkov, Y., Rastogi, P., Dyer, C.: Problems with evaluation of word embeddings using word similarity tasks. arXiv preprint (2016). arXiv:1605.02276
8. Finkelstein, L., Gabrilovich, E., Matias, Y., Rivlin, E., Solan, Z., Wolfman, G., Ruppin, E.: Placing search in context: the concept revisited. In: Proceedings of the 10th International Conference on World Wide Web, pp. 406–414. ACM (2001)

9. Gurevych, I.: Using the structure of a conceptual network in computing semantic relatedness. In: Dale, R., Wong, K.-F., Su, J., Kwong, O.Y. (eds.) IJCNLP 2005. LNCS, vol. 3651, pp. 767–778. Springer, Heidelberg (2005). doi:10.1007/11562214_67
10. Harris, Z.S.: Distributional structure. Word **10**(2—-3), 146–162 (1954)
11. Levy, O., Goldberg, Y.: Neural word embedding as implicit matrix factorization. In: Advances in Neural Information Processing Systems, pp. 2177–2185 (2014)
12. Li, Y., Xu, L., Tian, F., Jiang, L., Zhong, X., Chen, E.: Word embedding revisited: a new representation learning and explicit matrix factorization perspective. In: Proceedings of the Twenty-Fourth International Joint Conference on Artificial Intelligence, IJCAI, pp. 25–31 (2015)
13. Lund, K., Burgess, C.: Producing high-dimensional semantic spaces from lexical co-occurrence. Behav. Res. Meth. Instrum. Comput. **28**(2), 203–208 (1996)
14. Luong, T., Socher, R., Manning, C.D.: Better word representations with recursive neural networks for morphology. In: CoNLL, pp. 104–113 (2013)
15. Mikolov, T., Chen, K., Corrado, G., Dean, J.: Efficient estimation of word representations in vector space. arXiv preprint (2013). arXiv:1301.3781
16. Mikolov, T., Yih, W.T., Zweig, G.: Linguistic regularities in continuous space word representations. In: HLT-NAACL, vol. 13, pp. 746–751 (2013)
17. Mnih, A., Hinton, G.E.: A scalable hierarchical distributed language model. In: Advances in Neural Information Processing Systems, pp. 1081–1088 (2009)
18. Pennington, J., Socher, R., Manning, C.D.: Glove: global vectors for word representation. EMNLP **14**, 1532–1543 (2014)
19. Schnabel, T., Labutov, I., Mimno, D., Joachims, T.: Evaluation methods for unsupervised word embeddings. In: Proceedings of EMNLP (2015)
20. Schutze, H.: Dimensions of meaning. In: Proceedings of Supercomputing 1992, pp. 787–796. IEEE (1992)
21. Turian, J., Ratinov, L., Bengio, Y.: Word representations: a simple and general method for semi-supervised learning. In: Proceedings of the 48th Annual Meeting of the Association for Computational Linguistics, pp. 384–394. Association for Computational Linguistics (2010)
22. Wu, Y., Li, W.: Overview of the NLPCC-ICCPOL 2016 shared task: chinese word similarity measurement. In: Lin, C.-Y., Xue, N., Zhao, D., Huang, X., Feng, Y. (eds.) ICCPOL/NLPCC -2016. LNCS, vol. 10102, pp. 828–839. Springer, Cham (2016). doi:10.1007/978-3-319-50496-4_75
23. Zesch, T., Gurevych, I.: Automatically creating datasets for measures of semantic relatedness. In: Proceedings of the Workshop on Linguistic Distances, pp. 16–24. Association for Computational Linguistics (2006)
24. Zipf, G.K.: Human behavior and the principle of least effort (1950)

A Pipelined Pre-training Algorithm for DBNs

Zhiqiang Ma(✉), Tuya Li(✉), Shuangtao Yang(✉), and Li Zhang(✉)

College of Information Engineering, Inner Mongolia University of Technology, Hohhot, China
675898486@qq.com, 2297854548@qq.com, 60130107@qq.com, 2550896731@qq.com

Abstract. Deep networks have been widely used in many domains in recent years. However, the pre-training of deep networks is time consuming with greedy layer-wise algorithm, and the scalability of this algorithm is greatly restricted by its inherently sequential nature where only one hidden layer can be trained at one time. In order to speed up the training of deep networks, this paper mainly focuses on pre-training phase and proposes a pipelined pre-training algorithm because it uses distributed cluster, which can significantly reduce the pre-training time at no loss of recognition accuracy. It's more efficient than greedy layer-wise pre-training algorithm by using the computational cluster. The contrastive experiments between greedy layer-wise and pipelined layer-wise algorithm are conducted finally, so we have carried out a comparative experiment on the greedy layer-wise algorithm and pipelined pre-training algorithms on the TIMIT corpus, result shows that the pipelined pre-training algorithm is an efficient algorithm to utilize distributed GPU cluster. We achieve a 2.84 and 5.9 speed-up with no loss of recognition accuracy when we use 4 slaves and 8 slaves. Parallelization efficiency is close to 0.73.

Keywords: Component · Deep networks · Pre-training · Greedy layer-wise · RBM · Pipelined

1 Introduction

Recently, deep networks have been widely used in many domains because of its powerful modeling capacity, including speech recognition [1], image recognition [2] and natural language processing [3]. However, deep neural networks have not been discussed much in machine learning literature before Hinton et al. introduced a greedy layer-wise unsupervised pre-training algorithm to train such multi-layer neural networks, a reasonable explanation is that there were no efficient algorithms to train such deep neural networks, since gradient-based optimization starting from random initialization appears helpless [4]. The greedy layer-wise unsupervised pre-training algorithm can quickly find a fairly good set of parameters by greedily training one layer at a time, even with millions of parameters and many hidden layers. Reference [5] successfully trained a deep belief networks for MNIST digit classification and achieved better digit classification than any discriminative learning algorithms. Then this greedy layer-wise

M. Sun et al. (Eds.): CCL 2017 and NLP-NABD 2017, LNAI 10565, pp. 48–59, 2017.
https://doi.org/10.1007/978-3-319-69005-6_5

algorithm was analyzed and extended in [6] which made it become a general algorithm to initialize deep networks.

Since Greedy layer-wise pre-training algorithm was proposed, it proved to be effective by lots of successful practices. However, scalability of greedy layer-wise pre-training algorithm is greatly restricted by its inherently sequential nature and only one hidden layer can be trained at one time because of data dependency. As the training data and the depth of deep networks continue to grow, the pre-training of deep networks becomes more and more time-consuming, despite the use of high performance GPU and other optimization strategies [7].

In order to speed up the training of deep networks, this paper proposes a pipelined pre-training algorithm for distributed cluster, which can significantly reduce the pre-training time at no loss of recognition accuracy. It's more efficient than the greedy layer-wise pre-training algorithm and it speeds up the training of deep networks obviously by using the computational resources of distributed cluster. The outline of this paper is as follows: Sect. 2 mainly discusses previous works on parallelization of deep networks training. Section 3 briefly introduces restricted Boltzmann machine deep belief networks and greedy layer-wise pre-training algorithm. In Sect. 4 there is a detail description of pipelined pre-training algorithm. In Sect. 5, the experiments are conducted and discussed. Section 6 summarizes the works in this paper and gives some suggestions on future works.

2 Related Work

Many efforts have been devoted to using the distributed cluster in order to accelerate the training of deep networks. In previous works, parallelization of deep networks training mainly includes model parallelism and data parallelism [8].

To facilitate the training of super large deep networks, Google developed a framework that is called DistBelief, it supports parallel training of super large deep networks on CPU cluster [9]. The success of DistBelief shows that the parallel performance advantage depends on the model's connection structure and computing requirements. Reference [10] developed a neural-net training framework which adopted different versions of data parallelism. Each slave node in the framework has a copy of the entire model and has a different randomly selected subset of SGDs on the copy. After all slaves process a fixed number of training data, the copies across all slaves will be averaged and re-distributed to each slave for further training until all training cases are processed.

GPU-based distributed parallelization is more common compared to CPU-based distributed parallelization, because the use of a smaller number of GPU cards can achieve satisfactory acceleration. However, a number of existing deep learning frameworks do not support distributed GPU parallelization across multiple machines currently, most of them just can take advantage of GPUs on the same machine, such as Torch [9] and Theano [10]. In order to enhance these distributed GPU popular framework. Spark Net [11] was proposed, which supports to train deep networks in Spark and it achieves a 4–5 times speedup with 10 machines equipped GPU cards. In order to overcome the difficulty of parallelize back-propagation algorithm, asynchronous stochastic gradient descent algorithm (ASCD) was used in fine-tune the DNN on multi-GPU cards in [12]. Each GPU computes gradient on the latest parameters independently and updates the parameters asynchronously. In this way, a 3.2 times speedup was achieved with 4 GPU cards without any performance loss. In order to speed up the training of Multilingual DNN on multiple GPU cards, [13] proposes two distribution frameworks which is called DistModel and DistLang. Each GPU trains an instance of the multilingual DNN by a part of training data in DistModel, and these parallel model instances are averaged periodically after a pre-defined number of mini-batches. The multilingual DNN instances are trained separately by languages without any communications in DistLang. In essence, these two distribution frameworks are both belong to data parallelism.

Besides model parallelism and data parallelism, there are also other parallel strategies have been proposed for deep networks training. Reference [14] found that the pipelined back-propagation can update models with delayed gradient and allow training layers parallel. Experiments showed that the pipelined BP is an efficient way of utilizing multiple GPUs in a single machine. It achieved 1.9 and 3.3 times speed-up with 2 and 4 GPUs at no loss of recognition accuracy. However, this strategy is only suitable for discriminative training. Different from above acceleration strategies, [15] diverted its attention to the per-training phase and proposed a synchronized greedy layer-wise algorithm. The synchronized algorithm allows training different layer parallel by multiple threads running on different cores with regular synchronization. Experiments on dimensionality reduction of MNIST showed that this algorithm achieved 26% speed-up compared to greedy layer-wise pre-training algorithm with the same reconstruction accuracy.

3 DBN and Greedy Layer-Wise Algorithm

DBN is a deep generative model with many layers of hidden causal. It can be learned efficiently by stacking multiple RBMs from bottom to top with greedy layer-wise pre-training algorithm. The pre-training of DBNs mainly include three steps as shown in Fig. 1 (from left to right).

Left: construct a RBM with an input layer v and a hidden layer L_1. The number of units in input layer depends on the dimensionality of input data, then use CD-1algorithm to train this RBM. It will obtain one layer representation from input data after the training is finished, and the representation will be used as input for second

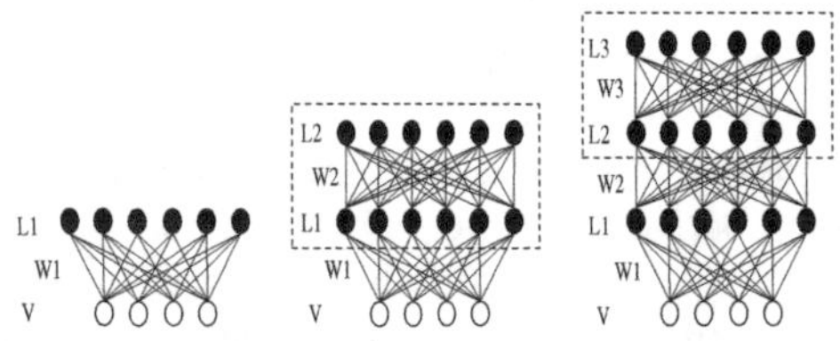

Fig. 1. Greedy layer-wise pre-training of DBNs.

RBM. In this paper, the activations of each hidden unit are chosen as the representations.

Middle: Hidden layer L_2 is newly added layer and the second RBM is constructed by L_1 and L_2. Then train it like the first RBM, the only difference is that input for the second RBM is computed according to Eq. (1) from input data according to RBM.

$$p(h_j = 1|v) = \sigma\left(b_j + \sum\nolimits_i v_i w_{ij}\right) \quad (1)$$

Right: continue to stack new hidden layers on the top and train it as previous until the DBNs are all trained.

Since greedy layer-wise algorithm was proposed, it has been proved to be effective through lots of successful practices [7]. However, scalability of greedy layer-wise algorithm is greatly restricted. L_2 has to wait until L_1 have finished all training task, because L_2 needs the output from L_1 as input. The greedy layer-wise algorithm is quite simple, as illustrated in Algorithm 1. Function RBM update means the training of RBM with CD-1.

```
Algorithm 1: Greedy Layer-wise algorithm
ϵ: learning rate for CDK algorithm
L: number of hidden layers
W^i: weight matrix
b^i : bias vector for hidden layer
-----------------------------------------
split dataset into batches[]
initialize
For = 1 to do
  Initialize =0, =0
  For e = 1 to epoch do
For mini-batch in batches
RBMupdate (mini-batch, ϵ, W^i , b^i , b^(i-1) )
End for
  End for
End for
```

4 Pipelined Pre-training Algorithm

The data dependency between adjacent hidden layers makes it hard to parallel the pre-training of DBNs. In order to achieve the parallelization, it is necessary to overcome the inherently sequential nature of Greedy Layer-wise algorithm. This paper proposes a pipelined pre-training algorithm with this intent, which is more efficient than the greedy layer-wise pre-training algorithm and it speeds up the training of deep networks obviously by using the computational resources of distributed cluster.

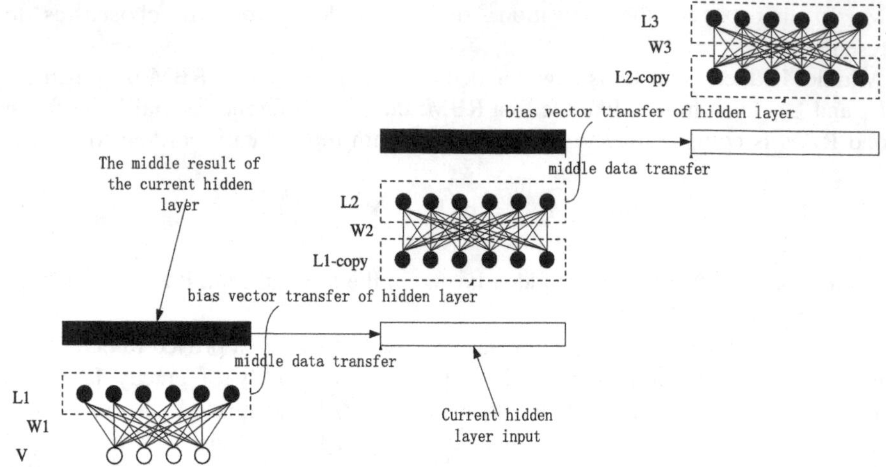

Fig. 2. Data transfer in DNN pipelined pre-training

A new concept called middle result is proposed in pipelined pre-training algorithm, that is shown in Fig. 2.

When using CD-1 to train the first RBM in Fig. 1, the middle result is calculated. It computes the activation probability of each hidden unit via Eq. (1) again, and get the binary state vector h1, which is the reconstruction for h0. At this point, all the parameters can be updated via Eqs. (2), (3) and (4).

$$\Delta w_{ij} = \epsilon\left(\langle v_i h_j \rangle_{data} - \langle v_i h_j \rangle_{recon}\right) \tag{2}$$

$$\Delta a_i = \epsilon\left(\langle v_i \rangle_{data} - \langle v_i \rangle_{recon}\right) \tag{3}$$

$$\Delta b_j = \epsilon\left(\langle h_j \rangle_{data} - \langle h_j \rangle_{recon}\right) \tag{4}$$

The middle result can be used as input for the second RBM. Thus, hidden layer L_1 and L_2 are trained in parallel. In order to make a detailed description of the proposed algorithm, we make following statements:

L_i is the ith hidden layer, L_0 is the input layer.
B_i is the bias vector of L_i.
L_{i-copy} is the copy of hidden layer L_i.
L_{i-1} and form RBM_i that is trained at M_i.
L_{i-copy} and L_{i+1} form RBM_{i+1} that is trained at M_{i+1}.

Generally, the pipelined pre-training algorithm mainly does three things:

1. Segment DBNs into multiple RBMs and assign each RBM to an exclusive computer. For example, as shown in Fig. 3 (left), RBM1 and RBM2 are adjacent and share the hidden layer L_1. In order to make RBM1 and RBM2 independent of each

other, we use the copy of L_1 instead of L_1 to construct RBM2, thus RBM2 is formed by L_{i-copy} and L_2.

2. Start pre-training from RBM1 which is formed by input layer and hidden layer L_1. Transmit B_1 and the middle result to RBM2 after RBM1 finishes a training of K mini-batches, initializing the bias of L_{1-copy} with B_1 at the first when RBM2 receives them and then start the training of RBM2 with middle result. The transmission of biases and middle results is achieved by message communication between computers, which is indicated by dotted line in Fig. 3 (right).
3. Train RBM_{i+1} with B_i and the middle result from RBM_i until all hidden layers are trained. Collecting all parameters in each RBM after pre-training is finished and begin to fine tune the entire network.

It should be pointed out that RBM_i is composed of hidden layer L_i and hidden layer L_{i-1} of the DBN. The pseudo-code of pipelined pre-training algorithm is shown in Algorithm 2.

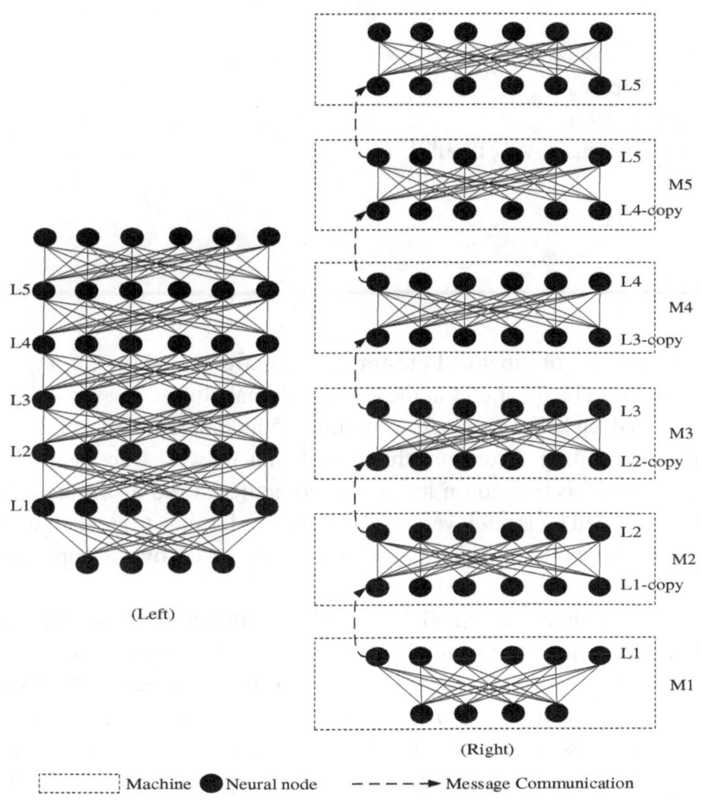

Fig. 3. Pipelined per-training of DBNs

Algorithm 2: Pipelined pre-training algorithm
ϵ: learning rate for CDK algorithm
L: number of hidden layers
W^i: weight matrix
b^i : bias vector for hidden layer
o_e^i:middle result of hidden layer at epoch e

```
Master:
Initialize cluster
split DBNs to slaves
Slave:
Fori = 1 to L parallel do
InitializeW^i , b^i
  For e = 1 to epoch do
If i = 1
batches[] = split from dataset
   Initializeb^0
Else
receive o_e^{i-1} , b^{i-1} from L_{i-1}
batches[] = split from o_e^{i-1}
For mini-batch in batches
RBMupdate (mini-batch, ε, W^i , b^i ,b^{i-1} )
End for
Send o_e^i , b^i to L_{i+1}
    End for
End for
```

The training process of pipelined pre-training algorithm is shown in Fig. 3 (Right), all hidden layers are trained parallel in the computational cluster. As shown in Fig. 3, in order to pre-train a deep belief networks containing 5 hidden layers (L1, L2, L3, L4, L5) with pipelined pre-training algorithm, the deep belief networks are segmented into 5 RBMs, and each RBM is trained on its special computer in the distributed cluster. For example, RBM1 formed by input layer and hidden layer L1, it is trained on machine M1, RBM2 formed by the copy of hidden layer L1 (represented by L1-copy) and hidden layer L2, it is trained on Machine M2.

In pipelined pre-training, when RBM1 finishes a training of K mini-batches every time, it will produce a number of middle results, and update B_1 (biases of hidden layer L1) K times. Then, these middle result and B_1 will be transmitted to RBM2 through message communication. It first sets the biases of L1-copy to B_1 according to the rule that biases of the copy should always be consistent with the biases of its original after RBM2 receives the middle result and B_1, and then begins the training with received middle result. Actually, every time RBM2 finishes a training of K mini-batches, it also produces some middle results, and updates the biases of L1-copy. But these updates will not be transmitted backward to RBM1 and the updated biases of L1-copy only survive to next communication. The biases of the L1-copy will always be set to B_1 that received from RBM1, because RBM1 has been trained with more training data, the biases of L1 is more suitable to training data.

5 Experiment

In order to better understand the advantage brought by pipelined pre-training algorithm, experiments are performed on TIMIT corpus with the task of speech recognition. TIMIT is a popular corpus of speech recognition, and many recognition experiments have been conducted on this popular corpus, and greedy layer-wise algorithm is also evaluated on it. So, it's ideal for evaluating pipelined pre-training algorithm.

In the TIMIT corpus experiment, this paper carries on the contrast experiment of the greedy layer-wise unsupervised pre-training algorithm and the pipelined pre-training algorithm in different hidden layers. The experimental data for TIMIT are shown in Table 1.

Table 1. Import parameters.

Parameter name	Parameter value
Activation function	tanh
Number of neural units in hidden layer	1024
Initial learning rate of pre-training	0.015
The final learning rate	0.002
K value of CD-K algorithm	1
Pre-training cycle times	20
Mini-batch size	256

In order to conduct pipelined pre-training of DBNs, a distributed parallel framework oriented distributed cluster is introduced, and the architecture is shown in Fig. 4. This paper only makes a brief introduction about this framework. It adopts master-slave structure, the master node is responsible for the schedule and monitor of entire DBNs during pre-training, slaves are responsible for the training of each hidden layer. In each slave, training work is done by Theano, and middle results are transmitted through message communication. All slaves (eight slaves) are equipped with four 3.20 GHz CPU and one GPU card GeForce GTX 660. All distributed experiments are conducted in this framework.

5.1 Recognition Accuracy

Three deep belief networks are pre-trained using greedy layer-wise and pipelined pre-training algorithm respectively, and the sentence recognition error rate shown in Table 2.

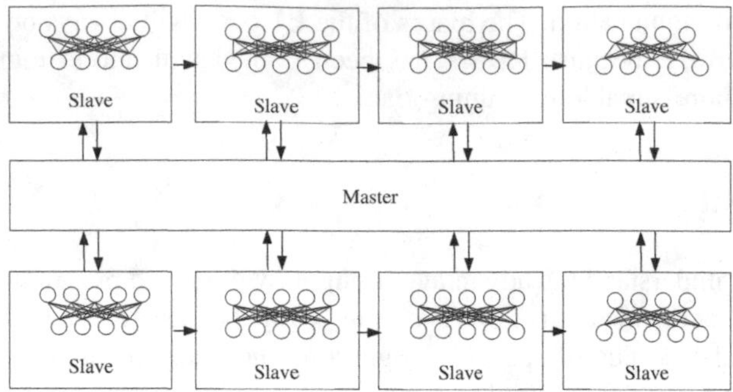

Fig. 4. Distributed experiment framework

Table 2. Recognition error rate of each DBN

Platform	Algorithm	The number of layers of hidden layers	Sentence recognition error rate
Theano	Greedy layer-wise algorithm	4	22.81%
		5	19.92%
		6	18.35%
Pipelined pre-training framework	Pipelined pre-training algorithm	4	23.43%
		5	20.02%
		6	18.72%
Kaldi	Greedy layer-wise algorithm	4	22.81%
		5	19.92%
		6	18.35%

5.2 Time Complexity of Pipelined Pre-training Algorithm

Under the premise of no loss of recognition accuracy, pipelined pre-training algorithm is more efficient and it speeds up the pre-training of deep networks obviously by using the computational cluster. Time of all pre-trainings is shown in Table 3. Before discussion, it should be pointed out that all pre-trainings using pipelined pre-training algorithm are trained with enough computers, which means that each hidden layer is trained on an exclusive computer.

In Table 3, L indicates the number of hidden layers in deep belief networks and M indicates the number of computers in distributed cluster. The first row (red units) is the pre-training time for DBNs on a single machine (single GPU) using greedy layer-wise pre-training algorithm. Second row (yellow units) is the pre-training time for DBNs on a single machine (single GPU) using pipelined pre-training algorithm. Other rows (green units) are the pre-training time for DBNs in a distributed cluster with pipelined pre-training algorithm, each slave in the distributed cluster has only one GPU card. These blank units in Table 3 means there are no experiments conducted.

Table 3. Time of each pre-training.

M	L				
	4	5	6	7	8
1	68.68	90.3	113.67	139.78	166.17
1	67.89	90.12	112.71	139.82	168.02
4	24.17				
5		25.09			
6			25.95		
7				26.69	
8					28.15

As shown in Table 3, the pre-training time grows sharply with the increase of hidden layers when using greedy layer-wise algorithm to pre-train DBNs on a single computer. A DBN having 4 hidden layers can be trained with 68.68 min, but it needs 166.17 min to pre-train a 8-hidden layers DBN, the pre-training time increases by 97.49 min. Pipelined pre-training can significantly reduce the pre-training time compared to greedy layer-wise algorithm, increasing the number of hidden layers does not lead to a dramatic increase in the training time anymore. And the increase in training time using pipelined pre-training algorithm is slow and gentle. For example, pre-training time of a DBN with 4 hidden layers is 24.17 min and it's 28.15 in a 8-hidden layers DBN, there is only a 3.98 minutes-growth.

When using pipelined pre-training algorithm to pre-train a deep belief networks with N hidden layers (represented by L1, L2, …, LN), training process is shown in Fig. 5. As shown in Fig. 5, Blank rectangle indicates a training of K mini-batches in current RBM. Solid line with arrow indicates the beginning of next K mini-batches pre-training in current RBM. Dotted line indicates the transmission of middle result and biases between original hidden layer and its copy. The trainings between these RBMs are not completely parallel. Upper layer will have a short delay compared to lower layer, because it has to wait for the lower layer to finish a K mini-batches training, transmit middle results and biases. For example, R2 has a short delay compared to R1, R3 has a short delay compared to R2, and the delay nearly equals to the time of a K mini-batches pre-training, this is why there exists a tiny growth in Table 3.

5.3 Speed-Up of Pipelined Pre-training Algorithm

The speed up of pipelined pre-training algorithm is shown in Fig. 6, which is calculated from Table 3.

The acceleration of pipelined pre-training algorithm mainly benefits the simple connectivity structure. Each slave node only connects two other slave nodes, which greatly reduce the communication overheads of the cluster during the per-training. There is few data needs to be transmitted between slaves compared to other

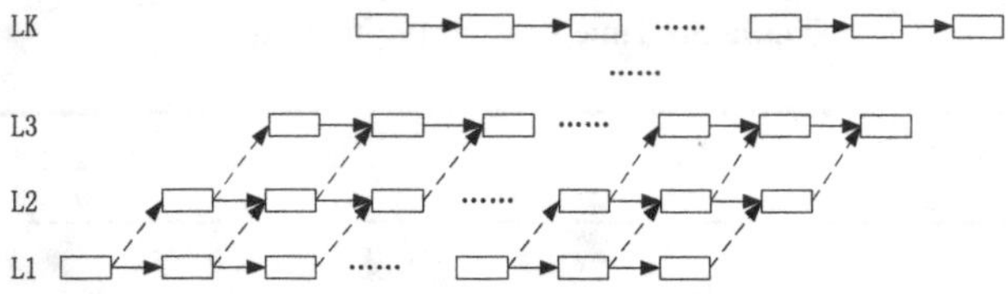

Fig. 5. Pipelined pre-training of a k hidden layers

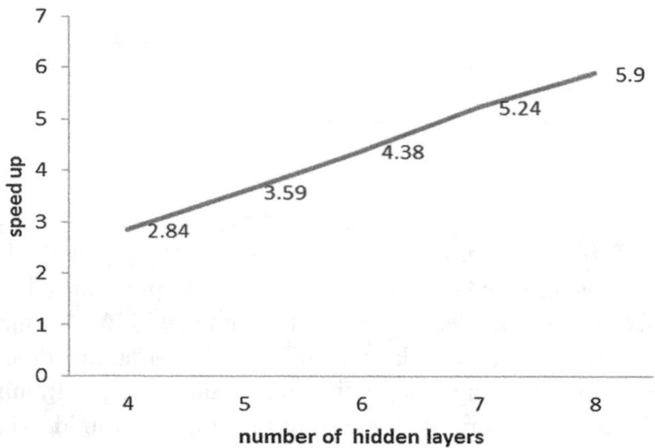

Fig. 6. Speed up of pipelined pre-training algorithm

parallelisms. The data that needs to be transmitted between slaves in every communication only contains K mini-batches middle results and a bias vector, which are surprisingly few compared to the entire model.

6 Conclusion

In order to accelerate the training of deep networks, many efforts have been devoted to leveraging distributed cluster to speed up the training of deep networks, but previous works mainly concentrate on the fine-tuning phase. In order to overcome the inherently sequential nature of greedy layer-wise algorithm, a pipelined pre-training algorithm is proposed, which is more efficient than the greedy layer-wise pre-training algorithm and it speeds up the training of deep networks obviously by using distributed cluster. For the above experimental results through the TIMIT corpus, we know that speed up of the proposed algorithm get a linear increase with the number of slave node and the parallelization efficiency is close to 0.73 compared to greedy layer wise algorithm. In addition, Pipelined pre-training algorithm is more suitable for distributed cluster, it's easy to implement. Although all experiments in this paper are conducted on GPU, the proposed algorithm also supports CPU pre-training well.

However, there are still lots of works to do in the future. We will mainly concentrate on two things: (1) Expands pipelined pre-training algorithm to other types of deep networks. (2) Parallel the training of a hidden layer to more computers rather a single machine.

Acknowledgments. Funding project: National Natural Science Foundation of China (61650205). Inner Mongolia Autonomous Region Natural Sciences Foundation project (2014MS0608). Inner Mongolian University of Technology key Fund (ZD201118).

References

1. Dahl, G.E., et al.: Context-dependent pre-trained deep neural networks for large-vocabulary speech recognition. IEEE Trans. Audio Speech Lang. Process. **20**(1), 30–42 (2012)
2. Krizhevsky, A., Sutskever, I., Hinton, G.E.: Imagenet classification with deep convolutional neural networks. In: Advances in Neural Information Processing Systems (2012)
3. Sarikaya, R., Hinton, G.E., Deoras, A.: Application of deep belief networks for natural language understanding. IEEE/ACM Trans. Audio Speech Lang. Process. **22**(4), 778–784 (2014)
4. Bengio, Y.: Learning deep architectures for AI. Found. Trends® Mach. Learn. **2**(1), 1–127 (2009)
5. Hinton, G.E., Osindero, S., Teh, Y.-W.: A fast learning algorithm for deep belief nets. Neural Comput. **18**(7), 1527–1554 (2006)
6. Bengio, Y., et al.: Greedy layer-wise training of deep networks. In: Advances in Neural Information Processing Systems, vol. 19, p. 153 (2007)
7. Dean, J., et al.: Large scale distributed deep networks. In: Advances in Neural Information Processing Systems (2012)
8. Seide, F., et al.: On parallelizability of stochastic gradient descent for speech DNNs. In: 2014 IEEE International Conference on Acoustics, Speech and Signal Processing (ICASSP). IEEE (2014)
9. Collobert, R., Kavukcuoglu, K., Farabet, C.: Torch7: a matlab-like environment for machine learning. In: BigLearn, NIPS Workshop. No. EPFL-CONF-192376 (2011)
10. Bergstra, J., et al.: Theano: deep learning on gpus with python. In: NIPS 2011, BigLearning Workshop, Granada, Spain (2011)
11. Moritz, P., et al.: SparkNet: Training Deep Networks in Spark (2015). arXiv preprint: arXiv: 1511.06051
12. Zhang, S., et al.: Asynchronous stochastic gradient descent for DNN training. In: 2013 IEEE International Conference on Acoustics, Speech and Signal Processing (ICASSP). IEEE (2013)
13. Miao, Y., Zhang, H., Metze, F.: Distributed learning of multilingual DNN feature extractors using GPUs (2014)
14. Chen, X., et al.: Pipelined back-propagation for context-dependent deep neural networks. In: INTERSPEECH (2012)
15. Santara, A., et al.: Faster learning of deep stacked autoencoders on multi-core systems using synchronized layer-wise pre-training (2016). arXiv preprint: arXiv:1603.02836

Enhancing LSTM-based Word Segmentation Using Unlabeled Data

Bo Zheng, Wanxiang Che(✉), Jiang Guo, and Ting Liu

Research Center for Social Computing and Information Retrieval,
Harbin Institute of Technology, Harbin, China
{bzheng,car,jguo,tliu}@ir.hit.edu.cn

Abstract. Word segmentation problem is widely solved as the sequence labeling problem. The traditional way to this kind of problem is machine learning method like conditional random field with hand-crafted features. Recently, deep learning approaches have achieved state-of-the-art performance on word segmentation task and a popular method of them is LSTM networks. This paper gives a method to introduce numerical statistics-based features counted on unlabeled data into LSTM networks and analyzes how it enhances the performance of word segmentation model. We add pre-trained character-bigram embedding, pointwise mutual information, accessor variety and punctuation variety into our model and compare their performances on different datasets including three datasets from CoNLL-2017 shared task and three datasets of simplified Chinese. We achieve the state-of-the-art performance on two of them and get comparable results on the rest.

Keywords: Word segmentation · Statistics-based features · Neural network · Unlabeled data

1 Introduction

Most of the natural language processing tasks are processed in the units of words. In order to do downstream tasks, word segmentation is basic and important in those languages like Chinese and Japanese which are written in continuous sequences of characters, without delimiters between words. For Vietnamese, there are two kinds of white spaces between characters, one is inside words, the other one is between words. The goal of word segmentation for Vietnamese is to recognize these two kinds of white spaces. Word segmentation problem is widely solved as the sequence labeling problem. The traditional way to this kind of problem is machine learning method like conditional random field [5] with hand-crafted features. Neural network-based models have been extensively used in natural language processing during recent years, due to their strong capability of automatical feature learning. LSTM networks is a popular method on word segmentation task. A meaningful way to improve the performance of existing approaches is introducing more helpful features into the basic model or finding new ways to introduce these existing features.

M. Sun et al. (Eds.): CCL 2017 and NLP-NABD 2017, LNAI 10565, pp. 60–70, 2017.
https://doi.org/10.1007/978-3-319-69005-6_6

Previous researchers have tried to use auto-segmented result of large scale unlabeled data [13] or statistical magnitudes like mutual information [6], accessory variety [2] to help the supervised learning system. Performance improvement is achieved in their works. However, those previous works use the statistical results as discrete features while it may cause the problem of missing information. For example, [10] only uses the integer part of the mutual information, which will lose the information of the fractional part. To the best of our knowledge, there hasn't been any work that feeds numerical statistics-based features into LSTM networks. We think it is worth to study since numerical features seem more suitable than discrete features in LSTM networks. In this work, we present an approach that directly uses numerical statistics-based features [10] counted on unlabeled data to enhance word segmentation based on LSTM networks. The statistics-based features we utilize include pointwise mutual information, accessor variety and punctuation variety [10]. We also use pre-trained character-bigram embeddings to replace randomly initialized ones. We conduct our experiments on six datasets including three datasets from CoNLL-2017 shared task and three datasets of simplified Chinese. We achieve the state-of-the-art performance on two of them and get comparable results on the rest of them.

2 Related Work

Neural network approaches are popular in word segmentation task, [9] used a tensor neural network to achieve extensive feature combinations, capturing the interaction between characters and tags. [7] combined semi-CRF with neural network to solve NLP segmentation tasks, their experiments show that their neural semi-CRF model benefits from representing the entire segment. [14] proposed a transition-based neural word segmentation model, they replaced the manually-designed discrete features the neural features in a word-based segmentation framework. Both [14] and [7] used word-level information. [1] proposed a novel neural network framework which thoroughly eliminates context windows and can utilize complete segmentation history.

Using unlabeled data to enhance Chinese word segmentation has also been widely applied. [10] proposed a unified solution to include features derived from unlabeled data to a discriminative learning model based on conditional random field. The feature set includes mutual information, accessor variety, punctuation variety and other statistics-based features. Their experiments are based on conditional random field. Our model uses several features from this paper and combines them together with a neural network model.

3 Methodology

The word segmentation task is usually solved by character-level sequence labeling algorithm. Specifically, given a character sequence x, our model generates a corresponding y, where y belongs to the collection of {'B', 'I', 'E', 'S'}. 'B' denotes the beginning position, 'I' denotes the middle position, 'E' denotes the ending positions of a word and 'S' denotes this position is a word of a single character. We use y to segment the sequence.

Table 1 shows an example of word segmentation on a Chinese sentence "中国外长将访问加拿大/The Chinese Foreign Minister will visit Canada".

Table 1. An example of word segmentation on a Chinese sentence.

中	国	外	长	将	访	问	加	拿	大
B	E	B	E	S	B	E	B	I	E

In this section, we first describe the features we utilize in this work and give the proposed feature-rich LSTM-based model.

3.1 Pretrained Character-Bigram Embedding

Previous works show that using pre-trained word embeddings helps the model to converge to better results compared to randomly initialized word embeddings in many NLP tasks. Similarly, we use pre-trained character-bigram embeddings instead of randomly initialized ones. An intuitive explanation is the pre-trained character-bigram embeddings carry more semantic information due to they are obtained on a large corpus. To the best of our knowledge, there hasn't been any work that uses pre-trained character-bigram embedding on word segmentation task.

The character-unigram embeddings we utilize are initialized randomly. To obtain the pre-trained character-bigram embeddings, we first convert the original character sequence to a bigram sequence. For example, the bigram sequence of sentence "我是中国人。" will be "我是 是中 中国 国人 人。". Then we can train bigram embeddings readily using word2vec [8] toolkit on the resulting bigram sequences.

3.2 Statistics-Based Features

Statistics-based features have been shown helpful for word segmentation task [10]. We'll introduce three kinds of statistics-based features we utilize in this part, including pointwise mutual information, accessor variety and punctuation variety.

We scale all the raw scores of statistics-based features with their z-scores, the z-score of raw score x is $\frac{x-\mu}{\sigma}$, where μ and σ are the mean and standard deviation of the raw score distribution, respectively. z-score measures the distance between the raw score and the population mean in the units of standard deviation. A z-score reflects the position of the original value in all values. It is a linear transformation of the original score and does not change the distribution of the original score.

Pointwise Mutual Information. PMI (pointwise mutual information) is very helpful for word segmentation because word boundaries are more likely to occur between two characters with low PMI than high PMI. It has the ability to measure the closeness between characters. It has been used on word segmentation task in previous works.

The PMI values are computed through:

$$\texttt{PMI}\left(c_1, c_2\right) = \log \frac{P\left(c_1 c_2\right)}{P\left(c_1\right) P\left(c_2\right)} \tag{1}$$

where $P(c_1)$, $P(c_2)$ and $P(c_1c_2)$ are counted on the big corpus of raw data. $P(s)$ denotes the probability string s appears in the raw data.

Table 2 shows a snapshot of z-scored PMI, we find that two characters with high PMI tend to belong to the same word, Otherwise they tend to belong to different words.

Table 2. A snapshot of z-scored point mutual information.

Character Pair	PMI	Is a word?
中国 (China)	1.8448	yes
豚鼠 (Guinea pig)	2.9991	yes
我病 (I sick)	-0.9099	no
你去 (You go)	0.9693	no

Accessor Variety. Accessor variety evaluates how independent a string is used, if a string is surrounded by a variety of different characters, it is very likely to be a word. This idea is introduced for identifying meaningful Chinese words in [2]. Given a string s, which consist of $l(2 \leq l \leq 3)$ characters, the *left accessor variety* $L^l_{av}(s)$ is defined as the number of distinct characters that precede s in a corpus. Similarly, the *right accessor variety* $R^l_{av}(s)$ is defined as the number of distinct characters that succeed s.

We obtained the accessor variety values from the large corpus of unlabeled data, and replaced their original values with their z-scored values, Table 3 shows a snapshot of z-scored accessor variety, the string with larger accessor variety value has more probability of being a word. Since the values are too large, they cannot be utilized by neural network models. We normalize them to $[-1, 1]$ before using. The accessor variety we input at position i is shown as follows:

- Accessor variety of strings with length 2:
  $L^2_{av}(c_{[i:i+1]})$,$L^2_{av}(c_{[i+1:i+2]})$,$R^2_{av}(c_{[i-1:i]})$,$R^2_{av}(c_{[i-2:i-1]})$;
- Accessor variety of strings with length 3:
  $L^3_{av}(c_{[i:i+2]})$,$L^3_{av}(c_{[i+1:i+3]})$,$R^3_{av}(c_{[i-2:i]})$,$R^3_{av}(c_{[i-3:i-1]})$;

Table 3. A snapshot of z-scored accessor variety.

Character String	$L^l_{av}(s)$	$R^l_{av}(s)$	Is a word?
中国 (China)	36.8096	46.8093	yes
我们 (We)	27.4731	34.6770	yes
我病 (I sick)	0.5088	-0.0234	no
悄悄话 (Whispering)	0.9689	0.4563	yes

Punctuation Variety. Punctuation variety is used to measure how often a string appears next to a punctuation mark, since punctuation marks are symbols that indicate the structure and organization of written language, if a string always appears next to the punctuation, it has more possibility of being a word. The definition of punctuation variety is very similar to the accessor variety. As defined by the previous work of [10], the punctuation variety $L^l_{pv}(s)$ if defined as the number of punctuation marks that precede string s. Similarly, $R^l_{pv}(s)$ is defined as the number of punctuation marks that succeed string s.

Table 4 shows a snapshot of z-scored punctuation variety obtained from large corpus of unlabeled data, the string with larger punctuation variety value has more probability of being a word. Since the values of punctuation variety are also too large for neural network models, we normalize them to $[-1, 1]$ before using. We have two different kinds of features which can be the input feature of position i:

- Punctuation variety of strings with length 2:
  $L^2_{pv}(c_{[i:i+1]})$,$R^2_{pv}(c_{[i-1:i]})$;
- Punctuation variety of strings with length 3:
  $L^3_{pv}(c_{[i:i+2]})$,$R^3_{pv}(c_{[i-2:i]})$;

Table 4. A snapshot of z-scored punctuation variety.

Character String	$L^l_{pv}(s)$	$R^l_{pv}(s)$	Is a word?
中国 (China)	240.9068	61.6721	yes
我们 (We)	92.0613	1.4849	yes
我病 (I sick)	-0.0286	-0.0452	no
悄悄话 (Whispering)	0.1021	0.1086	yes

3.3 LSTM-based Model

Our model is based on bidirectional LSTM networks [3], which is very popular for sequence labeling tasks. A basic idea is feeding the character-unigram embedding to LSTM-based model and get the predicted label at position t using the corresponding hidden state h_t of bidirectional LSTM.

However, to most languages, a single character may not carry sufficient semantic information, so we decide to add character-bigram embedding into our model. And because of the size limitation of the labeled data, external information may be very useful to our model, we decide to add some statistics-based features which we have discussed in the previous part of this section to get our proposed feature-rich LSTM-based model.

Our input unit representation is calculated by concatenating character-unigram embedding, character-bigram embedding and all numerical features together, and pass it through a non-linear neural network layer, which can be represented as follows:

$$x_t = max\left\{0, W[B_{t-1}, B_t, U_t, \texttt{PMI}(c_{t-1}, c_t), \texttt{PMI}(c_t, c_{t+1}), ...] + b\right\} \tag{2}$$

where B_t denotes character-bigram embedding at position t, U_t denotes character-unigram embedding at position t, PMI denotes point mutual information between characters and other numerical features are omitted here.

Finally, we calculate the probability of label y_i at position t by the following equation:

$$p\left(y_i|h_t\right) = \frac{exp\left(g_i^T h_t + q_i\right)}{\sum_j exp\left(g_j^T h_t + q_j\right)} \tag{3}$$

where h_t is hidden state of bidirectional LSTM at position t, g_i is a column vector representing the embedding of the label i and q_i is a bias term for label i.

The architecture of our bidirectional LSTM-based model is illustrated in Fig. 1.

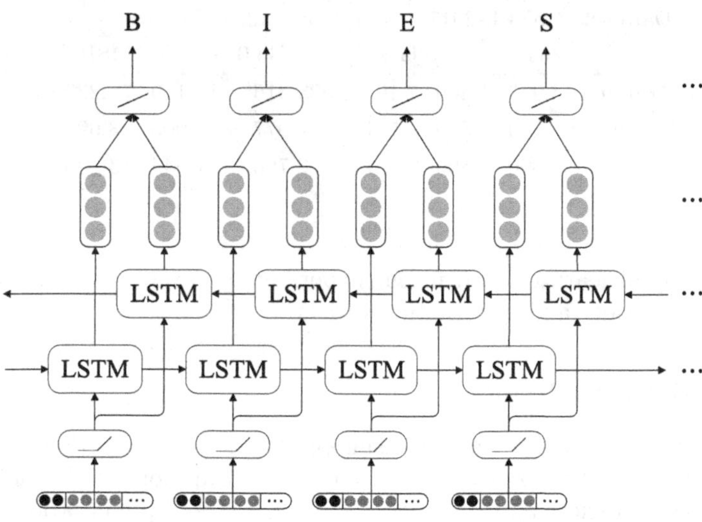

Fig. 1. An illustration of the LSTM-based model. The concatenated character-unigram embedding, two character-bigram embeddings and other numerical features are used as the input of the neural network after passed through an non-linear neural network layer.

4 Experiments

4.1 Data and Settings

We conduct experiments on three languages on CoNLL-2017 shared task [1] including traditional Chinese (zhT), Vietnamese (vi) and Japanese (ja). And we do further experiments on three simplified Chinese datasets: PKU and MSR from 2nd SIGHAN backoff and Chinese Treebank 6.0 (CTB6.0). For the PKU and MSR datasets, last 10% of the training data are used as development data as [9] does. For CTB6.0 data, recommended data split is used. We covert all the double byte digits and letters into a single byte and then convert all continuous digits into one token '<Digit>' as our preprocess. The performance of our word segmentation model is evaluated by F-score. The statistics-based features and pre-trained character-bigram embeddings of three datasets from CoNLL-2017 shared task and three datasets of simplified Chinese are obtained from the raw data of Wikipedia provided by CoNLL-2017 shared task and the Chinese Gigawords, respectively. We use both character-unigram embedding and character-bigram embedding of 100 dimensional. The input dimension and hidden dimension of LSTM networks is set to 100 and 128, respectively. Table 5 shows the number of instances in each dataset.

Table 5. The number of instances in training, development and test data of 6 different datasets.

Data set	CoNLL-2017			Simplified Chinese		
	zhT	vi	ja	CTB6.0	PKU	MSR
Training	3,997	1,400	7,164	23,416	17,149	78,232
Devel.	500	800	511	2,077	1,905	8,692
Test	500	800	557	2,796	1,944	3,985

Our numerical features used in our experiments are all z-scored, including PMI, accessor variety and punctuation variety.

4.2 Experimental Results

On the following tables, 'Pre' denotes using pre-trained character-bigram embedding, 'PMI' denotes using z-scored point mutual information, 'AV' denotes using z-scored accessor variety and 'PV' denotes using z-scored punctuation variety.

[1] The data could be downloaded at http://universaldependencies.org/conll17/data.html.

Results on Development Dataset. Table 6 shows the results on development dataset, evaluated by F-score. From Table 6, we can see numerical features obtained on unlabeled data have improvement on small dataset (e.g. zhT and vi from CoNLL-2017 shared task) and have less effect on dataset with enough training data. All of point mutual information, accessor variety and punctuation variety are able to improve the performance of our model in a different level. We can also see, PMI is the most helpful feature especially on smaller dataset while the other two features get smaller improvement.

Table 6. Results on development dataset, using different sets of features, evaluated by F-score. The numbers in parentheses denote the number of instances in corresponding training dataset.

Data set	CoNLL-2017			Simplified Chinese		
	zhT (3,997)	vi (1,400)	ja (7,164)	CTB6.0 (23,416)	PKU (17,149)	MSR (78,232)
Baseline	92.00	89.29	93.70	95.09	96.04	97.06
Pre	94.27	91.81	94.28	95.53	96.46	97.13
Pre+PMI	95.22	93.07	94.83	95.56	96.57	97.30
Pre+PMI+AV	**95.77**	**93.57**	94.72	95.58	96.64	97.49
Pre+PMI+PV	95.56	93.31	94.81	**95.69**	96.65	**97.50**
Pre+PMI+AV+PV	95.47	93.34	**95.13**	95.62	**96.67**	97.39

We evaluate the Out-of-vocabulary (OOV) recall rate on the development dataset. As shown in Table 7, adding numerical statistics-based features significantly increases the OOV recall rate regardless of the size of the training dataset. The improvement is more obvious when the size of training dataset is smaller. All of pre-trained character-bigram embeddings, pointwise mutual information, accessor variety and punctuation variety have the ability to help the model to recognize more OOV words. For dataset which has high OOV rate, introducing more statistics-based features also gives more information which the model cannot learn in the training dataset. Increasing OOV recall rate directly improves the performance of the model.

Results on Evaluation Dataset. At last, we compare our LSTM-based model with other state-of-the-art models in Table 8. The first block of Table 8 shows the non-neural CWS models and the second block shows the neural models. Both [7] and [14] used word-level information which we didn't use in this work. [13] use auto-segmented result of large scale unlabeled data. Our work tries to feed numerical statistics-based features to LSTM networks and gets competitive results. From Table 8 we can see that our model achieves the state-of-the-art performance on traditional Chinese and Vietnamese word segmentation dataset of CoNLL-2017 shared task, which has less training instances compared with other datasets. And on the other four datasets, we have comparable results to state-of-the-art performance.

Table 7. OOV recall rate on development dataset, using different sets of features. The numbers in parentheses denote the OOV rate of corresponding development dataset.

Data set	CoNLL-2017			Simplified Chinese		
	zhT (12.1)	vi (14.7)	ja (8.5)	CTB6.0 (5.4)	PKU (3.8)	MSR (2.7)
Baseline	63.9	63.4	67.2	75.4	67.6	60.9
Pre	79.4	71.9	73.2	76.0	69.8	62.9
Pre+PMI	82.9	75.1	73.8	77.6	68.2	71.6
Pre+PMI+AV	**85.1**	**78.1**	72.7	75.5	71.5	71.1
Pre+PMI+PV	83.6	76.5	74.3	**78.2**	**72.5**	**71.7**
Pre+PMI+AV+PV	83.2	76.3	**75.3**	76.6	71.5	70.1

Table 8. Comparison with the state-of-the-art word segmentation systems, evaluated by F-score. We still don't know the methods of 1st systems of CoNLL-2017 shared task official evaluation. The 1st system on Japanese of CoNLL-2017 shared task is an in-house system.

Genre	Model	CoNLL-2017			Simplified Chinese		
		zhT	vi	ja	CTB6.0	PKU	MSR
Non-NN	[Tseng 2005] [12]	-	-	-	-	95.0	96.4
	[Zhang and Clark 2007] [15]	-	-	-	-	95.1	97.2
	[Sun *et al.* 2009] [11]	-	-	-	-	95.2	97.3
	[Wang *et al.* 2011] [13]	-	-	-	**95.7**	-	-
NN	[Zheng *et al.*, 2013] [16]	-	-	-	-	92.4	93.3
	[Pei *et al.* 2014] [9]	-	-	-	-	94.0	94.9
	[Pei *et al.* 2014] w/bigram [9]	-	-	-	-	95.2	97.2
	[Kong *et al.* 2015] [4]	-	-	-	-	90.6	90.7
	[Liu *et al.* 2016] [7]	-	-	-	95.48	95.67	97.58
	[Zhang *et al.* 2016] [14]	-	-	-	-	**95.7**	**97.7**
	[Cai *et al.* 2016] [1]	-	-	-	-	95.5	96.5
	1st on official evaluation	94.57	87.30	**98.59***	-	-	-
Our best		**95.49**	**91.96**	95.09	95.26	95.44	97.32

5 Conclusion and Future Work

In this paper, we scale the value of statistic-based features in previous works with their z-scored values and feed the new values into our LSTM-based model as numerical features. Experiments show that it significantly improves the F-score on smaller datasets and it can also slightly enhance the performance on larger datasets. Also, this method shows greater generalization than those methods without statistic-based features counted on unlabeled data. We analyze the effect of statistic-based features by giving the OOV recall rate of each development dataset with different sets of features. Our model achieves state-of-the-art performance on two datasets of CoNLL-2017 shared task. And we have comparable results to state-of-the-art performance on the other datasets.

We plan to add more effective numerical features into neural network model and to try some new methods other than z-score method to get the numerical features.

Acknowledgements. We thank the anonymous reviewers for their valuable suggestions. This work was supported by the National Key Basic Research Program of China via grant 2014CB340503 and the National Natural Science Foundation of China (NSFC) via grant 61370164 and 61632011.

References

1. Cai, D., Zhao, H.: Neural word segmentation learning for Chinese. In: Proceedings of the 54th Annual Meeting of the Association for Computational Linguistics, (vol. 1: Long Papers), pp. 409–420. Association for Computational Linguistics, Berlin, August 2016
2. Feng, H., Chen, K., Deng, X., Zheng, W.: Accessor variety criteria for Chinese word extraction. Comput. Linguist. **30**(1), 75–93 (2004)
3. Hochreiter, S., Schmidhuber, J.: Long short-term memory. Neural Comput. **9**(8), 1735–1780 (1997)
4. Kong, L., Dyer, C., Smith, N.A.: Segmental recurrent neural networks. arXiv preprint (2015). arXiv:1511.06018
5. Lafferty, J., McCallum, A., Pereira, F.: Conditional random fields: probabilistic models for segmenting and labeling sequence data. In: ICML, vol. 1, pp. 282–289 (2001)
6. Liang, P.: Semi-supervised learning for natural language. Ph.D. thesis, Massachusetts Institute of Technology (2005)
7. Liu, Y., Che, W., Guo, J., Qin, B., Liu, T.: Exploring segment representations for neural segmentation models, pp. 2880–2886 (2016)
8. Mikolov, T., Chen, K., Corrado, G., Dean, J.: Efficient estimation of word representations in vector space. In: International Conference on Learning Representations (ICLR) Workshop (2013)
9. Pei, W., Ge, T., Chang, B.: Max-margin tensor neural network for Chinese word segmentation. In: ACL (1), pp. 293–303 (2014)
10. Sun, W., Xu, J.: Enhancing Chinese word segmentation using unlabeled data. In: Proceedings of the Conference on Empirical Methods in Natural Language Processing, pp. 970–979. Association for Computational Linguistics (2011)
11. Sun, X., Zhang, Y., Matsuzaki, T., Tsuruoka, Y., Tsujii, J.: A discriminative latent variable Chinese segmenter with hybrid word/character information. In: Proceedings of Human Language Technologies: The 2009 Annual Conference of the North American Chapter of the Association for Computational Linguistics, pp. 56–64. Association for Computational Linguistics (2009)
12. Tseng, H., Chang, P., Andrew, G., Jurafsky, D., Manning, C.: A conditional random field word segmenter for Sighan bakeoff 2005. In: Proceedings of the Fourth SIGHAN Workshop on Chinese Language Processing, vol. 171. Citeseer (2005)
13. Wang, Y., Jun'ichi Kazama, Y.T., Tsuruoka, Y., Chen, W., Zhang, Y., Torisawa, K.: Improving Chinese word segmentation and POS tagging with semi-supervised methods using large auto-analyzed data. In: IJCNLP, pp. 309–317 (2011)

14. Zhang, M., Zhang, Y., Fu, G.: Transition-based neural word segmentation. In: Proceedings of the 54nd ACL (2016)
15. Zhang, Y., Clark, S.: Chinese segmentation with a word-based perceptron algorithm. In: Annual Meeting-Association for Computational Linguistics, vol. 45, p. 840 (2007)
16. Zheng, X., Chen, H., Xu, T.: Deep learning for Chinese word segmentation and POS tagging. In: EMNLP, pp. 647–657 (2013)

Machine Translation and Multilingual Information Processing

Context Sensitive Word Deletion Model for Statistical Machine Translation

Qiang Li(✉), Yaqian Han, Tong Xiao, and Jingbo Zhu

NiuTrans Laboratory, School of Computer Science and Engineering, Northeastern University, Shenyang, China
liqiangneu@gmail.com, hanyaqianneu@gmail.com
{xiaotong,zhujingbo}@mail.neu.edu.cn

Abstract. Word deletion (WD) errors can lead to poor comprehension of the meaning of source translated sentences in phrase-based statistical machine translation (SMT), and have a critical impact on the adequacy of the translation results generated by SMT systems. In this paper, first we classify the word deletion into two categories, wanted and unwanted word deletions. For these two kinds of word deletions, we propose a maximum entropy based word deletion model to improve the translation quality in phrase-based SMT. Our proposed model are based on features automatically learned from a real-word bitext. In our experiments on Chinese-to-English news and web translation tasks, the results show that our approach is capable of generating more adequate translations compared with the baseline system, and our proposed word deletion model yields a +0.99 BLEU improvement and a −2.20 TER reduction on the NIST machine translation evaluation corpora.

Keywords: Natural language processing · Statistical machine translation · Word deletion

1 Introduction

Recently, although researchers have shown an increasing interest in neural machine translation (NMT) [1–4], statistical machine translation (SMT) also draw a lot of attention. SMT has been applied to many applications, and the phrase-based translation model has been widely used in modern SMT systems due to its simplicity and strong performance [5,6]. To evaluate the quality of machine translation systems, we often consider both adequacy and fluency [7], and measure the number of edits required to change a system output into one of the references [8]. For poor translation results with low adequacy, the problem is mainly caused by word deletion problems, word insertion problems, and incorrect word choices. Word insertion problems are not common during translation [9]. Incorrect word choices are eliminated by improving translation model [10,11] or using domain adaptation [12]. As word deletion (WD) problems have not gotten enough attention in research community, in this paper we propose a context sensitive word deletion model to address these problems.

M. Sun et al. (Eds.): CCL 2017 and NLP-NABD 2017, LNAI 10565, pp. 73–84, 2017.
https://doi.org/10.1007/978-3-319-69005-6_7

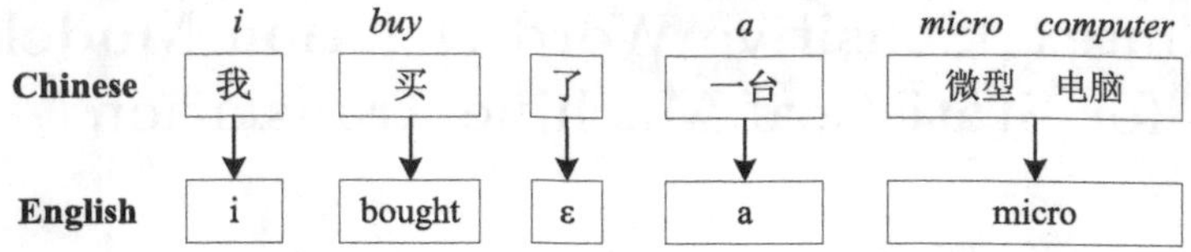

Fig. 1. Example of wanted and unwanted word deletion.

Table 1. Statistics of unwanted word deletion determined by human evaluators from 200 randomly selected machine-translated sentences on the news translation task.

Corpus		Unwanted WD	
# Sentences	# Words	Frequency	Ratio
200	3,293	450	13.67%

There are two kinds of word deletions. First, every language has some *spurious* words that do not need to be translated, referred to as *wanted word deletion*. It is correct that the source spurious words are not translated during translation. See Fig. 1 for an example. The source Chinese spurious word 了 has no counterparts in the other language and will be translated to empty word ϵ by decoder. It is possible to learn phrase pairs '了, ϵ' for wanted word deletion from a word aligned bilingual training corpus. Consequently, SMT systems realize the function of wanted word deletion. However, *unwanted word deletion* appears along with wanted word deletion during phrase extraction. For example, the phrase pair '微型 电脑, micro' in Fig. 1 is an unwanted word deletion as the source *meaningful* word '电脑' has no counterparts in the target language and results in a translation error. An unwanted word deletion seriously influences the adequacy of translation results generated by SMT systems. Unwanted word deletion is very common in SMT systems, from Table 1 we can see that the ratio of unwanted word deletion is as high as 13.67% of all 3,293 words in our 200 randomly selected sentences determined by human evaluators, and there are about 2.5 meaningful words that are not translated at all in each sentence on average. In this paper, we try to explore the research into wanted and unwanted word deletions for the phrase-based SMT system.

To address wanted and unwanted word deletion problems, first of all, we should judge whether a source word is a spurious or meaningful word. For a source spurious word, we do not want to translate it during translation, which is referred to as 'deleted'. On the contrary, a source meaningful word that we want it to be correctly translated is referred to as 'reserved'. Obviously, this problem can be cast as a binary classification problem. Consequently, we propose a novel maximum entropy based context sensitive model to improve the translation quality. The proposed word deletion model based on maximum entropy automatically learns features from a real-world bitext. During decoding, our proposed model is embedded inside a log-linear phrase-based model of translation. Finally, experimental results demonstrate that our proposed methods achieve significant improvements in BLEU [7] and TER [8] score on the Chinese-to-English news and web translation tasks. For example, it yields a +0.99 BLEU improvement and a −2.20 TER reduction on the NIST MT evaluation corpora.

2 Statistical Machine Translation

The goal of machine translation is to automatically translate from a source string f_1^J to a target string e_1^I. In SMT, this problem can be stated as: we find a target string $\hat{e}_1^I$ from all possible translations by the following equation:

$$\hat{e}_1^I = \arg\max_{e_1^I}\{Pr\left(e_1^I|f_1^J\right)\} \tag{1}$$

where $Pr\left(e_1^I|f_1^J\right)$ is the probability that e_1^I is the translation of the given source string f_1^J. To model the posterior probability $Pr\left(e_1^I|f_1^J\right)$, our decoder utilizes the log-linear model [13]. $Pr\left(e_1^I|f_1^J\right)$ is calculated as follows:

$$Pr\left(e_1^I|f_1^J\right) = \frac{\exp(\sum_a \lambda_a h_a(f_1^J, e_1^I))}{\sum_{e_1^{I^*}} \exp(\sum_a \lambda_a h_a(f_1^J, e_1^{I^*}))} \tag{2}$$

where $\{h_a(f_1^J, e_1^I)|a = 1, ...\}$ is a set of features, and λ_a is the feature weight corresponding to the a-th feature. $h_a(f_1^J, e_1^I)$ can be regarded as a function that maps each pair of source string f_1^J and target string e_1^I into a non-negative value, and λ_a can be regarded as the contribution of $h_a(f_1^J, e_1^I)$ to $Pr\left(e_1^I|f_1^J\right)$. Ideally, λ_a indicates the pairwise correspondence between the feature $h_a(f_1^J, e_1^I)$ and the overall score $Pr\left(e_1^I|f_1^J\right)$. A positive value of λ_a indicates a positive correlation between $h_a(f_1^J, e_1^I)$ to $Pr\left(e_1^I|f_1^J\right)$, while a negative value indicates a negative correlation.

In a general pipeline of SMT, λ is learned on a tuning data set to obtain an optimized weight vector λ^*. To learn the optimized weight vector λ^*, λ is usually optimized according to a certain objective function. The objective function should take the translation quality into account and can be automatically learned from MT outputs and reference translations. Therefore, we use BLEU to define the error function and learn optimized feature weights using the minimum error rate training method [14].

3 Context Sensitive Word Deletion Model

3.1 Word Deletion Model

As mentioned in Sect. 2, all the features used in our system are combined in a log-linear fashion. So, Given a derivation v, the corresponding model score is calculated as follows:

$$Pr\left(e_1^I, v|f_1^J\right) = \prod_{(f_{j_1}^{j_2}, e_{i_1}^{i_2})\in v} Pr^l(f_{j_1}^{j_2}, e_{i_1}^{i_2}) \times Pr_r(v)^{\lambda_r} \times Pr_{lm}(e_1^I)^{\lambda_{lm}} \times \mathrm{WD}^{\lambda_{\mathrm{WD}}} \tag{3}$$

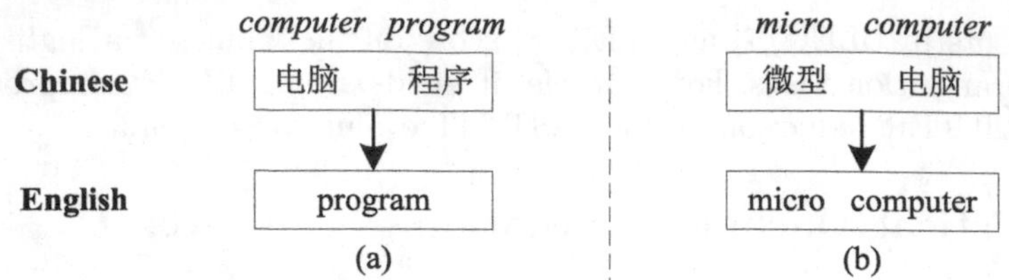

Fig. 2. Example of phrase pairs for illustrating context condition.

where $1 \leq i_1, i_2 \leq I$, $1 \leq j_1, j_2 \leq J$, $Pr_r(v)$ is the maximum entropy based reordering model proposed in [15], and λ_r is its weight. $Pr_{lm}(e_1^I)$ is the n-gram language model score, and λ_{lm} is its weight. We use $Pr^l(f_{j_1}^{j_2}, e_{i_1}^{i_2})$ to calculate the probability of the lexical rule.

$$\begin{aligned} Pr^l(f_{j_1}^{j_2}, e_{i_1}^{i_2}) = & p(e_{i_1}^{i_2}|f_{j_1}^{j_2})^{\lambda_1} \times p(f_{j_1}^{j_2}|e_{i_1}^{i_2})^{\lambda_2} \times \\ & p_{lex}(e_{i_1}^{i_2}|f_{j_1}^{j_2})^{\lambda_3} \times p_{lex}(f_{j_1}^{j_2}|e_{i_1}^{i_2})^{\lambda_4} \times \\ & exp(1)^{\lambda_5} \times exp(|e_{i_1}^{i_2}|)^{\lambda_6} \end{aligned} \quad (4)$$

where $p(\cdot)$ are the phrase translation probabilities in both directions, $p_{lex}(\cdot)$ are the lexical translation probabilities in both directions, and $exp(1)$ and $exp(|e_{i_1}^{i_2}|)$ are the phrase penalty and word penalty, respectively.

WD in Eq. 3 is our proposed context sensitive word deletion model, and λ_{WD} is its weight. For the word deletion model WD, we define it on source word f_j, context context(f_j) and deletion $d \in \{deleted, reserved\}$. WD is defined as follows:

$$\text{WD} = f(d, f_j, \text{context}(f_j)) \quad (5)$$

where f_j is a source word that needs to be translated. context(f_j) is the context words around the source word f_j. d is deletion or not that based on the word alignments between the source sentence s_1^I and the target sentence t_1^J, which covers the value over *deleted* and *reserved*. If f_j is a source spurious word and we do not want to translate it during translation, $d = deleted$. On the other hand, if f_j is a source meaningful word and we want it to be correctly translated, $d = reserved$. We will describe the proposed model in the next section.

3.2 Maximum Entropy Based Word Deletion Model

In this section, first, we will explain why we use context to address word deletion problems. Through data analysis determined by human evaluators, we can see that incorrect context condition is the main cause for the incorrect word deletion. See Fig. 2 for an example. The phrase pair '电脑 程序, program', whose source meaningful word ' 电脑' is translated to ϵ based on this context, is correct. ' 电脑' that can be regarded as a spurious source word based on this context is referred to as wanted word deletion. If our bilingual training corpus contains this phrase pair, then the phrase pair '电脑, ϵ' will be produced during phrase extraction. But for phrase pairs '微型 电脑, micro computer', '电脑' can not be translated to ϵ based on current context. During translation, '微型 电脑' will be translated into 'micro' if the phrase pair '电脑, ϵ' is selected by the decoder. Then an unwanted word deletion occurs. Consequently, based on the context of a given source word, we want to automatically learn correct wanted and unwanted word deletion models. Therefore, we propose a context sensitive word deletion model to address word deletion problems.

As described above, we defined the word deletion model WD on three factors: source word f_j, context(f_j), and the word deletion d. The central problem is that given f_j and context(f_j), how to predict $d \in \{deleted, reserved\}$. This is a typical problem of two-class classification. To be consistent with the whole model, the conditional probability $p(d|f_j, \text{context}(f_j))$ is calculated. A good way to this problem is to use features of source lexical words and word alignments between source and target sentence as word deletion evidences. It is very straight to use maximum entropy model to integrate features to predicate word deletions of the source word f_j. Under the maximum entropy based model, we have:

$$\text{WD} = p_\theta(d|f_j, \text{context}(f_j)) = \frac{\exp(\sum_b \theta_b h_b(d, f_j, \text{context}(f_j)))}{\sum_{d^*} \exp(\sum_b \theta_b h_b(d^*, f_j, \text{context}(f_j)))} \tag{6}$$

where the functions $h_b \in \{0, 1\}$ are model features and the θ_b are weights of the model features which can be trained by different algorithms [16].

3.3 Word Deletion Examples and Features

If we want to extract high-precision word deletion examples, first we should have a bilingual corpus with high-precision word alignments. We obtain the word alignments using the way in [15]. After running GIZA++ in both directions [17], we apply the *grow-diag-final-and* refinement rule on the intersection alignments for each sentence pair.

A *word deletion example* is a triple $(d, f_j, \text{context}(f_j))$. In the bilingual training corpus with high-precision word alignments, for the source word f_j, if there exists a target word e_i that is aligned to f_j, $d = reserved$. Otherwise, $d = deleted$.

With the extracted word deletion examples, we can obtain features for our maximum entropy based context sensitive word deletion model. See Fig. 3 for an example, we want to justify if the current source word '一台' or '了' should be deleted or reserved. The feature templates for our method is shown here:

- the lexical form of the source word f_j itself, here is '一台' or '了'
- the lexical forms f_{j-2}, f_{j-1}, f_{j+1}, and f_{j+2}. Where f_{j-2} and f_{j-1} are the two words to the left of f_j, and f_{j+1}, and f_{j+2} are the two words to the right of f_j.

Then we can obtain two word deletion examples for the source spurious and meaningful words, respectively:

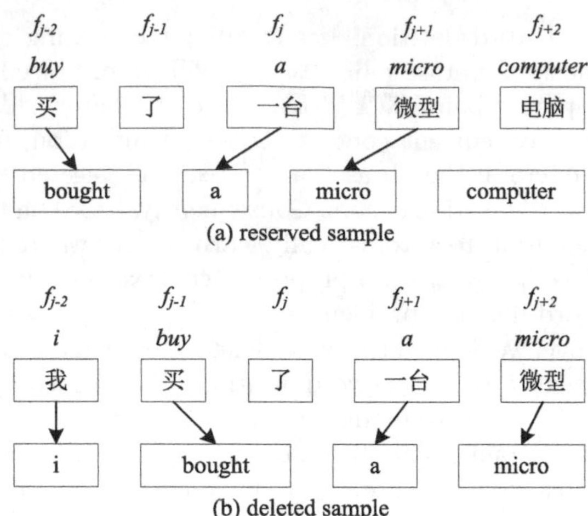

Fig. 3. The lexical form of words in rectangle are the features that used in maximum entropy word deletion model.

- d=reserved, f_j =一台, f_{j-2} =买, f_{j-1} =了, f_{j+1} =微型, f_{j+2} =电脑
- d=deleted, f_j =了, f_{j-2} =我, f_{j-1} =买, f_{j+1} =一台, f_{j+2} =微型

We first extract word deletion evidences from our 2.43M bilingual training data with word alignments. Then, we use the MaxEnt toolkit[1] to tune the feature weights. Finally, the proposed maximum entropy based WD model is integrated into the standard log-linear model used by our decoder in Eq. 3.

3.4 Decoder

After training the context sensitive word deletion model WD with the maximum entropy approach, we integrate it into our log-linear phrase-based model during decoding. Here, the source sentence f_1^J that is needed to be translated is '我买了一台微型电脑', after tokenization we can get a string '我 买 了 一台 微型 电脑' For every word $f_{j_1}^{j_2}$ in f_1^J, $1 \leq j_1, j_2 \leq J$, we will use WD model to justify if it is needed to be *deleted* or *reserved*.

When we translate the Chinese source word '了', the WD model shows that it is more likely to be spurious word and needed to be 'deleted' based on current context during translation. When the decoder selects the phrase '买 了, bought' in Fig. 4(a) that contains source word '了' and does not have any correspondences for '了' in the target side, then the WD feature will be active during translation. But when the decoder selects the phrase in Fig. 4(b) that contains source word '了' and the target word 'a' is aligned to '了', then the WD feature will be inactive for the phrase (买 了, bought a) during translation.

[1] http://homepages.inf.ed.ac.uk/lzhang10/maxent.html.

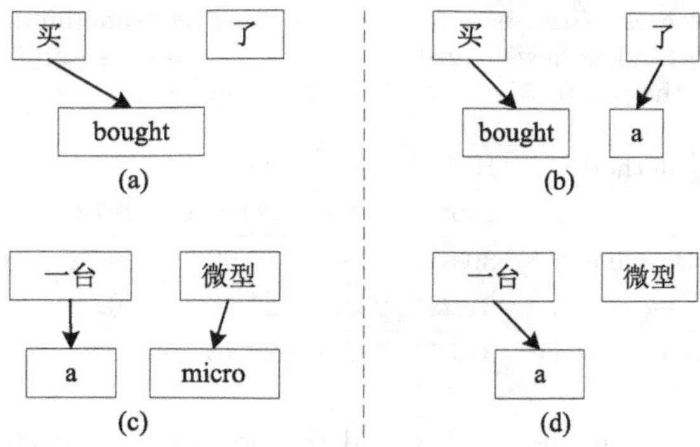

Fig. 4. Sample phrases pairs used during decoding.

Now we switch to the source meaningful word. When we translate the Chinese source word '微型', the context sensitive model shows that it is more likely to be meaningful word and needed to be 'reserved' based on this context. When the decoder selects the phrase (一台 微型, a micro) in Fig. 4(c) that the target word 'micro' is aligned to the source word '微型', then the WD feature will be active during decoding. Otherwise, the WD feature will be inactive if the decoder selects the phrase (一台 微型, a) in Fig. 4(d) as there are no correspondences for the Chinese source meaningful word '微型'.

4 Evaluation

In this section, we describe our method of evaluating the context sensitive word deletion model to address word deletion issues in SMT. We applied the proposed methods to a state-of-the-art phrase-based SMT system [18] and carried out experiments on Chinese-to-English news and web translation tasks.

4.1 Experiment Setup

We developed a CKY style decoder that employed a beam search and cube pruning to build our phrase-based SMT system [19]. Our SMT system used all standard features adopted in the current state-of-the-art phrase-based system, including bidirectional phrase translation probabilities, bidirectional lexical weights, an n-gram language model, target word penalty and phrase penalty. In addition, the ME-based lexicalized reordering model was employed in our system [15]. The reordering limit was set to 8 and the beam size was set to 30. The maximum length of source and target phrases were limited to 5 words.

Our experiments were conducted on two Chinese-to-English translation tasks: news and web domains. In both domains, our bilingual data consisted of 2.43 million sentence pairs selected from the NIST portion of the bilingual data of NIST MT 2008 Evaluation. The 5-gram language model for both translation

Table 2. BLEU4 scores of the baseline and the proposed maximum entropy based model in Chinese-to-English news translation. Here, * indicates significantly better on test performance at the $p = 0.05$ level compared to the baseline method.

Method	BLEU on News Data [%]			
	2006	2008	2008 pro	2012
Baseline	30.58	29.60	27.22	29.42
$+\epsilon$	31.28*	29.68	27.46	30.08*
$+\epsilon$+maxent	31.57*	30.25*	28.13*	30.28*

Table 3. BLEU4 scores of the baseline and the proposed maximum entropy based model in Chinese-to-English web translation. Here, * indicates significantly better on test performance at the $p = 0.05$ level compared to the baseline method.

Method	BLEU on Web Data [%]			
	2006	2008	2008 pro	2012
Baseline	28.03	21.28	22.41	19.68
$+\epsilon$	28.44	21.68	22.78	19.95
$+\epsilon$+maxent	28.77*	21.99*	23.01*	19.91

tasks was trained on the Xinhua portion of English Gigaword corpus (16.28 M) in addition to the target side of the bilingual data. For the news domain, we used the NIST 2006 news MT evaluation set as our development set (616 sentences) and the NIST 2008 news, 2008 progress news, and 2012 news MT evaluation sets as our test sets (691, 688, and 400 sentences). For the web domain, we used the NIST 2006 webdata MT evaluation set as our development set (483 sentences) and the NIST 2008 web, 2008 progress web, and 2012 web MT evaluation sets as our test sets (666, 682, and 420 sentences).

The GIZA++ tool was used to perform the bidirectional word alignment between the source and target sentences [17]. After running GIZA++ in both directions, we applied the *grow-diag-final-and* refinement rule on the intersection alignments for each sentence pair.

4.2 Results

Tables 2 and 3 depict the BLEU scores of the baseline approach (Row 'baseline') and the maximum entropy based WD model (Row '$+\epsilon$+maxent') on Chinese-to-English news and web translation tasks. In order to compare with the method proposed by Li et al. [20] to address spurious source word translation, a specific empty symbol ϵ on the target language side is posited and any source word is allowed to translate into ϵ (Row '$+\epsilon$'). This symbol is just visible in phrase table. That is, ϵ is not counted when calculating language model score, word penalty and any other feature values, and it is omitted in the final translation results.

Table 4. TER scores of various methods in news translation. For TER, lower is better.

Method	TER on News Data [%]			
	2006	2008	2008 pro	2012
Baseline	76.31	59.65	60.30	60.54
+ϵ+maxent	74.15	58.20	59.10	58.34

Table 5. TER scores of various methods in web translation. For TER, lower is better.

Method	TER on Web Data [%]			
	2006	2008	2008*pro*	2012
Baseline	62.31	63.92	63.06	66.95
+ϵ+maxent	60.33	62.33	61.31	65.53

For our proposed context sensitive WD model, any source word is also allowed to translate into ϵ.

On the Chinese-to-English news translation in Table 2, first we can see that, when empty symbol ϵ is posited on the target language side (Row '+ϵ'), the baseline system achieved BLEU score increase of 0.70, 0.08, 0.24, and 0.66 on NIST 2006 news, 2008 news, 2008 progress news, and 2012 news, respectively. From this we can say that it is better to improve translation quality in BLEU score when any source words are allowed to translated to empty word ϵ. Second, we can see that our proposed context sensitive WD model significantly improve the BLEU score on both development and test sets (Row '+ϵ+maxent'). Our proposed method achieved BLEU score increase of 0.99, 0.65, 0.91, and 0.86 on development and test datasets, respectively.

When we switch to Chinese-to-English web translation in Table 3, the experimental results are similar to those in Table 2. When introduced empty symbol ϵ (Row '+ϵ'), the baseline system achieved BLEU score increase of 0.41, 0.40, 0.37, and 0.27 on NIST 2006 web, 2008 web, 2008 progress web, and 2012 web, respectively. For our proposed context sensitive model (Row '+ϵ+maxent'), the achievements are 0.74, 0.71, 0.60, and 0.23 points on the BLEU score for the NIST 2006 web, 2008 web, 2008 progress web, and 2012 web, respectively.

Translation Edit Rate (TER) is an error metric for machine translation that measures the number of edits required to change a system output into one of the references [8]. Snover et al. [8] showed that the single-reference variant of TER correlates as well with human judgments of MT quality as the four-reference variant of BLEU. So, in addition to use BLEU score to evaluate the translation quality for statistical machine translation system, we also use TER metric to evaluate our proposed context sensitive WD model for the word deletion problems. Different from BLEU score, the lower is better for TER metric. Tables 4 and 5 depict the TER scores of the baseline approach and the proposed methods on Chinese-to-English news and web translation tasks. On news translation in

Table 4, we can see that our proposed method (Row '+ϵ+maxent') yields a gain of 2.16, 1.45, 1.20, and 2.20 TER score decrease on the development and test sets, respectively. When we switch to web translation in Table 5, the experimental results are similar to those in Table 4. For example, our proposed method (Row '+ϵ+maxent') achieved TER score decrease of 1.98, 1.59, 1.75 and 1.42 on the development and test sets, respectively. Therefore, we can conclude that our proposed maximum context sensitive word deletion model can significantly improve the translation quality in TER metric for Chinese-to-English news and web translation.

5 Related Work

Although researchers have shown an increasing interest in NMT [1–4], SMT also draw a lot of attention. There are many problems that SMT finds difficult to solve and the word deletion issue is among them. Several studies have addressed the word deletion problems, Li et al. [21] proposed four effective models to handle undesired word deletion. Parton et al. [22] presented a hybrid approach, APES, to target adequacy errors. Huck and Ney [23] investigated an insertion and deletion model that was implemented as phrase-level feature functions that counted the number of inserted or deleted word. Zhang et al. [24] focused on unaligned words only and applied hard deletion and optional deletion of the unaligned words on the source side before phrase extraction. Though easy to implement, this method introduced more noise into the phrase table. They showed that reducing the noise in phrase extraction is more effective than improving word alignment [25, 26]. Menezes and Quirk [27] presented an extension of the treelet translation method to include order templates with structural insertion and deletion. Li et al. [20] proposed three models to handle spurious source words. They utilized different methods to calculate the translation probability that the source words are translated into empty word ϵ.

In contrast to previous studies, we first categorize word deletion problems into wanted and unwanted word deletion. Second, we proposed maximum entropy based context sensitive word deletion model to address both the wanted and unwanted word deletions.

6 Conclusion

In this paper, we tackled the word deletion issue for the phrase-based SMT. First of all, we classified word deletion problems into two categories, wanted and unwanted word deletion. For these two kinds of word deletion problems, we proposed a context sensitive WD model to address them. The proposed WD model are based on features automatically learned from a real-word bitext. We evaluated our proposed methods on Chinese-to-English news and web translation tasks, and the experimental results demonstrated that our proposed context sensitive model achieved significant improvements in BLEU and TER scores. On the NIST Chinese-to-English evaluation corpora, it achieved a +0.99 BLEU improvement and a -2.20 TER reduction on top of a baseline system.

Acknowledgements. This work was supported in part by the National Science Foundation of China (61672138 and 61432013), the Fundamental Research Funds for the Central Universities, and the Opening Project of Beijing Key Laboratory of Internet Culture and Digital Dissemination Research.

References

1. Sutskever, I., Vinyals, O., Le, Q.V.: Sequence to sequence learning with neural networks. In: Advances in Neural Information Processing Systems 27: Annual Conference on Neural Information Processing Systems, 8–13 December 2014, Montreal, Quebec, Canada, pp. 3104–3112 (2014)
2. Luong, T., Pham, H., Manning, C.D.: Effective approaches to attention-based neural machine translation. In: Proceedings of the 2015 Conference on Empirical Methods in Natural Language Processing, EMNLP 2015, 17–21 September 2015, Lisbon, Portugal, pp. 1412–1421(2015)
3. Sennrich, R., Haddow, B., Birch, A.: Neural machine translation of rare words with subword units. In: Proceedings of the 54th Annual Meeting of the Association for Computational Linguistics, ACL, 7–12 August 2016, Berlin, Germany, vol. 1: Long Papers (2016)
4. Britz, D., Goldie, A., Luong, M., Le, Q.V.: Massive exploration of neural machine translation architectures. CoRR abs/1703.03906 (2017)
5. Koehn, P., Och, F.J., Marcu, D.: Statistical phrase-based translation. In: Human Language Technology Conference of the North American Chapter of the Association for Computational Linguistics, HLT-NAACL 2003, Edmonton, Canada, 27 May-1 June 2003 (2003)
6. Och, F.J., Ney, H.: The alignment template approach to statistical machine translation. Comput. Linguist. **30**(4), 417–449 (2004)
7. Papineni, K., Roukos, S., Ward, T., Zhu, W.: Bleu: a method for automatic evaluation of machine translation. In: Proceedings of the 40th Annual Meeting of the Association for Computational Linguistics, 6–12 July 2002, Philadelphia, PA, USA, pp. 311–318 (2002)
8. Snover, M., Dorr, B., Schwartz, R., Micciulla, L., Makhoul, J.: A study of translation edit rate with targeted human annotation. In: Proceedings of Association for Machine Translation in the Americas, vol. 200 (2006)
9. Vilar, D., Xu, J., d'Haro, L.F., Ney, H.: Error analysis of statistical machine translation output. In: Proceedings of LREC, pp. 697–702 (2006)
10. Chiang, D.: Hierarchical phrase-based translation. Comput. Linguist. **33**(2), 201–228 (2007)
11. Galley, M., Hopkins, M., Knight, K., Marcu, D.: What's in a translation rule? In: Human Language Technology Conference of the North American Chapter of the Association for Computational Linguistics, HLT-NAACL 2004, Boston, Massachusetts, USA, 2–7 May 2004, pp. 273–280 (2004)
12. Koehn, P., Schroeder, J.: Experiments in domain adaptation for statistical machine translation. In: Proceedings of the Second Workshop on Statistical Machine Translation. Association for Computational Linguistics, pp. 224–227 (2007)
13. Och, F.J., Ney, H.: Discriminative training and maximum entropy models for statistical machine translation. In: Proceedings of the 40th Annual Meeting of the Association for Computational Linguistics, 6–12 July 2002, Philadelphia, PA, USA, pp. 295–302 (2002)

14. Och, F.J.: Minimum error rate training in statistical machine translation. In: Proceedings of the 41st Annual Meeting of the Association for Computational Linguistics, 7–12 July, Sapporo Convention Center, Sapporo, pp. 160–167 (2003)
15. Xiong, D., Liu, Q., Lin, S.: Maximum entropy based phrase reordering model for statistical machine translation. In: ACL 2006, 21st International Conference on Computational Linguistics and 44th Annual Meeting of the Association for Computational Linguistics, Proceedings of the Conference, Sydney, Australia, 17–21 July 2006 (2006)
16. Malouf, R.: A comparison of algorithms for maximum entropy parameter estimation. In: Proceedings of the 6th Conference on Natural Language Learning, CoNLL 2002, Held in cooperation with COLING 2002, Taipei, Taiwan (2002)
17. Och, F.J., Ney, H.: Improved statistical alignment models. In: 38th Annual Meeting of the Association for Computational Linguistics, Hong Kong, China, 1–8 October 2000 (2000)
18. Xiao, T., Zhu, J., Zhang, H., Li, Q.: Niutrans: an open source toolkit for phrase-based and syntax-based machine translation. In: The 50th Annual Meeting of the Association for Computational Linguistics, Proceedings of the System Demonstrations, 10 July 2012, Jeju Island, Korea, pp. 19–24 (2012)
19. Huang, L., Chiang, D.: Forest rescoring: faster decoding with integrated language models. In: Annual Meeting-Association For Computational Linguistics, vol. 45, p. 144 (2007)
20. Li, C.H., Zhang, D., Li, M., Zhou, M., Zhang, H.: An empirical study in source word deletion for phrase-based statistical machine translation. In: Proceedings of the Third Workshop on Statistical Machine Translation. Association for Computational Linguistics, pp. 1–8 (2008)
21. Li, Q., Zhang, D., Li, M., Xiao, T., Zhu, J.: Better addressing word deletion for statistical machine translation. In: Lin, C.-Y., Xue, N., Zhao, D., Huang, X., Feng, Y. (eds.) ICCPOL/NLPCC -2016. LNCS, vol. 10102, pp. 91–102. Springer, Cham (2016). doi:10.1007/978-3-319-50496-4_8
22. Parton, K., Habash, N., McKeown, K., Iglesias, G., De Gispert, A.: Can automatic post-editing make mt more meaningful? In: Proceedings of the 16th Annual Conference of the European Association for Machine Translation, EAMT 2012, pp. 111–118 (2012)
23. Huck, M., Ney, H.: Insertion and deletion models for statistical machine translation. In: Proceedings of Human Language Technologies: Conference of the North American Chapter of the Association of Computational Linguistics, 3–8 June 2012, Montréal, Canada, pp. 347–351 (2012)
24. Zhang, Y., Matusov, E., Ney, H.: Are unaligned words important for machine translation? In: Proceedings of The 13th Annual Conference of the EAMT, vol. 226, p. 233 (2009)
25. Liu, Y., Liu, Q., Lin, S.: Discriminative word alignment by linear modeling. Computat. Linguist. **36**(3), 303–339 (2010)
26. Zhu, J., Li, Q., Xiao, T.: Improving syntactic rule extraction through deleting spurious links with translation span alignment. Nat. Lang. Eng. **21**(2), 227–249 (2015)
27. Menezes, A., Quirk, C.: Syntactic models for structural word insertion and deletion. In: Proceedings of the Conference on Empirical Methods in Natural Language Processing. Association for Computational Linguistics, pp. 735–744 (2008)

Cost-Aware Learning Rate for Neural Machine Translation

Yang Zhao, Yining Wang, Jiajun Zhang, and Chengqing Zong(✉)

National Laboratory of Pattern Recognition, Institute of Automation, CAS University of Chinese Academy of Sciences, Beijing, China
zhaoyang2015@ia.ac.cn
{yining.wang,jjzhang,cqzong}@nlpr.ia.ac.cn

Abstract. Neural Machine Translation (NMT) has drawn much attention due to its promising translation performance in recent years. The conventional optimization algorithm for NMT sets a unified learning rate for each gold target word during training. However, words under different probability distributions should be handled differently. Thus, we propose a cost-aware learning rate method, which can produce different learning rates for words with different costs. Specifically, for the gold word which ranks very low or has a big probability gap with the best candidate, the method can produce a larger learning rate and vice versa. The extensive experiments demonstrate the effectiveness of our proposed method.

Keywords: Neural machine translation · Cost-aware learning rate

1 Introduction

Neural Machine Translation (NMT) based on the encoder-decoder architecture proposed by [4,10] can achieve promising translation performance for several language pairs, such as English-to-German and English-to-French [1,14,23,25].

In general, we can train a NMT system by using maximum likelihood estimation with stochastic gradient descent and back propagation through time. However, this kind of optimization algorithm has a drawback that it sets a unified learning rate for each gold target word during training.

Actually, for a parallel sentence pair, gold target words have different prediction probability distributions (costs). Figure 1 shows an example. Given the gold target sentence $\{y_1, y_2, y_3, y_4\}$ during training, each gold target word has a different probability distribution. y_1 ranks first and this is the ideal case. y_2 ranks second and the gap with the best candidate is quite small (0.01), making y_2 only need a small boost. In contrast, although there exists a small gap (0.05) between y_3 and the top one, its ranking is relatively low (lower than the beam size in decoding). The ranking of y_4 is high (second) while there exists a huge gap (0.85) with the top one. Intuitively, y_3 and y_4 need a big boost to increase the ranking or reduce the gap.

We believe that it is more reasonable to assign different learning rates to words under different costs. Therefore, we propose a cost-aware learning rate

M. Sun et al. (Eds.): CCL 2017 and NLP-NABD 2017, LNAI 10565, pp. 85–93, 2017.
https://doi.org/10.1007/978-3-319-69005-6_8

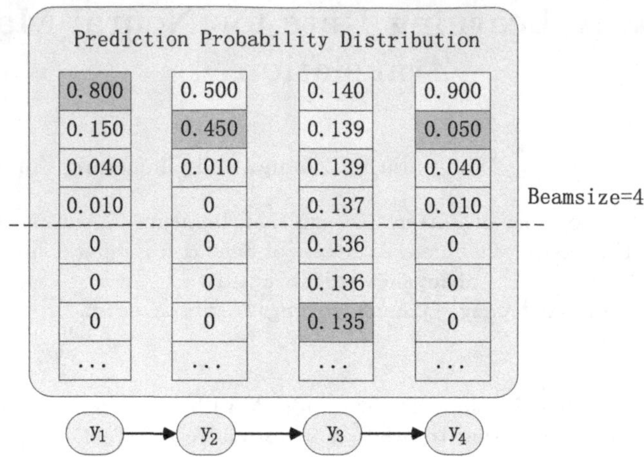

Fig. 1. For the target sentence y_1, y_2, y_3, y_4 in a parallel sentence pair, each gold target word (highlighted in yellow) has a different prediction probability distribution, and ideally dynamic learning rate is needed. In this example, we assume the beam size in decoding is set to 4. (Color figure online)

method, which can produce dynamic learning rates according to the probability distribution of the gold target words. More specifically, for the gold words which have a low probability ranking (lower than the beam size which is set in decoding) or have a big probability gap with the top candidate, the method will produce a larger learning rate and vice versa.

In this paper, we make the following contributions:

(1) To best of our knowledge, this is the first effort to propose a cost-aware learning rate to improve the training procedure of neural machine translation. According to the prediction probability distributions, we design different strategy to produce dynamic learning rates.
(2) Our empirical experiments on Chinese-English translation tasks show the efficacy of our methods and we can obtain an average improvement of 0.87 BLEU score on multiple evaluation datasets.

2 Neural Machine Translation

The goal of machine translation is to transform a sequence of source words $X = \{x_1, x_2, ..., x_{Tx}\}$ into a sequence of target words $Y = \{y_1, y_2, ..., y_{Ty}\}$. The NMT contains two parts, encoder and decoder. As the name suggests, encoder transforms the source sentence X into context vectors C. And decoder generates target translation Y from the context vectors C by maximizing the probability of $p(y_i|y_{<i}, C)$. And Fig. 2 shows the framework of the attention-based NMT proposed by Luong et al. [14], which utilizes stacked Long Short Term Memory (LSTM) [29] layers for both encoder and decoder.

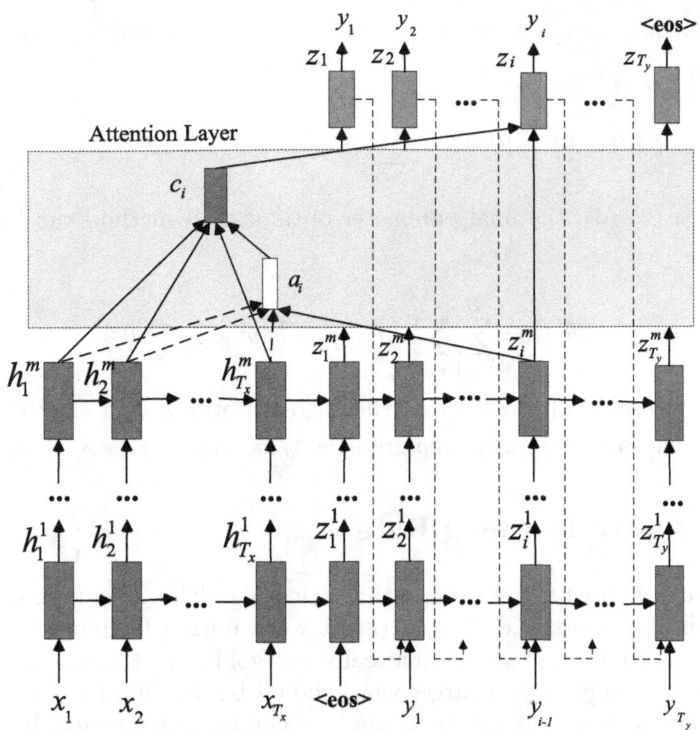

Fig. 2. The encoder-decoder framework for NMT.

Given the sentence aligned bilingual training data, the cost functions can be defined as the following conditional log-likelihood[1]:

$$L(\theta, D) = \frac{1}{N}\sum_{n=1}^{N}\sum_{i}^{T_y} log(p(y_i^{(n)}|p(y_{<i}^{(n)}, X^{(n)}, \theta)) \tag{1}$$

Then, we can use maximum likelihood estimation with stochastic gradient descent and back propagation through time to get the optimal parameters as follows:

$$\theta \leftarrow \theta + \eta * \bigtriangledown L(\theta, D) \tag{2}$$

where η is the learning rate, $\bigtriangledown L(\theta, D)$ is the gradient direction, and can be calculated as the sum of the gradients of the sentences in minibatch B:

$$\bigtriangledown L(\theta, D) = \sum_{n=1}^{B} \bigtriangledown L(\theta, (X^{(n)}, Y^{(n)})) \tag{3}$$

[1] Recently, evaluation metric oriented cost functions are investigated Shen et al. [21] and Wu et al. [25] and the cost-aware learning rate can also be applied. In this paper, we use log-likelihood costs as a case study.

The gradients of each sentences can be calculated as a sum of gradients per-step:

$$\triangledown L(\theta, (X^{(n)}, Y^{(n)})) = \sum_{i=1}^{T_y} \triangledown log(p(y_i^{(n)}|y_{<i}^{(n)}, X^{(n)}, \theta)) \quad (4)$$

From Eqs. (2)–(4), the final parameter optimization method can be defined as follows:

$$\theta \leftarrow \theta + \eta * \sum_{n=1}^{B} \sum_{i=1}^{T_y} \triangledown log(p(y_i^{(n)}|y_{<i}^{(n)}, X^{(n)}, \theta)) \quad (5)$$

It is easy to see from Eq. (5) that the current optimization algorithm sets a unified learning rate η for each step gradient $\triangledown log(p(y_i^{(n)}|y_{<i}^{(n)}, X^{(n)}, \theta))$.

3 Cost-Aware Learning Rate

In Sect. 2 we described the current optimization algorithm (Eq. (5)), which sets a unified learning rate for each gold target word during training. In fact, the probability distributions vary dramatically for gold target words in different training steps. Ideally, a gold target word should be penalized much more if it ranks very low or has a big gap with the best candidate. Accordingly, dynamic learning rate is needed. To achieve this goal, we design cost-aware learning rate as follows:

Step1: For each gold target word y_i in Y, we can get the ranking (denoted as r) of y_i based on the prediction probability distribution $p(V_t|y_{<i}, X, \theta)$, where V_t is all the target candidates.

Step2: We can also get the probability gap between y_i and the word with the maximum probability as follows:

$$g = max(p(V_t|y_{<i}, X, \theta)) - p(y_i|y_{<i}, X, \theta) \quad (6)$$

Step3: Then, we can calculate the cost aware learning rate λ_i for y_i as follows:

$$\begin{aligned} \lambda_i &= \alpha * f(r) + \beta * g + \gamma \\ f(r) &= \begin{cases} 1 & if\ r > b \\ 0 & if\ r \leq b \end{cases} \end{aligned} \quad (7)$$

where r is derived from Step 1, g is calculated as Eq. (6), b is the beam size which is set in decoding, α, β and γ are hyper parameters that can be used to adjust the respective weights. As shown in Eq. (7), our method has two functions:

(1) It can produce a larger learning rate for the word whose ranking is lower than the beam size. Here we explain the reason why we design our method like this. During decoding, we will use beam search to get the best target sentence. To make it possible, we should first guarantee that each gold target word could rank before beam size during training. Therefore, the algorithm will set a larger learning rate for the word whose ranking is lower than the beam size to boost its ranking.

(2) It can also produce a larger learning rate for the words which have a big probability gap with the top one. The process of involving g is important because we want to reduce the gap between the gold target words and the candidates with the maximum prediction probability.

After getting the cost-aware learning rate λ_i for y_i, our final parameter optimization method, extended from Eq. (5), can be described as follows:

$$\theta \leftarrow \theta + \eta * \sum_{n=1}^{B} \sum_{i=1}^{T_y} \lambda_i * \nabla log(p(y_i^{(n)} | y_{<i}^{(n)}, X^{(n)}, \theta)) \tag{8}$$

where λ_i is calculated as Eq. (7). We retain the unified learning rate η. When $\alpha = 0$, $\beta = 0$ and $\gamma = 1$ (Eq. (7)), our method falls back to the original optimization method.

4 Experimental Settings

4.1 Dataset

We test the proposed methods on Chinese-to-English with two data sets: (1) small data set, which includes 0.63 M[2] sentence pairs; (2) large-scale data set, which contains about 2.1 M sentence pairs. For validation, we choose NIST 2003 (MT03) dataset. For testing, we use NIST2004 (MT04), NIST 2005 (MT05), NIST 2006 (MT06) and NIST 2008 (MT08) datasets.

4.2 Training and Evaluation Details

We use the Zoph_RNN toolkit[3] to implement our described methods. The encoder and decoder include two stacked LSTM layers. The word embedding dimension and the size of hidden layers are all set to 1,000. We use a minibatch size of $B = 128$. We limit the vocabulary to 30 K most frequent words for both the source and target languages. Other words are replaced by a special symbol UNK. At test time, we employ beam search with beam size $b = 12$. We use case-insensitive 4-gram BLEU score as the automatic metric [18] for translation quality evaluation.

---

[2] LDC2000T50, LDC2002L27, LDC2002T01, LDC2002E18, LDC2003E07, LDC2003E14, LDC2003T17, LDC2004T07.

[3] https://github.com/isi-nlp/Zoph_RNN. We extend this toolkit with global attention.

4.3 Translation Methods

In the experiments, we compare our method with the conventional Statical Machine Translation (SMT) model and the baseline NMT model trained with the unified learning rate. We list all the translation methods as follows:

(1) **Moses:** It is the state-of-the-art phrase-based SMT system [11]. Our system is built using the default settings.
(2) **U_lr:** It is the baseline attention-based NMT system [14,28] trained with the unified learning rate. The initial unified learning rate η is set to 0.1, and the learning rate decay for η is set to 0.5.
(3) **C_lr:** It is similar to **U_lr** except that it is trained by our cost-aware learning rate method. The hyper parameters in Eq. (7) are respectively set to 0.2 (α), 0.8 (β) and 1 (γ), which are tuned on the validation dataset.

5 Translation Results

Table 1 reports the detailed translation results for different methods. Comparing the **Moses** and **U_lr**, it is very obvious that the attention-based NMT system **U_lr** substantially outperforms the phrase-based SMT system **Moses** on both small and large data, where average improvement on small data is up to 3.99 BLEU points (32.71 vs. 28.72) and on large data is 1.85 (36.74 vs. 34.89).

Table 1. Translation results (BLEU) for different methods on small and large-scale data. "*" indicates that it is statistically significant better ($p < 0.05$) than "**U_lr**" and "†" indicates $p < 0.01$.

Method	MT03	MT04	MT05	MT06	MT08	Ave
Moses(small)	28.35	30.02	29.10	32.92	23.20	28.72
U_lr(small)	34.20	36.96	32.60	33.85	25.96	32.71
C_lr(small)	35.01*	37.74*	33.71†	34.93†	26.51*	33.58
Moses(large)	38.54	39.01	36.55	35.59	24.76	34.89
U_lr(large)	39.07	40.49	37.26	38.04	28.83	36.74
C_lr(large)	39.73*	41.06*	38.24*	38.88*	29.49*	37.48

Compared to **U_lr** (row 2 in Table 1), our method (**C_lr**) improves the translation quality on all test sets and the average improvement is up to 0.87 BLEU points (33.58 vs. 32.71). It indicates that our cost-aware learning rate method can learn better network parameters for neural machine translation.

As our method tries to make more gold target words rank before beam size and reduce the probability gap between the gold word and the best candidate with the maximum prediction probability, we calculate in the training data the proportion of the gold target words which rank in top beam size and the average

Table 2. The proportion of gold target words whose rankings lie in the top beam size and the average gap between the gold target words and the best candidate.

Method	Ranking in top beam size	Gap
U_lr	92.73%	0.067
C_lr	95.92%	0.046

gap between the gold target word and the top one. As shown in Table 2, our method can indeed boost the rankings of the gold target words and narrow the gap with the best candidate.

Besides that, we conduct another experiment to find out whether or not is our method still very effective when we have much more bilingual data. As shown by the last two rows in Table 1, our model can also improve the NMT translation quality on all of the test sets and the average improvement can be up to 0.74 BLEU points (37.48 vs. 36.74).

6 Related Work

In order to get better parameters for NMT, most of the existing works mainly focus on using more monolingual data [3,7,20,27] or adding additional prior knowledge besides bilingual data [5,17,24,26], and designing better attentional mechanisms [2,6,13–16].

Our work attempts to improve the network parameter tuning for neural machine translation when the log-likelihood objective function is employed. There are two closely related studies: one resorts to redesign the loss functions and the other tries to optimize the beam search algorithm.

Shen et al. [21] applies the minimum risk training for NMT and achieves a significant improvement. Sam and Alexander [19] proposes a model using beam search training scheme to get sequence-level scores.

Several researchers improved the beam search method in decoding. He et al. [8] and Stahlberg et al. [22] rerank target word candidates with additional features. Li and Jurafsky [12] rescore the translation candidates on sentence-level by using the mutual information between target and source sides. Hoang et al. [9] converts the decoding from a discrete optimization problem to a continuous optimization problem.

The significant difference between our work and these studies lies in that our work focuses on improving the NMT training procedure from another perspective. We design a cost-aware learning rate method and set different learning rates for the words with different costs.

7 Conclusions and Future Work

In order to improve the current NMT optimization algorithm that used a unified learning rate for each gold target word during the whole training procedure, we proposed a cost-aware learning rate method, which aims at producing different learning rates for the gold target words under different probability distributions. The extensive experiments show that our method can achieve statistical significantly improvements on translation quality.

In the future, we plan to design more effective methods to calculate more appropriate learning rates for NMT training.

Acknowledgments. The research work has been supported by the Natural Science Foundation of China under Grant No. 61403379 and No. 61402478.

References

1. Bahdanau, D., Cho, K., Bengio, Y.: Neural machine translation by jointly learning to align and translate. In: Proceedings of ICLR 2015 (2015)
2. Cheng, Y., Shen, S., He, Z., He, W., Wu, H., Sun, M., Liu, Y.: Agreement-based joint training for bidirectional attention-based neural machine translation. In: Proceedings of IJCAI 2016 (2016)
3. Cheng, Y., Wei, X., He, Z., He, W., Hua, W., Sun, M., Liu, Y.: Semi-supervised learning for neural machine translation. In: Proceedings of ACL 2016, pp. 1965–1974 (2016)
4. Cho, K., van Merriënboer, B., Gulcehre, C., Bahdanau, D., Bougares, F., Schwenk, H., Bengio, Y.: Learning phrase representations using RNN encoder-decoder for statistical machine translation. In: Proceedings of EMNLP 2014, pp. 1724–1734 (2014)
5. Cohn, T., Vu Hoang, C.D., Vymolova, E., Yao, K., Dyer, C., Haffari, G.: Incorporating structural alignment biases into an attentional neural translation model. In: Proceedings of NAACL 2016, pp. 876–885 (2016)
6. Feng, S., Liu, S., Li, M., Zhou, M.: Implicit distortion and fertility models for attentionbased encoder-decoder NMT model. arXiv preprint arXiv:1601.03317 (2016)
7. He, D., Xia, Y., Qin, T., Wang, L., Yu, N., Liu, T., Ma, W.: Dual learning for machine translation. In: Proceedings of NIPS 2016 (2016)
8. He, W., He, Z., Hua, W., Wang, H.: Improved neural machine translation with Smt features. In: Proceedings of AAAI 2016, pp. 151–157 (2016)
9. Vu Hoang, C.D., Haffari, G., Cohn, T.: Decoding as continuous optimization in neural machine translation. arXiv preprint arXiv:1701.02854 (2017)
10. Kalchbrenner, N., Blunsom, P.: Recurrent continuous translation models. In: Proceedings of EMNLP 2013, pp. 1700–1709 (2013)
11. Koehn, P., Hoang, H., Birch, A., Callison-Burch, C., Federico, M., Bertoldi, N., Cowan, B., Shen, W., Moran, C., Zens, R., et al.: Moses: open source toolkit for statistical machine translation. In: Proceedings of ACL 2007, pp. 177–180 (2007)
12. Li, J., Jurafsky, D.: Mutual information and diverse decoding improve neural machine translation. arXiv preprint arXiv:1601.00372 (2016)
13. Liu, L., Utiyama, M., Finch, A., Sumita, E.: Neural machine translation with supervised attention. In: Proceedings of COLING 2016, pp. 3093–3102 (2016)
14. Luong, M.-T., Pham, H., Manning, C.D.: Effective approaches to attention based neural machine translation. In: Proceedings of EMNLP 2015, pp. 1412–1421 (2015)
15. Meng, F., Zhengdong, L., Li, H., Liu, Q.: Interactive attention for neural machine translation. In: Proceedings of COLING 2016, pp. 2174–2185 (2016)

16. Mi, H., Sankaran, B., Wang, Z., Ittycheriah, A.: A coverage embedding model for neural machine translation. In: Proceedings of EMNLP 2016, pp. 955–960 (2016)
17. Mi, H., Wang, Z., Ittycheriah, A.: Supervised attentions for neural machine translation. In: Proceedings of EMNLP 2016, pp. 2283–2288 (2016)
18. Papineni, K., Roukos, S., Ward, T., Zhu, W.: BLEU: a method for automatic evaluation of machine translation. In: Proceedings of ACL 2002, pp. 311–318 (2002)
19. Wiseman, S., Rush, A.M.: Sequence-to-sequence learning as beam-search optimization. In: Proceedings of EMNLP 2016, pp. 1296–1306 (2016)
20. Sennrich, R., Haddow, B., Birch, A.: Improving neural machine translation models with monolingual data. In: Proceedings of ACL 2016, pp. 86–96 (2016)
21. Shen, S., Cheng, Y., He, Z., He, W., Hua, W., Sun, M., Liu, Y.: Minimum risk training for neural machine translation. In: Proceedings of ACL 2015, pp. 1683–1692 (2015)
22. Stahlberg, F., Hasler, E., Waite, A., Byrne, B.: Syntactically guided neural machine translation. arXiv preprint arXiv:1605.04569 (2016)
23. Sutskever, I., Vinyals, O., Le, Q.V.: Sequence to sequence learning with neural networks. In: Proceedings of NIPS 2014, pp. 3104–3112 (2014)
24. Tang, Y., Meng, F., Lu, Z., Li, H., Yu, P.L.H.: Neural machine translation with external phrase memory. arXiv preprint arXiv:1606.01792 (2016)
25. Yonghui, W., Schuster, M., Chen, Z., Le, Q.V., Norouzi, M., Macherey, W., Krikun, M., Cao, Y., Gao, Q., Macherey, K., et al.: Bridging the gap between human and machine translation. arXiv preprint arXiv:1609.08144 (2016)
26. Zhang, J., Zong, C.: Bridging neural machine translation and bilingual dictionaries. arXiv preprint arXiv:1610.07272 (2016)
27. Zhang, J., Zong, C.: Exploiting source-side monolingual data in neural machine translation. In: Proceedings of EMNLP 2016, pp. 1535–1545 (2016)
28. Zoph, B., Knight, K.: Multi-source neural translation. In: Proceedings of NAACL 2016, pp. 30–34 (2016)
29. Hochreiter, S., Schmidhuber, J.: Long short-term memory. Neural Comput. **9**(8), 1735–1780 (1997)

Knowledge Graph and Information Extraction

Integrating Word Sequences and Dependency Structures for Chemical-Disease Relation Extraction

Huiwei Zhou[1(✉)], Yunlong Yang[1], Zhuang Liu[1], Zhe Liu[2], and Yahui Men[2]

[1] School of Computer Science and Technology, Dalian University of Technology, Dalian 116024, Liaoning, China
zhouhuiwei@dlut.edu.cn, {SDyyl_1949,zhuangliu1992}@mail.dlut.edu.cn

[2] School of Life Science and Medicine, Dalian University of Technology, Dalian 116024, Liaoning, China
dlutliuzhe@163.com, menyahui@mail.dlut.edu.cn

Abstract. Understanding chemical-disease relations (CDR) from biomedical literature is important for biomedical research and chemical discovery. This paper uses a *k*-max pooling convolutional neural network (CNN) to exploit word sequences and dependency structures for CDR extraction. Furthermore, an effective weighted context method is proposed to capture semantic information of word sequences. Our system extracts both intra- and inter-sentence level chemical-disease relations, which are merged as the final CDR. Experiments on the BioCreative V CDR dataset show that both word sequences and dependency structures are effective for CDR extraction, and their integration could further improve the extraction performance.

Keywords: CDR extraction · CNN · Word sequences · Dependency structures

1 Introduction

Extracting chemicals, diseases and their relationships are significantly important to biomedical research and healthcare [1]. Manual annotating chemical-disease relations (CDR) from the vast amount of published biomedical literature is expensive and time-consuming, and is impossible to keep up-to-date. Many automated CDR extraction methods have been proposed. To promote CDR research, the BioCreative V CDR task [2] provides a public dataset as a platform for comparing different methods. The task includes two subtasks: (i) disease named entity recognition and normalization (DNER) and (ii) chemical-induced diseases (CID) relation extraction. In this paper, we focus on the CID subtask with both intra- and inter-sentence levels.

Existing studies on CDR extraction contain rule-based [3] and machine learning-based [4–7] methods. Rule-based methods could make full use of syntactic information and have achieved good performance. But the rules are hard to develop to a new dataset. As for machine learning-based relation extraction, feature-based and

M. Sun et al. (Eds.): CCL 2017 and NLP-NABD 2017, LNAI 10565, pp. 97–109, 2017.
https://doi.org/10.1007/978-3-319-69005-6_9

kernel-based methods are widely used. Feature-based methods [4–6] focus on extracting effective features. However, the features are one-hot representations, which could not capture deep semantic information. Kernel-based methods [7] define a tree kernel over shallow parse tree representations of sentences, which is also hard to capture deep syntactic structure information.

With the development of neutral networks, some studies begin to exploit deep semantic information for relation extraction. Zhou et al. [7] simply adopt a long short-term memory (LSTM) model [8] and a convolutional neural network (CNN) model [9] to get semantic representations of surface sequence, and have achieved success for CDR extraction. CNN shows its superiority to other neutral networks on relation extraction task [9].

This paper develops a multiple layer CNN model to integrate sequences and dependency structures for CDR extraction. To capture more effective semantic and syntactic information, we use the *k*-max pooling [10] instead of the traditional max pooling. Besides, we propose an extended context representation inspired by Vu et al. [11]. The major difference between our method and Vu et al. [11] is that we concatenate the different context representations by different weights rather than concatenating them equally. Both intra- and inter-sentence level CDR are investigated in this paper to improve the extraction performance. Experiments on the BioCreative V CDR dataset demonstrate the effectiveness of our method. In the following section, we review the literature related to this paper from two aspects: CDR extraction and CNN for relation extraction.

2 Related Work

2.1 CDR Extraction

Lowe et al. [3] develop rules by manually identifying the key words that indicate the CDR. Their system is evaluated on the BioCreative V CDR Task, and achieves 60.75% F-score using gold-standard entities, 52.20% F-score using entities identified by their entity recognizer.

Feature-based methods focus on designing rich features. Gu et al. [5] use effective linguistic features to extract CDR with maximum entropy models. They achieve 58.3% F-score on the BioCreative V test data using gold-standard entities. Xu et al. [4] employ different drug-side-effect resources to generate knowledge-based features for both sentence-level and document-level CDR extraction, and achieve 67.16% F-score using gold-standard entities. Pons et al. [6] use rich prior knowledge features and achieve 70.2% F-score using gold-standard entities.

Kernel-based methods are effective for capturing syntactic structure information. Zhou et al. [7] exploit a shortest dependency path (SDP) tree kernel to capture the predicate-argument relations, which could achieve 50.11% F-score using gold-standard entities. Zhou et al. [7] also use two categories of neural networks, LSTM and CNN, to capture deep semantic representations. To further integrate lexical and syntactic information, two neural models are combined with feature-based model and kernel-based model by a linear combination respectively. Among different neural network models employed for relation extraction [9, 12], CNN is superior for relation extraction to the others.

2.2 CNN for Relation Extraction

Nguyen and Grishman [9] first employ CNN for relation extraction. To avoid the noise that originates from the feature extraction process, Zeng et al. [12] propose a piecewise CNN, which divides the convolution results into three segments based on the positions of the two entities, and returns the maximum value in each segment instead of a single maximum value over the entire sentence. Inspired by their work, we apply CNN model to capture both the word sequence-based representations and the dependency-based representations for CDR extraction.

3 Methods

The architecture of our system is shown in Fig. 1, which consists of a training phase and a testing phase. In the training phase, we construct the intra- and inter-sentence level instances from the training data. For intra-sentence level instances, we learn a sequence-based model and a dependency-based model by CNN respectively. For inter-sentence level instances, we learn a sequence-based model by CNN. In the testing phrase, the three models are applied to extract CDR respectively. And the predicted results of the three models are merged as the final results.

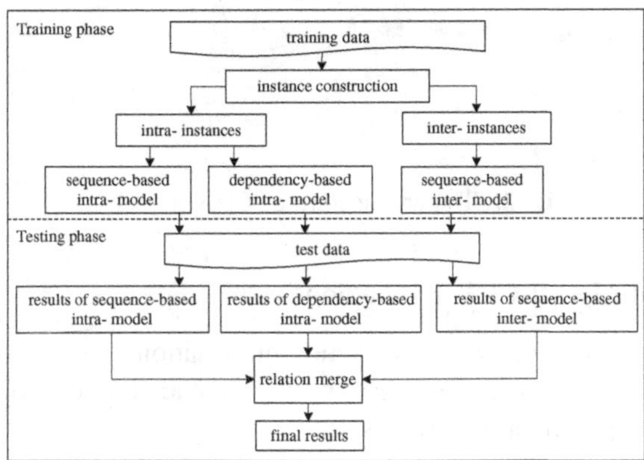

Fig. 1. Architecture of our system.

3.1 Convolutional Neural Network

The architecture of our CNN model are shown in Fig. 2. It consists with four main layers:

(i) the vector representation layer. The vector representation layer embeds each word in a sentence into a low dimensional space. Consider an input of word vector sequence $x = \{x_1, x_2, \ldots, x_n\}$, where $x_n \in \mathbb{R}^d$ is a d-dimensional word vector. Then the word vector sequence is fed into the convolution layer.

(ii) the convolution layer. The convolution operation with a filter $w \in \mathbb{R}^{h \times d}$ can be expressed as $c_i = f(w \cdot x_{i:i+h-1} + b)$, where h is a window size, b is a bias term, f is a non-linear function such as the hyperbolic tangent and $x_{i:j}$ refer to the subsequence of words from x_i to x_j. The filter is used to each possible window of words in the sequence $x = \{x_1, x_2, \ldots, x_n\}$ to produce a feature map: $\mathbf{c} = [c_1, c_2, \ldots, c_{n-h+1}]$ with $\mathbf{c} \in \mathbb{R}^{n-h+1}$. In our model, multiple filters with different window size are apply to obtain multiple features.

(iii) the k-max pooling layer. We use a k-max pooling operation instead of the max-pooling to take the k highest values as the features. The order of the k values in the sequence corresponds to their original order in $\mathbf{c}$. In particularly, when $k = 1$, the pooling operation becomes the max pooling operation.

(iv) the softmax output layer. The k-max feature vector $z = [c_{11}, c_{12}, \ldots, c_{1k}, \ldots, c_{mk}] \in \mathbb{R}^{m*k}$ is fed to a softmax layer to perform classification in the end. Note that here we have m filters and each filter select the k highest values during the pooling.

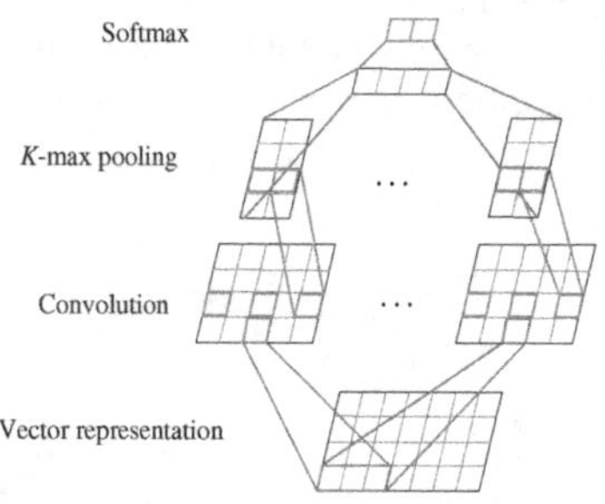

Fig. 2. The architecture of CNN model.

3.2 Intra-sentence Level CDR Extraction

To explore deep semantic and syntactic information behind CDR pairs of intra-sentence level instances, we learn word sequence-based representations and dependency-based representations by CNN.

Word Sequence-based Representations. The following representation methods based on word sequences are introduced and compared in this paper.

Word. This method inputs the word sequences between chemical and disease entities into CNN to capture semantic representations of CDR pairs. The dimension of word representation $xw \in \mathbb{R}^{d_1}$ is d_1. We regard this method as our baseline.

Word-position. Besides the word sequences, this method also inputs position tags of the word sequences. The relative distances from the current word to the two entities are transformed into representations. Then the representations of each word and its position tags are concatenated to form a vector representation $xw, xp \in \mathbb{R}^{d_1 + d_2 * 2}$.

Word-context. The **Word** method only includes internal context between chemical and disease entities. Motivated by Vu et al. [11], we introduce external context for relation extraction. The sentence is split into three disjoint regions based on the two entities: the left external context, the middle internal context and the right external context. Not only focusing on the middle internal context but also not ignoring the other external contexts, we use two contexts (1) *L*: a combination of the left external context, the left entity and the middle internal context; (2) *R*: a combination of the middle internal context, the right entity and the right external context. The difference between our model and Vu et al. [11] is that we do not connect the two contexts equally. Instead, we use the weight $\alpha, \beta \in [0, 1](\alpha + \beta = 1)$ to control the connection of the two contexts as follows:

$$z = [\alpha \cdot L_{11}, \alpha \cdot L_{12}, \ldots, \alpha \cdot L_{mk}, \beta \cdot R_{11}, \beta \cdot R_{12}, \ldots, \beta \cdot R_{mk}] \quad (1)$$

The weight α, β are the parameters that the network need to learn, which are both initialized as 0.5 at first. In order to compare the traditional connection method with the weighted concatenation, we name them as **Word-context** and **Word-weighted-context** respectively.

Dependency-based Representations. SDP is the shortest path linking the two entities in dependency tree. Taking Sentence 1 as an example, a chemical entity is denoted by wave line and three disease entities are denoted by underline. The chemical entity "*Lithium*" is associated with the three disease entities.

Sentence 1: *Lithium* also caused *proteinuria* and systolic *hypertension* in absence of *glomerulosclerosis*.

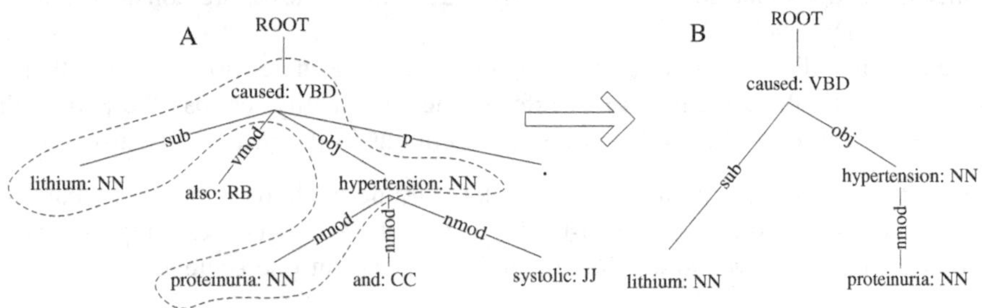

Fig. 3. Shortest dependency path tree (SDPT). (A) the fragment of dependency tree for Sentence 1. (B) shortest dependency path.

For the fragment of dependency tree (all words in Sentence 1 are transformed to lowercase) shown in Fig. 3A, SDP of the candidate "*lithium*" and "*proteinuria*" is shown in Fig. 3B. The following input methods are adopted to learn dependency-based representations.

SDP-word. This method inputs a sequence of words in the SDP into CNN to capture dependency semantic representations behind SDP. Note that the sequence follows the left-to-right order in SDP as shown in Fig. 4A.

SDP-dep. Compared with **SDP-word**, this method inputs the sequence consists both words and dependency relations of SDP as shown in Fig. 4B. The dimensions of word representations $xw \in \mathbb{R}^{d_1}$ and relation representations $xr \in \mathbb{R}^{d_1}$ are both d_1.

SDPSeq-word. Compared with **SDP-word**, this method also inputs a word sequence of SDP. However, the sequence follows the natural order of words in the sentence as shown in Fig. 4C. We consider that this order could reflect the actual semantic information in context.

SDPSeq-dep. This method also inserts the dependency relations into the **SDPSeq-word** as shown in Fig. 4D.

A lithium → caused → hypertension → proteinuria

B lithium → sub → caused → root → hypertension → obj → proteinuria → nmod

C lithium → caused → proteinuria → hypertension

D lithium → sub → caused → root → proteinuria →nmod →hypertension → obj

Fig. 4. SDP sequences. (A) **SDP-word.** (B) **SDP-dep.** (C) **SDPSeq-word.** (D) **SDPSeq-dep.**

3.3 Inter-sentence Level CDR Extraction

To reduce the inter-sentence level instances, the following heuristic filtering rules are applied on both training and testing datasets:

- Only the entities that not involved in any intra-sentence level are considered at the inter-sentence level.
- The sentence distance between two mentions in an instance should be less than 3.
- If there are multiple mentions that refer to the same entity, choose the pair of the inter-sentence level chemical and disease mentions in the nearest distance.

After that, the sequence-based intra- model learning method is applied to learn the inter- model based on these inter-CDR instances. **Word-context** representation methods are not employed since the two entities are not in one sentence.

3.4 Intra- and Inter- Level CDR Merge

The intra- and inter-sentence level extraction results are merged as the final relations. The CDR extracted by each level model are regarded as the true positives. Thus, the final CDR are consists with the following two parts:

- All the CDR extracted by the intra-sentence level model.
- The CDR extracted by the inter-sentence level model only if there are no intra-sentence level CDR find in the abstract.

3.5 Post-processing

To further pick more likely CDR and improve the performance, some rules are applied to help extract relations.

- **Focused rules for the post-processing.** If there are no CDR found in the abstract, all the chemicals in the title are associated with all the diseases in the entire abstract. When no chemical in the title, the chemical in the most occurrences number in the abstract is chosen to associate with all the diseases in the entire abstract.
- **Hypernym filtering for the post-processing.** There are hypernym or hyponym relationship between concepts of diseases or chemicals. However, the goal of the CID subtask aims to extract the relationships between the most specific diseases and chemicals. Therefore, we determine the hypernym relations based on the Mesh-controlled vocabulary [13] following the post-processing in Gu et al. [5]. Then we remove the positive instances that involve entities which are more general than other entities already extracted as the positive ones.

4 Experiments and Discussion

Dataset. Experiments are conducted on the BioCreative V CDR Task corpus. This corpus contains 1500 PubMed articles: 500 each for the training, development and test set. We combine the training and the development sets into the final training set and randomly select 20% of this set as the development set. We test our system on the test set with the golden standard entities. All sentences in the corpus are preprocessed with GENIA Tagger[1] and Gdep Parser[2] to get lexical information and dependency trees, respectively. The evaluation of CDR extraction is reported by official evaluation toolkit[3], which adopts Precision (*P*), Recall (*R*) and F-score (*F*) to measure the performance.

Hyperparameter Settings. For all the experiments below, 100 filters with the window size 3, 4 and 5 respectively are used in our system. In our experiments, we use Word2Vec tool[4] [14] to pre-train word representations on the datasets (about 8868 MB) downloaded from PubMed[5]. The dimension of word embeddings, dependency type embeddings and position embeddings are 100, 100 and 30 respectively.

---

1 http://www.nactem.ac.uk/GENIA/tagger/.

2 http://people.ict.usc.edu/~sagae/parser/gdep.

3 http://www.biocreative.org/tasks/biocreative-v/track-3-cdr.

4 https://code.google.com/p/word2vec/.

5 http://www.ncbi.nlm.nih.gov/pubmed/.

4.1 Effects of the *K*-Max Pooling

In this section, we compare the performance of the *k*-max pooling with the max pooling for CDR extraction. Several input methods are selected to learn representations. Table 1 shows the performance of different input methods with different *k*. We vary *k* from 1 to 4.

From Table 1, we can see that the trends of the three methods are similar. When we increase *k* from 1 (the max pooling) to 2, the performance of all methods is improved. This indicates that the *k*-max pooling could capture more effective information and produce deep semantic representations than the max pooling method. However, when *k* increases to 2 and 4, the performance drops. The reason may be that too much noise features are select during the pooling, which could harm model performance. We set $k = 2$ in the following experiments.

Table 1. Performance of different *k* values.

Methods	*k* = 1 (%)			*k* = 2 (%)			*k* = 3 (%)			*k* = 4 (%)		
	P	*R*	*F*	*P*	*R*	*F*	*P*	*R*	*F*	*P*	*R*	*F*
Word	47.41	57.60	52.01	49.78	54.50	**52.04**	48.99	54.50	51.60	51.70	51.31	51.51
Word-position	52.68	49.81	51.89	55.19	49.81	**52.36**	50.65	50.84	51.30	55.74	46.90	51.61
SDP-word	55.36	51.88	53.56	51.78	55.91	**53.77**	53.26	52.81	53.04	53.20	52.91	53.06

4.2 Performance of the Intra-sentence CDR Extraction

In this section, we evaluate the word sequence-based and dependency-based representations for the intra-sentence CDR extraction.

Performance of the word sequence-based representations. The detailed performances of the word sequence-based methods are summarized in Table 2. From the results, we can see that:

- The **Word** method with only the word sequence has achieved an acceptable result, which demonstrates the superiority of CNN for relation extraction.
- When the position embeddings are added to the word sequence, the performance of **Word-position** is improved. This indicates that encoding the relative distances to the entity pairs is effective for CDR extraction.
- The **Word-context** method shows a better result than the **Word** method. The reason may be that the trigger words which indicate the CID relation would occur not only in the middle contexts but also in the left or the right contexts.
- The **Word-weighted-context** improves the performance further. It is believed that given different weights to the contexts could reduce the noise data, and result in higher F-score. The best performance is obtained with $\alpha = 0.589$ during the training process.

Table 2. Performance of word sequence-based representations.

Methods	*P* (%)	*R* (%)	*F* (%)
Word	49.78	54.50	52.04
Word-position	55.19	49.81	52.36
Word-context	57.40	50.18	53.55
Word-weighted-context	53.98	53.47	**53.72**

Performance of the dependency-based representations. Table 3 shows the performance of the dependency-based methods on the CDR extraction. From this table, we can see that:

- The **SDP-word** get a better result than the **Word** in Table 2. Thus, it can be seen that SDP could capture the most direct semantic representation connecting the two entities and provide the strong hints for the relation extraction.
- When we add the dependency type in the **SDP-word**, the F-score of the **SDP-dep** improves to 53.90%. The dependency type can reflect the syntactic relation between two words, which lead to improvement in extraction precision.
- However, the **SDPSeq-dep** fails to catch up the **SDP-dep**, and the **SDPSeq-word** fails to catch up the **SDP-word** similarly, which suggest that the natural order of words may lose the structure information and is hard for CNN to capture the semantic representations.

After getting both the sequence-based representations and dependency-based representations, we combine the best sequence-based (**Word-weighted-context**) and dependency-based (**SDP-dep**) models as the final intra-sentence level model. Then for each intra-sentence instance x in the test set, the predicted relation label y is calculated by $y = \arg\max_{l \in \{0,1\}}(P_{seq}(l|x) + P_{dep}(l|x))$, where $P_{seq}(l|x)$ and $P_{dep}(l|x)$ represent the predicted probabilities of the sequenced-based and dependency-based models with the relation label $l \in \{0, 1\}$. This method is called **Combination.** The result reaches 55.15% F-score as shown in Table 3. This indicates that both the sequence-based model and the dependency-based model have their own advantages and could capture different information for CDR extraction. Their combination could further improve the performance.

Table 3. Performance of dependency-based representations.

Methods	*P* (%)	*R* (%)	*F* (%)
SDP-word	51.78	55.91	53.77
SDP-dep	54.74	53.10	53.90
SDPSeq-word	53.27	51.88	52.57
SDPSeq-dep	51.04	54.88	52.89
Combination	53.07	57.41	**55.15**

4.3 Performance of the Inter-sentence CDR Extraction

From Table 4 we can see that the performance of inter-sentence is quite low. The reason may be that:

- The inter-sentence level relations need more features and information to classify these implicit discourse relations. Only the raw word sequence may fail to capture some important information.
- It may be hard to learn the sequence representations between several sentences and the noise data also make confuse to the model.

Table 4. Performance of the Inter-sentence level methods.

Methods	*P* (%)	*R* (%)	*F* (%)
Word	24.80	14.16	18.03
Word-position	33.49	13.79	**19.53**

4.4 Results of the CDR Merging and Post-processing

Then we merge the best intra-sentence level relations (**Combination**) and the best inter-sentence level relations (**Word-position**) to obtain the final CDR. The merging results are shown in Table 5. From the Table, we can see that adding inter-sentence level relation improves the F-score from 55.15% to 59.16%. After applying the post-processing rules to the system, the F-score achieves to 61.35%. In particular, the post-processing could help the system to pick up some missed CDR from the abstract and remove some false positives involving hypernym entities. As a supplement to the system, post-processing has a very strong effectiveness.

Table 5. Results of the CDR merging and post-processing.

System	*P* (%)	*R* (%)	*F* (%)
Combination	53.07	57.41	55.15
CDR merging	60.19	58.16	59.16
+focused rules	55.48	66.41	60.46
+hypernym filter	58.38	64.63	**61.35**

4.5 Comparison with Related Work

Table 6 compares our system with the related work in the BioCreative V CDR task. All the systems are evaluated by the golden standard entities.

Table 6. Comparison with related work.

System	*P* (%)	*R* (%)	*F* (%)
Xu et al. [4]	60.86/65.80*	53.10/68.57*	56.71/67.16*
Gu et al. [5]	62.00	55.10	58.30
Lowe et al. [3]	59.29	62.29	60.75
Zhou et al. [7]	55.56	68.39	61.31
Ours	58.38	64.63	**61.35**

For CDR extraction, Xu et al. [4] use large-scale prior knowledge database, Comparative Toxicogenomics Database (CTD), to extract the domain knowledge features. With the golden entities, they achieve the highest F-score 67.16% with CTD features (with the symbol '*') while the other result without CTD features. The features derived from the CTD provide the improvement from 56.71% to 67.16%. The knowledge databases play a critical role in CDR extraction as it could help extract the relations not exist in the training corpus effectively. Our system does not utilize large-scale knowledge bases, and could not achieve comparable performance using knowledge-based features in Xu et al. [4]. Recently, researchers have leveraged large-scale knowledge bases to learn knowledge representations, which show good performance for relation extraction [15]. We would like to leave the effect of knowledge representations as a problem for future work.

Gu et al. [5] use many lexical and dependency features with the maximum entropy classifiers. Compared with Gu et al. [5], our system does not need extensive feature engineering but achieves better performance. The reason may be that our CNN model could capture both sequence and dependency information more effectively. Lowe et al. [3] find CDR by a rule-based system and achieve 60.75% F-score. Their system is simple and effective. However, the handcrafted rules are hard to develop to a new dataset. Zhou et al. [7] integrate a feature-based model, a kernel-based and a neural network model into a uniform framework. Our system only uses the CNN, but achieve a slightly better results 61.35% F-score than their 61.31% F-score.

4.6 Error Analysis

We perform an error analysis on the output of our final results (row 4 in Table 5) to detect the origins of false positives (FP) and false negatives (FN) errors, which are categorized in Fig. 5.

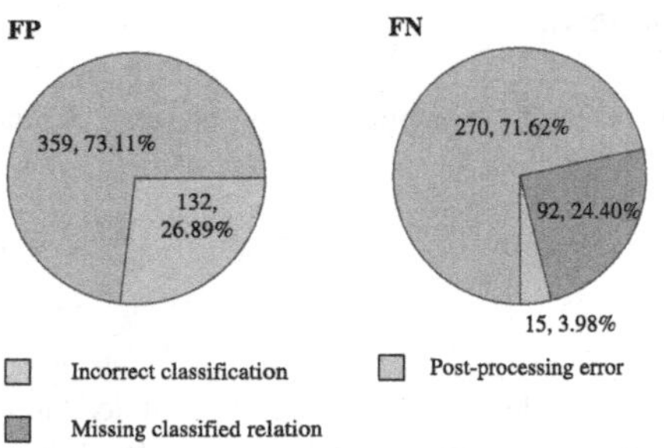

Fig. 5. Origins of FP and FN errors.

For FP in Fig. 5, two main error types are listed as follows:

- Incorrect classification: In spite of the detailed semantic representations, 73.11% FP come from the incorrect classification made by the intra- and inter- model. The main reason may be that sentence structure is complicated for both intra- and inter- level instances.

- Post-processing error: The focused rules bring 132 false CDR, with a proportion of 26.89%.

For FN in Fig. 5, three main error types are listed as follows:

- Incorrect classification: Among the 377 CDR that have not been extracted, 71.61% is caused by incorrect classification. Since it is difficult to find the relations spanning several sentences.
- Post-processing error: The hypernym filter removes 15 real CDR, with a proportion of 3.98%.
- Missing classified classification: 92 inter-sentence level instances are removed by the heuristic filtering rules in Sect. 3.3, which are not classified by our system at all. Because the sentence distance between the chemical and disease entities are more than 3.

5 Conclusion

Both semantic and syntactic information are effective for CDR extraction. Benefiting from the superior property of k-max pooling CNN, these information are well captured from word sequences and dependency structures for both intra- and inter-sentence level relation extraction. Furthermore, we propose weighted context representations for the sequence-based model to introduce external context of the two entities, which outperforms traditional context representations. Experiments on the BioCreative V CDR dataset show the effective of our sequence-based model, dependency-based model and their combination. In the future, we would like to encourage large-scale prior knowledge such as CTD and Wikipedia to improve extraction performance based on knowledge representation learning.

Acknowledgements. This research is supported by Natural Science Foundation of China (No. 61272375).

References

1. Dogan, R.I., Murray, G.C., Névéol, A., Lu, Z.Y.: Understanding PubMed user search behavior through log analysis. Database (2009), doi:10.1093/database/bap018
2. Wei, C.H., Peng, Y.F., Leaman, Ret al.: Overview of the biocreative v chemical disease relation (CDR) task. In: The Fifth BioCreative Challenge Evaluation Workshop, pp. 154–166 (2015)
3. Lowe, D.M., O'Boyle, N.M., Sayle, R.A.: Efficient chemical-disease identification and relationship extraction using Wikipedia to improve recall. Database (2016), doi:10.1093/database/baw039

4. Xu, J., Wu, Y.H., Zhang, Y.Y., Wang, J.Q., Lee, H., Xu, H.: CD-REST: a system for extracting chemical-induced disease relation in literature. Database (2016), doi:10.1093/database/baw036
5. Gu, J.H., Qian, L.H and Zhou, G.D.: Chemical-induced disease relation extraction with various linguistic features. Database (2016), doi:10.1093/database/baw042
6. Pons, E., Becker, B.F.H., Akhondi, S.A., Afzal, Z., van Mulligen, E.M., Kors, J.A.: Extraction of chemical-induced diseases using prior knowledge and textual information. Database (2016), doi:10.1093/database/baw046
7. Zhou, H.W., Deng, H.J., Chen, L., Yang, Y.L., Jia, C., Huang, D.G.: Exploiting syntactic and semantics information for chemical-disease relation extraction. Database (2016), doi:10.1093/database/baw048
8. Gers, F.A., Schmidhuber, J.: Recurrent nets that time and count. In: Neural Networks: Como, vol. 3, pp. 189–194 (2000)
9. Nguyen, T.H., Grishman, R.: Relation extraction: perspective from convolutional neural networks. In: The NAACL Workshop on Vector Space Modeling for NLP, pp. 39–48 (2015)
10. Kalchbrenner, N., Grefenstette, R., Blunsom, P.: A convolutional neural network for modelling sentences. In: Proceeding of ACL, pp. 655–665 (2014)
11. Vu, N.T., Adel, H., Gupta, P., Schütze, H.: Combining recurrent and convolutional neural networks for relation classification. In: Proceedings of NAACL-HLT, pp. 534–539 (2016)
12. Zeng, D.J., Liu, K., Chen, Y.B., Zhao, J.: Distant supervision for relation extraction via piecewise convolutional neural networks. In: Proceedings of EMNLP, pp. 1753–1762 (2015)
13. Coletti, M.H., Bleich, H.L.: Medical subject headings used to search the biomedical literature. J. Am. Med. Inform. Assoc. **8**, 317–323 (2011)
14. Mikolov, T., Sutskever, I., Chen, K., Corrado, G.S., Dean, J.: Distributed representations of words and phrases and their compositionality. In: Proceedings of NIPS, pp. 3111–3119 (2013)
15. Xie, R.B., Liu, Z.Y., Sun, M.S.: Representation learning of knowledge graphs with hierarchical types. In: Proceedings of AAAI, pp. 2965–2971 (2016)

Named Entity Recognition with Gated Convolutional Neural Networks

Chunqi Wang[1,2](✉), Wei Chen[2], and Bo Xu[2]

[1] University of Chinese Academy of Sciences, Beijing, China
[2] Institute of Automation, Chinese Academy of Sciences, Beijing, China
chqiwang@126.com, {wei.chen.media,xubo}@ia.ac.cn

Abstract. Most state-of-the-art models for named entity recognition (NER) rely on recurrent neural networks (RNNs), in particular long short-term memory (LSTM). Those models learn local and global features automatically by RNNs so that hand-craft features can be discarded, totally or partly. Recently, convolutional neural networks (CNNs) have achieved great success on computer vision. However, for NER problems, they are not well studied. In this work, we propose a novel architecture for NER problems based on GCNN — CNN with gating mechanism. Compared with RNN based NER models, our proposed model has a remarkable advantage on training efficiency. We evaluate the proposed model on three data sets in two significantly different languages — SIGHAN bakeoff 2006 MSRA portion for simplified Chinese NER and CityU portion for traditional Chinese NER, CoNLL 2003 shared task English portion for English NER. Our model obtains state-of-the-art performance on these three data sets.

1 Introduction

Named entity recognition (NER) is a challenging task in natural language processing (NLP) community. On the one hand, there is only very small amount of data for supervised training in most languages and domains. On the other hand, there are few constraints on the kinds of words that can be a name entity so that the distribution of name entities are sparse. Sparse distribution is typically difficult for models to generalize. NER is also a popular NLP task and plays a vital role for downstream systems, such as machine translation systems and dialogue systems.

Traditional NER systems are often linear statistical models, such as Hidden Makov Models (HMM), Support Vector Machines (SVM) and Conditional Random Fields (CRF) [18,21,24]. These models rely heavily on hand-craft features and language dependent resources. For example, gazetteers are widely used in NER systems. However, such features and resources are costly to develop and collect.

Recent years, non-linear neural networks are getting more and more interests. Collobert [6] proposed a unified architecture for sequence labeling tasks,

M. Sun et al. (Eds.): CCL 2017 and NLP-NABD 2017, LNAI 10565, pp. 110–121, 2017.
https://doi.org/10.1007/978-3-319-69005-6_10

including NER, chunking and part-of-speech (POS) tagging, semantic role labeling (SRL). They introduced two approaches — a feed-forward neural network (FNN) approach and a convolutional neural network (CNN) [16] approach. Neural networks are able to learn features automatically and thus alleviate reliance on hand-craft features. Besides, large scale of unlabeled corpus can be used to boost performance in a multi-task manner. Recently, recurrent neural networks (RNNs), together with its variants long short-term memory (LSTM) [10] and gated recurrent unit (GRU) [5], have shown great success in NLP community [2,28,29]. As for NER, there are a series of works that are based on RNN [4,8,11,15,19]. Ma [19] proposed an end-to-end model that requires no hand-craft feature or data preprocessing. Despite the excellent performance of RNN based models, they are difficult to parallelize over sequence. In this perspective, CNNs have great advantages. In this paper, we propose a novel architecture for NER problems based on CNN. Instead of recurrent layers, we adopt hierarchical convolutional layers to extract features from raw sentence. We also introduce gating mechanism into the convolutional layer to allow more flexible information control. Compared to RNN based models, our model is training faster, and perform better.

We evaluate the proposed model on three benchmark data sets for two significantly different languages — SIGHAN bakeoff 2006 MSRA portion for simplified Chinese NER, SIGHAN bakeoff 2006 CityU portion for traditional Chinese NER and CoNLL 2003 shared task English portion for English NER. Our model obtains state-of-thc-art performance on these three data sets. Contributions of this work are: (i) We propose a novel architecture for NER problems. (ii) We evaluate our model on three benchmark data sets for two significantly differently languages — Chinese and English. (iii) Our model obtains state-of-the-art performance on these three data sets.

2 Architecture

In this section, we describe our network architecture from bottom to top.

2.1 CNN for Encoding English Word Information

In this work, we focus on two significantly different languages: Chinese and English. In Chinese, there is no separator between words in sentences. There are mainly two approaches to handle it. One of them is to use an upstream system to segment words and feed the words into NER systems. The other is to feed the characters directly into the systems. We choose the latter approach to cut off the dependence with upstream systems. In English, unlike Chinese, there are separators, i.e. blanks, between words, therefore we adopt words as the basic input unit.

For Chinese, characters are transformed to character embeddings. Similarly, for English, words are transformed to word embeddings. However, information about word morphology is not included in word embedding, which is often crucial for various NLP tasks. Several previous works [4,19,26,27] have shown that CNN is effective in extracting morphological features from characters. In this work, we adopt a similar network. The network accepts characters (of a word) as inputs and output a fixed dimention vector. Architecture of the network is shown in Fig. 1. The output vector is concatenated with the word embedding and fed into upper layers. Note that for Chinese, we do not need the network.

2.2 Deep CNN with Gating Mechanism

Currently, for NER problems, the main-stream approach is to consider a sentence as a sequence of tokens (characters or words) and to process them with a RNNs [4,8,11,15,19]. In this work, we adopt a novel strategy which is significantly different from previous works. Instead of RNN, we use hierarchical CNN to extract local and context information. We introduce gating mechanism into the convolutional layer. Dauphin [7] have shown that gating mechanism is useful for language modeling tasks. Figure 2 shows the structure of one gated convolutional layer.

Formally, we define the number of input channels as N, the number of output channels as M, the length of input as L and kernel width as k. A gated convolutional layer can be written as

$$F_{gating}(X) = (X * W + b) \otimes \sigma(X * V + c) \tag{1}$$

where $*$ denotes row convolution, $X \in R^{L \times N}$ is the input of this layer, $W \in \mathbb{R}^{k \times N \times M}$, $b \in \mathbb{R}^N$, $V \in \mathbb{R}^{k \times N \times M}$, $c \in \mathbb{R}^N$ are parameters to be learned, σ is the sigmoid function and $\otimes$ represent element-wise product. We make $F_{gcnn}(X) \in \mathbb{R}^{L \times M}$ by augmenting X with padding.

Multiple gated convolutional layers are stacked to capture long distance information. On the top of the last layer, we use a linear transformation to transform output of the network to unnormalized scores of labels $E \in \mathbb{R}^{L \times C}$, where L is the length of a given sentence and C is the number of labels.

2.3 Linear Chain CRF

Though deep neural networks have the ability to capture long distance information, it has been verified that considering the correlations between adjacent labels can be very beneficial in sequence labeling problems [6,11,15,19].

Correlations between adjacent labels can be modeled as a transition matrix $T \in \mathbb{R}^{C \times C}$. Given a sentence

$$\mathcal{S} = (w_1, w_2, ..., w_L) \tag{2}$$

we have corresponding scores $E \in \mathbb{R}^{L \times C}$ given by the CNN. For a sequence of labels $y = (y_1, y_2, ..., y_L)$, we define its unnormalized score to be

$$s(\mathcal{S}, y) = \sum_{i=1}^{L} E_{i,y_i} + \sum_{i=1}^{L-1} T_{y_i,y_{i+1}} \tag{3}$$

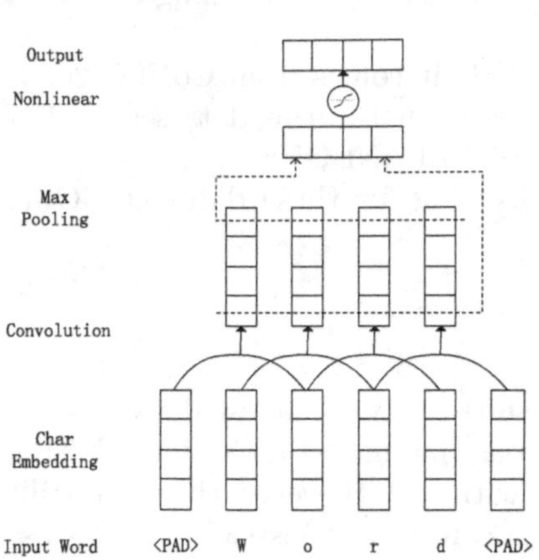

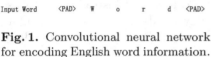

Fig. 1. Convolutional neural network for encoding English word information.

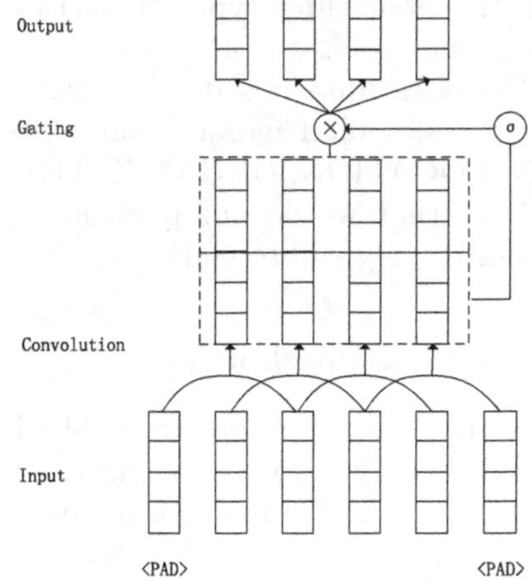

Fig. 2. Structure of one convolutional layer with gating mechanism.

Probability of the sequence of labels then be defined as

$$P(y|\mathcal{S}) = \frac{e^{s(\mathcal{S},y)}}{\sum_{y\prime \in \mathcal{Y}} e^{s(\mathcal{S},y\prime)}} \tag{4}$$

where $\mathcal{Y}$ is the set of all valid sequences of labels. This formulation is actually linear chain conditional random field (CRF) [14]. The final loss of the proposed model then be defined as the negative log-likelihood of the ground-truth sequence of labels y^*

$$\mathcal{L}(\mathcal{S}, y^\star) = -logP(y^\star|\mathcal{S}) \tag{5}$$

During training, the loss function is minimized by back propagation. During test, Veterbi algorithm is applied to find the label sequence with maximum probability.

3 Experimental Setup

3.1 Data Sets

We evaluate our model on three data sets. Two of them are Chinese and another is English.

MSRA is a data set for simplified Chinese NER. It comes from SIGHAN 2006 shared task for Chinese NER [17]. There are three types of entities tagged in this data set: PERSON, LOCATION and ORGANIZATION. Within the training data, we hold the last $\frac{1}{10}$ for development.

CityU is a data set for traditional Chinese NER. Same with the first data set, it also comes from SIGHAN 2006 shared task for Chinese NER and is tagged with the same three types of entities. We hold the last $\frac{1}{10}$ of training data for development.

CoNLL-2003 is a data set for English NER. It comes from CoNLL 2003 shared task [30]. There are four types of entities tagged in this data set: PERSON, LOCATION, ORGANIZATION and MISCELLANEOUS.

Note that we do not perform any preprocessing for these data sets. Our system is truly end-to-end.

3.2 LSTM Baseline

Since there is no appropriate public LSTM results for two Chinese data sets — MSRA and CityU, we implemented a LSTM baseline model for Chinese NER. Our baseline LSTM model is almost the same with [11]. However, there are still some differences: (i) Our baseline model accepts characters instead of words as input. (ii) Our baseline model does not use any hand-craft features. (iii) Our baseline model adopts dropout [9] in the same way with [31]. (iv) Our baseline model has more than one layer.

3.3 Dropout

Dropout [9] is a very efficient and simple way for preventing overfitting, especially when the data set is small. We apply dropout to our model on the top of all convolutional layers and embedding layers (including character embedding layer and word embedding layer) with a fixed dropout rate. We observed remarkable improvement when dropout was applied.

3.4 Tagging Scheme

We didn't pay much attention to tagging scheme. For two Chinese data sets, we use simple IOB format (Inside, Outside, Beginning). For another English data set, we use IOBES format (Inside, Outside, Beginning, End, Singleton) to keep consistent with previous works [4,15,19].

3.5 Pretrained Embeddings

Following Collobert [6], we use pretrained embeddings. For simplified Chinese data set MSRA, we train the character embeddings on news corpus collected by Sogou [1] with an open source tool word2vec [20]. For traditional Chinese data set CityU, we train the character embeddings on wikipiedia corpus, also by word2vec. As for English data set CoNLL-2003, we use Standford's publicly available Glove word embeddings [2] trained on 6 billion words from Wikipedia and web text [22].

We fine-tune the embeddings while training with normal back propagation.

---

[1] http://www.sogou.com/labs/resource/ca.php.

[2] http://nlp.stanford.edu/projects/glove/.

3.6 Hyper-parameters

We tune the hyper-parameters on development set by random search for each data set. For MSRA and CityU, we select the size of character embeddings from $\{100, 200\}$. For CoNLL-2003, we select the size of word embeddings from $\{100, 200\}$, the size of character embeddings from $\{20, 40, 60, 80\}$. For all data sets, we select the number of convolutional channels from $\{100, 200\}$, the kernel size from $\{3, 5\}$, the dropout rate from $\{0.2, 0.5\}$ and the network depths from $\{3, 7, 11, 15\}$. The selected hyper-parameters are shown in Table 1.

We use the same way to tune hyper-parameters of our baseline LSTM model. We list these hyper-parameters in Table 2.

Table 1. Hyper-parameters we choose for our model on three data sets. SZ_wemb refer to the size of word embeddings. SZ_cemb refer to the size of character embeddings. N_channels refer to the number of convolutional channels. SZ_kernel refer to the size of convolutional kernel. Depth refer to the number of convolutional layers.

Data Set	SZ_wemb	SZ_cemb	N_channels	SZ_kernel	Dropout	Depth
MSRA	-	200	200	3	0.2	15
CityU	-	200	200	3	0.2	11
CoNLL-2003	100	60	200	3	0.5	3

Table 2. Hyper-parameters we choose for our LSTM baseline model on two Chinese data sets. SZ_cemb refer to the size of character embedding. SZ_hidden refer to the size of LSTM hidden state. Depth refer to the number of bi-directional LSTM layers.

Data Set	SZ_cemb	SZ_hidden	Dropout	Depth
MSRA	200	200	0.2	4
CityU	200	200	0.2	3

3.7 Optimization

For MSRA and CityU, parameter optimization is performed with Adam [13] and the initial learning rate are is to 0.001. We set the batch size to 100. This setting behaves well on both data sets. For CoNLL-2003, we use stochastic gradient descent (SGD) with a fixed learning rate 0.005 and a smaller batch size 20. We tried Adam on this data set, with a larger batch size. However, severe overfitting was obeserved.

We adopt weight normalization [25] — a simple but effective method, on all convolutional layers to accelerate the training procedure.

4 Experimental Result

4.1 Main Result

Tables 3 and 4 give performances of the proposed model (GCNN) on three data sets. For comparison, we also list the scores of some other models. To make the comparison between our model and others fair, we mark the models that use external labeled data. On MSRA data set, our model outperforms the LSTM baseline in a large margin (1.05 in F1). On CItyU and CoNLL-2003 data sets, our model outperforms baseline slightly. Our model abtains state-of-the-art performance on three data sets without any data preprocessing, hand-craft features and external labeled data.

It seems unbelievable that our model can outperform LSTM based models. Intuitively, our model can only see a local window with limited size at every moment[3] , while LSTM based models can see the whole sentence. It is well known that a fully connected one hidden layer neural network can in principle learn any real-valued function, but much better results can be obtained with a deep problem-specific architecture which develops hierarchical representations. CNNs for computer vision are examples of this. Analogously, deep CNNs may surpass RNNs in NER problems despite the fact that RNNs have strong ability for sequence modeling.

We also explore the impact of gating mechanism, CRF and pretrained embeddings. For each data set, We train other three models with same hyper-parameters but with the absence of gating mechanism, CRF and pretrained embeddings, respectively. The differences between them and the original model are descirbed below:

CNN (-gating) We remove gating mechanism and instead use rectified linear unit (ReLU). Formally, the layer is defined as

$$F_{relu}(X) = Relu(X * W + b) \tag{6}$$

GCNN (-crf) We remove transition scores from Eq. 3. Specifically, we substitute Eq. 3 with

$$s(\mathcal{S}, y) = \sum_{i=1}^{L} E_{i,y_i} \tag{7}$$

GCNN (-pretrain) We use random initialized embeddings instead of pre-trained embeddings.

As shown in Tables 3 and 4, pretrained embeddings give us the biggest improvement in all of the three data sets (+5.18 in average). Gating mechanism and CRF also give us remrakable improvement (+0.54 and +0.68 respectively).

[3] The window size equals to $d \times (k-1) + 1$, where d is the network depth and k is the kernel size.

Table 3. Comparison with previous works on MSRA and CityU data set. * indicates models trained with the use of external labeled data.

Model	MSRA			CityU		
	Precision	Recall	F1	Precision	Recall	F1
Zhou [12]	88.94	84.20	86.51	-	-	-
Zhou [12]*	90.76	89.22	89.99	-	-	-
Chen [3]	91.22	81.71	86.20	92.66	84.75	88.53
Zhao [32]	-	-	86.30	-	-	89.18
Zhou [33]	91.86	88.75	90.28	92.33	87.37	89.78
LSTM	91.14	89.24	90.18	92.01	89.27	90.62
CNN (-gating)	91.56	90.02	90.78	91.42	89.19	90.29
GCNN (-crf)	91.06	89.50	90.27	91.51	89.07	90.27
GCNN (-pretrain)	89.59	83.55	86.46	89.76	86.26	87.98
GCNN	**92.34**	**90.15**	**91.23**	**92.68**	**88.71**	**90.65**

Table 4. Comparison with previous works on CoNLL-2003 data set. * indicates models trained with the use of external labeled data.

Model	Precision	Recall	F1
Huang [11]	-	-	90.10
Luo [18] *	91.50	91.40	91.20
Passos [21]	-	-	90.90
Lample [15]	-	-	90.94
Ma [19]	91.35	91.06	91.21
CNN (-gating)	90.02	90.86	90.44
GCNN (-crf)	90.37	90.69	90.53
GCNN (-pretrain)	83.55	83.45	83.50
GCNN	**91.39**	**91.09**	**91.24**

Table 5. The sum of training time and validation time of 100 epoches of various models on MSRA data set.

Model	Depth	Time (hour)	F1
LSTM	1	20	88.36
	2	36	90.07
	3	46	90.00
	4	60	90.18
GCNN	3	6	89.84
	7	12	89.64
	11	16	90.96
	15	21	**91.23**

4.2 Network Depth

With the network grows deeper, the network has stronger representation ability in principle and can see a larger context and thus higher performance is expected. Figure 3 shows the F1 scores on three data sets with different network depth settings. With the network grows deeper, the performance of the network has a rising trend on MSRA and CityU data sets. However, we can also observe a degradation phenomenon. On CoNLL-2003 data set, a deeper network with 7 layers has a much lower score than the shallow one with only 3 layers. We leave this phenomenon for further research.

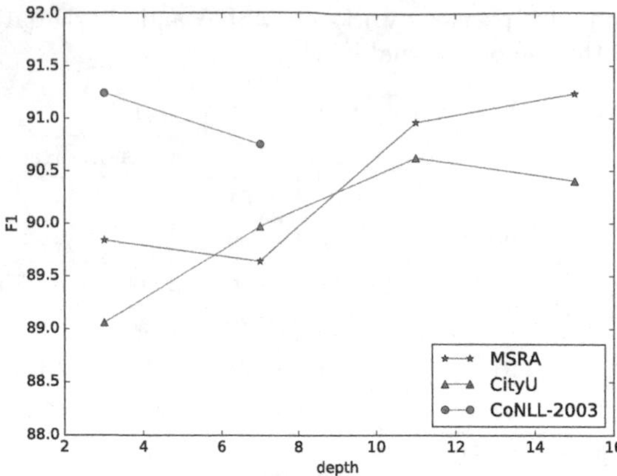

Fig. 3. Performance of our model with various depth on three data sets. On CoNLL-2003 data set, we observed severe degradation phenomenon as we increase network depth from 3 to 7, so we didn't try further depth.

4.3 Training Efficiency

In this section, we show that our proposed model has a remarkable advantage on training efficiency compared to LSTM based models. Table 5 give summaries of the training time of 100 epoches for these models on MSRA data set. We train each model in a single K20 GPU with the same batch size (100 sentences per batch) and platform (*tensorflow* [1]), therefore the statistics is reliable. Our proposed model with 15 convolutional layers consumed roughly the same amount of time with the LSTM based model with 1 bi-directional LSTM layer. However, the former outperforms the latter in a large margin (2.87 in F1). Moreover, the LSTM based model with the best performance has 4 bi-directional LSTM layers and consumed 60 h but the performance is much lower than our CNN based model with 11 convolutional layers, which only consumed 16 h. Our proposed model has much higher training efficiency than LSTM based models in that LSTMs are extremely deep if we unroll them over the whole sequence.

5 Related Work

There are primarily two kinds of approaches for NER problems. One is linear models, like CRF and SVM, together with carefully designed hand-craft features, as well as external knowledges. The other kind is neural network based models. Recent years, neural network based models take over the dominate position. Collobert [6] proposed a unified architecture based on FNN for sequence labeling problems, including part-of-speech (POS) tagging, NER and chunking. Their model utilizes word embeddings and thus large amount of unlabeled data can be used to pretrain the embeddings to boost NER performance. dos [26] extend their architecture for NER problems with character embeddings. Our model can be seen as an extension of their model, where the FNN is replaced with a deep CNN. Collobert [6] also proposed a CNN based model. However, their model is significantly different from ours since theirs adopt max-pooling to encode the whole sentence into a fixed size vector and use position embeddings to demonstrate which word to be tagged while ours does not use max-pooling and thus position embeddings are not required.

Recently, RNN based approaches, together with LSTM, are prevailing. Huang [11] used bi-directional LSTM for word-level feature extraction and CRF for sequence prediction. Their model didn't take character-level information into consideration. Chiu [4] also used bi-directional LSTM for word-level feature extraction. Besides, they utilized CNN for character-level feature extraction. Unlike Huang [11], they didn't use CRF. Lample [15] proposed a model that utilizes a bi-directional LSTM for word-level feature extraction and another bi-directional LSTM for character-level feature extraction, as well as a CRF layer for sequence prediction. Ma [19] proposed a model similar with Lample [15] but use CNN instead of bi-directional LSTM for character-level feature extraction. Gillick [8] applied RNN based encoder-decoder architecture Sutskever [29] for NER problems.

Our model is significantly different with previous RNN based models in that we only use CNN for feature extraction. For English NER, we adopt CNN for character-level feature extraction, which is simillar with dos [26], Chiu [4] and Ma [19]. We also adopt CRF for sentence level prediction as Collobert [6], dos [26], Huang [11], Lample [15] and Ma [19] did.

Our work is also inspired by works on language modeling [7,23]. Pham [23] applied CNN for language modeling and their model outperforms RNNs but is below state of the art LSTM based models. Dauphin [7] extended CNN with gating mechanism for language modeling and achieved a new state of the art on WikiText-103 as well as a new best single-GPU result on the Google Billion Word benchmark.

6 Conclusion and Future Work

We proposed a novel architecture based on gated CNN for solving NER problems of different languages. We evaluated our model on three benchmark data sets in two significantly different languages — Chinese and English, and achieved state-of-the-art performance on all of the three data sets. Compared to prevailing LSTM based models, our model abtains better performance and has a remarkable advantage on training efficiency.

There are two future works worth studying. One is to make the network deeper without degradation so that larger context can be utilized by the network and thus may yield better performance. The other interesting direction is to apply the architecture to other sequence labeling tasks, like POS tagging, chunking etc.

Acknowledgement. This work is supported by the National Key Research & Development Plan of China (No.2013CB329302). Thanks anonymous reviewers for their valuable suggestions. Thanks Wang Geng, Zhen Yang and Yuanyuan Zhao for their useful discussions.

References

1. Abadi, M., Agarwal, A., Barham, P., Brevdo, E., Chen, Z., Citro, C., Corrado, G.S., Davis, A., Dean, J., Devin, M., et al.: Tensorflow: Large-scale machine learning on heterogeneous distributed systems. arXiv preprint (2016). arXiv:1603.04467
2. Bahdanau, D., Cho, K., Bengio, Y.: Neural machine translation by jointly learning to align and translate. Computer Science (2014)
3. Chen, A., Peng, F., Shan, R., Sun, G.: Chinese named entity recognition with conditional probabilistic models, pp. 173–176 (2006)
4. Chiu, J.P.C., Nichols, E.: Named entity recognition with bidirectional lstm-cnns. Computer Science (2015)
5. Chung, J., Gulcehre, C., Cho, K., Bengio, Y.: Empirical evaluation of gated recurrent neural networks on sequence modeling. arXiv preprint (2014). arXiv:1412.3555
6. Collobert, R., Weston, J., Bottou, L., Karlen, M., Kavukcuoglu, K., Kuksa, P.: Natural language processing (almost) from scratch. J. Mach. Learn. Res. **12**(1), 2493–2537 (2011)
7. Dauphin, Y.N., Fan, A., Auli, M., Grangier, D.: Language modeling with gated convolutional networks (2016)
8. Gillick, D., Brunk, C., Vinyals, O., Subramanya, A.: Multilingual language processing from bytes. arXiv preprint (2015). arXiv:1512.00103
9. Hinton, G.E., Srivastava, N., Krizhevsky, A., Sutskever, I., Salakhutdinov, R.R.: Improving neural networks by preventing co-adaptation of feature detectors. Comput. Sci. **3**(4), 212–223 (2012)
10. Hochreiter, S., Schmidhuber, J.: Long short-term memory. Neural Comput. **9**(8), 1735–1780 (1997)
11. Huang, Z., Xu, W., Yu, K.: Bidirectional lstm-crf models for sequence tagging. arXiv preprint (2015). arXiv:1508.01991
12. Junsheng, Z., Liang, H., Xinyu, D., Jiajun, C.: Chinese named entity recognition with a multi-phase model. In: COLING ACL 2006, p. 213 (2006)
13. Kingma, D., Ba, J.: Adam: A method for stochastic optimization. Computer Science (2014)
14. Lafferty, J., McCallum, A., Pereira, F.: Conditional random fields: probabilistic models for segmenting and labeling sequence data. In: Proceedings of the eighteenth international conference on machine learning, ICML, vol. 1, pp. 282–289 (2001)
15. Lample, G., Ballesteros, M., Subramanian, S., Kawakami, K., Dyer, C.: Neural architectures for named entity recognition (2016)
16. LeCun, Y., Boser, B., Denker, J., Henderson, D.: Backpropagation applied to handwritten zip code recognition. Neural Comput. **1**(4), 541–551 (1989)
17. Levow, G.A.: The third international chinese language processing bakeoff: word segmentation and named entity recognition. In: Proceedings of the Fifth SIGHAN Workshop on Chinese Language Processing, pp. 108–117 (2006)
18. Luo, G., Huang, X., Lin, C.Y., Nie, Z.: Joint entity recognition and disambiguation. In: Conference on Empirical Methods in Natural Language Processing, pp. 879–888 (2015)

19. Ma, X., Hovy, E.: End-to-end sequence labeling via bi-directional lstm-cnns-crf (2016)
20. Mikolov, T., Sutskever, I., Chen, K., Corrado, G., Dean, J.: Distributed representations of words and phrases and their compositionality. Adv. Neural Inf. Process. Syst. **26**, 3111–3119 (2013)
21. Passos, A., Kumar, V., Mccallum, A.: Lexicon infused phrase embeddings for named entity resolution. Computer Science (2014)
22. Pennington, J., Socher, R., Manning, C.: Glove: Global vectors for word representation. In: Conference on Empirical Methods in Natural Language Processing, pp. 1532–1543 (2014)
23. Pham, N.Q., Kruszewski, G., Boleda, G.: Convolutional neural network language models. In: Proceedings of EMNLP (2016)
24. Ratinov, L., Roth, D.: Conll 09 design challenges and misconceptions in named entity recognition. In: CoNLL 2009: Proceedings of the Thirteenth Conference on Computational Natural Language Learning, pp. 147–155 (2009)
25. Salimans, T., Kingma, D.P.: Weight normalization: A simple reparameterization to accelerate training of deep neural networks (2016)
26. dos Santos, C., Guimaraes, V., Niterói, R., de Janeiro, R.: Boosting named entity recognition with neural character embeddings. In: Proceedings of NEWS 2015 The Fifth Named Entities Workshop, p. 25 (2015)
27. dos Santos, C.N., Zadrozny, B.: Learning character-level representations for part-of-speech tagging. In: ICML, pp. 1818–1826 (2014)
28. Sundermeyer, M., Schlüter, R., Ney, H.: Lstm neural networks for language modeling. In: Interspeech, pp. 194–197 (2012)
29. Sutskever, I., Vinyals, O., Le, Q.V., Sutskever, I., Vinyals, O., Le, Q.V.: Sequence to sequence learning with neural networks. Adv. Neural Inf. Process. Syst. **4**, 3104–3112 (2014)
30. Sang, E.F.T.K., De Meulder, F.: Introduction to the conll-2003 shared task: language-independent named entity recognition. Comput. Sci. **21**(08), 142–147 (2003)
31. Zaremba, W., Sutskever, I., Vinyals, O.: Recurrent neural network regularization. arXiv preprint (2014). arXiv:1409.2329
32. Zhao, H., Kit, C.: Unsupervised segmentation helps supervised learning of character tagging for word segmentation and named entity recognition. In: IJCNLP, pp. 106–111. Citeseer (2008)
33. Zhou, J., Qu, W., Zhang, F.: Chinese named entity recognition via joint identification and categorization. Chin. J. Electron. **22**(2), 225–230 (2013)

Improving Event Detection via Information Sharing Among Related Event Types

Shulin Liu[1,2](✉), Yubo Chen[1], Kang Liu[1], Jun Zhao[1,2], Zhunchen Luo[3], and Wei Luo[3]

[1] National Laboratory of Pattern Recognition Institute of Automation, Chinese Academy of Sciences, Beijing 100190, China
[2] University of Chinese Academy of Sciences, Beijing 100049, China
[3] China Defense Science and Technology Information Center, Beijing 100142, China
{shulin.liu,yubo.chen,kliu,jzhao}@nlpr.ia.ac.cn
zhunchenluo@gmail.com, htqxjj@126.com

Abstract. Event detection suffers from data sparseness and label imbalance problem due to the expensive cost of manual annotations of events. To address this problem, we propose a novel approach that allows for information sharing among related event types. Specifically, we employ a fully connected three-layer artificial neural network as our basic model and propose a type-group regularization term to achieve the goal of information sharing. We conduct experiments with different configurations of type groups, and the experimental results show that information sharing among related event types remarkably improves the detecting performance. Compared with state-of-the-art methods, our proposed approach achieves a better F_1 score on the widely used ACE 2005 event evaluation dataset.

1 Introduction

In the ACE (Automatic Context Extraction) event extraction program, an event is represented as a structure consisting of an event trigger and a set of arguments. This paper tackles with the task of event detection (ED), which is a crucial component in the overall task of event extraction. The goal of ED is to identify event triggers and their corresponding event types from the given documents.

The dominative approaches to ED follow the supervised learning paradigm which exploits a set of labeled instances to train diverse models. However, the available annotated data is insufficient and highly imbalanced due to the expensive cost of manual annotations of events. ACE event evaluation program defines 33 event types (under eight coarse types), whereas the widely used dataset ACE 2005 corpus only contains 599 annotated documents, which is insufficient to train satisfying models. Even worse, ACE 2005 is highly imbalanced due to the significant occurrence difference between common and uncommon events. Table 1 shows the statistical information about the most frequent and infrequent labeled events in ACE 2005 corpus. From the table, we observed that the frequency of

M. Sun et al. (Eds.): CCL 2017 and NLP-NABD 2017, LNAI 10565, pp. 122–134, 2017.
https://doi.org/10.1007/978-3-319-69005-6_11

the most frequent events is 73 times (3009/41) more than that of the infrequent events. For common events, which typically occurs frequently in the real world, such as *Attack* and *Transport*, there are hundreds of labeled instances. By contrast, there are only few instances for uncommon events, where types *Extradite*, *Acquit* and *Release-Parole* contain even less than 10 labeled samples. Apparently, it is difficult to yield a satisfying performance using such a small scale of training data.

Table 1. The most frequent and infrequent event types and their frequencies of labeled samples in ACE 2005 corpus.

Frequent events		Infrequent events	
Type	Frequency	Type	Frequency
Attack	1367	*Merge-Org*	14
Transport	659	*Nominate*	12
Die	540	*Extradite*	7
Meet	262	*Acquit*	6
End-Position	181	*Release-Parole*	2
Total	3009	Total	41

In the ED task, events are associated with each other. For example, *Injure* and *Die* events are more likely to co-occur with *Attack* events than others, whereas *Marry* and *Born* events are unlikely to co-occur with *Attack* events. This information is very useful for the ED task. For example, in the sentence "*He* ***left*** *the company, and planned to* ***go*** *home directly.*", the trigger word **left** may trigger a *Transport* (a person left a place) event or an *End-Position* (a person retired from a company) event. However, if we take the following event triggered by **go** into consideration, we are confident to judge it as a *Transport* event rather than an *End-Position* event. Several existing approaches have been proposed to exploit the aforementioned information for the ED task. [21] proposed a two-pass cross-event method to employ event-event association information. [20] proposed a sentence-level joint model to capture the combinational features of triggers and arguments. [23] proposed a two staged approach based on the probabilistic soft logic model (PSL) [2,18] to utilize the association information among events. In these methods, the aforementioned information is encoded as features and learnt from the training data.

The main weakness of these methods is that they could not tackle with the data sparseness and label imbalance problem. The reasons are twofold. On the one hand, all these methods encode the event association information as features and learn them from the training data, however it is difficult to learn useful information for sparse events. On the other hand, from the perspective of the model (ignoring the features they used), all these methods treat events of various types independently and ignore the event-event association. On the contrast, in this paper we propose an approach to exploit the event-event association information from the perspective of the model, which allows related events to share information in the procedure of training. Specifically, we first divide all the event types into several groups. Then, we employ a three-layer Artificial Neural Networks (ANNs) [13] based event detection model to automatically learn features and propose a type-group regularization term to encourage events in the same group to share information in training process. In this way, events of sparse types are expected to benefit from that of dense types in the same group. Our idea is inspired by multi-task learning approaches [6,10], where multiple related prediction tasks are learned jointly, sharing information across the tasks.

Recently, [22] addressed this problem by leveraging FrameNet [3,11]. Contrast with their approach, our solution does not need any external resources. Moreover, our approach can be applied to theirs (see Sect. 2.2 for details). In summary, the contributions of this paper are as follows.

- To our knowledge, this is the first work to address the data sparseness and imbalance problem without using external resource for the ED task.
- We propose two event-type grouping strategies and apply them in our proposed detecting model. We also conduct a set of experiments to illustrate their performances.
- We conduct experiments using the widely used ACE 2005 dataset and its expanded version published by [22]. The experimental results on both datasets demonstrate that the proposed appraoch is effective for the ED task. Our approach outperforms state-of-the-art methods.

2 Background

2.1 Task Description

The ED task is a subtask of the ACE event evaluations. We first introduce the ACE event extraction task. In ACE evaluations, an event is defined as a specific occurrence involving one or more participants. Event extraction task requires that certain specified types of events, which are mentioned in the source language data, be detected. We introduce some ACE terminologies to facilitate the understanding of this task:

Entity: an object or a set of objects in one of the semantic categories of interests.

Entity mention: a reference to an entity (typically, a noun phrase).

Event trigger: the main word that most clearly expresses an event occurrence.

Event arguments: the mentions that are involved in an event (participants).

Event mention: a phrase or sentence within which an event is described, including the trigger and arguments.

The 2005 ACE evaluation included 8 supertypes of events, with 33 types. Consider the following sentence:

He ***died*** *in the hospital.*

An event extractor should detect a *Die* event mention, along with the trigger word "*died*", the victim "*He*" and the place "*hospital*".

Unlike the standard ACE event extraction task, event detection task concentrates only on trigger identification and event type classification, which implies that in the previous example, our task is to identify that the token "*died*" is an event trigger and that its type is *Die*.

2.2 Related Work

Event extraction is an increasingly hot and challenging research topic in NLP. Many approaches have been proposed to this task. Nearly all of the reported ACE event extraction approaches use supervised paradigm. We further divide supervised approaches to feature-based methods, structure-based methods and representation-based methods.

In feature-based methods, a diverse set of strategies have been exploited to convert classification clues (such as sequences and parse trees) into feature vectors. [1] uses the lexical features (e.g., full word, pos tag), syntactic features (e.g., dependency features) and external-knowledge features (WordNet) to extract events. Inspired by the hypothesis of "One Sense Per Discourse" [16,28] combined global evidence from related documents with local decisions for the event extraction. To capture more clues from the texts, [12,15,21] proposed the cross-event and cross-entity inference for the ACE event task. [23] proposed a global inference approach to employ both latent and global information for event detection. Although these approaches achieve high performance, feature-based methods suffer from the problem of selecting a suitable feature set when converting the classification clues into feature vectors.

In structure-based methods, researchers treat event extraction as the task of predicting the structure of the event in a sentence. [24] cast the problem of biomedical event extraction as a dependency parsing problem. [20] presented a joint framework for ACE event extraction based on structured perceptron with beam search. To use more information from the sentence, [19] proposed to extract entity mentions, relations and events in ACE task based on the unified structure.

In representation-based methods, candidate event mentions are represented by embedding, which typically are fed into neural networks. Several related approaches have been proposed to event detection [8,26,27]. [27] employed Convolutional Neural Networks (CNNs) to automatically extract sentence-level features for event detection. [8] proposed dynamic multi-pooling operation on CNNs to better capture sentence-level features. These methods yield relatively high performance. However, they all ignored the data sparseness and label imbalance problem.

Recently, [22] leveraged FrameNet to alleviate the data sparseness problem for event detection. They added the events automatically detected from FrameNet to the ACE corpus to achieve the goal of alleviating the data sparseness problem. They used FrameNet because of the highly similar structures and definitions of frames and events. The idea is simple but effective. Contrast with them, we try to solve the data sparseness problem by exploiting event-type consistency rather than using external resources. Moreover, our approach could be applied to theirs (via applying the proposed approach on the expanded ACE 2005 corpus generated by their method).

3 Methodology

[7] proved that performing trigger identification and classification in a unified manner is superior to handling them separately. Similar to previous work, we model these activities as a word classification task. Each word of a sentence is a trigger candidate, and our objective is to classify each of these candidates into one of the target classes (including a NEGATIVE class).

3.1 Basic Event Detection Model

We employ a fully connected three-layer (a input layer, a hidden layer and a soft-max output layer) Artificial Neural Networks (ANNs) [13] as the basic event detection model, which has been demonstrated very effective for the event detection task by [22].

Embedding Learning. Word embeddings learned from large amount of unlabeled data have been shown to be able to capture the meaningful semantic regularities of words [5,9]. This paper uses unsupervised pre-trained word embedding as the source of base features. In this work, we use the Skip-gram model [25] to pre-train the word embedding. This model is the state-of-the-art model in many NLP tasks [4,8]. The Skip-gram model trains the embeddings of words $w_1, w_2, ..., w_m$ by maximizing the average log probability,

$$\frac{1}{m}\sum_{t=1}^{m}\sum_{-c\leq j\leq c, j\neq 0}\log p(w_{t+j}|w_t) \tag{1}$$

where c is the size of the training window, m is the size of the unlabeled text. In this paper, we use the NYT corpus[1] to train word embeddings.

Model Training. Given a sentence, we concatenate the embedding vector of the candidate trigger and the average embedding vector of the words in the sentence as the input to the basic event detection model. Finally, for a given input sample $\mathbf{x}$, the ANNs with parameter θ outputs a vector $\mathbf{O}$, where the i-th value o_i in $\mathbf{O}$ is the confident score of classifying $\mathbf{x}$ to the i-th event type. To obtain the conditional probability $p(i|\mathbf{x}, \theta)$, we apply a softmax operation over all event types:

$$p(i|\mathbf{x}, \theta) = \frac{e^{o_i}}{\sum_{k=1}^{m} e^{o_k}} \tag{2}$$

[1] https://catalog.ldc.edu/LDC2008T19.

Given all of our (suppose T) training instances $(\mathbf{x^{(i)}}; y^{(i)})$, we can then define the negative log-likelihood loss function

$$J(\theta) = -\sum_{i=1}^{T} \log p(y^{(i)}|\mathbf{x^{(i)}}, \theta). \tag{3}$$

We train the model using a simple optimization technique called stochastic gradient descent (SGD) over shuffled mini-batches with the Adadelta rule [29]. Regularization is implemented by a dropout [14,17].

3.2 Type Group Regularization

As mentioned in Introduction, we want to encourage related types (which are indicated by the given type groups, and the grouping strategy will be introduced in the next subsection) to share information when training the model. To achieve this goal, a regularization term is proposed to the loss function,

$$R(\theta) = \sum_{\mathbf{g}\in\mathbf{G}} \frac{1}{|\mathbf{g}|} \sum_{k=1}^{|\mathbf{g}|} \frac{1}{\log(n^{(g,k)})} ||\mathbf{W_o^{(g,k)}} - \overline{\mu}_{\mathbf{g}}||^2 \tag{4}$$

$$\overline{\mu}_{\mathbf{g}} = \frac{1}{|g|} \sum_{j=1}^{|g|} \mathbf{W_o^{(g,j)}} \tag{5}$$

where $\mathbf{G}$ is type groups; $\mathbf{g}$ is one group in $\mathbf{G}$; $n^{(g,k)}$ is the instance amount of the k-th event type in $\mathbf{g}$; $\mathbf{W_o}$ is the weight matrix in the output layer (soft-max layer); $\overline{\mu}_{\mathbf{g}}$ is the average weight vector of all types in $\mathbf{g}$ (see Eq. 5) and $\mathbf{W_o^{(g,j)}}$ is the weight vector of the j-th event type in $\mathbf{g}$.

The hypothesis behind this intuition is that similar event types should have similar weight vectors in $\mathbf{W_o}$. The quadratic term in Eq. 4 encourages weight vectors of types in the same group to be similar. And the coefficient of it states that types with more labeled instances are less penalized by this term, which means that types with sufficient labeled instances should keep their own weight vectors. By contrast, for types which have less labeled instances, they should learn more from the group. In this way, sparse types are expected to benefit from tense types, which enables our model to alleviate the data sparseness and label imbalance problems for event detection.

Our final loss function $J^{'}(\theta)$ is defined as follows:

$$J^{'}(\theta) = J(\theta) + \alpha R(\theta) \tag{6}$$

where α is a hyper-parameter for trade-off between J and R. Akin to the basic event detection model, we minimize the loss function $J^{'}(\theta)$ using SGD over shuffled mini-batches with the Adadelta update rule.

3.3 Grouping Event Types

In this paper, we focus on alleviating the data sparseness and label imbalance problem, which means that our main goal is to improve the performance of sparse types. We can not learn type groups from the labeled corpus because it contains only a few instances of our target event types. A good choice is to manually group all the event types based on prior knowledge about events and their types. We propose two grouping strategies as follows.

G1: Positive vs. Negative. Our first grouping strategy is based on the hypothesis that all the positive events share some common characteristics to a certain extent compared with negative events (labeled with NEGATIVE). Thus, we divide all the event types into two groups. One of them contains all the positive event types, and the other only contains the NEGATIVE type.

G2: ACE Event Taxonomy. It is obvious that the first grouping strategy is too coarse, because not all the positive events share common characteristics to the same extent. For example, *Start-Org* events should share more common characteristics with *End-Org* events than with *Marry* events. Based on the above observation, we propose our second grouping strategy. We use the event taxonomy defined by ACE to group the event types.

All 33 positive event types in the ACE 2005 event evaluation program are grouped into eight supertypes (see Table 2). We obtained our event groups via slightly modifying these groups by moving the event types *Die* and *Injure* from supertype *Life* to *Conflict* because events of these two types often co-occur with events of type *Attack* and *Demonstrate*, which are in the supertype *Conflict.*

Table 2. Event taxonomy in ACE 2005 corpus.

Supertype	Type
Personal	*Start-Position, End-Position, Nominate, Elect*
Life	*Be-Born, Marry, Divorce, Injure, Die*
Movement	*Transport*
Contact	*Meet, Phone-Write*
Conflict	*Attack, Demonstrate*
Business	*Start-Org, End-Org, Merge-Org, Declare-Bankruptcy*
Transaction	*Transfer-Money, Transfer-Ownership*
Justice	*Arrest-Jail, Execute, Pardon, Release-Parole, Fine, Convict, Acquit, Appeal, Trial-Hearing, Charge-Indict, Sentence, Sue, Extradite*

4 Experiments

4.1 Data Set and Experimental Setup

ACE 2005 Corpus. We performed experiments on the ACE 2005 corpus. For the purpose of comparison, we followed the evaluation of [8,20,23]: randomly selected 30 articles from different genres as the development set, and subsequently conducted a blind test on a separate set of 40 ACE 2005 newswire documents. We used the remaining 529 articles as our training data set.

ExtACE 2005 Corpus. [22] used the events automatically detected from FrameNet as extra training data to alleviate the datasparseness problem for event detection. For simplicity sake, we denoted the ACE2005 corpus extended with FrameNet as ExtACE 2005 corpus. To investigate the effects of applying our approach to theirs, we also perform experiments on ExtACE2005 corpus. [22] published the events automatically detected from FrameNet, which can be easily obtained[2]. Note that, the development and test datasets hold the same as introduced in ACE 2005 corpus.

Evaluation Metrics. Following previous work [8,20,27], we use the following criteria to evaluate the results:

(1) A trigger is correctly identified if its offset matches a reference trigger.
(2) A trigger is correctly classified if both its event type and offset match a reference trigger. Finally, we use *Precision (P), Recall (R) and F meansure* (F_1) as the evaluation metrics.

Hyper-parameter Setting. Hyper-parameters are tuned by grid search on the development data set. We observed an interesting phenomenon when tuning parameters. For CNNs, updating word embeddings in the training procedure usually improves performances [8,27]. However, it is false for ANNs. Figure 1 shows the training curves on development data set. We observe that *UWE* (***U****pdating* ***W****ord* ***E****mbedding*) outperforms *NUWE* (***N****ot* ***U****pdating* ***W****ord* ***E****mbedding*) in the first five iterations. However, the situation is opposite in the remaining iterations. We believe the reason is that updating word embedding causes ANNs overly fit the training data and thus hurts the performances on development data. We apply regularization strategies to try to address this issue, but still fail to make *UWE* achieve good performances. In this work, word embeddings are not updated in training process.

In our experiments, we set the size of the hidden layer to 300, the size of word embeddings to 200, the batch size to 100 and the dropout rate to 0.5. The hyper-parameter α in Eq. 6 is various for different grouping strategies, we will give its setting in the next section.

[2] https://github.com/subacl/acl16.

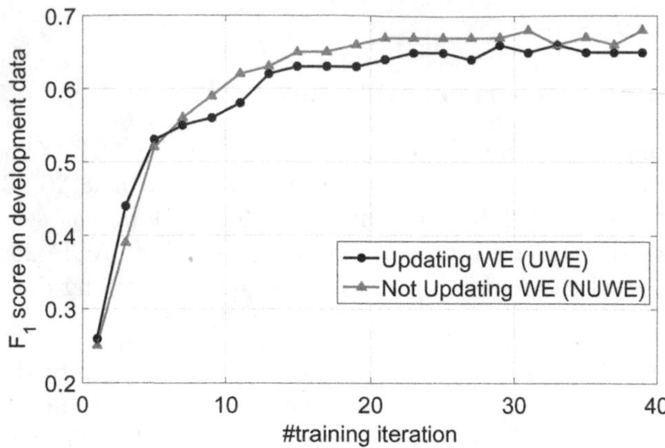

Fig. 1. Training curves on development data. UWE is short for "updating word embedding" whereas NUWE is short for "not updating word embedding".

4.2 Systems

In this section, we introduce the systems implemented in this work.

ANN is the basic event detection model, in which the hyper-parameter α is set to 0. In this system, event types do not share information.

ANN-G1 uses the first type grouping strategy G1 introduced in Subsect. 3.3. We use the development data set to tune the hyper-parameter α, and the final assignment is 2.56e-4.

ANN-G2 uses the second type grouping strategy G2 and the hyper-parameter α is set to 5.12e-5.

4.3 Experiments on ACE 2005 Corpus

We select the following state-of-the-art methods for comparison.

(1) *Li's joint model* is the method proposed by [20], which extracts events based on structure prediction. It is the best-reported structured-based system.
(2) *Ngyuen's CNN* is the method proposed by [27], which employs CNNs to detect events.
(3) *Chen's DMCNN* is the method proposed by [8], which employs dynamic multi-pooling operations on CNNs to extract events.
(4) *Liu's PSL* is the method proposed by [23], which employ both latent local and global information for event detection. It is the best-reported feature-based system.

Table 3 presents the experimental results on ACE 2005 corpus. The first group illustrates the performances of state-of-the-art approaches, and the second group illustrates the performances of our systems. Based on these results, we make the following observations:

Table 3. Experimental results on ACE 2005 corpus

Methods	Identification (%)			Classification (%)		
	P	R	F_1	P	R	F_1
Li's joint model (2013)	76.9	65.0	70.4	73.7	62.3	67.5
Nguyen's CNN (2015)	N/A			71.8	66.4	69.0
Chen's DMCNN (2015)	80.4	67.7	73.5	75.6	63.6	69.1
Liu's PSL (2016)	N/A			75.3	64.4	69.4
ANN (Ours)	83.1	63.5	72.0	79.7	60.9	69.0
ANN-G1 (Ours)	81.7	67.1	**73.7**	76.7	63.0	69.2
ANN-G2 (Ours)	82.0	64.7	72.3	78.9	62.2	**69.6**

(1) Information sharing among event types makes both *ANN-G1* and *ANN-G2* outperform the basic event detection model *ANN*, which demonstrates the effectiveness of our proposed approach.
(2) It is evident that the first grouping strategy G1 enables the event detection model to achieve more improvements for identification (whether it triggers an event or not) than for classification (what event type it triggers) (1.7% vs. 0.2%), and the second grouping strategy G2 is versa (0.3% vs. 0.6%). This phenomenon is easy to understand. Since G1 only differentiate positive events from negative events, it is reasonable to bring more improvements for identification than for classification. Whereas, G2 contains detail information for specific event types, thus it is more helpful for classification.
(3) Compared with state-of-the-art approaches, *ANN-G2* outperforms all of them with remarkable improvements. We also perform a t-test ($p \leqslant 0.05$), which indicates that our method significantly outperforms all of the compared methods.

4.4 Experiments on ExtACE 2005 Corpus

Recently, [22] used the events automatically detected from FrameNet as extra training data to alleviate the data sparseness problem for event detection. To investigate the effects of applying our method to theirs, we also perform experiments on ExtACE 2005 corpus, which is obtained by adding the events automatically detected from FrameNet to the ACE 2005 training data. Table 4 presents the experimental results. Consistent with the results reported in the above section, G1 makes *ANN-G1* achieve remarkable improvements for identification compared with *ANN* (74.0% vs. 72.9%). However, G2 fails to bring as much improvements as it performs on ACE 2005 corpus. The reason may be that the data sparseness problem in ExtACE 2005 corpus is less serious than that in ACE 2005. Nevertheless, the results demonstrate that information sharing among event types is also helpful for the ExtACE 2005 corpus.

Table 4. Experimental results on ExtACE 2005 corpus

Methods	Identification (%)			Classification (%)		
	P	R	F_1	P	R	F_1
ANN	79.2	67.5	72.9	76.8	65.5	70.7
ANN-G1	77.4	70.9	**74.0**	73.7	67.5	70.5
ANN-G2	78.5	69.1	73.5	75.6	66.6	**70.8**

4.5 Performances on Sparse Event Types

Our proposed approach allows for information sharing among related event types, which is expected to help the sparse types to benefit from dense types. To demonstrate the effectiveness of this intuition, we evaluate the proposed approach on the top 15 sparse event types[3].

Table 5. Performances of *ANN/ANN-G1/ANN-G2* on the top 15 sparse event types.

Dataset	Methods	Identification (%)			Classification (%)		
		P	R	F_1	P	R	F_1
ACE 2005	ANN	93.5	49.2	64.4	90.3	47.5	62.2
	ANN-G1	92.4	52.2	**66.7**	87.1	49.2	62.9
	ANN-G2	93.0	50.9	65.8	90.9	49.7	**64.3**
ExtACE 2005	ANN	91.8	50.6	65.2	88.8	48.9	63.1
	ANN-G1	91.4	53.3	***67.3***	86.6	50.5	63.8
	ANN-G2	92.0	52.6	66.9	89.0	50.8	***64.7***

Table 5 shows the experimental results, from which we could observe the following two results. (1) all systems achieve poor recall scores on sparse events. This is not difficult to understand: few training labeled data prevents the model to predict test samples to sparse types, which consequently causes poor recall scores. (2) Compared with *ANN*, *ANN-G1* and *ANN-G2* respectively improve the performances of identification and classification with remarkable gains on both datasets, which demonstrates that our approach is effective for sparse types.

5 Conclusions

We propose a novel approach for event detection that allows for information sharing among related event types. The proposed method uses given event type groups to decide which events should share information. In this paper, we explore

[3] *Appeal, Start-Org, Fine, Divorce, Execute, Merge-Org, Nominate, Extradite, Acquit, Declare-Bankruptcy, Pardon, End-Org, Be-Born, Sue* and *Release-Parole.*

two strategies, which are respectively denoted by G1 and G2, to group event types. To demonstrate the effectiveness of the proposed method, we conduct experiments on ACE 2005 corpus and its expanded version named ExtACE 2005. The results on both datasets demonstrate that the proposed approach is effective for the event detection task, and our approach outperforms all compared methods.

Acknowledgments. This work was supported by the Natural Science Foundation of China (No. 61533018) and the National Basic Research Program of China (No. 2014CB340503). And this research work was also supported by Google through focused research awards program.

References

1. Ahn, D.: The stages of event extraction. In: Proceedings of the Workshop on Annotating and Reasoning about Time and Events, pp. 1–8 (2006)
2. Bach, S.H., Huang, B., London, B., Getoor, L.: Hinge-loss Markov random fields: Convex inference for structured prediction. In: Proceedings of Uncertainty in Artificial Intelligence (UAI) (2013)
3. Baker, C.F., Fillmore, C.J., Lowe, J.B.: The berkeley framenet project. In: Proceedings of 17th Annual Meeting of the Association for Computational Linguistics, pp. 86–90 (1998)
4. Baroni, M., Dinu, G., Kruszewski, G.: Dont count, predict! a systematic comparison of context-counting vs. context-predicting semantic vectors. In: Proceedings of the 52nd Annual Meeting of the Association for Computational Linguistics, vol. 1, pp. 238–247 (2014)
5. Bengio, Y., Ducharme, R., Vincent, P., Janvin, C.: A neural probabilistic language model. J. Mach. Learn. Res. **3**, 1137–1155 (2003)
6. Caruana, R.: Multitask learning. Mach. Learn. **28**(1), 41–75 (1997)
7. Chen, C., Ng, V.: Joint modeling for Chinese event extraction with rich linguistic features. In: COLING, pp. 529–544 (2012)
8. Chen, Y., Xu, L., Liu, K., Zeng, D., Zhao, J.: Event extraction via dynamic multi-pooling convolutional neural networks, pp. 167–176. Association for Computational Linguistics (2015)
9. Erhan, D., Bengio, Y., Courville, A., Manzagol, P.A., Vincent, P., Bengio, S.: Why does unsupervised pre-training help deep learning? J. Mach. Learn. Res. **11**, 625–660 (2010)
10. Evgeniou, T., Micchelli, C.A., Pontil, M.: Learning multiple tasks with kernel methods. J. Mach. Learn. Res. **6**(4), 615–637 (2005)
11. Fillmore, C.J., Johnson, C.R., Petruck, M.R.: Background to framenet. Int. J. Lexicogr. **16**(3), 235–250 (2003)
12. Gupta, P., Ji, H.: Predicting unknown time arguments based on cross-event propagation. In: Proceedings of ACL-IJCNLP, pp. 369–372 (2009)
13. Hagan, M.T., Demuth, H.B., Beale, M.H., et al.: Neural Network Design. PWS Publishing, Boston (1996)
14. Hinton, G.E., Srivastava, N., Krizhevsky, A., Sutskever, I., Salakhutdinov, R.R.: Improving neural networks by preventing co-adaptation of feature detectors. arXiv preprint. arXiv:1207.0580 (2012)

15. Hong, Y., Zhang, J., Ma, B., Yao, J., Zhou, G., Zhu, Q.: Using cross-entity inference to improve event extraction. In: Proceedings of ACL, pp. 1127–1136 (2011)
16. Ji, H., Grishman, R.: Refining event extraction through cross-document inference. In: Proceedings of ACL, pp. 254–262 (2008)
17. Kim, Y.: Convolutional neural networks for sentence classification. In: Proceedings of the 2014 Conference on Empirical Methods in Natural Language Processing, pp. 1746–1751 (2014)
18. Kimmig, A., Bach, S., Broecheler, M., Huang, B., Getoor, L.: A short introduction to probabilistic soft logic. In: Proceedings of NIPS Workshop, pp. 1–4 (2012)
19. Li, Q., Ji, H., Hong, Y., Li, S.: Constructing information networks using one single model. Association for Computational Linguistics (2014)
20. Li, Q., Ji, H., Huang, L.: Joint event extraction via structured prediction with global features. In: Proceedings of ACL, pp. 73–82 (2013)
21. Liao, S., Grishman, R.: Using document level cross-event inference to improve event extraction. In: Proceedings of ACL, pp. 789–797 (2010)
22. Liu, S., Chen, Y., He, S., Liu, K., Zhao, J.: Leveraging framenet to improve automatic event detection. In: Proceedings of ACL (2016)
23. Liu, S., Liu, K., He, S., Zhao, J.: A probabilistic soft logic based approach to exploiting latent and global information in event classification. In: Proceedings of the thirtieth AAAI Conference on Artificail Intelligence (2016)
24. McClosky, D., Surdeanu, M., Manning, C.D.: Event extraction as dependency parsing, pp. 1626–1635. Association for Computational Linguistics (2011)
25. Mikolov, T., Chen, K., Corrado, G., Dean, J.: Efficient estimation of word representations in vector space. arXiv preprint. arXiv:1301.3781 (2013)
26. Nguyen, H.T., Grishman, R.: Modeling skip-grams for event detection with convolutional neural networks. In: Proceedings of the 2016 Conference on Empirical Methods in Natural Language Processing, pp. 886–891. Association for Computational Linguistics (2016)
27. Nguyen, T.H., Grishman, R.: Event detection and domain adaptation with convolutional neural networks. Association for Computational Linguistics (2015)
28. Yarowsky, D.: Unsupervised word sense disambiguation rivaling supervised methods. In: Proceedings of ACL, pp. 189–196 (1995)
29. Zeiler, M.D.: ADADELTA: An adaptive learning rate method. arXiv preprint. arXiv:1212.5701 (2012)

Joint Extraction of Multiple Relations and Entities by Using a Hybrid Neural Network

Peng Zhou[1,2], Suncong Zheng[1,2], Jiaming Xu[1], Zhenyu Qi[1(✉)], Hongyun Bao[1], and Bo Xu[1,2]

[1] Institute of Automation, Chinese Academy of Sciences, Beijing, China
[2] University of Chinese Academy of Sciences, Beijing, China
{zhoupeng2013,suncong.zheng,jiaming.xu zhenyu.qi,hongyun.bao,xubo}@ia.ac.cn

Abstract. This paper proposes a novel end-to-end neural model to jointly extract entities and relations in a sentence. Unlike most existing approaches, the proposed model uses a hybrid neural network to automatically learn sentence features and does not rely on any Natural Language Processing (NLP) tools, such as dependency parser. Our model is further capable of modeling multiple relations and their corresponding entity pairs simultaneously. Experiments on the CoNLL04 dataset demonstrate that our model using only word embeddings as input features achieves state-of-the-art performance.

Keywords: Information extraction · Neural networks

1 Introduction

Entity and relation extraction is to detect entities and recognize their semantic relations from the given sentence. It plays a significant role in various NLP tasks, such as question answering [7] and knowledge base construction [16].

Traditional systems treat this task as a pipeline of two separated tasks, i.e., Named Entity Recognition (NER) [4] and Relation Classification (RC) [24]. Although adopting such a pipeline based method would make a system comparatively easy to assemble, it may encounter some limitations: First, the combination of these two components through a separate training way may hurt the performance. Consequently, errors in the upstream components (e.g., NER) are propagated to the downstream components (e.g., RC) without any feedback. Second, it over-simplifies the problem as multiple local classification steps without taking cross-task dependencies into consideration.

Recent studies show that joint modeling of entities and relations [9,12] is critical for achieving a high performance, since relations interact closely with entities. For instance, to recognize the triplet $\{\textbf{Chapman}_{e1}, \textbf{Kill}_{r}, \textbf{Lennon}_{e2}\}$ in the following sentence:

Lennon was murdered by Chapman outside the Dakota on Dec. 8, 1980.

M. Sun et al. (Eds.): CCL 2017 and NLP-NABD 2017, LNAI 10565, pp. 135–146, 2017.
https://doi.org/10.1007/978-3-319-69005-6_12

It may be useful to identify the relation *Kill* in this sentence, which constrains its arguments to be *Person* (or at least, not to be *Location*) and helps to enforce that **Lennon** and **Chapman** are likely to be *Person*, while **Dakota** is not.

However, most existing joint models are feature-based systems. They need complicated feature engineering and heavily rely on the supervised NLP toolkits, such as dependency parser, which might also lead to error propagation.

Recently, deep learning methods provide an effective way of reducing the number of handcrafted features. Miwa and Bansal [11] proposed an effective Recurrent Neural Networks (RNN) model that requires little feature engineering to detect entities first and then combines these two entities to detect relations. However, the sentence may contain lots of entities, and these entities will form too many entity pairs, as each two entities can form an entity pair. Normally, the number of relations is less than the number of entities in the sentence.[1] If the relations are detected first and used to recognize entity pairs, this will not only reduce the computational complexity but also extract triplets more exactly.

RNN also has disadvantages. Despite its ability to account for word order and long distance dependencies of an input sentence, RNN suffers from the problem that the later words make more influence on the final sentence representation than the former ones, ignoring the fact that important words can appear anywhere in the sentence. Though Convolutional Neural Networks (CNN) can relieve this problem by giving largely uniform importance to each word in the sentence, the long range dependency information in the sentence would be lost.

Most state-of-the-art systems [24] treat relation classification as a multi-class classification problem and predict one most likely relation for an input sentence. However, one sentence may contain multiple relations, and it is helpful to identify entity pairs by providing every possible relation.

Based on the analysis above, this paper presents a novel end-to-end model, dubbed BLSTM-RE, to jointly extract entities and relations. Firstly, Bidirectional Long Short-Term Memory Networks (BLSTM) is utilized to capture long-term dependencies and obtain the whole representation of an input sentence. Secondly, CNN is used to obtain a high level feature vector, which will be given to a sigmoid classifier. In this way, one or more relations can be generated. Finally, the whole sentence representation generated by BLSTM and the relation vectors generated by the sigmoid classifier are concatenated and fed to another Long Short-Term Memory Networks (LSTM) to predict entities. Our contributions are described as follows:

- This paper presents a novel end-to-end model BLSTM-RE to combine the extraction of entity and relation. It employs BLSTM and CNN to automatically learn features of the input sentence without using any NLP tools such as dependency parser. Therefore, it is simpler and more flexible.
- BLSTM-RE can generate one or more relations for an input sentence. Therefore it is capable of modeling multiple relations and their corresponding entity pairs simultaneously.

[1] The above example contains one relation and three entities, and these entities will form three entity pairs (or six entity pairs if the direction of relation is considered).

- Experimental results on the CoNLL04 dataset show that BLSTM-RE achieves better performance compared to the state-of-the-art systems.

2 Related Works

The task we address in this work is to extract triplets that are composed of two entities and the relation between these two entities. Over the years, a lot of models have been proposed, and these models can be roughly divided into two categories: the pipeline based method and the end-to-end based method. The former treats this task as a pipeline of two separated tasks, i.e., NER and RC, while the latter jointly models entities and relations.

2.1 Named Entity Recognition

NER, as a classical NLP task, has drawn research attention for a few decades. Most existing NER models are linear statistical models which include Conditional Random Fields (CRF) [21], and their performances rely on hand-crafted features extracted by NLP tools and external knowledge resources.

Recently, several neural network based models have been successfully applied to NER. Huang et al. [4] first proposed LSTM stacked with a CRF for sequential tagging tasks, including tagging Part Of Speech (POS), chunking and NER tasks, and produced state-of-the-art (or close to) accuracies. Lample et al. [8] applied character and word embeddings in LSTM-CRF and generated good results on NER for four languages.

2.2 Relation Classification

As to relation classification, besides traditional feature-based [18] and kernel-based approaches [23], several neural models have been proposed, including CNN and RNN. Zeng et al. [24] utilized CNN to extract lexical and sentence level features for relation classification; Zhang et al. [25] employed RNN to learn temporal features, long range dependency between nominal pairs. Vu et al. [19] combined CNN and RNN using a voting process to improve the results of RC.

This paper also implements a pipeline based model. It utilizes BLSTM to obtain the representation of a sentence, and then concatenates relation vectors, which are generated by the pre-trained relation classification model, just like CR-CNN proposed by Santos et al. [14], to extract entity pairs from the sentence.

2.3 Joint Extraction of Entities and Relations

As to end-to-end extraction of relations and entities, most existing models are feature-based systems, which include integer linear programming [20], card-pyramid parsing [6], global probabilistic graphical systems [17] and structured prediction [9,12]. Such models rely on handcrafted features extracted from NLP tools, such as POS. However, designing features manually is time-consuming, and using NLP tools may result in the increase of computational and additional propagation errors. Recently, deep learning methods provide an effective way of reducing the number of handcrafted features.

To reduce the manual work in feature extraction, three neural network based models have been proposed. Gupta et al. [1] utilized a unified multi-task RNN to jointly model entity recognition and relation classification tasks with a table representation. It needs to label $n(n+1)/2$ cells for a sentence of length n, while BLSTM-RE only needs to predict $m_r(n+1)$ tags, which are m_r different relations, n entity tags and one relation type, and m_r is less than the number of relations in the sentence. Miwa et al. [11] utilized both bidirectional sequential and bidirectional tree-structured RNN to jointly extract entities and relations in a single model, which depended on a well-performing dependency parser. BLSTM-RE does not rely on the dependency parser, so it is more straightforward and flexible. Zheng et al. [26] proposed a hybrid neural network model to extract entities and relations. However they only joined the loss of NER and RC without considering the interactions between them, which may still hurt the performance.

To verify the effect of the sigmoid classifier, this paper proposes another joint model BLSTM-R. Different from BLSTM-RE, BLSTM-R treats relation classification as a multi-class classification problem and employs a softmax classifier to conduct relation classification instead of using a sigmoid classifier.

3 Model

As shown in Fig. 1, BLSTM-RE consists of five components: Input Layer, Embedding Layer, BLSTM Layer, RC Module and NER Module. The details of different components will be described in the following sections.

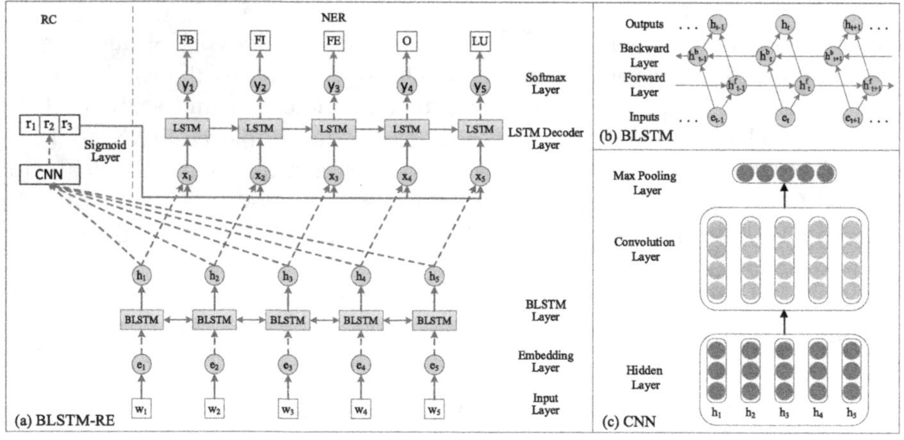

Fig. 1. An illustration of our model. (a): the overall architecture of BLSTM-RE, (b): BLSTM is utilized to capture sentence features, (c): CNN is utilized to capture a high level sentence representation. The dashed lines represent dropout.

3.1 Word Embeddings

If the input sentence consists of l words $s = [w_1, w_2, \ldots, w_l]$, every word w_i is converted into a real-valued vector e_i. For each word in s, we first look up the embedding matrix $W^{wrd} \in \mathbb{R}^{d \times |V|}$, where V is a fixed-sized vocabulary and d is the dimension of word embeddings. The matrix W^{wrd} is a parameter to be learned, and d is a hyper-parameter to be chosen by user. We transform a word x_i into its word embeddings e_i by using the matrix-vector product:

$$e_i = W^{wrd} v^i, \tag{1}$$

where v^i is a one-hot vector of size $|V|$. Then the sentence is fed to the next layer as a real-valued matrix $emb_s = \{e_1, e_2, \ldots, e_l\} \in \mathbb{R}^{l \times d}$.

3.2 BLSTM Layer

LSTM [3] was proposed to overcome the gradient vanishing problem of RNN. The underlying idea is to introduce an adaptive gating mechanism, which decides the degree to which that LSTM units keep the previous state and memorize the extracted features of the current data input. From Embedding Layer, we obtain a real-valued matrix $emb_s = \{e_1, e_2, \ldots, e_l\}$, which will be processed by LSTM step by step. At time-step t, the memory c_t and the hidden state h_t are updated based on the following equations:

$$\begin{bmatrix} i_t \\ f_t \\ o_t \\ \hat{c}_t \end{bmatrix} = \begin{bmatrix} \sigma \\ \sigma \\ \sigma \\ \tanh \end{bmatrix} W \cdot [h_{t-1}, e_t], \tag{2}$$

$$c_t = f_t \odot c_{t-1} + i_t \odot \hat{c}_t, \tag{3}$$

$$h_t = o_t \odot \tanh(c_t), \tag{4}$$

where e_t is the input at the current time-step, i_t, f_t and o_t are the input gate, forget gate and output gate respectively, $\hat{c}$ is the current cell state, $\cdot$, σ and $\odot$ denote dot product, the sigmoid function and element-wise multiplication respectively.

For the sequence modeling tasks, it is beneficial to have access to the past context as well as the future context. Schuster et al. [15] proposed BLSTM to extend the unidirectional LSTM by introducing a second hidden layer, where the hidden to hidden connections flow in the opposite temporal order. Therefore, BLSTM can exploit information from both the past and the future.

This paper also utilizes BLSTM to capture the past and the future information. As shown in Fig. 1(b), the network contains two sub-networks for the forward and backward sequence context respectively. The output of the tth word is shown in the following equation:

$$h_t = [\overrightarrow{h_t} \oplus \overleftarrow{h_t}]. \tag{5}$$

Here, the element-wise sum is used to combine the forward and backward pass outputs. In this paper, we set the hidden units of LSTM to the same size with word embeddings.

3.3 Relation Classification Module

As shown in Fig. 1, RC Module consists of three parts: Convolution Layer, Max Pooling Layer and Sigmoid Layer. The following sections will discuss each of the three layers in detail.

Convolution Layer. The hidden matrix $H = \{h_1, h_2, \ldots, h_l\} \in \mathbb{R}^{l \times d}$ is obtained from the BLSTM Layer, which contains the past and the future information of the input sentence s, and then is fed to the Convolution Layer. In this paper, one-dimensional narrow convolution [5] is utilized to extract higher level features of the sentence s. A convolution operation involves a filter $m \in \mathbb{R}^{k \times d}$, which is applied to a window of k words to produce a new feature. For example, a feature c_i is generated from a window of words $H_{i:i+k-1}$ by

$$c_i = f(m \cdot H_{i:i+k-1} + b), \tag{6}$$

here, $b \in \mathbb{R}$ is a bias term, and f is a non-linear function such as hyperbolic tangent. This filter is applied to each possible window of words in the sentence s to produce a feature map:

$$c = [c_1, c_2, \ldots, c_{l-k+1}]. \tag{7}$$

Max Pooling Layer. From Convolution Layer, we get a feature map $c \in \mathbb{R}^{l-k+1}$. Then, we employ the max-over-time pooling to select the maximum value of the feature map by

$$\hat{c} = max(c), \tag{8}$$

as the feature corresponding to the filter m. In RC Module, n filters with different window sizes k are utilized to learn complementary features. And the final vector z is formed as:

$$z = [\hat{c}_1, \hat{c}_2, \ldots, \hat{c}_n]. \tag{9}$$

Sigmoid Layer. To find out whether a sentence contains multiple relations, we utilize a sigmoid classifier instead of a softmax classifier to classify the relations based on the feature z, which is defined as:

$$\hat{p}\,(y|s) = sigmoid\,(W_R \cdot z + b_R)\,, \tag{10}$$

$$\hat{y} = \hat{p}\,(y|s) > \delta, \tag{11}$$

where $W_R \in \mathbb{R}^{n_r \times n}$, n_r is the number of relations, $b_R \in \mathbb{R}$ is a bias term, and δ is a hyper-parameter to be chosen by user.

3.4 Named Entity Recognition Module

As shown in Fig. 1(a), NER module consists of two parts: LSTM Decoder Layer and Softmax Layer. Both of these two layers will be described in the following sections.

LSTM Decoder Layer. We treat entity detection as a sequential token tagging task and apply the *BIEOU* tagging scheme, where each tag means a token is the **B**egin, **I**nside, **E**nd, **O**utside and **U**nit of an entity mention respectively.

Note that relations are directed, and the same relation with opposite directions is considered to be two different classes. For example, compared to *Kill (Chapman, Lennon)*, *Kill (Lennon, Chapman)* expresses the opposite meaning that *Chapman* is murdered by *Lennon* in Sect. 1. This paper uses two different letters F and L to represent the former entity mention and the latter entity mention in the relation respectively. For example in Fig. 1(a), we assign FB, FI, FE and LU to two different entity mentions.

To extract entity pairs of different relations, we combine the relation vectors obtained by the RC Module to generate entity tags. If the sentence only contains one relation, at each time-step t, the output h_t of the BLSTM Layer and the relation vector r are concatenated and fed to the LSTM Decoder Layer.

$$y_t = LSTM(concat(h_t, r)), \tag{12}$$

here, $y_t \in \mathbb{R}^d$, $concat(h_t, r) \in \mathbb{R}^{d+n}$ represents x_t in Fig. 1(a).

Softmax Layer. From the LSTM Decoder Layer, we get a real-valued matrix $O = \{y_1, y_2, \dots, y_l\} \in \mathbb{R}^{l \times d}$. Then it is passed to the Softmax Layer to predict the named entity tags as follows:

$$\hat{p}(y|s) = softmax(W_T \cdot O + b_T), \tag{13}$$

$$\hat{y} = \arg\max_y \hat{p}(y|s), \tag{14}$$

where $W_T \in \mathbb{R}^{n_t \times d}$, n_t is the number of entity tags, and $b_T \in \mathbb{R}$ is a bias term. In this way, we can get one relation and its possible entity pairs. If the sentence contains multiple relations, this process will be repeated several times, each time using a different relation vector.

4 Experimental Setups

In this section, we introduce the dataset, the evaluation metrics and the hyper-parameters used in this paper.

Table 1. Summary statistics of the dataset. Sent, Ment and Rel represent the number of sentences, entity mentions and relation instances respectively, L: average sentence length, M: maximum sentence length.

Data	Sent	Ment	Rel	L	M
Train	1,153	7,935	1,626	29.07	114
Test	288	2,025	422	28.94	118

4.1 Dataset

The primary experiments are conducted on a public dataset CoNLL04 [13][2]. The corpus defines four named entity types (*Location*, *Organization*, *Person* and *Other*) and five relation types (*Kill*, *Live_In*, *Located_In*, *OrgBased_In* and *Work_For*). Besides, it contains $1,441$ sentences that contain at least one relation. We randomly split these into training $(1,153)$ and test (288), as same as Gupta et al. [1][3]. Summary statistics of the dataset are shown in Table 1.

4.2 Metric and Hyper-parameter Settings

We use the standard $F1$ measure to evaluate the performance of entity extraction and relation classification. An entity is considered correct if one of its tokens is tagged correctly. A relation for a word pair is considered correct if its relation type and its two entities are both correct.

We update the model parameters including weights, biases, and word embeddings using gradient based optimizer AdaDelta [22] to minimize binary cross-entropy loss for relation classification and cross-entropy loss for entity detection. As there is no standard development set, we randomly select 20% of the training data as the development set to tune the hyper-parameters. The final hyper-parameters are as follows.

The word embeddings are pre-trained by Miklov et al. [10], which are 300-dimensional. The number of hidden units of LSTM is 300. We use 300 convolution filters each for the window size of 3. We set the mini-batch size as 10 and the learning rate of AdaDelta as the default value 1.0. We set the threshold δ of the sigmoid classifier to 0.5, which is selected from $\{0.1, 0.2, \cdots, 0.9\}$ based on the performance of the development set. To alleviate overfitting, we use Dropout [2] on Embedding Layer, BLSTM Layer and Convolution Layer with a dropout rate of 0.3, 0.2 and 0.2 respectively. We also utilize $l2$ penalty with coefficient $1e^{-5}$ over the parameters.

5 Overall Performance

As other systems did not show the result of joint extraction of entities and relations on the CoNLL04 dataset, we only compare our models with two state-

[2] conll04.corp at cogcomp.cs.illinois.edu/page/resource_view/43.

[3] https://github.com/pgcool/TF-MTRNN/tree/master/data/CoNLL04.

Table 2. Comparison with previous results.

Model	Settings	P	R	F1
TF	pipeline	.647	.522	.577
	end-to-end	**.760**	.509	.610
TF-MT	pipeline	.641	.545	.589
	end-to-end	.646	.531	.583
Ours	pipeline	.643	.390	.485
	BLSTM-R	.691	.481	.567
	BLSTM-RE	.747	**.548**	**.632**

Table 3. Comparison of our models on the task of entity detection.

Model	P	R	F1
pipeline	.597	.410	.486
BLSTM-R	.779	.648	.708
BLSTM-RE	.883	.652	.750

Table 4. Comparision for relation classification on the CoNLL04 dataset.

	[Kate & Mooney]			[Miwa & Sasaki]			[Gupta & Schutze]			LSTM-RE		
	P	R	F1	P	R	F1	P	R	F1	P	R	F1
OrgBase_In	.662	.641	.647	.768	.572	.654	**.831**	.562	.671	.761	**.783**	**.771**
Live_In	.664	.601	.629	**.819**	.532	.644	.727	.640	.681	.797	**.739**	**.767**
Kill	.775	.815	.790	.933	.797	.858	.857	**.894**	.875	**.952**	.870	**.909**
Located_In	.539	.557	.513	.821	.549	.654	**.867**	.553	.675	.804	**.732**	**.766**
Work_For	.720	.423	.531	.886	.642	.743	**.945**	.671	.785	.845	**.790**	**.817**
Average	.672	.607	.622	**.845**	.618	.710	.825	.664	.737	.832	**.783**	**.806**

of-the-art systems TF [12] and TF-MT [1]. Both TF and TF-MT mapped the entity and relation extraction task to a simple table-filling problem. And the table filling method needs to label $n(n+1)/2$ cells for a sentence of length n, while our models only need to predict $m_r(n+1)$ tags, where m_r is much less than $n/2$. BLSTM-RE boosts the $F1$ score by 2.2%. Compared with these two models, our model BLSTM-RE is simpler and more effective.

Table 2 also indicates that both BLSTM-RE and BLSTM-R perform better than the pipeline model, mainly because that the pipeline model trains entities and relations separately without considering the interaction between them, while BLSTM-R and BLSTM-RE learn entities and relations simultaneously.

BLSTM-RE achieves better results than BLSTM-R, the reason is that the input sentence may contain many relations as shown in Table 1. The softmax classifier only generates one most likely relation, while the sigmoid classifier can generate several relations at a time. In this situation, BLSTM-R only models one triplet, while BLSTM-RE can model multiple triplets simultaneously.

5.1 Analysis of NER and RC

This section summarizes the performance of NER and RC individually, which means that an entity is considered correct if one of its tokens is tagged correctly and a relation is considered correct if its relation type is correct. Because these three systems [1,6,12] assumed that the entity boundaries were given and only recognized entity types, while we only recognize entity boundaries. Therefore, we only compare the effect of RC with them as shown in Table 4.

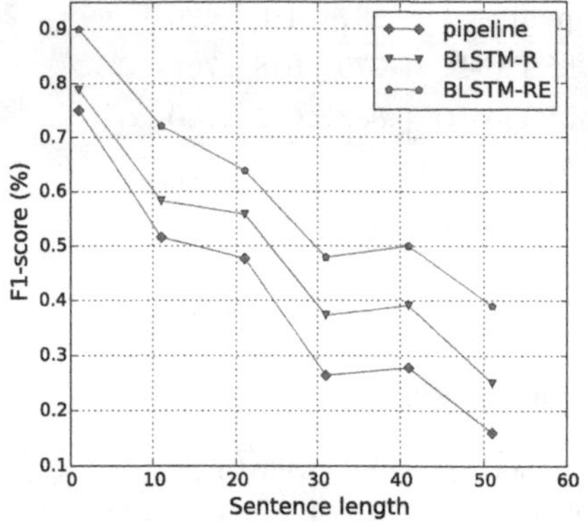

Fig. 2. Results *vs.* sentence length.

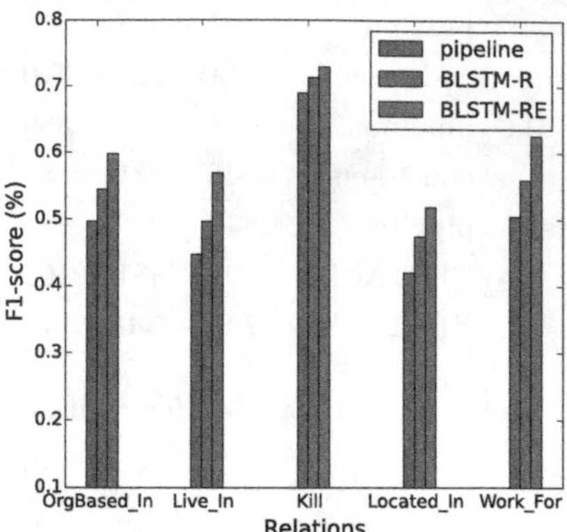

Fig. 3. Results *vs.* relations.

Table 3 shows the results of our three models on the task of NER. BLSTM-R and BLSTM-RE both have better performance than the pipeline model, which means that relation vectors are useful for the extraction of entities. Furthermore, BLSTM-RE is better than BLSTM-R, which shows that multi-label classification can effectively recognize relations than multi-class classification in this work.

The first two works [6,12] performed 5-fold cross-validation on the complete corpus. However, the folds were not available. We follow Gupta et al. [1] and report results on the same dataset. Since the standard divisions of the corpus are not the same, we cannot directly compare the results with the first two works [6,12]. But compared with TF-MT [1], BLSTM-RE shows an improvement of 6.9% in average $F1$ score.

5.2 Effect of the Sentence Length

Figure 2 depicts the performance of our models on sentences of different length. The x-axis and the y-axis represent sentence length and $F1$ score respectively. The sentences collected in the test set are no longer than 60 words. The $F1$ score is the average value of the sentences with length in the window $[n, n+9]$, where $n = \{1, 11, \ldots, 51\}$. Each data point is a mean score over five runs.

BLSTM-RE outperforms the other two models, and this suggests that learning multiple relations and entity pairs corresponding to the relations simultaneously can effectively extract triplets from sentences. At the same time, it shows that the $F1$ score declines with the length of sentence increasing. In the future work, we would like to investigate neural mechanisms to preserve long distance dependencies of sentences.

5.3 Effect of the Relations

Figure 3 depicts the performance of our models on different relations. The x-axis and y-axis represents relations and $F1$ score respectively. As the same as in Fig. 2, each data point is a mean score over five runs.

Different from Table 4, the $F1$ score involves entity and relation, which means that a relation is marked correct if the named entity boundaries and relation type are both correct. The figure shows that our models have different performance on different relations, and BLSTM-RE performs better than the other two models. All models perform better on relation *Kill* than the other four relations. There may be two main reasons. One is that all test sentences containing relation *Kill* do not contain other relations, and most of them contain keywords such as "kill", "death", and "assassinate", and therefore most of these sentences can be classified correctly when extracting relations. The other is that more than 80% of test sentences containing relation *Kill* only contain two entities. Thus, it is easy to recognize these entities.

6 Conclusions

This paper presents a novel end-to-end model BLSTM-RE to extract entities and relations. This model exploits BLSTM and CNN to automatically learn features from word embeddings without using any NLP tools. Thus, it is more straightforward and flexible. It treats relation classification as a multi-label classification problem and utilizes a sigmoid classifier to generate one or more relations. Therefore, it can model multiple relations and entity pairs at the same time. The effectiveness of BLSTM-RE is demonstrated by evaluating the model on the CoNLL04 dataset, and our model performs better than the pipeline based models and other end-to-end models. The experiment results also show that relation vectors obtained by RC Module are useful for the extraction of entities.

Acknowledgments. This research was supported by the National High Technology Research and Development Program of China (No. 2015AA015402) and the National Natural Science Foundation of China (No. 61602479). We thank the anonymous reviewers for their insightful comments.

References

1. Gupta, P., Schutze, H., Andrassy, B.: Table filling multi-task recurrent neural network for joint entity and relation extraction. In: COLING (2016)
2. Hinton, G.E., Srivastava, N., Krizhevsky, A., Sutskever, I., Salakhutdinov, R.R.: Improving neural networks by preventing co-adaptation of feature detectors. Comput. Sci. **3**(4), 212–223 (2012)
3. Hochreiter, S., Schmidhuber, J.: Long short-term memory. Neural Comput. **9**(8), 1735–1780 (1997)
4. Huang, Z., Xu, W., Yu, K.: Bidirectional LSTM-CRF models for sequence tagging. Comput. Sci. (2015)

5. Kalchbrenner, N., Grefenstette, E., Blunsom, P.: A convolutional neural network for modelling sentences. In: ACL (2014)
6. Kate, R.J., Mooney, R.J.: Joint entity and relation extraction using card-pyramid parsing. In: ACL (2010)
7. Kumar, A., Irsoy, O., Ondruska, P., Iyyer, M., Bradbury, J., Gulrajani, I., Zhong, V., Paulus, R., Socher, R.: Ask me anything: dynamic memory networks for natural language processing. Comput. Sci. (2016)
8. Lample, G., Ballesteros, M., Subramanian, S., Kawakami, K., Dyer, C.: Neural architectures for named entity recognition. In: NAACL-HLT, pp. 260–270 (2016)
9. Li, Q., Ji, H.: Incremental joint extraction of entity mentions and relations. In: ACL, pp. 402–412 (2014)
10. Mikolov, T., Sutskever, I., Chen, K., Corrado, G., Dean, J.: Distributed representations of words and phrases and their compositionality. In: NIPS (2013)
11. Miwa, M., Bansal, M.: End-to-end relation extraction using LSTMs on sequences and tree structures. In: ACL, pp. 1105–1116 (2016)
12. Miwa, M., Sasaki, Y.: Modeling joint entity and relation extraction with table representation. In: EMNLP, pp. 944–948 (2014)
13. Roth, D., Yih, W.: A linear programming formulation for global inference in natural language tasks. Technical report, DTIC Document (2004)
14. Santos, C.N.D., Xiang, B., Zhou, B.: Classifying relations by ranking with convolutional neural networks. Comput. Sci. (2015)
15. Schuster, M., Paliwal, K.K.: Bidirectional recurrent neural networks. IEEE Trans. Signal Process. **45**(11), 2673–2681 (1997)
16. Shin, J., Wu, S., Wang, F., De Sa, C., Zhang, C., Ré, C.: Incremental knowledge base construction using deepdive. VLDB Endowm. **8**(11), 1310–1321 (2015)
17. Singh, S., Riedel, S., Martin, B., Zheng, J., Mccallum, A.: Joint inference of entities, relations, and coreference. In: The Workshop on Automated Knowledge Base Construction, pp. 1–6 (2013)
18. Suchanek, F.M., Ifrim, G., Weikum, G.: Combining linguistic and statistical analysis to extract relations from web documents. In: SIGKDD, pp. 712–717 (2006)
19. Vu, N.T., Adel, H., Gupta, P., et al.: Combining recurrent and convolutional neural networks for relation classification. In: NAACL-HLT, pp. 534–539 (2016)
20. Yang, B., Cardie, C.: Joint inference for fine-grained opinion extraction. In: ACL, pp. 1640–1649 (2013)
21. Yao, L., Sun, C., Li, S., Wang, X., Wang, X.: CRF-based active learning for Chinese named entity recognition. In: IEEE International Conference on Systems, Man and Cybernetics, pp. 1557–1561 (2009)
22. Zeiler, M.D.: ADADELTA: an adaptive learning rate method. Comput. Sci. (2012)
23. Zelenko, D., Aone, C., Richardella, A.: Kernel methods for relation extraction. J. Mach. Learn. Res. **3**(3), 1083–1106 (2010)
24. Zeng, D., Liu, K., Lai, S., Zhou, G., Zhao, J., et al.: Relation classification via convolutional deep neural network. In: COLING, pp. 2335–2344 (2014)
25. Zhang, D., Wang, D.: Relation classification via recurrent neural network. Comput. Sci. (2015)
26. Zheng, S., Hao, Y., Lu, D., Bao, H., Xu, J., Hao, H., Xu, B.: Joint entity and relation extraction based on a hybrid neural network. Neurocomputing (2017)

A Fast and Effective Framework for Lifelong Topic Model with Self-learning Knowledge

Kang Xu[(✉)], Feng Liu, Tianxing Wu, Sheng Bi, and Guilin Qi

School of Computer Science and Engineering, Southeast University, Nanjing, China
{kxu,fengliu,wutianxing,bisheng,gqi}@seu.edu.cn

Abstract. To discover semantically coherent topics from topic models, knowledge-based topic models have been proposed to incorporate prior knowledge into topic models. Moreover, some researchers propose lifelong topic models (LTM) to mine prior knowledge from topics generated from multi-domain corpus without human intervene. LTM incorporates the learned knowledge from multi-domain corpus into topic models by introducing the Generalized Polya Urn (GPU) model into Gibbs sampling. However, GPU model is nonexchangeable so that topic inference for LTM is computationally expensive. Meanwhile, variational inference is an alternative approach to Gibbs sampling and tend to be faster than Gibbs sampling. Moreover, variational inference can also be flexible for inferring topic models with knowledge, i.e., regularized topic model. In this paper, we propose a fast and effective framework for lifelong topic model, called Regularized Lifelong Topic Model with Self-learning Knowledge (RLTM-SK), with lexical knowledge automatically learnt from the previous topic extraction, then design a variational inference method to estimate the posterior distributions of hidden variables for RLTM-SK. We compare our method with 5 state-of-the-art baselines on a dataset of product reviews from 50 domains. Results show that the performance of our method is comparable to LTM and other knowledge-based topic models. Moreover, our model is consistently faster than the best baseline method, LTM.

Keywords: Variational inference · Lifelong topic model · Knowledge-based topic model

1 Introduction

Topic models, such as pLSA (probabilistic Latent Semantic Analysis) [13] and LDA (Latent Dirichlet Allocation) [4], are popular content analysis techniques. Topic models are purely data-driven where topics are generated based on high-order word co-occurrence. However, some researchers find that the produced topics may not conform to human judgements [16]. One key problem is that the objective functions of topic models (e.g., LDA), which are fully based on implicit word co-occurrence patterns [18], often do not correlate well with human judgements [5].

M. Sun et al. (Eds.): CCL 2017 and NLP-NABD 2017, LNAI 10565, pp. 147–158, 2017.
https://doi.org/10.1007/978-3-319-69005-6_13

To alleviate the above problem, some researchers try to leverage knowledge-based models which incorporate external knowledge to guide topic modeling. The existing knowledge-based topic models mainly incorporate lexical knowledge. For example, Dirichlet Forest-Latent Dirichlet Allocation (DF-LDA) [1] utilizes domain-specific lexical knowledge in the form of must-links to discover topics in accordance with domain knowledge. Thereinto, Must-link (u,v) represents two words u,v have a similar probability within any topics. A Must-link can be a word-pair with semantic association (e.g., "large" and "big"), or a word-pair occur in the same phrases (e.g., "battery" and "life") [1]. Chen et al. [8–11] expand domain-specific lexical knowledge to multi-domain knowledge. In their work, words in the same semantic-set share the same word sense. Each semantic-set is viewed as a must-link. However, all the knowledge based on lexicon are static and general, a majority of knowledge is not flexible for topic modeling in a specific domain, while domain-related knowledge is not covered in the lexicon. Chen et al. [6,7,17] further propose a method to mine Must-link knowledge automatically and incorporate these knowledge into topic models. LTM incorporates the learned knowledge from multi-domain corpus into topic models by introducing the Generalized Polya Urn (GPU) model into Gibbs sampling. There exist some disadvantages of Gibbs sampling approaches for LTM: (1) words in the same documents and topics influence each other during topic inference, hence it is difficult to conduct inference in parallel for large-scale corpus; (2) Gibbs sampling is computationally expensive. Based on Gibbs sampling method, only GPU model can be utilized for incorporating knowledge in LTM. However, GPU model is nonexchangeable so that topic inference for LTM is more expensive than Gibbs sampling. An optimal alternative to Gibb sampling is variational inference [3]. Variational methods use optimization to find a distribution over the latent variables that is close to the expected posterior of interest [20]. For variational methods, each iteration of variational inference is difficult and it requires the computation of complicated functions [4]; however, it only needs dozens of iterations to converge. Moreover, variational methods are flexible for incorporating Must-link knowledge in a fast and effective way, i.e., by appending regularized terms into lower bound function of topic models.

In this paper, we propose a new framework, Regularized Lifelong Topic Model with Self-learning Knowledge (RLTM-SK), which can be divided into two main steps: knowledge mining with topic models and knowledge-constrained topic modeling. Our process for mining high-quality topics from multi-domain documents involves first mining frequent co-occurred word-pairs (knowledge) based on topics mined from multi-domain corpus in advance, and then incorporating these knowledge into topic models for the next round of topic extraction. For lifelong topic model with self-learning knowledge, we will repeat the two steps alternately until convergence.

There exist three main contributions of RLTM-SK: (1) We propose a fast and effective framework for RLTM-SK, which contains the method for automatically mining Must-link knowledge and the method of incorporating Must-links into topic modeling, via appending a regularized term into lower bound function of

LDA model. (2) We design a gradient descent approach for parameter estimation of RLTM-SK. (3) We implement experiments on a product review dataset from 50 domains to evaluate the effectiveness and efficiency of topic extraction in RLTM-SK.

2 Related Work

Topic Models, e.g. pLSA [13] and LDA [4], modeled semantic relations among words in an unsupervised way. The primitive topic models do not introduce any prior knowledge or other external resources, and topic models produce topics with uncontrolled quality. Nowadays, some researchers tried to leverage the domain knowledge of words to promote topic modeling. All the knowledge based topic models incorporated lexical (word-level) knowledge into topic models. The DF-LDA topic model [1] used tree-based priors to encode domain-specific expert knowledge on topic models in the form of must-links and cannot-links. Thereinto, a must-link indicates that two words must be assigned to the same topic, while a cannot-link states that two words should not be in the same topic. In [19], a factor graph framework was proposed to incorporate prior knowledge into topic models, where prior knowledge is modeled as sparse constraints (must-links and cannot-links) to speed up model training. In [2,15], they all incorporated domain knowledge into topic modeling in the form of first-order logic.

Recently, Chen et al. [6–11] proposed a series of research works that incorporated prior lexical knowledge from multi-domains into topic models. Thereinto, the first related work is MDK-LDA (LDA with Multi-Domain Knowledge) [11], a framework that exploited prior knowledge (must-links) from the past domains in topic models to bias topic assignment in the new domains. MC-LDA (LDA with M-set and C-set) [10] is the extension of MDK-LDA which used must-links and cannot-link prior knowledge. In GK-LDA (General Knowledge based LDA) [9], the model not only incorporated the general prior knowledge, but also handled incorrect knowledge without user input. Further they proposed AKL (Automated Knowledge LDA) [8] and LTM (Lifelong Topic Model) [7] that learned prior knowledge automatically from multiple domains to produce more coherent topics. All the knowledge-based topic models are based on Gibbs sampling, which is computationally intensive and cannot be scaled to large dataset [3]. Based on Gibbs sampling, LTM used GPU model for incorporating lexical knowledge. However, GPU model is nonexchangeable, the inference for LTM can be more computationally expensive than Gibbs sampling due to the non-exchangeability of words [6].

3 Lifelong Topic Model with Self-learning Knowledge

To extract topical words that satisfy our desired requirements, we propose a framework that can be divided into two main steps: knowledge-mining with topic models and knowledge-constrained topic modeling. Our process for transforming documents into high-quality topics involves first mining frequent co-occurred word-pairs (knowledge), and then incorporating these knowledge into topic models for the next round of topic mining. For lifelong topic model with self-learning knowledge, we will repeat the two steps alternately until convergence. In this section, we firstly make a brief review of LDA; then describe the process of knowledge mining and utilization; finally introduce the regularized topic model with self-learning knowledge.

3.1 Brief Review of LDA

LDA assumes that a document is a mixture of topics where a topic is a multinomial distribution over words in the vocabulary. The generative process is as follows:

1. For topic index $k \in \{1, ..., K\}$
   i. Choose a word distribution $\beta_k \sim \text{Dir}(\eta)$
2. For document $d \in \{1, ..., D\}$
   i. Choose a topic distribution $\theta_d \sim \text{Dir}(\alpha)$
   ii. For $n \in \{1, ..., N_d\}$ word
      a. Choose a topic assignment $z_{d,n} \sim \text{Multi}(\theta_d)$
      b. Choose a word $w_{d,n} \sim \text{Multi}(\beta_{z_{d,n}})$

In this process, $Mult()$ is a multinomial distribution, and $Dir()$ is a Dirichlet distribution which is a prior distribution of $Mult()$, α and η are hyper-parameters. The total probability of LDA is as Eq. 1.

$$p(\theta, \beta, z, w|\alpha, \eta) = \prod_{d=1}^{D} P(\theta_d; \alpha) \prod_{n=1}^{N} P(z_{d,n}|\theta_d) P(w_{d,n}|z_{d,n}, \beta) \prod_{k=1}^{K} P(\beta_k; \eta) \quad (1)$$

The mean-field variational distribution q for LDA breaks the relevance between words and documents, the detailed q is shown in Eq. 2. Based on Eq. 2, we can get lower bound on the likelihood $\mathbf{L}$ as Eq. 3, the object is to maximize $\mathbf{L}$ with respect to λ, γ and ϕ, where λ, γ and ϕ are utilized for estimating the objective posteriors.

$$q(\theta, \beta, z) = \prod_{d=1}^{D} q(\theta_d|\gamma_d) q(z_{d,n}|\phi_{d,n}) \prod_{k=1}^{K} q(\beta_k|\lambda_k) \quad (2)$$

$$\begin{aligned} \mathbf{L} = & E_{q(\theta,\beta,z)} \log \left[p(\theta|\alpha) \cdot p(\beta|\eta) \cdot p(z|\theta) \cdot p(w_n|z, \beta)\right] \\ & - E_{q(\theta,\beta,z)} \log \left[q(\theta|\gamma) \cdot q(\beta|\lambda) \cdot q(z|\phi)\right] \end{aligned} \quad (3)$$

3.2 Knowledge Mining and Utilization

The key object of LTM-SK is to extract Must-link knowledge from topics mined in the previous topic modeling. These knowledge contains word-pairs with semantic association (e.g., "large" and "big"), or word-pairs occur in the same phrases (e.g., "battery" and "life"). By incorporating these self-learning knowledge into topic modeling, we can mine more coherent topics.

Multi-domain Knowledge Mining. Given a set of documents $D = [D_1, ..., D_n]$ from n domains, LTM-SK mine knowledge from these documents with 3 main steps:

(1) Topic models are utilized to produce a set of topics S. In the initial phrase of topic modeling, LDA (Variational Inference) is utilized to mine topics, in the latter phrase of topic modeling, when knowledge has been learnt, we use Topic Model with Self-learning Knowledge to generate topics. (2) Topics are mined from multi-domain corpus, so many topics are not semantically related. If we mine knowledge from all the topics, much noisy knowledge will be introduced. To reduce noise in knowledge mining, we only mine knowledge in semantically similar topics from multi-domain documents, hence K-means clustering algorithm [12] is used to cluster topics. Thereinto, each topic in S corresponds to a word distribution, in our work, we choose the word distribution as the feature of the topic for clustering. (3) Only topics in the same clusters are utilized for mining knowledge together. In this step, we aim to mine Must-links from topics S, i.e., word-pairs co-occur multiple times in topics from multi-domain corpus. Here, each topic is represented as a list of words ranked with top-T probabilities in the topic-word distribution. To generate Knowledge Base (KB), i.e., a set of Must-links, from topics in different clusters, we use frequent itemset mining (FIM) [14] to mine Must-links. FIM is stated as follows: Given a set of transactions (topics) X, where each transaction (topic) $x_i \in X$ is a set of items (words). The goal of FIM is to discover every itemset (a set of items) that stratifies user-specified frequency threshold (i.e., minimum support), which the minimum times of an itemset must occur in X. Such itemsets are $frequentitemsets$, i.e., KB we need to learn. These $frequentitemsets$ are frequently co-occurred words in our work. To guarantee the quality of knowledge, we only use $frequentitemsets$ with 2-length, i.e., Must-links in our context. Must-links can be word-pairs with semantic association (e.g., "large" and "big"), or word-pairs occur in the same phrases (e.g., "battery" and "life")

Specific-Domain Knowledge Utilization. Must-links are mined from multi-domain topics, however, these Must-links are only applicable in a specific domain. For example, Must-link "battery" and "life" is useful for topic modeling in the domain of *Phone*, but it is inapplicable in the domain of *Book*, even it can be adverse for topic modeling in the domain of *Book*. Hence, to measure the correlation of Must-links in the current domain, we use Pointwise Mutual Information (PMI) to estimate the correctness of the Must-link towards the current domain, i.e., it measure the extent of two words, in a Must-link, co-occur in the current domain. The PMI of words w_1 and w_2 is $PMI(w_1, w_2) = log\frac{P(w_1,w_2)}{P(w_1)P(w_2)}$, where $P(w)$ denotes the probability of seeing word w in a document, and $P(w_1, w_2)$ denotes the probability of seeing both words co-occurring in a document. These probabilities are empirically estimated from the current domain D^t, where $\#D^t(w)$ is the number of documents in D^t that contains words w and $D^t(w_1, w_2)$ is the number of documents that contain both words w_1 and w_2. $\#D^t$ is the total number of documents in D^t.($P(w) = \frac{\#D^t(w)}{\#D^t}$, $P(w_1, w_2) = \frac{\#D^t(w_1,w_2)}{\#D^t}$) A high PMI value implies a true semantic correlation of words in the current domain.

3.3 Regularized Lifelong Topic Model with Self-learning Knowledge (RLTM-SK)

This model is an extension of LDA, the generative process of RLTM-SK is the same as LDA. Hence, as is shown in Eq. 3, the objective function of LDA is lower bound of the total probability of LDA model. Two words u,v in a Must-link have a similar probability within any topics, i.e., $\lambda_{k,u} \approx \lambda_{k,v}$ for each topic $k = 1, ..., T$. It means two words in the same Must-link have a high similarity over their topic distribution, where the similarity is measured by vector inner product between λ_u and λ_v. λ_u and λ_v are topic distributions of words u and v. The more likely two words exist in a Must-link, the more similar topics of two words are. As the aforementioned discussion, words in a Must-link will influence the topic assignment of the two words and then influence the topic distribution of a document.

$$
\begin{aligned}
&\mathbf{L_{RLTM-SK}} = \mathbf{L} + \mathbf{L_{KRT}} \\
&= \sum_{d=1}^{D}(\log \Gamma(\sum_{k=1}^{T} \alpha) - \sum_{k=1}^{T} \log \Gamma(\alpha) + \sum_{k=1}^{T}(\alpha - 1)[\Psi(\gamma_{dk}) - \Psi(\sum_{j=1}^{T} \gamma_{dj})]) \\
&+ \sum_{k=1}^{T}(\log \Gamma(\sum_{v=1}^{V} \eta) - \sum_{v=1}^{V} \log \Gamma(\eta) + \sum_{v=1}^{V}(\eta - 1)[\Psi(\lambda_{kv}) - \Psi(\sum_{j=1}^{V} \lambda_{kj})]) \\
&+ \sum_{d=1}^{D}(\sum_{n=1}^{N}\sum_{k=1}^{T} \phi_{dnk} \cdot [\Psi(\gamma_{dk}) - \Psi(\sum_{j=1}^{T} \gamma_{dj})]) \\
&+ \sum_{d=1}^{D}(\sum_{n=1}^{N}\sum_{k=1}^{T} w_{d,n} \cdot \phi_{dnk} \cdot [\Psi(\lambda_{k,w_{dn}}) - \Psi(\sum_{j=1}^{V} \lambda_{kj})]) \\
&- \sum_{d=1}^{D}((\log \Gamma(\sum_{j=1}^{T} \gamma_{dj}) - \sum_{k=1}^{T} \log \Gamma(\gamma_{dk}) + \sum_{k=1}^{T}(\gamma_{dk} - 1)[\Psi(\gamma_{dk}) \\
&- \Psi(\sum_{j=1}^{T} \gamma_{dj})])) - \sum_{k=1}^{T}((\log \Gamma(\sum_{v=1}^{V} \lambda_{kv}) - \sum_{v=1}^{V} \log \Gamma(\lambda_{kv}) + \sum_{v=1}^{V}(\lambda_{kv} - 1) \\
&[\Psi(\lambda_{kv}) - \Psi(\sum_{j=1}^{V} \lambda_{kj})])) - \sum_{d=1}^{D}(\sum_{n=1}^{N}\sum_{k=1}^{T} \phi_{dnk} \log(\phi_{dnk}))\{\mathbf{L}\} \\
&+ \sum_{(u,v)\in KB} PMI(u, v) * log \sum_{k=1}^{K} (\lambda_{k,u} * \lambda_{k,v})\{\mathbf{L_{KRT}}\}
\end{aligned} \tag{4}
$$

To guarantee the words in a Must-link share similar topics, the similarity of two words in a Must-link, $log \sum_{k=1}^{K} (\lambda_{k,u} * \lambda_{k,v})$, is introduced into the objective function **L** as regularized item $\mathbf{L_{KRT}}$. Since Must-links are learnt from multi-domain corpus, Must-links are not flexible in all the domains. In our work, we use $PMI(u,v)$ to measure the flexibility of a Must-link in the current domain. Hence, $PMI(u,v)$ is set as a weight of $log\sum_{k=1}^{K}(\lambda_{k,u}*\lambda_{k,v})$, $PMI(u,v)*log\sum_{k=1}^{K}(\lambda_{k,u}*\lambda_{k,v})$. The bigger the value of $PMI(u,v)$ is, the more similar of two words u and v in a Must-link are. The objective function of regularized lifelong topic model is shown in Eq. 4.

Inference for RLTM-SK

$$\gamma_{d,k} = \alpha + \sum_{n=1}^{N} \phi_{dnk} \tag{5}$$

$$\phi_{d,n,k} \propto exp([\Psi(\gamma_{dk}) + \Psi(\lambda_{k,w_{d,n}}) - \Psi(\sum_{j=1}^{V} \lambda_{kj})]) \tag{6}$$

$$\lambda_{k,v} = \eta + \sum_{d=1}^{D}\sum_{n=1}^{N} w_{dn} \cdot \phi_{dnk} \tag{7}$$

$$\begin{aligned}\frac{\mathrm{d}L}{\mathrm{d}\lambda_{k,v}} &= [\Psi^{'}(\lambda_{k,v}) - \Psi^{'}(\sum_{j=1}^{V}\lambda_{k,j})][\eta + \sum_{d=1}^{D}\sum_{n=1}^{N} w_{d,n} * \phi_{d,n,k} - \lambda_{k,v}] \\ &+ \sum_{(v,u)\in KB} PMI(v,u) * \frac{1}{\sum_{k=1}^{K}\lambda_{k,v}*\lambda_{k,u}} * \sum_{k=1}^{K}\lambda_{k,u}\end{aligned} \tag{8}$$

Through the adjusting of variational parameters based on LDA, the distributions can maximize Eq. 4. The inference of γ and ϕ are shown as Eqs. 5 and 6. The computation of $\lambda_{k,w}$ is divided into two conditions: if $w \notin KB$, the equation is shown as Eq. 7; otherwise, a gradient-based optimization method is adopted to get the optimized $\lambda_{k,w}$ as Eq. 8. The whole procedure, named variational inference for RLTM-SK, is shown in Algorithm 1.

4 Experiment Results

This paper evaluated the proposed RLTM-SK model and compares it with six state-of-the-art baselines: **LDA-GS** (Latent Dirichlet Allocation -Gibbs Sampling), **LDA-VB** (Latent Dirichlet Allocation -Variational Inference) [4], **DF-LDA** (Dirichlet Forest LDA) [1], **GK-LDA** (General Knowledge LDA) [9], **AKL** [8] (Automated Knowledge LDA), **LTM** [7] (Lifelong Topic Model).

Algorithm 1. Mean-field variational inference for RLTM-SK

Require: $\alpha, \eta, K, iterNum$
Ensure: λ, γ, ϕ
  if $i < iterNum$ **then**
    for each topic k and vocabulary v **do**
      if $w_i \notin$ KB **then**
        Update $\lambda_{k,v}$ Using Eq. 7
      end if
      if $w_i \in$ KB **then**
        Update $\lambda_{k,v}$ by gradient-based optimization with derivate in Eq. 8
      end if
    end for
    for each document d **do**
      Update $\gamma_{d,k}$ Using Eq. 5
      for each document d **do**
        Update $\phi_{d,n,k}$ Using Eq. 6
      end for
    end for
  end if

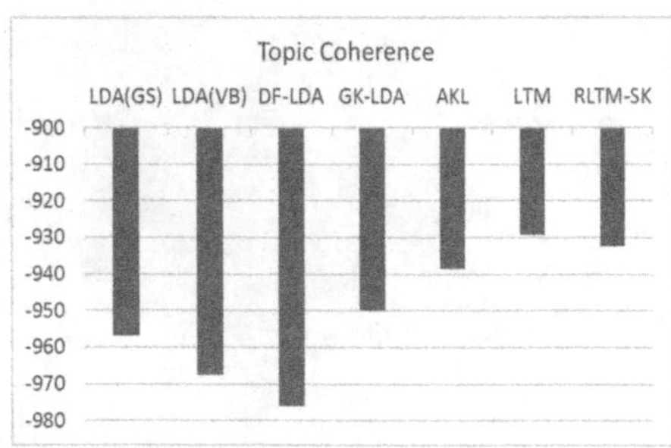

(a) Average coherence score in 50 domains

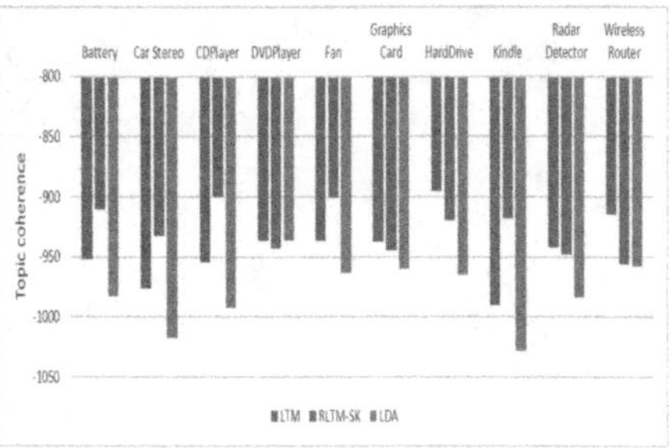

(b) Coherence score in 10 domains

Fig. 1. (a) Average coherence score on the top 10 words in the 15 topics discovered on 50-domains product reviews. (b) Coherence score on the top 10 words in the 15 topics in the selected 10 domains.

4.1 Datasets and Methods for Comparison

We used a large dataset containing 50 review collections from 50 product domains from Amazon.com as LTM [7], where each domain has 1000 reviews. The pre-process of the dataset was the same as LTM.

Parameter Settings. As the setting of LTM [7], we also set $\alpha = 1, \beta = 0.1$ and $K = 15$. For parameters of other baselines were set as their paper suggested. In all the baseline methods, Gibbs sampling was run for 2,000 iterations with 200 burn-in periods. For our variational inference method, the number of iterations was set as 200 (The variational inference method can converge faster than the Gibbs sampling method [20]). As LTM, the top 15 words of each topic were used to represent the topic for frequent itemset mining. For the number of clusters, $|S|$ is 10. The minimum support threshold was empirically set to max (5,0.4*$\#Trans$) where $\#Trans$ is the size of Transactions in each cluster (as LTM).

4.2 Topic Coherence

Another goal of RLTM-SK is to extract coherent topics from document collection and evaluate the effectiveness of topics captured by our models. In order to conduct quantitative evaluation of topic coherence, we used an automated metric proposed in [16], $C(t;V^{(t)}) = \sum_{m=2}^{M}\sum_{l=1}^{m-1} log\frac{D(v_m^{(t)},v_l^{(t)})+1}{D(v_l^{(t)})}$, where topic coherence, denoted as $D(v)$, is the document frequency of word v, $D(v,v^{'})$ is the co-document frequency of word v and $v^{'}$ and $V^{(k)} = (v_1^{(k)},...,v_T^{(k)})$ is a list of the T most probable words in topic k. The key idea of the coherence score is that if a word pair is related to the same topic, they will co-occur frequently in the corpus. In order to quantify the overall coherence of the discovered topics, the average coherence score, $\frac{1}{K}\sum^{k} C(z_k;V^{(z_k)})$, was utilized. The topic coherence is bigger, the topic quality is better. Here we compared RLTM-SK with six knowledge-based topic models: LDA(GS), LDA(VB), DF-LDA, GK-LDA, AKL and LTM. The result is shown in Fig. 1(a). From the topic coherent results, the overall topic coherence score is close to the best baseline, LTM, and better than other baseline methods. We randomly selected 10 domains to compare the topic coherence score with LTM, which is shown in Fig. 1(b). In domain Battery, Car Stereo, CD player, Fan and Kindle, our model performed better than LTM in topic coherence; in other domains, LTM performed better than our model. Because the applicability of knowledge varied in different domains, topic coherence didn't perform better than LTM in all domains consistently. It is clear that the performance of our simple framework can be comparable with computationally expensive LTM.

4.3 Human Evaluation

As our objective is to discover more coherent topics, so we chose to evaluate the topics manually which is based on human judgement. Without enough knowledge, the annotation will not be credible. Following [16], we asked two human judges, who are familiar with common knowledge and skilled in looking up the test tweet dataset, to annotate the discovered topics manually. To ensure the annotation reliable, we labeled the generated topics by all the baseline models and our proposed model at learning iteration 10.

Here we only compared with our model with the best baseline and LDA model in human evaluation. Following [16], we asked the judges to label each topic as *coherent* or *incoherent* (a topic as *coherent* when at least half of top 15 words were related to the same semantic-coherent concept; others were *incoherent*). Then we chose *coherent* topics which were judged before and asked judges to

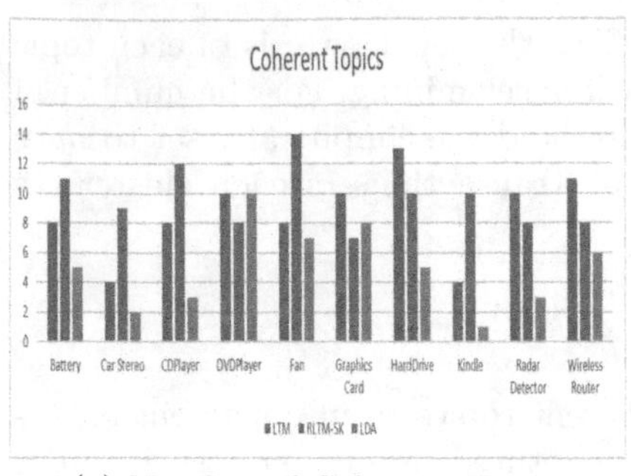

(a) Number of Coherent Topics

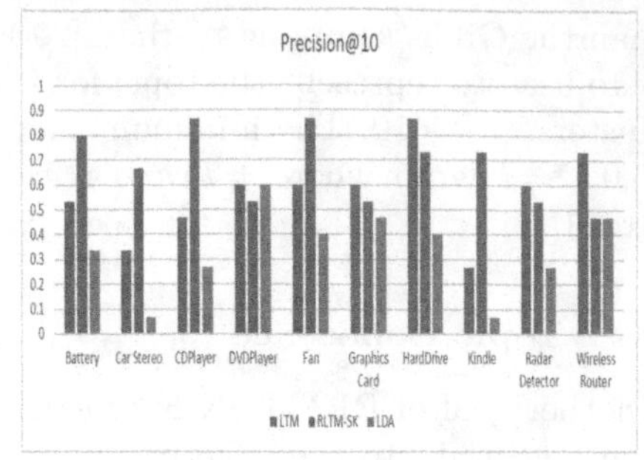

(b) Precision of Coherent Topics

Fig. 2. (a) Proportion of *coherent* topics generated by each model (b) Average Precision @10 (p@10) of words in *coherent* topics

label each word of the top 15 words among these *coherent* topics. When a word was in accordance with the main semantic-coherent concept that represents the topic, the word was annotated as *correct* and others were *incorrect*. Figure 2(a) shows that, in 5 of 10 domains, RLTM-SK can discover more *coherent* topics than LTM and LTM can perform better in 4 domains. Figure 2(b) shows that, in 5 of 10 domains, RLTM-SK performed better than LTM in Precision. In summary, our model, RLTM-SK, can perform better than LTM on human evaluation in the randomly selected 10 domains.

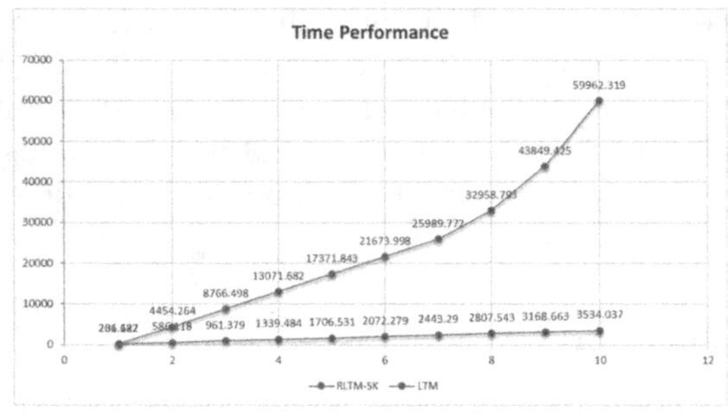

Fig. 3. The plot above demonstrates the speed of LTM and RLTM-SK.

4.4 Scalability

In the result of topic coherence and human evaluation, our model can achieve a competitive performance. Moreover, the significant advantages of our model are simplicity, efficiency and easily scalable. To understand the run-time complexity of our framework, which contains two main separate procedures, i.e., knowledge mining with topic models and knowledge-constrained topic modeling. The framework first involves topic modeling with self-learning knowledge by RLTM-SK model. However, there exists no prior knowledge initially, hence we use basic LDA to modeling topics. The second step is take the learnt topics as the input for knowledge mining, By jointly timing these two steps in our framework, we can empirically analyze the expected runtime of each iteration. Figure 3 shows the runtime of LTM, which is a previous lifelong topic model, and RLTM-SK over learning iterations. For our framework, with the growth of the learning iteration, the time cost did not increase significantly; On the contrary, LTM increases with a significant growth. When the iteration is 10, the run-time of LTM is far more than RLTM-SK. It shows that our framework can run lifelong topic model within a relatively short time, hence RLTM-SK can be much more easily scaled to large-scale corpus than LTM.

5 Conclusion and Future Work

In this paper, we propose a fast and effective framework for lifelong topic modeling. In our framework, we firstly mined knowledge automatically from topics extracted from multi-domain corpus and give different weights to knowledge so as to make knowledge adapting to a specific domain. Then, we used a variational inference method, which is fast and flexible for incorporating domain-adaptation knowledge, to infer parameters of topic models during lifelong topic modeling. Experimental results on 50-domains product reviews showed that our framework can consume much shorter time than LTM (the best baseline method), and it can perform as well as LTM in topic extraction. As future work, we plan to transfer this framework for jointly modeling sentiment and topic. Meanwhile, we can mine complex knowledge to improve topic modeling.

Acknowledgements. This work is supported in part by the National Natural Science Foundation of China (NSFC) under Grant No. 61672153, the 863 Program under Grant No. 2015AA015406 and the Fundamental Research Funds for the Central Universities and the Research Innovation Program for College Graduates of Jiangsu Province under Grant No. KYLX16_0295.

References

1. Andrzejewski, D., Zhu, X., Craven, M.: Incorporating domain knowledge into topic modeling via Dirichlet forest priors. In: Proceedings of ICML, pp. 25–32. ACM (2009)
2. Andrzejewski, D., Zhu, X., Craven, M., Recht, B.: A framework for incorporating general domain knowledge into latent Dirichlet allocation using first-order logic. In: Proceedings of IJCAI, pp. 1171–1192. AAAI (2011)
3. Blei, D.M., Kucukelbir, A., McAuliffe, J.D.: Variational inference: a review for statisticians. CoRR, abs/1601.00670 (2016)
4. Blei, D.M., Ng, A.Y., Jordan, M.I.: Latent Dirichlet allocation. J. Mach. Learn. Res. **3**, 993–1022 (2003)

5. Chang, J., Gerrish, S., Wang, C., Boyd-Graber, J.L., Blei, D.M.: Reading tea leaves: how humans interpret topic models. In: Proceedings of NIPS, pp. 288–296. MIT Press (2009)
6. Chen, Z.: Lifelong machine learning for topic modeling and beyond. In: Proceedings of NAACL-HLT, pp. 133–139 (2015)
7. Chen, Z., Liu, B.: Topic modeling using topics from many domains, lifelong learning and big data. In: Proceedings of ICML, pp. 703–711. ACM (2014)
8. Chen, Z., Mukherjee, A., Liu, B.: Aspect extraction with automated prior knowledge learning. In: Proceedings of ACL, pp. 347–358. ACL (2014)
9. Chen, Z., Mukherjee, A., Liu, B., Hsu, M., Castellanos, M., Ghosh, R.: Discovering coherent topics using general knowledge. In: Proceedings of CIKM, pp. 209–218. ACM (2013)
10. Chen, Z., Mukherjee, A., Liu, B., Hsu, M., Castellanos, M., Ghosh, R.: Exploiting domain knowledge in aspect extraction. In: Proceedings of EMNLP, pp. 1655–1667. ACL (2013)
11. Chen, Z., Mukherjee, A., Liu, B., Hsu, M., Castellanos, M., Ghosh, R.: Leveraging multi-domain prior knowledge in topic models. In: Proceedings of IJCAI, pp. 2071–2077. AAAI (2013)
12. Hartigan, J.A., Wong, M.A.: Algorithm as 136: a k-means clustering algorithm. Appl. Stat. **28**, 100–108 (1979)
13. Hofmann, T.: Probabilistic latent semantic indexing. In: Proceedings of SIGIR, pp. 50–57. ACM (1999)
14. Koronacki, J., Ras, Z.W., Wierzchon, S.T., Kacprzyk, J. (eds.): Advances in Machine Learning II, Dedicated to the Memory of Professor Ryszard S. Michalski. SCI, vol. 263. Springer, Heidelberg (2010)
15. Mei, S., Zhu, J., Zhu, J.: Robust Regbayes: selectively incorporating first-order logic domain knowledge into Bayesian models. In: Proceedings of ICML, pp. 253–261. ACM (2014)
16. Mimno, D., Wallach, H.M., Talley, E., Leenders, M., McCallum, A.: Optimizing semantic coherence in topic models. In: Proceedings of EMNLP, pp. 262–272. ACL (2011)
17. Wang, S., Chen, Z., Liu, B.: Mining aspect-specific opinion using a holistic lifelong topic model. In: Proceedings of the 25th International Conference on World Wide Web, WWW 2016, Montreal, Canada, 11–15 April 2016, pp. 167–176 (2016)
18. Yan, X., Guo, J., Lan, Y., Cheng, X.: A biterm topic model for short texts. In: Proceedings of WWW, pp. 1445–1456. Springer (2013)
19. Yang, Y., Downey, D., Evanston, I.L., Boyd-Graber, J.: Efficient methods for incorporating knowledge into topic models. In: Proceedings of EMNLP, pp. 308–317. ACL (2015)
20. Zhai, K., Boyd-Graber, J.L., Asadi, N., Alkhouja, M.L.: LDA: a flexible large scale topic modeling package using variational inference in mapreduce. In: Proceedings of WWW, pp. 879–888 (2012)

Collective Entity Linking on Relational Graph Model with Mentions

Jing Gong[1], Chong Feng[1(✉)], Yong Liu[2], Ge Shi[1], and Heyan Huang[1]

[1] Beijing Institute of Technology University, Beijing 100081, China
{gongjing, fengchong, hhy63}@bit.edu.cn,
shige713@126.com
[2] State Key Lab, Beijing 100081, China
24787806@qq.com

Abstract. Given a source document with extracted mentions, entity linking calls for mapping the mention to an entity in reference knowledge base. Previous entity linking approaches mainly focus on generic statistic features to link mentions independently. However, additional interdependence among mentions in the same document achieved from relational analysis can improve the accuracy. This paper propose a collective entity linking model which effectively leverages the global interdependence among mentions in the same source document. The model unifies semantic relations and co-reference relations into relational inference for semantic information extraction. Graph based linking algorithm is utilized to ensure per mention with only one candidate entity. Experiments on datasets show the proposed model significantly out-performs the state-of-the-art relatedness approaches in term of accuracy.

Keywords: Collective entity linking · Entity disambiguation · Relational graph

1 Introduction

The Entity Linking (EL) is crucial for information extraction and knowledge base population [1–3]. Given a document and a list of extracted mentions such as people, locations, organizations, entity linking targets at mapping the mention to an entity from reference knowledge base (KB) like Wikipedia, DBpedia, or YAGO etc. For example, considering the sentence posted to a news story: "Browne and Caldwell talked about the ongoing security crackdown in Baghdad". The mentions "*Browne*" and "*Caldwell*" should be mapped to the entities "*Sam Browne*" and "*Reche Caldwell*" respectively. The mentions are ambiguous because most of people are "*Browne*" and "*Caldwell*".

Most of earlier EL approaches focused on generic statistical features, which were later enhanced with a certain level of global reasoning. But essentially most approaches fail to acquire and exploit context semantic information in source documents. For

M. Sun et al. (Eds.): CCL 2017 and NLP-NABD 2017, LNAI 10565, pp. 159–171, 2017.
https://doi.org/10.1007/978-3-319-69005-6_14

example, "*He is supporting Gordon Brown, David Cameron is also backing Brown*", the mention "*Brown*" should be mapped to "*Gordon Brown*". If we notice that the latter "*Brown*" refers to the first Gordon "*Brown*", it will be much easier to link the latter mention to the corresponding entity instead of linking it to the dominant "*Brown*" (like most existing entity link systems did). The main idea of this intuition is to understand that the relationship between the two "*Brown*" is a pair of co-reference. Similarly, other relationship between the mentions will also provide us efficient semantic features for the linking task.

To address the shortcomings of features-based method, it is intuitive to consider the analysis of context semantic information and make fully use of relations between mentions and entities. An example of our method is shown in Fig. 1, which illustrates the map between mentions and entities from reference knowledge base. Through analyzing the context, the mentions in the same document are semantically related to each other. We also exploit the relationship among entities in the knowledge base, which stores a huge amount of explicit information. To the end, we utilize a graph based algorithm in term of these relations to disambiguate the entities. Our collective EL methods jointly exploit the interdependence between mentions in the same document, while non-collective approaches linking each mention independently.

This paper is organized as follows. Section 2 describes related work. Section 3 discuss how to exploit the semantic relations and co-reference relations in source documents. The construction of relational graph and a graph based linking algorithm are presented to disambiguate entities in Sect. 4. The experimental results are given and discussed in Sect. 5.

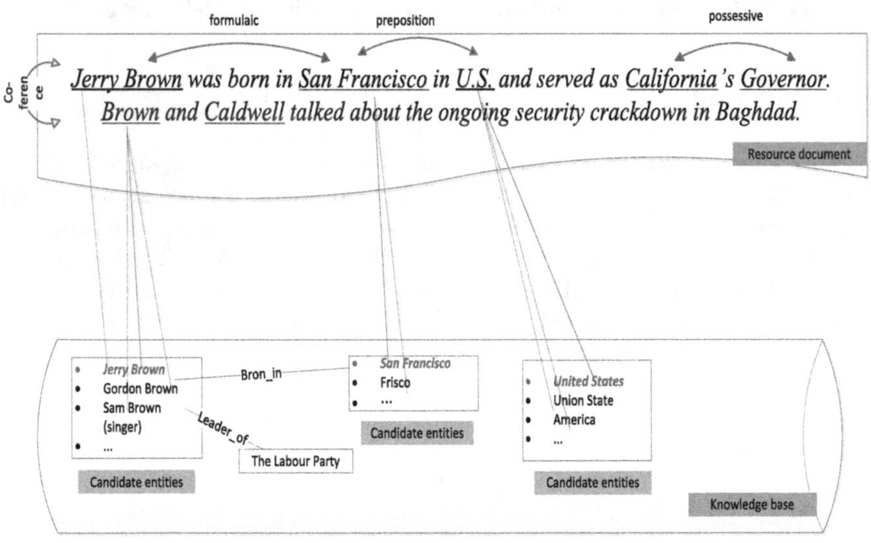

Fig. 1. The example of Entity Linking.

2 Related Work

Early works on entity linking often formulated the task as a Word Sense Disambiguation (WSD) problem [8, 9], which determined the correct sense of a multi-meaning word in a text according to its context information. The EL approaches can be divided into the following three major categories:

(1) **Local and Global Compatibility based Approaches:** The *local* compatibility method focused on context discriminative features to map a mention to the entity which has the highest contextual similarity. Fader et al. [5] defined a similarity measure that compared the context of a mention to the Wikipedia categories of an entity candidate. The *global* compatibility method focused on all mentions in a document simultaneously to arrive at a coherent set of disambiguation and utilized the link structure information to estimate coherence. Ratinov et al. [4], Cucerzan et al. [6], proposed to emphasize different coherence measures between the titles of the disambiguated mentions in the same document and the relatedness of common noun phrases in a mention's context. Milne and Witten [7] leveraged semantic relatedness between a mention's candidate entities and the unambiguous mentions in the textual context. While these features pointed towards semantic coherence and were still limited to mapping each mention separately. Even though these local and global compatibility based approaches had a competitive coverage rate, it would not work well on highly ambiguous surface strings.

(2) **Relational based Approaches:** The *relational* based approaches focused on computing the relationship of candidate entity-to-candidate entity and mention-to-candidate entity. Their motivation utilized the coherent and interdependent mentions in the same document. Dutta et al. [8] proposed a joint model combining cross-document co-reference resolution and entity linking, which also focused on co-occurring mentions allowing for global context and feature propagation. Zheng et al. [9] applied a dynamically joint inference method to improve within-document co-reference resolution. However, these approaches did not exploit the global interdependence among mentions in the same document and suffered on high computational costs even if for an approximate solving of the optimization model.

(3) **Graph based Approaches**: Navigli and Lapata et al. [10] proposed the graph connectivity metrics method, in which nodes were ranked with respect to their local importance of centrality measures such as in-degree, centrality, PageRank or HITS, etc. Blanco et al. [11] made a connection between graph problem and the Maximum Capacity Representative Set. Aharonu et al. [12] leveraged queries, websites and Wikipedia ideas collaboratively for getting to know generic search space intents and assemble a heterogeneous graph to characterize a number of kinds of relationships between them. Han et al. [13] and Liu et al. [14] proposed the graph-based collective entity linking algorithm, which utilized structured relationship of the knowledge base and external knowledge sources. While these approaches ignore the semantic information between mentions in the same document, which could improve the entity linking accuracy.

3 Relation Extraction

The primary challenge in incorporating relational analysis into the entity linking task is to systematically construct the relational constraints. We explore semantic relations and co-reference relations for relational inference. Not only the textual relations are extracted from the text, but also the weights are assigned to these semantic relations. Different from previous work on relation extraction [21], which are mainly conducted on ACE2004 (Automatic Content Extraction) or Relation Detection and Characterization (RDC) dataset, our method utilize large scale knowledge resources effectively, such as Wikipedia and YAGO.

3.1 Derivation of the Semantic Relations

The relation types in knowledge base are categorized into 4 semantic relations [15], which are {*premodifiers, possessive, preposition, formulaic*}. More detailed description of the four structures are as followings:

(1) **Premodifiers:** modifies the proper adjective or proper noun. E.g.: [the [Chinese] building]
(2) **Possessive:** indicates the first mention. E.g.: [[California]'s Governor]
(3) **Preposition:** indicates two semantically related mentions by the existence of a preposition. E.g.: [[The Great Wall] in [China]]
(4) **Formulaic:** indicates formulaic relations according to the ACE04 annotation guideline. E.g.: [The Great Wall], [China].

The process of semantic relations extraction is illustrated in algorithm (Fig. 2). Before employing the algorithm of semantic relations extraction, a pre-processing phase is necessary to improve the accuracy. The processing of mentions is aided by mention expansion and segmentation. Since some entities may have different names, aliases, acronyms and abbreviations, we use regular expressions to match abbreviations and longer surface forms that are often incorrectly segmented or ignored by NER due to different annotation standards.

3.2 Derivation of the Semantic Relations

Understanding of co-reference relations are also important for entity linking. Considering the following example:

> *"Jerry Brown was born in San Francisco in U.S. and served as California's Governor, Brown and Caldwell talked about the ongoing security crackdown in Baghdad.".*

The mention "*Brown*" should be mapped to the entity "*Jerry Brown*", but all existing EL approaches would map the popular page of *Brown.*

Thus, besides semantic relations, the co-reference relations are encountered to cover the common cases, where two or more co-reference mentions are mapped to the same entity. In this process, the input is the set of candidate entities mapped by mentions, and the output is the cluster C of co-reference relations. The entities, that share tokens or be acronyms of others, are clustered in the following algorithm (Fig. 3).

Algorithm 1 Exploiting Semantic Relations

```
Input: M = {m_1, m_2 ... m_k} is the set of mention. S= {premodifiers,
possessive, preposition, formulaic}.M_train is the set of annotated

gold mentions in training data. D_g = {(m_i, m_j} ∈ M_train × M_train D_s = ∅

Output: cluster R = ∅ of syntactic relations.

RE_base = RE classifier trained on D_g;

foreach (m_i, m_j) ∈ M do:

  p= structure inference on (m_i, m_j) using patterns;

if p ∈ S ∨ (m_i, m_j) was annotated with a S structure do:

D_s = D_s ∪ (m_i, m_j)
RE_s = RE classifier trained on D_s;

for each (m_i, m_j) ∈ M do:

  p = structure inference on (m_i, m_j) using patterns;
  if p∈ S do:

    r = relation for (m_i, m_j) using RE_s;
    R = R∪ r;
  else do:

    r = relation for (m_i, m_j) using RE_base;
    R = R∪ r;
return R
```

Fig. 2. The algorithm of exploiting syntactic relations

Algorithm 2 Exploiting the Co-reference Relations

```
Input: M = {m_1, m_2 ... m_k} is the set of mention. θ is the cutoff
threshold.
Output: co-reference cluster C.

        For all m_i, m_j ∈ M do:

            If C[m_i] ≠ C[m_j] and Sim(C[m_i], C[m_j]) > θ do:

            Merge (C[m_i], C[m_j], C) ;
        end for
        return C
```

Fig. 3. The algorithm of exploiting the co-reference relations

An issue occurs that the correct co-referent candidate entity might not exist in the candidate list in the cluster. To resolve the problem, we ignore candidate entities generated from short surface strings and give it the same candidate list as the head mentions in its cluster. The processing of longer and shorter mentions are different because the shorter mentions are inherently more ambiguous. The longer mentions should collectively refer to shorter mentions once a co-referent relation is determined.

3.3 Global Optimization of Relations by Integer Linear Programming

Our objective function of relational inference can be defined as following:

$$\Gamma = \sum_i \sum_k P(t_i^k|m_i)e_i^k + \sum_i \sum_k Z\alpha sim(\sigma|m_i)r_{ij}^{(k,l)} \quad (1)$$

Where

- m_i: the i-th mention.
- t_i^k: the k-th candidate title being chosen for mention m_i.
- $P(t_i^k|m_i)$: the initial score for the k-th candidate title being chosen for mention m_i.

$e_i^k \in \{0,1\}\left(\forall i \sum_k e_i^k = 1\right)$ is used to denote whether we disambiguate $\boldsymbol{m_i}$ to t_i^k.

The relation is denoted as $r_{ij}^{(k,l)} \in \{0,1\}\left(r_{ij}^{(k,l)} = e_i^k \wedge e_j^l, 2r_{ij}^{(k,l)} \leq e_i^k + e_j^l\right)$ whether title t_i^k and t_j^l are chosen simultaneously. Its value depends on the textual relation type and on how coherent it is with our existing knowledge.

Z is a normalization factor that normalizes all $\sum_i \sum_k Z\alpha sim(\sigma|m_i)$ to the range [0, 1]. The symbol α. the weight of implicit relations with explicit predicate, whose range is [1, 5].

$\sigma = (t_i, \mathrm{p}, t_j)$ is the set of triples obtained from indexing all Wikipedia links and DBpedia relations. The arguments t_i, t_j are tokenized, stemmed and lowercased, p is a relation predicate from the DBpedia ontology or the predicate linking indicating a hyperlink relation.

The integer linear programming problem is a mathematical optimization or feasibility program in which some or all of the variables are restricted to be integers. The objective function and the constraints (other than the integer constraints) are linear.

4 Entity Disambiguation on Relational Graph

4.1 Construction of Relational Graph

A weighted, undirected relational graph G = <V, E> is constructed, where $\mathrm{V} = \{v_1, v_2 \ldots v_m\}$ is the set of nodes, namely mentions and candidate entities, and $\mathrm{E} = \{e_1, e_2 \ldots e_n\}$ is the set of edges. The goal of this relational graph is to identify a dense sub-graph that contains merely one mention-entity edge for each mention.

Mention-Mention Graph

To avoid abusing linguistic knowledge from the source documents, we construct a collective mention-mention graph, whose edges are the selected semantic relations and co-reference relations. Figure 4 depicts a constructed mention-mention graph, which contains a set of vertices representing the mentions extracted from the source document and a set of undirected edges. The weights of the edges are calculated by Eq. (1).

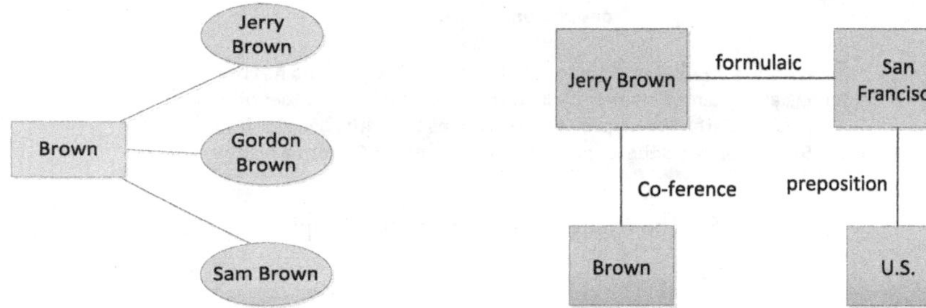

Fig. 4. The example of Mention-Mention Graph.

Fig. 5. The example of Mention-Entity Graph.

Mention-Entity Graph

We construct the mention-entity graph with mentions and its candidate entities as vertexes, whose weights of edges are calculated by the context similarity between mentions and its corresponding candidate entities such as $sim\left(context(m_i), context\left(t_i^k\right)\right)$, the $context(m_i)$ denotes the context window around mention m_i, the $context\left(t_i^k\right)$ denotes the context window around the anchor of candidate entity in the Wikipedia page (Fig. 5).

Entity-Entity Graph

We utilize the semantic relations of types and classes between entities in knowledge base to construct the entity-entity graph. The weights of edges are calculated by the equation $P\left(e_i, e_j\right) = 1 - \frac{\log\left(\max\left(\left|IN_{e_i}\right|, \left|IN_{e_j}\right|\right)\right) - log\left(\left|IN_{e_i} \cap IN_{e_j}\right|\right)}{\log(|N|) - log\left(\min\left(\left|IN_{e_i}\right|, \left|IN_{e_j}\right|\right)\right)}$, IN_{e_i} denotes the number of incoming links of candidate entity e_i. Figure 6 presents a sub-graph containing the relevant entities in the *Jerry Brown* example.

4.2 Graph Based Linking Algorithm

The goal of this graph based linking algorithm is to calculate a dense sub-graph which would ideally contain all mention nodes and exactly one mention-entity edge for each mention. The challenge of this task is how to specify a notion of density which is best suited for capturing the coherence of the resulting entity nodes (Fig. 7).

Hence we need to pay attention to the weak links in the collective entity set of the desired sub-graph. We regard the value of relational inference between nodes in the graph as the total weights of its incident edges. The density of a sub-graph could be regarded as the minimum weighted degree among its nodes. Based on an

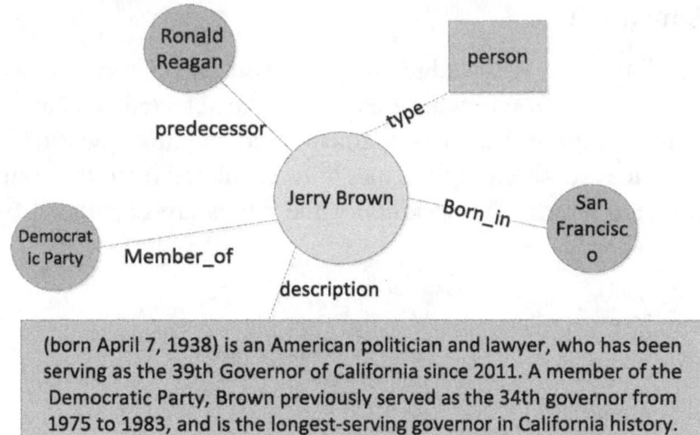

Fig. 6. The example of Entity-Entity Graph

Algorithm 3 Graph based Linking Algorithm

Input: the relational graph *G*, the set of mentions *M*, the set of candidate entities *E*.
Output: result graph with one edge per mention.
  For each mention **do**
    Calculate W_{m_i,m_j} , m_i *is connected with* m_j;
  for each candidate entity **do:**
    if the candidate entity is isolated and the weight is minimum, drop the nodes;
    keep the closest(5*mentions_count) candidate entities, drop others;
  while each mention has more than one candidate entity **do:**
    if m_i *and* m_j *has edge* & e_i^k*and* e_j^l*has edge***do**
      $S = S \cup \{e_i^k, e_j^l\}$;
    else
      Set the candidate entity with highest weighted degree to S;

Fig. 7. Graph based Linking Algorithm

approximation algorithm proposed by Sozio et al. [16], this paper propose a graph based linking algorithm to find strongly interconnected, size-limited groups in the graph.

Let S be equal to the set of candidate entities per mention in relational graph. The definition of e_i^k is a candidate entity of m_i, and let N_{m_i} be the number of all mentions. Let N_{m_i,e_i^k} be the number of candidate entities of m_i.

5 Experiments and Analysis

5.1 Experiments System

The process of entity linking contains three steps which is illustrated in the following. Firstly, we generate initial mentions M = {mi} from source documents and candidate entities C = {ci} from knowledge base, then extract semantic and co-reference relations from source documents with regular expressions. Finally, we leverage the integer linear programming to integrate the semantic information and disambiguate mentions in term of graph based linking algorithm.

5.2 Preparation of Dataset

To evaluate the performance of our method, we conduct experiments on 4 datasets used in Ratinov et al. [4]. The ACE dataset is a subset of ACE2004 Coreference documents and MSNBC is from Cucerzan et al. [6]. The AQUAINT dataset is introduced in Milne and Witten [7] and the Wiki dataset is a subset of Wikipedia. The detailed statistics are presented in Table 1.

Table 1. The description of 4 datasets

Dataset	The number of Text	The number of Linking
ACE	57	620
MSNBC	20	150
AQUAINT	50	449
Wiki	80	700

For each mention, we check whether the KB entity returned by EL approach is correct or not. Standard metrics is adopted in the following to evaluate the experimental performance. Let M* be the golden standard set of the linked mentions, M be the set of linked mentions outputted by EL system. We get Precision (P), Recall (R) and F1 score (F1) through equations as follows:

$$\mathrm{P} = \frac{|M \cap M*|}{|M|}, \mathrm{R} = \frac{|M \cap M*|}{|M*|}, \mathrm{F1} = \frac{2(P+R)}{P*R} \tag{2}$$

5.3 Comparison of Different Approaches of Entity Linking

We evaluate and compare our results with five approaches, which are *Tf-idf, Wikification* [17], *Aida* [18], *M&W* [7], *R&R* [4], *List-only* [21]. ***LGSCR*** (Entity Linking with Reference Graph Model) represents method proposed by this paper.

(1) ***Tf-idf:*** A simple *local compatibility* based method using the context similarity between mentions and candidate entities.

(2) ***Wikification:*** This approach identified entity relations and interdependence among mentions. Then incorporates these relations into an integer linear programming formulation.
(3) ***Aida:*** This is an integrated EL method which unifies prior probability and text similarity into a weighted *graph model*. The Aida utilizes robustness tests for self-adaptive behavior to avoid some specific situations.
(4) ***M&W:*** Milne&Witten utilized *simple relational features* between candidate entities and the context mentions.
(5) ***R&R:*** Ratinov utilized *local and global features* for entity disambiguation to Wikipedia.
(6) ***List-only:*** Lin selected seed mentions by *collective inference* to bridge the gap between mentions and non-informative target entities.
(7) ***LGSCR:*** Our approach utilize collective inference to link a set of coherent mentions simultaneously, which combines semantic relations with co-reference relations, integrating these relations into a graph based linking algorithm.

As Table 2 demonstrates, our collective EL method significantly outperforms other approaches. The ***LGSCR*** scored 2.41% higher than *aida* system in F1 score, which jointly exploits the global interdependence among mentions for entity disambiguation. By utilizing the semantic relations between mentions and entities, the *Wikification* achieve a higher performance over the generic statistical based baseline *tf-idf*.

Through the investigation of the four systems we find that the statistical method *tf-idf* does not suffice to the specific situations. For example, the sentence "*Instead of Los Angeles International, for example, consider flying into Burbank or John Wayne Airport in Orange County, Calif.*", the mention "*Burbank*" can be mapped to the wrong entity "*Burbank, California*" with high *tf-idf*, however, our EL system map the correct entity "*Bob_Hope_Airport*" according to the semantic relations.

Moreover, the performance in ***LGSCR*** is higher than other EL approaches, which is probably because they mainly reflect the relations among mentions and not the importance of the word itself just as position and frequency do. Consequently, this experiment not only demonstrates the effectiveness of graph based linking algorithm, but also reveals the importance of global interdependence structure among mentions to entity linking.

Table 2. Accuracy (%) of different methods on test set

Approaches	ACE	MSNBC	AQUAINT	Wiki	TAC2014
Tf-idf	73.52	72.99	73.75	79.77	73.02
Wikification	84.25	83.83	84.91	89.68	87.11
Aida	85.77	85.10	86.43	88.76	86.23
M&W	82.44	84.06	83.55	87.45	82.09
R&R	83.22	85.03	85.67	90.01	85.28
List-only	84.65	83.83	85.87	88.49	85.92
LGSCR	**85.98**	**87.35**	**86.96**	**92.44**	**87.57**

5.4 Analysis of Features

In this section, we incrementally add five components to the system and explore their impacts on the linking performance. We chose five groups of features: *local features, global features* [4], *semantic relations, co-reference relations,* and *relational graph.*

(1) *Local* features capture the context similarity between the vector of mention context and candidate entity context.
(2) *Global* features are refinements of similarity measures among Wikipedia titles, which leverage the incoming or outgoing link structure in Wikipedia. Thus we utilize a well-known Pointwise Mutual Information (PMI) relatedness measure. Given a Wikipedia title collection W, titles t1 and t2 with a set of incoming links L1, and L2 respectively, PMI is computed as follows:

$$\mathrm{PMI}(\mathrm{L}_1, L_2) = \frac{|\mathrm{L}_1 \cap L_2|/|W|}{|\mathrm{L}_1|/|W||L_2|/|W|}$$

(3) *Semantic relations* include global interdependence between mentions in the same source document. The algorithm of exploiting semantic relations is presented in Sect. 3.1.
(4) *Co-reference relations* include different surface mentions mapped to a same entity. An algorithm of exploiting the co-reference relations is illustrated in Sect. 3.2.
(5) *Relational Graph* integrates semantic relations and co-reference relations into graph based linking algorithm. The construction of relational graph and the graph based linking algorithm are given in Sect. 4.

Table 3 shows the performance of our EL system with different features. The final results are highly improved after adding relations among mentions and entities, which is probably because the relational inference can explore the implied semantic information and the interdependence among mentions. Compared with the local and global features, the semantic and co-reference relations of interdependence among mentions can significantly improve the F1 measure by 3.10%. By exploiting the relational graph model, our EL method can further improve the performance by 2.44% than the measure of semantic and co-reference relations.

Error analysis in many cases has shown that the summaries of the different disambiguation candidates for the same surface forms are very similar. The disadvantage of this approach is that irrelevant candidates are inevitably added to the disambiguation context, which would create noises. Different characteristics show somewhat consequently different gains from the various aspects of our approach.

Table 3. Results of entity linking with different groups of features (F1%)

Methods	ACE	MSNBC	AQUAINT	Wiki	TAC2014
LR	81.71	81.12	83.33	87.91	81.21
LGR	83.54	83.02	84.65	88.28	83.32
LGSR	84.59	84.14	85.97	89.86	84.42
LGSCR	**86.73**	**85.44**	**86.78**	**90.14**	**87.36**

LR: local features + relational graph.
LGR: local features + global features + relational graph.
LGSR: local + global features + semantic relations features + relational graph.
LGSCR: local + global + semantic relations features + co-reference relations features + relational graph.

6 Conclusions and Future Work

This paper propose a novel collective entity linking method, which jointly exploit the interdependence among mentions by selecting the most coherent set of entity candidates on the KB side. The model effectively incorporates semantic relations and co-reference relations into a graph based linking algorithm. The experiment results reveal that it performs better than all other state-of-art approaches with different features. In the future, more relations such as temporal relations and conjunction relations could be considered for entity linking task.

Acknowledgement. The research of this paper is partially supported by National 863 project 2015AA015404 and open project of State key lab. Smart manufacturing for special vehicles and transmission system.

References

1. Ji, H., Grishman, R., Dang, H.T., et al.: Overview of the TAC 2010 knowledge base population track. In: Text Analysis Conference (2010)
2. http://nlp.cs.rpi.edu/kbp/2016/taskspec.pdf
3. Ji, H., Grishman, R.: Knowledge base population: successful approaches and challenges. In: Proceedings of ACL, Portland, Oregon, USA, 19–24 June 2011
4. Ratinov, L., Dan, R., Downey, D., et al.: Local and global algorithms for disambiguation to Wikipedia. In: Proceedings of ACL, Portland, Oregon, USA, 19–24 June 2011, pp. 1375–1384 (2011)
5. Fader, A., Soderland, S., Etzioni, O.: Scaling Wikipedia-based named entity disambiguation to arbitrary web text. In: Proceedings of Wikiai (2009)
6. Cucerzan, S.: TAC entity linking by performing full-document entity extraction and disambiguation. In: 2011 Proceedings of the Text Analysis Conference (2011)
7. Milne, D., Witten, I.H.: Learning to link with Wikipedia. In: Proceedings of the 17th ACM Conference on Information and Knowledge Management, pp. 509–518. ACM (2008)
8. Dutta, S., Weikum, G.: C3EL: a joint model for cross-document co-reference resolution and entity linking. In: Proceedings of EMNLP (2015)
9. Zheng, J., Vilnis, L., Singh, S., et al.: Dynamic knowledge-base alignment for coreference resolution. In: Proceedings of the Seventeenth Conference on Computational Natural Language Learning, pp. 153–162 (2013)
10. Navigli, R., Lapata, M.: An experimental study of graph connectivity for unsupervised word sense disambiguation. IEEE Trans. Pattern Anal. Mach. Intell. **32**(4), 678–692 (2010)
11. Blanco, R., Boldi, P., Marino, A.: Using graph distances for named-entity linking. Sci. Comput. Program. **130**, 24–36 (2015)

12. Aharonu, M., Kale, M.R.: Entity linking based graph models for Wikipedia relationships. Int. J. Eng. Trends Technol. **18**(8), 380–385 (2014)
13. Han, X., Sun, L., Zhao, J.: Collective entity linking in web text: a graph-based method. In: SIGIR, pp. 765–774. ACM (2011)
14. Qiao, L., Yun, Z., Yang, L., et al.: Graph-based collective chinese entity linking algorithm. J. Comput. Res. Dev. (2016)
15. Chan, Y.S., Roth, D.: Exploiting syntactico-semantic structures for relation extraction. In: Proceedings of ACL: Proceedings of the Conference on Human Language Technologies, Portland, Oregon, USA, 19–24 June 2011, pp. 551–560 (2011)
16. Sozio, M., Gionis, A.: The community-search problem and how to plan a successful cocktail party. In: ACM SIGKDD International Conference on Knowledge Discovery and Data Mining, pp. 939–948. ACM (2010)
17. Cheng, X., Roth, D.: Relational inference for Wikification. In: Proceedings of EMNLP, pp. 1787–1796. ACL (2013)
18. Hoffart, J., Yosef, M.A., Bordino, I., et al.: Robust disambiguation of named entities in text. In: Proceedings of EMNLP, pp. 782–792. ACL (2011)
19. Flanigan, J., Thomson, S., Carbonell, J., et al.: A discriminative graph-based parser for the abstract meaning representation. In: Proceedings of ACL, pp. 1426–1436 (2014)
20. Ji, H., Nothman, J., Hachey, B.: Overview of TAC-KBP2014 entity discovery and linking tasks. In: Proceedings of Text Analysis Conference (TAC 2014), November 2014
21. Lin, Y., Lin, C.-Y., Ji, H.: List-only entity linking. In: Proceedings of ACL, pp. 536–541 (2017)

XLink: An Unsupervised Bilingual Entity Linking System

Jing Zhang, Yixin Cao, Lei Hou, Juanzi Li(✉), and Hai-Tao Zheng

Department of Computer Science and Technology, Tsinghua University, Beijing 100084, People's Republic of China
zhangjinglavener@gmail.com , caoyixin2011@gmail.com, greener@gmail.com, lijuanzi@tsinghua.edu.cn, zheng.haitao@sz.tsinghua.edu.cn

Abstract. Entity linking is a task of linking mentions in text to the corresponding entities in a knowledge base. Recently, entity linking has received considerable attention and several online entity linking systems have been published. In this paper, we build an online bilingual entity linking system XLink, which is based on *Wikipeida* and *Baidu Baike*. XLink conducts two steps to link the mentions in the input document to entities in knowledge base, namely mention parsing and entity disambiguation. To eliminate dependency of language, we conduct mention parsing without any named entity recognition tools. To ensure the correctness of linking results, we propose an unsupervised generative probabilistic method and utilize text and knowledge joint representations to perform entity disambiguation. Experiments show that our system gets a state-of-the-art performance and a high time efficiency.

Keywords: Entity linking system · Entity disambiguation · Mention detection

1 Introduction

Entities, which describe specific concepts or represents real-world objects, play an important role in Web document, e.g., *persons*, *locations* and *organizations* record key elements of news articles. Unfamiliar entities may affect text understanding. Fortunately, large knowledge bases contain rich information about world's entities, including their semantic classes and mutual relationships. To make Web text more understandable, a critical step is to linking the entity mentions with their corresponding entities in a knowledge base, which is entity linking. Besides text understanding, it can facilitate many different tasks such as question answering [22,25], knowledge base population [19].

In recent years, various entity linking systems have been published, such as Wikify! [14], AIDA [12], DBpedia Spotlight [13], TagMe [9], Linkify [23]. These systems commonly have two components: mention detection and entity linking. For mention detection, AIDA [12] and Linkify [23] depend on Names Entity Recognition (NER) tools. However, NER tools depend on language heavily [10]

M. Sun et al. (Eds.): CCL 2017 and NLP-NABD 2017, LNAI 10565, pp. 172–183, 2017.
https://doi.org/10.1007/978-3-319-69005-6_15

and only recognize three types of named entities: *persons*, *locations* and *organizations*, far from covering the types of entities in knowledge base. To address the problem of ambiguity and variation in entity linking, the simplest way is to choose the most prominent entity (i.e., the candidate with the largest number of incoming or outcoming links in Wikipedia) for the given mention. However, different context of mentions leads to different linking results, which is too complex to be solved through entity priority. An alternative idea calculates the contextual similarity for single mention linking, and further employs the topical coherence to collectively link all mentions within a document. But few of these systems considers the features in a unified and effective way. Moreover, these systems mainly use Wikipedia as the knowledge base and rarely handle Chinese documents. Additionally, there emerge many large-scale Chinese encyclopedias, e.g., Baidu Baike, and it's time to conduct entity linking in both Chinese and English.

To address the above issues, we develop a bilingual online entity linking system named XLink. It conducts a language independent process for both Chinese and English documents on-the-fly via two phases: mention parsing and entity disambiguation. Mention parsing detects mentions in input documents and generates candidate entities for each mention. Entity disambiguation phase chooses the correct entity in the candidate set. XLink aims to provide users an online service of linking all important mentions in text to entities in knowledge base correctly and efficiently. In particular, we first use a parsing algorithm to search a pre-built dictionary to detect mentions instead of using NER tagger. Secondly, we design a generative probabilistic entity disambiguation method which models contextual feature, coherence feature and prior feature jointly to guarantee the accuracy of disambiguation. For the system efficiency, we use Aho-Corasick algorithm to parse mentions and introduce word and entity embeddings to ensure the time efficiency of disambiguation phase. In addition, the disambiguation method is unsupervised so that it is easy to deploy the system online.

In summary, the main contributions of this paper can be described as follow:

1. We utilize a pre-built dictionary rather than a NER tagger to detect mentions to avoid language dependency and recognize entities of more types.
2. We propose an unsupervised generative probabilistic model to disambiguate entities for the detected mentions. *Context* of mentions and *entity coherence* as well as *priority* are employed to promote the performance of disambiguation. Experiment shows that the disambiguation algorithm significantly outperforms the state-of-the-art unsupervised approaches.
3. We construct a web service of XLink. Users can enter a text fragment of any types (e.g., news, tweets) in Chinese or English, and XLink adds URLs to the mention labels for visualization on the web page and ranks the results according to disambiguation confidence score.

The rest of this paper is organized as follow. In Sect. 2 we present the definitions. In Sect. 3, we describe the framework of XLink and details of the methods. In Sect. 4, we present evaluations of our system. In Sect. 5 we discuss the related work and finally in Sect. 6 we present our conclusions and future work.

2 Problem Definition

We introduce some concept definitions and problem formulation in this section.

Definition 1. *A **knowledge base** $\mathcal{KB}$ contains a set of entities $\mathcal{E} = \{e_j\}$. Each entity corresponds a page containing title, textual description, hyperlinks pointing to other entities, infobox, etc.*

Definition 2. *A **text corpus** $\mathcal{D}$ contains a set of words $\mathcal{D} = \{w_1, w_2, ..., w_{|\mathcal{D}|}\}$. A mention m is a word or phrase in $\mathcal{D}$ which may refer to an entity e in $\mathcal{KB}$. In this paper, we pre-train word and entity representations, and use low-dimensional vectors v_w and v_e to denote the embedding of word w and entity e in $\mathcal{KB}$.*

Definition 3. *An **anchor** $a \in \mathcal{A}$ is a hyperlink in $\mathcal{KB}$ articles, which links its surface text mention m to an entity e. $\mathcal{A}_{e,m}$ denotes the set of anchors of mention m pointing to entity e. Anchor Dictionary is the dictionary that we build through utilizing all the anchors in $\mathcal{KB}$. Each a in the anchor dictionary may refer to a set of entities $\mathcal{E}_m = \{e_j\}$.*

Definition 4. ***Problem Definition.*** *Given a document $\mathcal{D} = \{w_1, w_2, ..., w_{|\mathcal{D}|}\}$ and $\mathcal{KB}$, the task is to find out the mentions in $\mathcal{D}$ and link them to their referent entities. We resolve the problem into two phases. In Mention Parsing, we detect mentions $\mathcal{M} = \{m_1, m_2, ..., m_{|\mathcal{M}|}\}$ and generate a candidate entity set $\mathcal{C} = \{e_1, e_2, ..., e_{|\mathcal{C}|}\}$ for each mention m_j. In Entity Disambiguation, we select the most probable entity e_j^* in the candidate set $\mathcal{C}$ for each mention m_j.*

3 The Anatomy of XLink

Figure 1 shows the framework of our proposed XLink system. It receives a textual document $\mathcal{D}$, and tries to link the mentions in $\mathcal{D}$ to entities in $\mathcal{KB}$ in two steps, mention parsing and entity disambiguation. *Mention Parsing* detects mentions by searching the pre-built *Anchor Dictionary*, and generates candidate entities

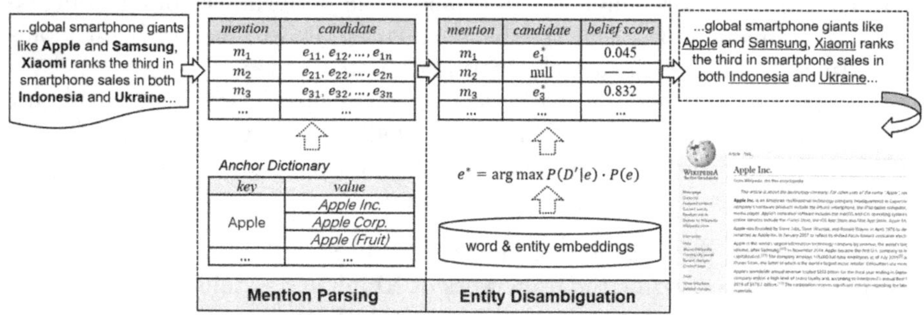

Fig. 1. Illustration of XLink

to be disambiguated. *Entity Disambiguation* utilizes a generative probabilistic method to determine which candidate entity e should be linked to the corresponding mention m, and pre-trained representations are employed to calculate probabilities.

3.1 Mention Parsing

Mention parsing detects the possible entity mentions in the input document $\mathcal{D}$ by searching a pre-built anchor dictionary. Therefore, dictionary building and parsing algorithm are the major problems.

Dictionary Building. In Wikipedia and Baidu Baike, the anchor text of a hyperlink pointing to an entity page provides useful name variations of the pointed entity. An anchor can be a synonym, abbreviation or title of an entity. For example, anchor text "Apple" may point to the page of *Apple Inc.*, *Apple Corps.* or *Apple (fruit)* in different documents. Inversely, the entity *Apple Inc.* also has other anchor texts, such as "Apple Computer Inc.". By extracting anchor texts and their corresponding hyperlinks from $\mathcal{KB}$ articles, we can construct an anchor dictionary, where the keys are mentions and values are candidate entities, as shown in Table 1. A mention may refer to several entities and an entity may have several mentions. Thus, we can generate the candidate entities referred by a mention easily by querying the dictionary.

Table 1. Examples of Anchor Dictionary

Wikipedia		Baidu Baike	
key	*value*	*key*	*value*
Microsoft	*Microsoft*	微软	微软
Microsoft Corporation	*Microsoft*	微软公司	微软
Apple	*Apple Inc.* *Apple*	苹果	苹果公司 苹果
Apple Computer Inc.	*Apple Inc.*	苹果电脑公司	苹果公司

We define $link(a)$ as the times anchor a occurs as a hyperlink in the $\mathcal{KB}$ articles, and $freq(a)$ as the times that a occurs as either a hyperlink or a plain text. $link\_prob(a) = link(a)/freq(a)$ denotes the probability that an anchor a occurs as a hyperlink and points to some entities in $\mathcal{KB}$. To make the dictionary clean, we filter the useless anchors according to the following rules: (1) the anchors with only one character since they usually convey little information; (2) the anchors with low absolute linked frequency ($link(a) < 2$) since it indicates the entity the anchors point to are not popular enough; (3) the anchors with low relative linked frequency ($link\_prob(a) < 0.01\%$) since it implies that the anchors are usually used as general terms. Finally, we also merge the *redirect* information in the anchor dictionary. *Redirect* maps from misspelling, abbreviation or other frequent forms of entity names to the exact entities.

Parsing Algorithm. To accelerate parsing process, we use a fast string searching algorithm to parse mentions in anchor dictionaries, *Aho-Corasick Algorithm*[1]. It is a kind of dictionary-matching algorithm that locates elements of a finite set of strings (the "dictionary") within an input text and it matches all strings simultaneously. Informally, the algorithm constructs a finite state machine that resembles a trie with additional links between the various internal nodes. With the pre-built anchor dictionary, we could construct the automaton off-line. In particular, the complexity of the algorithm is linear in the length of the strings plus the length of the searched text plus the number of output matches, which is efficient for online process.

However, because the automaton find all matches simultaneously, there could be a quadratic number of conflicts (substrings and overlaps). To solve the problem, we design an algorithm to choose a match which could be most probable to be an entity mention. For two conflicting mentions m_1 and m_2, if m_1 is much longer, we regard m_1 to be more specific than m_2. For example, the mention " 香港特别行政区 " is more specific than " 香港 ". Besides, if m_1 has the same length with m_2, we choose the one with greater link probability. We assume a mention name with greater link probability is more likely to be linked in text and has less ambiguity intuitively. Furthermore, the parsing algorithm detects mentions iteratively until there is no conflicting mentions in the text, and experiment shows the algorithm can be terminated after a smaller number of iterations. Finally, we could generate candidate entity set $\mathcal{C} = \{e_1, e_2, ..., e_{|\mathcal{C}|}\}$ for mention m_j.

3.2 Entity Disambiguation

With the candidate set $\{e_1, e_2, ..., e_{|\mathcal{C}|}\}$ for each mention m_j, *Entity Disambiguation* selects the most suitable entity e_j^*. Inspired by the works of Han et al. [11], we propose a generative probabilistic method to model the context, coherence and priorities jointly. In the following, we present the model details and representations of words and entities.

Joint Embedding of Words and Entities. We utilize the models proposed by [24], jointly learning the embeddings of words and entities and mapping words and entities into the same continuous vector space. It consists of three models based on skip-gram model: (1) the conventional skip-gram model that learns to predict neighboring words given the target word in text corpora; (2) the knowledge base graph model that learns to estimate neighboring entities given the target entity in the link graph of the knowledge base. (3) the anchor context model that learns to predict neighboring words given the target entity using anchors and their context words in the knowledge base. Essentially, the knowledge graph model learns the relatedness of entities and the anchor context model aims to align vectors such that similar words and entities occur close to one another in the vector space. Hence, we can measure the similarity between any pairs of words and entities, which are used to estimate probability distributions.

Disambiguation Model. We resolve the entity disambiguation as a generative model. Different from the works of Han et al. [11], we use coherence instead of mention name because experiments show that sometimes mention name leads to wrong disambiguation (details in Sect. 4). Given the mention m, we first choose a referent entity e from $\mathcal{KB}$, according to the entity prior popularity distribution $P(e)$, then estimate its context according to the textual context distribution $P(\hat{\mathcal{C}}|e)$, and finally generate the coherent entities of the referent entity via the distribution of related entities $P(\mathcal{N}|e)$. Hence, the probability of m referring to a specific entity e in $\mathcal{KB}$ can be inferred as:

$$P(m,e) = P(e) \cdot P(\hat{\mathcal{C}}|e) \cdot P(\mathcal{N}|e) \tag{1}$$

Given the mention $m \in \mathcal{M}$ in a document $\mathcal{D}$, the final entity we need to find is the one maximizing the post-prior $P(e|m)$. Thus, entity disambiguation can be resolved as following:

$$\begin{aligned} e^* &= \underset{e \in \mathcal{C}}{argmax} \frac{P(m,e)}{P(m)} \\ &= \underset{e \in \mathcal{C}}{argmax}\, P(e) \cdot P(\hat{\mathcal{C}}|e) \cdot P(\mathcal{N}|e) \end{aligned} \tag{2}$$

where $\hat{\mathcal{C}}$ is the set of textual context around mention m, $\mathcal{N}$ is the set of disambiguated entities in $\mathcal{D}$, $\mathcal{C} = \{e_1, e_2, ..., e_{|\mathcal{M}|}\}$ is the candidate set.

$P(e)$ is the distribution of entity prior. Especially, we define the entity prior as the probability it is referred in the whole corpus. In large corpus, the more times an entity is referred, the more popular this entity tends to be. However, entities have different prior probabilities in different domains. Thus we introduce a parameter $\alpha \in [0,1]$to control the influence of prior:

$$P(e) = (\frac{|\mathcal{A}_{e,*}|}{|\mathcal{A}_{*,*}|})^{\alpha} \tag{3}$$

where $\mathcal{A}_{e,*}$ is the set of anchors pointing to entity e and $\mathcal{A}_{*,*}$ is the set of all the anchors in $\mathcal{KB}$. $\alpha = 0$ denotes entity prior has no impact on the result and $\alpha = 1$ indicates the case without no control of entity prior.

$P(\hat{\mathcal{C}}|e)$ is the textual context distribution given e. An entity is more likely to appear in a context similar with its sense. For example, in text "In 2001, Michael Jordan and others resigned from the Editorial Board of Machine Learning", we can know the mention "Michael Jordan" refers to the professor *Michael I. Jordan* from the context "Machine Learning". Hence, following [24], we use a cosine similarity of context word vector and entity vector to estimate the distribution. We average the vectors of context words to represent the context vector:

$$\vec{v_{\hat{c}}} = \frac{1}{|W_{\hat{C}}|} \sum_{w \in W_{\hat{C}}} \vec{v_w} \tag{4}$$

where $W_{\hat{C}}$ is the set of context words. We obtain the words of context via searching a pre-built word dictionary which is indexed to a trie using Aho-Corasick algorithm. The word dictionary is the same as the words corpus used to train the word embeddings.

$P(\mathcal{N}|e)$ is the distribution of context entities given e. Entities in context share one or few same topics, and related entities are close in vector space. Thus the distribution can be seen as the topical *coherence*. Similar to [18,24], we adopt a two-step method to calculate *coherence* iteratively. Firstly, we find unambiguous entities as context entities with a popularity $P(e|m) > \varepsilon$, where $P(e|m) = |\mathcal{A}_{e,m}|/|\mathcal{A}_{*,m}|$, and we set ε to 0.95 empirically. Secondly, we use the predicted unambiguous entities as context entities to calculate $P(\mathcal{N}|e)$ again. To estimate $P(\mathcal{N}|e)$, we use cosine similarity between the vector of context entities and the vector of target entity, namely,

$$\vec{v_N} = \frac{1}{|E_N|} \sum_{e \in E_N} \vec{v_e} \tag{5}$$

where E_N is the unambiguous entities.

It should be noted that there are two ways to perform disambiguation according to the ordering of candidates, namely L2R (left to right) and S2C (simple to complex). L2R is more efficient to apply because there is no need to rank the candidate lists. While S2C need to rank candidate lists again according to the size of candidate list of each mention.

4 Experiments

4.1 Dataset and Settings

We use CoNLL, a popular named entity disambiguation dataset [12], to test the performance of XLink. It is based on NER data from CoNLL 2003 shared task, and consists of 946, 216 and 231 training, development and test documents respectively. Because our disambiguation method is unsupervised, we test on the entire dataset, including mentions having valid entries to Wikipedia and we ignore mentions with NIL entities. To make the comparison fair, we use a public dataset PPRforNED[1] [17] to generate candidates for the entity disambiguation.

The version of Wikipedia dump we use is Apr. 1, 2016. In preprocess, we first tokenize the Chinese corpus using ANSJ[2] and we discard tokens that appears lower than 5 times. Finally, we learn the representations of 2.9 million words and 5.1 million entities in Wikipedia, 4.5 million words and 5.7 million entities in Baidu Baike. For both Wikipedia and Baiku corpus, the dimension of embedding vectors is 300 and the window size is 10 as suggested by [24]. Negative samples $g = 5$ and learning rate η is set to 0.025 which linearly decreases with the iterations of training. We train the models by iterating the corpus 10 times.

4.2 Evaluation of Mention Parsing

We build anchor dictionaries for both Wikipedia and Baidu Baike separately, and achieve 3,922,720 mention-candidates entries in Wikipedia and 2,210,817

[1] https://github.com/masha-p/PPRforNED.
[2] https://github.com/NLPchina/ansj_seg.

entries in Chinese. Because both corpora are comprehensive encyclopedias with lots of general terms, the mentions detected may have redundancy, which are not as helpful as specific entities. Thus, we discard the detected mentions simply via a threshold of $link\_prob(m)$. As Fig. 2 shows, with threshold grows, the precision decreases and the recall increases. And when the threshold is around 0.04, we have the best F1 score while precision is 0.672 and recall is 0.691.

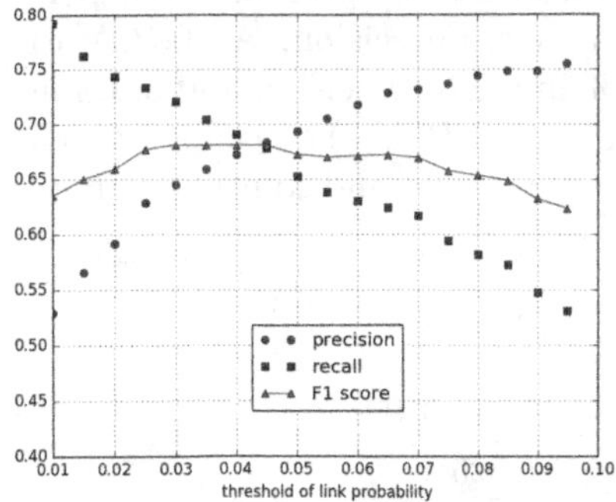

Fig. 2. Evaluation of Mention Parsing

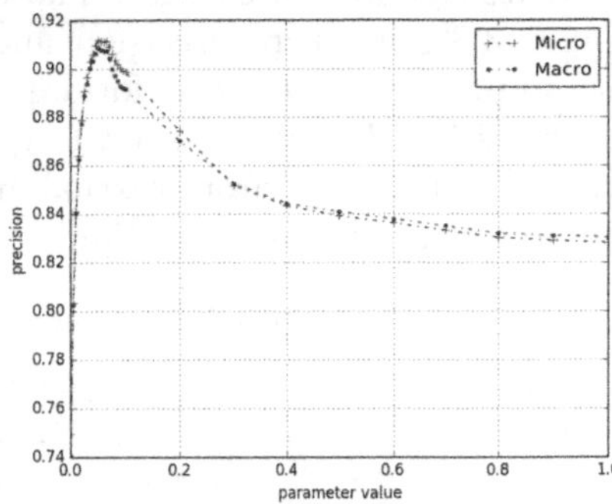

Fig. 3. Impact of prior parameter α

4.3 Evaluation of Disambiguation Entities

To compare our results with state-of-the-art methods, we report Hoffart et al.'s results [12] as they reimplemented two other systems and also ran them over the CoNLL dataset. We also compare with Alhelbawy and Gaizauskas [2] and Shirakawa et al. [20] who carried out their experiments using the same dataset. Additionally, we compare the result in macro-(aggregates over all documents) and micro-(aggregates over all mentions) accuracies. Table 2 shows that our disambiguation result outperforms these state-of-the-art unsupervised methods, and there is no significant difference between L2R and S2C for our system.

Table 2. Performance of Unsupervised Methods

	Cucerzan	Kulkarni	Hoffart	Shirakawa	Alhelbaway	XLink(L2R)	XLink(S2C)
MicroP@1	0.510	0.729	0.818	0.823	0.842	0.911	0.912
MacroP@1	0.437	0.767	0.819	0.830	0.875	0.908	0.909

Observing the results, we find our method works well on the cases with bias of popular entities, but can not handle the extreme situations. For example, in text *"Australia will defend the Ashes in a six-test series against England"*, mention "England" refers to the entity *England_cricket_team* but is linked to the entity *England*. Although the value of $P(\mathcal{N}|England\_cricket\_team)$ is 0.9 and $P(\mathcal{N}|England)$ is 0.7 which means the entity has high similarities with context and topical coherence, however, the prior of *England* is 0.032, 46 times of *England cricket team*, thus leading to an error case. Also, we test the performance with the mention name knowledge incorporated in our model. The performance will decline about 2% overall, and the main reason is that it misleads the decisions of entities with priority bias.

Furthermore, to analyze the reason of effectiveness of our model, we conduct experiments to understand how different distributions impact the results. As shown in Table 3, the distribution of $P(e)$ is the major part which achieves the micro-precision of 82.1%. This makes sense because most entities in the dataset are well-known entities. The distribution of $P(\hat{\mathcal{C}}|e)$ promotes the performance 3.8% in micro precision and 3.4% in macro-precision. And $P(\mathcal{N}|e)$ gives a improvement of the performance for 5.3% in micro-precision and 5.0% in macro-precision. The results show that both $P(\hat{\mathcal{C}}|e)$ and $P(\mathcal{N}|e)$ can capture rich information of context, from textual and coherent aspects, and jointly promote the performance of disambiguation.

Table 3. Compact of different distributions

	MicroP@1	MacroP@1
$P(e)$ only	0.821	0.825
$P(e)\&P(\hat{\mathcal{C}}\|e)$	0.859	0.859
$P(e)\&P(\hat{\mathcal{C}}\|e)\&P(\mathcal{N}\|e)$	0.912	0.909

As we analyzed before, the prior probability greatly affects the result of entity disambiguation. Thus we introduce a parameter to control the importance to the overall probability. Figure 3 shows the disambiguation precision under different values of α on the dataset of CoNLL, and we can see both micro and macro precision increase a lot with increasing of α and decrease quickly after the peaks. Thus we set α to 0.05 experimentally.

4.4 Evaluation of Time Efficiency

We test time efficiency of mention parsing and entity disambiguation separately as shown in Fig. 4. In mention parsing, the time required is linear of amount of mentions $|\mathcal{M}|$ in the documents. In entity disambiguation, the time needed is linear of the amount of all candidates in a document which is the amount of mentions $|\mathcal{M}|$ multiply average candidate sets size $|\mathcal{C}|$. Thus, the overall time complexity is $\mathcal{O}(|\mathcal{M}| + |\mathcal{M}| \cdot |\mathcal{C}|)$.

5 Related Work

As far as we know, the first Web-scale entity linking system is SemTag, built by Dill et al. [8]. With the knowledge sharing communities appearing, such as Wikipedia, and the development of information extraction techniques, such as instance matching [26] and knowledge linking [16], more and more knowledge bases have been constructed automatically, such as YAGO [21], DBpedia [3] and Freebase [4]. These knowledge bases are usually used as resources for entity linking task and many entity linking systems are based on them. Wikify! [14] and

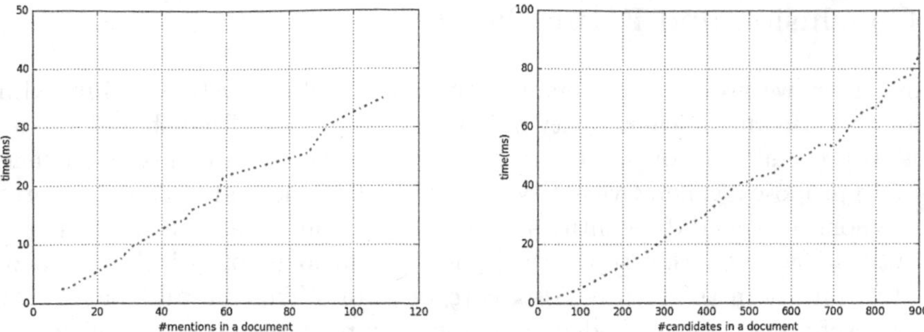

Fig. 4. Time cost of Mention Parsing (left) and Entity Disambiguation (right)

Cucerzan [7] are early works employing Wikipedia to identify and link entities. Wikify! firstly proposed *link probability* to extract keywords as a preprocess of entity disambiguation. Miline&Witten [15] proposed an approach that yielded considerable improvements by hinging on two main ingredients: (1) a measure of relatedness of two pages based on overlap between their in-linking pages in Wikipedia; (2) a notion of coherence between a page and unambiguous pages. Following [15], Ferragina ans Scaiella [9] designed and implemented TagMe, which annotates a short plain-text with pertinent hyperlinks to Wikipedia pages efficiently, and proposed a vote scheme to capture the collective agreement among the entities referred that utilizes the method to compute relatedness in [15]. TagMe showed its competitive performance in short text disambiguation compared with Miline&Witten. Meanwhile, another entity linking system based on DBpedia, called DBpedia Spotlight [13], was proposed, taking full advantage of the DBpedia ontology for specifying which entity should be annotated. It used a part of speech tagger to disregard any spots that are only composed of verbs, adjectives, adverbs and prepositions while spotting. In disambiguation, it weighted the resources of DBpedia using product of term frequency and inverse candidate frequency based on a vector space model. Linkfy [23] is implemented as a script emphasizing the helpfulness of entity linking systems, using supervised machine-learning methods with a broad set of features, including link probability features, entity features, entity class features, topical coherence features, textual features and mention occurrence features. However, it relies on NER tools to recognize entities compared with other systems.

As representation learning becoming a base method to represent semantic elements in nature language preprocessing, increasingly more researchers focus on modeling words and entities to a united space to address the task of entity linking. Yamada et al. [24] learns the embeddings of words and entities separately, then maps them to one space via anchors in Wikipedia. Following, Cao [5] proposes a method to model the representation of mentions, which learns multiple sense embeddings for each mention by jointly modeling words from textual contexts and entities. Compared with traditional methods, representation based methods show their competitiveness in entity disambiguation tasks as our experiments show.

6 Conclusion and Future Work

In this paper, we present a bilingual online entity linking system XLink. XLink provides precise and efficient entity linking service in both English and Chinese. We use a pre-built anchor dictionary to detect mentions instead of NER tagger tools, and propose a generative entity disambiguation method to choose a correct entity among the candidate entities. Currently, XLink regards mention parsing and entity disambiguation separately, and we will focus on jointly optimizing these two phases in the future. Also, categories of Wikipedia and Baidu Baike conveys useful domain knowledge, and how to exploit the category information for domain specific entity linking [6] is an interesting future direction.

Acknowledgements. The work is supported by 973 Program (No. 2014CB340504), NSFC key project (No. 61533018, 61661146007), Fund of Online Education Research Center, Ministry of Education (No. 2016ZD102), THUNUS NExT Co-Lab, National Natural Science Foundation of China (Grant No. 61375054) and Natural Science Foundation of Guangdong Province (Grant No. 2014A030313745).

References

1. Aho, A.V., Corasick, M.J.: Efficient string matching: an aid to bibliographic search. Commun. ACM **18**(6), 333–340 (1975)
2. Alhelbawy, A., Gaizauskas, R.J.: Graph ranking for collective named entity disambiguation. In: ACL, vol. 2, pp. 75–80 (2014)
3. Auer, S., Bizer, C., Kobilarov, G., Lehmann, J., Cyganiak, R., Ives, Z.: DBpedia: a nucleus for a web of open data. In: Aberer, K., Choi, K.-S., Noy, N., Allemang, D., Lee, K.-I., Nixon, L., Golbeck, J., Mika, P., Maynard, D., Mizoguchi, R., Schreiber, G., Cudré-Mauroux, P. (eds.) ASWC/ISWC -2007. LNCS, vol. 4825, pp. 722–735. Springer, Heidelberg (2007). doi:10.1007/978-3-540-76298-0_52
4. Bollacker, K., Evans, C., Paritosh, P., Sturge, T., Taylor, J.: Freebase: a collaboratively created graph database for structuring human knowledge. In: Proceedings of the 2008 ACM SIGMOD International Conference on Management of Data, pp. 1247–1250 (2008)
5. Cao, Y., Huang, L., Ji, H., Chen, X., Li, J.: Bridging text and knowledge by learning multi-prototype entity mention embedding. In: Proceedings of ACL (2017)
6. Cao, Y., Li, J., Guo, X., Bai, S., Ji, H., Tang, J.: Name list only? target entity disambiguation in short texts. EMNLP **15**, 654–664 (2015)
7. Cucerzan, S.: Large-scale named entity disambiguation based on wikipedia data. In: Proceedings of the 2007 Joint Conference on Empirical Methods in Natural Language Processing and Computational Natural Language Learning, pp. 708–716 (2007)
8. Dill, S., Eiron, N., Gibson, D., Gruhl, D., Guha, R., Jhingran, A., Kanungo, T., Rajagopalan, S., Tomkins, A., Tomlin, J.A., et al.: Semtag and seeker: Bootstrapping the semantic web via automated semantic annotation. In: Proceedings of the 12th International Conference on World Wide Web, pp. 178–186 (2003)
9. Ferragina, P., Scaiella, U.: Fast and accurate annotation of short texts with wikipedia pages. IEEE Softw. **29**(1), 70–75 (2012)

10. Finkel, J.R., Grenager, T., Manning, C.: Incorporating non-local information into information extraction systems by gibbs sampling. In: Proceedings of the 43rd Annual Meeting on Association for Computational Linguistics, pp. 363–370 (2005)
11. Han, X., Sun, L.: A generative entity-mention model for linking entities with knowledge base. In: Proceedings of the 49th Annual Meeting of the Association for Computational Linguistics: Human Language Technologies, vol. 1, pp. 945–954 (2011)
12. Hoffart, J., Yosef, M.A., Bordino, I., Fürstenau, H., Pinkal, M., Spaniol, M., Taneva, B., Thater, S., Weikum, G.: Robust disambiguation of named entities in text. In: Proceedings of the Conference on Empirical Methods in Natural Language Processing, pp. 782–792 (2011)
13. Mendes, P.N., Jakob, M., García-Silva, A., Bizer, C.: Dbpedia spotlight: shedding light on the web of documents. In: Proceedings of the 7th International Conference on Semantic Systems, pp. 1–8 (2011)
14. Mihalcea, R., Csomai, A.: Wikify!: linking documents to encyclopedic knowledge. In: Proceedings of the Sixteenth ACM Conference on Conference on Information and Knowledge Management, pp. 233–242 (2007)
15. Milne, D., Witten, I.H.: Learning to link with wikipedia. In: Proceedings of the 17th ACM Conference on Information and Knowledge Management, pp. 509–518 (2008)
16. Pan, L., Wang, Z., Li, J., Tang, J.: Domain specific cross-lingual knowledge linking based on similarity flooding. In: Lehner, F., Fteimi, N. (eds.) KSEM 2016. LNCS, vol. 9983, pp. 426–438. Springer, Cham (2016). doi:10.1007/978-3-319-47650-6_34
17. Pershina, M., He, Y., Grishman, R.: Personalized page rank for named entity disambiguation. In: HLT-NAACL, pp. 238–243 (2015)
18. Ratinov, L., Roth, D., Downey, D., Anderson, M.: Local and global algorithms for disambiguation to wikipedia. In: Proceedings of the 49th Annual Meeting of the Association for Computational Linguistics: Human Language Technologies, vol. 1, pp. 1375–1384 (2011)
19. Shen, W., Wang, J., Han, J.: Entity linking with a knowledge base: Issues, techniques, and solutions. IEEE Trans. Knowl. Data Eng. **27**(2), 443–460 (2015)
20. Shirakawa, M., Wang, H., Song, Y., Wang, Z., Nakayama, K., Hara, T., Nishio, S.: Entity disambiguation based on a probabilistic taxonomy. Microsoft Research, Seattle, WA, USA, Tech. Rep. MSR-TR-2011-125 (2011)
21. Suchanek, F.M., Kasneci, G., Weikum, G.: Yago: a core of semantic knowledge. In: WWW (2007)
22. Weston, J., Bordes, A., Chopra, S., Rush, A.M., van Merriënboer, B., Joulin, A., Mikolov, T.: Towards ai-complete question answering: a set of prerequisite toy tasks. arXiv preprint arXiv:1502.05698 (2015)
23. Yamada, I., Ito, T., Usami, S., Takagi, S., Takeda, H., Takefuji, Y.: Evaluating the helpfulness of linked entities to readers. In: Proceedings of the 25th ACM Conference on Hypertext and Social Media, pp. 169–178 (2014)
24. Yamada, I., Shindo, H., Takeda, H., Takefuji, Y.: Joint learning of the embedding of words and entities for named entity disambiguation. arXiv preprint arXiv:1601.01343 (2016)
25. Yao, X., Van Durme, B.: Information extraction over structured data: question answering with freebase. In: ACL, vol. 1, pp. 956–966 (2014)
26. Zhang, Y., Jin, H., Pan, L., Li, J.Z.: Rimom results for OAEI 2016. In: OM@ ISWC, pp. 210–216 (2016)

Using Cost-Sensitive Ranking Loss to Improve Distant Supervised Relation Extraction

Daojian Zeng(✉), Junxin Zeng, and Yuan Dai

Hunan Provincial Key Laboratory of Intelligent Processing of Big Data on Transportation, School of Computer and Communication Engineering, Changsha University of Science and Technology, Changsha 410004, People's Republic of China

zengdj@csust.edu.cn

{zeng_jx,daiy}@stu.csust.edu.cn

Abstract. Recently, many researchers have concentrated on using neural networks to learn features for Distant Supervised Relation Extraction (DSRE). However, these approaches generally employ a softmax classifier with cross-entropy loss, and bring the noise of artificial class *NA* into classification process. Moreover, the class imbalance problem is serious in the automatically labeled data, and results in poor classification rates on minor classes in traditional approaches.

In this work, we exploit cost-sensitive ranking loss to improve DSRE. It first uses a Piecewise Convolutional Neural Network (PCNN) to embed the semantics of sentences. Then the features are fed into a classifier which takes into account both the ranking loss and cost-sensitive. Experiments show that our method is effective and performs better than state-of-the-art methods.

1 Introduction

There has been many methods proposed for relation extraction. In these methods, the supervised paradigm has been shown to be effective and yield relatively high performance [8,19]. However, a large labeled training data is often required for this task, and manually annotating large labeled training data is a time-consuming and labor intensive task.

To address the shortcomings of supervised paradigm, distantly supervised [11] paradigm is proposed to automatically generate training data. Traditional methods have typically applied supervised models to elaborately handcrafted features when obtained the labeled data through distant supervision [5,11,14,15]. These features are often derived from preexisting Natural Language Processing (NLP) tools, thus inevitably have errors. With the recent revival of interest in neural networks, many researchers have investigated the possibility of using neural networks to automatically learn features for relation classification [7,9,17,18]. The neural networks based methods achieve substantial improvements in the task, however, they still have the following deficiencies.

M. Sun et al. (Eds.): CCL 2017 and NLP-NABD 2017, LNAI 10565, pp. 184–196, 2017.
https://doi.org/10.1007/978-3-319-69005-6_16

Table 1. The distribution of the data that is generated through distant supervision strategy.

Relations	Number of Samples
NA	158513
/location/location/contains	2966
/people/person/place_lived	792
/people/person/nationality	711
/business/person/company	498
/people/person/place_of_birth	483
/people/deceased_person/place_of_death	263
/location/neighborhood/neighborhood_of	177
/business/company/founders	87

First, it brings the noise of artificial class *NA* into the classification process. Previous methods usually employ a Convolutional Neural Network (CNN) to embed the semantics of sentences. The learned vectors are subsequently fed into a softmax classifier and the whole network is learned to minimize a categorical cross-entropy loss function. Unfortunately, the artificial class *NA* is very noisy since it groups many different infrequent relation types. Table 1 shows the distribution of the training data that is generated through distant supervision strategy. The samples corresponding to *NA* account for vast majority of the illustrated relations. Thus, the noise in *NA* cannot be ignored.

Second, it has class imbalance problem in the automatically labeled training data, and shows poor classification rates. From Table 1, we can observe that the class imbalance problem is indeed serious. For example, the number of samples corresponding to */location/location/contains* is about 34 times that of */business/company/founders*. It tends to be biased toward the major classes when using the training data generated through distant supervision.

In this paper, we exploit a cost-sensitive ranking loss function to address the two problems described above. We use a PCNN to automatically learn relevant features and incorporates multi-instance To address the noise of artificial class *NA*, the PCNN is followed by a ranking-based classifier instead of a softmax classifier. In the classifier, we adopt a pairwise ranking loss function and do not learn the class embedding for *NA*. Moreover, we incorporate cost-sensitive in the loss function to alleviate the class imbalance problem. In this work, we give different margins to different classes in order to achieve cost-sensitive classification. The experimental results show that our model achieves significant and consistent improvements as compared with the baseline systems.

2 Related Work

Relation extraction is one of the most important topics in NLP. Supervised approaches are the most commonly used methods for relation extraction and yield relatively high performance [2,16,19]. In the supervised paradigm, relation extraction is considered to be a multi-class classification problem and may suffer from a lack of labeled data for training. To address this issue, [11] adopts Freebase to perform distant supervision. As described in Sect. 1, the algorithm for training data generation is sometimes faced with the wrong label problem. To address this shortcoming, [5,14,15] develop the relaxed distant supervision assumption for multi-instance learning. [12] utilize relation definitions and Wikipedia documents to improve their systems

The methods mentioned above have been shown to be effective for DSRE. However, their performance depends strongly on the quality of the designed features. Recently, many researchers attempt to use deep neural networks in DSRE without handcrafted features. [18] adopts CNNs to embed the semantics of the sentences. Moreover, [4] proposes a pairwise ranking loss function in the CNNs to reduce the impact of artificial class. These methods build classifier based on sentence-level annotated data, which cannot be directly applied for DSRE since multiple sentences corresponding to a fact may be achieved in the data generating procedure. Therefore, [17] incorporates multi-instance learning with neural network model, which can build relation extractor based on distant supervision data. Although the method achieves significant improvement in relation extraction, it only selects the most likely sentence for each entity pair in their multi-instance learning paradigm. To address this issue, [9] proposes sentence level attention over multiple instances in order to utilize all informative sentences. [7] employs cross-sentence max-pooling to select features across different instances, and then aggregates the most significant features for each entity pair.

The aforementioned works, especially neural networks, have greatly promoted the development of relation extraction. However, these works do not pay attention to the noise of artificial class and the class imbalance problem, which are unfortunately very common in DSRE. In this work, we use cost-sensitive ranking loss to address these problems in DSRE. Different from [4], we incorporate cost sensitive in the loss function and our approach involves the problem of instance selection as well.

3 Methodology

Figure 1 shows the neural network architecture used in this work. It consists of two parts: PCNNs Module and Ranking Based Classifier Module. We describe these parts in details below.

3.1 PCNNs Module

This module is used to extract feature vector of an instance (sentence) in a bag. PCNNs differs from traditional CNN by devising piecewise max pooling layer instead of the single max pooling layer.

Vector Representation. The inputs of our network are raw word tokens. When using neural networks, we typically transform word tokens into low-dimensional vectors. In this paper, the "word token" refers to word and entity. In the following, we do not distinguish them and call them "word". In our method, each input word token is transformed into a vector by looking up pre-trained word embeddings. Moreover, we use Position Features (PFs) [17,18] to specify entity pairs, which are also transformed into vectors by looking up position embeddings.

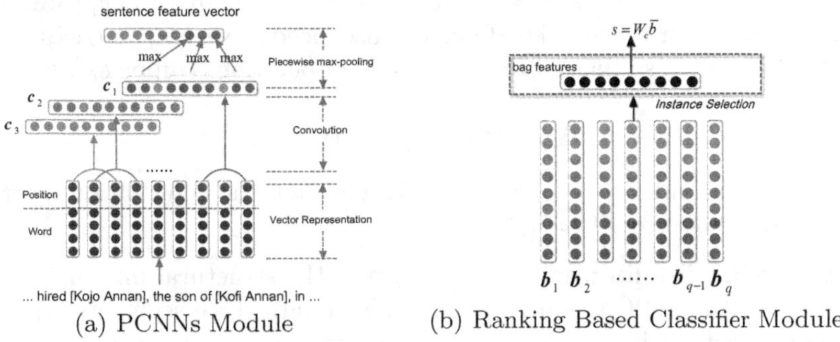

(a) PCNNs Module (b) Ranking Based Classifier Module

Fig. 1. The architecture used in this work.

Word Embeddings. Word embeddings are distributed representations of words that map each word in a text to a 'k'-dimensional real-valued vector. They have recently been shown to capture both semantic and syntactic information about words very well, setting performance records in several word similarity tasks [10,13]. Using word embeddings that have been trained a priori has become common practice for enhancing many other NLP tasks [6]. In the past years, many methods for training word embeddings have been proposed [1,3,10]. We employ the method [10] to train word embeddings and denote it by **E**.

Position Embeddings. [17] has shown the importance of PFs in relation extraction. Similar to their works, we use PFs to specify entity pairs. A PF is defined as the combination of the relative distances from the current word to entity e_1 and entity e_2. We randomly initialize two position embedding matrices $\mathbf{PF}_i (i = 1, 2)$ (for e_1 and e_2), and transform the relative distances into vectors by looking them up.

We concatenate the word representation and position representation as the input of the network (shown in Fig. 1(a)). Assume that the size of word representation is k_w and that of position representation is k_d, then the size of a word vector is $k = k_w + 2k_d$.

Convolution. Assume that $\mathbf{A} = (a_{ij})_{m \times n}$ and $\mathbf{B} = (b_{ij})_{m \times n}$, then the convolution of $\mathbf{A}$ and $\mathbf{B}$ is defined as $\mathbf{A} \otimes \mathbf{B} = \sum_{i=1}^{m} \sum_{j=1}^{n} a_{ij} b_{ij}$.

We denote the input sentence by $S = \{s_1, s_2, \cdots, s_{|S|}\}$ where s_i is the i-th word, and use $\boldsymbol{s}_i \in \mathbb{R}^k$ to represent its vector. We use $\mathbf{S}_{i:j}$ to represent the matrix concatenated by sequence $[\boldsymbol{s}_i : \boldsymbol{s}_{i+1} : \cdots : \boldsymbol{s}_j]$ ($[\boldsymbol{x}_1 : \boldsymbol{x}_2]$ denotes the horizontal concatenation of $\boldsymbol{x}_1$ and $\boldsymbol{x}_2$). We denote the length of filter by w (Fig. 1(a) shows an example of $w = 3$), then the weight matrix of the filter is $\mathbf{W} \in \mathbb{R}^{w \times k}$. Then the convolution operation between the filter and sentence S results in another vector $\boldsymbol{c} \in \mathbb{R}^{|S|-w+1}$:

$$c_j = \mathbf{W} \otimes \mathbf{S}_{(j-w+1):j} \tag{1}$$

where $1 \leq j \leq |S| - w + 1$.

In experiments, we use $n (n > 1)$ filters (or feature maps) to capture different features of an instance. Therefore, we also need n weight matrices $\mathbf{W}_c = \{\mathbf{W}_1, \mathbf{W}_2, \cdots, \mathbf{W}_n\}$, so that all the convolution operations can be expressed by

$$c_{ij} = \mathbf{W}_i \otimes \mathbf{S}_{(j-w+1):j} \tag{2}$$

where $1 \leq i \leq n$ and $1 \leq j \leq |S| - w + 1$. Through the convolution layer, we obtain the results vectors $\mathbf{C} = \{\boldsymbol{c}_1, \boldsymbol{c}_2, \cdots, \boldsymbol{c}_n\}$.

Piecewise Max Pooling. In order to capture the structural information and fine-grained features, PCNNs divides an instance into three segments according to the given entity pair (two entities cut the sentence into three parts) and do max-pooling operation on each segment. For the result vector $\boldsymbol{c}_i$ of convolution operations, it can be divided into three parts $\boldsymbol{c}_i = \{\boldsymbol{c}_{i,1}, \boldsymbol{c}_{i,2}, \boldsymbol{c}_{i,3}\}$. Then piecewise max-pooling procedure is $p_{ij} = \max(\boldsymbol{c}_{i,j})$, where $1 \leq i \leq n$ and $j = 1, 2, 3$. After that, we can concatenate all the vectors $\boldsymbol{p}_i = [p_{i,1}, p_{i,2}, p_{i,3}] (i = 1, 2, \cdots, n)$ to obtain vector $\boldsymbol{p} \in \mathbb{R}^{3n \times 1}$. Figure 1(a) displays an example of $n = 3$, in which the gray circles are the positions of entities. Finally, we compute the feature vector $\boldsymbol{b}_S = \tanh(\boldsymbol{p})$ for sentence S.

3.2 Ranking Based Classifier Module

The PCNNs module extracts the feature vector for each sentence. The ranking based classifier module is responsible for selecting the most appropriate instance in a bag and predicting the most likely relation.

Classifier. To compute the score for each relation, the feature vector of each instance is fed into a ranking based classifier. Given the distributed vector representation of an instance $\boldsymbol{b}$, the network computes the score for a class label t_i by using the dot product:

$$s_{t_i} = \mathbf{w}_{t_i} \boldsymbol{b} \tag{3}$$

where $\mathbf{w}_{t_i} \in \mathbb{R}^{1 \times 3n}$ is the class embedding for class label t_i. All the class embeddings $\mathbf{w}_{t_i}$ $(i = 1, \cdots, T)$ constitute the class embedding matrix $\mathbf{W}_T \in \mathbb{R}^{T \times 3n}$ whose rows encode the distributed vector representations of the different class labels. T is equal to the number of possible relation types for the relation extraction system. Note that the number of dimensions in each class embedding must be equal to the size of the distributed vector representation of the input bag $3n$. The class embedding matrix $\mathbf{W}_T$ is a parameter to be learned by the network.

Instance Selection. Distant supervised relation extraction suffers from wrong label problem [14]. The core problem that needs to be solved in the multi-instance learning is to get the corresponding bag feature vector from all the instance feature vectors in the bag. In fact, the problem is the instance selection strategy. We employ an instance selection strategy borrowed from [17]. Different from [17], we randomly select an instance from the bag with *NA* label since our model do not give score for *NA* class (see Sect. 3.2). In addition, we choose the instance which has the highest score for the bag label except for *NA*. The scores are computed using Eq. (3). Therefore, our instance selection strategy will not be disturbed by the noise in *NA*. Assume that there is a bag $B_i = \{b_1^i, b_2^i, \cdots, b_{q_i}^i\}$ that contains q_i instances with feature vectors $\{\boldsymbol{b}_1^i, \boldsymbol{b}_2^i, \cdots, \boldsymbol{b}_{q_i}^i\}$ and the bag label is r_i ($r_i \neq NA$). The j-th instance b_j^i is selected and the j is constrained as follows:

$$j = \arg\max\{s_{r_i}^1, s_{r_i}^2, \cdots, s_{r_i}^{q_i}\} \;\; 1 \leq j \leq q_i \tag{4}$$

where $s_{r_i}^j = \mathbf{w}_{r_i} \boldsymbol{b}_j^i$ $(1 \leq j \leq q_i)$ is computed using Eq. (3).

Cost-Sensitive Ranking Loss. As mentioned in Sect. 1, the cross-entropy loss brings the noise of artificial class into the classification process. This phenomenon is mainly due to the noise of artificial class *NA*. To address this shortcoming, we propose a pairwise ranking loss instead of cross-entropy which is often used for softmax classifier.

In our model, the network can be stated as a tuple $\theta = (\mathbf{E}, \mathbf{PF}_1, \mathbf{PF}_2, \mathbf{W}_c, \mathbf{W}_T)$. Assume that there are N bags in training set $\{B_1, B_2, \cdots, B_N\}$, and their labels are relations $\{r_1, r_2, \cdots, r_N\}$. After the instance selection, we get a representative instance and its corresponding feature vector is considered as the bag feature vector $\bar{\boldsymbol{b}}$. The input for each iteration round is a bag feature vector and the class label. In the pairwise ranking, the loss function is defined on the basis of pairs of objects whose labels are different. We can get the ranking loss function through selecting a class label that is different from the input one. In this work, we choose the negative class with the highest score among all incorrect classes. For example, when the i-th bag with label $r_i = t_j$ is fed into the network, we select a negative class t_k which obtains highest score except class t_j. Using Eq. (3), we can get the classification scores of the i-th bag $s_{t_j}^i$ and $s_{t_k}^i$ for class t_j and t_k, respectively. The ranking loss function is define as follows:

$$\begin{aligned} \mathcal{L} = \sum_{i=1}^{N} \{ &\log(1 + \exp(\lambda(m^+ - s_{t_j}^i))) \\ &+ \log(1 + \exp(\lambda(m^- + s_{t_k}^i)))\} \end{aligned} \tag{5}$$

where $t_k \neq t_j$ and $j, k \in \{1, 2, \cdots, T\}$. λ is a scaling factor that magnifies the difference between the scores. m^+ and m^- are the margin for correct and incorrect class, respectively.

DSRE confronts with another problem is the class imbalance. To alleviate this shortcoming, we incorporate cost-sensitive in the loss function and different margins are given to different classes. The margins are computed as follows:

$$m_{t_i} = \gamma \times \frac{\log(\#t_i)}{\sum_{j=1}^{T} \log(\#t_j)} \tag{6}$$

where $\gamma > 0$ is a constant term. $\#t_j$ represents the number of samples corresponding to relation t_j. Substituting m_{t_i} into Eq. (5), the cost-sensitive ranking loss function is shown as follows:

$$\begin{aligned} \mathcal{L} = &\sum_{i=1}^{N} \{\log(1 + \exp(\lambda(m_{t_j} - s^i_{t_j}))) \\ &+ \log(1 + \exp(\lambda(m_{t_k} + s^i_{t_k})))\} \end{aligned} \tag{7}$$

From the cost-sensitive ranking loss function, we can observe that the first term in the right side of Eq. (7) decreases as the score s_{t_j} increases and the second term decreases as the score s_{t_k} decreases. The cost-sensitive ranking loss function aims to give scores greater than m_{t_j} for the correct class t_j and smaller than m_{t_k} for incorrect class t_k. When the minor classes are incorrectly classified, our model gives them more penalties than the major classes. We use the backpropagation algorithm and stochastic gradient descent (SGD) to minimize the loss function with respect to θ.

It is very difficult to learn patterns for the artificial class *NA*. Therefore softmax classifier often brings noise into the classification process of the natural classes. We can avoid explicitly leaning patterns for the artificial class when using ranking loss function. We omit the artificial class *NA* by setting the first term in the right side of Eq. (7) to zero and do not learn the class embedding for *NA*. Thus, our model does not give score for the artificial class *NA* and the noise in *NA* is alleviated. At prediction time, an instance is classified as *NA* only if all actual classes have negative scores. A bag is positively labeled if and only if the output of the network on at least one of its instances is assigned a positive label and we choose the class which has the highest score.

4 Experiments

In this section, we first introduce the dataset and evaluation metrics, then test several variants via cross-validation to determine the parameters used in our experiments, finally show the experimental results and analysis.

4.1 Dataset and Evaluation Metrics

We evaluate our method on a widely used dataset[1] that was developed by [14] and has also been used by [5,15,17]. This dataset was generated by aligning

[1] http://iesl.cs.umass.edu/riedel/ecml/.

Freebase relations with the NYT corpus, with sentences from the years 2005–2006 used as the training corpus and sentences from 2007 used as the testing corpus.

Following the previous work [11], we evaluate our approach using held-out evaluation. The held-out evaluation compares the extracted relation instances against Freebase relation data.

4.2 Experimental Settings

In this work, we use the Skip-gram model (word2vec)[2] to train the word embeddings on the NYT corpus. The tokens are concatenated using the ## operator when the entity has multiple word tokens. Position features are randomly initialized with uniform distribution between $[-1, 1]$. For convenience of comparing with baseline methods, the PCNNs module uses the same parameter settings as [17]. We use L2 regularization with regularization parameter $\beta = 0.001$ and set the max number of iteration to 200. We tune the proposed model using three-fold validation to study the effects of two parameters: the constant terms λ and γ used in the loss function. We use a grid search to determine the optimal parameters and manually specify subsets of the parameter spaces: $\lambda \in \{1, 2, \cdots, 10\}$ and $\gamma \in \{10, 20, \cdots, 100\}$. Table 2 shows all parameters used in the experiments.

Table 2. Parameters used in our experiments.

Parameters	Value
Window size	$w = 3$
Feature maps	$n = 230$
Word dimension	$d_w = 50$
Position dimension	$d_p = 5$
Batch size	$b_s = 50$
Adadelta parameter	$\rho = 0.95, \varepsilon = 1e^{-6}$
Constant term	$\lambda = 2, \gamma = 50$

4.3 Baselines

We select three previous works that use handcrafted features as well as the CNN-based methods as baselines. *Mintz* is proposed by [11] which extracts features from all instances; *MultiR* is a multi-instance learning method proposed by [5]; *MIML* is a multi-instance multi-labels method proposed by [15]; *PCNNs+MIL* is the method proposed by [17], which incorporates multi-instance learning with PCNNs to extract bag features; *CrossMax* is proposed by [7], which exploits PCNNs and cross-sentence max-pooling to select features across different instances.

[2] https://code.google.com/p/word2vec/.

4.4 Comparison with Baseline Methods

In this section, we show the experimental results and comparisons with baseline methods. In the following experiments, we use *Ours* to refer to the proposed model that use cost-sensitive ranking loss.

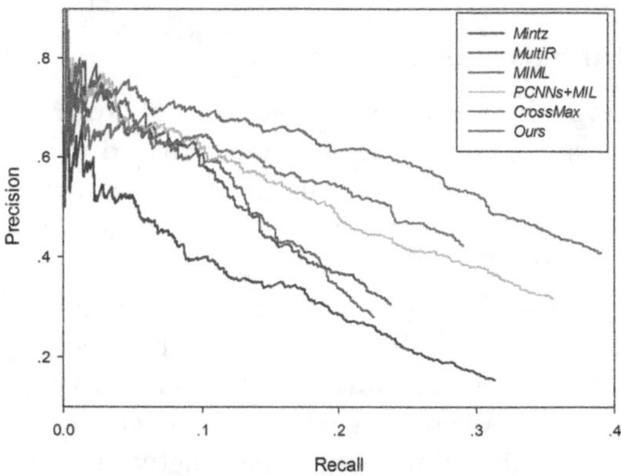

Fig. 2. Performance comparison of proposed method and baseline methods.

The held-out evaluation provides an approximate measure of precision without requiring costly human evaluation. Half of the Freebase relations are used for testing. The relation instances discovered from the test articles are automatically compared with those in Freebase.

For convenience of comparing with baseline methods, the prediction results are sorted by the classification scores and a precision-recall curve is created for the positive classes. Figure 2 shows the precision-recall curves of our approach and all the baselines. We can observe that our model outperforms all the baseline systems and improves the results significantly. It is worth emphasizing that the best of all baseline methods achieves a recall level of 36%. In contrast, our model is much better than the previous approach and enhances the recall to approximately 39%. The significant improvement can be contributed to the magic of ranking based classifier. The ranking based classifier use ranking loss which avoids explicitly learning the patterns for *NA*. Thus, our model will not trend to classify the samples as *NA* compared to sofmax classifier and recalls more positive samples.

Furthermore, our model achieves a large improvement in precision especially at higher recall levels. From Fig. 2, we can see that our model achieves precision of 40% when recall is 39%. In contrast, when *PCNNS* and *CrossMax* achieve such precision, the recalls are decreased to approximately 24% and 29%, respectively. Thus, our approach is advantageous from the point of view of precision. This improvement can be contributed to the cost-sensitive. The class imbalance problem is alleviated through cost-sensitive, and the precision is improved.

Also note that our model does not show advantages in the precision when the recall is very low. This phenomenon is mainly due to the fact that when using held-out evaluation, some examples with high classification score are false negatives and are actually true relation instances. Therefore, we can conclude that our model outperforms all the baseline systems and improves the results significantly in terms of both precision and recall.

4.5 Effects of Cost-Sensitive and Ranking Loss

In order to validate the effects of cost-sensitive, we compute the confusion matrix and analyze the detail of some relations in Table 3. From Table 3, we can see that: (1) It achieves better results in the majority of relations when using cost-sensitive; (2) The F1 score is lower in */people/person/place_lived* and */people/person/place_of_birth*, mainly due to the fact that these two relations are more difficult to separate from each other. Nonetheless, the cost-sensitive helps to improve the performance in this case.

Table 3. Precision, recall and F1 score of some relations. *Ours-CS* means that do not use cost sensitive.

Relations	*Ours-CS*			*Ours*		
	P	R	F1	P	R	F1
/location/location/contains	35.45	43.44	39.04	**36.67**	**43.50**	**39.79**
/people/person/place_lived	12.87	18.67	15.24	**16.31**	**17.86**	**17.05**
/people/person/nationality	**47.79**	24.53	32.42	46.54	**25.32**	**32.80**
/business/person/company	35.41	**52.48**	**42.29**	**36.48**	49.87	42.14
/people/person/place_of_birth	11.45	16.82	13.62	**15.66**	**17.77**	**16.65**
/people/deceased_person/place_of_death	26.31	22.22	24.09	**26.43**	**24.59**	**25.47**
/location/neighborhood/neighborhood_of	37.50	29.34	32.92	**38.55**	**31.81**	**34.86**
/business/company/founders	47.05	**28.76**	**35.70**	**47.23**	28.42	35.49

The precision-recall curves with and without cost-sensitive are illustrated in Fig. 3, from which we can also observe that it brings better performance when adding cost-sensitive in the loss function. After removing the cost-sensitive ranking loss, our model degrades to *PCNNs+MIL*. In order to further validate the effects of ranking loss, the *PCNNs+MIL* result is illustrated in Fig. 3. As we expected, ranking loss take effects and *Ours-CS* can get better performance compared with *PCNNS*. The superiority of our approach indicates that using cost-sensitive ranking loss function can effectively improve DSRE.

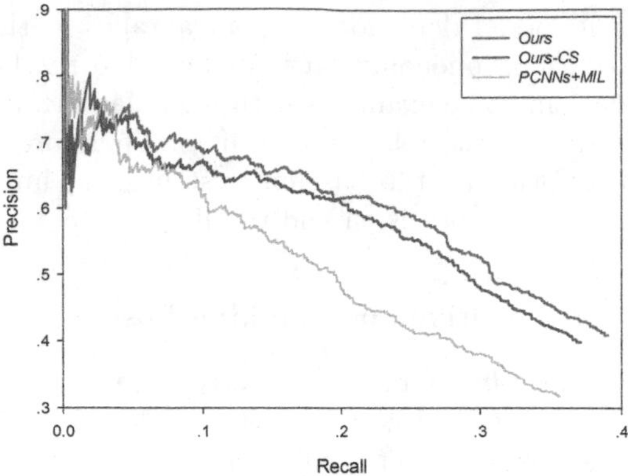

Fig. 3. Effects of cost-sensitive. *Ours-CS* means that do not use cost sensitive.

5 Conclusions

In this paper, we exploit cost sensitive ranking loss to improve DSRE. We pay attention to the noise of artificial class *NA* and the class imbalance problem in DSRE. Experimental results show that the proposed approach offers significant improvements over comparable methods. The noise of artificial class and the class imbalance problem can be effectively addressed by using cost-sensitive ranking loss. In the future, we would like to further investigate how different loss functions and different cost-sensitive strategies influence performance.

Acknowledgments. This work was supported by the National Natural Science Foundation of China (No. 61602059), Hunan Provincial Natural Science Foundation of China (No. 2017JJ3334), the Research Foundation of Education Bureau of Hunan Province, China (No. 16C0045), and the Open Project Program of the National Laboratory of Pattern Recognition (NLPR). We thank the anonymous reviewers for their insightful comments.

References

1. Bengio, Y., Ducharme, R., Vincent, P., Janvin, C.: A neural probabilistic language model. J. Mach. Learn. Res. **3**, 1137–1155 (2003)
2. Bunescu, R., Mooney, R.J.: Subsequence kernels for relation extraction. In: Weiss, Y., Schoelkopf, B., Platt, J. (eds.) Advances in Neural Information Processing Systems. Proceedings of the 2005 Conference on NIPS, vol. 18 (2006)
3. Collobert, R., Weston, J., Bottou, L., Karlen, M., Kavukcuoglu, K., Kuksa, P.: Natural language processing (almost) from scratch. J. Mach. Learn. Res. **12**, 2493–2537 (2011)

4. dos Santos, C.N., Xiang, B., Zhou, B.: Classifying relations by ranking with convolutional neural networks. In: Proceedings of ACL (2015)
5. Homann, R., Zhang, C., Ling, X., Zettlemoyer, L., Weld, D.S.: Knowledge-based weak supervision for information extraction of overlapping relations. In: Proceedings of the 49th Annual Meeting of the Association for Computational Linguistics: Human Language Technologies, HLT 2011, vol. 1, pp. 541–550. Association for Computational Linguistics, Stroudsburg (2011)
6. Huang, F., Ahuja, A., Downey, D., Yang, Y., Guo, Y., Yates, A.: Learning representations for weakly supervised natural language processing tasks. Comput. Linguist. **40**(1), 85–120 (2014)
7. Jiang, X., Wang, Q., Li, P., Wang, B.: Relation extraction with multi-instance multi-label convolutional neural networks. In: Proceedings of COLING, pp. 1471–1480 (2016)
8. Kambhatla, N.: Combining lexical, syntactic, and semantic features with maximum entropy models for extracting relations. In: Proceedings of the ACL 2004 on Interactive Poster and Demonstration Sessions, ACLdemo 2004. Association for Computational Linguistics, Stroudsburg (2004)
9. Lin, Y., Shen, S., Liu, Z., Luan, H., Sun, M.: Neural relation extraction with selective attention over instances. In: Proceedings of ACL, pp. 2124–2133. Association for Computational Linguistics, Stroudsburg (2016)
10. Mikolov, T., Chen, K., Corrado, G., Dean, J.: Efficient estimation of word representations in vector space (2013)
11. Mintz, M., Bills, S., Snow, R., Jurafsky, D.: Distant supervision for relation extraction without labeled data. In: Proceedings of the Joint Conference of the 47th Annual Meeting of the ACL and the 4th International Joint Conference on Natural Language Processing of the AFNLP, ACL 2009, vol. 2, pp. 1003–1011. Association for Computational Linguistics, Stroudsburg (2009)
12. Nguyen, T.-V.T., Moschitti, A.: End-to-end relation extraction using distant supervision from external semantic repositories. In: Proceedings of the 49th Annual Meeting of the Association for Computational Linguistics: Human Language Technologies: Short Papers, HLT 2011, vol. 2, pp. 277–282. Association for Computational Linguistics, Stroudsburg (2011)
13. Pennington, J., Socher, R., Manning, C.D.: Glove: global vectors for word representation. In: Proceedings of EMNLP 2014, pp. 1746–1751 (2014)
14. Riedel, S., Yao, L., McCallum, A.: Modeling relations and their mentions without labeled text. In: Balcázar, J.L., Bonchi, F., Gionis, A., Sebag, M. (eds.) ECML PKDD 2010. LNCS, vol. 6323, pp. 148–163. Springer, Heidelberg (2010). doi:10.1007/978-3-642-15939-8_10
15. Surdeanu, M., Tibshirani, J., Nallapati, R., Manning, C.D.: Multi-instance multi-label learning for relation extraction. In: Proceedings of the 2012 Joint Conference on Empirical Methods in Natural Language Processing and Computational Natural Language Learning, EMNLP-CoNLL 2012, pp. 455–465. Association for Computational Linguistics, Stroudsburg (2012)
16. Zelenko, D., Aone, C., Richardella, A.: Kernel methods for relation extraction. J. Mach. Learn. Res. **3**, 1083–1106 (2003)

17. Zeng, D., Liu, K., Chen, Y., Zhao, J.: Distant supervision for relation extraction via piecewise convolutional neural networks. In: Proceedings of EMNLP, pp. 17–21. Association for Computational Linguistics, Stroudsburg (2015)
18. Zeng, D., Liu, K., Lai, S., Zhou, G., Zhao, J.: Relation classification via convolutional deep neural network. In: Proceedings of COLING, pp. 2335–2344 (2014)
19. GuoDong, Z., Jian S., Jie Z., Min Z.: Exploring various knowledge in relation extraction. In: Proceedings of the 43rd Annual Meeting on Association for Computational Linguistics, ACL 2005, pp. 427–434. Association for Computational Linguistics, Stroudsburg (2005)

Multichannel LSTM-CRF for Named Entity Recognition in Chinese Social Media

Chuanhai Dong[1,2(✉)], Huijia Wu[1,2], Jiajun Zhang[1,2], and Chengqing Zong[1,2,3]

[1] CASIA, National Laboratory of Pattern Recognition, Beijing, China
[2] University of Chinese Academy of Sciences, Beijing, China
[3] CAS Center for Excellence in Brain Science and Intelligence Technology, Shanghai, China
{chuanhai.dong,huijia.wu,jjzhang,cqzong}@nlpr.ia.ac.cn

Abstract. Named Entity Recognition (NER) is a tough task in Chinese social media due to a large portion of informal writings. Existing research uses only limited in-domain annotated data and achieves low performance. In this paper, we utilize both limited in-domain data and enough out-of-domain data using a domain adaptation method. We propose a multichannel LSTM-CRF model that employs different channels to capture general patterns, in-domain patterns and out-of-domain patterns in Chinese social media. The extensive experiments show that our model yields 9.8% improvement over previous state-of-the-art methods. We further find that a shared embedding layer is important and randomly initialized embeddings are better than the pretrained ones.

Keywords: Multichannel · Named entity recognition · Chinese social media

1 Introduction

Named Entity Recognition is a fundamental technique for many natural language processing applications such as information extraction [2] and entity linking [13]. With the development of Internet, more and more researches turn towards NER in social media [10,31]. Social media texts are informal and mixed with strong noise which makes it more challenging to recognize named entities. Research on NER in English has narrowed the gap between social media and formal domains [4], but NER in Chinese social media is still hard [26].

One important reason that limits NER in Chinese social media is that there is rare annotated data for supervised learning. For example, the training set of Weibo NER corpora [26], which come from Sina Weibo service (comparable in size and popularity to Twitter), is less than 1/30 of MSRA training set in the third SIGHAN Bakeoff Chinese NER shared task [21] in size. It's difficult to achieve comparable results using such rare data, let alone its informality and strong noise. However, since manual annotation is time consuming and costs expensive, we choose to use out-of-domain annotated data to improve in-domain NER results using domain adaptation method.

M. Sun et al. (Eds.): CCL 2017 and NLP-NABD 2017, LNAI 10565, pp. 197–208, 2017.
https://doi.org/10.1007/978-3-319-69005-6_17

We consider domain adaptation method for NER in Chinese social media. Generally, we would train a model on all available data for a given task and test it on the same domain. However, MSRA data and Weibo data are from different domains [25,32]. The former comes from news and the latter comes from social media. In this case, distribution changes in the different input domains make generalizing across them difficult [28].

There have been much progress in domain adaptation [1,8,33]. A notable example is the feature augmentation method [7], whose key insight is that if we partition the model parameters to those that handle general patterns and those that handle domain-specific patterns, the model is forced to learn from all domains yet preserve domain-specific knowledge [19].

In this paper, we extend the feature augmentation method to multichannel LSTM-CRF for NER in Chinese social media. We make the following contributions:

- We propose three LSTM channels where one captures general patterns and the other two capture source domain patterns and target domain patterns, respectively. After concatenating three LSTM channels to a shared hidden layer, we propose domain-specific CRF layers to decode for different domains.
- We find that a shared embedding layer is important for improving performance. Randomly initialized embeddings are better than pretrained embeddings for multichannel architecture.
- We improve model's generalization ability using multichannel LSTM-CRF and achieve significant performance improvement.

2 Related Work

The problem of NER requires both boundary identification and type classification [3]. As the DEFT ERE Annotation Guidelines[1] shows, there are five entity types: person (PER), titles (TTL), organizations (ORG), geopolitical entities (GPE) and locations (LOC). A mention is a single occurrence of a name (NAM), nominal phrase (NOM) or pronominal phrase (PRO) that refers to or describes a single entity [16]. In Weibo NER dataset [26], which comes from Chinese social media, PER, ORG, GPE and LOC are considered, all including NAM and NOM mentions. In the third SIGHAN Bakeoff Chinese NER shared task [21] MSRA dataset, which comes from news, there are three types: PER, ORG and LOC, only in NAM mentions. In this paper, we focus on named entities mentions: PER, ORG and LOC.

Most related research regards NER as a sequence tagging task. Hidden Markov Model (HMM), Support Vector Machine (SVM) and Conditional Random Field (CRF) once achieved good results [12,14,22]. These classic methods need delicate hand-crafted features to obtain good results. In recent years, neural architectures show great learning power both for English NER [5,6,18,20,23] and Chinese NER [9]. These neural architectures don't need hand-crafted features

[1] Entities V1.7, Linguistic Data Consortium, 2014.

and some are end-to-end models which can be easily applied to other languages or similar tasks without data preprocessing. As Chinese words have no natural word boundaries, character-based tagging strategy simplifies NER without results of Chinese Word Segmentation (CWS) compared to word-based strategy. [9] achieve state-of-the-art performance on MSRA dataset using character-based LSTM-CRF architecture. We use character-based LSTM-CRF as our basic channel for a single domain.

Methods mentioned above have been restricted to formal text, e.g. news. It is difficult for NER in social media because of its informality and strong noise. There are many abbreviations, typos, novel words and ungrammatical constructions in social media. Chinese presents additional challenges, since it lacks of explicit word boundaries and other clues that indicate a named entity, e.g. capitalizations in English.

Related works on NER in Chinese social media focus on supervised learning using rare annotated corpora. [26] first release a Chinese social media corpora, namely Weibo NER data. They explore several types of embeddings using a CRF model and propose joint training objectives for embeddings and NER. [27] use Chinese word segmentation representation as features to improve NER. [15] propose a F-score driven training method through adding sentence level F-score to its label accuracy loss function. These methods only utilize rare in-domain corpora and get good precision but low recall rate, which is less than half of the recall rate trained on enough corpora [9]. [16] combine cross-domain supervised learning using out-of-domain annotated data with semi-supervised learning using in-domain unannotated data to achieve performance improvement. We extend feature augmentation method to multichannel LSTM-CRF and improve model's generalization ability with only out-of-domain data.

The feature augmentation method is first considered for sparse binary-valued features which underlie conventional NLP systems. They conjoin feature types with domain indicators as a kind of data preprocessing and use them alongside the original feature types. They extend the feature augmentation method to semi-supervised learning in [8]. [19] try a neural extension of the feature augmentation method on English slot tagging task and different domains in their task have different labels. Our work applies feature augmentation method to NER in Chinese social media using a novel multichannel LSTM-CRF model, which captures not only general patterns across formal and informal domains but also domain-specific patterns.

3 Model

We use character-based LSTM-CRF described in [9] as our single channel tagger. The architecture is shown in Fig. 1. We then extend it to multichannel LSTM-CRF with three LSTMs and two CRFs. These LSTMs respectively capture general patterns, source domain patterns and target domain patterns. Similarly, two CRF decoders are designed for source domain and target domain separately.

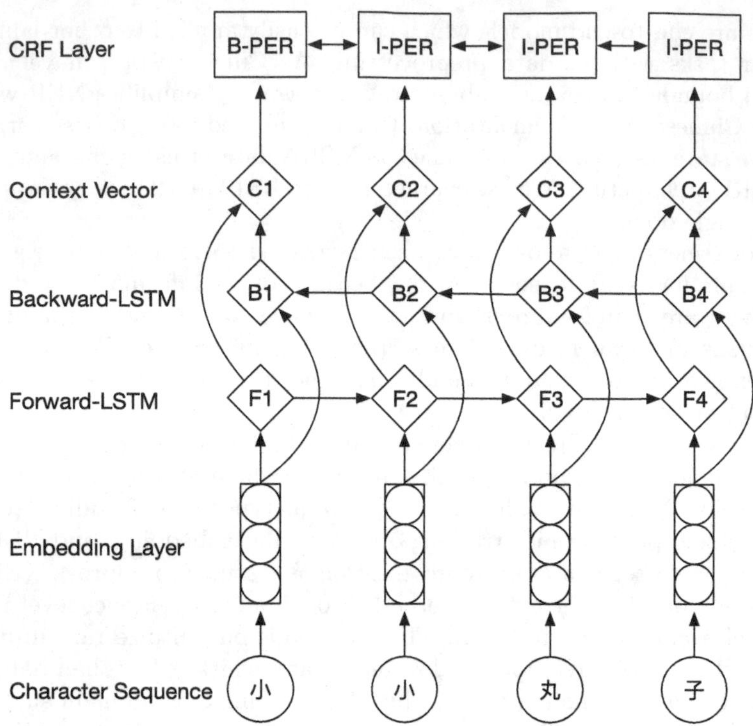

Fig. 1. The architecture of our character-based single channel BLSTM-CRF. The example means "little meat ball", a name in Chinese social media.

3.1 Multichannel LSTM-CRF

[7] propose the feature augmentation method for domain adaptation. All they do is to take each feature in the original problem and make three versions of it: a general version, a source-specific version and a target-specific version. The augmented source data contain general and source-specific versions. The augmented target data contain general and target-specific versions.

Formally, $\boldsymbol{x}$ is the input spaces; D^s is the source domain data set and D^t is the target domain data set. Define mappings Φ^s, Φ^t for mapping the source and target data to feature spaces respectively. Then after feature augmenting,

$$\Phi^s(\boldsymbol{x}) = \langle \boldsymbol{x}, \boldsymbol{x}, \mathbf{0} \rangle, \quad \Phi^t(\boldsymbol{x}) = \langle \boldsymbol{x}, \mathbf{0}, \boldsymbol{x} \rangle$$

where $\mathbf{0} = \langle 0, 0, ..., 0 \rangle$ is the zero vector. This approach can be easily applied to multi domains.

In our multichannel LSTM-CRF model, we use three LSTM channels: one general LSTM, one source domain LSTM and one target domain LSTM in Fig. 2. As there are general, source domain and target domain data, we try different pretrained embeddings (left part in Fig. 2). Each LSTM uses a domain-specific embedding layer which means different character vectors are put into different

LSTMs. All three LSTM outputs are concatenated through a mask vector. If the input data is from source domain, mask vector $m = [\vec{1}, \vec{1}, \vec{0}]$. Otherwise, if the input data is from target domain, mask vector $m = [\vec{1}, \vec{0}, \vec{1}]$. In this way, source domain training data help to learn general and source LSTM parameters and character embeddings, and target domain training data help to learn general and target LSTM parameters and character embeddings. We apply similar mask operation to CRF layer with two CRF decoders. Instinctively, source domain data and target domain data should have different transition probabilities between tags.

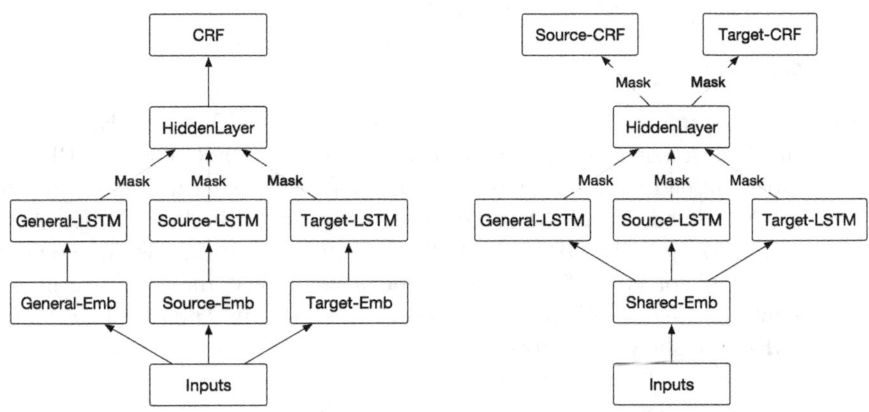

Fig. 2. The architecture of our model. First we use three embedding layers and LSTMs to learn general, source domain and target domain patterns (as shown in the left part). Then we adopt a shared embedding layer and 2 domain CRF decoders (as shown in the right part). We will explain the mask vector in Sect. 3.1.

3.2 Sharing Parameters

Our first model shares hidden layer and CRF layer parameters in the neural architecture. When the training sentence is from source domain, target domain embeddings and LSTM parameters are not updated. We notice that there is severe imbalance between source and target domain training data. Target domain training data is less than 1/30 of source domain training data. It means that most of the time during training, target channel LSTM is not trained. Related experiment is shown in Sect. 4.6.

To make our model share more parameters and make target channel learn more, we adjust our original architecture. We propose shared embedding layer but still keep multichannel LSTMs. No matter which domain the training sentence is from, the shared embedding layer can get updates. Meanwhile, multichannel LSTMs learn different domain patterns all the same. The proposed model can remember general, source and target patterns through multichannel

LSTMs and can be trained more effectively. At the same time, we use 2 different CRF layers respectively for source and target domain. The right part in Fig. 2 shows our improved architecture.

4 Experiments

To demonstrate the correctness and effectiveness of our framework, we do some experiments on NER datasets. We will describe the details of datasets, tagging scheme, pretrained embeddings, baselines, settings and results in our experiments.

4.1 Datasets

We use the same annotated corpora[2] as [16] which is called Weibo NER dataset for NER in Chinese social media. Weibo NER contains PER, ORG, GPE and LOC for both named and nominal mention. We use the training set of the third SIGHAN Bakeoff MSRA NER dataset as out-of-domain data. MSRA NER dataset contains only PER, ORG and LOC for named mention. We merge GPE and LOC as LOC for consistency. As we focus on named mention, we ignore nominal mention. The details of Weibo NER are shown in Table 1. The details of MSRA NER are shown in Table 2.

4.2 Tagging Scheme

As we use a character-based tagging strategy, we need to assign a named entity label to every character in a sentence. Many named entities span multiple characters in a sentence. Sentences are usually represented in the IOB format (Inside, Outside, Beginning). In this paper, we use IOBES tagging scheme. Using this scheme, more information about the following tag is considered [9,20]. Related works show that using a more expressive tagging scheme like IOBES improves performance [11,29].

4.3 Pretrained Embeddings

Previous works show that both pretrained word embeddings for English and pretrained character embeddings for Chinese improve performance significantly than randomly initialized embeddings [9,20]. We first use different embedding layers for different LSTM channels, because these LSTM channels tend to capture different domain patterns. For source domain, which is from news, we use unlabeled texts from the People's Daily (1994–2003) to pretrain Chinese character embeddings. Here we use gensim[3] [30], which contains a python version

[2] We just fix four obvious annotating errors with starting PER character tagged as 'I-PER' in the training set.

[3] https://radimrehurek.com/gensim/index.html.

Table 1. Details of Weibo NER dataset.

	Named Entity	Sentence
Train Set	957	1350
Dev Set	153	270
Test Set	211	270

Table 2. Details of MSRA NER dataset.

Entity Type	Train Set	Test Set
PER	17615	1973
LOC	36517	2877
ORG	20571	1331
Sentence	46364	4365

implementation of word2vec [24]. After simple preprocessing, such as unifying different styles of punctuations, we use CBOW model to train the embeddings because it is faster than skip-gram model. For target domain, which is from social media, we use the character embeddings in [26], which are pretrained using 2,259,434 unlabeled Weibo messages. Although [26] report 3 kinds of Chinese embeddings, we use the character embeddings without position information in order to be consistent with the other two domain pretrained embeddings. For general domain, we use the character embeddings in [9], which are pretrained using unlabeled Chinese Wikipedia backup dump of 20151201. All the embeddings have a dimension of 100. Source and general embeddings are trained using the same parameters while target embeddings is directly adopted from [26].

4.4 Baselines

We regard character-based single channel LSTM-CRF (described in Fig. 1) as baseline, which achieves state-of-the-art performance in news dataset [9]. We use the same LSTM block in all experiments and other settings are showed in Sect. 4.5.

4.5 Settings

We use dropout training [17] before the input to LSTM layer with a probability of 0.5 in order to avoid overfitting. We train our network using the back-propagation algorithm updating our parameters on every training example, one at a time. We use stochastic gradient decent (SGD) algorithm with a learning rate of 0.05 for 100 epochs on all training sets. Dimension of LSTM is 100. Dimension of Chinese character embeddings is also 100. Fine tuning is applied in all experiments to adjust the character embeddings. We adopt these hyper parameters according to [9,20].

4.6 Results

Multichannel and Embeddings: To demonstrate the effectiveness of our proposed multichannel LSTMs with shared embedding layer and 2 CRF layers, we compare results of variants in Table 3. We adopt single channel LSTM-CRF

Table 3. Results of variants. 'S' stands for source domain training data. 'T' stands for target domain training data. 'S+T' means using merged data for training. 'random' means using randomly initialized embeddings. '3random' means using 3 different randomly initialized embeddings. '1news' '1weibo' '1wiki' '1random' respectively means a shared pretrained embeddings using news, weibo, wikipedia texts and a shared randomly initialized embeddings. '3embs' means using 3 pretrained embeddings together. '2CRF' stands for 2 domain-specific CRF decoder and '1CRF' stands for a shared CRF decoder. '2 channels' removes general LSTM.

ID	Models	Precision	Recall	F1
1	Single channel (T, random)	55.90	50.00	52.78
2	Single channel (S+T, random)	55.25	45.87	50.13
3	Multichannel (S+T, 3random, 1CRF)	64.50	50.00	56.33
4	Multichannel (S+T, 3embs, 1CRF)	58.25	54.30	56.21
5	Multichannel (S+T, 1news, 1CRF)	58.82	54.30	56.47
6	Multichannel (S+T, 1weibo, 1CRF)	57.14	48.87	52.68
7	Multichannel (S+T, 1wiki, 1CRF)	58.25	52.94	55.19
8	Multichannel (S+T, 1random, 1CRF)	66.48	54.75	60.05
9	Multichannel (S+T, 1random, 2CRF)	65.45	**56.56**	**60.68**
10	2 channels (S+T, 1random, 1CRF)	**71.14**	47.96	57.30

described in Fig. 1 as baselines (#1)(#2). (#1) only uses source domain training data and (#2) uses mixed source and target data. We can find that using mixed training data without distinction leads to the model bias to large source domain and the model labels less target domain entities in test data with a decline of recall.

(#3) and (#4) use different initialized character embeddings with the same multichannel architecture. Pretrained embeddings have important effect on single domain NER [9,20], but (#4) shows no improvement in overall F1. One possible reason is that three pretrained embeddings are not in the same vector space. Another important reason we have verified is that target channel parameters are not trained enough due to the imbalance source/target ratio. We can measure the changes of a character vector before (randomly initialized) and after training (fine tuned) using cosine similarity. We respectively compute the sum of cosine similarity of top 10 characters appeared with a tag of 'B-PER', which means Chinese family name, in source domain and target domain in (#3). The bigger cosine similarity means the less changes compared to randomly initialized vector. We can see target domain cosine similarity sum is much greater than source domain in Table 4. We find target parameters are not updated enough times because there is such few target domain training data.

Nearly all the multichannel architectures ((#3)$\sim$(#9)) perform better than single channel LSTM-CRF model. With general LSTM capturing general patterns on both source and target data, these multichannel architectures get better recall rate which is the main bottleneck that limits NER performance in

Table 4. Top 10 family name character embeddings changes before and after training in form of cosine similarity sum.

	Cosine Similarity Sum
Top 10 in Source	0.714075
Top 10 in Target	5.229697

Chinese social media. Through comparing (#8)(#9) to (#5)∼(#7), we find that randomly initialization gets better results than using pretrained embeddings as initialization. It is different from single domain supervised NER because it's hard to define a domain corpora to pretrain embeddings, especially when the pretrained embeddings are shared to three different domain LSTMs. But we can learn the shared embeddings with random initialization instead of pretraining one. (#6) has poor performance because we directly use the Weibo embeddings provided in [26]. It uses different training parameters. After using shared embedding layer which is randomly initialized in (#8)(#9), we achieve good results on F1 with improvement on both precision and recall. (#9) uses domain-specific CRF decoders which gain more improvement on recall.

We remove general LSTM in (#8) and thus get a 2 channels architecture (#10). The dramatic fall of recall rate in (#10) shows the importance of general LSTM on improving model's generalization ability.

Our multichannel LSTM-CRF (#9) exceeds overall F1 by +10.55 than baseline (#2). Multichannel variants gain widespread better recall rate.

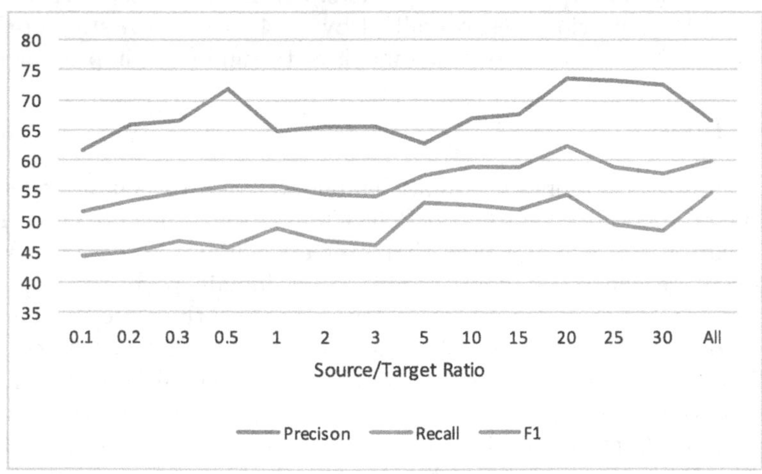

Fig. 3. Results of different source/target ratios.

Effects of Ratios: Source domain data are more than 30 times of target domain data in size. It's important to know the effects of ratios. We keep the size of target data unchanged and gradually increase the size of source data. We compare results with different amount source/target rations in Fig. 3. We use multichannel LSTM model with shared embeddings and CRF layer in this experiment. We can see that F1 goes up in overall along with more source training data adding in, then F1 reaches 62.50% as maximum when source/target ratio equals 20. We notice that the maximum ratio is nearly 35 and results may be different if more source data are used.

Table 5. Results compared to other works. * indicates results using out-of-domain annotated data.

Models	Precision	Recall	F1
[26] Peng2015	**74.78**	39.81	51.96
[27] Peng2016	66.67	47.22	55.28
[15] He2016	66.93	40.67	50.60
[16] He2017*	61.68	48.82	54.50
Our Model*	65.45	**56.56**	**60.68**

Compared with Other Works: Table 5 shows results compared with other works[4]. [15,26,27] just use in-domain annotated data for training and large unlabeled Weibo messages for pretraining. Except out-of-domain annotated data, [16] also use unlabeled Weibo messages for semi-supervised learning. We can see that we get the best result which owns a good recall rate due to the use of general LSTM and domain-specific CRF decoders. Our model exceeds previous best recall by +7.74 and previous best overall F1 by +5.4. We achieve state-of-the-art performance on NER in Chinese social media with significant improvement.

5 Conclusion

In this paper, we have proposed a multichannel LSTM-CRF neural model using out-of-domain annotated data for NER in Chinese social media. Three LSTM channels sharing the same Chinese character embedding are designed respectively to capture general, in-domain and out-of-domain patterns. The experiments demonstrate that our model achieves significantly better performance compared to the previous state-of-the-art methods on NER in Chinese social media. Through deep analysis, we find that different channels sharing the same character embedding is important for performance improvement. And randomly initialized embeddings perform better than the pretrained ones for multichannel architecture. Domain-specific CRF decoders also help to improve recall rate.

Acknowledgments. The research work has been supported by the Natural Science Foundation of China under Grant No. 61403379 and No. 61402478.

[4] [26,27] update their results here http://www.cs.jhu.edu/~npeng/papers/golden_horse_supplement.pdf.

References

1. Blitzer, J., McDonald, R., Pereira, F.: Domain adaptation with structural correspondence learning. In: Proceedings of the 2006 conference on empirical methods in natural language processing, pp. 120–128. Association for Computational Linguistics (2006)
2. Chang, C.Y., Teng, Z., Zhang, Y.: Expectation-regulated neural model for event mention extraction. In: Proceedings of the 2016 Conference of the North American Chapter of the Association for Computational Linguistics: Human Language Technologies, pp. 400–410. Association for Computational Linguistics, San Diego, California, June 2016
3. Chen, Y., Zong, C., Su, K.Y.: On jointly recognizing and aligning bilingual named entities. In: Proceedings of the 48th Annual Meeting of the Association for Computational Linguistics, pp. 631–639. Association for Computational Linguistics (2010)
4. Cherry, C., Guo, H.: The unreasonable effectiveness of word representations for twitter named entity recognition. In: HLT-NAACL, pp. 735–745 (2015)
5. Chiu, J.P., Nichols, E.: Named entity recognition with bidirectional lstm-cnns. arXiv preprint (2015). arXiv:1511.08308
6. Collobert, R., Weston, J., Bottou, L., Karlen, M., Kavukcuoglu, K., Kuksa, P.: Natural language processing (almost) from scratch. J. Mach. Learn. Res. **12**(Aug), 2493–2537 (2011)
7. Daumé III., H.: Frustratingly easy domain adaptation. arXiv preprint (2009). arXiv:0907.1815
8. Daumé III., H., Kumar, A., Saha, A.: Frustratingly easy semi-supervised domain adaptation. In: Proceedings of the 2010 Workshop on Domain Adaptation for Natural Language Processing, pp. 53–59. Association for Computational Linguistics (2010)
9. Dong, C., Zhang, J., Zong, C., Hattori, M., Di, H.: Character-Based LSTM-CRF with Radical-Level Features for Chinese Named Entity Recognition. In: Lin, C.-Y., Xue, N., Zhao, D., Huang, X., Feng, Y. (eds.) ICCPOL/NLPCC -2016. LNCS, vol. 10102, pp. 239–250. Springer, Cham (2016). doi:10.1007/978-3-319-50496-4_20
10. Dredze, M., McNamee, P., Rao, D., Gerber, A., Finin, T.: Entity disambiguation for knowledge base population. In: Proceedings of the 23rd International Conference on Computational Linguistics, pp. 277–285. Association for Computational Linguistics (2010)
11. Dyer, C., Ballesteros, M., Ling, W., Matthews, A., Smith, N.A.: Transition-based dependency parsing with stack long short-term memory. arXiv preprint (2015). arXiv:1505.08075
12. Fu, G., Luke, K.K.: Chinese named entity recognition using lexicalized hmms. ACM SIGKDD Explor. Newslett. **7**(1), 19–25 (2005)
13. Gottipati, S., Jiang, J.: Linking entities to a knowledge base with query expansion. In: Proceedings of the Conference on Empirical Methods in Natural Language Processing, pp. 804–813. Association for Computational Linguistics (2011)
14. Han, A.L.-F., Wong, D.F., Chao, L.S.: Chinese Named Entity Recognition with Conditional Random Fields in the Light of Chinese Characteristics. In: Kłopotek, M.A., Koronacki, J., Marciniak, M., Mykowiecka, A., Wierzchoń, S.T. (eds.) IIS 2013. LNCS, vol. 7912, pp. 57–68. Springer, Heidelberg (2013). doi:10.1007/978-3-642-38634-3_8
15. He, H., Sun, X.: F-score driven max margin neural network for named entity recognition in chinese social media. arXiv preprint (2016). arXiv:1611.04234

16. He, H., Sun, X.: A unified model for cross-domain and semi-supervised named entity recognition in chinese social media. In: Thirty-First AAAI Conference on Artificial Intelligence (2017)
17. Hinton, G.E., Srivastava, N., Krizhevsky, A., Sutskever, I., Salakhutdinov, R.R.: Improving neural networks by preventing co-adaptation of feature detectors. arXiv preprint (2012). arXiv:1207.0580
18. Huang, Z., Xu, W., Yu, K.: Bidirectional lstm-crf models for sequence tagging. arXiv preprint (2015). arXiv:1508.01991
19. Kim, Y.B., Stratos, K., Sarikaya, R.: Frustratingly easy neural domain adaptation. In: Proceedings of COLING 2016, the 26th International Conference on Computational Linguistics: Technical Papers. The COLING 2016 Organizing Committee, Osaka, Japan, pp. 387–396, December 2016
20. Lample, G., Ballesteros, M., Subramanian, S., Kawakami, K., Dyer, C.: Neural architectures for named entity recognition. arXiv preprint (2016). arXiv:1603.01360
21. Levow, G.A.: The third international chinese language processing bakeoff: Word segmentation and named entity recognition. In: Proceedings of the Fifth SIGHAN Workshop on Chinese Language Processing, pp. 108–117 (2006)
22. Li, L., Mao, T., Huang, D., Yang, Y.: Hybrid models for chinese named entity recognition. In: COLING• ACL 2006, p. 72 (2006)
23. Ma, X., Hovy, E.: End-to-end sequence labeling via bi-directional lstm-cnns-crf. arXiv preprint (2016). arXiv:1603.01354
24. Mikolov, T., Sutskever, I., Chen, K., Corrado, G.S., Dean, J.: Distributed representations of words and phrases and their compositionality. In: Advances in neural information processing systems, pp. 3111–3119 (2013)
25. Pan, S.J., Yang, Q.: A survey on transfer learning. IEEE Trans. Knowl. Data Eng. **22**(10), 1345–1359 (2010)
26. Peng, N., Dredze, M.: Named entity recognition for chinese social media with jointly trained embeddings. In: EMNLP, pp. 548–554 (2015)
27. Peng, N., Dredze, M.: Improving named entity recognition for chinese social media with word segmentation representation learning. In: Proceedings of the 54th Annual Meeting of the Association for Computational Linguistics, vol. 2, pp. 149–155 (2016)
28. Peng, N., Dredze, M.: Multi-task multi-domain representation learning for sequence tagging. arXiv preprint (2016). arXiv:1608.02689
29. Ratinov, L., Roth, D.: Design challenges and misconceptions in named entity recognition. In: Proceedings of the Thirteenth Conference on Computational Natural Language Learning, pp. 147–155. Association for Computational Linguistics (2009)
30. Rehurek, R., Sojka, P.: Software framework for topic modelling with large corpora. In: Proceedings of the LREC 2010 Workshop on New Challenges for NLP Frameworks. Citeseer (2010)
31. Ritter, A., Clark, S., Etzioni, O., et al.: Named entity recognition in tweets: an experimental study. In: Proceedings of the Conference on Empirical Methods in Natural Language Processing, pp. 1524–1534. Association for Computational Linguistics (2011)
32. Weiss, K., Khoshgoftaar, T.M., Wang, D.: A survey of transfer learning. J. Big Data **3**(1), 1–40 (2016)
33. Yang, Z., Salakhutdinov, R., Cohen, W.W.: Transfer learning for sequence tagging with hierarchical recurrent networks. arXiv preprint (2017). arXiv:1703.06345

Language Resource and Evaluation

Generating Chinese Classical Poems with RNN Encoder-Decoder

Xiaoyuan Yi(✉), Ruoyu Li, and Maosong Sun

State Key Laboratory of Intelligent Technology and Systems,
Tsinghua National Laboratory for Information Science and Technology,
Department of Computer Science and Technology,
Tsinghua University, Beijing, China
yi-xy16@mails.tsinghua.edu.cn, liruoyu@6estates.com,
sms@tsinghua.edu.cn

Abstract. We take the generation of Chinese classical poetry as a sequence-to-sequence learning problem, and investigate the suitability of recurrent neural network (RNN) for poetry generation task by various qualitative analyses. Then we build a novel system based on the RNN Encoder-Decoder structure to generate quatrains (*Jueju* in Chinese), with a keyword as input. Our system can learn semantic meaning within a single sentence, semantic relevance among sentences in a poem, and the use of structural, rhythmical and tonal patterns jointly, without utilizing any constraint templates. Experimental results show that our system outperforms other competitive systems.

Keywords: Chinese poetry generation · Neural network · Machine learning

1 Introduction

Chinese classical poetry is undoubtedly the largest and brightest pearl, if Chinese classical literature is compared to a crown. As a kind of literary form starting from the Pre-Qin Period, classical poetry stretches more than two thousand years, having a far-reaching influence on the development of Chinese history. Poets write poems to record important events, express feelings and make comments. There are different kinds of Chinese classical poetry, in which the quatrain with huge quantity and high quality must be considered as a quite important one. In the most famous anthology of classical poems, *Three Hundred of Tang Poems* [8], quatrains cover more than 25%, whose amount is the largest.

The quatrain is a kind of classical poetry with rules and forms which means that besides the necessary requirements on grammars and semantics for general poetry, quatrains must obey the rules of structure and tone. Figure 1 shows a quatrain generated by our system. A quatrain contains four sentences, each consists of seven or five characters. In Ancient Chinese, characters are divided into two tone categories, namely Ping (level tone) and Ze (oblique tone). Characters of particular tone must be in particular positions, which makes the poetry

M. Sun et al. (Eds.): CCL 2017 and NLP-NABD 2017, LNAI 10565, pp. 211–223, 2017.
https://doi.org/10.1007/978-3-319-69005-6_18

一声秋雁连天远，(*P*ZPPZ)
The twitter of a wild goose comes from the distant horizon.
万里归帆隔水遥。(*ZPPZZP)
The homebound ships are still ten thousand miles away from the destination.
惆怅旧游零落处，(*Z*PPZZ)
I am so sad to be the place where I said goodbye to my travelling companions.
白头萧瑟满江桥。(*P*ZZPP)
There is nothing here, but a gloomy spectacle and the old me in the bridge.

Fig. 1. A 7-char quatrain generated by our system with the keyword "秋雁" (autumn wild goose) as input. The tone of each character is shown in parentheses. P, Z and * represent Ping tone, Ze tone and either respectively. Rhyming characters are underlined.

cadenced and full of rhythmic beauty. Meanwhile, in term of the vowels, characters are divided into different rhyme categories. The last character of the first (optional), second and last sentence in a quatrain must belong to the same rhyme category, which enhances the coherence of poetry.

In this paper, we mainly focus on the automatic generation of quatrains. Nowadays, Deep Learning opens a new door to it, making computer no longer rely on prepared templates, and try to learn the composition method automatically from a large number of excellent poems. Poetry composition by machine is not only a beautiful wish. Based on the poem generation system, interesting applications can be developed, which can be used for education of Chinese classical poetry and the literary researches.

Different from the semantically similar pairs in machine translation tasks, the pair of two adjacent sentences in a quatrain is semantically relevant. We conduct various qualitative experiments to show RNN Encoder-Decoder structure can capture and learn the semantic relevance in Chinese classical poetry well. Based on these observations, consequently we take poem generation as a sequence-to-sequence learning problem, and use RNN Encoder-Decoder to learn the semantic meaning within a single sentence, the semantic relevance among sentences and the use of tonal patterns jointly. Furthermore, we use attention mechanism to capture character associations to improve the relevance between input and output sentences. Consisting of three independent sentences generation modules (word-to-sentence, sentence-to-sentence and context-to-sentence), our system can generate a quatrain with a user keyword. Both automatic and manual evaluations show our system outperforms other generation systems.

The rest of this paper is organized as follows. Section 2 introduces the related methods and systems. Section 3 gives the models in our system and analyses the suitability of them for poetry generation task by various qualitative experiments. Section 4 introduces our poetry generation system. Then Sect. 5 gives the evaluation experiments design and results. In Sect. 6 we draw a conclusion and point out future work.

2 Related Work

The research about poetry generation started in 1960s, and has been a focus in recent decades. Manurung [7] proposed three criteria for automatically generated poetry: grammaticality (the generated sentences must obey grammar rules and be readable), meaningfulness (the sentences should express something related to the theme) and poeticness (generated poems must have poetic features, such as the rhythm, cadence and the special use of words).

The early methods are based on rules and templates. For example, ASPERA [3] uses the changes of accent as the templates to fill with words. Haiku generation system [11] expands the input queries to haiku sentences in term of rules extracted from the corpus. Such methods are mechanical, which match the requirements of grammaticality, but perform poorly on meaningfulness and poeticness.

One important approach is generating poems with evolutionary algorithms. The process of poetry generation is described as natural selection. Then through genetic heredity and variation, good results are selected by the evaluation functions [6,7]. However, the methods depend on the quality of the evaluation functions which are hard to be designed well. Generally, the sentences perform better on meaningfulness but can hardly satisfy the poeticness.

Another approach is based on the methods for the generation of other kinds of texts. Yan et al. [12] generate poems with the method of automatic summarization. While SMT is first applied on the task of couplets generation by Jiang and Zhou [5]. They treat the generation of the couplets as a kind of machine translation tasks. He et al. [4] apply the method on quatrain generation, translating the input sentence into the next sentence. Sentences generated with such method is good at the relevance, but cannot obey the rules and forms.

With the cross field of Deep Learning and Natural Language Process becoming focused, neural network has been applied on poetry generation. Zhang and Lapata [13] compress all the previous information into a vector with RNN to produce the probability distribution of the next character to be generated.

Our work differs from the previous work mainly as follows. Firstly, we use RNN Encoder-Decoder as the basic structure of our system, compared with the method in [4]. Moreover, in He's system the rhythm is controlled externally and the results perform poorly on tonal patterns, while our system can learn all these things jointly. Secondly, compared with [13], our model is based on bi-directional RNN with gated units instead of the simple RNN. Besides, Zhang [13] compress all context information into a small vector, losing useful information in some degree. Thus they need two more translation models and another rhythm template to control semantic relevance and tones. The outputs of our system can obey these constraints naturally. Finally, we use attention mechanism to capture character associations and we also find reversing target sentences in training can improve performance.

3 Models and Qualitative Analyses

In machine translation tasks, the sentence pairs are semantically similar, from which the model learns the corresponding relations. While in Chinese classical quatrains, there is a close semantic relevance between two adjacent sentences. We use RNN Encoder-Decoder to learn the relevance which is then used to generate the next sentence given the preceding one. In this section, we introduce the models in our system and show why they are suitable for this semantic-relevant learning by several qualitative experiments.

3.1 Sentence Poetry Module (SPM)

We call the first model SPM (Sentence Poetry Module), which is used for sentence-to-sentence generation. Taking the first sentence as input, we use SPM to generate the second sentence in poem. As shown in Fig. 2, we use bi-directional RNN with attention mechanism proposed in [1] to build SPM. Denote the four sentences in a quatrain are L_1, L_2, L_3, L_4, then three pairs are extracted, $<L_1, L_2>$, $<L_2, L_3>$ and $<L_3, L_4>$, to train SPM.

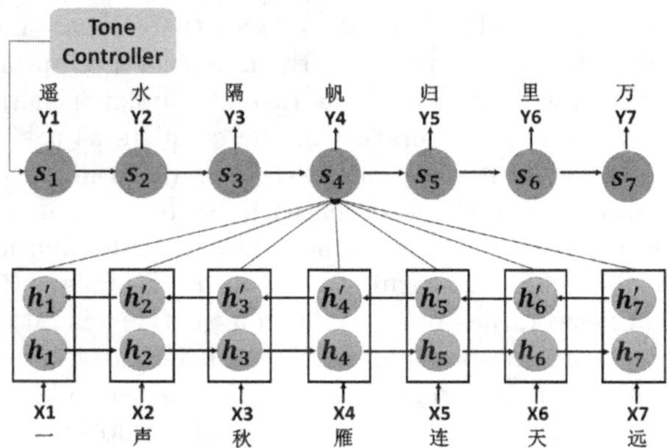

Fig. 2. An illustration of SPM. The tone controller is used to keep the last character of the second sentence level-toned.

Let us denote an input poetry sentence by $X = (x_1, x_2, ..., x_{T_x})$, and an output one by $Y = (y_1, y_2, ..., y_{T_y})$. $e(x_t)$ is the word-embedding of the t-th character x_t. h_t and $h_t^{'}$ represent the forward and backward hidden states in Encoder respectively.

In Encoder:

$$d_t = tanh(U[h_{t-1} \odot r_t] + We(x_t)) \quad (1)$$

$$u_t = \sigma(U_u h_{t-1} + W_u e(x_t)) \quad (2)$$

$$r_t = \sigma(U_r h_{t-1} + W_r e(x_t)) \quad (3)$$

$$h_t = (1 - u_t) \odot h_{t-1} + u_t \odot d_t \tag{4}$$

$$g_t = [h_t; h_t^{'}] \tag{5}$$

(1)–(5) are formulas for the computation of forward hidden states. The computation of backward hidden states is similar. $\odot$ is element-wise multiplication. g_t is the final hidden state of t-th character in Encoder. r_t and u_t are the reset gate and update gate respectively introduced in [2]. The formulas in decoder are similar. The difference is that a context vector c_t of attention mechanism is used to calculate the hidden state s_t of t-th character in Decoder. c_t is computed as:

$$c_t = \sum_{i=1}^{T_x} \alpha_{t,i} g_i \tag{6}$$

$$\alpha_{t,i} = \frac{exp(v_{t,i})}{\sum_{j=1}^{T_x} exp(v_{t,j})} \tag{7}$$

$$v_{t,i} = v_a^T tanh(W_a s_{t-1} + U_a g_i) \tag{8}$$

3.2 Target Sentences Reversing

As shown in Fig. 2, when training SPM we reverse the target sentences for two reasons. First, the final character of second sentence must be level-tone. However, if the final character of input sentence is level-tone, SPM can't determine the tone of the final character of output sentence because of some special tonal patterns in training pairs. Thus we add a tone controller into SPM. Obviously, this control will do harm to the semantic meaning of the outputs. Therefore we reverse the target sentences in training so that SPM can generate the tail character first, which will decrease the damage on meaningfulness as possible.

Furthermore, we find reversing target sentences can improve the performance. In [9], Sutskever et al. find reversing source sentences can improve the LSTM's performance on machine translation. But in Sect. 5, by quantitative evaluation, we show that reversing source sentences makes little improvement in our task. We think this is because we use a bi-directional Encoder, which handles the problem Sutskever points out in some degree.

Besides, we think the improvement of reversing target sentences is because of the attributive structure in Chinese classical poetry. There are many words with the structure *attributive + central word* in Chinese poetry. For example, "青草" (green grass), the character "青" (green) is attributive and the character "草" (grass) is central word. In normal generation order, "青" will be generated earlier than "草". But there are many other characters can be central word of "青", such as "青山" (green mountain), "青云" (green cloud), "青烟" (green smoke), which increases the uncertainty in the generation of "草". Whereas reversing target sentence can reduce this uncertainty since the attributive of "草" is often "青" in Chinese classical poetry.

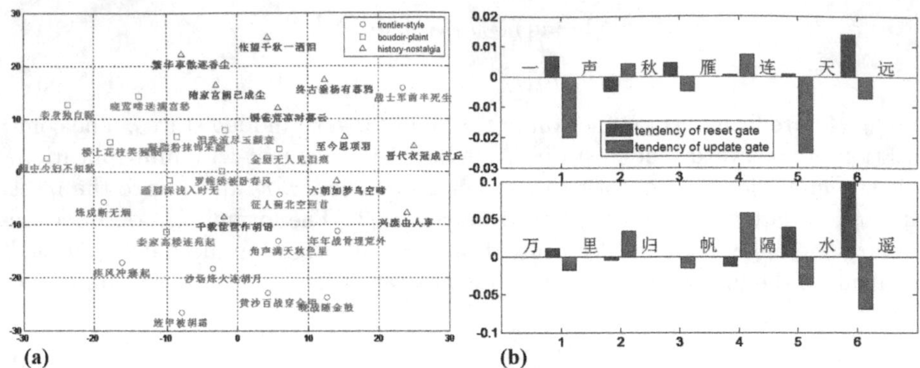

Fig. 3. (a) 2-D visualization of the learned poem sentences representations. The circle, square and triangle represent frontier-style, boudoir-plaint and history-nostalgia poetry sentences respectively. (b) An example of word boundaries recognition by gated units. Between every two adjacent characters, the first and the second bars show the reset and update tendencies respectively. The upper plot is the input sentence and the lower one is the output one.

3.3 Qualitative Analyses of SPM

Poem Sentence Representations. We used the average of g_t in formula (5) as sentence representation. We selected three types of classical poetry: frontier-style poetry (poetry about the wars), boudoir-plaint poetry (poetry about women's sadness) and history-nostalgia poetry (poetry about history). For each type, we obtained ten sentences and used Barnes-Hut-SNE [10] to map their representations into two-dimensional space. As shown in Fig. 3(a), sentences with the same type gather together, which shows these representations can capture the semantic meanings of poetry sentences well.

Gated Units in Word Boundary Recognition. The training and generation are based on characters (because there is no effective word segmentation algorithm for Chinese classical poetry) without any explicit word boundaries in the sequences, but we find gated units can recognize the word boundaries roughly. As in formula (2) and formula (3), when r_t tends to be zero and u_t tends to be one, the gated units tend to use current input to update the hidden state, whereas gated units tend to keep previous hidden states. We used the average value of every elements in r_t as the reset value of t-th character. Along the direction of hidden states propagation, we calculated the difference between reset values of two adjacent characters to get the reset tendency. Similarly, we got the update tendency.

As shown in Fig. 3(b), higher reset tendency and lower update tendency mean that the two characters tend to be an entirety (a whole word). Whereas they tend to be separated. In sentence "一声秋雁连天远", "一声" and "秋雁" are both words. We can see the reset tendency and update tendency reflect the word boundaries roughly. Furthermore, the tendency of gated units in Decoder is similar with that in Encoder. This nature makes the vector representations contain information of whole words and makes output sentences keep the similar structures as input ones.

Attention Mechanism in Capturing Associations. Different from word alignments in translation task, attention mechanism can capture the implicit associations between two characters. Figure 4 shows the visualizations of $\alpha_{t,i}$ in formula (8).

The top two plots show the associations between input and output sentences generated by a SPM trained with reversed target sentences. The bottom two plots are the results of SPM trained with normal target sentences.

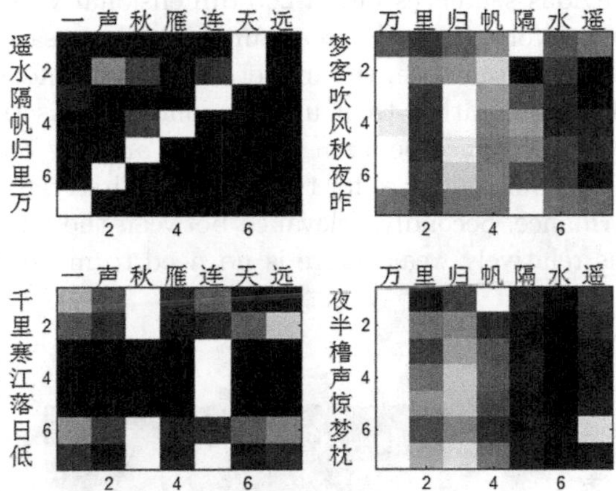

Fig. 4. Examples of attention visualizations. Each pixel shows the association (0: black, 1: white) between characters in input sentences (horizontal) and in output sentences (vertical). Outputs on the top two plots are reversed for the reasons described in Sect. 3.2. (Color figure online)

In the top left plot, each character in output sentence focuses on the semantic relevant character in input sentence, such as "水" (sea) and "天" (sky), "万" (ten thousand) and "一" (one), "帆" (sail) and "雁" (wild goose).

Also, in the top right plot, besides the first character, output sentence mainly focuses on the second character "归" (return), since the input is about home-bound ships and the output is about the travellers.

Besides, we get a great improvement by reversing the target sentences in training. There are no obvious associations in the bottom two plots compared with results in the top two plots, which shows reversing target sentences improves attention performance and thus leads to better generation performance. Detailed quantitative evaluation results please refer to Sect. 5.

3.4 Context Poetry Module (CPM)

To utilize more context information, we build another Encoder-Decoder called CPM (Context Poetry Module). The structure of CPM is similar with that of SPM. The difference is that we concatenate two adjacent sentences in a quatrain as a long input sequence, and use the next sentence as the target sequence in training. We extract two pairs from each quatrain, $<L1L2, L3>$, $<L2L3, L4>$ to train CPM. By this means, the model can utilize information of previous two sentences when generating current sentence.

The final characters of the second and the fourth sentence must rhyme and the final character of the third sentence must not. When generating the fourth sentence, SPM can't determine the rhyme category. By taking the second sentence into consideration, CPM can capture the rhyme pattern. Thus we use CPM to generate the third and the fourth sentences. Zhang [13] utilizes context by compressing all previous sentences into a 200-dimensional vector, which causes some loss to semantic information. Whereas our method can save all information. When generating current sentence, the model can learn to focus on important characters with attention, rather than use all context indiscriminately, which will improve semantic relevance between the inputs and the outputs. We don't concatenate more previous sentences for two reasons. Firstly, too long sequences result in low performance. Secondly, relevance between the fourth sentence and the first sentence is relatively weak, there is no need to make the system more complicated.

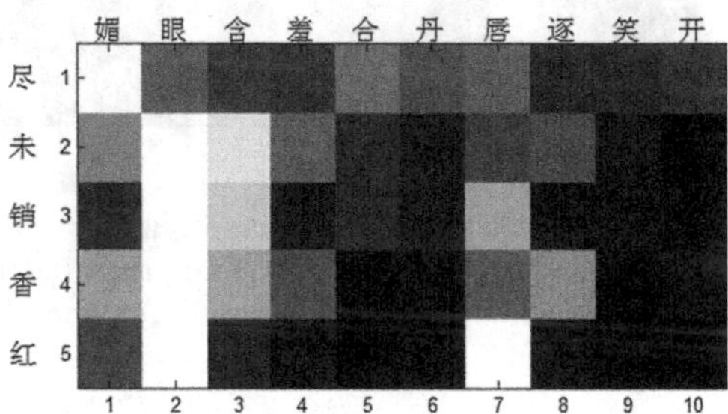

Fig. 5. An attention visualization example of CPM. The input are two concatenate sentences and each consists of five characters. The output is reversed.

Figure 5 shows an attention visualization of CPM. As we can see, because the input sentence is a description of a beautiful woman, attention mechanism focuses on two characters, "眼" (eyes) and "唇" (lips). Though there is a color word "丹" (red) in the input sentence, attention mechanism chooses to focus on "眼" and "唇" instead of "丹" for generating the character "红" (also means red color) since in Chinese classical poetry, "红" is often used to describe the beauty of women. Compared with the simple alignments of words with same semantic meanings in translation task, attention mechanism can learn the associations and helps the model to focus on the most relevant information instead of all context, which results in a stronger relevance between input and output sentences.

3.5 Word Poetry Module (WPM)

A big shortcoming of SMT-based methods is that they need another model to generate the first sentence. For example, He [4] expands user keywords, then uses constraint templates and a language model to search for a sentence.

For RNN Encoder-Decoder, words and sentences will be mapped into the same vector space. Since our system is based on characters, words can be considered as short sequences. Ideally, SPM will generate a relevant sentence taking a word as input. But the training pairs are all long sequences, it won't work well when the input is a short word.

Therefore, we train the third Encoder-Decoder, called Word Poetry Module (WPM). In detail, we pre-trained a SPM, then extracted some <word, sentence> pairs (e.g. <'明月','床前明月光'>) and trained the SPM with these pairs for several epoches, improving the ability of generating long sequences with short sequences.

4 Poetry Generation System

Based on observations above, we use RNN Encoder-Decoder to learn the relevance which is then used to generate the next sentence given the previous one. To utilize context information in different levels, we use three generation modules, Word Poetry Module (WPM), Sentence Poetry Module (SPM) and Context Poetry Module (CPM) to generate a whole quatrain.

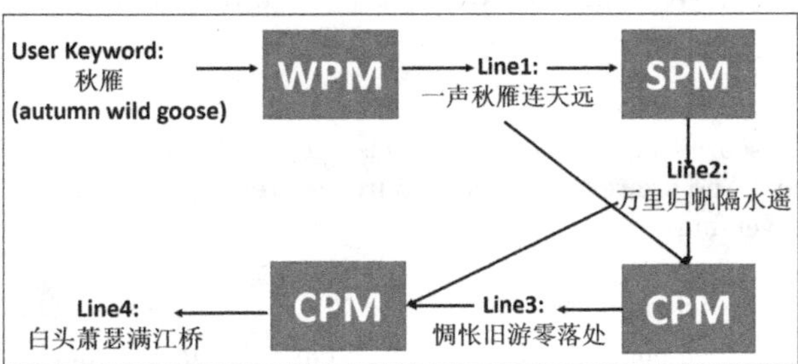

Fig. 6. An illustration of poem generation process with the keyword "秋雁" as input.

As illustrated in Fig. 6, the user inputs a keyword to show the main content and emotion the poem should convey. Firstly, WPM generates the first sentence relevant to the keyword. Then SPM takes the first sentence as input and generates the relevant second sentence. CPM generates the third sentence with the first two sentences as input. Finally, CPM takes the second and third sentences as input and generates the last sentence.

We train the model and generate poems based on Chinese characters, since there are no effective segmentation tools for Ancient Chinese. Fortunately, the length of Chinese classical poem sentences is fixed five or seven characters. And most words in Chinese classical poetry consist of one or two Chinese characters. Therefore, this method is feasible.

5 Experiments

5.1 Data and Settings

Our corpus contains 398,391 poems from Tang Dynasty to the contemporary. We extracted three pairs from each quatrain to train SPM, and extracted two pairs from each quatrain to train CPM. For training WPM, we selected 3000 words, and for each word we got 150 sentences which the word appears in. Finally we obtained 450,000 word-to-sentence pairs (half are 5-char and the other half are 7-char). We built our system based on GroundHog.[1]

5.2 Evaluation Design

BLEU Score Evaluation. Referring to He [4] and Zhang [13], we used BLEU-2 score to evaluate our model automatically. Since most words in Chinese classical poetry consist of one or two characters, BLEU-2 is effective. It's hard to obtain human-authored references for poetry so we used the method in [4] to extract references automatically. We first selected 4,400 quatrains from corpus (2,200 of them are 5-char and other 2,200 are 7-char) and extracted 20 references for each sentence in a quatrain (except the first sentence). Then the left quatrains are used as training set. We compared our SPM (with different strategies) with the system in [4].

Table 1. BLEU-2 scores on quatrains. SPM0 is the structure without reversing source or target sentences. And src reverse means source sentence reversing; trg reverse means target sentence reversing.

Models	Sentence2		Sentence3		Sentence4		Average	
	5-char	7-char	5-char	7-char	5-char	7-char	5-char	7-char
SMT	0.526	0.406	0.262	0.214	0.432	0.314	0.407	0.311
SPM0	0.773	0.956	0.478	0.728	0.831	1.450	0.694	1.045
SPM0 + src reverse	0.739	1.048	0.671	1.049	0.876	1.453	0.762	1.183
SPM0 + trg reverse	**1.126**	**1.900**	**1.251**	**1.441**	**1.387**	**2.306**	**1.255**	**1.882**

[1] https://github.com/lisa-groundhog/GroundHog.

Table 2. Human evaluation results. The Kappa coefficient of the two groups' scores is 0.62.

Models	Fluency		Coherence		Meaningfulness		Poeticness		Entirety	
	5-char	7-char	5-char	7-char	5-char	7-char	5-char	7-char	5-char	7-char
SMT	1.65	1.56	1.52	1.48	1.42	1.33	1.69	1.56	1.48	1.42
DX	2.53	2.33	2.19	1.96	2.31	2.00	2.52	2.31	2.29	2.08
PG	3.75	3.92	3.42	3.48	3.50	3.50	3.50	3.67	3.60	3.67
Human	3.92	3.96	3.81	4.10	4.08	4.13	3.75	4.02	3.96	4.21

Human Evaluation. Since poetry is a kind of creative text, human evaluation is necessary. Referring to the three criteria in [7], we designed five criteria: Fluency (are the sentences fluent and well-formed?), Coherence (does the quatrain has consistent topic across four sentences?), Meaningfulness (does the poem convey some certain messages?), Poeticness (does the poem have poetic features?), Entirety (the reader's general impression on the poem). Each criterion was scored from 0 to 5.

We evaluated four systems. **PG**, our system. **SMT**, He's system [4].[2] **DX**, the DaoXiang Poem Creator.[3] DX system is the pioneer for Chinese classical poetry generation. It has been developed for 15 years and been used over one hundred million times. **Human**, the poems of famous ancients poets containing the given keywords.

We selected 24 typical keywords and generated two quatrains (5-char and 7-char) for each keyword using the four systems. By this means, we obtained 192 quatrain (24*4*2) in total. We invited 16 experts on Chinese classical poetry to evaluate these quatrains. Each expert evaluated 24 quatrains. The 16 experts were divided into two groups and each group completed the assessments of the 192 poems. Thus we got two scores for each quatrain and used the average score.

5.3 Evaluation Results

Table 1 shows the BLEU-2 scores. Because DX system generates poetry as a whole, we only compared our system with SMT on single sentence generation task. In Chinese classical poetry, the relevance between two sentences in a pair is related to the position. Therefore He et al. [4] use pairs in different positions to train corresponding position-sensitive models. Because of the limited training data, we used pairs in all positions to train SPM. Even so, we got much higher BLEU scores than SMT in all positions. Moreover, 95% of the sentences generated by our system obey tonal constraints, but only 31% of SMT's outputs obey the constraints.

We can also see that reversing source sentences made a little change while reversing target sentences led to great improvement.

[2] http://duilian.msra.cn/jueju/.
[3] http://www.poeming.com/web/index.htm.

As shown in Table 2, our system got higher scores than other systems, expect the Human. For SMT and DX, the scores of 7-char poems are lower than that of 5-char poems in all criteria (both in Human evaluation and BLEU evaluation) because the composition of 7-char quatrains is more difficult. But the poems generated by PG got higher scores on 7-char poems, benefiting from gated units and attention mechanism. Scores of PG is closed to that of Human, though there is still a gap.

We also asked the experts to select a best sentence from the evaluated quatrains. 37% of the selected 5-char sentences are our system's and 42% are poets'. And 45% of the selected 7-char sentences are our system's, 45% are poets'. This indicates that our system has little difference with poets in generating meaningful sentences at least. More poems generated by our system are shown in Fig. 7.

梦断中秋月，
When I woke up from the dream suddenly, I saw the mid-autumn moon.
天寒咽暮蝉。
It was too cold for the cicadas to sing in the evening.
不堪送归客，
I couldn't bear the pain of seeing my friends off.
寂寞对床眠。
The only thing I could do was trying to fall asleep with loneliness.

谁怜两地中秋月，
Who will feel sympathy for the separated us? Only the autumn moon will.
独照西窗一夜凉。
The moonlight through the window is so lonely on the cold night.
行到故园应怅望，
Maybe your are overlooking and trying to find where I am in the distance.
哀词遗恨满潇湘。
While I can only put my missing and sadness in my poems, and let the melancholy fill the Xiao River and the Xiang River.

Fig. 7. Another two poems generated by our system with keyword "秋月" (autumn moon).

6 Conclusion and Future Work

In this paper, we take the generation of poem sentences as a sequence-to-sequence learning problem, and build a novel system to generate quatrains based on RNN Encoder-Decoder. Compared with other methods, our system can jointly learn semantic meanings, semantic relevance, and the use of rhythmical and tonal patterns. Both automatic and human evaluations show that our system outperforms other systems.

We show that RNN Encoder-Decoder is also suitable for the learning tasks on semantically relevant sequences. The attention mechanism can capture character associations, and gated units can recognize word boundaries roughly. Moreover, reversing target sentences in training will lead to better performance.

There are lots to do for our system in the future. We will improve our system to generate other types of Chinese poetry, such as Songci and Yuefu. We also hope our work could be helpful to other related work, such as the building of poetry retrieval system and literature researches.

References

1. Bahdanau, D., Cho, K., Bengio, Y.: Neural machine translation by jointly learning to align and translate. In: Proceedings of the 2015 International Conference on Learning Representations, San Diego, CA (2015)
2. Cho, K., Merriënboer, B., Gulcehre, C., Bahdanau, D., Bougares, F., Schwenk, H., Bengio, Y.: Learning phrase representations using RNN encoder–decoder for statistical machine translation. In: Proceedings of the 2014 Conference on Empirical Methods in Natural Language Processing, Doha, Qatar, pp. 1724–1734 (2014)
3. Gervás, P.: An expert system for the composition of formal Spanish poetry. In: Macintosh, A., Moulton, M., Coenen, F. (eds.) Applications and Innovations in Intelligent Systems VIII, pp. 19–32. Springer, London (2001). doi:10.1007/978-1-4471-0275-5_2
4. He, J., Zhou, M., Jiang, L.: Generating chinese classical poems with statistical machine translation models. In: Proceedings of the 26th AAAI Conference on Artificial Intelligence, Toronto, Canada, pp. 1650–1656 (2012)
5. Jiang, L., Zhou, M.: Generating chinese couplets using a statistical MT approach. In: Proceedings of the 22nd International Conference on Computational Linguistics, Manchester, UK, pp. 377–384 (2008)
6. Levy, R.P.: A computational model of poetic creativity with neural network as measure of adaptive fitness. In: Proceedings of the ICCBR-01 Workshop on Creative Systems (2001)
7. Manurung, H.M.: An evolutionary algorithm approach to poetry generation. Ph.D. thesis, University of Edinburgh (2003)
8. Sun, Z.: Three hundred Poems of the Tang Dynasty (《唐诗三百首》) (1764)
9. Sutskever, I., Vinyals, O., Le, Q.V.: Sequence to sequence learning with neural networks. Adv. Neural Inf. Process. Syst. **4**, 3104–3112 (2014)
10. van der Maaten, L.: Barnes-hut-SNE. In: Proceedings of the First International Conference on Learning Representations (ICLR 2013), Scottsdale, Arizona (2013)
11. Wu, X., Tosa, N., Nakatsu, R.: New hitch haiku: an interactive renku poem composition supporting tool applied for sightseeing navigation system. In: Proceedings of the 8th International Conference on Entertainment Computing, Paris, France, pp. 191–196 (2009)
12. Yan, R., Jiang, H., Lapata, M., Lin, S.-D., Lv, X., Li, X.: I, poet: automatic chinese poetry composition through a generative summarization framework under constrained optimization. In: Proceedings of the 23rd International Joint Conference on Artificial Intelligence, Beijing, China, pp. 2197–2203 (2013)
13. Zhang, X., Lapata, M.: Chinese poetry generation with recurrent neural networks. In: Proceedings of the 2014 Conference on Empirical Methods in Natural Language Processing, Doha, Qatar, pp. 670–680 (2014)

Collaborative Recognition and Recovery of the Chinese Intercept Abbreviation

Jinshuo Liu[1], Yusen Chen[1], Juan Deng[2](✉), Donghong Ji[1], and Jeff Pan[3]

[1] Computer School, Wuhan University, Wuhan 430072, China
[2] International School of Software, Wuhan University, Wuhan 430072, China
dengjuan@whu.edu.cn
[3] University of Aberdeen, Aberdeen AB24 3FX, UK

Abstract. One of the important works of Information Content Security is evaluating the theme words of the text. Because of the variety of the Chinese expression, especially of the abbreviation, the supervision of the theme words becomes harder. The goal of this paper is to quickly and accurately discover the intercept abbreviations from the text crawled at the short time period. The paper firstly segments the target texts, and then utilizes the Supported Vector Machine (SVM) to recognize the abbreviations from the wrongly segmented texts as the candidates. Secondly, this paper presents the collaborative methods: Improve the Conditional Random Fields (CRF) to predict the corresponding word to each character of the abbreviation; To solve the problems of the 1:n relationship, collaboratively merge the ranking list from the predict steps with the matched results of the thesaurus of abbreviations. The experiments demonstrate that our method at the recognizing stage is 76.5% of the accuracy and 77.8% of the recall rate. At the recovery step, the accuracy is 62.1%, which is 20.8% higher than the method based on Hidden Markov Model (HMM).

Keywords: Collaborative recovery · Improved CRF · Chinese abbreviation

1 Introduction

The most important information content security supervision methods is to match the sensitive words and rules of the text, which needs to manually or semi- automated build up the corpus and the thesaurus of rules. There are 2 challenging tasks for supervision. ① To avoid the supervision and management, the theme words or kernel phrases are sometimes substituted by the abbreviation, which cannot be found through preprocessing of the data. ② The manually built up corpus although is accurate, but needs to be continuously updated. So it is another tough job to quickly automated update the corpus via recognizing the recovering the related phrases from the relatively texts crawled in a short time.

This paper is supported by National Science Foundation of China (NOs.61672393, U1536204).

M. Sun et al. (Eds.): CCL 2017 and NLP-NABD 2017, LNAI 10565, pp. 224–236, 2017.
https://doi.org/10.1007/978-3-319-69005-6_19

The abbreviation is one of the most important forms to substitute the original phrases. So the recognition and recovery of the abbreviation is very important to public supervision. Because of the complexity of the Chinese and difference with English, the research for Chinese abbreviation is hard.

Chinese abbreviation means intercepting, abridging, concluding, changing the order of the original length of word without changing the meaning [1]. There are three type of abbreviation, intercept abbreviation, abridged abbreviation and concluding abbreviation. The intercept abbreviation only keeps the kernel morphemes to represent the original phrase. For example, "北大" (BěiDà) means the "北京大学" (Beijing University), which is the most important ways to avoid the supervision.

This paper is to quickly and accurately discover the intercept abbreviations from the texts crawled in the short time period. The paper firstly recognizes the abbreviations via SVM from the wrongly segmented texts. Secondly, this paper presents the collaborative recovery methods of the abbreviation. Predict the corresponding word to each character of the abbreviation with the improved CRF. The abbreviation—originate lookup table can also be updated finally.

The structure of the paper is listed as followings: Part 1 introduces the challenges of the Chinese abbreviation for network security. Part 2 is the related research work. Part 3 is our main methods. Part 4 introduces the experiments including performance experiments and comparison experiments. Part 5 is the conclusion.

2 Related Works

The recognition and recovery of abbreviations cannot be separated from the study of informal words because the abbreviations account for about 20% of informal words [2].

In study of the informal word recognition, Wang et al. [2] employ a factorial conditional random field to model both tasks of informal word recognition and Chinese word segmentation jointly. Besides that, Wang et al. [3] also use a large-scale corpus to select the formal equivalents of informal words according to context semantic similarity, and then formalize the task of informal word recovery as a binary classification problem. This method is feasible but can't achieve a rather high accuracy. Li et al. [4] classify the words into three classes: IV (in-vocabulary) correct-OOV (out-of-vocabulary) and ill-OOV, and proposed a non-standard word detection method based on the maximum entropy classifier. Monroe et al. [5] extend an existing Modern Standard Arabic segmenter with a simple domain adaptation technique and new features in order to segment informal and dialectal Arabic text.

For the recovery of abbreviation, Chang et al. [7] consider the original word is in a hidden state. And they map this problem to a HMM. Although, this method has a good result in intercepted abbreviations, it doesn't utilize the contextual features well. Roack et al. [8] focus on abbreviation recovery for text-to-speech synthesis and they use an n-gram model and SVM model to classify the candidate expansion of the abbreviation.

In study of the abbreviation prediction, Yan Jiao et al. [9] use conditional random field to generate a number of candidates, then they re-score the candidates according to the results from web search engine. And the one with the highest score is selected as the abbreviation. Kailong Zhang et al. [10] introduce the minimum semantic unit to capture word level information based on the CRF and use an integer linear programming formulation to recode the abbreviation from the generated candidates. Besides that, they also propose a two-stage method [11] to find the corresponding abbreviation. First they use a large scale corpus to generate candidates and get a coarse-grained ranking through graph random walk. Then re-rank the candidates according to the feature. Chen H et al. [12] propose a novel abbreviation generation method using first-order logic and markov logic network frameworks. Yangyang shi et al. [13] use a RNN model with maximum entropy extension in abbreviation prediction and generation.

All approach mentioned above builds on an important part: generate an abbreviation lookup table. Although this method can build a corpus quickly and efficiently, it may have high false detection rate for the reason of abbreviations' ambiguity.

3 Collaborative Recognition and Recovery

The paper devises three stages for recognizing and recovering the Chinese Abbreviation: pre-process, recognition and recovery. The framework of our method is listed as Fig. 1.

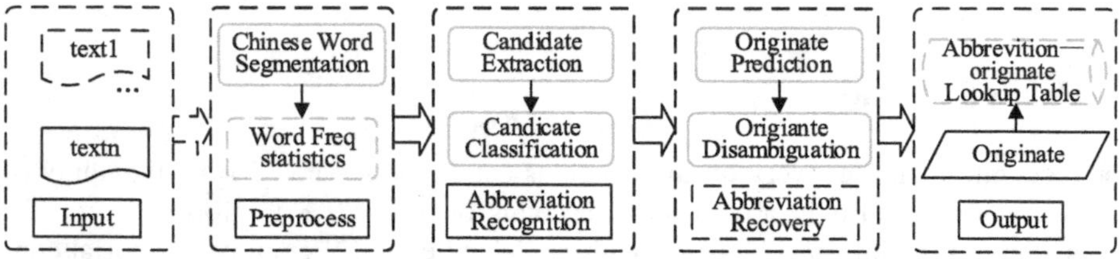

Fig. 1. The framework of abbreviation collaborative recognition and recovery

Preprocess. The text need to be segmented into a word sequence. As the unlogged words, abbreviations cannot be correctly segmented, but be left as the text slices or wrongly cut into 1-gram sequences.

Recognition. This paper selects the 1-gram sequences or long text slice as the candidate abbreviations and utilizes the information and context of the abbreviation as the features. The abbreviation can be classified into 2 sets, 'yes' or 'no', using SVM. 'yes' is the true abbreviations.

Recovery. This paper converts the problem of recovering the abbreviation into the prediction of each character. The traditional abbreviation-originate lookup table is utilized to assist in the originate disambiguation. The final originates are gotten through the the cosine similarity computation of candidate originates.

3.1 Rule and Context Based Abbreviation Recognition

This paper utilizes two filtering stage for recognizing the abbreviations. The first stage extracts the candidate abbreviations from the unlogged text slices. The second stage uses the SVM classifier to classify the candidates into two classes according to the features of rules and context. (Shown as Fig. 2)

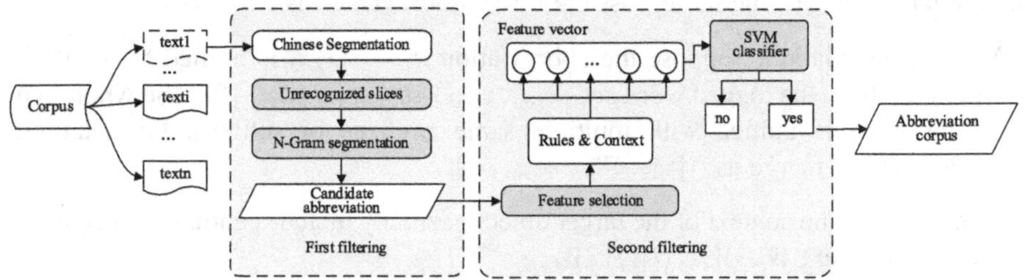

Fig. 2. Rule and context based recognition of abbreviation

Extraction of the unrecognized slices. Abbreviation as the unlogged words cannot be correctly segmented finely as the word sequences. After preprocessing the corpus, select the incorrectly segmented slices or consecutive unigram as the candidate abbreviation.

N-gram segmentation. Normally speaking, the abbreviation is 2 to 4 characters long. The ratio of length of abbreviation over 4 is very small. The single character abbreviation basically represents the capital in Chinese. So this paper utilizes the 2–4 characters long abbreviations as our candidates. Since the initial candidates normally are long, and need to be segmented further, we use the N-gram segmentation method to segment the candidates, and select 2 or 4 words as the final candidates. For example, "计生委" as the coarse candidate, and further segmented as "计生", ""生委"" and "计生委"。

Feature selection. This paper selects following three types of features:

Information feature. Define the abbreviation $x_1^n = x_1x_2...x_n$ as the sequences with length n, $2 \leq n \leq 4$.

- *Length m.* According to the statics, the proportion of bi-gram type is 55%, tri-gram is also normal, and quad-gram is the least. So we set the length as one feature.
- *Number.* numbers and the positions of them are also import discriminate features in Chinese. Normally speaking, number is very important to record the related words in the abbreviation. For example, "二" (second) of "第二次世界大战" (the Second World War) is so important, and is kept as "二战".
- *Prefix and suffix.* In the abbreviations, some Chinese characters are used as the start and end of the abbreviations. For examples, "局" is the end of the abbreviation such as "国安局" etc. We utilize the prefix and suffix with frequency as features and represented as 'word bag model'.
- *The probability of the positions* $\mathrm{P_{pos}}\left(\mathrm{x_1^n}\right)$.

$$P_{pos}(x_1^n) = \prod\nolimits_{x \in X} P(pos, x) \tag{1}$$

Where $P(pos, x)$ is the probability vector of character x at position pos. We limit the the value of pos to begin, middle and end. In Chinese, some characters "局、会、部" often appear at the end of the abbreviations. Some characters such as "中、北、东" often appear at the start or the middle of the abbreviations. So the higher one unpredicted abbreviation is, the more possible a real abbreviation is.

- Morph-abbreviation. Suppose the abbreviation $x_1^3 = x_1x_2x_3$ is unified by x_1, x_2, x_3, which are from the logged word set $\{x_1x_2, x_1x_3\}$ or $\{x_1x_3, x_2x_3\}$ [9]. The whole type of the word is unified with multiple same prefixes or suffixes. For example, "中医、西医" merge as "中西医".

Context feature. The context of the target object normally includes enough information. Define the slice text $W_{i-2}W_{i-1}x_1^nW_{i+1}W_{i+2}$.

- *The frequency of the abbreviation tf.* If an abbreviation is a real abbreviation, then the occurrence of them is definitely higher than other candidates.
- *Bigram information entropy.* The entropy of the bigram information entropy is represented by:

$$BH2(x_1^n) = -\sum\nolimits_{w \in W} \frac{C(w, x_1^n)}{n_c} \log \frac{C(w, x_1^n)}{n_c} \tag{2}$$

Where n_c is the occurrence of thé abbreviation x_1^n, W is the left or right word set of x_1^n , $C(w, x_1^n)$ is the co-occurrence of word w and x_1^n. The left and right entropy of the words evaluate the frequency of the left and right words. [14] The entropy can be bigger and bigger with the frequency of the combination of the words get higher and higher.

- *Tri-gram information entropy.* It is the information entropy of combination words, $W_{i-2}W_{i-1}x_1^n$, $W_{i-1}x_1^nW_{i+1}$ and $x_1^nW_{i+1}W_{i+2}$

Global features. The higher global information a candidate abbreviation holds, the more possible a real abbreviation is.

- *Frequency of the abbreviation in the corpus tfc.*
- *The number of the text containing the abbreviation idf.*

Classifier. We choose the Support Vector Machine (SVM). SVM is based on the least risk and more suitable for small sample set. Since the abbreviation is sparse with small training set.

3.2 Multi-Label Sparse Conditional Random Field Based Recovery

After the abbreviation has been recognized, we need to recover it to the corresponding originate. Using the feature that the abbreviations and originates have the 1:1 mapping relationship, we convert the problem of recovering the abbreviation into the prediction of each character and achieve the word-sequence prediction based on multi-label sparse conditional random field (SCRF). If the probability of all prediction results are low, we obtain the matched originate from the abbreviation-originate lookup table and put it together with the predicted originates as originate candidates. All candidates is ranked through the cosine similarities to obtain the final originate that is best for the current context to achieve the abbreviation disambiguation. Finally, record the new originates to extend the lookup table. The concrete process is shown in Fig. 3.

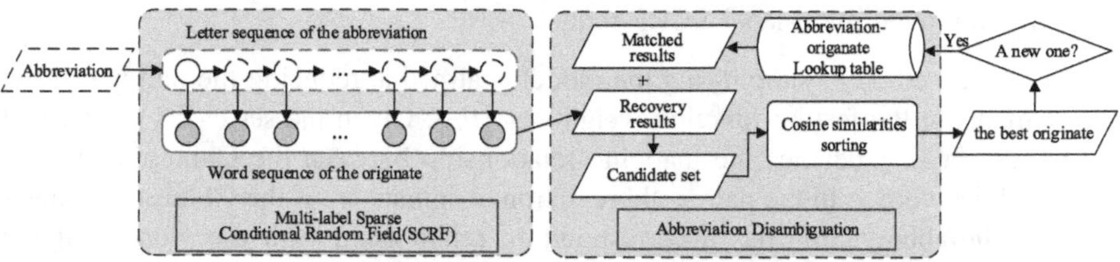

Fig. 3. The abbreviation recovery based on multi-label sparse conditional random field

Multi-label sparse conditional random field. This paper adopts the linear chain conditional random field model to achieve the abbreviation recovery. Take the abbreviation sequence x_1^n as the input sequence, and $x_i \in X$ is the Chinese character set. Take the originate sequence y_1^n as the output sequence, and $y_i \in Y$ is the word set. The conditional probability distribution $P(y_1^n|x_1^n)$ of the sequence y_1^n constitutes the conditional random field which satisfies Markov property

$$P(y_i|x_1^n, y_1, y_2 \ldots y_n) = P(y_i|x_1^n, y_{i-1}, y_{i+1}) \tag{3}$$

Then we call $P(y_1^n|x_1^n)$ the linear chain conditional random field. Under the given input sequence x_1^n, the conditional probability distribution of the output sequence y_1^n is as follows:

$$P(y_1^n|x_1^n) = \frac{1}{Z(x_1^n)} exp\left(\sum_{t=1}^{n} \sum_{k=1}^{K} \theta_k f_k(y_{t-1}, y_t, x_t,)\right) \tag{4}$$

$$Z(x_1^n) = \sum_y exp\left(\sum_{t=1}^{n} \sum_{k=1}^{K} \theta_k f_k(y_{t-1}, y_t, x_t,)\right) \tag{5}$$

In above formulas, f_k is the feature function, θ_k is the corresponding weight, and $Z(x_1^n)$ is the normalization factor. From the Formula (4), we can see that the number of the feature function is related to the state set X and the label set Y, and the parameter K satisfies the equation:

$$K = |Y|^2 \times |X|_{train} \tag{6}$$

$|X|_{train}$ denotes the number of all Chinese characters of the abbreviations in the training set, and $|Y|$ is the number of all words of the corresponding originates. It is obvious that X and Y contain a large number of elements, so the scale of the feature function set $\{f_k\}$ will be extremely large, which makes the learning difficulty of the CRF model grow exponentially.

This paper adopts a series of methods to simplify the model learning process, the main goal of which is to reduce the scale of the feature weight set $\{\theta_k\}$ and then to obtain the improved multi-label SCRF model.

(1) The first method of simplifying the model is aimed at reducing the number of the elements in the feature function weight set $\{\theta_k\}$. Given the set $\phi(x,y) \in M$, and $\phi(x,y) : x \rightarrow y$ denotes the mapping relationship between the Chinese character x and the word y. In the pair < abbreviation, originate > , if the Chinese character x of the abbreviation has a corresponding relationship with the word y of the originate, then the mapping relationship $\phi(x,y)$ holds. It is easy to know that after a Chinese character in the abbreviation set is recovered, the corresponding word set Y_x only contains a few words and there is no relations between the other words in the set Y. Therefore, given $x \in X$ and $y \in Y$, if there is no mapping relationship between x and y in the training set, then the features of x and y will be ignored which is achieved by setting the corresponding feature weights as $-\infty$, as shown in Formula (7).

$$\theta_k(y_i, x_j, i) = -\infty, \theta_k(y_i, x_j, i) \in \{\theta_k\}, s.t. \phi(x,y) \notin M \tag{7}$$

(2) The second method of simplifying the model is aimed at reducing the computational complexity of the model learning. This paper adopts the regularization term ℓ_1 to enhance the sparse degree of the model. This method tends to create less but more useful features in the model and lets most of the feature weights be zero, which will reduce the memory usage and optimize the forward-backward calculation in the model, and it greatly simplifies the model learning process to some degree.

Therefore, this paper takes the improved SCRF model as the abbreviation recovery method at last, and adopts the block-coordinate descent method [17] to achieve the model learning process.

Feature Selection. This paper selects features according to the related information of each Chinese character of abbreviations when recovering the abbreviations. If the abbreviation sequence $x_1^n = x_1 x_2 \ldots x_n$ is given, and x_i denotes the ith Chinese character of the abbreviation, then the selected features are as follows:

- *The Chinese character and Chinese phonetic alphabet of* x_i *and* x_{i-1}. The pronunciation of the Chinese character is related to its corresponding originate, which means that the Chinese character in the corresponding word has the same pronunciation as the original Chinese character in the abbreviation. For example, in the abbreviation “中行” (BOC) and in its corresponding originate “中国银行” (BANK OF CHINA), the two “行”s have the same pronunciation “háng” in the Chinese phonetic alphabet.

- *The word with the highest frequency in all short words that contain the Chinese character x_i in the text, its length and phonetic alphabet.* An abbreviation can be recovered to several different originates under different contexts. For example, the abbreviation “南大” (NU) can be recovered to “南京大学” (Nanjing University) and “南昌大学” (Nanchang University). It's found in researches that as for this kind of abbreviations, the corresponding word of the polysemantic Chinese character tends to appear in the context several times to help readers disambiguate, and its word frequency is higher than other words that contain the same Chinese character.
- *Whether x_i and x_{i-1} is a number or not.*
- *Morph-abbreviation.*

Abbreviation Disambiguation. There is a one-to-many relationship between the abbreviations and corresponding originates. Sometimes all the prediction results have a lower probability than 0.6, which means the best originate may be not in the prediction results. In this case, this paper chooses the top five originates with the highest prediction probabilities as the recovery candidate set. At the same time, according to the abbreviation-originate lookup table, we obtain the matching candidate set by matching the abbreviation in the lookup table. All the candidate originates will be evaluated according to the cosine similarity of context. We choose the sentence of the target abbreviation as context of candidate originates. The originate with highest score is the best result. Finally, add the new corresponding relationship to the dictionary, which automatically extends the dictionary. The calculation method of the cosine similarity is as follows:

$$\cos(context1, context2) = \frac{\sum_{i=1}^{n} c_{1i} \times c_{2i}}{\sqrt{\sum_{i=1}^{n} c_{1i}^2} \times \sqrt{\sum_{i=1}^{n} c_{2i}^2}} \quad (8)$$

4 Experiment and Analysis

4.1 Dataset

Abbreviations dataset. The abbreviated dataset used in this paper is mainly obtained in three ways, the Institute of Computational Linguistics, Peking University[1], Baidu Encyclopedia and the microblogging corpus.

We get an abbreviation-originate lookup table which includes 14372 pairs of abbreviations-originate. Table 1 represents the proportion of each type of abbreviations and we choose the intercepting abbreviation as the dataset for this experiment.

[1] http://www.icl.pku.edu.cn/icl_groups/corpus/.

Table 1. Comparison of the abbreviations of each category

	Intercepting	Abridging	Concluding
PKU	5846	1679	634
Baidu	3527	1034	355
Microblog	985	234	78

Corpus dataset. In this paper, we select about 20000 documents containing abbreviations from the text classification corpus released by Sogou Lab[2] as the corpus dataset of our experiment.

4.2 Experiment Setup

Experiment 1: Performance experiment.
We divide the procedure of Chinese abbreviations into two problems, the recognition and the recovery of abbreviations, and perform two independent performance experiments.
Abbreviation recognition. This paper uses the NLPIR[3] tokenizer of the Chinese Academy of Science to implement the Chinese word segmentation. We selected the decision tree (DT) model, the logical regression (LR) model and the support vector machine (SVM) model as the binary classifier and use 10-fold cross validation to train the abbreviated recognition model.

Abbreviation recovery. Experiment preprocesses about 10,000 pairs of abbreviations – originates, which form a 1-to-1 word mapping for each character in the abbreviation. In the stage of feature extraction, because the eigenvalue of CRF can only be discrete, we use the equal frequency method to discretize the continuous eigenvalue. Finally, 10-fold cross validation is used in the training of the abbreviated recovery model.

Experiment 2: Comparison experiment.
To validate the universal property of our model, we compare our abbreviation recovery method based on the sparse condition random field with the abbreviation recovery method based on the hidden Markov model [7]. We implement two methods and conduct the comparison experiment over the same dataset.

4.3 Results

4.3.1 Performance Experiment

The performance of the abbreviation recognition algorithm and the abbreviation recovery algorithm are verified respectively.

[2] http://www.sogou.com/labs/resource/.

[3] NLPIR: http://ictclas.nlpir.org/.

Abbreviations recognition method performance experiments
The DT, LR and SVM are compared shown in Table 2. To validate different kernel functions in SVM model, the Linear, POLY and RBF kernel are also compared. The experimental results of the different kernel functions are shown in Table 3.

Table 2. The experimental results of different classifiers in abbreviation identification methods

Classifier	Precision	Recall	F-value
DT	0.738	0.748	0.743
LR	0.734	0.769	0.751
SVM	**0.765**	**0.778**	**0.771**

Table 3. The experimental results of different kernel functions in SVM model

Kernel	Precision	Recall	F-value
Linear	0.761	0.771	0.766
Polynomial	0.758	0.766	0.762
RBF	**0.765**	**0.778**	**0.771**

It can be seen from Table 2 that the SVM model has a better effect than the LR model and the DT model. SVM model has higher improvement in precision than the other two models, but the LR model is similar to SVM model in recall rate and F value. In addition, it can be seen from Table 3 that although the SVM model with RBF kernel has higher precision, the SVM model with linear kernel is similar in precision to the other two kernel functions. Considering the data factors, the three kernel functions are not much different in terms of performance, which may be related to the higher feature dimension of the experiment.

Abbreviations recognition method performance experiments
We divide the selected features into basic and extended features. The basic feature is all the features except the phonetic symbols in Sect. 3. The extended feature is the phonetic alphabet of each Chinese character in the abbreviation. The experimental results are shown in Table 4. Top-n indicates whether the correct results are included in the first n most likely results of the selected model.

As can be seen from Table 4, the precision of the CRF model using basic features has been relatively high. In the basic features of the combination of expansion features for the precision has no significant improvement. This paper consider the expansion features because the Chinese characters have multiple pronunciations in different words, which will affect the meanings of the words. Therefore, we believe that the phonetic feature can improve the prediction ability of CRF model. Experiments show that the expansion feature of the abbreviation does a little help. We consider that the above situation may have a lower probability of appearing in the abbreviation dataset.

Table 4. The results of abbreviations recovery experiments based on improved CRF

Features	Top-N	Precision
basic features	1	0.617
	2	0.688
	all	0.934
basic features + extended features	1	**0.621**
	2	**0.691**
	all	**0.934**

4.3.2 Comparison Experiments Results

The result of the comparative experiment on two abbreviation recovery method is shown in Table 5.

Table 5. The result of the comparison between HMM method and CRF method

Model	Top-N	Precision
CRF	1	**0.621**
	2	**0.691**
	all	**0.934**
HMM	1	0.413
	2	0.525
	all	0.886

From Table 5, we can see that the HMM-based abbreviation recovery method has similar performance to CRF on Top-all results, but is significantly worse in Top-1 and Top-2 than the proposed method in this paper. Since the abbreviations have a one-to-many mapping relationship, and the same abbreviations in different documents may express different meanings. While the HMM method does not consider the current context of the abbreviations for each word when the word is recovered. Thus, for abbreviations with different contexts, predicted result using the HMM-based abbreviation recovery method is always the similar. Experiments show that the proposed recovery algorithm based on improved CRF in this paper can obtain more stable results than the comparative test method in different situations.

5 Conclusion

In order to solve the challenging problem of network supervision, the theme word substituted by abbreviation, this paper proposes a collaborative recognition and recovery method of intercept abbreviations. Firstly preprocess the texts by segmentation, and then further cut the incorrectly segmented texts, to get the candidate abbreviations. Secondly, use SVM to determine the candidate abbreviations with the devised statistic features. Thirdly, at recovery stage, use our improved CRF and statistic features of Chinese abbreviation to finally infer the corresponding originates. The experiments demonstrate that our model is effective and can get better results compared with other methods.

Our method can be used at other Chinese text content security analysis either. For example, improve the Chinese segmentation tool, automated update the vocabulary of the segmentation tool etc. In the future, we will try to improve the model to recognize and recover the abridged and concluded abbreviations.

References

1. Wang, H.F.: Survey: abbreviation processing in chinese text. J. Chin. Inf. Process. **25**(5), 60–67 (2011)
2. Wang, A.: Mining informal language from chinese microtext: joint word recognition and segmentation. In: Proceedings of the 51st Annual Meeting of the Association for Computational Linguistics, pp. 731–741. ACL, Sofia (2013)
3. Wang, A.: Chinese informal word normalization: an experimental study. In: The 6th International Joint Conference on Natural Language Processing (IJCNLP), pp. 127–135. ACL, Nagoya (2013)
4. Li, C.: Improving named entity recognition in tweets via detecting non-standard words. In: Proceedings of the 53rd Annual Meeting of the Association for Computational Linguistics, pp. 929–938. ACL, Beijing (2015)
5. Monroe, W.: Word segmentation of informal arabic with domain adaptation. In: Proceedings of the 52nd Annual Meeting of the Association for Computational Linguistics, pp. 206–211. ACL, Baltimore (2014)
6. Barrena, A.: Alleviating poor context with background knowledge for named entity disambiguation. In: Proceedings of the 54th Annual Meeting of the Association for Computational Linguistics, pp. 1903–1912. ACL, Berlin (2016)
7. Chang, J.S.: A preliminary study on probabilistic models for chinese abbreviations. In: Proceedings of the 3rd SIGHAN workshop on Chinese language learning, pp. 9–16. ACL, Barcelona (2004)
8. Roark, B.: Hippocratic abbreviation expansion. In: Proceedings of the 52nd Annual Meeting of the Association for Computational Linguistics, pp. 364–369. ACL, Baltimore (2014)
9. Jiao, Y.: Abbreviation Prediction Using Conditional Random Field and Web Data. J. Chin. Inf. Process. **26**(2), 62–68 (2012)
10. Zhang, L.K.: Predicting chinese abbreviations with minimum semantic unit and global constraints. In: Proceedings of the 2014 Conference on Empirical Methods in Natural Language Processing (EMNLP), pp. 1405–1414. ACL, Doha (2014)
11. Zhang, L.K.: Coarse-grained candidate generation and fine-grained re-ranking for chinese abbreviation prediction. In: Proceedings of the 2014 Conference on Empirical Methods in Natural Language Processing (EMNLP), pp. 1881–1890. ACL, Doha (2014)
12. Chen, H.: Chinese named entity abbreviation generation using first-order logic. In: The 6th International Joint Conference on Natural Language Processing (IJCNLP), pp. 320–328. ACL, Nagoya (2013)
13. Shi, Y.Y.: Cluster based Chinese Abbreviation Modeling. In: 15th Annual Conference of the International Speech Communication Association, pp. 273–277. COLIPS, Singapore (2014)
14. Chen, F.: Open Domain New Word Detection Using Condition Random Field Method. Ruan Jian Xue Bao/J. Softw. **24**(5), 1051–1060 (2013)
15. Lavergne, T.: From n -gram-based to CRF-based translation models. In: Proceedings of the 6th Workshop on Statistical Machine Translation, pp. 542–553. ACL, Edinburgh (2011)

16. Tsuruoka, Y.: Stochastic gradient descent training for L1-regularized log-linear models with cumulative penalty. In: Proceedings of the 47th Annual Meeting of the ACL and the 4th IJCNLP of the AFNLP, pp. 477–485. AFNLP, Suntec (2009)
17. Sokolovska, N.: Efficient learning of sparse conditional random fields for supervised sequence labeling. IEEE J. Sel. Top. Sign. Process. **4**(6), 953–964 (2010)
18. Yin, Q.: A joint model for ellipsis identification and recovery. J. Comput. Res. Dev. **52**(11), 2460–2467 (2015)
19. Sun, X.: Learning abbreviations from chinese and english terms by modeling non-local information. ACM Trans. Asian Lang. Inf. Process. (TALIP) **12**(2), 5:1–5:17 (2013)
20. Kenyon-Dean, K.: Verb phrase ellipsis resolution using discriminative and margin-infused algorithms. In: Proceedings of the 2016 Conference on Empirical Methods in Natural Language Processing (EMNLP), pp. 1734–1743. ACL, Austin (2016)

Semantic Dependency Labeling of Chinese Noun Phrases Based on Semantic Lexicon

Yimeng Li, Yanqiu Shao(✉), and Hongkai Yang

Beijing Language and Culture University, Beijing 100083, China
liyimengblcu@126.com, yqshao163@163.com

Abstract. We have presented a simple algorithm to noun phrases interpretation based on hand-crafted knowledge-base containing detailed semantic information. The main idea is to define a set of relations that can hold between the words and use a semantic lexicon including semantic classifications and collocation features to automatically assign relations to noun phrases. We divide the NPs into two kinds of types: NPs with one verb or non-consecutive verbs and NPs with consecutive verbs, and design two different labeling methods according to their syntactic and semantic features. For the first kind of NPs we report high precision, recall and F-score on a dataset with nine semantic relations, and for the second type the results are also promising on a dataset with four relations. We create a valuable manually-annotated resource for noun phrases interpretation, which we make publicly available with the hope to inspire further research in noun phrases interpretation.

Keywords: Noun relations · Semantic dependency · Noun phrases

1 Introduction

The automatic semantic dependency analysis of complex noun phrases such as "饮料/n 质量/n 监督/v 抽查/v" (the supervision and spot check of beverage quality), "文化/n 展示/v 活动/v 开幕式/n" (the opening ceremony of cultural exhibition) and "商业/n 调查/v 统计/v 工作/v" (business investigation and statistical work) is a difficulty in different languages. However, an important step towards being able to ascertain sentence meaning is to analyze the meaning of such NPs more generally. This kind of NPs have three basic properties which pose difficulties for their interpretation: (1) the compounding process is extremely productive; (2) the semantic relationship between the head and its modifier is implicit; (3) the interpretation can be influenced by variety of contextual and pragmatic factors [1]. The problem becomes more complicated when there are more than one "verbs" in the nominalization such as "节能/v 监督/v 管理/v 工作/v" (supervision and management of energy-saving) which is a noun phrase but constituted of "verbs", because verbs and verb phrases in Chinese can be nominalized without overt marker for it.

Semantic Dependency Analysis is a kind of deep semantic analysis, which describes the relations that hold between each word in a sentence. Therefore, basically the semantic dependency analysis of NPs is to explore the semantic relations that hold between nouns or verbal nouns. Interpretation of noun compounds (NCs) is highly

M. Sun et al. (Eds.): CCL 2017 and NLP-NABD 2017, LNAI 10565, pp. 237–248, 2017.
https://doi.org/10.1007/978-3-319-69005-6_20

dependent on lexical information [2]. One of the theme of SemEval-2007 is the interpretation of nominalizations and the researches based on different methods prove the importance of lexical resources [3]. So we explore the possibility of using an existing hand-crafted semantic knowledge-base (SKCC, Semantic Knowledge-base of Contemporary Chinese) for the purpose of placing words from a noun phrase into categories, and using the semantic classifications and collocation features to determine the relations that hold between nouns. The introduction of the semantic knowledge-base is aimed to add knowledge to the interpretation of complex NPs, because the process is highly dependent on encyclopedic knowledge. Our goal is to extract propositional information from the NPs, so the NPs extracted for the present study consist of at least one verbal noun.

In the following sections we will discuss the characteristics of the semantic knowledge-base SKCC that is used for the classification of semantic relations, the method to determine the relations, the evaluation of the results and some conclusions.

2 Related Work

We focus on the methods that analyze semantic relations in noun phrases. Rosario and Hearst [4] use a machine learning algorithm and a domain-specific lexical hierarchy achieving more than 60% accuracy on a dataset with 16 semantic relations. Hearst and Fillmore [2] continue the study by placing the words from a two-word compound from biomedical domain into categories, and then using this category membership to determine the relations that hold between nouns, obtaining classification accuracy of approximately 90% on a dataset with 35 semantic relations. Girju and Moldovan [5] use machine learning tools such as SVM, semantic scattering to explore noun relations with attributes extracted from ComLex and VerbLex. It turns out that SVM achieves the highest accuracy of 72% on a dataset with 35 semantic relations. Nastase and Szpakowicz [6] use the machine learning tools such as decision trees, instance-based learning and Support Vector Machines, with attributes respectively extracted from WordNet and corpus. The F-measure reaches a maximum of 82.47% on a dataset with 5 semantic relations after the introduction of the WordNet word meaning. Tratz and Hovy [7] use Maximum Entropy Classifier and $\text{SVM}^{\text{multiclass}}$ to classify semantic relations between English noun compounds and obtain an accuracy of 79.3% and 79.4% respectively. Their dataset comprises 17509 compounds with a new taxonomy of 43 semantic relations. Dima and Hinrichs [8] use neutral network classifier implemented in the Torch7 scientific computing framework for the automatic classification of noun compound semantic relations. The F-measure reaches a maximum of 79.48% on a dataset with 12 semantic relations.

Lijie Wang [9] focuses on the automatic analysis of Chinese sentences using Graph-based algorithm combined with knowledge from dependency parsing. The experiment achieves an accuracy of 66.83% on a dataset with 19 semantic relations. Ding Yu [10] automatically labels Chinese sentences based on the dependency graph. On the basis of the results obtained from dependency tree, she uses SVM to construct the dependency graph and achieves an accuracy of 69.37% on a dataset with 32 relations.

3 The Semantic Classification: SKCC

The semantic interpretation of complex NPs requires a great deal of world knowledge, and semantic lexicon can provide a certain background knowledge for automatic semantic analysis. There are mainly two forms of semantic knowledge [11]: (1) category knowledge, which can be expressed in the form of "attribute: value". For example, the simple description of the semantic attribute of a word: [semantic class: food] or the description of the semantic relations between two or more words: {Agent [semantic class: people | animal]}; (2) rule- based knowledge, which can be described in the form of "condition - > action". If the semantic properties of a noun and the semantic requirements of a verb's object argument are consistent, then the noun and the verb can make a verb-argument structure. The above category knowledge, together with rule-based knowledge, can be used to explain the difference between "eating apples" and "eating circles" (unacceptable). The dictionary-based approach is designed to use the semantic category to determine the acceptability of phrases or sentences.

The Semantic Knowledge-base of Contemporary Chinese (SKCC) is a large scale of bilingual semantic resource developed by Chinese Department of Peking University. It provides quite amount of semantic information such as semantic classification and collocation features for 66539 Chinese words and their English counterparts [12, 13]. It has three dictionaries including noun, adjective and verb. Each dictionary is organized in hierarchy with respect to semantic classes. Nouns are divided into four general semantic classes: entity, abstraction, time and space, and each of the category is further divided into multiple subcategories. The noun dictionary has three components: the word, the part of speech and the semantic class. For example: "金属" (metal), (metal, n, material). The verb dictionary is a six-point group: the word, the part of speech, the semantic class, the argument quantity, the subject and the object. For example the verb "切削" (cut), (cut, v, body function, 2, person, entity). Here is an example for analyzing, "金属/n 切削/v 机床/n" (metal cutting machine tool). Firstly we respectively map the words of the NP into the noun and verb dictionary, and then match the semantic class of "金属" (metal) to that of the subject and object of "切削" (cut). It turns out that "金属" (metal) could be an object of "切削" (cut), because the semantic class of "金属" (metal), i.e., "material" is a hyponym of the object of "切削" (cut), i.e., "entity". The specific semantic label will be further determined according to the semantic classes of the nouns and verbs. The method will be elaborated in Sect. 4.

4 Method and Evaluation

4.1 The Dataset of NPs

In the paper, we divide the noun phrases into two types: NPs with one verb (verbal noun) or non-consecutive verbs and NPs with consecutive verbs. The dataset for the study of noun phrases with one verb or non-consecutive verbs consists of 1035 noun phrases, and the one for NPs with consecutive verbs consists of 525 noun phrases. These NPs are automatically extracted from BLCU-HIT Semantic Dependency Graph Bank and Dynamic Circulation Corpus (DCC) and then checked manually. We run a part-of-speech tagger on LTP (Language Technology Platform) and a program that extracts only sequences of units tagged as nouns and verbs. The data are further inspected manually to create a dataset of only NPs.

4.2 Labeling NPs with One "Verb" of Non-consecutive "Verbs"

Firstly we will discuss the annotation method of NPs with one "verb" or non-consecutive "verbs" such as "尾气/n排放/v标准/n" (vehicle emission standard) and "垃圾/n运输/v车辆/n管理/n" (waste vehicles management). Given a NP with one "verb" or non-consecutive "verbs":

a. map the nouns and verbs to the noun and verb dictionary respectively;
b. match the verbs and arguments based on collocation features;
c. choose specific semantic labels according to the semantic classes of nouns and verbs;

As is illustrated in Fig. 1, first we map the nouns "垃圾" (garbage) and "车辆" (vehicle) to the noun dictionary finding their semantic classes respectively fall into "artifact" and "tool"; and then map the verbs "运输" (transport) and "管理" (manage) to the verb dictionary getting following information:

(transport, v, motion, 2, person | vehicle, entity),
(manage, v, other event, 2, person, entity | abstraction | process)

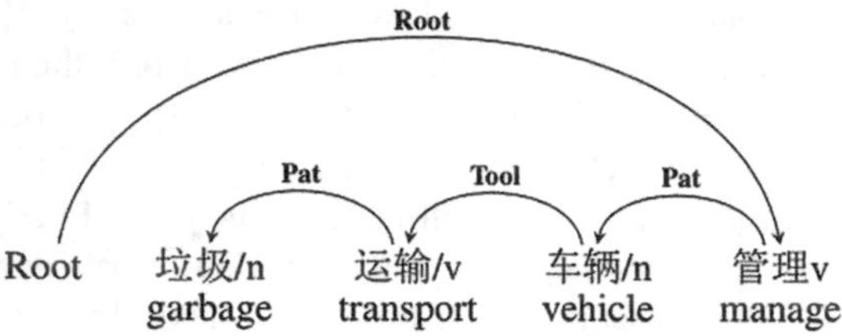

Fig. 1. An example for NPs with one verb or non-consecutive verbs.

Second we identify that "垃圾" (garbage) and "车辆" (vehicle) are the objects of the verbs "运输" (transport) and "管理" (manage) respectively, because the semantic classes of "垃圾" (garbage) is "artifact" which is a subclass of the object of "运输" (transport), i.e., "entity", and similarly the semantic class of "车辆" (vehicle) is "tool" which is a subclass of the object of "管理" (manage), i.e., "entity". Lastly we identify the specific labels according to the semantic classes of words, as is shown in Table 1. We think that the relations between words can be tentatively displayed by the word meaning. Take the subject as an example, organism that can act consciously could be an "Agent" while the subject that is described is an "Experiencer". Similarly, verbs in the SKCC are divided into 13 categories according to the semantic classes, and we design different relations such as "Patient", "Content" and "Product" according to the meaning of the verb. For example, "部门交流" (communication between departments) and

"部门直属" (directly subordinate to), since the semantic class of the subject are the same, we turn to that of verbs. "交流" (communication) falls into "Communication" while "直属" (directly subordinate to) falls into "State". It is true that "Communication" has to be done intentionally while "State" is a description of state, and thus the first relation is "Agt" and the second is "Exp". Therefore, The specific semantic label is determined by the semantic classes of nouns and verbs of the NPs.

Table 1. Semantic labels categorized by semantic classes.

Semantic class of nouns				Rel	Remark
1 Things	1.1 Entity	1.1.1 Organism	1.1.1.1 Person	Agt/Exp/Aft, Pat/Cont/Link	
			1.1.1.2 Animal	Agt/Exp/Aft, Pat/Cont/Link	
			1.1.1.3 Plant	Exp, Pat/Cont/Prod/Link	
			1.1.1.4 Microbe	Exp, Pat/Cont/Prod/Link	
		1.1.2 Object		Exp, Pat/Cont/Prod/Link	Tool: Tool
		1.1.3 Part		Exp, Pat/Cont/Prod/Link	
	1.2 Abstraction	1.2.1 Attribute 1.2.2 Info 1.2.3 Field ……		Exp, Pat/Cont/Prod/Link	
2 Time				Time	
3 Space				Loc	

4.3 Labeling NPs with Consecutive "Verbs"

The NPs with consecutive "verbs" in Chinese such as "学生/n 申诉/v 处理/v 制度/n" (processing system of student's appeal), "疾病/n 预防/v 控制/v 中心/n" (centers for disease control and prevention) and "分管/v 工作/v 完成/v 情况/n" (the completion of the work that is in charge of) is a common linguistic phenomenon. These are nominalizations with verbal nouns. Because there is no inflection in Chinese, the part-of speech taggers of the verbal nouns are also "verbs", which poses a difficulty for automatic acquisition of semantic relations. After annotating 525 such NPs manually, we find that there are four kinds of relations that hold between the verbal nouns.

a. Case Relation: one of the "verb" is an object of the other, such as "污染/v 处理/v 设备/n" (anti-pollution devices),

"电子/n 产品/n 污染/v 控制/v 管理/v 办法/n" (measures of the management and control of the electronic product), "防汛/v 抢险/v 物资/n 运输/v 保障/v 演习/v" (the exercise of ensuring the transportation of relief supplies), as is illustrated in Fig. 2. The semantic labels are "Pat", "Cont", "Prod";

b. Attribute Modifier: one of the nominalization is a modifier of the other, such as "加工/v 贸易/v 比重/v" (portion of processing trade), "上网/v 服务/v 营业/v 场所/n" (business site for Internet service), "节水/v 教育/v 读本/n" (water-saving education reader), as is illustrated in Fig. 3. The semantic label between them is "Desc";

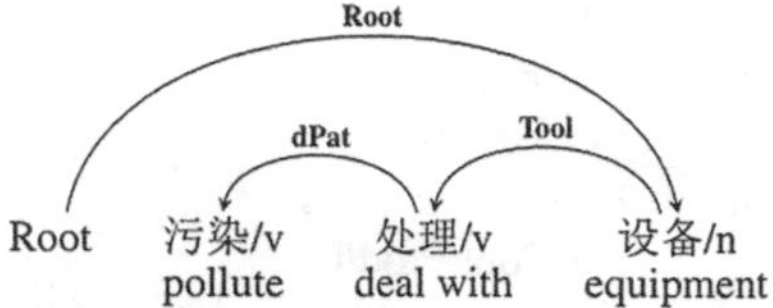

Fig. 2. Case relation.

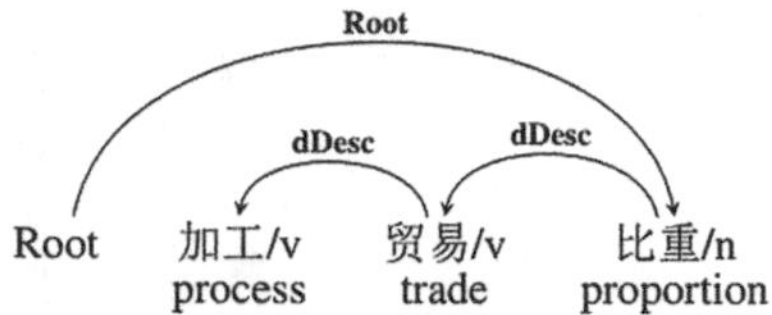

Fig. 3. Attribute relation.

c. Coordinating Relation: the two nominalizations function equally syntactically, such as "疾病/n预 防/v控制/v中心/n" (centers for disease control and prevention), "投诉/v举报/v中心/v" (complaint center), "生产/v加工/v企业/n" (production and processing enterprises), as is illustrated in Fig. 4. The semantic label between them is "eCoo";

d. Adverbial Modifier: the former nominalization describe the manner when the latter act is done, such as "全封闭式/n 无菌/v 操作/v" (totally enclosed aseptic operation), "燃煤/v 采暖/v 锅炉房/n" (coal heating boiler), "跨境/v 采访/v 报道/v 活动/v" (cross border coverage), as is illustrated in Fig. 5. The semantic relation between them is "Mann".

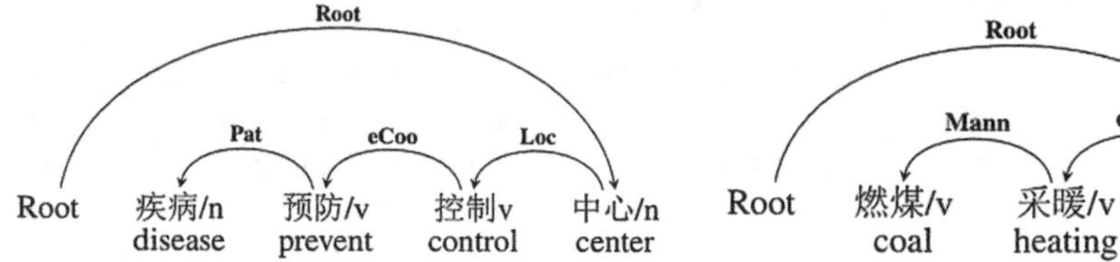

Fig. 4. Coordinating relation.

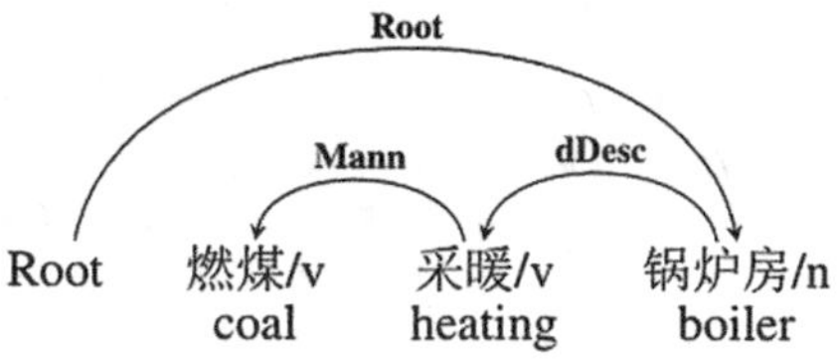

Fig. 5. Adverbial relation.

The method to label the NPs with consecutive "verbs" is a little different from the one mentioned above as is shown in Fig. 6:

a. map the nouns and verbs to thc noun and verb dictionary respectively to obtain the semantic classes;

b. match the semantic class of the object of each "verb" with that of the noun before them;
c. if the noun could be an argument of all the "verbs", the relation that holds between them is labeled "eCoo";
d. if the semantic class of the noun's and that of the "verbs" can not match totally, then eliminate the last "verb" and continue to match the semantic class of the noun with that of the rest of objects until all the objects are considered;
e. if there is no case relation found after all the objects are considered, the first "verb" is degraded as an "abstraction" noun, and then identified if it could be an argument of the latter "verbs"; this process is like the one in step b;

For example, "电子/n 产品/n 污染/v 控制/v 管理/v 办法/n" (measures of the management and control of the electronic product), firstly, we map the nouns and verbs of the NPs into dictionaries to obtain their semantic classes. Here are the semantic classes these words fall into:

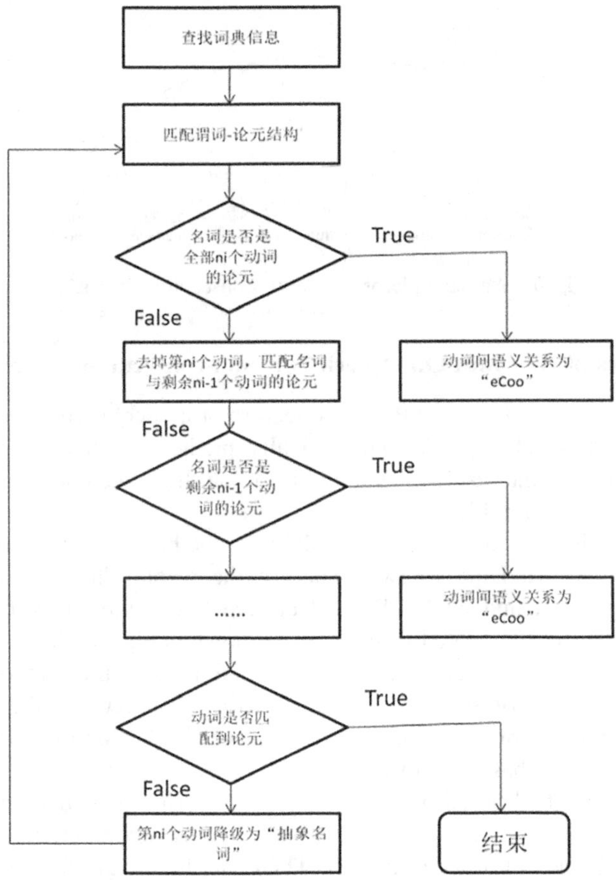

Fig. 6. The method to label the NPs with consecutive "verbs".

(电子 (electronics), n, substance)
(产品 (product), n, artifact)
(污染 (pollute), v, other event, 2, entity, space | natural object)
(控制 (control),v, other event, 2, person, entity | abstraction | event)
(管理 (manage), v, other event, 2, person, entity | abstraction | process)
(方法 (measure), n, process)

Secondly, we match the semantic class of the noun "产品" (product) with that of the objects of the three "verbs", and it turns out that "产品" (product) is an subject of "污染" (pollute), while it is an object of other "verbs". Since the relations between the noun and the "verbs" are not the same, the first "verb" "污染" (pollute) is degraded as an "abstraction" noun which could be an argument of both "控制" (control) and "管理" (manage) after being matched with the semantic classes of the rest of objects, as is shown in Fig. 7.

It is worth noting that the dependency arcs here are set to "Division" [14] by default, which means that the current word's father node is the word after it. And then the dependency arcs will be adjusted according to the labeling of relations.

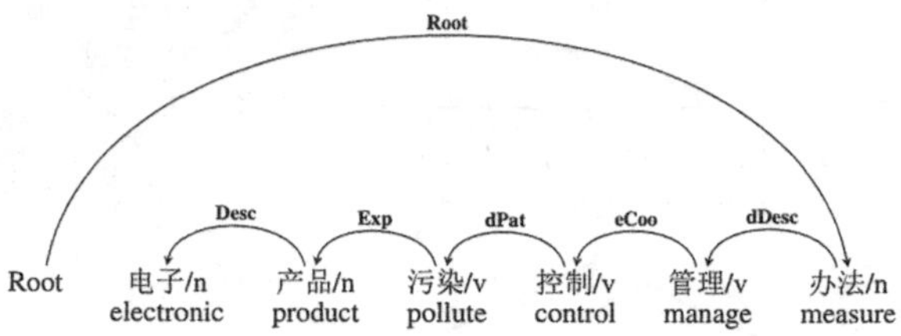

Fig. 7. An example of NPs with consecutive "verbs".

4.4 Accuracies of NPs with One "Verb" or Non-consecutive "Verbs"

We automatically extracted 1035 NPs with one verb or non-consecutive verbs, and use the algorithm mentioned above to automatically predict which relations should be assigned. We checked the results manually and found high accuracies in most of the relations, as is shown in Table 2.

Because there is no similar research in Chinese, the baselines we choose are from Lijie Wang [8] and Yu Ding [9] who analyze the whole Chinese sentence using Graph-based algorithm and SVM. We select five intersection tags (three tags of Graph-based method) to compare the results as is shown in Fig. 8. The task of semantic labeling the whole sentence is absolutely more difficult because the components, syntax structure and semantics of sentences are more complicated while the input in our program are only noun phrases through manual inspection which means it is easier to analyze, so our method based on rules performs better.

Generally the method based on semantic lexicon performs well when it comes to the identification of case relation, because in our case this is done literally according to the semantic class and collocation features. There are three main factors affecting the accuracy of the case relation. Firstly, thc labeling of this relation is highly dependent on

Table 2. The accuracy, recall and F-measure of the NPs with one "verb" or non-consecutive "verbs".

Rel	Occur	Accuracy	Recall	F-measure	Examples
Agt	214 (16.7%)	79.18	81.77	80.45	管理部门
Pat	479 (37.6%)	90.75	65.55	76.11	垃圾处理
Exp	123 (9.6%)	93.33	68.29	80.37	经济运行
Prod	104 (8.2%)	90.47	91.34	90.89	汽车生产
Cont	72 (5.5%)	87.23	56.94	68.90	天体研究
Mann	84 (6.5%)	64.70	39.28	48.41	规模经营
Tool	21 (1.5%)	65.00	61.90	63.41	切削机床
Loc	161 (13%)	95.13	85.09	89.83	北京总部
Time	17 (1.3%)	80.00	70.58	74.99	雪天运输

the properties of the lexical hierarchy and collocation information. The case relation can not be found if the two words' collocation information does not match. For example, "废水收集装置" (waste water collection device), the semantic class of "废水" (waste water) falls into "attribute" while that of the object of "收集" (collect) is "entity"; Secondly, the present program is not able to deal with the reverse relations which means the head argument lies behind the verb, such as "接待/v 游客/n 数量/n" (the number of tourists); Thirdly, it is hard to identify the case relation between words without direct semantic arcs. For example, "土地/n 规模/n 经营/v" (land-scale management), "土地" (land) is an patient of "经营" (manage), but the program fails to identify because the semantic arcs are set "Division" by default.

Time and Loc also have high accuracies because the labeling of these are highly dependent on word meaning. As for the labeling of relation Tool and Mann, the accuracy is pretty low, so it proves that semantic lexicon helps little in identifying these relations of which interpretation highly depends on contexts and pragmatics.

4.5 Accuracies of NPs with Consecutive Verbs

As for the NPs with consecutive "verbs", in order to label such kind of NPs we extracted 525 such NPs. Following are the results checked by hand as is shown in Table 2. The distribution of the four relations is equal overall. The relation "Desc" has the largest proportion accounting for 32.5%. It is an coincidence that Case Relation and Coordinating Relation have the same number due to the data scarcity. The Adverbial Relation accounts for a minimum proportion of 14.9% (Table 3).

The result is pretty promising considering the difficulty of the task. The use of SKCC plays a significant role in the differentiation of relations between nominalizations. The factors affecting the Case Relation are basically the same with the NPs with one "verb" or non-consecutive "verbs". The main factor affecting the accuracy of Coordinating Relation firstly is the properties of collocation information. For example, "固定/a 资产/n 监督/v 管理/v" (the supervision and management of fixed assets) the

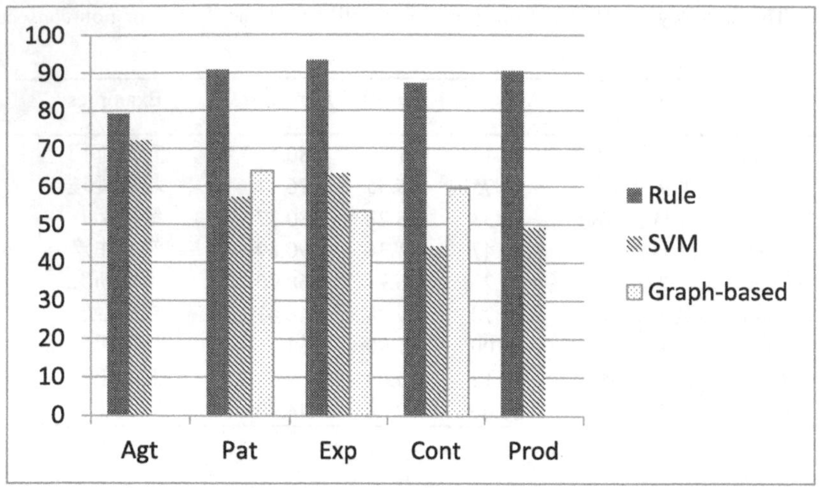

Fig. 8. The accuracy, recall and F-measure of the methods based on rules, SVM and Graph-based algorithm.

Table 3. The accuracy, recall and F-measure of the NPs with consecutive verbs.

Rel	Occur	Accuracy	Recall	F-measure	Examples
Case Rel	148 (26.3%)	72.88	58.10	64.65	支付保障
Desc	182 (32.5%)	76.73	54.96	64.04	节水教育
Coo	148 (26.3%)	68.70	68.24	68.46	生产经营
Mann	84 (14.9%)	60.75	55.95	58.25	应急处置

relation between "监督" (supervision) and "管理" (management) is coordination, but the "资产" (assets) and "监督" (supervision) has no case relation according to the collocation information. So the program fails to identify the correct relation between "监督" (supervision) and "管理" (management). Besides, some times words with semantic classes being different could be coordinating. For example, "宣传/v 教育/v 活动/v", though the objects' semantic classes of "宣传" (advocate) and "教育" (educate) fall into different classes, the two words are coordinating syntactically and semantically. As for Adverbial Relation we simply label the verbs that fall into semantic classes (Other Event, 1, Person) and (Change, 1, Person) "Mann", so the accuracy is not very ideal.

5 Conclusion

We have presented a simple algorithm to noun phrases interpretation based on semantic lexicon. The main idea is to define a set of relations that hold between the words and use a semantic lexicon with semantic classification and collocation features to automatically assign relations within noun phrases. We divide the NPs into two kinds of types, and respectively design annotation methods for them according to their structure features. Through annotating the NPs manually we find that there are four kinds of relations between Chinese verbal nouns: Case Relation, Coordinating Relation, Attribute Relation and Adverbial Relation and we further propose a method based on the semantic lexicon to automatically assign relations for such NPs. The method performs well when it comes to the identification of case relations but the performance is not very ideal as for the identification of "Mann" and "Tool" of which interpretation more depend on contexts and pragmatics. The semantic labels for the present study is not sufficient enough due to the limit of method, however our purpose is to create a manually annotated dataset of Chinese complex NPs which is used to provide support for machine learning. So our next job will be to explore the semantic relations of complex NPs through machine learning. We hope the combination of rules and machine learning could move the complex NPs a step further towards being generally understood. Understanding relations between multiword expressions is important for many tasks, including question answering, textual entailment, machine translation and information retrieval among others.

Acknowledgments. Thanks to National Natural Science Foundation of China (NSFC) via Grant 61170144, Major Program of China's National Linguistics Work Committee during the twelfth five-year plan (ZDI125-41), Young and Middle Aged Academic Cadre Support Plan of Beijing Language and Culture University (501321303), Graduate Innovation Foundation in 2017 (17YCX137).

References

1. Lapata, M.: The automatic interpretation of nominalizations. In: 17th National Conference on Artificial Intelligence and Twelfth Conference on Innovative Applications of Artificial Intelligence, pp. 716–721. AAAI Press (2000)
2. Rosario, B., Hearst, M., Fillmore, C.: The descent of hierarchy, and selection in relational semantics. In: Meeting on Association for Computational Linguistics, pp. 247–254. Association for Computational Linguistics, Philadelphia (2002)
3. Girju, N., et al.: SemEval-2007 Task 04: classification of semantic relations between nominals. In: 4th Proceeding of International Workshop on Semantic Evaluations (SemEval-2007), pp. 13–18. Association for Computational Linguistics, Prague (2007)
4. Rosario, B., Hearst, M., Fillmore, C.: Classifying the semantic relations in noun compounds via a domain-specific lexical hierarchy. In: Lee, L., Harman, D. (eds.) Proceedings of EMNLP (Empirical Methods in Natural Language Processing), pp. 247–254 (2001)

5. Girju, R., Giuglea, A.M., Olteanu, M., et al.: Support vector machines applied to the classification of semantic relations in nominalized noun phrases. In: Proceedings of the HLT-NAACL Workshop on Computational Lexical Semantics, pp. 68—75. Association for Computational Linguistics (2004)
6. Nastase, V., Sayyad-Shirabad, J., Sokolova, M., et al.: Learning noun-modifier semantic relations with corpus-based and WordNet-based features. In: National Conference on Artificial Intelligence, pp. 781–786. AAAI Press (2006)
7. Tratz, S., Hovy, E., et al.: A Taxonomy, dataset, and classifier for automatic noun compound interpretation. In: 48th Proceeding of the Annual Meeting of the Association for Computational Linguistics, pp. 678–687 (2010)
8. Dima, C., Hinrichs, E.: Automatic noun compound interpretation using deep neutral networks and embeddings. In: 11th Proceeding of the International Conference on Computational Semantics, pp. 173–183 (2015)
9. Lijie, W.: Research on Chinese semantic dependency analysis. Doctoral dissertation. Harbin Institute of Technology (2010)
10. Yu, D.: Dependency graph based Chinese semantic parsing. Doctoral dissertation. Harbin Institute of Technology (2014)
11. Weidong, Z.: Principles of determining semantic categories and the relativity of semantic categories. World Chin. Teach. **2**, 3–13 (2001)
12. Hui, W.: Structure and application of the semantic knowledge-base of modern Chinese. Appl. Linguist. **2**(1), 134–141 (2006)
13. Hui, W., Weidong, Z.: New progress of the semantic knowledge-base of contemporary Chinese. In: 7th Joint Academic Conference on Computational Linguistics, Harbin (2003)
14. Li, Y., Shao, Y.: Annotating Chinese noun phrases based on semantic dependency graph. In: 21st International Conference on Asian Language Processing, pp. 18–21. IEEE, Tainan (2016)

Information Retrieval and Question Answering

Bi-directional Gated Memory Networks for Answer Selection

Wei Wu, Houfeng Wang(✉), and Sujian Li

Key Laboratory of Computational Linguistics, Ministry of Education,
School of Electronics Engineering and Computer Science,
Peking University, No. 5 Yiheyuan Road, Haidian District,
Beijing 100871, China
{wu.wei,wanghf,lisujian}@pku.edu.cn

Abstract. Answer selection is a crucial subtask of the open domain question answering problem. In this paper, we introduce the Bi-directional Gated Memory Network (BGMN) to model the interactions between question and answer. We match question ($\boldsymbol{P}$) and answer ($\boldsymbol{Q}$) in two directions. In each direction(for example $\boldsymbol{P} \rightarrow \boldsymbol{Q}$), sentence representation of $\boldsymbol{P}$ triggers an iterative attention process that aggregates informative evidence of $\boldsymbol{Q}$. In each iteration, sentence representation of $\boldsymbol{P}$ and aggregated evidence of $\boldsymbol{Q}$ so far are passed through a gate determining the importance of the two when attend to every step of $\boldsymbol{Q}$. Finally based on the aggregated evidence, the decision is made through a fully connected network. Experimental results on SemEval-2015 Task 3 dataset demonstrate that our proposed method substantially outperforms several strong baselines. Further experiments show that our model is general and can be applied to other sentence-pair modeling tasks.

Keywords: Question Answering · Attention mechanism · Memory networks

1 Introduction

Answer selection is a long-standing challenge in NLP and catches many researchers' attention. Given a question and a set of corresponding answers, the task is to classify the answers as '*Good*', '*Potential*' and '*Bad*' according to the degree to which they can answer the question. Neural network based methods have made tremendous progress in this area, one of the key factors in these achievements has been the use of attention mechanism which emphasizes specific parts of one sentence which are relevant to the other sentence.

Table 1 lists an example question and its two corresponding answers. A question usually includes a title which gives a brief summary of the question and a body which describes the question in detail. Answer 1 is a good answer, because it provides helpful information, such as *'check it to the traffic dept'*. Although Answer 2 is relevant to the question, it does not contain any useful information for the question so it is regarded as a bad answer.

M. Sun et al. (Eds.): CCL 2017 and NLP-NABD 2017, LNAI 10565, pp. 251–262, 2017.
https://doi.org/10.1007/978-3-319-69005-6_21

From this example we can see why the attention mechanism is useful in answer selection task, one important characteristic is redundancy and noise [29] in both question and answer which may act as a distraction. In order to better model the relationship between question and answer, we must focus on the more informative parts from the question (*'check the history of the car'* in this example) and the more informative parts from the answer (*'check it to the traffic dept.'* in this example).

Table 1. An example question and answers for answer selection from SemEval-2015 Task 3 English dataset

Question title	Checking the history of the car
Question body	How can one check the history of the car like maintenance, accident or service history. In every advertisement of the car, people used to write "Accident Free", but in most cases, car have at least one or two accident, which is not easily detectable through Car Inspection Company. Share your opinion in this regard
Answer 1	Depends on the owner of the car.. if she/he reported the accident/s i believe u can check it to the traffic dept.. but some owners are not doing that especially if its only a small accident.. try ur luck and go to the traffic dept..
Answer 2	How about those who claim a low mileage by tampering with the car fuse box? In my sense if you're not able to detect traces of an accident then it is probably not worth mentioning...For best results buy a new car

Attention mechanisms in most prior works typically have one of these limitations: First, they only match question to answer but neglecting the other direction. Thus, they can not neglect useless segments from a potentially long question like the above example. Second, they only use a single-iteration attention mechanism which may not find the information useful enough to determine the answer quality. In the above example, single-iteration attention may find *car, detect, accident* to be relevant in answer 2 with the question thus making a wrong decision.

In this paper, to tackle these limitations, we introduce the Bi-directional Gated Memory Network (BGMN), an end-to-end neural network for answer selection. We use bi-directional attention mechanism to extract useful information from both directions. In order to refine attention representation iteratively we adopt the mechanism of revisiting question and answer multiply times. Furthermore, to improve the performance of memory mechanism in this task, an additional gate is added to determine the relative importance between the memory of one sentence and the representation of the other sentence, thus obtain a more focused relevance vector which can be used both in attention and formation of memory vector. Like the gating mechanism in LSTM [10] that optionally let information through cell state, this additional gate can control the extent to which the memory of one sentence and the representation of the other sentence can flow into the next iteration and generate the memory representation.

Our model consists of three parts: (1) the recurrent network to encode question and answer separately, (2) the gated memory network to iteratively aggregate evidence that is useful for answer selection, (3) the fully connected network to estimate the probability of labels representing the relationship between question and answer. The main contribution of our work can be summarized as follows:

- We apply the memory mechanism which can iteratively aggregate evidence from both directions to the answer selection task.
- We add an additional gate to memory networks to account for the fact that the memory of one sentence and the representation of the other sentence are of different importance when used in attention.
- Our proposed model yields state-of-the-art result on data from SemEval-2015 Task3 on Answer Selection in Community Question Answering.
- Our model achieves competitive result on the Stanford Natural Language Inference (SNLI) corpus demonstrating its effectiveness in the overall sentence-pair modeling task.

2 Related Works

2.1 Answer Selection

Answer selection task has been widely studied by many previous work. The methods using statistic classifiers ([18,24,28]) rely heavily on feature engineering, linguistic tools or external resources. While these methods show effectiveness, they might suffer from the availability of additional resources and errors of many NLP tools. Recently there are many works using deep learning architecture to represent the question and answer in the same hidden space, and then the task can be converted into a classification or learning-to-rank problem using these hidden representations. Among them, [8] models question and answer separately with multi-layer CNN, [22] proposes an attention-based RNN model which introduces question attention to answer representation. Simple as their model may be, they have not consider the interaction between question and answer thus only match question to answer but neglect the other direction. The single iteration attention mechanism also may not find relevant information to determine the relationship between question and answer.

2.2 Attention and Memory

A recent trend in deep learning research is the application of attention and memory mechanism. Attentive neural networks have been proved to be useful in a wide range of tasks ranging from machine translation [2], reading comprehension [9,17,27], and sentence summarization [16]. The idea is that instead of encoding each sentence as a fixed-length vector, we can focus on useful segments of text and neglect meaningless segments [22].

Memory network is a new class of attention model which can reason with inference components combined with a long-term memory component. It is first proposed in [25] where they use a memory component to answer questions via chaining facts. Despite being an effective system, their model requires that supporting facts to be labeled during training. In view of this defect, [21] proposes a memory network model that is end-to-end trainable. Their model is similar to the attention mechanism only that it makes multiple hops over the memory. [12,27] propose the dynamic memory network which is a general architecture for a variety of applications, including text classification, question answering, sequence modeling and visual question answering. In addition to the single-direction attention discussed above, one important defect of all these models is that they treat the memory of one sentence and the representation of the other sentence equally when used in attention and formation of memory vector. We argue that adding a gate for these two vectors can force the network to focus on the more important one, thus improving the effectiveness of the memory mechanism.

3 Method

In this section, we describe the architecture of our Bi-directional Gated Memory Network (BGMN) in detail. For notation, we denote scalars with italic lower-case (e.g. s_t^i), vectors with bold lower-case (e.g. $\boldsymbol{w}_t^p$), matrices with bold upper-case (e.g. $\boldsymbol{H}_p$) and sets with cursive upper-case (e.g. $\mathcal{Y}$). We assume words have already been converted to one-hot vectors. For answer selection, we are given a question $\boldsymbol{P}$ and an answer $\boldsymbol{Q}$, where $\boldsymbol{P} = \{\boldsymbol{w}_t^p\}_{t=1}^m$ is a sentence with length m, $\boldsymbol{Q} = \{\boldsymbol{w}_t^q\}_{t=1}^n$ is a sentence with length n, our task is to predict a label $y \in \mathcal{Y}$ representing the relationship between $\boldsymbol{P}$ and $\boldsymbol{Q}$, $\mathcal{Y} = \{good, potential, bad\}$ where *good* indicates $\boldsymbol{Q}$ is definitely relevant to $\boldsymbol{P}$, *potential* indicates $\boldsymbol{Q}$ is potentially useful to $\boldsymbol{P}$, *bad* indicates $\boldsymbol{Q}$ is bad or irrelevant to $\boldsymbol{P}$. Our model estimates the conditional probability distribution $Pr(y|\boldsymbol{P}, \boldsymbol{Q})$ through the following modules.

3.1 Sentence Encoder

Consider two sentences $\boldsymbol{P} = \{\boldsymbol{w}_t^p\}_{t=1}^m$ and $\boldsymbol{Q} = \{\boldsymbol{w}_t^q\}_{t=1}^n$. We first convert words to their respective word embeddings ($\{\boldsymbol{d}_t^p\}_{t=1}^m$ and $\{\boldsymbol{d}_t^q\}_{t=1}^n$), and then use a bi-directional RNN to incorporate contextual information into the representation of each time step of $\boldsymbol{P}$ and $\boldsymbol{Q}$ respectively, The output at each time step is the concatenation of the two output vectors from both directions, i.e. $\boldsymbol{h}_t = \overrightarrow{\boldsymbol{h}_t} \| \overleftarrow{\boldsymbol{h}_t}$. The representation of each sentence ($\boldsymbol{v}_p$ and $\boldsymbol{v}_q$) is formed by the concatenation of the last vectors on both directions ($\boldsymbol{v}_p = \overrightarrow{\boldsymbol{h}_m^p} \| \overleftarrow{\boldsymbol{h}_1^p}$, $\boldsymbol{v}_q = \overrightarrow{\boldsymbol{h}_n^q} \| \overleftarrow{\boldsymbol{h}_1^q}$):

$$\boldsymbol{h}_t^p = BiRNN(\boldsymbol{h}_{t-1}^p, \boldsymbol{d}_t^p) \tag{1}$$

$$\boldsymbol{h}_t^q = BiRNN(\boldsymbol{h}_{t-1}^q, \boldsymbol{d}_t^q) \tag{2}$$

3.2 Bi-directional Gated Memory Network

This is the core layer within our model. The goal of this module is to iteratively refine the memory of each sentence with newly relevant information about that sentence. The memory of one sentence means the informative evidence about that sentence when used for determining sentence-pair relationship, it can be iteratively refined using attention mechanism. It was initialized with the representation of that sentence ($\boldsymbol{m}_p^0 = \boldsymbol{v}_p, \boldsymbol{m}_q^0 = \boldsymbol{v}_q$). In each iteration, as is shown in Fig. 1, we attend the two sentences $\boldsymbol{P}$ and $\boldsymbol{Q}$ in two directions: from $\boldsymbol{P}$ to $\boldsymbol{Q}$ and from $\boldsymbol{Q}$ to $\boldsymbol{P}$. In each direction, for example $\boldsymbol{P} \rightarrow \boldsymbol{Q}$, we add an additional gate to determine the importance of the memory of one sentence and the representation of the other sentence when used to attend, thus obtaining the relevance vector $\boldsymbol{r}_q^i$ for sentence $\boldsymbol{Q}$ in iteration i:

$$\boldsymbol{r}_q^i = sigmoid\left(\boldsymbol{W}_r\left[\boldsymbol{v}_p, \boldsymbol{m}_q^i\right]\right) \odot \left[\boldsymbol{v}_p, \boldsymbol{m}_q^i\right] \tag{3}$$

We then use an attention mechanism similar to [9], the attentional representation $\boldsymbol{e}_q^i$ of sentence $\boldsymbol{Q}$ in iteration i is formed by a weighted sum of outputs from the above sentence encoder layer $\boldsymbol{H}^q = \{\boldsymbol{h}_t^q\}_{t=1}^n$, these normalized weights $\boldsymbol{s}^i$ are interpreted as the degree to which the network attends to a particular token in the answer when answering the question in iteration i:

$$\begin{aligned} \boldsymbol{n}_t^i &= tanh\left(\boldsymbol{W}_n\left[\boldsymbol{h}_t^q, \boldsymbol{r}_q^i\right]\right) \\ s_t^i &= softmax\left(\boldsymbol{W}_s \boldsymbol{n}_t^i\right) \\ \boldsymbol{e}_q^i &= \boldsymbol{H}^q \odot \boldsymbol{s}^i \end{aligned} \tag{4}$$

Finally, following [27], we use a ReLU layer to update memory with newly relevant information from iteration i:

$$\boldsymbol{m}_q^{i+1} = ReLU\left(\boldsymbol{W}_m\left[\boldsymbol{e}_q^i, \boldsymbol{r}_q^i\right]\right) \tag{5}$$

Above describes one iteration of the BGMN model, it can be applied multiple times to aggregate more information required to determine the relationship between the sentence-pair. The number of iterations is a hyper-parameter to be tuned on the development set. Empirically three or four iterations can result in good performance.

3.3 Output Layer

This layer is employed to evaluate the conditional probability distribution $Pr(y|\boldsymbol{P}, \boldsymbol{Q})$ given memory $\boldsymbol{m}_p$ and $\boldsymbol{m}_q$ from the last iteration. For that purpose, we use a two layer fully-connected neural network and apply the $softmax$ function in the last layer.

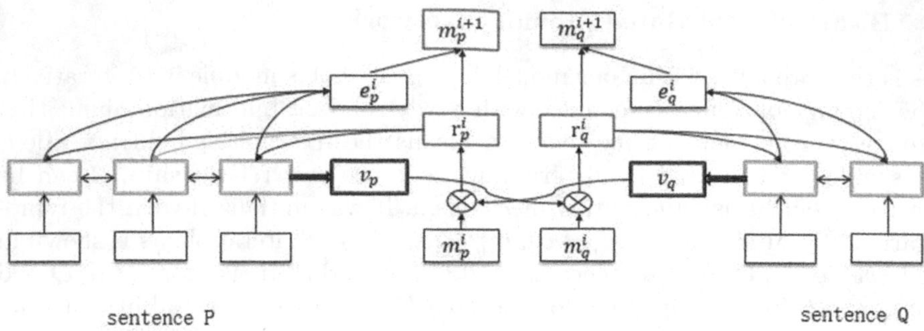

Fig. 1. Illustration for one iteration of our Bi-directional gated memory network

4 Experiments

In this section, we evaluate our BGMN model on the SemEval-2015 cQA dataset. We will first introduce the basic information about this dataset in Subsect. 4.1 and the general setting of our model in Subsect. 4.2. Then we compare our model with state-of-the-art models in Subsect. 4.3 and demonstrate the properties of our model through some ablation study in Subsect. 4.4. Finally, since our BGMN model essentially models the relationship between sentences, we also test its effectiveness on another sentence-pair modeling task: textual entailment recognition in Subsect. 4.5.

4.1 Dataset Description

We conduct experiments on subtask A of SemEval-2015 task 3 [1]: Answer Selection in Community Question Answering to validate the effectiveness of our model. The corpus contains data from the *QatarLiving* forum[1], and is publicly available on the task's website[2]. The dataset consists of questions and a list of answers for each question. Every question consist of a short title and a more detailed description. There are also some metadata associated with them, e.g., user ID, date of posting, the question category. We do not use these metadata because we think raw texts from question and answer are enough to determine the relationship between these two sentences. Answers are required to be classified as *Good*, *Bad*, or *Potentially relevant* with respect to the question. Some statistics about the dataset are shown in Table 2.

The performance is measured by two metrics in official scorer[3]: Macro-averaged F1 and accuracy.

---

[1] http://www.qatarliving.com/forum.

[2] http://alt.qcri.org/semeval2015/task3/.

[3] http://alt.qcri.org/semeval2015/task3/data/uploads/semeval2015-task3-english-arabic-scorer.zip.

Table 2. Statistics of the SemEval-2015 cQA English dataset.

Category	Train	Dev	Test
Questions	2,600	300	329
Answers	16,541	1,645	1,976
- *Good*	8,069	875	997
- *Potential*	1,659	187	167
- *Bad*	6,813	583	812

4.2 Experiment Setup

We use the tokenizer from NLTK [4] to preprocess each sentence. All word embeddings in the sentence encoder layer are initialized with the 300-dimensional GLoVe [14] word vectors trained on Wikipedia 2014 + Gigaword 5 and embeddings for out-of-vocabulary words are set to zero. Gated Recurrent Unit (GRU) [6] is chosen in our experiment because it performs similarly to LSTM [10] but is computationally cheaper. The hidden size of GRU is set to 200. To prevent our model from overfitting, a dropout [20] rate of 0.2 is used for all GRU layers and the fully-connected network before softmax. We use ADAM [11] for optimization with a first momentum coefficient of 0.9 and a second momentum coefficient of 0.999. We perform a small grid search over combinations of initial learning rate [1E-6, 3E-6, 1E-5], L2 regularization parameter [1E-7, 3E-7, 1E-6] and number of iterations [2, 3, 4]. We take the best configuration based on performance on the validation set, and only evaluate that configuration on the test set. In order to mitigate class imbalance problem, we use median frequency balancing as in [7] to reweight each class in the cross-entropy loss, thus the rarer a class is in training set, the larger weight it will get in the cross entropy loss.

4.3 Model Comparison

In order to analyze the performance of our BGMN model more precisely, we compare with some baselines and state-of-the-art models on this dataset. These models are introduced as follows:

- **Baseline: always 'Good'** is a basic baseline method, which assigns the most common label in training set (in this case *Good*) to every answer in the test set.
- **Baseline: BiLSTM** encodes question and answer separately with Bi-directional LSTM and sentence vectors are generated by the last hidden states from both directions, two sentence vectors are passed through a fully-connected layer to determine the sentence-pair relationship.
- **Baseline: BiLSTM-attention** resembles **Baseline: BiLSTM** but sentence vectors are generated by the attentive pooling of all hidden states [22].
- **JAIST** [23] ranks first in the evaluation of this SemEval task, it used a supervised feature rich approach, which includes topic models and word vector representation, with an SVM classifier.

- **R-CNN** [31] applies CNN to learn the joint representation of question-answer pair firstly, and then uses the joint representation as input of LSTM to learn the answer sequence of a question for labeling the matching quality of each answer.
- **KEHNN** [26] uses question categories as prior knowledge to help identify useful information and filter out noise in order to match long text.

Table 3 shows the performances of above models and our model. The results of **JAIST**, **R-CNN** and **KEHNN** are from original papers. **Baseline: always 'Good'** is the worst because it did not use any information from the test set. **Baseline: BiLSTM** performs quite well in terms of accuracy demonstrating its strong power in modeling sequences. **Baseline: BiLSTM-attention** performs better in terms of Macro-F1 but worse in terms of accuracy than **Baseline: BiLSTM**. A closer look into the result show that **Baseline: BiLSTM-attention** can better model the samples in relatively less class '*Potential*' which improves the Macro-average result but may hurt overall accuracy. The more complicated **R-CNN** is only slightly better than **Baseline: BiLSTM-attention** and **KEHNN** is only slightly better than **BiLSTM**, demonstrating that there are much room to be improved. We can see that our model achieves the state-of-the-art performance for this community question answering task despite its simplicity over **R-CNN** and **KEHNN**.

Table 3. Results on the SemEval-2015 cQA English dataset.

Models	Macro F1	Accuracy
baseline: always 'Good'	22.36	50.46
baseline: BiLSTM	51.94	74.75
baseline: BiLSTM-attention	55.61	71.26
JAIST [23]	57.19	72.67
R-CNN [31]	56.14	-
KEHNN [26]	-	74.8
Our BGMN model	**58.55**	**75.81**

4.4 Ablation Study

In this subsection, we conduct a series of studies to evaluate the effectiveness of each model features. We build several ablation models by removing one feature at a time. Table 4 shows the performance of all ablation models and our full BGMN model on the SemEval-2015 Task 3 dataset. We can see that removing any component from the BGMN model decreases the performance significantly. Removing question-to-answer attention induces more performance loss than removing answer-to-question attention, demonstrating question-to-answer attention is more important in answer selection task. Among all the features, gating is the most crucial feature for our full model to achieve good performance. When we set the number of iterations to 1 in our model, accuracy drops significantly, demonstrating the necessity of the memory component.

Table 4. Ablation study on the SNLI test set.

Models	Accuracy
w/o question-to-answer attention	74.13
w/o answer-to-question attention	74.80
w/o gating[a]	71.82
w/o memory	73.15
Our BGMN model	**75.81**

[a]We just set relevance to be the concatenation of two input vectors.

4.5 Further Study on Sentence-Pair Modeling

Our model can achieve state-of-the-art result on answer selection task, but due to the nature of our model is classification of relationship between a pair of sentences, we also experiment on textual entailment recognition task. Experiment results show the effectiveness of our model for this task.

Recognizing Textual Entailment. Recognizing Textual Entailment is essential in tasks ranging from information retrieval to semantic parsing to commonsense reasoning. For natural language inference task, $\boldsymbol{P}$ is a premise sentence, $\boldsymbol{Q}$ is a hypothesis sentence, and $\mathcal{Y} = \{entailment, neural, contradiction\}$ where *entailment* indicates $\boldsymbol{Q}$ can be inferred from $\boldsymbol{P}$, *neural* indicates $\boldsymbol{P}$ and $\boldsymbol{Q}$ are irrelevant, *contradiction* indicates $\boldsymbol{Q}$ can not be true condition on $\boldsymbol{P}$. Previous works often stuck in employing engineered NLP pipelines, extensive manual creation of features, as well as various external resources (e.g. [3,13,30]). [15] proposes a sentence-by-word attentive LSTM model that reads two sentences to determine entailment, and extended that model with a word-by-word neural attention mechanism that encourages reasoning over entailments of pairs of words and phrases. However, its sentence-by-word model performs poorly and word-by-word model is computational expensive. Despite being a much simpler attention mechanism, our proposed model still outperforms their word-by-word attentive model by more than 1 point.

Experiments on Textual Entailment Recognition. In this subsection, we conduct experiments on the SNLI dataset [5]. It is a large corpus with over 55K training sentence pairs and its labels are more balanced and is publicly available[4]. Table 5 shows the performances of some competitive models and our model. All baseline results are from original paper. We can see that the performance of our model is on par with some state-of-the-art models. Especially when compared

[4] https://nlp.stanford.edu/projects/snli/.

with [15], our model is much more concise than their word-by-word attention model but achieves a more impressive result. Therefore, our model is also effective for natural language inference task.

Table 5. Results on the SNLI test set.

Models	Accuracy
100D LSTM encoders [5]	77.6
Attention, two-way [15]	82.4
Word-by-word attention [15]	83.5
MKAL [19]	84.2
Our BGMN model	84.15

5 Conclusion

We propose the Bi-directional Gated Memory Network(BGMN), an end-to-end neural network architecture for answer selection. Our model uses an iterative process to aggregate more relevant information which is useful to identify the relationship between question and answer. Experiment results show that our model achieves state-of-the-art performance in SemEval-2015 cQA task. Ablation study show that all features of our model are crucial for good performance. Further experiments on the SNLI dataset demonstrate that our model is general and can be applied to more sentence-pair modeling tasks. Future work involves incorporating label dependency in answers of the same question in answer selection and extend our model to a more suitable ranking-based answer selection task.

Acknowledgement. Our work is supported by National Natural Science Foundation of China (No. 61370117, No. 61433015 & No. 61572049).

References

1. Nakov, P., Marquez, L., Magdy, W., Moschitti, A., Glass, J., Randeree, B.: Semeval-2015 task 3: answer selection in community question answering. In: SemEval-2015, p. 269 (2015)
2. Bahdanau, D., Cho, K., Bengio, Y.: Neural machine translation by jointly learning to align and translate. CoRR, abs/1409.0473 (2014)
3. Beltagy, I., Roller, S., Cheng, P., Erk, K., Mooney, R.J.: Representing meaning with a combination of logical form and vectors (2015). arXiv preprint: arXiv:1505.06816
4. Bird, S.: Nltk: the natural language toolkit. In: Proceedings of the COLING/ACL on Interactive Presentation Sessions, pp. 69–72. Association for Computational Linguistics (2006)
5. Bowman, S.R., Angeli, G., Potts, C., Manning, C.D.: A large annotated corpus for learning natural language inference. In: EMNLP (2015)

6. Cho, K., van Merrienboer, B., Gülehre, C., Bahdanau, D., Bougares, F., Schwenk, H., Bengio, Y.: Learning phrase representations using RNN encoder-decoder for statistical machine translation. In: EMNLP (2014)
7. Eigen D., Fergus, R.: Predicting depth, surface normals and semantic labels with a common multi-scale convolutional architecture. In: Proceedings of the IEEE International Conference on Computer Vision, pp. 2650–2658 (2015)
8. Feng, M., Xiang, B., Glass, M.R., Wang, L., Zhou, B.: Applying deep learning to answer selection: a study and an open task. In: ASRU (2015)
9. Hermann, K.M., Kocisky, T., Grefenstette, E., Espeholt, L., Kay, W., Suleyman, M., Blunsom, P.: Teaching machines to read and comprehend. In: Advances in Neural Information Processing Systems, pp. 1693–1701 (2015)
10. Hochreiter, S., Schmidhuber, J.: Long short-term memory. Neural Comput. **9**(8), 1735–1780 (1997)
11. Kingma, D., Ba, J.: Adam: a method for stochastic optimization (2014). arXiv preprint: arXiv:1412.6980
12. Kumar, A., Irsoy, O., Ondruska, P., Iyyer, M., Bradbury, J., Gulrajani, I., Zhong, V., Paulus, R., Socher, R.: Ask me anything: dynamic memory networks for natural language processing. In: ICML (2016)
13. Lai, A., Hockenmaier, J.: Illinois-lh: a denotational and distributional approach to semantics. In: Proceedings of SemEval, 2:5, pp. 329–334 (2014)
14. Pennington, J., Socher, R., Manning, C.D.: Glove: global vectors for word representation. In: EMNLP, vol. 14, pp. 1532–1543 (2014)
15. Rocktäschel, T., Grefenstette, E., Hermann, K.M., Kocisky, T., Blunsom, P.: Reasoning about entailment with neural attention. In: International Conference on Learning Representations (ICLR) (2016)
16. Rush, A.M., Chopra, S., Weston, J.: A neural attention model for abstractive sentence summarization. In: EMNLP (2015)
17. Seo, M., Kembhavi, A., Farhadi, A., Hajishirzi, H.: Bidirectional attention flow for machine comprehension (2016). arXiv preprint: arXiv:1611.01603
18. Severyn, A., Moschitti, A.: Automatic feature engineering for answer selection and extraction. In: EMNLP, vol. 13, pp. 458–467 (2013)
19. Sha, L., Li, S., Chang, B., Sui, Z.: Recognizing textual entailment via multi-task knowledge assisted LSTM. In: Sun, M., Huang, X., Lin, H., Liu, Z., Liu, Y. (eds.) CCL/NLP-NABD -2016. LNCS, vol. 10035, pp. 285–298. Springer, Cham (2016). doi:10.1007/978-3-319-47674-2_24
20. Srivastava, N., Hinton, G.E., Krizhevsky, A., Sutskever, I., Salakhutdinov, R.: Dropout: a simple way to prevent neural networks from overfitting. J. Mach. Learn. Res. **15**(1), 1929–1958 (2014)
21. Sukhbaatar, S., Weston, J., Fergus, R., et al.: End-to-end memory networks. In: Advances in Neural Information Processing Systems, pp. 2440–2448 (2015)
22. Tan, M., Xiang, B., Zhou, B.: LSTM-based deep learning models for non-factoid answer selection. CoRR, abs/1511.04108 (2015)
23. Tran, Q.H., Tran, V., Vu, T., Nguyen, M., Pham, S.B.: Jaist: combining multiple features for answer selection in community question answering. In: Proceedings of the 9th International Workshop on Semantic Evaluation, SemEval, vol. 15, pp. 215–219 (2015)
24. Wang, M., Smith, N.A., Mitamura, T.: What is the jeopardy model? A quasi-synchronous grammar for QA. In: EMNLP-CoNLL, vol. 7, pp. 22–32 (2007)
25. Weston, J., Chopra, S., Bordes, A.: Memory networks (2014). arXiv preprint: arXiv:1410.3916

26. Wu, Y., Wu, W., Li, Z., Zhou, M.: Knowledge enhanced hybrid neural network for text matching (2016). arXiv preprint: arXiv:1611.04684
27. Xiong, C., Zhong, V., Socher, R.: Dynamic coattention networks for question answering (2016). arXiv preprint: arXiv:1611.01604
28. Yih, W.-T., Chang, M.-W., Meek, C., Pastusiak, A., Yih, S.W.-T., Meek, C.: Question answering using enhanced lexical semantic models (2013)
29. Zhang, X., Li, S., Sha, L., Wang, H.: Attentive interactive neural networks for answer selection in community question answering. In: Thirty-First AAAI Conference on Artificial Intelligence (2017)
30. Zhao, J., Zhu, T.T., Lan, M.: Ecnu: one stone two birds: ensemble of heterogenous measures for semantic relatedness and textual entailment. In: Proceedings of the SemEval, pp. 271–277 (2014)
31. Zhou, X., Hu, B., Chen, Q., Tang, B., Wang, X.: Answer sequence learning with neural networks for answer selection in community question answering. In: ACL (2015)

Generating Textual Entailment Using Residual LSTMs

Maosheng Guo[(✉)], Yu Zhang, Dezhi Zhao, and Ting Liu

School of Computer Science and Technology, Harbin Institute of Technology, Harbin 150001, China
{msguo, zhangyu, dzzhao, tliu}@ir.hit.edu.cn

Abstract. Generating textual entailment (GTE) is a recently proposed task to study how to infer a sentence from a given premise. Current sequence-to-sequence GTE models are prone to produce invalid sentences when facing with complex enough premises. Moreover, the lack of appropriate evaluation criteria hinders researches on GTE. In this paper, we conjecture that the unpowerful encoder is the major bottleneck in generating more meaningful sequences, and improve this by employing the residual LSTM network. With the extended model, we obtain state-of-the-art results. Furthermore, we propose a novel metric for GTE, namely EBR (Evaluated By Recognizing textual entailment), which could evaluate different GTE approaches in an objective and fair way without human effort while also considering the diversity of inferences. In the end, we point out the limitation of adapting a general sequence-to-sequence framework under GTE settings, with some proposals for future research, hoping to generate more public discussion.

Keywords: Generating textual entailment · Natural language generation · Natural language processing · Artificial intelligence

1 Introduction

The ability of reasoning in natural language is necessary for many information access applications such as question-answering systems, where the answer to a question should be inferred from the supporting text. The reasoning relationship in texts is defined as textual entailment [4]. There are two major tasks to study this relationship: Recognizing Textual Entailment (RTE) and Generating Textual Entailment (GTE).

Compared with RTE which is well studied, GTE is a rather new task which was formally proposed very recently to overcome the shortcomings when applying RTE techniques in downstream NLP tasks, such as question answering and text summarization, where only one source sentence is available and models need to come up with their own hypotheses by inference according to commonsense knowledge [7].

In GTE settings, the system is asked to produce a new sentence called hypothesis (e.g. S2 in Fig. 1) according to a given text known as a premise (e.g. S1). Rule-based algorithms [6, 9] and sequence-to-sequence LSTM model [7] were proposed to generate inferences.

M. Sun et al. (Eds.): CCL 2017 and NLP-NABD 2017, LNAI 10565, pp. 263–272, 2017.
https://doi.org/10.1007/978-3-319-69005-6_22

S1. A group of people prepare hot air balloons for takeoff.
S2. A group of people are outside.

Fig. 1. An example of generating textual entailment.

We found three limitations in previous studies on GTE (which are analyzed detailedly in the related work section):

1. Rule-based methods often lack adequate coverage. Moreover, the process of formulating inference rules is inefficient and requires special knowledge.
2. Current sequence-to-sequence models are prone to produce simple and short hypotheses which are fragile when faced with more complex premises, although they have gotten rid of dependence on hand-crafted rules.
3. All previous works on GTE were evaluated by an inappropriate metric, i.e. BLEU, or non-objective human annotators which make horizontal comparison among GTE models inconvenient.

To circumvent these limitations, we firstly improve the sequence-to-sequence model by using residual LSTM which is a more potent encoder, leading to a state-of-art result with an improvement of correct rate by 3% over strong baseline models; and secondly propose a new assessment metric called EBR, which could evaluate different GTE models in an objective and fair way without human effort while also considering the diversity of generated hypotheses.

Moreover, we point out the limitation of the current sequence-to-sequence framework in GTE tasks, with some proposals for future research, hoping to generate more public discussion.

In the rest of this paper, we will describe the details of our improved GTE model in Sect. 2; propose the EBR metric which is then compared with previous evaluation criteria on GTE, i.e. BLEU and human annotation, in Sect. 3; introduce our experiments settings and results analyses in Sect. 4; draw conclusions and discuss future research directions in the last section.

2 The Improved Sequence-to-Sequence Model for GTE

2.1 A Generic Encoder-Decoder Framework

The encoder-decoder framework was proposed by Cho et al. [3] for sequence-to-sequence NLP tasks, such as machine translation and dialogue generation. Similarly, it is intuitive to employ this model to generate textual entailment.

Figure 2 shows a generic encoder-decoder framework for GTE. Each box in the illustration represents a cell of LSTM, around which arrows with a solid line indicate its inputs and outputs. The first three cells that share weights constitute the encoder whose duty is to "remember" the semantic information of the premise, while the remaining forms the decoder which is responsible for inferring a hypothesis. At each time step, the encoder takes a word in the premise as input and pass the cell states to the next step. After receiving the encoding represented by a dense vector, the decoder starts to infer the first token of hypothesis and then takes the word just generated as input to produce more tokens until reaching a <EOS>.

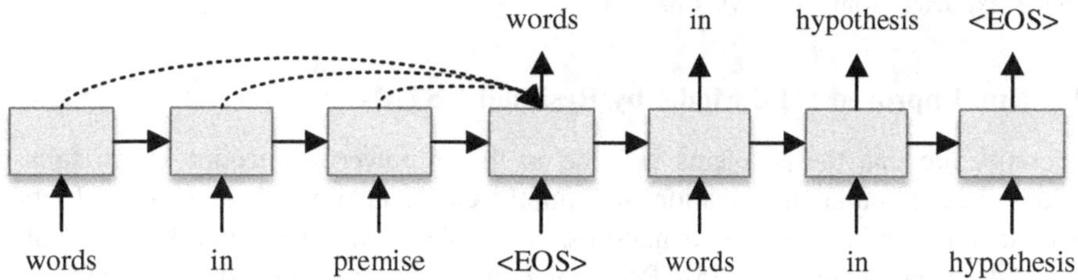

Fig. 2. Encoder-decoder framework for generating textual entailment.

2.2 Problems in Current Models

The above describes the basic architecture for generating inference from a single text. However, the memory of a fixed length vector is limited. Kolesnyk et al. [7] improved it by adding the word-by-word attention (the arrows with a dotted line[1]) which let the decoder reference the outputs of the encoder at each time step when generating tokens. By this mean, the decoder receives more information from the premise, which improved the correctness of inference.

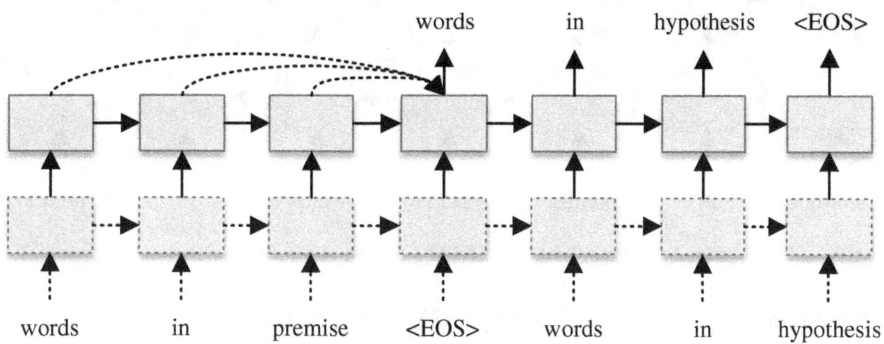

Fig. 3. 2-layer LSTM GTE model [7].

We reimplemented the model proposed by Kolesnyk as our baseline, which is a 2-layer unidirectional LSTM sequence-to-sequence model, as depicted in Fig. 3. After reviewing the produced premise-hypothesis pairs, we found that the baseline model is prone to generate invalid sentences, e.g. S4 in Fig. 4, when faced with complex enough premises, e.g. S3, although it performs well on simple input sentences.

[1] For clarity, only one step of attention is drawn in figures.

S3.	A female gymnast in black and red being coached on bar skill.
S4.	A female is in a bar.

Fig. 4. Examples of invalid sentence pairs generated by the baseline model. (Sentence pair S3-S4 is extracted from Kolesnyk's paper.)

2.3 Our Improved GTE Model by Residual LSTMs

We conjecture that the problems may lie in the unpowerful encoder which fails to encode some essential information and finally cause an invalid generating. In fact, when stacking multiple layers of neurons, such as LSTMs, the network often suffers from a degradation problem [5]. Residual connections are proved to be helpful to overcome this issue in an encoder-decoder framework [12]. We suspect that the degradation problem might be the major factor causing the invalid generating and add residual connections (arrows with a dashed line) to our sequence-to-sequence model, as shown in Figs. 5 and 6(b). We will show by experiments that this modification is effective to alleviate the degradation problem, leading to a more informative generating with a much higher correct rate.

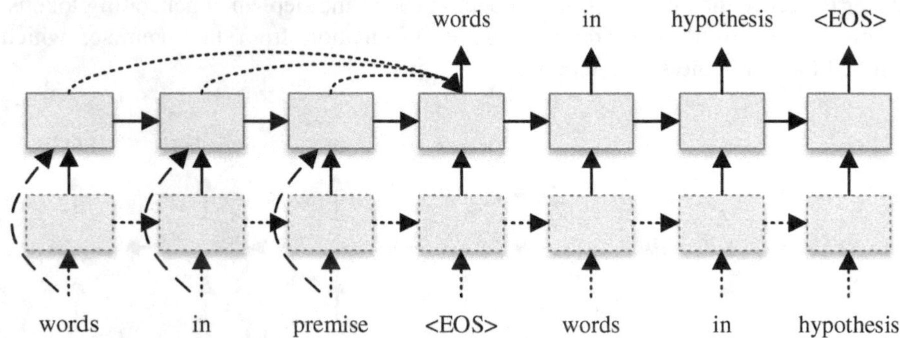

Fig. 5. 2-layer residual LSTM GTE model (our model).

We improve the original 2-layered LSTM network (see Fig. 6(a)) by adding a residue shortcut connection. In our case, the residual connection performs an identity mapping $I(\cdot)$, followed by a pointwise addition (see Fig. 6(b), Eq. (2)).

Formally, the output of a 2-layered Residual LSTM at timestep t is

$$output^t_{ResLSTM} = LSTM^t_2\left(x^t_2\right) \tag{1}$$

$$x^t_2 = LSTM^t_1\left(x^t_1\right) + I\left(x^t_1\right) \tag{2}$$

where $I\left(x^t_1\right) = x^t_1$.

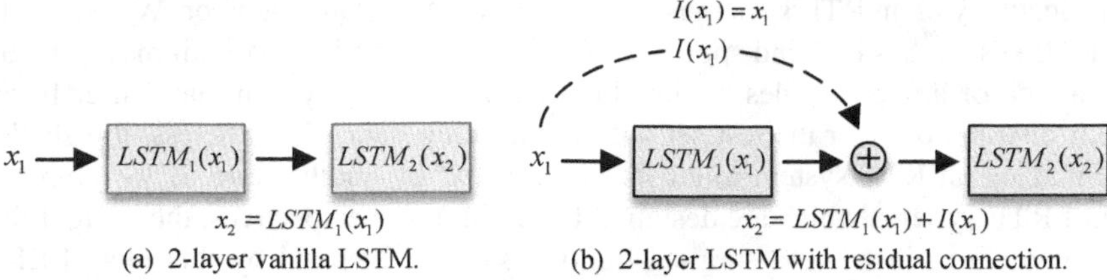

(a) 2-layer vanilla LSTM.

(b) 2-layer LSTM with residual connection.

Fig. 6. Residual connection for LSTMs at one timestep.

3 An Objective and Fair Metric for GTE: EBR

All the previous works on GTE use either human judgment or BLEU to evaluate the generated hypotheses by their models.

BLEU is designed as a metric to evaluate machine translation [10]. It considers exact matching between system generated translations and reference translations by counting n-gram overlaps. However, compared with machine translation, generated hypotheses have a greater diversity in both sentential form view and semantic view. As shown in Fig. 7, sentence S6 and S7 are both valid hypotheses inferred from the premise S5. However, there is no overlap n-gram between them, which leads to a zero-valued BLEU score. This phenomenon makes the use of BLEU in GTE settings problematic.

On the other hand, annotation by a human is inefficient when the test set contains thousands of examples, and random sampling may lead to instability of the evaluation results.

S5. Two young children in blue jerseys, one with the number 9 and one with the number 2 are standing on wooden steps in a bathroom and washing their hands in a sink.
S6. Two kids wearing numbered jerseys wash their hands.
S7. The children are in a bathroom.

Fig. 7. Examples of various valid hypotheses inferred from a single text.

To overcome these limitations, we propose our novel evaluation metric EBR, which is an abbreviation of Evaluation By RTE. As the name implies, we employ recognizing textual entailment systems to evaluate whether the generated hypotheses could be inferred from given premises.

Compared with BLEU, the diversity of hypotheses is considered instinctively by the design of RTE systems. Most RTE systems could adapt to the variety of hypotheses inferred from a single premise in both sentential form view and semantic view.

Thanks to modern hardware and optimized algorithms, EBR could validate GTE results more efficiently than human judgment. However, a possible shortage in EBR is that the accuracy of an RTE system is often lower than human annotator. We admit that every RTE system has its blind spot, e.g., knowledge-based RTE system may get stuck due to a lack of inference rules, while classifier-based RTE system may suffer from a different distribution over the test set with the training data. Nevertheless, the shallow left behind by an RTE system might be illuminated by another one. If we employ a bunch of RTE systems which are designed from different perspectives, they might light up the whole area just like a surgical lighting system. Inspired by this idea, EBR is designed to use an ensemble of existing RTE systems to measure the correctness of generated hypotheses.

The choice of RTE systems is essential to evaluate the produced hypotheses. After a survey of public available RTE systems, we choose the Excitement Open Platform (EOP) as our testbed [8]. The EOP is an open source state-of-the-art RTE platform including several heterogeneous RTE algorithms: transformation-based (BIUTEE), edit-distance based (EDIT), and classifier-based (TIE). In addition to these out-of-the-box EDAs, we use an ensemble version of them by majority voting (MAJOR). Finally, our EBR metric consists of a tuple of scores: {BIUTEE, EDIT, TIE, MAJOR}. Also, it is easy to extend EBR by employing more RTE techniques.

Another benefit brought by EBR is the independence on reference hypotheses, which make it possible to evaluate GTE results on unlabeled data.

4 Experiments and Analyses

4.1 Dataset

Our dataset is extracted from the Stanford Natural Language Inference (SNLI) corpus [1], which contains about 560K sentence pairs labeled as entailment, contradiction and neutral. We only use the entailment-labeled part, which contains 183,416 premise-hypothesis pairs in the training set, 3,329 pairs in the validation set, and 3,368 pairs in the test set.

4.2 Experiment Settings

We adapt glove 840B 300d vectors [11] as our word representation, with out-of-vocabulary words randomly initialized by sampling values uniformly from $\left[-\sqrt{3}, \sqrt{3}\right]$. Dropout (= 0.5) is applied after each LSTM layer. Greedy decoding is used at test time. The dimension of LSTM units is fixed to 300 across all models, which are trained by the SGD algorithm (learning rate 0.3) with the mini-batch size of 64. All RTE systems in the EBR metric are executed by loading the pre-trained model published in their official website without retraining or fine-tuning.

4.3 Baseline Models

We implemented the GTE model proposed by Kolesnyk as our first baseline, which is a 2-layer unidirectional LSTM sequence-to-sequence model, as shown in Fig. 3. Furthermore, Bidirectional LSTM encoder (as depicted in Fig. 8) which is popular in RTE tasks [2] is also implemented as another baseline.

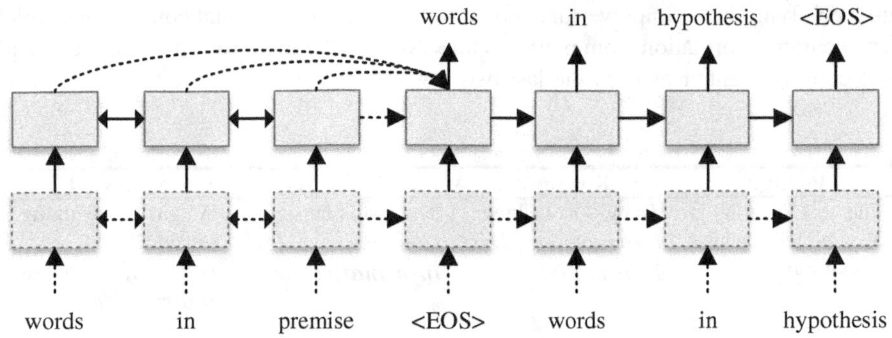

Fig. 8. 2-layer BiLSTM GTE model (Inspired by Chen et al. [2]).

Table 1. Correct rate (%) of GTE models.

Models	EBR				Manual
	BIUTEE	EDIT	TIE	MAJOR	
Nevěřilová	-	-	-	-	47.06
Kolesnyk	65.41	73.21	69.83	71.61	80.00
BiLSTM	66.26	74.34	72.13	74.02	81.00
ResLSTM	**67.39**	**78.24**	**75.31**	**77.14**	**84.00**

4.4 Results and Analyses

Table 1 shows the GTE results evaluated by EBR and human judgment[2], where Nevěřilová[3] represents a rule-based GTE approach [9]; Kolesnyk (2-layer unidirectional LSTM, Fig. 3) and BiLSTM (see Fig. 8) are our baseline models; ResLSTM is our improved sequence-to-sequence model. It is ideal to employ annotators to assess all the generated sentences, but due to the huge volume of our test dataset, human assessment is done by random sampling 300 produced hypotheses (100 for each approach).

The results demonstrate that our improved model outperforms other baseline models on both EBR and Manual metrics. Another conclusion drawn from the table is that EBR metric behaves in a rather consistent way with a human annotator, where they all believe ResLSTM performs better than BiLSTM and then a unidirectional one. This phenomenon suggests that EBR is a more reasonable replacement for inefficient human annotators.

After reviewing the hypotheses produced by all approaches above, we found that hypotheses generated by our residual model (e.g. the last column in Fig. 9) usually keep more accurate information from the same premises (e.g. the first column in Fig. 9) than baselines (e.g. the middle columns in Fig. 9), which confirms our conjecture of

[2] BELU, which is proved to be inappropriate in the context of GTE (See Sect. 3), is excluded.

[3] This model is not reimplemented. The number 47.06 is obtained from the original paper.

bottleneck lying in the unpowerful encoder. In addition, the residual connections which keep accurate information from premises make our model more robust when faced with some complex sentences (e.g. the last two rows in Fig. 9).

Premise	Kolesnyk	BiLSTM	ResLSTM
The girl wearing a brown jacket whilst walking in snow.	The girl is walking. *(correct, **less informative**)*	The girl is outside. *(correct, **less informative**)*	A girl is walking outside. *(correct, more informative)*
Three young women perform a dance in a crowded hall.	Three women dance. *(correct, **less informative**)*	Three women are dancing. *(correct, **less informative**)*	Three women dance in a crowded room. *(correct, more informative)*
Two middle-aged police officers watch over a parking lot, at night.	Two police are watching a race. ***(incorrect)***	The police officers are at night. *(correct, **less informative**)*	Two police officers are looking at a parking lot. *(correct, more informative)*
A mass of people looking and moving in the same general direction.	People are in the distance. ***(incorrect)***	The people are in the area. ***(incorrect)***	A group of people are in the same direction. *(correct)*

Fig. 9. Examples of generated hypotheses from the same premise.

5 Related Work

To the best of our knowledge, Jia [6] is the first researcher to study how to produce an entailed sentence from a given premise. He proposed a naïve rule-based algorithm repeating pattern matching and applying sentence rewriting rules developed by experts. Although these rules are reliable, the process of formulating entailment rules requires special knowledge and is inefficient. According to the author, only ten rules could be made up manually by an expert in one hour, which make it unacceptable in practical applications. Nevěřilová [9] developed a similar rule-based method which also suffers from the lack of inference knowledge, with the result that only 47.06% of generated hypotheses are correct.

Sequence-to-sequence recurrent neural networks were first proposed for machine translation by Cho et al. [3]. They use an LSTM network to encode the sentence in source language as a fixed-length vector, and then another LSTM network to decode the target translation from it. Their method is an end-to-end approach so that no rules are involved, which exactly meet our needs to eschew the lack of inference rules. Kolesnyk et al. [7] adapted the sequence-to-sequence framework from Cho for the GTE task. Furthermore, they employed a word-by-word attention, which allows the decoder to search in the encoder's outputs to avoid the memory bottleneck of the vanilla LSTM networks. Their model gets rid of the dependence on human-crafted inference rules, which makes it possible in practical applications. However, after reviewing their generated sentences, we found that the hypotheses produced by their model are often short and fragile when faced with more complex premises. We suspect that the problem may lie in the unpowerful sentence encoder, and our experiments confirm our assumption.

Prakash et al. [12] first proposed the stacked residual LSTM networks as sentence encoder by adding residual connections between vertically stacked multi-layer LSTM networks where the output of the previous layer of LSTM is fed to the input of the next one. Toderici et al. [13] used residual GRU to show an improvement in image compression rates for a given quality over JPEG. Our improved model is highly inspired by these RNN networks with residual connections.

All the works above on GTE use either human judgment or BLEU to evaluate the generated hypotheses by their models.

6 Conclusion and Future Work

In this paper, we described an improved sequence-to-sequence model with stacked residual LSTM networks and a novel evaluation metric EBR for the task of generating textual entailment. Experiments show that our improved model obtains state-of-the-art results and the EBR metric could validate various GTE models' performance efficiently in an objective and fair way.

We notice that there are also limitations in current sequence-to-sequence GTE models:

Firstly, hypotheses produced by current models are short for variety. Compared with the large space of possible valid hypotheses (see Fig. 9), only one sentence could be decoded by current sequence-to-sequence architecture, which is undesirable. Thus, how to increase the diversity of generation is a topic worthy of study.

Secondly, the hypotheses are generated blindly. In other words, the generation is performed without a purpose. For example, considering sentence S5 in Fig. 9, if the question is "what are the children doing?", sentence S6 should be generated. However, if the question is "where are the kids?", then a generation of S7 is more acceptable. Therefore, how to produce a hypothesis to meet some predefined requirements is another subject worthwhile to research.

As for the EBR metric, there is an inherent limitation – the correctness is upper-bounded by the correctness of the underlying classifiers. Although this problem is partially alleviated by an ensemble of heterogeneous RTE systems, a recognizing technique of reasoning relations with higher accuracy is always desirable.

We plan to study further along these directions.

Acknowledgements. This paper was supported by the National Natural Science Foundation of China (Grant No. 61472105, 61472107), The National High Technology Research and Development Program of China (863 Program) (2015AA015407).

References

1. Bowman, S.R., et al.: A large annotated corpus for learning natural language inference. In: Proceedings of the 2015 Conference on Empirical Methods in Natural Language Processing (EMNLP). Association for Computational Linguistics (2015). doi:10.18653/v1/d15-1075
2. Chen, Q., et al.: Enhancing and Combining Sequential and Tree LSTM for Natural Language Inference (2017). arXiv:160906038 Cs
3. Cho, K., et al.: Learning Phrase Representations using RNN Encoder-Decoder for Statistical Machine Translation (2014). arXiv:14061078 Cs Stat. doi:10.3115/v1/d14-1179
4. Dagan, I., Glickman, O., Magnini, B.: The PASCAL recognising textual entailment challenge. In: Quiñonero-Candela, J., Dagan, I., Magnini, B., d'Alché-Buc, F. (eds.) MLCW 2005. LNCS, vol. 3944, pp. 177–190. Springer, Heidelberg (2006). doi:10.1007/11736790_9
5. He, K., et al.: Deep residual learning for image recognition. In: 2016 IEEE Conference on Computer Vision and Pattern Recognition, CVPR (2016). doi:10.1109/cvpr.2016.90
6. Jia, J.: The generation of textual entailment with NLML in an intelligent dialogue system for language learning CSIEC. In: International Conference on Natural Language Processing and Knowledge Engineering, NLP-KE 2008, pp. 1–8. IEEE (2008). doi:10.1109/nlpke.2008.4906806
7. Kolesnyk, V., et al.: Generating Natural Language Inference Chains (2016). arXiv preprint: arXiv:160601404
8. Magnini, B., et al.: The excitement open platform for textual inferences. In: ACL (System Demonstrations), pp. 43–48 (2014). doi:10.3115/v1/p14-5008
9. Nevěřilová, Z.: Paraphrase and textual entailment generation. In: Sojka, P., Horák, A., Kopeček, I., Pala, K. (eds.) TSD 2014. LNCS, vol. 8655, pp. 293–300. Springer, Cham (2014). doi:10.1007/978-3-319-10816-2_36
10. Papineni, K., et al.: BLEU: a method for automatic evaluation of machine translation. In: Proceedings of the 40th Annual Meeting on Association for Computational Linguistics, pp. 311–318. Association for Computational Linguistics (2002). doi:10.3115/1073083.1073135
11. Pennington, J., et al.: Glove: global vectors for word representation. In: EMNLP, pp. 1532–1543 (2014). doi:10.3115/v1/d14-1162
12. Prakash, A., et al.: Neural Paraphrase Generation with Stacked Residual LSTM Networks (2016). arXiv:161003098 Cs
13. Toderici, G., et al.: Full Resolution Image Compression with Recurrent Neural Networks (2016). arXiv preprint: arXiv:160805148

Unsupervised Joint Entity Linking over Question Answering Pair with Global Knowledge

Cao Liu[1,2(✉)], Shizhu He[1], Hang Yang[1], Kang Liu[1], and Jun Zhao[1,2]

[1] National Laboratory of Pattern Recognition, Institute of Automation, Chinese Academy of Sciences, Beijing 100190, China
{cao.liu,shizhu.he,hang.yang,kliu,jzhao}@nlpr.ia.ac.cn
[2] University of Chinese Academy of Sciences, Beijing 100049, China

Abstract. We consider the task of entity linking over question answering pair (QA-pair). In conventional approaches of entity linking, all the entities whether in one sentence or not are considered the same. We focus on entity linking over QA-pair, in which question entity and answer entity are no longer fully equivalent and they are with the explicit semantic relation. We propose an unsupervised method which utilizes global knowledge of QA-pair in the knowledge base(KB). Firstly, we collect large-scale Chinese QA-pairs and their corresponding triples in the knowledge base. Then mining global knowledge such as the probability of relation and linking similarity between question entity and answer entity. Finally integrating global knowledge and other basic features as well as constraints by integral linear programming(ILP) with an unsupervised method. The experimental results show that each proposed global knowledge improves performance. Our best F-measure on QA-pairs is **53.7%**, significantly increased **6.5%** comparing with the competitive baseline.

Keywords: Joint entity linking · Question answering pair · Global knowledge · Integral linear programming

1 Introduction

Entity Linking (EL) plays an important role in natural language processing, which aims to link text span or name **mention** with **entity** in the knowledge bases [2,5,7,9,10,16]. Entity linking is widely used in Information Extraction(IE), knowledge-based question answering(KB-QA), and some other AI applications. Recently, we witness many large-scale knowledge bases(KBs), such as Freebase [3], DBpedia [1], WikiData[1]. Although they contain lots of structured knowledge in the form of triple(*head entity, relation, tail entity*), there is much missing knowledge in the knowledge bases. On the one hand, entity linking contributes to expanding knowledge bases by extracting unstructured text. On the other hand, entity linking is a key step for developing current knowledge bases to other NLP tasks.

[1] https://www.Wikidata.org/wiki/Wikidata:Main_Page.

M. Sun et al. (Eds.): CCL 2017 and NLP-NABD 2017, LNAI 10565, pp. 273–286, 2017.
https://doi.org/10.1007/978-3-319-69005-6_23

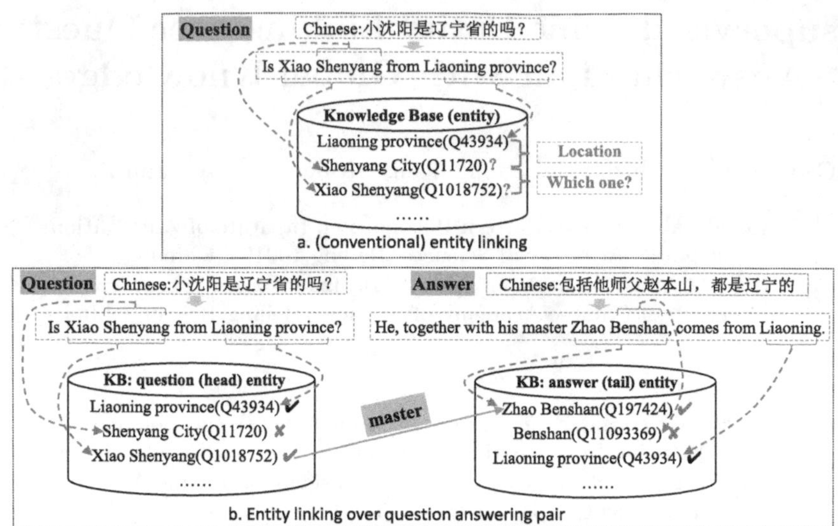

Fig. 1. An illustration of entity linking and entity liking over question answering pair

We focus on entity linking over QA-pair, in which the answer is a fluency, correct and coherent response(e.g., answer in Fig. 1(b) *He, together with his master Zhao Benshan, comes from Liaoning.*), rather than the solitary entity or phrase. Such answer provides a friendly interaction for human-machine. Furthermore, it provides some explanation of answering process which could be used to answering verification and is better to support downstream tasks such as synthetic speech [12]. These QA-pairs widely appears in community website, such as Quara[2], Wiki.answer[3], Baidu Zhidao[4] and so on. Yin et al. proposed generative natural answers in sequence-to-sequence Generative-QA based on Chinese community website including Baidu Zhidao [20]. Entity linking over QA-pair, as a kind of entity linking, not only contributes to the development of entity linking, but also benefits to choose QA-pairs which suit for answering automaticly [20].

Entity linking over QA-pair is different from conventional entity linking. Firstly, entity linking is multi-sentences and multi-entities linking, which inputs at least two sentences including question and answer. So the number of entities is uncertain. The significant difference, entity linking over QA-pair considers the explicit semantic relation in the KB between question entity(entity in the question) and answer entity(entity in the answer), while traditional (collective) entity linking takes the coherent topic or semantic into consideration [9,10], and all entities whether in one sentence or not are considered the same. Therefore, it is lack of constraints on the explicit semantic relation. As for the question *Is Xiao Shenyang from Liaoning province?* shown in Fig. 1(a), mention *Xiao Shenyang*,

[2] https://www.quora.com/.
[3] http://www.answers.com/Q/.
[4] https://zhidao.baidu.com/.

Shenyang and *Liaoning province* correspond entity *Xiao Shenyang(Q1018752)*, *Shenyang City (Q11720)* and *Liaoning province(Q43934)* in the KB respectively. Both of *Shenyang City(Q11720)* and *Liaoning province(Q43934)* are locations, and they are close in the topic space. So it is likely to link the wrong entity *Shenyang City(Q11720)* rather than *Xiao Shenyang(Q1018752)* for conventional entity linking. As for entity linking over QA-pair, question entity and tail entity are constrained on the explicit semantic relation, e.g., triple *(head entity, relation, tail entity)*. One basic hypothesis is that question entity is one of *head entity* and *tail entity*, and the answer entity is the other. In most cases, question entity and answer entity are *head entity* and *tail entity* respectively [20]. So question entity and answer entity are no longer fully equivalent. As shown in Fig. 1(b), there is relation *master* between question entity *Xiao Shenyang(Q1018752)* and answer entity *Zhao Benshan(Q197424)*. If taking such explicit semantic relation into consideration, it is more likely to link the correct entity *Xiao Shenyang(Q1018752)* rather than *Shenyang City(Q11720)*.

In this paper, firstly, we collect 5,546,743 QA-pairs from Baidu Zhidao and get their corresponding triples in Wikidata for all the QA-pairs. Furthermore, we exploit global knowledge of QA-pair in the KB for entity linking. The most significant global knowledge are: 1) The probability of relation between question entity and answer entity. The higher probability means that these entities are more likely to be linked. We train TransE [4] to represent the entity, then using multi-layer perceptrons to calculate the probability of relation between question entity and answer entity. 2) Linking similarity between question entity and answer entity in the KB. We count the same entities which for question entity and answer entity linked to. Finally, Integral linear programming(ILP)[11,18] integrates the above as well as some other basic features and constraints. Specifically, ILP is unsupervised and convenient to increase or decrease features and constraints. The experimental results show that each proposed knowledge improves performance. Our best F-measure on QA-pairs is **53.7%**, significantly increased **6.5%** comparing with the competitive baseline.

2 Task and Data

2.1 Task Description

The input, task of entity linking over QA-pairs, is natural question and answer. All mention-entity pairs in the QA-pair should be returned. e.g., as shown in Fig. 1(b), **Question:** *Is Xiao Shenyang from Liaoning province?* and **Answer:** *He, together with his master Zhao BenShan, comes from Liaoning*. Mention-entity: *Xiao Shenyang-Xiao Shenyang(Q1018752)* for question, *Liaoning(province)-Liaoning province(Q43934)* for question and answer, and *Zhao BenShan-Zhao BenShan(Q197424)* for answer should be returned. Other mentions such as *Shenyang* and *BenShan* are noise. In fact, their entity *Shenyang City(Q11720)* is nearly to *Liaoning province(Q43934)* in semantic space, and the *Benshan(Q11093369)* is another entity of person.

2.2 Data

To research the task of entity linking over QA-pair, we construct a new database collected from the Internet. The dataset and extracted process as follows:

1. **QA-pairs**: We crawl HTML files from Baidu Zhidao and extract QA-pairs from them. We obtain 5,546,743 QA-pairs(Table 1) after filtering these which either question or answer is longer than 50 in the number of characters. As for the task of entity linking, if question or entity do not contain entity, discarding it.
2. **Candidate mention and entity**: We use the tool FEL [2,16] to get the mentions, entities and their scores($Score_{fel}$). Especially, one mention may correspond more than one entity. Each entity is one to one correspondence on Wikipedia. All of them as candidates.
3. **Knowledge base**: We extract structured triple*(head entity, relation, tail entity)* from Wikidata. In particular, Wikidata is public and convenient to obtain. It is language-independent, which links to hundreds of languages and makes up to the lack of KB in Chinese. We totally get 80,421,642 triples and 22,450,412 entities. Some entities of Wikidata correspond to Wikipedia entity with simplified or complex Chinese. Fortunately, the entity outputted on the Tool *FET* is Wikipedia entity too. So, our entity in QA-pair links to Wikidata by Wikipedia entity. Eventually, these QA-pairs match 3,581,158 triples and 1,069,593 different entities.

Table 1. Dataset of QA-pairs and KB

Baidu Zhidao	Extracted knowledge base		KB corresponding to QA-pairs	
#QA-pairs	#triples	#entities	#triples	#entities
5,546,743	80,421,642	22,450,412	3,581,158	1,069,593

After getting QA-pairs, candidate mentions and entities, the key challenge in entity linking is to choose appropriate mentions and their corresponding entities from candidates. Due to the lack of labeled data, it's hard to use supervised or semi-supervised methods. To make use of the question, answer and knowledge bases with unsupervised way, we take advantage of integral linear programming(ILP) to integrate global knowledge between question entity and answer entity on the next section.

3 Methodology

Overall structure of integral linear programming for entity linking over QA-pair illustrates in Fig. 2. As for each QA-pair, all candidate mentions and entities are the variables which equal 0 or 1. The objective function contains different

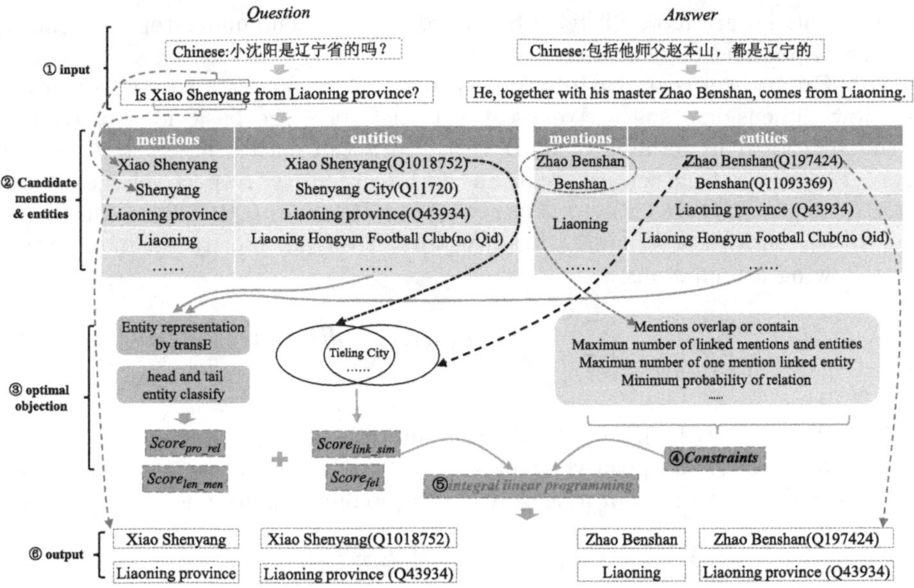

Fig. 2. Overall structure of integral linear programming for entity linking over QA-pair

features to guarantee that the selected mention or entity are relevant, consistent, correct. Because ILP is unsupervised, we can design different features and constraints to decide which of them are effective. We consider two important features as global knowledge: (1) The probability of relation between question entity and answer entity(noted as $Score_{pro\_rel}$). If there is the semantic relation between question entity and answer entity, such as *(question entity, relation, answer entity)*, these entities are more likely to be linked. (2) Linking similarity between question entity and answer entity($Score_{link\_sim}$). The more same entities which question entity and answer entity link to, the higher possibility that linking to these entities. Beside, there are some basic features: the score of FEL($Score_{fel}$), and the length of mention($Score_{len\_men}$). As for constraints, we consider as follows: Selected mention can not contain or overlap, the maximum number of linked mentions and entities in the question or answer, the number of one mention corresponds an entity at most and so on. Finally, combining all scores of features as optimized objections and constraints to ILP, then obtaining the linked mentions and entities.

3.1 Features

The Probability of Relation Between Question Entity and Answer Entity. This step aims to calculate the probability of relation between question entity and answer entity. The better probability means that the question entity and answer entity exist more semantic relation in the knowledge base, the two entities are more likely to be linked entities. The main steps are entity representation and classification.

(a) Entity representation: Entity representation aims to embed entity into low dimensional space. We use the transE [4]. The basic idea of transE is the relational hypothesis of head entity and tail entity: $h + r \approx t$, where h, r, t denotes head entity, relation and tail entity respectively, such as $Xiao\,Shenyang(Q1018752) + master \approx Zhao\,BenShan(Q197424)$. After getting all the entities to Wikidata for QA-pairs. We train the transE model with the following formulations:

$$L = \sum_{(h,r,t)\in S} \sum_{(h',r,t')\in S'_{h,r,t}} [\gamma + d(h,r,t) - d(h',r,t')]_+ + \alpha\|\theta\| \tag{1}$$

where $[x]_+$ is $max(0,x)$, $\gamma(\gamma>0)$ denotes margin hyperparameter. $\|\theta\|$ is the regular term. S is the positive triples (h,r,t), while S' is negative triple by random replacing h or t, but a negative example only replace one of h and t, as:

$$S' = \{(h',r,t)\} \cup \{(h,r,t')\} \tag{2}$$

The distance between h, r and t notes $d(h,r,t)$, and:

$$d(h,r,t) = \sum_{i\in D}(h_i + r_i - t_i) \tag{3}$$

where D is the dimensionality of entity, we calculate errors of h, r, t directly.

(b) Calculating the probability of relation by classifying question entity and answer entity: Entity representation by transE is used to the input of calculating probability of relation. For triple*(head entity, relation, tail entity)*, we view *head entity* combined with *tail entity* as the positive instance, and their expected probability of relation is 1. We random sample negative example by replacing one of head entity and tail entity, and their expected probability is 0.

Here, a *softmax* classifier with two-layer MLP(multi-layer perceptron) is used to calculate the probability of relation. The middle layer used the rectified linear unit (ReLU) as activation function. Finally, we get the score of *head entity* and *tail entity* with relation, noted as $Score_{pro\_rel}$.

We consider question entity and answer entity are head entity and tail entity respectively. Each question entity and answer entity pair, can get the probability of relation. As shown in Fig. 2, because of the triple *(Xiao Shenyang(Q1018752), master, Zhao BenShan(Q197424))*, the $Score_{pro\_rel}$ for either question entity *Xiao Shenyang(Q1018752)* or answer entity *Zhao BenShan(Q197424)* is high.

Linking Similarity Between Question Entity and Answer Entity: The probability of relation between question entity and answer entity consider the direct relation. Besides, the same entities which link to both question entity and answer entity are another feature for entity linking. For example (shown in Fig. 2), *Xiao Shenyang(Q1018752)* links to *Tieling city(Q75268)*, and *Tieling city(Q75268)* links *Zhao Benshan(Q197424)* too. We count the mutual linked entity for question entity and answer entity. One question entity may correspond more than one answer entities, such as question entity *Xiao Shenyang(Q1018752)* corresponds different answer entities *Zhao Ben-Shan(Q197424)*, *BenShan(Q11093369)* and so on, which each of them is with linking similarity. So do other entities. Extracting the maximum as $Score_{link\_sim}$.

Basic Features: Besides the probability of relation and linking similarity. There are some other features. Firstly, the FEL tool gives each mention-entity pair a confident score when getting the candidate of mention and entity. The score is negative, the more approaching zero means better confident score. Adding a constant and becoming to the positive number. The confidence of FEL notes as $Score_{fel}$. Secondly, the length of mention contributes to entity linking. Intuitively, most entities are linked by mentions which are not too long. While long mentions link to entities usually possess high performance. Basing on the above observation, we add the length of mention as another feature, marked as $Score_{len\_men}$.

3.2 Model: Entity Linking over QA-pair by Integral Linear Programming(ILP)

Integral Linear Programming(ILP) is optimal problem under constraint condition. *'Integral'* means the variable is integral. The variable is usually binary. The binary variable represents selecting the variable or not. The definition of ILP with mathematical formula [15] as follows:

$$\begin{aligned} maximize \quad & c^T x \\ subject\ to \quad & Ax \leq b \\ & x \in \{0,1\} \end{aligned} \tag{4}$$

x is the variable which constraint in 0 or 1. Under the constraint $Ax \leq b$, getting the maximize objection $c^T x$.

As for entity linking over QA-pair by ILP, the above features(Score) can be the optimal objection of ILP. Adding some constraints to constitute the whole ILP. Integrating the different scores for question and answer. The mathematical optimizational objection is:

$$maximize \quad Score_{question} + Score_{answer} \tag{5}$$

where, $Score_{question}$ and $Score_{answer}$ are the total score of question and answering respectively, calculated as follows:

$$Score = c^T [Score_{fel}, Score_{len\_men}, Score_{link\_sim}, Score_{pro\_rel}] \tag{6}$$

c is the weight of features. The constrains of question and answer are:

1. **Mentions overlap or contain**: Selecting overlap or contain mentions is forbidden. For example, the mention *Xiao Shenyang* contains the mention *Shenyang*, so the two mentions are selected one at most, eventually.
2. **Maximun number of linked mentions and entities**: Choosing too many mentions or entities is more likely to bring noisy mentions and entities. It is necessary to set an appropriate threshold for maximum number of mentions and entities. Due to the unsupervised character of ILP, it is easy to change the threshold for different applications.
3. **Maximun number of one mention linked entities**: If mention links more than one entity, the ambiguity still exists. So a mention links one entity at most.
4. **Minimum probability of relation:** If the probabilities of relation for question entity to each answer entity are low, the most possibility is that the candidate question entity is improper. So does the answer entity. For example (shown in Fig. 2), the question mention *Shenyang* has a candidate entity *Shenyang Taoxian International Airport.* This entity is low probability of relation to all answer entities. In fact, it is wrong to link it. In our experiment, if the maximum probability of relation is small and less than the threshold, discard it.

Above are the optimal objection and their constraints. They can combine, remove and add randomly. If the entity as well as it's corresponding mention variable equals to 1, these mention-entity pairs are the final outputs.

4 Experiment

4.1 Dataset and Evaluation Metric

We extracted QA-pairs from Baidu Zhidao as the dataset. Due to the unlabeled mentions and entities, we invited the volunteer to label data for evaluation. Different mentions may link to the same entity, such as mention *Liaoning* and *Liaoning Province* are linked to entity *Liaoning province(Q43934)*. To be convenient for evaluation, we just label linked entity on QA-pairs. In fact, if the final entity is correct, the mention is less important. The volunteer labels 200 QA-pairs in total. To evaluate the performance in the question and answer, labeling question entity and answer entity respectively. In special, for testing system on one mention corresponding to one or multi candidate entities(such as: mention *Liaoning* links 2 candidate entities: *Liaoning Province* and *Liaoning Hongyun Football Club*, some mention may correspond only one entity). That one linked mention corresponds to multi-entities notes as **1-m**. And that one linked mention corresponds to only one candidate entity is **1-1**. We distinguish **1-m** and **1-1** in the question and answer by splitting QA-pairs as: (1) **QA:1-1** All linked mentions are one to one for entities in QA-pair. (2) **Q:1-m** Existing **1-m** only in the question. (3) **A:1-m** Existing **1-m** only in the answer. (4) **QA:1-m** Existing **1-m** in both question and answer. Each of them is 50 QA-pairs.

4.2 Evaluation Metric

We utilize standard precision, recall and F-measure to evaluate entity linking performance[5]. Where precision is the proportion for correctly returned entities to all returned entities, recall is the correctly returned entities to all labeling entity, F-measure reconciles precision and recall, they are:

$$precision = \frac{\|List_{return} \bigcap List_{label}\|}{\|List_{return}\|} \tag{7}$$

$$recall = \frac{\|List_{return} \bigcap List_{label}\|}{\|List_{label}\|} \tag{8}$$

$$F_1 = \frac{2 \cdot precision \cdot recall}{precision + recall} \tag{9}$$

4.3 Comparison Models

Our candidate mention-entity comes from FEL [2,16]. Mention-entity of FEL as well as confident score is pretty good. ILP with $Score_{fel}$ and constraints(except probability of relation) for candidate mention-entity of FEL is our baseline, noted *FEL* in following Table. *+len_men* uses $Score_{fel}$ and $Score_{len\_men}$ as optimal objection. *+link_sim* optimize $Score_{fel} + Score_{len\_men} + Score_{link\_sim}$. While *pro_rel* continues to add optimal objection $Score_{pro\_rel}$. In particular, each question(or answer) entity corresponds more than one probabilities of relation. That calculating the sum, maximum and average are make sense. If no special explaination, probability of relation is the average. *Questions* and *Answers* stand for evaluating in the question and answer respectively, while *QA-pairs* represent performance on both question and answer. By the way, all the performance is percentage(%). Specially, we compare different methods on QA-pair, single question or answer on the four label datasets.

4.4 Overall Performance

We evaluate the performance of different methods on the *Questions*, *Answers* and *QA-pairs*. The overall performance on test data is shown in Table 2. The conclusions are:

1. Each feature improves performance on *QA-pairs*. Taking the length of mention into consideration improves prominently.
2. ***+link_sim*** as well as ***+pro_rel*** contribute to improve performance. Both of them are global knowledge of QA-pair as well as their knowledge in the KB.
3. The entity linking performance on the *Questions* is superior to the *Answers* for the whole data. Intuitively, QA-pairs come from the community website. Asking the question aims at solving the question, The question is usually specific while the answer is uncertain. So entity linking in the *Questions* is easier than entity linking in the *Answers*.

[5] http://nlp.cs.rpi.edu/kbp/2014/scoring.html.

Table 2. Overall performance

Methods	*Questions*			*Answers*			*QA-pairs*		
	P	R	F	P	R	F	P	R	F
FEL	46.3	61.7	52.9	33.1	53.3	40.8	39.9	58.0	47.2
+len_men	51.8	68.7	59.0	34.8	56.2	43.0	43.5	63.2	51.5
+link_sim	51.9	**69.2**	**59.3**	36.5	59.2	45.2	44.4	**64.8**	52.7
+pro_rel	**52.5**	65.0	58.0	40.2	**62.1**	**48.8**	**46.4**	63.7	**53.7**

4. The best F-measure on QA-pairs is **53.7%**, improving apparently **6.5%** compared with *FEL* **47.2%**.

4.5 Performance on One Mention Corresponding to Different Number of Entities

To evaluate performance of **1-m** on the question and answer respectively, we compare our model on **QA:1-1**, **Q:1-m**, **A:1-m** and **QA:1-m**. The detail results are shown in Table 3. We can get:

Table 3. Performance on mention corresponding different number of entities

Methods	Datas	QA:1-1			Q:1-m			A:1-m			QA:1-m		
		P	R	F	P	R	F	P	R	F	P	R	F
FEL	*Questions*	55.1	69.0	61.3	50.0	62.2	55.4	44.8	60.6	51.5	44.3	62.3	51.8
	Answers	36.8	53.3	43.5	26.9	44.6	33.6	37.8	54.0	44.4	34.8	**62.0**	44.6
	QA-pairs	46.0	61.8	52.8	38.4	54.6	45.1	41.4	57.5	48.1	39.8	62.2	48.5
+len_men	*Questions*	60.7	76.1	67.5	55.4	68.9	61.5	51.6	69.0	59.0	48.5	*68.1*	**56.6**
	Answers	43.7	63.3	51.7	32.3	53.6	40.3	37.4	54.0	44.2	34.8	**62.0**	44.6
	QA-pairs	52.3	70.2	59.9	43.8	62.3	51.4	44.6	61.9	51.9	41.9	65.6	51.2
+link_sim	*Questions*	57.3	71.8	63.8	**59.8**	**74.3**	**66.3**	49.0	66.2	56.3	47.4	66.7	55.4
	Answers	39.8	58.3	47.3	32.3	53.6	40.3	**44.6**	**65.1**	**52.9**	32.6	58.0	41.7
	QA-pairs	48.6	65.7	55.8	**46.0**	**65.4**	**54.0**	46.8	65.7	54.7	40.3	**63.0**	49.2
+pro_rel	*Questions*	**67.9**	**80.3**	**73.6**	46.6	55.4	50.6	**61.8**	**77.5**	**68.8**	**48.9**	62.3	54.8
	Answers	**47.1**	**66.7**	**55.2**	**37.4**	**60.7**	**46.3**	44.0	63.5	52.0	**39.2**	**62.0**	**48.1**
	QA-pairs	**57.4**	**74.1**	**64.7**	41.9	57.7	48.5	**52.8**	**70.9**	**60.5**	**44.3**	62.2	**51.8**

1. Simple situation (**QA:1-1**) gets better than complex cases (**Q:1-m**, **A:1-m** and **QA:1-m**) for all methods on F-measure. It proves that **1-m** is more challenge than **1-1**.
2. When adding linking similarity, performance on *Questions* improved much for **Q:1-m** while performance on *Answers* is in low level, and performance on *Answers* of **A:1-m** achieved the best performance while performance of *Questions* is low. However, ***+pro_rel*** improves performance on one of *Questions* and *Answers*, and the other maintains good relatively at the same time. It implies that ***+pro_rel*** keeps the balanced performance on the *Questions* and *Answers* when improving one of them.

3. On most of situations, ***+pro_rel*** achieved the best performance. Which proved again that all of our features are effective. Especially, the probability of relation improves performance at last.

4.6 Performance on Different Forms to the Probabilities of Relation Between Question Entity and Answer Entity

The above experiments show that the probability of relation is an important feature. $Score_{pro\_rel}$ can be the sum, maximum and average (noted ***pro_rel_sum***, ***pro_rel_max*** and ***pro_rel_ave*** respectively) when question(answer) entity calculates the probability of relation with different answer (question) entities. Table 4 shows the results on different form to calculate the probability of relation. ***pro_rel_ave*** achieved the best performance on the whole situations as well as different evaluation metrics. Intuitively, the sum may bring some noise and the maximum will get good performance. While ***pro_rel_max*** superiors ***pro_rel_sum*** a little and inferiors to ***pro_rel_ave***. One guess is that the maximum is influenced largely by noise. We look forward the performance on the probability of relation between question entity and answer entity. The precisions are 85.6% for positive example, 86.6% for negative example, respectively. Although the performance is pretty good, it still exists noise which make the maximum bad performance.

Table 4. Performance on different forms to the probabilities of relation

Methods	*Questions*			*Answers*			*QA-pairs*		
	P	R	F	P	R	F	P	R	F
pro_rel_sum	50.8	62.6	56.1	39.9	61.5	48.4	45.3	62.1	52.4
pro_rel_max	51.7	64.0	57.2	39.9	61.5	48.4	45.8	62.9	53.0
pro_rel_ave	**52.5**	**65.0**	**58.0**	**40.2**	**62.1**	**48.8**	**46.4**	**63.7**	**53.7**

5 Related Work

Entity linking is a foundational research in natural language processing. Many works researched on entity linking. Mihalcea & Csomai use cosine distance to calculate between mention and entity [6]. Milne et al. calculate the mention-to-entity compatibility by using inter-dependency of mention and entity [14]. Zhou et al. propose ranking-based and classification-based resolution approaches which disambiguate both entities and word senses [22]. While it is lack of global constraints. Han et al. propose Structural Semantic Relatedness and collective entity linking [9,10]. Medelyan et al. take the semantic relatedness of candidate entity as well as contextual entities into consideration [13]. These semantic relations of this work are relatively simple. Blanco et al. multilingual entity extraction and linking with fast speed(named as fast entity linking(FEL)) and high performance

[2,16]. It divides entity linking into mention detection, candidate entity retrieval, entity disambiguation for mentions with multiple candidate entities and mention clustering for mentions that do not link to any entity. This paper utilizes less feature to realize multilingual, fast and unsupervised entity linking with high performance.

As for entity linking on question answering over knowledge base, [17] using Smart (Structured Multiple Additive Regression Trees) tool [19] for entity linking, which returned all the possible candidate entity for freebase by surface matching and ranking via statistical model. Dai et al. realize the importance of entity linking on KB-QA [8]. They explore entity priority or relation priority. The candidate entities are large, while relation is with a small number. Determining firstly relation contributes to entity linking for reducing candidates. Yin et al. come up with active entity linker by sequential labeling to search surface pattern in the entity vocabulary lists [21].

In short, these methods consider all entities whether in one sentence or not are the same. However, question entity and answer entity in QA-pair usually represent head entity and tail entity respectively with the explicit semantic relation. So we take the semantic relation of question entity and answer entity into consideration.

6 Conclusion

This paper proposes a novel entity linking over question answer pair. Differring from traditional entity linking which considers the coherent topic or semantic and all the entity are the same. Question entity and answer entity are no longer fully equivalent, and they are constrained with the explicit semantic relation. We collect a large-scale Chinese QA-pairs along with their corresponding triples as knowledge base, and propose unsupervised integral linear programming to get the linked entities of QA-pair. The main steps of our method: (1) Retrieving candidate mentions and entities, (2) Setting optimal objection. The main objections are the probability of relation and linking similarity between question entity and answer entity, which are the global knowledge of QA-pair and could be used to semantic constraints. (3) Adding some constraints of mention and entity. (4) Combining optimal objection and constraints to integer linear programming, and obtaining target mention and entity. The experimental results show that each proposed global knowledge improves performance. Our best F-measure on QA-pairs is **53.7%**, significantly increased **6.5%** comparing with the competitive baseline.

Acknowledgements. This work was supported by the Natural Science Foundation of China (No. 61533018) and the National Basic Research Program of China (No. 2014CB340503). And this research work was also supported by Google through focused research awards program.

References

1. Auer, S., Bizer, C., Kobilarov, G., Lehmann, J., Cyganiak, R., Ives, Z.: DBpedia: a nucleus for a web of open data. In: Aberer, K., Choi, K.-S., Noy, N., Allemang, D., Lee, K.-I., Nixon, L., Golbeck, J., Mika, P., Maynard, D., Mizoguchi, R., Schreiber, G., Cudré-Mauroux, P. (eds.) ASWC/ISWC -2007. LNCS, vol. 4825, pp. 722–735. Springer, Heidelberg (2007). doi:10.1007/978-3-540-76298-0_52
2. Blanco, R., Ottaviano, G., Meij, E.: Fast and space-efficient entity linking in queries. In: Proceedings of the Eight ACM International Conference on Web Search and Data Mining, WSDM 15, NY, USA. ACM, New York (2015)
3. Bollacker, K., Evans, C., Paritosh, P., Sturge, T., Taylor, J.: Freebase: a collaboratively created graph database for structuring human knowledge. In: Proceedings of the 2008 ACM SIGMOD International Conference on Management of Data, pp. 1247–1250. AcM (2008)
4. Bordes, A., Usunier, N., Garcia-Duran, A., Weston, J., Yakhnenko, O.: Translating embeddings for modeling multi-relational data. In: Advances in Neural Information Processing Systems, pp. 2787–2795 (2013)
5. Bunescu, R.C., Pasca, M.: Using encyclopedic knowledge for named entity disambiguation. Eacl **6**, 9–16 (2006)
6. Csomai, A., Mihalcea, R.: Linking documents to encyclopedic knowledge. IEEE Intell. Syst. **23**(5) (2008)
7. Cucerzan, S.: Large-scale named entity disambiguation based on wikipedia data (2007)
8. Dai, Z., Li, L., Xu, W.: CFO: conditional focused neural question answering with large-scale knowledge bases. arXiv preprint arXiv:1606.01994 (2016)
9. Han, X., Sun, L., Zhao, J.: Collective entity linking in web text: a graph-based method. In: Proceedings of the 34th International ACM SIGIR Conference on Research and Development in Information Retrieval, pp. 765–774. ACM (2011)
10. Han, X., Zhao, J.: Named entity disambiguation by leveraging wikipedia semantic knowledge. In: Proceedings of the 18th ACM Conference on Information and Nowledge Management, pp. 215–224. ACM (2009)
11. Khachiyan, L.G.: Polynomial algorithms in linear programming. USSR Comput. Mathe. Mathe. Phys. **20**(1), 53–72 (1980)
12. McTear, M., Callejas, Z., Griol, D.: The Conversational Interface. Springer, Cham (2016)
13. Medelyan, O., Witten, I.H., Milne, D.: Topic indexing with Wikipedia. In: Proceedings of the AAAI WikiAI workshop, vol. 1, pp. 19–24 (2008)
14. Milne, D., Witten, I.H.: Learning to link with Wikipedia. In: Proceedings of the 17th ACM Conference on Information and knowledge Management, pp. 509–518. ACM (2008)
15. Papadimitriou, C.H., Steiglitz, K.: Combinatorial optimization: algorithms and complexity. Courier Corporation (1982)
16. Pappu, A., Blanco, R., Mehdad, Y., Stent, A., Thadani, K.: Lightweight multilingual entity extraction and linking. In: Proceedings of the Tenth ACM International Conference on Web Search and Data Mining, WSDM 17, NY, USA. ACM, New York (2017)
17. Xu, K., Reddy, S., Feng, Y., Huang, S., Zhao, D.: Question answering on freebase via relation extraction and textual evidence. arXiv preprint arXiv:1603.00957 (2016)

18. Yahya, M., Berberich, K., Elbassuoni, S., Ramanath, M., Tresp, V., Weikum, G.: Natural language questions for the web of data. In: Proceedings of the 2012 Joint Conference on Empirical Methods in Natural Language Processing and Computational Natural Language Learning, pp. 379–390. Association for Computational Linguistics (2012)
19. Yang, Y., Chang, M.W.: S-mart: novel tree-based structured learning algorithms applied to tweet entity linking. arXiv preprint arXiv:1609.08075 (2016)
20. Yin, J., Jiang, X., Lu, Z., Shang, L., Li, H., Li, X.: Neural generative question answering. In: Proceedings of the Twenty-Fifth International Joint Conference on Artificial Intelligence (IJCAI-16) Neural (2016)
21. Yin, W., Yu, M., Xiang, B., Zhou, B., Schütze, H.: Simple question answering by attentive convolutional neural network. arXiv preprint arXiv:1606.03391 (2016)
22. Zhou, Y., Nie, L., Rouhani-Kalleh, O., Vasile, F., Gaffney, S.: Resolving surface forms to Wikipedia topics. In: Proceedings of the 23rd International Conference on Computational Linguistics, pp. 1335–1343. Association for Computational Linguistics (2010)

Hierarchical Gated Recurrent Neural Tensor Network for Answer Triggering

Wei Li and Yunfang Wu(✉)

Key Laboratory of Computational Linguistics (Peking University), Ministry of Education, School of Electronic Engineering and Computer Science, Peking University, Beijing, China
{liweitj47,wuyf}@pku.edu.cn

Abstract. In this paper, we focus on the problem of answer triggering addressed by Yang et al. (2015), which is a critical component for a real-world question answering system. We employ a hierarchical gated recurrent neural tensor (HGRNT) model to capture both the context information and the deep interactions between the candidate answers and the question. Our result on F value achieves 42.6%, which surpasses the baseline by over 10 %.

Keywords: Answer Triggering · Question Answering · Hierarchical gated recurrent neural tensor network

1 Introduction

Answer triggering is a crucial subtask of the open domain question answering (QA) system. It is first brought up by Yang et al. (2015), where the goal is first to detect whether there exist answers in a set of candidate sentences for a question, and if so return the correct answer. This problem is similar to answer selection (AS) in the way that they all include selecting sentence(s) out of a paragraph. The difference is that AS tasks guarantee that there is at least one answer. Trec-QA (Wang et al. 2007) and WikiQA (Yang et al. 2015) have been the benchmark for such problems.

However, the assumption that at least one answer can be found in the candidate sentences may not be true for real-world applications. In many cases, none of the candidate sentences in the retrieved paragraph can answer the question. As reported by Yang et al. (2015), about 2/3 of the questions don't have any correct answers in the related paragraph in the WikiQA dataset. Therefore they claim that answer triggering task is essential in a real-world QA system. Unfortunately, most of the previous researchers neglect this problem and only concentrate on those questions that have correct answers. They either get rid of the unanswerable questions during the data construction procedure (Wang et al. 2007) or omit the unanswerable questions directly when predicting, for instance, Wang and Jiang (2016); Wang et al. (2016, 2017).

Although recent works that focus on measuring the similarity between an individual candidate answer and its corresponding question have reached very good MRR and MAP scores, they ignore the fact that these candidate answer sentences are continuous text in a paragraph in the setting of WikiQA. These sentences are not separate

M. Sun et al. (Eds.): CCL 2017 and NLP-NABD 2017, LNAI 10565, pp. 287–294, 2017.
https://doi.org/10.1007/978-3-319-69005-6_24

fragments, but under a common topic. Based on this observation, we assume that by bringing the context information of the sentences into consideration, we can get better results in the answer triggering problem. This assumption is verified by our experiments. The F score reaches 42.6% in the answer triggering problem of WikiQA, which surpasses the baseline in Yang et al. (2015) by 10%.

Our contributions lie in the following two aspects:

1. We bring attention to the problem of answer triggering, which is very important but has not been thoroughly studied. We improve the F score by 10% over the original baseline model.
2. We employ a hierarchical recurrent neural tensor (HGRNT) model to take context information into consideration when predicting whether a sentence is a correct answer towards the question. Our experiments demonstrate that the context information consistently increases the F score no matter what sentence encoder structures are used.

2 Related Work

In the previous studies, researchers tend to focus on the ranking part of the answer selection (AS) problem, what they need to do is to extract the most probable one from a set of pre-selected sentences. Traditional approaches calculate the similarity of two sentences based on hand crafted features (Yao et al. 2013; Heilman and Smith 2010; Severyn and Moschitti 2013). As deep learning thrives, researchers turn to deep learning methods. At the early stage, they apply neural networks like recurrent neural networks (RNN) or convolutional neural networks (CNN) to encode each of the sentences into a fixed length vector, and then compare the question and answer by calculating the semantic distance between these two vectors (Feng et al. 2015; Wang and Nyberg 2015).

Recent works focus on bringing attention mechanism into the question answering problem inspired by the success of attention based machine translation (Bahdanau et al. 2014). Hermann et al. (2015) and Tan et al. (2015) introduced attention into the RNN encoder in the QA setting. From then on, researchers have tried many kinds of ways to improve the attention mechanism on QA, like Yin et al. (2015); dos Santos et al. (2016); Wang et al. (2016). Wang et al. (2016) made a very successful attempt at doing impatient inner attention instead of the traditional outer attention over the hidden states of the sentences. They claim that this can make use of both the local word/phrase information and the sentence information. Wang and Jiang (2016) and Wang et al. (2017) apply a compare and aggregate framework on AS, and compare various ways to compute similarities between question and answer.

3 Our Approach

As is described in Yang et al. (2015), when they construct the WikiQA dataset, they first ask the annotators to decide whether the retrieved paragraph can answer the question. If so, the annotator is further asked to select which of the sentences can answer the question individually. Otherwise, each of the sentences in the paragraph is marked as *No*. Based on this observation, we assume that the overall information of the paragraph can be of help to predict the answer. Therefore, we propose our HGRNT model that aims to take the context information into consideration when calculating the confidence score of each candidate sentence.

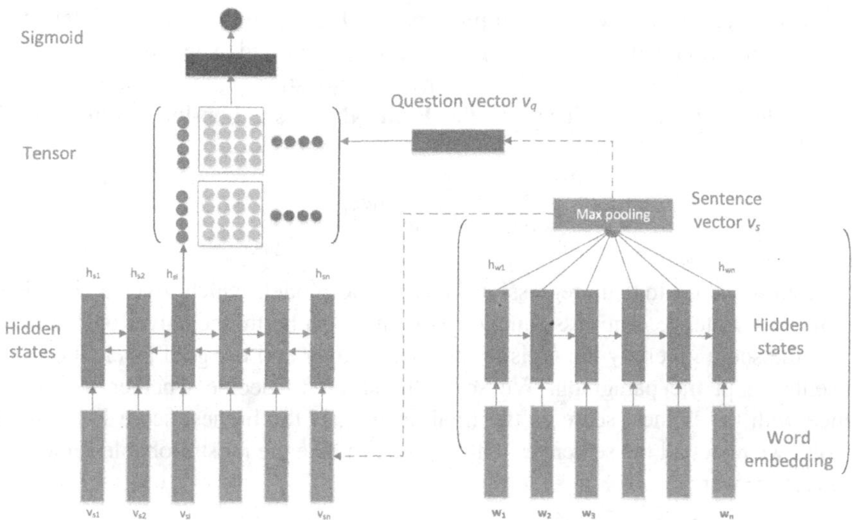

Fig. 1. Hierarchical gated recurrent neural tensor model for answer triggering problem

3.1 Hierarchical Gated Recurrent Neural Tensor model

Our approach is depicted in Fig. 1, we first encode the question sentence into a fixed length vector v_q with the simple Gated Recurrent Neural Network (GRNN) (Cho et al. 2014). Then we encode answer sentences into vectors v_s with another encoder. Different strategies of this answer sentence encoder can be applied. We will show the results of some models that have achieved state-of-the-art results on the AS problem in the next subsection[1]. The objectives of these models are very similar to our task except that they focus on the relative ranking scores of the sentences. In the bottom right part of Fig. 1, we present the encoder that gives the best result. Both the question encoder and the answer encoder are GRNN with max pooling. The dashed line in Fig. 1

[1] We re-implement the model as the paper described, but we were not able to get as good as the original MRR and MAP result they claim. But this is not the focus of our paper.

between max-pooling layer and v_s or v_q indicates that there is no transformation between these two parts.

After we get the vectors of the candidate sentences v_s, we go over the vector of each sentence in the paragraph with bidirectional gated recurrent neural networks (BiGRNN), which lets the context information flow between answer sentences. Each sentence vector is treated as one time step in the BiGRNN. We denote the hidden states of the BiGRNN as h_s, which capture the context information. We use BiGRNN because we think that context from both directions are important, and the gate mechanism can filter out the irrelevant information.

As is testified in Qiu and Huang (2015), neural tensor network is very effective in modelling the similarity between two sentences. After we get the answer sentence representation h_s produced by BiGRNN, we connect h_s with the question vector v_q by a neural tensor layer as is shown in the top left part of Fig. 1, so that the deep interactions between the question and candidate sentences can be captured. The tensor layer can be calculated with Eq. 1, where v_q is the vector of the question, h_s is the hidden states of the candidate sentence s produced by the BiGRNN, f is a non-linear function, like *sigmoid*.

$$\mathrm{T}(q, a) = f\left(v_q M^{[1:r]} h_a\right) \tag{1}$$

At last, we add a logistic regression layer to the model, which gives a confidence score of each sentence. The loss function is then set to be the negative log-likelihood between the score given by the logistic regression layer and the gold label (0 or 1) for each sentence in the paragraph. We set a threshold to decide whether to take the sentence with the highest score as the final answer. If the highest score is below the threshold, we reject all the sentences. Otherwise, we take the most probable sentence as the correct answer.

3.2 Sentence Encoder

The encoder of candidate sentences can be of various structures, which is not the focus of our paper. Here we list the ones we applied.

- Gated RNN: As is shown in the bottom right of Fig. 1, we use GRNN to go over each word embedding in the sentence, then max pooling is applied over the sentence length. The parameters of both candidate sentences and questions are shared.
- IARNN-Gate (Wang et al. 2016): This model is very similar to the GRNN model except that the question vector is first calculated and then is added to compute the gates of the answers. The details can be found in the original paper.
- Compare Aggregate model[2]: This model first performs word-level (context-level) matching, followed by aggregation using either CNN or RNN.

[2] This kind of model is some what sophistecated, so we can only give a brief description. Please refer to Wang and Jiang (2016) and Wang et al. (2017) for detail.

4 Experiment

In this paper, we conduct experiments on the WikiQA data. This data has already been split into train (70%), dev (10%) and test (20%) data. There are 3,047 questions in total, only 1,473 of which have answers. Each question is attached with a set of candidate sentences in a Wikipedia article.

All the hyper-parameters are tuned on the dev set. The word embeddings are pre-trained on the WikiQA corpus without fine-tuning by word2vec (Mikolov et al. 2013) tool-kit. We do our experiments using Tensorflow package (Abadi et al. 2015). The parameters in the model are all trained with Adam stochastic optimization method (Kingma and Ba 2014). We use GRNN as the aggregate part for the Compare Aggregate model.

Table 1. Results compared with (Yang et al. 2015), IARNN-Gate (Wang et al. 2016), Compare and Aggregate (Wang and Jiang 2016)

Model	Prec	Rec	F
Yang et al. (2015)	27.96	37.86	32.17
IARNN - Gate	25.94	42.39	32.19
+ context & tensor	36.82	44.86	40.45
compare aggregate	27.64	39.92	32.65
+ context & tensor	29.71	50.62	37.44
GRNN	38.03	25.51	30.54
+ context & tensor	40.91	44.44	42.6

Table 2. Effect of adding context information and tensor

Model	Prec	Rec	F
GRNN	38.03	25.51	30.54
+ tensor	39.36	30.45	34.34
+ context	37.55	42.80	39.99
+ context & tensor	40.91	44.44	42.6

4.1 Compare with Baselines

From Table 1 we can see, all the baseline models, even with state of the art MRR and MAP, get rather low F values which is the concern of our task. However, when these models are incorporated into our HGRNT framework, all of their F values are increased by a big margin. We think that this is because these models are only good at comparing the relative rank of sentences, but short at the ability to decide whether to accept the most probable sentence to be the answer. Context information becomes important in this situation. Additionally, these complicated models perform worse than our simple HGRNT, perhaps because they are affected by the scale of the corpus. Since the number of training samples is far from enough for such complicated neural models.

4.2 Effect of Context information

In this subsection, we analyze the effect of adding context information and tensor. As is shown in Table 2, the original GRNN model gives a poor result, with an F score of 30.54. However, both tensor network and context information give big improvements over the basic model. It is also worth noticing that the context information gives a significant gain in recall. This observation is consistent both with (30.45–44.44) and without (25.51–42.8) the tensor layer. We think that this is because with the help of context information our model can get hold of an overall idea about the whole retrieved paragraph. In the next subsection, we will give an example of how this global information facilitates the predicting of individual sentences.

4.3 Case Study

In this subsection, we make a detailed analysis on two examples. We choose the neural tensor model without context information as the baseline, so that the effect of context information can be highlighted.

1. **Question:** *what is korean money called*
   Candidates: ①←*the won (sign:; code: krw) is the currency of south korea.* ②←*a single won is divided into 100 jeon, the monetary subunit.* ③ *the jeon is no longer used for everyday transactions, and appears only in foreign exchange rates.*
2. **Question:** *where to write to mother angelica*
   Candidates: ①←*mother mary angelica of the annunciation, pcpa (born rita antoinette rizzo on april 20, 1923) is an american franciscan nun best known as a television personality and the founder of the eternal word television network.* ② *in 1944, she entered the poor clares of perpetual adoration, a franciscan religious order for women, as a postulant, and a year later she was admitted to the order as a novice.* ③ *she went on to find a new house for the order in 1962 in irondale, alabama, where the ewtn is headquartered, and in 1996 she initiated the building of the shrine of the most blessed sacrament and our lady of the angels monastery in hanceville, alabama.* ④←*mother angelica hosted shows on ewtn until she suffered a stroke in 2001.* ⑤ *she is a recipient of the pro ecclesia et pontifice award granted by pope benedict xvi and lives in the cloistered monastery in hanceville.*

Table 3. Scores given by the Gated recurrent tensor model and HGRNT in Example 1

Id	Golden label	Tensor	HGRNT
1	1	0.2432	0.4924
2	0	0.0622	0.1362
3	0	0.0588	0.0073

From Table 3 we can see that in Example 1, although the relative rank of both models are the same, our HGRNT model gives a higher score on the first sentence, which is exactly the correct answer. In the example, we can observe that these three candidate sentences are all about Korean currency. The first sentence points out the

Table 4. Scores given by the Gated recurrent tensor model and HGRNT in Example 2

Id	Golden label	Tensor	HGRNT
1	0	0.3045	0.0237
2	0	0.0243	0.0132
3	0	0.0846	0.0588
4	0	0.0104	0.0075
5	0	0.1	0.0183

answer, while the second sentence confirms the fact to be true by further dictating the relation between *won* and *jeon*, which are two Korean monetary subunits. This example shows that the context information can help predicting the score of individual sentences. It also explains why the recall rate is improved by a big margin when context information is added, as shown in Table 2. Additionally, from this example we can see that the models giving the same MRR and MAP may differ in F value, which explains why the state of the art models on answer selection task don't work well in our task (Table 4).

In Example 2 we can see that both models give very low scores on the second to the last sentences. The difference is that our HGRNT model makes the right decision by giving a rather low score on the first sentence. We think this is because the hierarchical structure can capture the context information and detect that the whole paragraph doesn't contain information about '*writing*' in the question.

5 Conclusion

In this paper, we employ a Hierarchical gated recurrent neural tensor model to deal with the answer triggering problem, which introduces the context information into our model. Our experiment result surpasses the baseline by over 10 %.

In the future we hope to develop a more sensible method to judge whether to accept a candidate sentence instead of setting a strict threshold. Additionally, the WikiQA corpus is too small for sophisticated models to work, and we hope to make use of abundant unlabeled raw data to help resolve this problem.

Acknowledgement. This work is supported by the National Key Basic Research Program of China (2014CB340504), the National Natural Science Foundation of China (61371129, 61572245).

References

Abadi, M., Agarwal, A., Barham, P., Brevdo, E., Chen, Z., Citro, C., Corrado, G.S., Davis, A., Dean, J., Devin, M., Ghemawat, S., Goodfellow, I., Harp, A., Irving, G., Isard, M., Jia, Y., Jozefowicz, R., Kaiser, L., Kudlur, M., Levenberg, J., Man´e, D., Monga, R., Moore, S., Murray, D., Olah, C., Schuster, M., Shlens, J., Steiner, B., Sutskever, I., Talwar, K., Tucker, P., Vanhoucke, V., Vasudevan, V., Vi´egas, F., Vinyals, O., Warden, P., Wattenberg, M., Wicke, M., Yu, Y., Zheng, X.: TensorFlow: large-scale machine learning on heterogeneous systems. Software available from tensorflow.org (2015). http://tensorflow.org/

Bahdanau, D., Cho, K., Bengio, Y.: Neural machine translation by jointly learning to align and translate. arXiv preprint arXiv:1409.0473 (2014)

Cho, K., Van Merriënboer, B., Gulcehre, C., Bahdanau, D., Bougares, F., Schwenk, H., Bengio, Y.: Learning phrase representations using RNN encoder-decoder for statistical machine translation. arXiv preprint arXiv:1406.1078 (2014)

dos Santos, C.N., Tan, M., Xiang, B., Zhou, B.: Attentive pooling networks. CoRR, abs/1602.03609 (2016)

Feng, M., Xiang, B., Glass, M.R., Wang, L., Zhou, B.: Applying deep learning to answer selection: a study and an open task. In: 2015 IEEE Workshop on Automatic Speech Recognition and Understanding (ASRU). IEEE, pp. 813–820 (2015)

Heilman, M., Smith, N.A.: Tree edit models for recognizing textual entailments, paraphrases, and answers to questions. In: Human Language Technologies: The 2010 Annual Conference of the North American Chapter of the Association for Computational Linguistics. Association for Computational Linguistics, pp. 1011–1019 (2010)

Hermann, K.M., Kocisky, T., Grefenstette, E., Espeholt, L., Kay, W., Suleyman, M., Blunsom, P.: Teaching machines to read and comprehend. In: Advances in Neural Information Processing Systems, pp. 1693–1701 (2015)

Kingma, D., Ba, J.: Adam: a method for stochastic optimization. arXiv preprint arXiv:1412.6980 (2014)

Mikolov, T., Sutskever, I., Chen, K., Corrado, G.S., Dean, J.: Distributed representations of words and phrases and their compositionality. In: Advances in Neural Information Processing Systems, pp. 3111–3119 (2013)

Qiu, X., Huang, X.: Convolutional neural tensor network architecture for community based question answering. In: IJCAI, pp. 1305–1311 (2015)

Severyn, A., Moschitti, A.: Automatic feature engineering for answer selection and extraction. In: EMNLP, vol. 13, pp. 458–467 (2013)

Tan, M., dos Santos, C., Xiang, B., Zhou, B.: LSTM-based deep learning models for non-factoid answer selection. arXiv preprint arXiv:1511.04108 (2015)

Wang, B., Liu, K., Zhao, J.: Inner attention based recurrent neural networks for answer selection. In: The Annual Meeting of the Association for Computational Linguistics (2016)

Wang, D., Nyberg, E.: A long short-term memory model for answer sentence selection in question answering. In: ACL, (2), pp. 707–712 (2015)

Wang, M., Smith, N.A., Mitamura, T.: What is the jeopardy model? A quasi synchronous grammar for QA. In: EMNLP-CoNLL, vol. 7, pp. 22–32 (2007)

Wang, S., Jiang, J.: A compare aggregate model for matching text sequences. arXiv preprint arXiv:1611.01747 (2016)

Wang, Z., Hamza, W., Florian, R.: Bilateral multi-perspective matching for natural language sentences. arXiv preprint arXiv:1702.03814 (2017)

Yang, Y., Yih, W., Meek, C.: Wikiqa: a challenge dataset for open-domain question answering. In: EMNLP. Citeseer, pp. 2013–2018 (2015)

Yao, X., Van Durme, B., Callison-Burch, C., Clark, P.: Answer extraction as sequence tagging with tree edit distance. In: HLTNAACL. Citeseer, pp. 858–867 (2013)

Yin, W., Schütze, H., Xiang, B., Zhou, B.: ABCNN: attention-based convolutional neural network for modeling sentence pairs. arXiv preprint arXiv:1512.05193 (2015)

Question Answering with Character-Level LSTM Encoders and Model-Based Data Augmentation

Run-Ze Wang, Chen-Di Zhan, and Zhen-Hua Ling(✉)

National Engineering Laboratory for Speech and Language Information Processing, University of Science and Technology of China, Hefei, China
{wrz94520,cdzhan}@mail.ustc.edu.cn, zhling@ustc.edu.cn

Abstract. This paper presents a character-level encoder-decoder modeling method for question answering (QA) from large-scale knowledge bases (KB). This method improves the existing approach [9] from three aspects. First, long short-term memory (LSTM) structures are adopted to replace the convolutional neural networks (CNN) for encoding the candidate entities and predicates. Second, a new strategy of generating negative samples for model training is adopted. Third, a data augmentation strategy is applied to increase the size of the training set by generating factoid questions using another trained encoder-decoder model. Experimental results on the SimpleQuestions dataset and the Freebase5M KB demonstrates the effectiveness of the proposed method, which improves the state-of-the-art accuracy from 70.3% to 78.8% when augmenting the training set with 70,000 generated triple-question pairs.

Keywords: Question answering · Knowledge base · Long short-term memory · Encoder-Decoder

1 Introduction

As the scale of structured knowledge bases (KB) grows, how to take full advantage of them gets more and more attention. One of the popular research topics is knowledge base-based question answering (KB-QA), which aims to answer natural language factoid questions using the triples in knowledge bases. Developing a high-accuracy KB-QA system has a lot of applications, such as the next generation searching engines, digital assistants, and so on.

The existing approaches to KB-QA can be summarized into three main categories. The first is the semantic parsing-based approach [1,7,11,14–16]. This approach usually constructs a semantic parser to translate natural language queries into structured expressions, i.e., logic-forms, and then derives answers from large-scale KBs using these generated query expressions. The second is the information retrieval-based approach [13]. This approach usually uses the information conveyed in questions to search answers from KBs, and adopts ranking techniques to make final selection among candidate answers. The third is the vector space modeling-based approach [3,6]. This approach maps both natural

M. Sun et al. (Eds.): CCL 2017 and NLP-NABD 2017, LNAI 10565, pp. 295–305, 2017.
https://doi.org/10.1007/978-3-319-69005-6_25

language questions and all triples in KBs into low-dimensional embedding vectors. An input question is answered by finding the triple in the KB which has the highest similarity score with the question in the embedding vector space. At training time, the model parameters are estimated to maximize the similarity scores for the question-answer pairs in the training set.

With the rapid development of deep learning techniques in natural language processing, some researchers have started to introduce deep structured neural networks into the vector space modeling-based approach to KB-QA in recent years. Various neural network architectures, such as memory networks [4] and convolutional neural networks (CNN) [8], have been employed to derive the vector representations for questions and triples and to measure the similarity scores between them. A character-level encoder-decoder modeling method for KB-QA was proposed [9]. In this method, character-level encoders were adopted to deal with the data sparsity issue of using word-level encoders. Long short-term memory (LSTM) models [10] and convolutional neural networks were applied to encode input questions and triple elements (i.e., entities and predicates) respectively. An LSTM model with attention was built to decode the optimal entities and predicates according to the encoding results. All model parameters were estimated in an end-to-end manner using a training set of question-triple pairs. This method achieved the state-of-the-art performance on the SimpleQuestions dataset without use of ensembles.

This paper improves this character-level encoder-decoder modeling method [9] from three aspects. First, LSTMs are adopted to replace CNNs for encoding the candidate entities and predicates. Second, a new strategy of generating negative samples for model training is adopted. Third, inspired by the recently proposed encoder-decoder-based question generation method [12], a data augmentation strategy is applied to increase the size of the training set by generating factoid questions from KB triples to further alleviate the data sparsity issue. Experimental results on the SimpleQuestions dataset [4] with the Freebase KB [2] demonstrates the effectiveness of our proposed method. Before data augmentation, this method achieves an accuracy of 77.5% in the Simplequestions setting, outperforming previous state-of-the-art accuracy of 70.3% [9] by 7.2%. Furthermore, an accuracy of 78.8% is obtained when augmenting the training set with 70,000 generated triple-question pairs.

2 Character-Level Attention Model with LSTM Encoders

This paper works on single-relation question answering. Thus, the aim of the character-level attention model is to decode every natural language question into an entity and a predicate, which can uniquely determine a triple in the KB. Let q denote the input question, $\{e\} = e_1, ..., e_N$ and $\{p\} = p_1, ..., p_M$ denote a set of candidate entities and predicates respectively. This model calculates the probability of $p(e_i, p_j|q)$ for each $i \in 1...N$ and $j \in 1...M$.

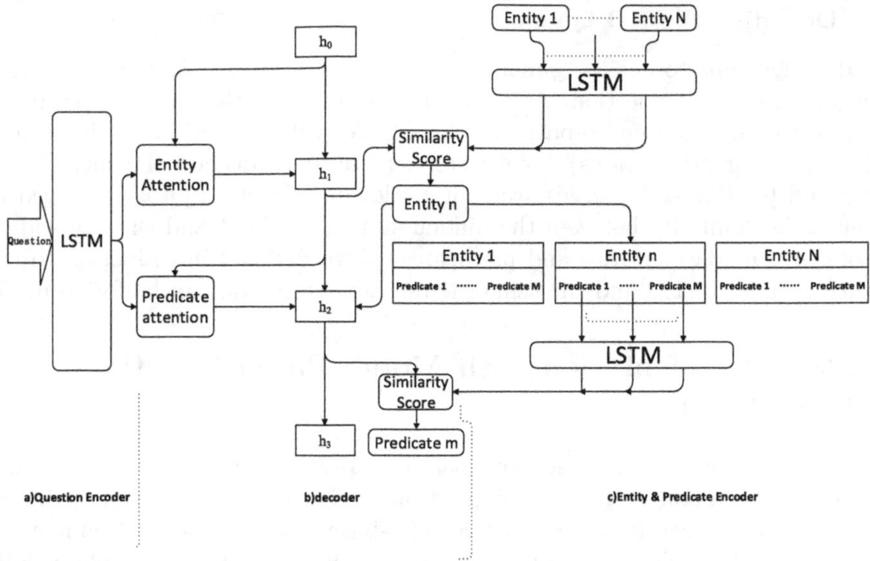

Fig. 1. The model structure of question answering with character-level LSTM encoders.

The model structure is shown in Fig. 1. Three character-level LSTM encoders are adopted to transform question texts, entity names and predicate names into embedding vectors. An LSTM decoder with attention mechanism is employed to calculate the similarity scores between the input question and candidate triple elements. These similarity scores are used to calculate $p(e_i, p_j|q)$ in order to find the most likely (entity, predicate) pair for question answering. This model structure is very similar to the one proposed in Golub's work [9]. The difference is that LSTMs are adopted to replace the CNNs for encoding the names of candidate entities and predicates. Compared with CNNs, LSTMs are expected to be more capable of sequence modeling. The details of each component in Fig. 1 are briefly described in the following subsections.

2.1 Encoding the Question, Entity and Predicate

Two steps are taken to encode the question, entity and predicate. First, three groups of one-hot encoding vectors are extracted to represent each character in question texts, entity names and predicate names respectively. Then, three LSTM encoders are built to accept these character-level encoding vectors as input. When encoding questions, we keep the outputs at all time steps and get a sequence of embedding vector for each input question. When encoding entities and predicates, we choose the output vector at the last time step or conduct average pooling along time axis to get the embedding vectors.

2.2 Decoding the KB Query

The decoder aims to get the single entity and predicate for deriving the right answer to the input question. As shown in Fig. 1, the entity and the predicate are decoded in two steps separately. An LSTM with attention mechanism is built and the hidden states at each step are used to decode the most likely entity and predicate. A pairwise semantic relevance function [9] is employed to measure the similarity between the hidden states of LSTM and the embedding vectors of candidate entities and predicates. More detailed introduction to the attention-based LSTM and the semantic relevance function can be found in [9].

3 Data Augmentation with Model-Based Question Generation

The performance of neural network-based KB-QA methods are always constrained by the amount of available question-answer or question-triple pairs for model training. Recently, an encoder-decoder-based question generation method was proposed [12]. This method considered the mapping from a triple in KBs to a natural language question as a translating process and adopted an encoder-decoder framework to achieve it. The encoder transformed each triple into a vector using embedding matrices pre-trained by TransE [5]. In TransE, the predicate of a triple (*topic entity, predicate, answer entity*) in the KB is considered as a transformation between the topic entity and the answer entity. The objective function of TransE training is to make the sum of the topic entity vector and the predicate vector close to the answer entity vector. The estimated TransE model can easily transform each triple in the KB into a vector as its output. Then, the vector of the output of TransE was fed into an LSTM-decoder to generate a natural language question. All model parameters were estimated using human annotated question-triple pairs. It was reported that this method can generate questions indistinguishable from real human-generated ones [12].

Inspired by this question generation method, this paper presents a data augmentation strategy to increase the size of the training set by generating factoid questions from KB triples and to alleviate the data sparsity issue for QA model training.

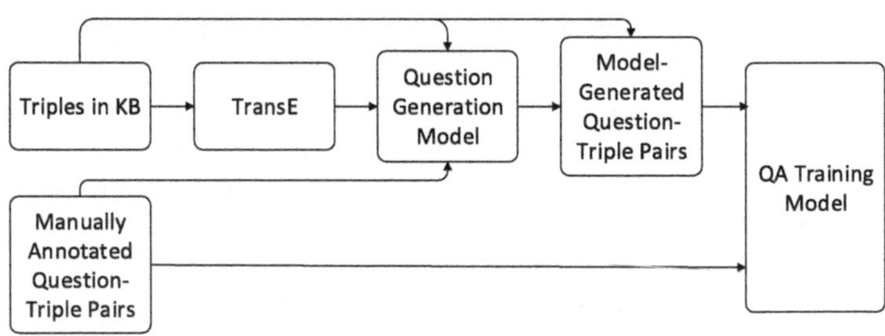

Fig. 2. The flowchart of data augmentation with model-based question generation.

The flowchart of this strategy is shown in Fig. 2. Given a training set with human-annotated question-triple pairs and a large-scale KB for KB-QA, we first train a TransE model to get the embedding matrices for all entities and predicates in the KB. Then, An encoder-decoder-based question generation model is built using the pre-trained TransE model and the human-annotated question-triple pairs following the method proposed in [12]. Finally, a large amount of questions can be produced using the question generation model and the triples in the KB. These model-generated questions are combined with the human-annotated ones for training the QA model introduced in Sect. 2.

4 Experiments

4.1 Experimental Conditions

We evaluated our proposed method on the SimpleQuestions dataset and the Freebase5M KB [4]. The original dataset consist of 108,442 single-relation questions and their corresponding triples formed as (*topic entity, predicate, answer entity*). It is usually split into 75,910 question-triple pairs for training, 10,845 pairs for validation, and the remaining 21,687 pairs for test. In our implementation, we removed the pairs whose topic entity can not find a name string in the Freebase5M KB. Therefore, we finally got 75,519 training samples, 10,787 validation samples, and 21,573 test samples respectively.

For an input question, we took the entities in the Freebase5M KB whose name matched an n-gram substring of the question as candidate entities. Simple statistics showed that the number of matched entity names for all questions in the SimpleQuestions dataset was less than 7. Thus, we fixed the number of candidate entity names to 7 and added some candidate entity names randomly for the questions whose matched entity names were less than 7. For each candidate entity name, the entity in the Freebase5M whose name was identical to this candidate entity name were added to the set of candidate entity. If the number of entity matching a candidate entity name was larger than 10, we sorted these entity by the number of facts they had in the KB and the top-10 entity were added to the set of candidate entity. For each candidate entity, the predicates in the triples whose topic entity was in these candidate entity were appended to the set of candidate predicates. We fixed the number of candidate predicates to 150 for each candidate entity name and also added candidate predicates randomly for these entity names with less than 150 linked predicates. Finally, the number of candidate pairs of (topic entity name, predicate) for each question was 7×150.

When building our character-level attention model with LSTM encoders, the character-level encoding vectors were 200-dimensional and the three LSTM encoders for questions, entities, and predicates all had one hidden layer of size 200. When encoding entities and predicates, we either chose the output vector at the last time step or calculated the average of the outputs at all time steps as the embedding vectors. The LSTM decoder also had a hidden layer of size 200. The model parameters were estimated using AdaDelta with the learning rate of 0.0001.

4.2 Comparison on Negative Sample Generation Methods

In Golub's work [9], the candidate entities and predicates for model training both consisted of a true answer and 50 randomly sampled answers. In our implementation, we adopted the candidate generation process introduced in Sect. 4.1 to produce the negative samples for model training. We compared the performance of using Golub's method and the proposed candidate generation method for producing negative samples. The results are shown in Table 1, from which we can see that the proposed candidate generation method achieved an accuracy of 76.7% and outperformed the random generation method by 5.11%.

Table 1. QA accuracy (%) of using different negative sample generation methods for model training.

Negative sample generation	Joint acc.	Entity acc.	Predicate acc.
Golub's method [9]	71.59	91.76	71.68
Proposed method	76.70	91.80	76.79

4.3 Comparison on Pooling Methods of LSTM Encoders for Entities and Predicates

In our proposed model structure shown in Fig. 1, the LSTM encoders for entities and predicates are required to produce a single vector representation for each entity or predicate. Since the raw outputs of LSTMs are sequential, a pooling procedure is necessary. In this experiment, we compared the performance of using the output vector at the last time step or the average of all output vectors as the encoding results. The results are shown in Table 2. From this table, we can see that using average pooling achieved a better accuracy than using the last vector. This is reasonable because the averaged vector may convey more global information of the text string than the last vector given by LSTM encoders. Thus, this average pooling strategy were adopted in the following experiments.

Table 2. QA accuracy (%) of using different pooling ways of LSTM encoders for questions, entities and predicates.

Pooling methods	Joint acc.	Entity acc.	Predicate acc.
Last	76.70	91.80	76.79
Average	77.50	92.00	77.56

4.4 Effects of Data Augmentation

We built two augmented training sets for comparison. The *T_set* was composed of the original training set of SimpleQuestions and another 70,000 questions generated using a fixed template as "*What is the P of E ?*", where E denoted the entity name in a triple and P meant the predicate [4]. The *M_set* consisted of the original training set of SimpleQuestions and 70,000 questions produced by the encoder-decoder-based question generation method introduced in Sect. 3. Two models were built to achieve this model-based data augmentation.

1. The first one was a TransE [5] model as showed in Fig. 2. Due to the sparsity of triples in the SimpleQuestions training set, an augmented KB based on the SimpleQuestions training set and the Freebase5M KB was built for TransE training. Simple statistics showed that there were 7,523 predicates in Freebase5M while only 1,629 predicates in SimpleQuestions training set. We built an intermediate set by extracting those triples in Freebase5M whose predicates were in the SimpleQuesitons training set and totally got 16,561,736 triples. The final augmented KB for TransE training was composed of the triples in Freebase5M whose topic entities were in the intermediate set. There were 36,291,331 triples in the final augmented KB and the output KB embeddings given by TransE had 200 dimensions.
2. The second one was the encoder-decoder model for question generation built following the method proposed in [12]. The encoder part accepted the KB embeddings produced by the TransE model as inputs and generated a 600-dimensional representation vector for each input triple. Then, this vector was fed into the decoder part, which was a GRU-recurrent neural network (GRU-RNN) with attention. The hidden layer of the GRU-RNN had 600 units. The Simplequestions training set was used to train this encoder-decoder with a learning rate of 2.5×10^{-4}.

Both sets approximately doubled the original training set of SimpleQuestions. Two character-level attention models for KB-QA were built using the two augmented training sets and the results are shown in Table 3. It can be observed that the data augmentation strategy was helpful and the model-based question generation method achieved more performance improvement than the conventional template-based method.

Table 3. QA accuracy (%) of data augmentation.

Training set	Joint acc.	Entity acc.	Predicate acc.
SimpleQuestions	77.50	92.00	77.56
T_set	77.91	91.94	77.99
M_set	78.81	92.29	78.85

4.5 Comparison with Other Existing Methods

We compared the performance of our proposed methods and some existing methods. The results are shown in Table 4. Both methods (1) and (2) adopted memory networks [4] for KB-QA and built models at word-level. Method (2) used ensembles of multiple models and combined the WebQuestion training set and a paraphrase dataset to deal with the data-sparsity issue. The difference between our proposed method and Method (3) [9] in Table 4 has been discussed before. From this table, we can see that our proposed method achieved an accuracy of 77.5% in the Simplequestions setting without data augmentation, which outperformed other existing methods listed in Table 4. Furthermore, an accuracy of 78.8% was obtained when augmenting the training set with 70,000 generated triple-question pairs.

Table 4. QA accuracy (%) of proposed methods and some existing methods.

Method	Joint accuracy
(1) MenNN [4]	61.6
(2) MemNN-Ensemble [4]	63.9
(3) Character attention [9]	70.9
(4) Proposed method without data argumentation	77.5
(5) Proposed method with data argumentation	78.8

4.6 Analysis and Discussion

Comparison between using LSTMs or CNNs to encode entities and predicates. We compared the performance of using LSTMs or CNNs to encode entities and predicates in our implementation. The results are shown in Table 5. Here, the CNN had two alternating convolutional and fully-connected layers, followed by one fully-connected layer. The width of filters and the number of feature maps in convolution layers were set to 4 and 100 respectively. All the fully-connected layers had 200 output units. The other modules of the two systems were the same. Form this table, we can see the effectiveness of encoding entities and predicates using LSTMs.

Table 5. QA accuracy (%) of using LSTMs or CNNs to encode entities and predicates.

Model	Joint acc.	Entity acc.	Predicate acc.
CNN	73.1	91.7	73.2
LSTM	77.5	92.0	77.6

Discussion on negative sample generation method. As introduced in Sect. 4.1, randomly selected entities and predicates were used during candidate generation in order to achieve fixed numbers of candidate entities and predicates for each question. An experiment was also conducted to remove these randomly selected candidates for model testing, and the results are shown in Table 6. From this table, we can see that randomly adding candidates helped to achieve a better performance of question answering.

Table 6. QA accuracy (%) with or without adding random candidates.

Add random candidates	Joint acc.	Entity acc.	Predicate acc.
Yes	78.81	92.29	78.85
No	72.11	92.74	72.38

We made some further analysis to investigate the reason of the performance difference in Table 6. There were totally 21,573 questions in our test set. When using random candidate entities and predicates, there were 1,266 test questions whose target entity can not be found in the candidate entities and there were 480 test questions whose target entities were in the candidate set but predicates not. Without adding random candidates, these two numbers were 1,266 and 2,801 respectively. The number increase from 480 to 2,801 indicates the advantage of adding random candidates, which is to construct a candidate set with better coverage on the target predicates of test questions. We also tried to remove the test questions whose target entities or predicates were missing in the candidate sets and re-evaluated the two testing set in Table 6. The results are shown in Table 7. Comparing Table 6 with Table 7, we can see that the performance of both systems got improved when the candidate sets can provide an 100% coverage of the correct ones. In Table 7, the QA accuracy of using random candidates is lower than the one without using random candidates. This means that adding random candidates increases the difficulty of model inference when all correct answers are in the candidate set. Therefore, there exists a trade-off between the coverage of candidate sets and the difficulty of model inference in our implementation.

Table 7. QA accuracy (%) with or without adding random candidates. The test questions whose target entities or predicates were missing in the candidate sets were removed.

Add random candidates	Joint acc.	Entity acc.	Predicate acc.
Yes	85.75	98.04	85.79
No	88.86	98.52	89.20

5 Conclusion

This paper has proposed a new character-level encoder-decoder modeling method for simple question answering. We have improved the existing approach [9] by employing LSTMs to encode entities and predicates, introducing a new strategy to generate negative samples for model training, and augmenting training set with neural-network-based question generation method. Our proposed method has achieved a new state-of-the-art accuracy of 78.8% on the SimpleQuestions dataset and the Freebase5M KB. To investigate better candidate generation strategy, to build larger augmented training set and to combine the advantages of word-level and character-level modeling will be the tasks of our future work.

Acknowledgements. This paper was supported in part by the National Natural Science Foundation of China (Grants No. U1636201) and the Fundamental Research Funds for the Central Universities (Grant No. WK2350000001).

References

1. Berant, J., Chou, A., Frostig, R., Liang, P.: Semantic parsing on freebase from question-answer pairs. In: EMNLP, vol. 2, p. 6 (2013)
2. Bollacker, K., Evans, C., Paritosh, P., Sturge, T., Taylor, J.: Freebase: a collaboratively created graph database for structuring human knowledge. In: Proceedings of the 2008 ACM SIGMOD International Conference on Management of Data, pp. 1247–1250. ACM (2008)
3. Bordes, A., Chopra, S., Weston, J.: Question answering with subgraph embeddings. arXiv preprint arXiv:1406.3676 (2014)
4. Bordes, A., Usunier, N., Chopra, S., Weston, J.: Large-scale simple question answering with memory networks. arXiv preprint arXiv:1506.02075 (2015)
5. Bordes, A., Usunier, N., Garcia-Duran, A., Weston, J., Yakhnenko, O.: Translating embeddings for modeling multi-relational data. In: Advances in Neural Information Processing Systems, pp. 2787–2795 (2013)
6. Bordes, A., Weston, J., Usunier, N.: Open question answering with weakly supervised embedding models. In: Calders, T., Esposito, F., Hüllermeier, E., Meo, R. (eds.) ECML PKDD 2014. LNCS, vol. 8724, pp. 165–180. Springer, Heidelberg (2014). doi:10.1007/978-3-662-44848-9_11
7. Cai, Q., Yates, A.: Large-scale semantic parsing via schema matching and lexicon extension. In: ACL, vol. 1, pp. 423–433 (2013)
8. Dong, L., Wei, F., Zhou, M., Xu, K.: Question answering over freebase with multi-column convolutional neural networks. In: ACL, vol. 1, pp. 260–269 (2015)
9. Golub, D., He, X.: Character-level question answering with attention. arXiv preprint arXiv:1604.00727 (2016)
10. Hochreiter, S., Schmidhuber, J.: Long short-term memory. Neural Comput. **9**(8), 1735–1780 (1997)
11. Kwiatkowski, T., Choi, E., Artzi, Y., Zettlemoyer, L.: Scaling semantic parsers with on-the-fly ontology matching. In: Proceedings of EMNLP. Citeseer, Percy (2013)
12. Serban, I.V., García-Durán, A., Gulcehre, C., Ahn, S., Chandar, S., Courville, A., Bengio, Y.: Generating factoid questions with recurrent neural networks: the 30m factoid question-answer corpus. arXiv preprint arXiv:1603.06807 (2016)

13. Yao, X., Van Durme, B.: Information extraction over structured data: Question answering with freebase. In: ACL, vol. 1, pp. 956–966. Citeseer (2014)
14. Yih, S.W.t., Chang, M.W., He, X., Gao, J.: Semantic parsing via staged query graph generation: question answering with knowledge base (2015)
15. Zettlemoyer, L.S., Collins, M.: Learning context-dependent mappings from sentences to logical form. In: Proceedings of the Joint Conference of the 47th Annual Meeting of the ACL and The 4th International Joint Conference on Natural Language Processing of the AFNLP, vol. 2, pp. 976–984. Association for Computational Linguistics (2009)
16. Zettlemoyer, L.S., Collins, M.: Learning to map sentences to logical form: Structured classification with probabilistic categorial grammars. arXiv preprint arXiv:1207.1420 (2012)

Exploiting Explicit Matching Knowledge with Long Short-Term Memory

Xinqi Bao and Yunfang Wu(✉)

Key Laboratory of Computational Linguistics (Peking University), School of Electronic Engineering and Computer Science, Peking University, Beijing, China
wuyf@pku.edu.cn

Abstract. Recently neural network models are widely applied in text-matching tasks like community-based question answering (cQA). The strong generalization power of neural networks enables these methods to find texts with similar topics but miss detailed matching information. However, as proven by traditional methods, the explicit lexical matching knowledge is important for effective answer retrieval. In this paper, we propose an ExMaLSTM model to incorporate the explicit matching knowledge into the long short-term memory (LSTM) neural network. We extract explicit lexical matching features with prior knowledge and then add them to the local representations of questions. We summarize the overall matching status by using a bi-directional LSTM. The final relevance score is calculated using a gate network, which can dynamically assign appropriate weights to the explicit matching score and the implicit relevance score. We conduct extensive experiments for answer retrieval in a cQA dataset. The results show that our proposed ExMaLSTM model outperforms both the traditional methods and various state-of-the-art neural network models significantly.

Keywords: Lexical matching knowledge · LSTM · Question answering

1 Introduction

The community-based question answering (cQA) attracts considerable attention in recent years. Traditional question answering systems, driven by evaluations such as the Text REtrieval Conference (TREC), generally aim to retrieve short and factoid answers. But questions from cQA services tend to be more subjective and complex, and the answers are often in a causal style, including both fact description and subjective opinions. So the answer retrieval task in cQA is more challenging.

Traditional methods on cQA retrieval are mainly based on surface lexical matching, which suffer from the severe lexical gap problem. Recently, researchers have proposed various neural networks and semantic embedding based methods to overcome this problem (for example, Hu et al. 2014; Palangi et al. 2015; Zhou et al. 2015; Qiu and Huang 2015), which take advantage of the strong generalization power of neural networks. Generally speaking, these methods try to dive into the latent embedding

M. Sun et al. (Eds.): CCL 2017 and NLP-NABD 2017, LNAI 10565, pp. 306–317, 2017.
https://doi.org/10.1007/978-3-319-69005-6_26

space and then calculate the relevance score to find the pairs which are mostly like to match each other.

However, there are limitations for most of previous neural network methods in practice. First, a large amount of training data is required to learn appropriate parameters, which is unrealistic for some specified domains. Second, there exist out of vocabulary (OOV) words and unseen phrases, and it is hard to embed their latent semantics. Third, the strong generalization power enables these methods to find texts with similar topics, but they may miss or obscure the detailed matching information, so underestimate the relevance of those text spans with explicitly matched points.

Table 1 shows an example. The basic neural network model of this paper successfully captures the "delicious food" topic but loses the explicitly matched key point "spicy hot pot", which is rare or even unseen in the training data but is the semantic focus of this question. We can see that the traditional method of direct lexical matching still has its value.

Table 1. An example of a question and its related answers. The unexpected answer is returned by the basic LSTM model of this paper; the expected answer is the right answer.

Question: I want to know where is the most delicious spicy hot pot in Beijing?
Unexpected Answer: Beijing is the culinary capital where roasted duck, sauteed noodles with vegetables and other local snacks are easy available. Just please walk on the Wangfujing Snack Street to spend happy time with various delicious foods. The address is ……
Expected Answer: On a cold winter day, you may like to have something hot with your family. Then the spicy hot pot is perhaps the best choice for you. Now let's introduce the most famous hot pots in Beijing below ……

In this paper, we focus on exploiting such explicit matching information in question-answer pairs for answer retrieval. We propose an ExMaLSTM model, which extends the traditional LSTM model as follows.

- We extract explicit lexical matching features of question-answer pairs with prior knowledge, by using rich language resources.
- We incorporate these explicit matching features into the original word vector for each word in the question. The overall explicit matching status is summarized by a bi-directional LSTM, and then the explicit matching score is calculated via the summarized representation.
- We calculate the final relevance score by using a gate network, which can dynamically assign different weights to the explicit matching score and the implicit relevance score. The implicit relevance score is calculated by the basic LSTM model of this paper.

We conduct extensive experiments for answer retrieval in a Chinese cQA dataset. The experimental results show that our extended ExMaLSTM model outperforms various state-of-the-art neural network models significantly. It can well capture the explicit lexical matching information and assign appropriate weights to explicit and implicit scores.

2 Related Work

There are a lot of researches to utilize neural network based models in cQA retrieval. They can be clustered to the following two groups.

The first idea is to embed the question and answer separately into latent semantic spaces, and then calculate the implicit relevance score with embedded vectors. Studies include bag-of-words based embedding models (Wang et al. 2011), recursive neural network model (RNN) (Iyyer et al. 2014), convolutional neural network (CNN) model (Hu et al. 2014), long short-term memory network model (Palangi et al. 2015) and combined model (Zhou et al. 2015). Qiu and Hunag (2015) implemented a tensor transformation layer on CNN based embeddings to capture the interactions between question and answer more effectively.

The second idea is to conduct matching process with pairs of local embeddings and then calculate the overall relevance score. Works include enhanced lexical model (Yih et al. 2013), DeepMatch (Lu and Li 2013). Pang et al. (2016) calculated word similarity matrix from pairs of words between question and answer, and then built hierarchical convolution layers on it. Yin and Schutze (2015) proposed MultiGranCNN, which integrates multiple matching models with different levels of granularity. Wan et al. (2016) proposed Multiple Positional Sentence Representation (MPSR), which uses LSTM and interactive tensor to capture matching points with positional local context. The difference with our work is that they still depend on embeddings of local information, thus cannot fully capture the explicit matching information of question-answer pairs.

Some other works try to incorporate non-textual information into the basic neural cQA model. Hu et al. (2013) used a deep belief network (DBN) to learn joint representations for textual features and non-textual features. Bordes et al. (2014) learnt joint embeddings of words and knowledge base constituents with subgraph embedding method.

To the best of our knowledge, most of the neural network models in cQA retrieval pay little attention to the explicit lexical matching information of text pairs. Wang and Nyberg (2015) simply combined their LSTM neural network model with the exact keyword matching score, but their method is quite different from our work in the following aspects. (1) They only extract the cardinal numbers and proper nouns to do keyword matching, while our work extracts plenty of lexical matching information. (2) They use the traditional Okapi BM25 algorithm to calculate the keywords matching score, while we employ a bi-directional LSTM network to predict the explicit matching status. (3) They use an external gradient boosting decision tree (GBDT) method to combine features, while we exploit a gate network to dynamically assign different importance weights to the implicit relevance score and explicit matching score.

3 The Basic Model

We first describe the basic neural network model adopted in this paper for question-answer relevance calculation, which is depicted in Fig. 1. We utilize a bi-directional LSTM to represent questions, and propose a Sent-LDA model to represent answers. Then a three-way tensor is employed to model the interactions of question-answer pairs. Finally, a multilayer perception (MLP) is utilized to calculate the relevance score.

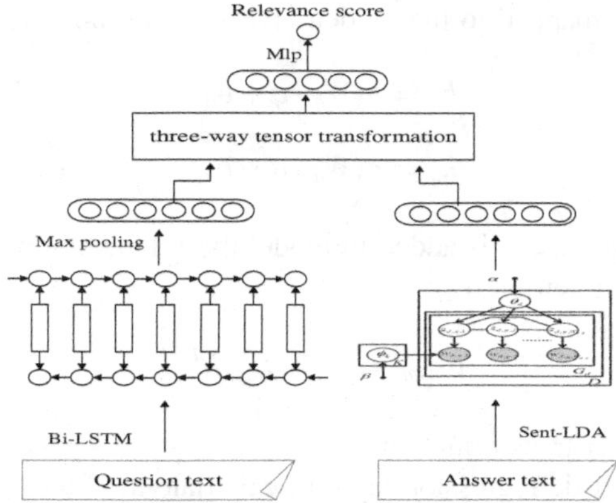

Fig. 1. The basic network model of this paper

3.1 Question Representation

Like Palangi et al. (2015), we use the bi-directional LSTM to embed questions into latent semantic representations, which can effectively capture the long-range dependencies of context information. We use max pooling through time to extract the final fixed-length representation for the question.

3.2 Answer Representation

We can also use LSTM to generate latent representations for answers. However, answers in a cQA forum often consist of multiple sentences and are much longer than questions, which makes the training process very time consuming. So, we utilize a sentence-level LDA (Sent-LDA), inspired by phrase-LDA (Kishky et al. 2014), to model sentence level information. It runs fast while achieves comparable results with neural based representations.

The Sent-LDA is the same with the classical LDA except that all words within a sentence are constrained to a unique topic. We treat each answer as a document and sample the topic assignments on it. Each sentence in the answer will get a topic that is consistent with the topic its words are assigned. This leads to a "bag of sentence topic" representation for multi-sentence answers, which can capture high level information rather than individual words. In our experiment, the sentences are segmented with Chinese punctuations (including comma), and the number of topic is set to 200.

3.3 Tensor Relevance Model

To model the relevance of question-answer pairs, we use a three-way tensor to transform the representations of question and answer into a semantic matching representation, like Qiu and Huang (2015). The representations of a question and its related answer are separately mapped to the hidden layers with a nonlinear transformation:

$$h_q = \sigma(W_h \cdot q + b_h) \quad (1)$$

$$h_a = \sigma(W_a \cdot a + b_a) \quad (2)$$

A new hidden layer h_{tensor} is added to model the interaction between question and answer via a three-way tensor W_{tensor}:

$$h_{tensor} = h_a W_{tensor}(h_q^T) \quad (3)$$

where T denotes tensor transformation.

We then use a logistic regression layer to calculate the final score:

$$score_{imp} = \sigma(W_{output} \cdot h_{tensor} + b_{output}) \quad (4)$$

where W_{output} and b_{output} are parameters of the regression layer.

4 The Extended Model ExMaLSTM

In cQA, the most appropriate answer to a question often explicitly mentions some key points of the question. However, as discussed above, we may lose this detailed matching information when embedding texts into the latent semantic space by using traditional neural network models. To overcome this limitation, we extend the basic LSTM neural network model (as shown in Fig. 1) to incorporate the explicit matching knowledge, and then calculate the question-answer relevance by combining both implicit relevance score and explicit matching score in a dynamic fashion. Our extended model ExMaLSTM is depicted in Fig. 2, where the notation 1, 2 and 3 are related to the following Subsects. 4.1, 4.2 and 4.3, respectively.

4.1 Extracting Explicit Matching Features

For each word in the question, we introduce the following explicit lexical matching features. These features describe how well each question word is explicitly matched in the answer as a possible key point.

In traditional lexical matching methods, only exact word matching features are used. In this paper, we extract explicit matching information from nine dimensions, by using external resources like synonym dictionary and word vectors pre-trained on a large corpus. So our explicit matching features have stronger power to capture the matching information in question-answer pairs.

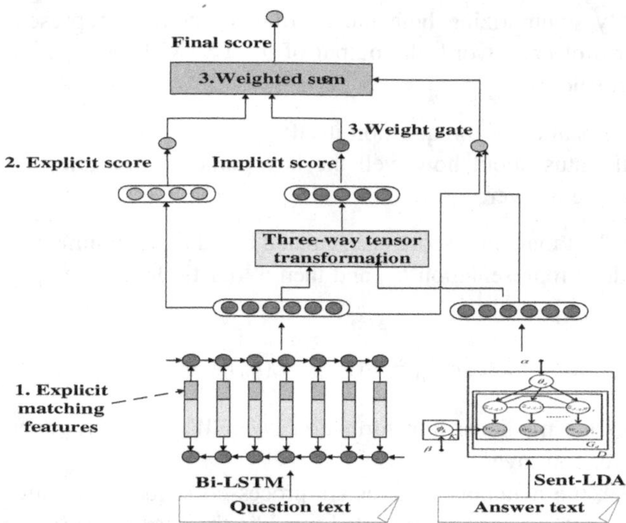

Fig. 2. Our extended ExMaLSTM model. The yellow parts denote our extensions with explicit matching knowledge, compared with the basic LSTM model in Fig. 1. (Color figure online)

- **word occurrence.** A boolean feature denoting whether the word occurs in the answer.
- **word occurrence count.** The number of occurrences of the word occurring in the answer.
- **synonym occurrence.** A boolean feature denoting whether any synonym of the word occurs in the answer. We use HIT-CIR Tongyici Cilin as our synonym dictionary.
- **synonym occurrence count.** The number of occurrences of synonyms occurring in the answer.
- **occurrence in the head.** A boolean feature denoting whether the word or its synonym occurs in the first sentence of the answer.
- **word2vec similarity.** The similarity score of the most similar word in the answer, which is calculated by cosine similarity between word vectors.
- **tf-idf score.** The tf-idf score of the word if any synonym or the word itself occurs in the answer.
- **content word.** A boolean feature denoting whether the word that occurs in the answer is a content word.
- **entity word.** A boolean feature denoting whether the word that occurs in the answer is an entity word (with POS tag NR, NT or NS).

4.2 Calculating Explicit Matching Score

For each word in the question, we form the new input representation of the LSTM layer by appending these lexical matching features to the original word vector. Then a bi-directional LSTM network is used to generate the semantic presentation h_q of a question text. By summarizing both the distributed semantic representation and the matching features of each word, the output of the LSTM layer h_q now captures two aspects of information:

(1) The latent semantics of the question itself;
(2) The overall status about how well the key points of the question are matched explicitly in the answer.

Then the explicit matching score is calculated by adding a nonlinear transformation layer on the hidden representation h_q, and then a logistic layer is employed to get the final output:

$$score_{exp} = \sigma(W_{exp} \cdot L(h_q) + b_{exp}) \tag{5}$$

where L denotes the nonlinear transformation layer, W_{exp} and b_{exp} denote the parameters of the regression layer.

In our model, the matching features are processed sequentially, thus the consecutively matched substrings can be extracted just like the Maximum Common Substring (MCS) method. Then they are treated as a whole to estimate the matching score. For example in Table 2, the Chinese word "spicy hot pot" is wrongly segmented into three words "spicy", "hot" and "pot", but our model can still capture the explicit matching information of this word by processing the consecutively matched fragments as a whole. So our model is robust to Chinese word segmentation errors, which is a non-trivial task for Chinese language processing in web texts like cQA.

Table 2. An example of a question-answer pair. The wrongly segmented fragments [spicy-hot-pot] are extracted by our model as a whole to estimate the matching score.

Question: I want to know where is the most delicious [**spicy-hot-pot**] in Beijing?
Expected Answer: On a cold winter day, you may like to have something hot with your family. Then the [**spicy-hot-pot**] is perhaps the best choice for you. Now let's introduce the most famous [**hot-pots**] in Beijing below…

4.3 Combining Implicit and Explicit Scores

We calculate the final relevance score by combing both the implicit relevance score and the explicit matching score to take advantage of both aspects of information.

$$score = g.score_{imp} + (1 - g).score_{exp} \tag{6}$$

Instead of using a fixed weight factor, we propose to utilize a dynamic scoring strategy that can dynamically assign appropriate weights to two relevance scores:

$$g = \sigma(W_{sel} \cdot [h_q, h_a] + b_{sel}) \quad (7)$$

Here, g is calculated via a gate network, which dynamically estimates the importance of two relevance scores based on the current hidden states. It avoids over-estimating or under-estimating the final score due to the arbitrary weight setting, since the question and answer with few matching words can be highly relevant, and vice versa, the question and answer with many common words may talk about different things.

5 Experiment

5.1 Experiment Setup

The dataset comes from Baidu Zhidao, which is one of the most popular cQA services in China. We have crawled 180,000 question-answer pairs under the "travelling" topic. The data was pre-processed with Chinese word segmentation and part of speech tagging using ICTCLAS (Zhang et al. 2003). We also trained a CRF-based entity recognizer to annotate the places with the label NS. We removed the pairs which have too short answer or question (<=5 words) or consist of only an URL string. Finally, there are 160,000 question-answer pairs remained. We picked 5,000 pairs for testing, 5,000 for validation, and the remaining 150,000 for training.

In our experiment, the word embeddings are pretrained using word2vec (Mikolov et al. 2013) on Baidu Zhidao corpus, including the whole data of 160,000 question-answer pairs. The dimension is set to 200. The hyper-parameters in the neural network are tuned using the validation data, and Table 3 shows these settings. We employ a large margin objective for model training, and the objective loss function is optimized using AdaGrad.

Table 3. Hyper-parameters in the neural network

Hyper-parameters	Value
h_q length	200
h_a length	200
Tensor rank	3
Tensor output length	100
Margin	0.2
λ of l2-norm	0.001

5.2 Baselines

We conduct extensive experiments on the dataset, including traditional bag-of-words methods and various neural network models.

- **Cosine similarity.** Calculate cosine similarity between vectors of question and answer using tf-idf weight.
- **KL divergence.** Construct the unigram language model M_q for a question and M_a for an answer, and then compute their KL-distance.
- **Word overlapping.** Simply count the number of overlapped words between question and answer.
- **DeepMatch.** We implement the DeepMatch network proposed by Lu and Li (2013). The number of latent topic is tuned to 200.
- **Bi-CNN models.** Both question and answer are embeded into the latent semantic space using convolutional neural network. This includes the Arc-1 model with multi-layer perception (Hu et al. 2014) denoted as "qCNN-aCNN-Mlp" and tensor model (Qiu and Huang 2015) denoted as "qCNN-aCNN-Tensor".
- **One side CNN models.** We replace the answer side CNN in the above models with the Sent-LDA method discussed in Sect. 3.2, thus form two models denoted as "qCNN-aTopic-Mlp" and "qCNN-aTopic-Tensor", respectively.
- **One side LSTM models.** We use the LSTM network on question side and the Sent-LDA topic representation on the answer side. The "qLSTM-aTopic-Cosine" model calculates the cosine similarity between hidden representations like Palangi et al. (2015), while our basic model in this paper "qLSTM-aTopic-Tensor" utilizes a tensor layer.
- **LSTM model + Cosine.** We combine the basic LSTM network score and cosine similarity score in a straightforward way $score = a \cdot score_{lstm} + (1 - a) \cdot score_{\cos ine}$, where the heuristic weight a is fine-tuned in the validation data.

5.3 Results

Table 4 reports the experimental results on answer retrieval in our cQA dataset. In general, the performances of traditional methods, including cosine similarity, KL-divergence and word overlapping are unsatisfying. However, we can still see that the simple exact word matching method like "Word over-lapping" retrieves correctly 32.3% answers in the 5,000 test data. It demonstrates that explicit lexical matching features play an important role for answer retrieval.

We get the following observations from Table 4. (1) The neural network models obtain considerably better results than traditional methods. (2) The tensor network gives an obvious improvement than the multi-layer perception. (3) Our Sent-LDA representation for answers obtains comparable results with CNN. (4) The bi-directional LSTM representation for questions achieves further improvement than CNN. (5) Among those neural network models with only implicit semantic relevance, the basic LSTM model in this paper performs the best with 46.8% on P@1 and 64.9% on MRR.

Table 4. The experimental results on answer retrieval. We implement various neural network models in our dataset: DeepMatch (Lu and Li 2013), qCNN-aCNN-Mlp (Hu et al. 2014), qCNN-aCNN-Tensor (Qiu and Huang 2015), qLSTM-aTopic-Cosine (like Palangi et al. 2015).

Method	P@1	MRR
Cosine similarity	34.2	53.8
KL-divergence	24.4	45.1
Word overlapping	32.3	52.0
DeepMatch	41.9	60.5
qCNN-aCNN-Mlp	43.5	61.7
qCNN-aCNN-Tensor	44.6	63.8
qCNN-aTopic-Mlp	43.2	62.5
qCNN-aTopic-Tensor	45.4	63.2
qLSTM-aTopic-Cosine	45.7	62.7
qLSTM-aTopic-Tensor	**46.8**	**64.9**
+Cosine	47.7	65.8
+ Explicit match (static)	48.4	66.3
+Explicit match (dynamic)	**49.1**	**66.9**

Our proposed ExMaLSTM model combines dynamically the implicit semantic relevance score and the explicit matching information, achieving the best performance with 2.3% increase on P@1 ($p < 0.01$) and 2.0% increase on MRR ($p < 0.01$).

5.4 Analysis

We will give a more detailed analysis on our extended model ExMaLSTM. The incorporation of the explicit matching features is denoted as "Explicit match" in Table 4. For the static version, we simply add up the explicit and implicit scores with a fixed weight, which is fine-tuned on the validation data. For the dynamic version, we use the gate network to automatically calculate the weight.

It can be seen that the explicit matching information do benefit, because even simply combining the score of our basic LSTM network model with the cosine similarity score achieves better results than individual methods. Both of two versions consistently outperform the basic LSTM model. The static version obtains 1.6% increase on P@1 ($p < 0.05$) and 1.4% increase on MRR ($p < 0.05$), and the dynamic version obtains 2.3% ($p < 0.05$) increase on P@1 and 2.0% increase on MRR ($p < 0.05$). The dynamic weighting strategy performs better because it can consider different contributions of the explicit and implicit scores through the gated weight.

We briefly analyze the computation process on the example in Table 1. Table 5 gives the intermediate values in the relevance computing process between the question and its expected and unexpected answers.

Although the unexpected answer lies in the same "food" topic with the question thus gets a high implicit relevance score 0.91, the explicit matching score is quite low with only 0.22. What's more, the gate network does not give the implicit score a high weight (only 0.53). Thus the final relevance score between the question and its

Table 5. The intermediate values in the relevance computing process.

Value	Expected Ans.	Unexpected Ans.
$score_{imp}$	0.64	0.91
$score_{exp}$	0.87	0.22
g	0.42	0.53
$score$	0.77	0.59

unexpected answer is only 0.59. However for the expected answer, it gets both a high explicit score (0.87) due to the lexical matching of "spicy hot pot" in this question-answer pair, and a high implicit score (0.64) by addressing the same "food" topic. Thus the final relevance score between the question and its expected answer is 0.77. In this way, our extended model ExMaLSTM successfully retrieves the expected answer but discards the unexpected answer.

6 Conclusion

In this paper, we propose an ExMaLSTM model to incorporate the explicit matching knowledge into the traditional LSTM neural network. First, we extract the explicit lexical matching knowledge by using rich linguistic information. Then, we incorporate these explicit matching features into the LSTM network to summarize the overall explicit matching status between a question and its related answers. Finally, we dynamically assign different weights to the explicit matching score and the implicit relevance score through a gate network, and sum up both scores to get the final relevance score. The experimental results show that our proposed ExMaLSTM model outperforms various state of-the-art neural network methods.

Acknowledgement. This work is supported by the National High Technology Research and Development Program of China (2015AA015403), the National Natural Science Foundation of China (61371129).

References

Kishky, A., Yanglei, S., Chi, Voss Clare, W., Jiawei, H.: Scalable topical phrase mining from text corpora. In: Proceedings of the VLDB Endowment, pp. 305–316 (2014)

Graves, A., Mohamed, A.R., Hinton, G.: Speech recognition with deep recurrent neural networks. In: IEEE International Conference on Acoustics, Speech and Signal Processing (ICASSP), pp. 6645–6649 (2013)

Hu, B., Lu, Z., Li, H., Chen, Q.: Convolutional neural network architectures for matching natural language sentences. In: Advances in Neural Information Processing Systems (NIPS), pp. 2042–2050 (2014)

Wang, B., Liu, B., Wang, X., Sun, C., Zhang, D.: Deep learning approaches to semantic relevance modeling for chinese question-answer pairs. ACM Trans. Asian Lang. Inf. Process. (TALIP) **10** (2011)

Dyer, C., Ballesteros, M., Ling, W., Matthews, A., Smith, N.A.: Transition based dependency parsing with stack long short-term memory. In: Proceedings of ACL, pp. 334–343 (2015)
Wang, D., Nyberg, E.: A long short-term memory model for answer sentence selection in question answering. In: Proceedings of ACL, pp. 707–712 (2015)
Hu, H., Liu, B., Wang, B., Liu, M., Wang, X.: Multimodal DBN for predicting high-quality answers in CQA portals. In: Proceedings of ACL, pp. 843–847 (2013)
Palangi, H., Deng, L., Shen, Y., Gao, J., He, X., Chen, J., Song, X., Ward, R.: Deep sentence embedding using the long short term memory network: analysis and application to information retrieval. IEEE/ACM Trans. Audio Speech Lang. Process., 694–707 (2015)
He, X., Chen, J., Song, X., Ward, R.: Deep sentence embedding using the long short term memory network: analysis and application to information retrieval. IEEE/ACM Trans. Audio Speech Lang. Process., 694–707 (2015)
Zhang, H.-P., Yu, H.-K., Xiong, D.-Y., Liu, Q.: HHMM-based chinese lexical analyzer ICTCLAS. In: SIGHAN 2003 Proceedings of the Second SIGHAN Workshop on Chinese Language Processing, vol. 17, pp. 184–187 (2003)
Pang, L., Lan, Y., Guo, J., Xu, J., Wan, S., Cheng, X.: Text matching as image recognition. In: Proceedings of AAAI (2016)
Iyyer, M., Boyd-Graber, J., Claudino, L., Socher, R., Daumé III, H.: A neural network for factoid question answering over paragraphs. In: Proceedings of EMNLP, pp. 633–644 (2014)
Hochreiter, S., Schmidhuber, J.: Long short term memory. Neural Comput. **9**(8), 1735–1780 (1997)
Wan, S., Lan, Y., Guo, J., Xu, J., Cheng, X.: A deep architecture for semantic matching with multiple positional sentence representations. In: Proceedings of AAAI (2016)
Mikolov, T., Chen, K., Corrado, G., Dean, J.: Efficient estimation of word representations in vector space. In: Workshop at ICLR (2013)
Yin, W., Schütze, H.: MultiGranCNN: an architecture for general matching of text chunks on multiple levels of granularity. In: Proceedings of ACL, pp. 63–73 (2015)
Yih, W.-T., Chang, M.-W., Meek, C., Pastusiak, A.: Question answering using enhanced lexical semantic models. In: Proceedings of ACL, pp. 1744–1753 (2013)
Zhou, X., Hu, B., Chen, Q., Tang, B., Wang, X.: Answer sequence learning with neural networks for answer selection in community question answering. In: Proceedings of ACL, pp. 713–718 (2015)
Qiu, X., Huang, X.: Convolutional neural tensor network architecture for community based question answering. In: Proceedings of IJCAI, pp. C1305–C1311 (2015)
Lu, Z., Li, H.: A deep architecture for matching short texts. In: Advances in Neural Information Processing Systems (NIPS), pp. 1367–1375 (2013)
Bordes, A., Chopra, S., Weston, J.: Question answering with subgraph embeddings. In: Proceedings of the 2014 Conference on Empirical Methods in Natural Language Processing (EMNLP), pp. 615–620. Doha, Qatar (2014)

Text Classification and Summarization

Topic-Specific Image Caption Generation

Chang Zhou([✉]), Yuzhao Mao, and Xiaojie Wang

School of Computer, Beijing University of Posts and Telecommunications, Beijing, China
{elani,maoyuzhao,xjwang}@bupt.edu.cn

Abstract. Recently, image caption which aims to generate a textual description for an image automatically has attracted researchers from various fields. Encouraging performance has been achieved by applying deep neural networks. Most of these works aim at generating a single caption which may be incomprehensive, especially for complex images. This paper proposes a topic-specific multi-caption generator, which infer topics from image first and then generate a variety of topic-specific captions, each of which depicts the image from a particular topic. We perform experiments on flickr8k, flickr30k and MSCOCO. The results show that the proposed model performs better than single-caption generator when generating topic-specific captions. The proposed model effectively generates diversity of captions under reasonable topics and they differ from each other in topic level.

Keywords: Image caption · Topic model · Encoder-decoder

1 Introduction

Image caption is a cross-modal task which links the visual and the natural language modality. It aims at generating textual descriptions for an image automatically, and have received attentions worldwide. Inspired by successful advances in neural machine translation [1,2], most image caption generators are based on the encoder-decoder framework and trained in an end-to-end fashion. In machine translation, an LSTM is used to encode the sentence in source language, and another LSTM is employed to decode the intermedia into target language. By replacing the encoder with a CNN, encouraging performance has been achieved in image caption [6–11].

Most image caption generators generate a single caption for an image. However, an image is rich of information and an individual caption may be insufficient to depict it, especially for complex images. On the other hand, when facing an image, human may focus on different aspects and describe it from various of angles, resulting in multiple captions for the same image. There are also demands for captioning image under particular topics in real life. Sometimes one is interested just in a particular aspect of the image. Textual information related to the target topic should be extracted and information beyond the topic should be omitted in this circumstance.

M. Sun et al. (Eds.): CCL 2017 and NLP-NABD 2017, LNAI 10565, pp. 321–332, 2017.
https://doi.org/10.1007/978-3-319-69005-6_27

To simulate the multi-caption results of human beings, as well as generate captions specific to particular topics, we propose a topic-specific multi-caption generator for image. It takes latent topic attributes of captions into account. We employ an unsupervised topic model to infer latent topics from captions first. Each topic is represented as an embedding and then integrated into the decoder, guiding the generating of topic-specific captions. We also propose a method of inferring topics from images to limit the range of topics to perform captioning. The results show that the topic-specific image caption generator effectively generates diverse captions under reasonable topics and each of them depicts the image in a particular aspect.

The remainder of the paper is organized as follows. Section 2 introduces some previous works in image caption generation. Detailed formulation and model structure are given in Sect. 3. Experimental settings, evaluation metrics and experimental results are shown in Sect. 4. Conclusion and discussion of future works are included in Sect. 5.

2 Related Work

As for image caption generating, there are various studies, from early pipeline methods [14,17,18] to the end-to-end models commonly used now [3–5,9–11]. Inspired by the success of the encoder-decoder framework in machine translation, Karpathy et al. [4] employed CNN as encoder to extract features from image and RNN is used as decoder to generate sentences. For the advantage of LSTM dealing with long distance dependence, Vinyals et al. [7] replaced the RNN generator with LSTM and made continuous improvement.

In order to pay additional attention to visual or semantic information, the attention mechanism is employed and improve the performance of image caption to a great extent. Xu et al. [9] use visual attention method to pay attention to particular parts of the image with different ratios at each time step. You et al. [10] and Zhou et al. [11] propose different semantic attention approaches separately. You et al. extract several key words as semantic attributes for each image and then integrate the semantic information into input and output. While Zhou et al. use image feature filtered by text feature (text-conditional image feature) as semantic guidance for the gLSTM decoder. Both of the two methods take current generated words into account and use them to impact input and output states, or filter image features.

Recently, a number of studies resulting in multi-captions generating arise. Johnson et al. [12] propose a dense image caption model to generate an individual caption for multiple objects separately. They add a dense localization layer between the CNN encoder and the RNN decoder to handle the localization and description task jointly. Captions in various granularities, namely words, phrases and sentences, are generated as bounding-box moving throw the image. Mao et al. [13] aim at generating unambiguous captions for similar objects in an image. They link descriptions to corresponding bounding-boxes and train the model by minimizing the max-margin loss between positive samples and negative samples.

Although the two models above can generate multi-captions for an image, they are object-driven essentially while ours are topic-driven. We aim at generating topic-specific multiple captions. Compared with generating results of previous models, our generation is more tendentious and diverse. The generated captions depict the image from various points of view which is more human-like.

3 Model

In this paper, we propose a model which can infer latent topics from image and generate multiple topic-specific captions based on the encoder-decoder framework. Remarkable results can be achieved by maximizing the probability of the captions conditioned on the given image together with the topic and minimizing the divergence between the predicted topic distribution and the real one for the image simultaneously.

We first formulize the topic-specific image generation task in Sect. 3.1. A overview of the architecture of the proposed model is given in Sect. 3.2. Detailed introduction of each sub module including the unsupervised topic model training, image-topic distribution predicting and topic-specific caption generating is presented in Sects. 3.3, 3.4 and 3.5 respectively. Finally, we address the loss function and the details of training in Sect. 3.6.

3.1 Problem Formulization

For single-caption generators, the target of the image caption is to maximize the probability of the description given an image. Suppose an image is presented as I and a caption is presented as S, the target is to maximize:

$$\log P(S|I) = \sum_{t=1}^{N_S} \log P(w_t|w_0, \ldots, w_{t-1}, I) \ . \tag{1}$$

where $S = \{w_0, \ldots, w_{N_s}\}$ is the caption of image I with N_s words.

Different from the traditional single-caption generator, we aim at inferring latent topics from an image first and then generating multiple topic-specific captions each of which depicts the image from a particular topic point of view. Based on the assumption that topic-caption pairs are independent, our target is to maximize the probability of all topic-caption pairs given an image as follows:

$$\log P(S, Z|I) = \sum_{k=1}^{N_K} \log P(s_k, z_k|I) \ . \tag{2}$$

where Z, S denote the topic set and the corresponding caption set for image I, z_k and s_k are the k-th topic and caption specific to it. N_K denotes the amount of the topic-caption pairs (s_k, z_k) which can be inferred from the image.

Note that each item in the summation can be decomposes as follows:

$$P(s_k, z_k|I) = P(s_k|z_k, I)P(z_k|I) \ . \tag{3}$$

We decompose the target into two parts, the second part $P(z_k|I)$ can be seen as an image-topic classifier, indicating whether the topic z_i can be inferred from the image. The first part $P(s_k|z_k, I)$ can be seen as a sentence generator similar to the traditional image caption generator, while with a topic restriction in addition. So the target can be represented as follows,

$$\log P(S, Z|I) = \sum_{k=1}^{N_K} \log P(z_k|I) + \sum_{k=1}^{N_K} \log P(s_k|z_k, I). \tag{4}$$

As shown above, the target of finding topic-caption pairs for a given image is divided into two parts, predicting topic distribution from the given image first and then predicting descriptions conditioned on the image and a particular topic.

3.2 Model Architecture

Following discussions above, we now depict the topic-specific image generating model. We employ the encoder-decoder framework, with CNN such as VggNet to encode the image and LSTM to decode image representation into a textual sentence. The decoding side mainly consists of three modules: topic extracting, topic distribution predicting and topic-specific caption generating. The topic

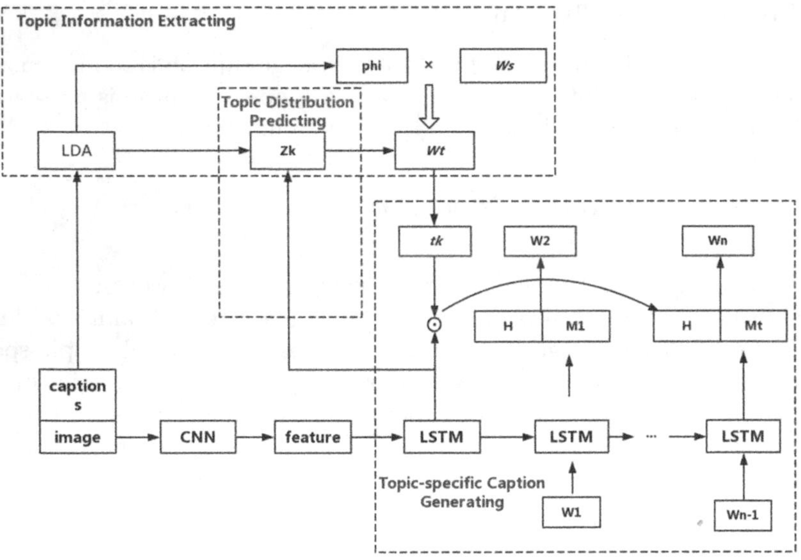

Fig. 1. The framework of the proposed topic-specific image caption generator. After applying LDA on textual captions, the topic distribution for each document (zk) and the word distribution for each topic (phi) can be gained. Then train the predictor to infer topic distributions and the generator for image caption. Ws denotes the word embedding matrix, Wt denotes the topic embedding matrix. A particular topic embedding t_k supervises the caption procedure along with the image.

extracting module employs an unsupervised topic model to extract topic information from the captions, such as topic distribution features among different captions and word distribution features among different topics. The topic distribution prediction module is an image-topic classifier essentially. It approximates the topic distribution in the image to the inferred results in the topic extracting module. The topic-specific caption generating module takes the image and a particular topic as input and generates caption with topic restriction. The model architecture is shown in Fig. 1. When generating captions for new images, topic predictor infers topic sets first. Each of the inferred topics is utilized separately, leading generating of topic-specific captions.

3.3 Topic Information Extracting

Topics are latent features in captions. As there is no image caption dataset offering captions with ground-truth topic label at present, we have to obtain the latent topic information in an unsupervised manner. LDA [15] is an unsupervised topic model which has been widely used in tasks such as document classification. It introduces latent topics into document-word distribution and can infer topic distribution of unlabeled corpus. Representing each caption as a bag of words, topic distribution of each caption and word distribution of each topic can be learnt by applying LDA. Each caption with the inferred topic label composes a topic-caption pair which is used in the subsequent training procedure. It's worth to notice that we take the average of the inferred topic distributions of all captions for the same image as the target topic distribution in topic-distribution prediction training.

3.4 Topic Distribution Predicting

To generate multiple topic-specific captions for an image, it is necessary to infer topics which are occurred in the image first. It can be solved as a multi-label classification task, while we tackle it in a more elaborated way. An image may contain more than one topics simultaneously with different probabilities. We train a probability distribution predictor which approximates the topic distribution of the image to the inferred one in topic information extracting period. If the probability of a topic is higher than a threshold, we believe that the topic exists in the image and a caption should be generated.

It is worth to notice that we take the output of the first LSTM unit in decoder as input to train the topic distribution predictor, which is represented as I afterwards. Commonly, the output of the encoder can be seen as the image representation and then fed to the first LSTM unit to initialize the decoder. While the output of the first LSTM unit carries visual feature as well. It can be seen as a more abstract representation of the original image and utilizing it results in better performance than the encoder output when training the topic distribution predictor.

As mentioned before, the target is to minimizing the divergence of the topic distributions between the predicted one and the inferred one by applying LDA.

We use sigmoid-entropy as loss function, and the loss function is shown below,

$$z^{'} = sigmoid(WI + b) . \tag{5}$$

$$L_{topic\_dist} = -\sum_{k=1}^{K}(z_k \log z_k^{'} + (1 - z_k)(1 - z_k^{'})) . \tag{6}$$

where I denotes the abstract representation of the image mentioned above, z_k denotes the probability of topic k inferred by LDA, and $z_k^{'}$ denotes the one predicted by topic-distribution predictor. W, b are training parameters.

3.5 Topic-Specific Caption Generator

Topic Embedding Construction. The topic label is represented as embedding before feeding into the decoder. For each topic in the topic sets, we represent it as a weighted sum of all word embeddings as follows:

$$topic_k = \sum_{k=1}^{K} \phi_{k,i} w_i . \tag{7}$$

where $\phi_{k,i}$ denotes the probability of the ith word in topic k, which can be learned by LDA, and w_i denotes the embedding form of the ith word which can be learnt from LSTM networks during training procedure.

Topic-Specific Caption Generator. As shown in Fig. 1, to generate a topic-specific caption for a given image, a simple but effective way is performing softmax function on a mixture of topic feature and the image feature when predicting words. To compute the probability of each candidate word in each time step with restriction of $topic_k$, we use following formulations,

$$H = W_I I \odot W_{topic} topic_k . \tag{8}$$

$$i_t = \sigma(W_{ix} x_t + W_{im} m_{t-1}) . \tag{9}$$

$$f_t = \sigma(W_{fx} x_t + W_{fm} m_{t-1}) . \tag{10}$$

$$o_t = \sigma(W_{ox} x_t + W_{om} m_{t-1}) . \tag{11}$$

$$c_t = f_t \odot c_{t-1} + i_t \odot h(W_{cx} x_t + W_{cm} m_{t-1}) . \tag{12}$$

$$m_t = o_t \odot c_t . \tag{13}$$

$$p_{t+1} = softmax(m_t, H) . \tag{14}$$

where I is the image representation mentioned above, H is the representation mixed with image and topic features, x_t is the input word embedding, m_t is the output of the LSTM unit, i_t, f_t, o_t are input, forget, output gates and c_t is the memory in LSTM unit. W matrices are trained parameters.

The basic idea behind the formulation is simply but reasonable. We take the first LSTM output as a more abstract representation of the image. Then construct a latent variable H which extracting intersection features of image and topic and concatenate it with the output of the LSTM unit at each time step. It results in a mixture which contains not only the predictions made by the language model, but also the intersection restriction of the image and the topic. Apply softmax function on the mixed output and choose the word with the maximum probability in vocabulary as the predicted one.

3.6 Loss Function

The deviation of the topic-specific caption generating model comes from two parts, namely the deviation of the language model (the LSTM generator), and the deviation of the topic distribution predictor. The loss function is shown below:

$$\log L(S, Z|I) = -\sum_{k=1}^{N_K}(z_k \log z_k^{'} + (1 - z_k)(1 - z_k^{'})) \tag{15}$$

$$-\sum_{k=1}^{N_K}\sum_{t=1}^{N_{S_k}} \log P(w_{k,t}|w_{k,0}, \ldots, w_{k,t-1}, I, z_k) \ .$$

where N_{S_k} denotes the length of the caption s_k specific to topic z_k and $w_{k,t}$ denotes the t-th word in caption s_k. Our model is trained by minimizing the loss function above with stochastic gradient descent. Batch size is set to 100 and learning rate is set to 0.0005. We also set dropout ratio to 0.5 for both the input embedding layer and output layer of the LSTM to combat overfitting.

4 Experiments

4.1 Datasets and Experimental Settings

Datasets. We test our model on 3 public datasets, which is flickr8k [16], flickr30k [19] and MS-COCO [20] with total images of 8000, 31000 and 123000 respectively. Five references are provided by human annotators for each image in both Flickr8k and Flickr30k dataset. As for MS-COCO dataset, some images have more than 5 references which for dataset consistency we retain only 5 of them. We use public splits [4] to perform train, validation and test.

Topic Model Training. In order to extract topic features from captions, LDA is applied in training set of the three dataset separately. We implement LDA with publicly available code, plda [21]. The parameters are set as $\alpha = 0.1$, $\beta = 0.01$. We train LDA with various topic numbers from 20 to 100 with varying step.

Image Features. For image representations, we adopt the pre-trained VggNet as encoder and take the penultimate layer with 4096 dimensions as encoder output. We don't fine-tune the encoder CNN during the experiment to be consistent with the compared models.

4.2 Evaluation Strategy

We carry out the evaluation in two steps: evaluating performance of the topic-distribution predictor first and then the topic-specific caption generator.

Image-topic Classification Evaluation. For each caption, we take the topic with the highest probability inferred by LDA as its topic label. For each image, the set of topic labels of all its captions can be regard as the latent topics for the image. When predicting topics from image, we filter topics with low probability and get predicted topics. We adopt two metrics, namely $F1$ score and one-recall to evaluate topic predicting performance. $F1$ score is calculated as below:

$$F = \frac{2PR}{P+R} \ . \tag{16}$$

where P denotes precision and R denotes recall of the classifier. One-recall measures the percentage of topic classification results which shoot at least one of the topics in the inferred ones by LDA. The higher the one-recall score is, the better the predictor performs.

Caption Generating Evaluation. We adopt four metrics to evaluate the generated captions, namely BLEU@N [22], METEOR [23], ROUGE-L [24], and CIDEr-D [25]. To check whether or not the multi-caption generator is able to generate captions inclining to a particular topic, captions and reference are compared grouping by topic in evaluation. Topics of references can be inferred by applying the pre-trained LDA model. Topic-specific captions can be generated guiding by the same LDA inferred topics.

It's worth to notice that our model can generate multiple captions each of which is specific to a particular topic. However, previous models only generate one single caption in the matter of "topic". In order to show the difference in topic point of view among captions, we are forced to fake the traditional image caption generator as a multiple one. We copy the best generation of the single-caption generator to all topics, based on the assumption that generations in all topics are always the same.

4.3 Results

Classification Results and Analysis. We evaluate the classification performance under different topic number settings. The result is shown in Fig. 2.

From the results we can see, the F1 score is unsatisfactory among all datasets. While the one-recall score is pretty high. It indicates that the predictor makes

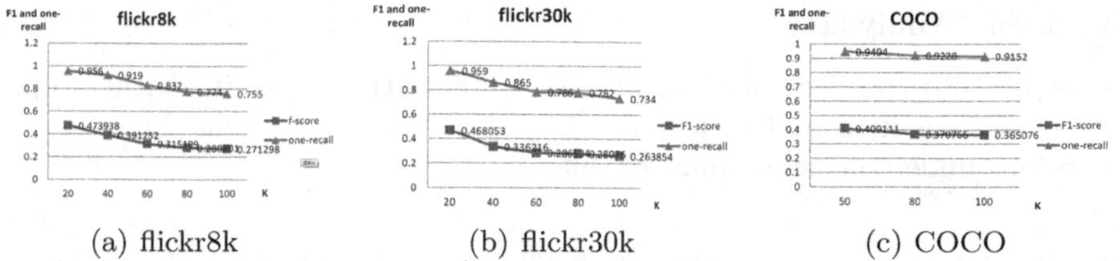

(a) flickr8k (b) flickr30k (c) COCO

Fig. 2. Image-topic classification performance with varying numbers of topic for three datasets. Classification performance declines with topic number increasing.

at least one correct prediction for most images though failing to infer all topics precisely. As the latent topics are obtained by applying LDA model, the performance of the topic model affects the classification performance to a certain extent. Note that most of the captions are short sentences with length no more than 10 words. Each caption is handled as a short document and topics underlying in short documents may not be well learnt by topic models like LDA.

Image Caption Results and Analysis. We compare our model with another two models without CNN fine-tuning: the Google NIC model [7] as baseline model and the glstm model [3]. Comparison results are shown in Table 1.

Table 1. Topic-specific caption generating results for flickr8k, flickr30k and COCO dataset. The proposed topic-specific model(TS) outperforms the baseline model and the glstm model in topic-specific image caption generating. Best performance is obtained when the topic number k is set to 100.

Datasets	Models	Bleu-1	Bleu-2	Bleu-3	Bleu-4	METEOR	ROUGE_L	CIDEr
flickr8k	baseline	0.348	0.204	0.125	0.078	0.128	0.311	0.403
	glstm	0.371	0.227	0.145	0.092	0.141	0.335	0.506
	TS	**0.379**	**0.241**	**0.156**	**0.101**	**0.154**	**0.366**	**0.662**
flickr30k	baseline	0.337	0.192	0.112	0.069	0.114	0.287	0.241
	glstm	0.34	0.204	0.128	0.082	0.122	0.311	0.385
	TS	**0.348**	**0.22**	**0.142**	**0.091**	**0.136**	**0.336**	**0.517**
COCO	baseline	0.426	0.265	0.168	0.109	0.145	0.356	0.54
	TS	**0.476**	**0.321**	**0.218**	**0.148**	**0.181**	**0.403**	**0.876**

As the results shown, our model surpasses both of the compared models in all metrics. With restriction of a particular topic, generations of the proposed model are more close to the human ones with the same topic. It indicates that the topic embedding captures latent topic features indeed. It guides the decoder to generate captions inclining to the target topic, depicting things related to the target topic and omitting the irrelevant ones.

4.4 Topic Analysis

Go deeper into the generated results, we confirm the topicality within topic-specific captions first, and then compare captions under different topics as well as captions under the same topic for different images.

Table 2. Topic consistency in flickr8k, flickr30k and COCO. The inferred topic is same as the supervised one most of the times.

Datasets	Accuracy
flickr8k	0.799068767908
flickr30k	0.845175766642
coco	0.78639553716

Topic Consistency. We take experiments to verify topic consistency between topic inferred by LDA and the supervised one used during generating. The topic label of each supervised topic in generating stage is recorded. After acquiring all topic-specific generations, we apply the pre-trained LDA model to them and infer topic distributions. Comparing the inferred topic with the supervised one and a good consistence occurs, as shown in Table 2.

The result shows that the inferred topic label is the same with the supervised one for nearly 80% of the generated descriptions, which indicates a good consistency. We can also confirm the rationality and effectiveness of the topic embedding.

A football player is holding a football during a football game.
A man wearing a red helmet is in front of a crowd.
Two men are playing basketball.

A man is making a turn on a motorcycle.
A man wearing a helmet is riding a bike.

Fig. 3. Similarity of captions among different images with the same topic and diversity of captions for the same image. Topics are represented as different colors. (Color figure online)

Generating Diversity. For image with rich topics, multiple captions can be obtained. Some examples are shown in Fig. 3. The topic-specific captions of the first image depict it from "sports" and "clothing" topics separately, and captions related with "action" and "clothing" are generated for the third one.

We also observe generation similarities among different images which are specific to the same topic. Both of the captions colored in green in Fig. 3 are generated under the same topic, which is obviously a topic related with sports.

5 Conclusion

In this paper, we proposed a topic-specific caption generator which can generate multiple captions each of which depict the image from a particular topic. Topic information is encoded in form of embedding and utilized to supervise generating topic-specific captions. Compared with results of single-caption generator, the generating results are more diverse and topic-specific.

As the experimental results show, the topic distribution predictor has great potential for improvement. In the future, we plan to train a multi-modal topic model which can capture topic features from image and texts jointly.

Acknowledgments. This paper is supported by 111 Project(No. B08004), NSFC(No. 61273365), Beijing Advanced Innovation Center for Imaging Technology, Engineering Research Center of Information Networks of MOE, and ZTE.

References

1. Cho, K., Van Merrienboer, B., Gulcehre, C., Bahdanau, D., Bougares, F., Schwenk, H., Bengio, Y.: Learning phrase representations using RNN encoder-decoder for statistical machine translation. arXiv preprint arXiv:1406.1078 (2014)
2. Sutskever, I., Vinyals, O., Le, Q.V.: Sequence to sequence learning with neural networks. In: Advances in Neural Information Processing Systems, pp. 3104–3112 (2014)
3. Jia, X., Gavves, E., Fernando, B., Tuytelaars, T.: Guiding the long-short term memory model for image caption generation. In: Proceedings of the IEEE International Conference on Computer Vision, pp. 2407–2415 (2015)
4. Karpathy, A., Fei-Fei, L.: Deep visual-semantic alignments for generating image descriptions. In: Proceedings of the IEEE Conference on Computer Vision and Pattern Recognition, pp. 3128–3137 (2015)
5. Kiros, R., Salakhutdinov, R., Zemel, R.: Multimodal neural language models. In: Proceedings of the 31st International Conference on Machine Learning (ICML 2014), pp. 595–603 (2014)
6. Mao, J., Xu, W., Yang, Y., Wang, J., Huang, Z., Yuille, A.: Deep captioning with multimodal recurrent neural networks (m-RNN). arXiv preprint arXiv:1412.6632 (2014)
7. Vinyals, O., Toshev, A., Bengio, S., Erhan, D.: Show and tell: a neural image caption generator. In: Proceedings of the IEEE Conference on Computer Vision and Pattern Recognition, pp. 3156–3164 (2015)
8. Wu, Q., Shen, C., Liu, L., Dick, A., van den Hengel, A.: What value do explicit high level concepts have in vision to language problems?. In Proceedings of the IEEE Conference on Computer Vision and Pattern Recognition, pp. 203–212 (2016)
9. Xu, K., Ba, J., Kiros, R., Cho, K., Courville, A., Salakhudinov, R., Zemel, R., Bengio, Y.: Show, attend and tell: neural image caption generation with visual attention. In: International Conference on Machine Learning, pp. 2048–2057, June 2015

10. You, Q., Jin, H., Wang, Z., Fang, C., Luo, J.: Image captioning with semantic attention. In: Proceedings of the IEEE Conference on Computer Vision and Pattern Recognition, pp. 4651–4659 (2016)
11. Zhou, L., Xu, C., Koch, P., Corso, J.J.: Image Caption Generation with Text-Conditional Semantic Attention. arXiv preprint arXiv:1606.04621 (2016)
12. Johnson, J., Karpathy, A., Fei-Fei, L.: Densecap: fully convolutional localization networks for dense captioning. In: Proceedings of the IEEE Conference on Computer Vision and Pattern Recognition, pp. 4565–4574 (2016)
13. Mao, J., Huang, J., Toshev, A., Camburu, O., Yuille, A.L., Murphy, K.: Generation and comprehension of unambiguous object descriptions. In Proceedings of the IEEE Conference on Computer Vision and Pattern Recognition, pp. 11–20 (2016)
14. Farhadi, A., Hejrati, M., Sadeghi, M.A., Young, P., Rashtchian, C., Hockenmaier, J., Forsyth, D.: Every picture tells a story: generating sentences from images. In: Daniilidis, K., Maragos, P., Paragios, N. (eds.) ECCV 2010. LNCS, vol. 6314, pp. 15–29. Springer, Heidelberg (2010). doi:10.1007/978-3-642-15561-1_2
15. Blei, D.M., Ng, A.Y., Jordan, M.I.: Latent dirichlet allocation. J. Mach. Learn. Res. **3**, 993–1022 (2003)
16. Hodosh, M., Young, P., Hockenmaier, J.: Framing image description as a ranking task: data, models and evaluation metrics. J. Artif. Intell. Res. **47**, 853–899 (2013)
17. Kulkarni, G., Premraj, V., Ordonez, V., Dhar, S., Li, S., Choi, Y., Berg, A.C., Berg, T.L.: Babytalk: understanding and generating simple image descriptions. IEEE Trans. Pattern Anal. Mach. Intell. **35**(12), 2891–2903 (2013)
18. Yang, Y., Teo, C.L., Daum III., H., Aloimonos, Y.: Corpus-guided sentence generation of natural images. In: Proceedings of the Conference on Empirical Methods in Natural Language Processing, pp. 444–454. Association for Computational Linguistics, July 2011
19. Young, P., Lai, A., Hodosh, M., Hockenmaier, J.: From image descriptions to visual denotations: new similarity metrics for semantic inference over event descriptions. Trans. Associat. Comput. Linguist. **2**, 67–78 (2014)
20. Lin, T.-Y., Maire, M., Belongie, S., Hays, J., Perona, P., Ramanan, D., Dollár, P., Zitnick, C.L.: Microsoft COCO: common objects in context. In: Fleet, D., Pajdla, T., Schiele, B., Tuytelaars, T. (eds.) ECCV 2014. LNCS, vol. 8693, pp. 740–755. Springer, Cham (2014). doi:10.1007/978-3-319-10602-1_48
21. Wang, Y., Bai, H., Stanton, M., Chen, W.-Y., Chang, E.Y.: PLDA: parallel latent dirichlet allocation for large-scale applications. In: Goldberg, A.V., Zhou, Y. (eds.) AAIM 2009. LNCS, vol. 5564, pp. 301–314. Springer, Heidelberg (2009). doi:10.1007/978-3-642-02158-9_26
22. Papineni, K., Roukos, S., Ward, T., Zhu, W.J.: BLEU: a method for automatic evaluation of machine translation. In: Proceedings of the 40th Annual Meeting on Association for Computational Linguistics, pp. 311–318. Association for Computational Linguistics, July 2002
23. Banerjee, S., Lavie, A.: METEOR: an automatic metric for MT evaluation with improved correlation with human judgments. In: Proceedings of the ACL Workshop on Intrinsic and Extrinsic Evaluation Measures for Machine Translation and/or Summarization, vol. 29, pp. 65–72, June 2005
24. Lin, C.Y.: Rouge: a package for automatic evaluation of summaries. In: Text Summarization Branches Out: Proceedings of the ACL 2004 workshop, vol. 8, July 2004
25. Vedantam, R., Lawrence Zitnick, C., Parikh, D.: Cider: consensus-based image description evaluation. In: Proceedings of the IEEE Conference on Computer Vision and Pattern Recognition, pp. 4566–4575 (2015)

Deep Learning Based Document Theme Analysis for Composition Generation

Jiahao Liu, Chengjie Sun(✉), and Bing Qin

Harbin Institute of Technology, Harbin 150001, China
{jhliu,qinb}@ir.hit.edu.cn, sunchengjie@hit.edu.cn

Abstract. This paper puts forward theme analysis problem in order to automatically solve composition writing questions in Chinese college entrance examination. Theme analysis is to distillate the embedded semantic information from the given materials or documents. We proposes a hierarchical neural network framework to address this problem. Two deep learning based models under the proposed framework are presented. Besides, two transfer learning strategies based on the proposed deep learning models are tried to deal with the lack of large training data for composition theme analysis problems. Experimental results on two tag recommendation data sets show the effect of the proposed deep learning based theme analysis models. Also, we show the effect of the proposed model with transfer learning on a composition writing questions data set built by ourself.

Keywords: Theme analysis · Deep learning · Transfer learning

1 Introduction

Automatically solving the material composition writing questions in a university's entrance examination like Gaokao [1] in China challenges natural language processing technology. Composition generation is a way to take up this challenge. Composition generation differs from text generation in that it needs to correctly analyze the theme firstly according to the specified materials. The target of text generation is to express the specified data in a natural language way. The specified data could be database records [2] or key words [3]. The key problem of text generation is language grounding [4], while the key problem for material composition generation is theme analysis.

How to analyze the theme from a given material? Because words are usually used to express the themes, theme analysis is related to key word extraction task [5]. Key words extraction methods can only output the words in the input text. However, the words expressing the theme of the material usually are not in the raw text and can capture the real semantic meaning behind the text. For example, the theme analysis results of the material in Fig. 1 could be {爱岗敬业, 尽职尽责, 责任心 } ({dedication, dutiful, responsibility}). Recently, [6] propose a deep keyphrase generation method, which attempts to capture the

M. Sun et al. (Eds.): CCL 2017 and NLP-NABD 2017, LNAI 10565, pp. 333–342, 2017.
https://doi.org/10.1007/978-3-319-69005-6_28

作文阅读下面的材料，根据要求写一篇不少于800字的文章。(60分)
船主请一位修船工给自己的小船刷油漆。修船工刷漆的时候，发现船底有个小洞，就顺手给补了。过了些日子，船主来到他家里道谢，送上去一个大红包。修船工感到奇怪，说："您已经给过工钱了。"船主说："对，那是刷油漆的钱，这是补洞的报酬。"修船工说："哦，那只是顺手做的一件小事……" 船主感激地说："当得知孩子们划船去海上之后，我才想起船底有洞这件事儿，绝望极了，觉得他们肯定回不来了。等到他们平安归来，我才明白是您救了他们。"
要求选好角度，确定立意，明确文体，自拟标题；不要脱离材料内容及含意的范围作文，不要套作，不得抄袭。

Read the following materials and write an essay of no less than 800 words. (60)
The owner of a boat asked a ship repairer to paint his boat. The repairer found that there was a small hole in the bottom of the boat during painting, he patched the hole by the way. A few days later, the owner came to thank him and gave him a big red envelope. The repairer felt surprised and said: "you have already paid." The owner said: "yes, that is for painting, this is the return to patch the hole." The repairer said: "Oh, just a little thing by the way......" The owner said gratefully: "when I heard that the children rowed out to the sea by the boat, I came to remember the bottom hole of the boat. I was so desperate and thought they couldn't come back. When they came back safely, I realized that you saved them."
Choose the right angle, determine the theme, make clear the genre, give the title; do not escape the scope of the content and meaning of the material, no plagiarism.

Fig. 1. An example of material composition question

deep semantic meaning of the content with a deep learning method. This work is also inspired by [6].

Another related task is tag recommendation [7]. Tag recommendation task has many similarities with this problem if we use tags to express the themes of materials. Both of them need to find tags to represent the meaning of a given text or materials. However one of the principle of making out the questions of Gaokao is to avoid similarity with history questions. So the successful collaborative filtering approaches in tag recommendation are not suitable for theme analysis for material composition question. Because themes are the distillation of materials, the theme analysis methods should have the ability to understand the materials.

Although there is still lack of clear explanation for the mechanism of deep learning, it does show the potential when dealing with semantic representation learning [8] and semantic reasoning [9]. Due to the promising of deep learning methods in natural language processing, deep learning based methods for document theme analysis required by composition generation are proposed in this work.

Deep learning models usually need large annotated training data to achieve good performance due to the numerous parameters in the models. However, no large annotated training data for theme analysis of material composition question is provided currently. One possible solution is to involve transfer learning [10] and some annotated training data for similarity tasks such as tag recommendation. Fortunately, the annotated training data for tag recommendation can be collected easily from some big social media websites such as Douban[1] and Zhihu[2]. Transfer learning for deep learning is also a hot research topic recently [11,12]. We try several transfer learning strategies based on the proposed deep learning models in this work to prompt the performance of theme analysis for material composition question.

2 Problem Definition

Most of the composition writing questions in Gaokao are material compositions. In a material composition question, a short essay is given and the students are required to write a composition based on the theme embedded in given material as shown in the example of Fig. 1. Theme analysis is the key step in the whole procedure of composition generation. It will be fail in this question if the theme is wrongly analyzed.

Theme analysis for material composition can be defined as following: given a short essay D, the target of theme analysis is to find a function F, which can map D to a word set $T = \{w_1, w_2, \cdots, w_n\}$. T represents the theme of D and can be used as the clue and input for composition generation.

Given the example in Fig. 1, the output T of theme analysis function F should be {爱岗敬业, 尽职尽责, 责任心 } ({dedication, dutiful, responsibility}). The words in T are the sublimation of the given essay, which can not be obtained through literal comprehension.

There are 3-fold challenges for theme analysis of material composition:

- lack of large annotated material-theme pairs training data.
- theme is the distillation of materials, not the surface expression of that.
- the expression of theme needs to be suitable for following procedure of composition Writing.

3 Method

In this work, a hierarchical neural network framework is proposed to learn the semantic representation V_{doc} of the give short essay D in material composition writing questions. With this representation, a predictor can be trained to output the confidence score $\delta(w_i|V_{doc})$ for each candidate theme word w_i. The theme analysis results for a material composition writing question consist of the words with the top N confidence score. N could be defined according to the requirements of applications. A theme word vocabulary T could be built in previous.

Two models are presented under this framework in the following. One is based on Gated Recurrent Unit (GRU) [13], named GRU-GRU model; The other is based on Convolutional Neural Networks (CNN) [14] and GRU, named CNN-GRU Model.

[1] https://www.douban.com/.
[2] https://www.zhihu.com/.

3.1 GRU-GRU Model

The GRU-GRU model architecture is shown in Fig. 2. In Fig. 2, the bottom two recurrent neural network (RNN) parts encode the input text into semantic representation. The unit of the RNN layers is Gated Recurrent Unit. The word embedding (word vector) of each word in D is taken as the input of the network.

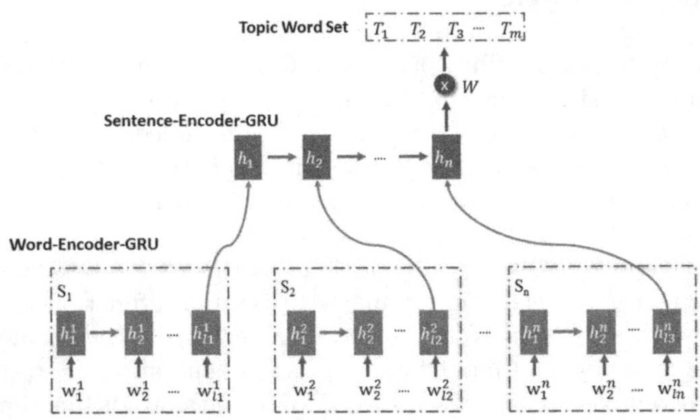

Fig. 2. GRU-GRU model architecture for theme analysis

The bottom part is a RNN word-sentence encoder. A "$\langle \backslash s \rangle$" is used to denote the end of a sentence. When encountering "$\langle \backslash s \rangle$", the hidden layer values of current RNN are taken as the sentence vector V_{s_i} of current sentence s_i. In this way, we can get $V_{s_1}, V_{s_2}, \cdots, V_{s_n}$ for a D with n sentences. The middle part is a RNN sentence-document encoder which takes V_{s_i} of each sentence s_i as input and outputs the semantic representation V_{doc} of D. The top part is a two-layer neural network. It takes document vector V_{doc} as input and output the confidence score δ_{w_i} of being theme word for each word w_i in T. δ_{w_i} is calculated by Eq. 1, Φ_{w_i} is a row of matrix W in Fig. 2. The size of matrix W is $|T| \times |V_{doc}|$.

$$\delta_{w_i} = Sigmoid(\Phi_{w_i} \cdot V_{doc}) \tag{1}$$

For a document D, the loss function of the network is defined as Eq. 2. In Eq. 2, T_D is the theme words set for D; M is the size of theme vocabulary T.

$$L = \sum_{i=1}^{M} [\sum_{w_i \in T_D} \log \delta_{w_i} + \sum_{w_i \notin T_D} \log(1 - \delta_{w_i})] \tag{2}$$

3.2 CNN-GRU Model

Convolutional Neural Networks (CNN) could better capture the local feature and has better performance when leaning the sentence semantic representation [15].

So, we propose CNN-GRU model by replacing the bottom layer in GRU-GRU model with CNN layer as shown in Fig. 3. Other parts of the model are same as what in GRU-GRU model.

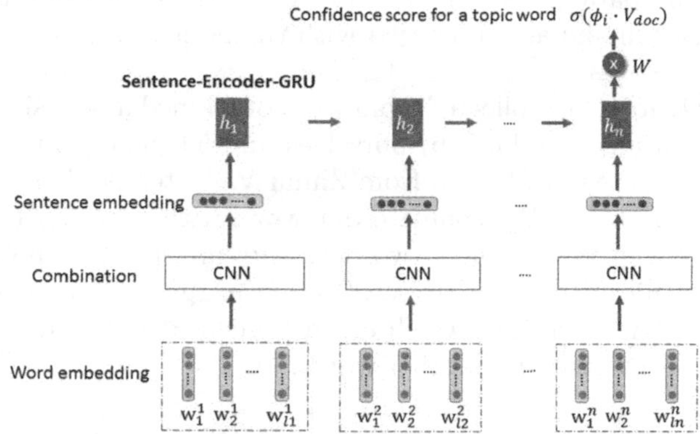

Fig. 3. CNN-GRU model architecture for theme analysis

3.3 Transfer Learning Strategies

In this section, two transfer learning strategies are proposed to overcome the shortage of theme analysis training data problem and boost the performance of theme analysis. Both of them are based on GRU-GRU model.

Feature Representation Based Transfer Learning. In GRU-GRU model, V_{doc} can be considered as a document representation. Inspired by [16], we propose a feature representation based transfer learning strategy, which train the GRU-GRU model with source domain training data and re-train the top part of Fig. 2 with target domain training data. Training data of source domain can be very large, so we can get a good document representation. Based on this transferred representation, better classifiers can be obtained by the small training data in the target domain.

Fine-Tuning Based Transfer Learning. In the proposed feature representation based transfer learning, only the parameters in the top part of Fig. 2 are modified by the target domain training data, which requires source domain and target domain have large similarities. While in fine-tuning based transfer learning, we first train the GRU-GRU model with source domain training data and then fine-tuning the whole network with the training data in target domain. In this way, all the parameters of GRU-GRU model learned from source domain will be adjusted to the target domain. When the differences between source domain and the target domain are large, this strategy may more suitable.

4 Data Set

Three data sets are used in this work: Composition, Zhihu and Douban. Table 1 shows samples of the three data set.

"Composition" data set is built by ourselves, which contains 1515 material composition problem and are annotated with theme-material pairs. The themes are expressed by words.

Zhihu and Douban are collected from two social media web sites: Zhihu and Douban. Zhihu data set are built by ourselves and 50,000 documents with their corresponding tags are downloaded from Zhihu Website. Douban data set came from Si [17] and Liu [18]. We compare our work with them on the same data set. The reasons why we use these two data sets are: (1) the shortage of large annotated material-theme pairs data set; (2) tags are given by users for numerous documents in the two websites, which could be considered as document theme words; (3) easy to compare with other works.

Table 1. Samples of Zhihu and Douban data set

Data Set	**Document**	**Tags**
Composition	滑雪是一种很好的运动项目，穿越林海雪原，飞速行进在都市中无缘得见的皑皑大地上，体会从山坡上急速滑降时那种风驰电掣般的感觉，真是无限乐趣在其中。但滑雪者都清楚地知道，要想轻松愉快地顺着山坡往下滑行，就必须先背负器材、一步步辛苦地登上山顶。	努力拼搏成功磨练困难克服困难
Zhihu	和朋友一起创办了一个补习班，可朋友现在很不用心，已经很多家长由于她的原因选择让孩子离开我们的补习班了。和她谈了几次，可还是不用心。因为是当初创办时的费用是一人一半的，而且没约定任何事情，现在她这样我很为难，想让她退出，哪怕我损失些钱也好，我该怎么和她说呢?	创业，合伙人，责任心
Douban	本书作者佩珀·怀特曾就读于MIT的机械工程系，他凭借睿智的眼光、情文并茂的描写，对自己早年在MIT辛酸的求学、生活和创业经历进行了全景式的回放，以"身在其中"的方式展示出MIT的独特风貌，带给读者关于人文精神的深刻反思。在与作者共同缅怀这段黄金岁月的过程中，相信每一个对MIT心存向往的人，都能够身临其境，切实体验到在MIT学习、生活的每一个平实的日子。	励志，我向往的学校，教育，传记，研究生，大学，MIT，经典，留学

5 Experimental Results

5.1 Experimental Settings

The experiments are designed for two purposes: (1) to show the theme analysis abilities of the two proposed deep learning models; (2) to verify the effect of the proposed transfer learning strategies.

Settings for Deep Learning Based Theme Analysis. 10,000 and 5,000 samples are randomly chosen from Zhihu data set as training data and test data respectively. The vocabulary T is built by collecting all the tag words in the training data. The embeddings of words are trained using the training data by word2vec[3] tools. The dimension of word vector is 200. In GRU-GRU model, the recurrent hidden layer of the word layer GRU contains 200 hidden units while sentences layer GRU contains 500. As to CNN-GRU model, we use three convolutional filters whose widths are 1, 2 and 3 to encode semantics of unigrams, bigrams and trigrams in a sentence. And the number of filters is 200, while the parameters of sentences layer GRU are the same as GRU-GRU model. Parameters of our model are randomly initialized over a uniform distribution with support $[-0.01, 0.01]$. The model is trained with the AdaDelta [19] algorithm.

The Top3 theme words given by the proposed models are used as the theme analysis results.

Precision, recall and F1-measure are taken as the evaluation criteria. The final evaluation scores are computed by micro-averaging (i.e. averaging on resources of test set). The tags given by users in the test data are taken as gold standard.

Settings for Transfer Learning. The Zhihu data set and Composition data set are taken as source domain and target domain respectively. The detail information about the data used in transfer learning experiments are shown in Table 2.

Table 2. Data settings for transfer learning

Data set	♯training	♯test	♯candidate tags
Composition (Target domain)	1415	100	694
Zhihu (Source domain)	10,000	5,000	5000

5.2 Experimental Results

Table 3 shows the results of the "GRU+GRU" and "CNN+GRU" models.

Table 3. Experimental results on Zhihu data set

Method	Precision	Recall	F1-measure
GRU+GRU	0.2762	0.3173	0.2766
CNN+GRU	0.2828	0.3247	0.2828

In order to better evaluate the performance of the proposed models, we compare their performances with TAM [17] and WTM [18] on Douban data set. With 49,050 documents with their corresponding tags from Douban as training data and 12,132 as test data, the comparison results are shown in Table 4.

[3] https://code.google.com/archive/p/word2vec/.

Table 4. Experimental results on Douban data set

Method	Precision	Recall	F1-measure
TAM	0.2971	0.3230	0.2676
WTM	0.3498	0.4182	0.3311
GRU+GRU	0.3680	0.4052	0.3337
CNN+GRU	0.3835	0.4213	0.3480

Due to no titles are given for essays in material composition writing questions, our models don't deal with the title of a document. That's the reason why we didn't compare the results with title information in [17,18].

From Table 4, it is obvious that two deep learning based models have better performance. The results indicate that deep learning based methods have better ability to understand the semantic of the documents than previous methods. Also, "CNN+GRU" model outperforms "GRU+GRU" model consistently on two data sets, which shows that CNN can use local information to obtain better sentence representation. Samples in Zhihu data set are more similar with material composition questions because most tags for a document can be found in the document in Douban data set. That's also the reason for the higher performance in Douban data set.

Table 5 shows the results of theme analysis on Composition data set with different methods. P@5 is used as the evaluation criteria. GRU+GRU model can only achieve 0.078 when we directly use 1415 training samples chosen from composition data set. The poor performance is largely due to the small number of training data compared with the results in Table 4. Two transfer learning methods can greatly boost the performance from 0.078 to more than 0.3. So transfer learning based on the deep learning model is a promising way to deal with theme analysis for material composition generation.

Table 5. Experimental results on Composition data set

Method	P@5
GRU+GRU	0.078
Feature representation	0.324
Fine-tuning	0.341

6 Conclusion

The first step of automatic composition generation for material composition questions in Gaokao is to identify the theme of the given materials, which is even a big challenge for most high school students. This work proposes a deep learning framework to solve this problem. The contributions of this work lie in:

(1) put forward theme analysis problem for material composition questions in Gaokao; (2) present two deep learning based methods to solve theme analysis problem and Show the potential of deep learning based theme analysis methods with two social media data sets; (3) propose transfer learning strategies to make the deep learning models trained on social media data set can be used to analyze material composition question data.

Acknowledgment. We would like to thank the anonymous reviewers for their thorough reviewing and proposing thoughtful comments to improve our paper. This work was supported by the National 863 Leading Technology Research Project via grant 2015AA015407, Key Projects of National Natural Science Foundation of China via grant 61632011.

References

1. Cheng, G., Zhu, W., Wang, Z., Chen, J., Qu, Y.: Taking up the gaokao challenge: an information retrieval approach. In: Proceedings of the Twenty-Fifth International Joint Conference on Artificial Intelligence, IJCAI 2016, New York, NY, USA, 9–15 July 2016, pp. 2479–2485 (2016)
2. Konstas, I., Lapata, M.: A global model for concept-to-text generation. J. Artif. Intell. Res. (JAIR) **48**, 305–346 (2013)
3. Uchimoto, K., Sekine, S., Isahara, H.: Text generation from keywords. In: 19th International Conference on Computational Linguistics, COLING 2002, Howard International House and Academia Sinica, Taipei, Taiwan, 24 August–1 September 2002 (2002)
4. Liang, P., Jordan, M.I., Klein, D.: Learning semantic correspondences with less supervision. In: ACL 2009, Proceedings of the 47th Annual Meeting of the Association for Computational Linguistics and the 4th International Joint Conference on Natural Language Processing of the AFNLP, Singapore, 2–7 August 2009, pp. 91–99 (2009)
5. Mihalcea, R., Tarau, P.: TextRank: bringing order into text. In: Proceedings of the 2004 Conference on Empirical Methods in Natural Language Processing, EMNLP 2004, A meeting of SIGDAT, a Special Interest Group of the ACL, Held in Conjunction with ACL 2004, Barcelona, Spain, 25–26 July 2004, pp. 404–411 (2004)
6. Meng, R., Zhao, S., Han, S., He, D., Brusilovsky, P., Chi, Y.: Deep keyphrase generation. In: ACL 2017 (2017)
7. Sigurbjörnsson, B., van Zwol, R.: FlicKR tag recommendation based on collective knowledge. In: Proceedings of the 17th International Conference on World Wide Web, WWW 2008, Beijing, China, 21–25 April 2008, pp. 327–336 (2008)
8. Bengio, Y., Courville, A.C., Vincent, P.: Representation learning: a review and new perspectives. IEEE Trans. Pattern Anal. Mach. Intell. **35**, 1798–1828 (2013)
9. Schmidhuber, J.: Deep learning in neural networks: an overview. CoRR abs/1404.7828 (2015)
10. Pan, S.J., Yang, Q.: A survey on transfer learning. IEEE Trans. Knowl. Data Eng. **22**(10), 1345–1359 (2010)
11. Zhuang, F., Cheng, X., Luo, P., Pan, S.J., He, Q.: Supervised representation learning: transfer learning with deep autoencoders. In: Proceedings of the Twenty-Fourth International Joint Conference on Artificial Intelligence, IJCAI 2015, Buenos Aires, Argentina, 25–31 July 2015, pp. 4119–4125 (2015)

12. Yosinski, J., Clune, J., Bengio, Y., Lipson, H.: How transferable are features in deep neural networks? In: Advances in Neural Information Processing Systems 27: 2014 Annual Conference on Neural Information Processing Systems, Montreal, Quebec, Canada, 8–13 December 2014, pp. 3320–3328 (2014)
13. Cho, K., van Merrienboer, B., Gülçehre, Ç., Bahdanau, D., Bougares, F., Schwenk, H., Bengio, Y.: Learning phrase representations using RNN encoder-decoder for statistical machine translation. In: Proceedings of the 2014 Conference on Empirical Methods in Natural Language Processing, EMNLP 2014, Doha, Qatar, 25–29 October 2014, A meeting of SIGDAT, a Special Interest Group of the ACL, pp. 1724–1734 (2014)
14. Kalchbrenner, N., Grefenstette, E., Blunsom, P.: A convolutional neural network for modelling sentences. In: ACL (2014)
15. Kim, Y.: Convolutional neural networks for sentence classification. In: Proceedings of the 2014 Conference on Empirical Methods in Natural Language Processing, EMNLP 2014, Doha, Qatar, 25–29 October 2014, pp. 1746–1751 (2014)
16. Razavian, A.S., Azizpour, H., Sullivan, J., Carlsson, S.: CNN features off-the-shelf: an astounding baseline for recognition. In: IEEE Conference on Computer Vision and Pattern Recognition, CVPR Workshops 2014, Columbus, OH, USA, 23–28 June 2014, pp. 512–519(2014)
17. Si, X., Liu, Z., Sun, M.: Modeling social annotations via latent reason identification. IEEE Intell. Syst. **25**(6), 42–49 (2010)
18. Liu, Z., Chen, X., Sun, M.: A simple word trigger method for social tag suggestion. In: Proceedings of the 2011 Conference on Empirical Methods in Natural Language Processing, EMNLP 2011, John McIntyre Conference Centre, Edinburgh, UK, 27–31 July 2011, A meeting of SIGDAT, a Special Interest Group of the ACL, pp. 1577–1588 (2011)
19. Zeiler, M.D.: ADADELTA: an adaptive learning rate method. CoRR abs/1212.5701 (2012)

UIDS: A Multilingual Document Summarization Framework Based on Summary Diversity and Hierarchical Topics

Lei Li, Yazhao Zhang(✉), Junqi Chi, and Zuying Huang

Center for Intelligence Science and Technology, School of Computer, Beijing University of Posts and Telecommunications, Beijing, People's Republic of China
{leili,yazhao}@bupt.edu.cn, 1709722796@qq.com, hpwthzy@126.com

Abstract. In this paper, we put forward UIDS, a new high-performing extensible framework for extractive MultiLingual Document Summarization. Our approach looks on a document in a multilingual corpus as an item sequence set, in which each sentence is an item sequence and each item is the minimal semantic unit. Then we formalize the extractive summary as summary diversity sampling problem that considers topic diversity and redundancy at the same time. The topic diversity is reflected using hierarchical topic models, the redundancy is reflected using similarity and the summary diversity is enhanced using Determinantal Point Processes. We then illustrate how this method encompasses a framework that is amenable to compute summaries for MultiLingual Single- and Multi-documents. Experiments on the MultiLing summarization task datasets demonstrate the effectiveness of our approach.

Keywords: Multilingual document summarization · Summary diversity · Determinantal point processes

1 Introduction

With the development of information communication technology, a large number of electronic documents are created on the Internet. Under this circumstance, it is an enormous challenge for users to find concise and relevant information, especially in the cross-language case. This motivates the development of methods to compute summaries for multiple languages.

Document summarization can generally be classified into extractive and abstractive ones. An abstractive summary can be seen as a reproduction of the original document in a new way. However, an extractive summary is generated by selecting a few relevant sentences from the original document.

The task on which we focus in this paper is extractive MultiLingual Document Summarization (MDS). The goal of MDS is to compute a summary for every document or document cluster in the multilingual corpus. The language of the summary is consistent with the language of the corresponding source

M. Sun et al. (Eds.): CCL 2017 and NLP-NABD 2017, LNAI 10565, pp. 343–354, 2017.
https://doi.org/10.1007/978-3-319-69005-6_29

text. And the summary length depends on the compressing rate which is mostly decided by users.

In this paper, our goal is to systematically explore an amenable unsupervised language independent sampling framework to automatically calculate diverse summaries (Unsupervised language Independent Diverse Summary method, UIDS) for multilingual corpus. According to our observation, a good summary should be diverse in latent semantics, including topic diversity (quality) and redundancy. The three main contributions of our work are:

1. We focus on the issue of Summary Diversity that contains *Topic Diversity* and *Redundancy* of extractive summarization.
2. We enhance the summary diversity of Multilingual documents using Determinantal Point Processes and multiple features including hierarchical topic models.
3. We propose an efficient extensible language independent framework to solve the Multilingual Document Summarization task.

The rest of this paper is organized as follows: Sect. 2 presents related works. Section 3 defines the summary diversity property and MultiLingual Document Summarization. Section 4 presents the system framework of UIDS based on hierarchical Topic Model (HTM) and Determinantal Point Processes(DPPs). A set of experiments are implemented on the MultiLingual datasets, described in Sect. 5. In Sect. 6, we conclude the paper with some pointers to future research directions.

2 Related Work

An extractive summary is often viewed as a machine learning problem: selecting a subset of sentences from a given document [9]. And several effective methods have been proposed to solve MDS problem.

In the method of [15], features were categorized as surface, content, relevance and event. They combined these four features to select sentences to compute a summary. In SIGDial 2015, UJF-Grenoble [2], CCS [7], EXB [20], NTNU [14] and UA-SLAI [21] all presented their systems on MSS task. CCS [7] used a term weighting method called OCCAMS [8] to compute the weight of each sentence and then choose the top few sentences to construct the summary.

Previous work also proved the effectiveness of Topic Models. [4] first proposed Latent Dirichlet Allocation (LDA) and used it into summarization. To relax the assumption that topic count of LDA is known and fixed, [3] extended LDA to exploit the hierarchical tree structure of topics, called hierarchical Latent Dirichlet Allocation, hLDA in short. It organizes the topics into a tree-like structure and supposes the topic count could grow with the dataset automatically. [6] provides a multi-document summarization based on supervised hLDA and obtains competitive results. [13] used hLDA based multiple feature combination method to compute MultiLingual Multi-Document Summarization.

The diversity property has been researched in many areas other than summarization, such as biodiversity, Shannon's diversity index and so on. [18] considered the diversity for summarization. They put forward a contrastive theme summarization based on hLDA and Structured Determinantal Point Processes (SDPPs). They use topic probability of word, under viewpoint to calculate qualities. But unfortunately, their focus on solving the sentiment diversity. Our method differs from the above methods by emphasizing the latent semantic diversity property implicated in summarization, which will be proved to be a novel solution for multilingual summarization.

3 Motivation and Formalization

3.1 Summary Diversity

As presented in classic topic models, a document can be represented using multiple latent topics. And each sentence belongs to a topic according to a certain probability. The consensus amongst the researchers of topic model is that each topic has some kind of latent semantic information implicated in articles. Besides, diversity is an instance of being composed of differing elements or qualities. Based on this, we believe that a good summary should be diverse in latent semantic level. That is to say a diverse summary should satisfy the following two requirements:

1. **Topic Diversity:** the summary should contain those important topics hidden in the document and each topic cannot be similar to others.
2. **Redundancy:** the summary should not contain two or more sentences that describe the same topic or aspect.

In general, our goal is to compute summaries with diversity. In extractive case, a summary may be a subset of sentences.

3.2 MultiLingual Document Summarization

Given a *document* D from a multilingual corpus, we can represent it using a sentence set $\{s_1, ..., s_n\}$, where n is the total number of sentences. Every *sentence* is a sequence of words $s_i = \{w_1, ..., w_m\}$. It is a big challenge to understand the specific meaning of every word, especially in the case of multiple languages. For English, a word is a sequence of letters. However, for Chinese, a word is one or more Chinese characters. In this paper, the "word" will be collectively referred to as an *item*. It represents the minimal semantic unit in a sentence that depends on its language.

Following the topic modeling customs, we define a *topic* in a document D to be a probability distribution over items. Different from "flat" topic model, we assume that the topics in D are organized as a tree-like hierarchy and every node is a topic. Every sentence s_i is assigned to a path c_j from the root node to a leaf node.

Given a document represented using items and topics, we define the *quality* of a sentence and the *similarity* between sentences. The *quality* of s_i determines the degree of its reflection on topics. However, the *similarity* determines the redundancy between sentences.

Finally, we define extractive MultiLingual Document Summary. Given a document $D = \{s_1, \ldots, s_n\}$ represented using items. The purpose of extractive summarization for MDS is to sample a subset $D' \subset D$ that gives consideration to both *quality* and *similarity*, thus generating a diverse summary covering more important information of the original document. And the sentence sampling method must be language independent.

4 *UIDS* Framework

In this section we describe our *UIDS* framework. It is presented as a *framework* rather than a singular approach because a number of the implementation details can very depending on the purpose of the task (Multi-document or Single document). And it provides a generic structure for building more specialized systems. Figure 1 shows the framework of our unsupervised language independent diverse summarization system (UIDS) based on Summary Diversity and DPPs. The line of dashes in Fig. 1 means that it can be modified according to specific tasks.

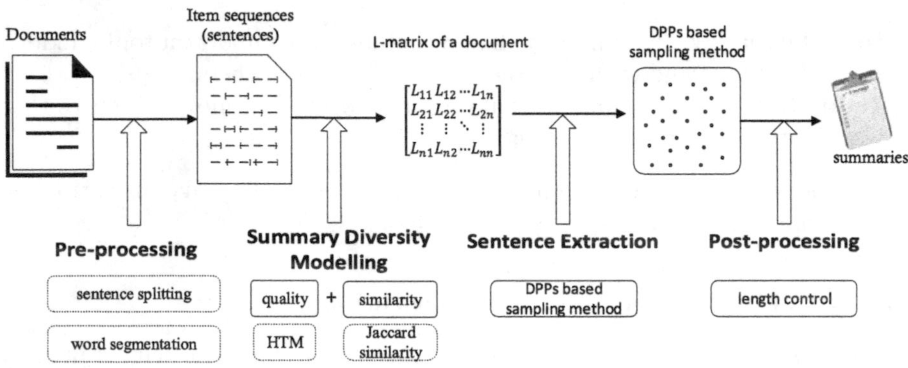

Fig. 1. Framework of UIDS system

4.1 Pre-processing

To deal with the linguistic difference and convert the documents into item sequences, we use the following steps to pre-process the original documents. (1) spilt document into sentences using period for every document; (2) use Rosette API [19] to tokenize the document of some languages, such as Chinese, Thai and Japanese; (3) calculate TF-IDF value of each item in every document; (4) model every document using hLDA [3].

4.2 Summary Diversity Modelling

Given the document and hierarchical topics calculated in Sect. 4.1, we estimate the quality (topic diversity) of each sentence using hierarchical topic information.

Hierarchical Topic Model (HTM): hLDA constructs a document to a tree-like structure. Based on this, we adapt the method that [13] proposed to use the information of hLDA for MSS task. HTM represents the level score of item calculated according to the topics in hLDA. We give the item higher score whose level distribution is more close to that of items in golden summary. We use Eq. (1) to calculate it.

$$q_{HTM} = \sum_{i=1}^{m}(\alpha_i T_i + Freq_i) \tag{1}$$

where T_i represents the distribution score of $item_i$ calculated by hLDA, α_i is the pre-defined weight of T_i according to our former experiments, $Freq_i$ is the frequency of $item_i$ in current hLDA node.

4.3 Determinantal Point Processes for Diverse Summary Extraction

Arisen in quantum physics and random matrix theory, DPPs are elegant probabilistic models of global, negative correlations [16]. In this paper, we will focus on discrete DPPs and follow the definition of Kulesza [1].

A point process P on a discrete set $Y = \{x_1, x_2, ..., x_n\}$ is a probability measure on 2^Y, the set of all subsets of Y. A Determinantal Point Process is a point process with a positive semidefinite matrix K, which is indexed by the elements of Y. That is the i-th row of K corresponds to the i-th element in Y. Thus the definition of DPP is:

Definition 1. *When Y is a random subset drawing according to point process P, we have, for every $A \subseteq Y$,*

$$P(A \subseteq \mathbf{Y}) = \det(K_A)$$

where $\det(K_A) = |K_{ij}|_{i,j \in A}$ *and we adopt* $\det(K_\Phi) = 1$.

As for K contains all information needed to compute the probability of any subset A being included in Y, we call it as *kernel matrix*. In order to model real data, we use L-ensemble [5] to construct DPPs. Thus we have

$$P_L(\mathbf{Y} = Y) = \frac{\det(L_Y)}{\det(L + I)}.$$

where L is a positive semidefinite matrix, $\det(L_Y) = |L_{ij}|_{i,j \in Y}$, I is the $N \times N$ identity matrix.

Using this representation, the entries of kernel L can be written as

$$L_{ij} = q_i \phi_i^\top \phi_j q_j$$

where $q_i \in R^+$ measures the *quality* of an element i, and $\phi_i^\top \phi_j$ is often regarded as a whole that measures the *similarity* between element i and element j.

To compute a summary, we adopt sampling algorithm proposed by Kulesza and Taskar to sample a sentence subset from a document, shown in Table 1. As we can see that the sampling algorithm is language independent.

Table 1. DPPs sampling method for diverse summary extraction, where S is the similarity matrix, D is the document, ω_0 is the parameter of sentence quality calculated using HTM

Input: HTM, S, D, max_len
$\rightarrow$ $quality_vec = \omega_0 *$HTM
$\rightarrow$ matrix_l = $quality\_vec * S * quality\_vec^T$
$\rightarrow$ $(\mathbf{v}_n, \lambda_n)$ = eigen_decompose(matrix_l)
$\rightarrow$ $J = \emptyset$
$\rightarrow$ **for** $n = 1, 2, \ldots, N$ **do**
$\rightarrow\rightarrow$ $J = J \cup \{n\}$ with prob. $\frac{\lambda_n}{\lambda_n + 1}$
$\rightarrow$ $V = \{\mathbf{v}_n\}_{n \in J}$
$\rightarrow$ $Y = \emptyset$
$\rightarrow$ **while** $\lvert V \rvert > 0$ and $len(Y) <$ max_len **do**
$\rightarrow\rightarrow$ Select i from Y with $Pr(i) = \frac{1}{\lvert V \rvert} \sum_{v \in V} (\mathbf{v}^\top \mathbf{e}_i)^2$
$\rightarrow\rightarrow$ $Y = Y \cup D[i]$
$\rightarrow\rightarrow$ $V = V_\perp$, an orthonormal basis for the subspace of V orthogonal to e_i
Output: summary Y

Besides, we use JACCARD to measure the sentence similarity (Redundancy), shown in Eq. (2)

$$r_{ij} = \frac{\lvert s_i \cap s_j \rvert}{\lvert s_i \cup s_j \rvert} \tag{2}$$

Thus each element L_{ij} can be calculated as follows.

$$L_{ij} = q_i r_{ij} q_j \tag{3}$$

Finally, we will truncate summary to human summary length and remove multiple white spaces to get our final summaries in the post-processing step.

5 Experiments

To test the capability of UIDS summarization framework, we also propose two contrast systems shown below.

Combined Features (CF): except *HTM* introduced in Sect. 4.2, we also propose four features to calculate the *score* of each sentence, then we select the top few sentences to construct the summary.

1. *Sentence Position (SP)*: Here we use Eq. (4) to calculate the score of sentence position.

$$q_{SP} = \frac{n-i+1}{n} \tag{4}$$

where n is the total sentence number of the document, i represents $i-th$ sentence in the document.

2. *Title Similarity (TS)*: Title Similarity is the cosine similarity of the sentence and the document title. We use Eq. (5) to calculate it.

$$q_{TS} = \frac{tf_{s_i} \times tf_{s_{title}}}{|tf_{s_i}||tf_{s_{title}}|} \tag{5}$$

where s_{title} and s_i represent the title and a sentence respectively.

3. *Sentence Length (SL)*: We define the sentence length as *item* number in s_i. Then we use Gaussian distribution to normalize the score, shown in Eq. (6).

$$q_{SL} = \frac{1}{\sqrt{2\pi}\sigma} e^{-\frac{(L_i-\mu)^2}{2\sigma^2}} \tag{6}$$

where L_i is the length of sentence i, μ is the average length and σ^2 is the variance of lengths.

4. *Sentence Coverage (SC)*: If an item appears in many sentences, then the sentence containing the item has a high probability of being selected as summary. Based on this, we can calculate SC using Eq. (7)

$$q_{SC} = \frac{\sum_{i=1}^{|s|} \frac{num_s(item_i)}{n}}{|s|} \tag{7}$$

where $num_s(item_i)$ is the sentence number that contains $item_i$, $|s|$ is the sentence length.
Given the five features (HTM, SP, TS, SL, SC), the score calculation method is shown below:

$$score_i = \sum_{k=1}^{5} \varphi_k q_{ki} \tag{8}$$

where $\varphi_k \in \{0,1\}$ is the combination proportion of corresponding features. q_{ki} represents the k-th quality feature of s_i.

Graphical Model: graphical model can obtain the summary in an unsupervised way, and it is also corpus and language independent. As a comparison, we use the LexRank algorithm [17] to obtain the score of sentence s_i. We then calculate the sentence order on the basis of sentence score. Finally, we select sentences one by one until the length of selected sentences exceeds the length limit. The method is shown in Table 2.

Table 2. Graphical Model Method for MSS, where sim_{ij} is the similarity of s_i, s_j, Φ is the edge threshold, max_inter is the max iteration times, d is the damping coefficient

Input: sim_{ij}, Φ, max_inter, d
for $i = 1, 2, \ldots, N$ **do:**
$\rightarrow$ **for** $j = 1, 2, \ldots, N$ **do:**
$\rightarrow\rightarrow$ **if** $sim_{ij} > \Phi$ **then:**
$\rightarrow\rightarrow\rightarrow$ $Edge_{ij} \leftarrow sim_{ij}$
$\rightarrow\rightarrow$ **else**
$\rightarrow\rightarrow\rightarrow$ $Edge_{ij} \leftarrow 0$
$\rightarrow$ $LR_i \leftarrow \frac{1-d}{N}$
$iter = 1$
while $iter < max\_iter$ **do**
$\rightarrow$ **for** $i = 1, 2, \ldots, N$ **do**
$\rightarrow\rightarrow$ $LR' = LR_i$
$\rightarrow\rightarrow$ **for** $j = 1, 2, \ldots, N$ **do**
$\rightarrow\rightarrow\rightarrow$ $LR_i \leftarrow \frac{1-d}{N} + d\frac{sim_{ji}}{\sum_{k=1}^{N} sim_{jk}} LR'_j$
Output: LR

5.1 Multilingual Single Document Summarization

We follow the MSS-2017 task [12] at MultiLing-2017 Workshop on Summarization and Summary Evaluation Across Source Types and Genres implemented within EACL 2017 (15th Conference of the European Chapter of the Association for Computational Linguistics), so as to measure the performance of our framework and methods.

The testing dataset contains 30 featured Wikipedia articles from each of 41 languages. All documents in testing dataset are provided by MSS-2017 task and formatted in both an XML format and raw text. The documents are in UTF-8 without mark-ups and images. And the target summary length is the same as the character length of the human summary.

Following existing models, we set predefined parameters (ω_0) of UIDS to the sum of the quality of every sentence (UIDS-HTM). In order to test the performance of HTM, we also use SP (UIDS-SP) and TS (UIDS-TS) to replace it to calculate the quality of sentences, and then construct matrix L. Besides CF and GM, there are two teams **SWAP** and **TeamMD** participated in the MSS task and they proposed nine summary methods. The organizer of MSS task has also provided three MSS systems for comparisons. **Oracle** uses the combinatorial covering algorithm in [8] by selecting sentences from its body text to cover the items in the human summary. Thus it can be considered as an upper bound approximation for every document. **Lead** just cuts the original document to summary length. **IWB** uses the structure of the document sections to extract sentences from sections and subsections. Table 3 shows the identifier of every method.

Table 3. System names and its supporting languages

Method name	Identifier	Method name	Identifier
IWB	B1	Combined feature	CF
Lead	B2	Graphical model	GM
Oracle	B3	TeamMD-1	T1
UIDS-HTM	S1	TeamMD-2	T2
UIDS-SP	S2	TeamMD-3	T3
UIDS-TS	S3	TeamMD-4	T4

Table 4 gives the ROUGE-2 F scores of 12 systems for 24 languages. The first column in both tables contain the ISO code for each language [10]. As shown in Table 4, S3 (UIDS-TS) performs much better than S2 (UIDS-SP) in 16 languages. And the phenomenon may due to the fact that titles of Wikipedia articles are highly summative. But anyway this illustrates that the performances of both TS and SP are deficient in stability. Fortunately, S1 (UIDS-HTM) performs much better than S2 and S3 in almost every language. This indicates that HTM based latent topic modeling method is more useful for latent topic diversity and sentence diversity sampling.

For more observation, Oracle ranks first in 24 languages with no doubt as it is the upper bound approximation of every document. With no consideration to Oracle, CF and GM methods give the worst performance in most languages. S1 performs better than other methods in 11 languages, and ranks top 3 in every language. This fully demonstrates the effectiveness of our framework.

We also notice that documents in az, bs, jv, li, lv, mr, tt, uk are much harder for summarization than others. Because MultiLing-2017 does not provide any training data for those languages. Our approach UIDS ranks top 2 in those languages and outperforms the B1 (IWB) baseline in 4 kinds of languages. This demonstrates the robustness of our framework. And this phenomenon may due

Table 4. ROUGE-2 results of all languages

lang	B1	B2	B3	S1	S2	S3	CF	GM	T1	T2	T3	T4
ar	5.982	4.916	8.958	**5.395**	3.98	4.61	3.03	2.999	4.523	4.008	3.887	3.706
az	4.79	3.928	11.216	**5.143**	4.422	4.143	2.636	1.64	4.249	3.886	4.151	3.875
bg	6.224	4.365	12.712	**6.009**	4.918	5.677	3.154	3.296	5.205	5.637	4.601	4.46
bs	4.407	3.485	9.053	**3.943**	3.03	3.403	2.74	3.617	3.192	3.815	2.881	3.446
cs	5.877	4.019	11.811	**5.442**	4.354	4.823	3.064	4.665	4.39	4.723	4.137	4.203
en	13.318	10.931	20.623	**13.985**	11.891	12.794	7.751	13.437	11.93	12.438	10.453	10.293
eo	8.331	6.916	12.682	**7.81**	6.934	7.554	4.868	3.17	6.729	6.973	5.662	5.823
fi	8.642	2.241	10.397	**5.148**	3.529	4.032	3.421	0	3.932	3.826	3.75	3.575
hr	4.475	3.196	8.704	**4.691**	3.006	3.05	3.1	2.973	3.123	3.714	3.47	3.126
id	9.206	6.437	14.354	**8.586**	7.682	7.969	5.153	7.973	8.362	7.599	7.082	6.821
jv	6.962	6.287	9.447	**8.309**	5.068	5.957	4.74	5.17	5.495	5.682	4.478	5.23
ko	2.792	2.387	6.763	2.385	**2.719**	2.144	1.805	1.602	1.838	1.954	2.013	2.079
li	4.365	3.405	6.103	**4.713**	3.286	3.059	3.357	3.831	4.596	4.504	3.744	3.344
lv	6.03	3.964	10.426	**4.594**	3.413	4.515	1.669	3.715	3.579	4.164	3.661	3.287
mr	18.84	17.787	27.584	**19.521**	17.24	16.986	10.654	18.411	19.427	18.469	16.725	16.547
ms	8.308	6.003	10.581	**7.033**	5.863	6.404	5.089	3.23	6.577	5.905	5.248	4.57
pl	6.302	4.03	11.981	**6.104**	4.462	5.673	4.02	3.934	4.685	4.63	4.641	4.233
pt	11.237	7.708	16.939	**10.453**	8.304	9.651	4.685	7.92	9.974	10.07	7.979	7.642
ro	8.751	6.113	15.281	**8.482**	7.955	7.496	4.092	7.541	7.794	7.961	6.936	7.096
sk	3.244	2.609	6.968	2.77	**2.844**	2.262	2.118	2.325	2.687	2.083	2.598	1.947
tr	6.928	6.072	12.409	**7.085**	6.765	6.316	4.27	6.108	5.419	4.797	5.834	5.429
tt	2.614	2.614	5.335	**2.787**	2.002	2.481	1.539	2.705	1.92	2.095	2.105	2.205
uk	3.462	1.855	6.782	**2.907**	1.829	1.644	1.14	1.253	2.041	1.649	1.456	1.769
zh	18.292	16.821	20.289	14.632	14.713	**15.128**	9.709	11.817	16.307	17.654	16.245	16.03

to the fact that in the generation of a good summarization, the latent central idea based sentence quality measurement and summary diversity property can partly replace the role played by training data.

5.2 MultiLingual Multi-document Summarization

The MultiLing hold annual workshops and adjoining competitions to encourage research in Multilingual Document Summarization. We present the results on the testing dataset of MultiLing-2015 MMS task (MMS-2015). MMS-2015 data is made up of from 10 to 15 sets of 10 news articles for each of 10 languages.

We report our results using the n-gram matching metric ROUGE following the setting of [11], shown in Table 5. *UIDS* is compared to several systems that participated in the MMS task. There are 7 systems in MultiLing2015 MMS task involving a human summarization. Despite using only HTM described in Sect. 4.2, *UIDS* performs best in Chinese, Czech and Hebrew. However, in Arabic, Greek, Hindi, the performance of our system is bad. Especially for Hindi, our results are far less than others. We need more experiments later to explore the reasons for this situation. But on the whole, our system is still competitive.

Table 5. ROUGE-2 results of MMS-2015 task, where - represents that the system does not participate the language

lang	ours	cist	esi	giau	human	mms3	occams	wbu
Arabic	0.10028	0.13729	0.18379	0.19055	0.49773	0.19645	0.21181	0.23783
Chinese	**0.20145**	0.04935	0.13445	-	0.55843	0.20097	0.06799	0.15947
Czech	**0.20914**	0.12686	0.14192	0.19723	0.46779	0.17239	0.18494	0.20409
English	0.12240	0.10529	0.16764	0.14924	0.46165	0.16849	0.17961	0.19215
French	0.19343	0.12148	0.19442	0.17381	0.4919	0.21797	0.20702	0.2484
Greek	0.12375	0.1206	0.12624	0.1755	0.44346	0.14829	0.15989	0.16623
Hebrew	**0.09428**	0.04968	0.09124	0.09653	0.37887	0.08192	0.07677	0.09337
Hindi	0.11192	0.24051	0.18841	0.25874	0.62603	0.27152	0.25877	0.28622
Romanian	0.12281	0.09476	0.1271	-	0.69859	0.14403	0.16013	0.18904
Spanish	0.23137	0.13581	0.22059	-	0.52141	0.24963	0.2444	0.28102

6 Conclusion and Future Work

In this paper, we have systematically explored an amenable language independent sampling framework to automatically calculate diverse summaries for multilingual corpus. We formalize MDS using summary diversity property, which includes topic diversity and redundancy. We have also detailed a basic implementation of MMS and MSS system that outperformed some of the most advanced methods described in the literature.

In the present description of *UIDS*, we use five classical features including HTM, SP, SL, SC, TS to calculate topic diversity and Jaccard similarity to model redundancy. This might not be feasible for a large-scale summary creation method. For this, we will pay more attention to DPPs. Then we will extend our system to social data summarization and so on.

Acknowledgements. This work was supported by the National Social Science Foundation of China under Grant 16ZDA055; National Natural Science Foundation of China under Grant 91546121, 71231002 and 61202247; EU FP7 IRSES MobileCloud Project 612212; the 111 Project of China under Grant B08004; Engineering Research Center of Information Networks, Ministry of Education; the project of Beijing Institute of Science and Technology Information; the project of CapInfo Company Limited.

References

1. Alex, K., Ben, T.: Determinantal point processes for machine learning. arXiv preprint arXiv:1207.6083 (2012)
2. Balikas, G., Amini, M.R.: The participation of UJF-grenoble team at multiling 2015 (2015)
3. Blei, D.M., Griffiths, T.L., Jordan, M.I.: The nested chinese restaurant process and bayesian nonparametric inference of topic hierarchies. J. ACM (JACM) **57**(2), 7 (2010)

4. Blei, D.M., Ng, A.Y., Jordan, M.I.: Latent dirichlet allocation. J. Mach. Learn. Res. **3**, 993–1022 (2003)
5. Borodin, A.: Determinantal point processes (2009)
6. Celikyilmaz, A., Hakkani-Tur, D.: A hybrid hierarchical model for multi-document summarization. In: Proceedings of the 48th Annual Meeting of the Association for Computational Linguistics, pp. 815–824. Association for Computational Linguistics (2010)
7. Conroy, J.M., Davis, S.T., Kubina, J.: Preprocessing and term weights in multilingual summarization (2015)
8. Davis, S.T., Conroy, J.M., Schlesinger, J.D.: OCCAMS-an optimal combinatorial covering algorithm for multi-document summarization. In: 2012 IEEE 12th International Conference on Data Mining Workshops (ICDMW), pp. 454–463. IEEE (2012)
9. Gambhir, M., Gupta, V.: Recent automatic text summarization techniques: a survey. Artif. Intell. Rev. **47**(1), 1–66 (2017)
10. Giannakopoulos, G., Conroy, J., Kubina, J., Rankel, P.A.: Multiling 2017 overview (2017)
11. Giannakopoulos, G., Kubina, J., Conroy, J.M., Steinberger, J., Favre, B., Kabadjov, M.A., Kruschwitz, U., Poesio, M.: Multiling 2015: multilingual summarization of single and multi-documents, on-line Fora, and call-center conversations. In: SIGDIAL Conference, pp. 270–274 (2015)
12. Giannakopoulos, G., Lloret, E., Conroy, M.J., Steinberger, J., Litvak, M., Rankel, P., Favre, B.: Proceedings of the MultiLing 2017 Workshop on Summarization and Summary Evaluation Across Source Types and Genres. Association for Computational Linguistics (2017). http://aclweb.org/anthology/W17-1000
13. Huang, T., Li, L., Zhang, Y.: Multilingual multi-document summarization based on multiple feature combination (2016)
14. Hung, H.T., Shih, K.W., Chen, B.: The NTNU summarization system at MultiLing 2015 (2015)
15. Kam-Fai, W., Mingli, W., Wenjie, L.: Extractive summarization using supervised and semi-supervised learning. In: Proceedings of the 22nd International Conference on Computational Linguistics, vol. 1, pp. 985–992. Association for Computational Linguistics (2008)
16. Matérn, B.: Stochastic previous models and their application to some problems in forest surveys and other sampling investigations. Medd. Statens Skogsforskningsinstitut **49**, 5 (1960)
17. Mihalcea, R., Tarau, P.: TextRank: bringing order into texts. Proc. EMNLP **2004**, 404–411 (2004)
18. Ren, Z., de Rijke, M.: Summarizing contrastive themes via hierarchical nonparametric processes. In: Proceedings of the 38th International ACM SIGIR Conference on Research and Development in Information Retrieval, pp. 93–102. ACM (2015)
19. Technology, B.: Rosette base linguistics (2016). https://www.rosette.com/function/tokenization/
20. Thomas, S., Beutenmüller, C., de la Puente, X., Remus, R., Bordag, S.: EXB text summarizer. In: 16th Annual Meeting of the Special Interest Group on Discourse and Dialogue, p. 260 (2015)
21. Vicente, M., Alcón, O., Lloret, E.: The university of alicante at multiling 2015: approach, results and further insights. In: 16th Annual Meeting of the Special Interest Group on Discourse and Dialogue, p. 250 (2015)

Conceptual Multi-layer Neural Network Model for Headline Generation

Yidi Guo[1,3](✉), Heyan Huang[1,2], Yang Gao[1,2], and Chi Lu[1,3]

[1] Beijing Institute of Technology, Beijing, China
{gyd409274478,hhy63,gyang,luchi}@bit.edu.cn

[2] Beijing Engineering Research Center of High Volume Language Information Processing and Cloud Computing Applications, Beijing, China

[3] Beijing Advanced Innovation Center for Imaging Technology, Capital Normal University, Beijing 100048, People's Republic of China

Abstract. Neural attention-based models have been widely used recently in headline generation by mapping source document to target headline. However, the traditional neural headline generation models utilize the first sentence of the document as the training input while ignoring the impact of the document concept information on headline generation. In this work, A new neural attention-based model called concept sensitive neural headline model is proposed, which connects the concept information of the document to input text for headline generation and achieves satisfactory results. Besides, we use a multi-layer Bi-LSTM in encoder instead of single layer. Experiments have shown that our model outperforms state-of-the-art systems on DUC-2004 and Gigaword test sets.

Keywords: Attention-based · Concept · Multi-layer Bi-LSTM

1 Introduction

Text summarization is the task of generating a short summary or headline that captures the subject content of a document. It is expected to understand the core meaning of the documents and then produce a coherent, informative but brief summarization of the source document. And We name the summarization task as headline generation [1] when the generated summary required to be a single sentence.

The main approaches of text summarization can be divided into two categories: extractive and generative. Most extractive summarization systems extract parts of the document (words or sentences) that are deemed interesting by some metric and joint them to form a summary. Despite of its simplicity, the summary always is awkward or grammatically strange. In contrast, generative summarization is to simply summarize as humans do. It aims at comprehending a document and generating a coherent and concise summary, which using some vocabulary unseen in the source document.

M. Sun et al. (Eds.): CCL 2017 and NLP-NABD 2017, LNAI 10565, pp. 355–367, 2017.
https://doi.org/10.1007/978-3-319-69005-6_30

Recently, sequence-to-sequence (seq2seq) model [2,3], which maps a sequential input into another sequential output, has been successfully applied on various natural language processing tasks. Especially, the seq2seq model with attention mechanism [4] has achieved overwhelming successes in machine translation (MT) and speech recognition. Since the superiority of the seq2seq model in sequential language generation that breaks the traditional gaps NLP area, it has also been successfully applied in text summarization [5,8,18] and creatively used in headline generation [14,17].

Despite of the identical objective of language generation for MT and our targeted headline generation task, there are still some differences. MT is a process of language generation, which has a strong one-to-one word-level alignment between input (source) and output (translation), and the length of output is typically close to the length of the input. But the output (headline) of headline generation is typically very short and does not depend on the length of the input. Headline generation is a process of information compression, which uses a lossy manner to compress the source document and preserve the key information. Therefore, The quality of information compression will directly affect the results of the final headline generation. Additionally, compare to the MT, headline generation is more subjective to what people are interested in. As such, a suitable headline should always adjust to some specific concepts. Specifically, the different concepts of news tend to use different words, fields and styles, which inspired us to use the concept information to play a guiding role in headline generation.

To integrate the concept of news for headline generation, in this paper, we propose a novel neural network framework that completes information compression and coherent language generation, specific to the concept sensitive headline generation. In this new model, called concept sensitive neural headline generation model (CNHG), a multi-layer Bi-LSTM encoder is extended by seamlessly adding document-based conceptual information construction model, which can guide the generation model in a manner of latent concept way. More specifically, in the encoding process, the key features was extracted from each document by TextRank algorithm, and then correspondingly maps to several regularized concepts by using probabilistic-based Probase knowledge database. In this way, the document-based concepts were extracted and embedded into the source information encoders. Empirical experiment results show that our model beats the state-of-the-art baseline on multiple English data sets.

The main contributions of this paper include: (i) The core of information compression and coherent language generation for headline generation is validated and accomplished in terms of using multi-layer of Bi-LSTM encoder of seq2seq attention model. (ii) The conceptual information is creatively incorporated into the encoder of the neural headline generation model as a latent guidance for generating more focused and desired headlines. (iii) We conducted extensive experiments to compare the effectiveness of our proposed CNHG model with other state-of-the-art models in benchmark datasets of DUC2004 and Gigaword.

2 Related Work

The task of headline generation was standardized around the DUC-2003 and DUC-2004 competitions [10]. Most of the work is focused on the extractive summarization before the development of the neural network, there has been little research on the generative summarization. The TOPIARY system [11] combines both linguistic and statistical information, which performed best in DUC-2004 Task-1. Later, syntactic and semantic features were used in headline generation [12,13]. And MOSES, a widely-used phrase-based machine translation system [16], was directly used as a method to generate headline which named MOSES+ by [5].

Recently, the seq2seq neural model has been applied successfully to various natural language processing tasks. For Headline generation task, Neural Headline Generation (NHG) model has been used widely. Rush et al. [5] proposed the method which combines a feed-forward neural language model with an attention-based encoder have shown significant performance. Chopra et al. [8] extended the model by [5] with a recurrent neural network and the attention mechanism to improve the performance. Method [14] incorporated the structural syntactic and semantic information in a baseline neural attention-based model to generate headline. Based on NHG model, more tricks or methods were added to improve the performance. Model [18] paid attention to vocabulary size and implemented a trick that constructs the vocabulary of documents in each mini-batch respectively. Besides, Gulcehre et al. [15] proposed a method to deal with the rare and unseen words in natural language generation.

However, to our knowledge, not any research has devoted to discover the effect of concept in NHG model. Therefore, in this work, we propose the CNHG model, implemented by a bidirectional recurrent neural network with a multi-layer Bi-LSTM encoder and also encoded by the concept information from source documents. The concept information plays an important role in training and guides the model learn the desired content and concise expression in saliency.

3 Model

Neural Headline Generation aims at generating a brief sentence from the source document. The framework of our proposed CNHG model is a multi-layer Bi-LSTM encoder and a mono-layer of LSTM decoder. Based on the model, conceptual embedding vectors are fed into the encoder to guide the headline generation process.

3.1 Multi-layer Encoder NHG

Compared to the traditional NHG model, we used a multi-layer Bi-LSTM encoder which means the output of previous encoder layer is the input of next encoder layer. The model we named 4-NHG includes a 4 layer Bi-LSTM encoder and a mono-layer LSTM decoder with the attention mechanism. Figure 1 shows the framework of the multi-layer Bi-LSTM encoder model.

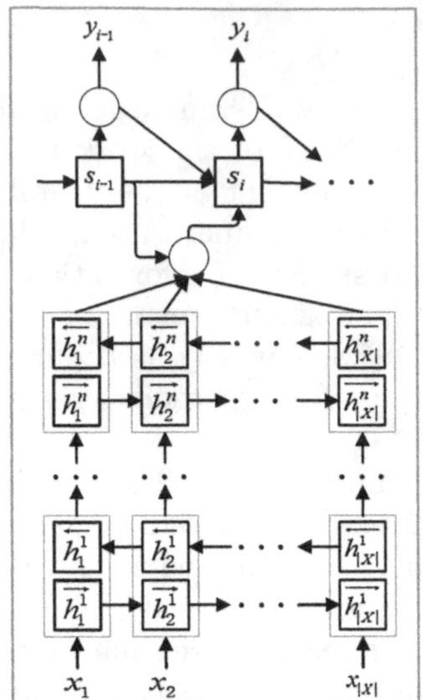

Fig. 1. The framework of the multi-layer Bi-LSTM encoder model

Long Short-Term Memory Networks. Long Short Term Memory (LSTM) was first proposed in [6] to address the issue that standard recurrent neural networks (RNNs) are unable to learn the long-term dependencies. LSTM is a special kind of recurrent neural networks, which are explicitly designed to avoid the long-term dependency problem.

The architecture of LSTM is controlled by a set of gates when it processes an input sequence $\mathbf{x} = \{x_1, x_2, \ldots, x_{|\mathbf{x}|}\}$ and generates a sequence of output states $\mathbf{h} = \{h_1, h_2, \ldots, h_{|\mathbf{x}|}\}$. The input gate i_t to control which part of new information would be used in current memory cell, the forget gate f_t to control what information would be throw away from the old memory cell, and the output gate o_t to control which part of the cell state would be output based on the memory cell. All those gates are combined to decide how to update the current memory cell c_t and the current hidden state h_t. At each time step, LSTM takes the input text x_t, previous hidden state h_{t-1}, previous cell c_{t-1} as input and generates c_t, h_t based on the following formulas:

$$\begin{aligned}
f_t &= \sigma(\mathbf{W}_f \cdot [h_{t-1}, x_t] + b_f) \\
i_t &= \sigma(\mathbf{W}_i \cdot [h_{t-1}, x_t] + b_i) \\
\widetilde{c}_t &= tanh(\mathbf{W}_c \cdot [h_{t-1}, x_t] + b_c) \\
o_t &= \sigma(\mathbf{W}_o \cdot [h_{t-1}, x_t] + b_o) \\
c_t &= f_t \odot c_{t-1} + i_t \odot \widetilde{c}_t \\
h_t &= o_t \odot tanh(c_t)
\end{aligned} \tag{1}$$

Here, σ and $tanh$ are activate functions which refer to the logistic sigmoid function and the hyperbolic tangent function. The symbols $\odot$ is an operation which denotes the element-wise multiplication.

Encoder-Decoder. The multi-layer Bi-LSTM encoder model encodes input text $\mathbf{x}$ into a sequence of hidden states $\{h_1, \ldots, h_{|\mathbf{x}|}\}$, and uses the attention mechanism to get the context vector c_i for decoder time step i based on $\{h_1, \ldots, h_{|\mathbf{x}|}\}$. The model generates the headline $\mathbf{y}$ by a decoder is based on the context vector c_i. Following a Markov process, the probability over the headline $\mathbf{y}$ is modeled by a product of individual conditional probabilities with parameters θ:

$$P(\mathbf{y}|\mathbf{x}, \theta) = \prod_{t=1}^{|\mathbf{y}|} p(y_t|\{y_1, \ldots, y_{t-1}\}, \mathbf{x}, \theta) \tag{2}$$

Decoder. The decoder is a mono-layer LSTM which is trained to predict the next output word y_i given the context vector c_i and decoder hidden state s_i for time step i. The above conditional probability is defined as

$$p(y_i|\{y_1, \ldots, y_{i-1}\}, \mathbf{x}, \theta) = g(s_i, c_i) \tag{3}$$

where s_i is computed by

$$s_i = g(s_{i-1}, y_{i-1}, c_i) \tag{4}$$

The context vector c_i depends on the output of the encoder module $\{h_1, h_2, \ldots, h_{|\mathbf{x}|}\}$. We computed the context vector c_i as

$$\begin{aligned} u_t^i &= f(s_{i-1}, h_t) \\ a_t^i &= softmax(u_t^i) \\ c_i &= \prod_{t=1}^{|\mathbf{x}|} a_t^i h_t \end{aligned} \tag{5}$$

Encoder. The encoder is a multi-layer bidirectional LSTM. With input text $\mathbf{x} = \{x_1, x_2, \ldots, x_{|\mathbf{x}|}\}$, the multi-layer forward LSTM calculates a sequence of *forward hidden states* $\mathbf{h}^{(f)} = (h_1^{(f)}, \ldots, h_{|\mathbf{x}|}^{(f)})$ while the multi-layer backward LSTM calculates a sequence of *backward hidden states* $\mathbf{h}^{(b)} = (h_1^{(b)}, \ldots, h_{|\mathbf{x}|}^{(b)})$. Then $\mathbf{h}^{(f)}$ and $\mathbf{h}^{(b)}$ are concatenated to get $\mathbf{h}$ as

$$\begin{aligned} h_t &= h_t^{(f)} \oplus h_t^{(b)} \\ \mathbf{h} &= \{h_1, h_2, \ldots, h_{|\mathbf{x}|}\} \end{aligned} \tag{6}$$

3.2 Concept Sensitive NHG

Each input text has a thematic concept information, we want to use this thematic concept information to provide a guiding role in the training process. Therefore, we combined the concept information with the above multi-layer encoder model to get a new model, namely Concept Sensitive NHG model. It includes two steps: obtaining concept information and training a concept sensitive model. The probability is defined as

$$P(\mathbf{y}|\mathbf{x}, \theta, \theta_c) = \prod_{t=1}^{|\mathbf{y}|} p(y_t|\{y_1, \ldots, y_{t-1}\}, \mathbf{x}, \theta, \theta_c) \quad (7)$$

where θ_c is the concept information of the input text $\mathbf{x}$, and the θ_c can be formed by the following concept generation process.

Concept Generation. Concept generation from a document can be conducted as two steps, which are keyword extraction and word-to-concept mapping. In this paper, TexRank is used to extract a list of keywords, and probabilistic-based Probase knowledge database[1] is used to map keywords to key concepts.

TextRank algorithm is a graph-based sorting algorithm for text. The basic idea of TextRank comes from Google's PageRank algorithm, which divides the text into several units (words and sentences) to establish the graph model and uses the voting mechanism to sort the important components in the text. TextRank algorithm only uses the information of a single document itself to implement keyword extraction, which greatly reduces the extraction time. We first construct a directed weighted graph $G = (V, E)$ for the input document and

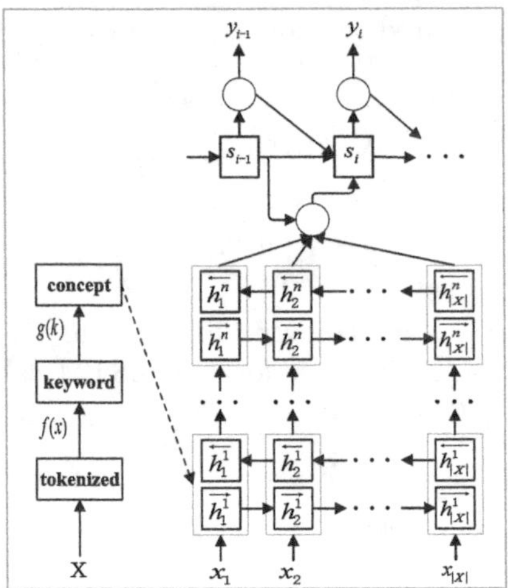

Fig. 2. The framework of concept sensitive NHG model with a multi-layer Bi-LSTM encoder

[1] It can be downloaded from https://concept.msra.cn.

then the set of keywords U is computed as

$$\begin{aligned} WS(V_i) &= (1-d) + d * \sum_{V_j \in In(V_i)} \frac{w_{ji}}{\sum_{V_k \in Out(V_j)} w_{jk}} WS(V_j) \\ U &= Top_n(WS(V_1), \ldots, WS(V_{|V|})) \end{aligned} \tag{8}$$

Here, d is the damping factor, $In(V_i)$ is a set of points pointing to V_i, $Out(V_i)$ is a set of points that V_i points to and $WS(V_i)$ is the score of V_i. The symbols Top_n is a function to obtain the highest score of n keywords, in there, we set up n as 5.

After obtaining the set of keywords, we use Probase to gain the concept information. The core version of IsA data in Probase was mined from billions of web pages, and this data contains more than 5.4 million unique concepts, 12.3 million unique instances. We took the 1,000 most frequently occurring concepts as a regularized set of concepts.

Probase calculates the concept based on the concept distribution of $p(c|w)$, which is a word-to-concept mapping. The concept information θ_c is computed follows the Eq. 9 and then we let $\theta_c \in \mathbb{R}^k$ be the k-dimensional word vector for encoding.

$$\begin{aligned} S(C_j) &= \sum_{w \in U} p(C_j|w) \\ \theta_c &= \max_{C_j}(S(C_j)), C_j \in C \end{aligned} \tag{9}$$

Here, C is the set of concepts.

Concept Sensitive Model. Figure 2 shows the framework of Concept Sensitive NHG model with a multi-layer Bi-LSTM encoder. The function $f(x)$ represents the keyword extraction from the input text and the function $g(k)$ represents the acquisition of concept information. In our model, the concept information of the input text is entered into the encoder along with source text, which will affect weight matrices in encoder. After encoder step, we obtain the output of hidden states $\mathbf{h}$ which contains the concept information. And we used $\mathbf{h}$ with attention mechanism in decoder to generate headline.

4 Experiments

The hypothesis of our model are: (1) The multi-layer encoder is more effective for information compression and language generation. (2) Concept information helps to generate better headlines and improve the results of multi-layer Bi-LSTM encoder model. We experimented the proposed CNHG model on the task of headline generation to verify our hypotheses.

4.1 Datasets and Evaluation Metrics

To demonstrate the effectiveness of our method, we used the English Gigaword Fifth Edition [7] corpus, which contains 9.5 million news articles with corresponding headlines[2] from various news services. We processed the data in the same way as [5], as a consequence, about 4 million examples are selected as our training set[3].

We evaluated our models on the DUC-2004 dataset[4]. It consists of 500 article-headline pairs, and each paired with 4 human-generated reference headlines. In addition, we also used Gigaword test data[5] used in [5] as our test set.

In this series of experiments, we utilized several versions of ROUGE [9] to evaluate the performance of headline generation. Similar to [5,8,18], for DUC-2004 test set, we reported 75 bytes capped (use the limited length with 75 bytes) recall scores of ROUGE-1, ROUGE-2 and ROUGE-L to evaluate our systems. And similar to [8,18], for Gigaword test set, we used full-length F1 scores of ROUGE-1, ROUGE-2 and ROUGE-L to evaluate our systems. In previous work, limited length recall was widely used, but that make it difficult for researchers to compare their results because of the choice of length limit varies with the corpus. The average length of headline in Gigaword test set is 8.3 words, that is significantly shorter than the summary in DUC-2004, and a shorter summary tends to get lower recall score. On the contrary, Full-length F1 makes evaluation unbiased to summary length and can penalize a longer summary. Thus, when testing on Gigaword test set, we report the full-length F1 scores.

4.2 Implementation Details

For all the models we discuss below, the word embeddings are randomly initialized with 128 dimension and then updated during training. We used stochastic gradient descent with mini-batches of 64 to minimize our loss and randomly shuffled the training data at every epoch. Besides, we set the vocabulary size to $150,000$ and the hidden unit size to 256. Since the vocabulary size is too large, we used sampled softmax method with the value of 4096 to speed up the training. We did not utilize any dropout or regularization, but gradient clipping used. For all our models, we initialized the learning rate to 0.15, and decayed the learning rate every $30,000$ batches with the decay rate to 0.95.

We trained all our models on a single GeForce GTX TITAN GPU. For 4-NHG it takes about 20 h for an epoch. For CNHG it takes about 24 h. At decoder time, we used beam search of size 8 to generate the headline, using a batch size of 1.

[2] We paired the first sentence of each article with its headline to form sentence-headline pairs. And Then we used the PTB tokenization to preprocess the pairs with tokenziation.

[3] The splits of Gigaword for training can be found at https://github.com/facebook/NAMAS.

[4] It can be downloaded from http://duc.nist.gov/ with permission.

[5] It can be obtained from https://github.com/harvardnlp/sent-summary.

5 Results and Analyses

Figure 3 shows the training loss of iterations, 1-NHG represents a mono-layer Bi-LSTM encoder model. At the beginning of training, the convergence speed of three models is similar, but gradually the CNHG model converges faster than the 4-NHG model and 1-NHG. When the number of iterations reaches about $200K$, the convergence speed of three models becomes slow and eventually tends to be stable. From the final training loss values, it can be seen that the CNHG model converges best and 4-NHG obtains better training effects than 1-NHG.

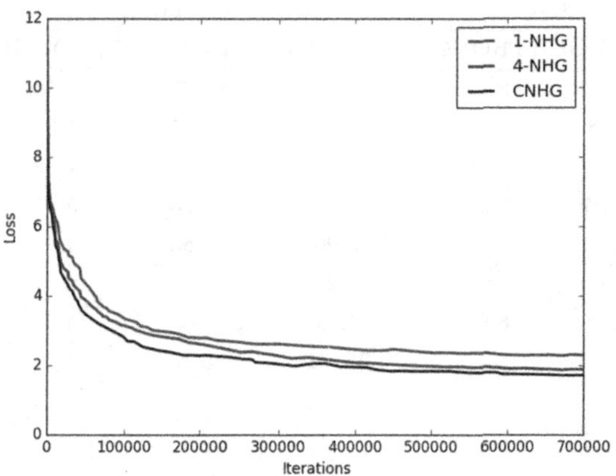

Fig. 3. Loss vs. iteration

Table 1 shows the results of 1-NHG and 4-NHG models on Gigaword English test set. AS we can see 4-NHG model outperforms 1-NHG model on Gigaword test set and achieves significant improvements. Combined with Fig. 3, we found that the multi-layer encoder is more effective for information compression and language generation than mono-layer encoder, which supports the hypothesis 1.

Table 1. Results of 1-NHG and 4-NHG models on Gigaword English test set.

Model	Gigaword		
	ROUGE-1	ROUGE-2	ROUGE-L
1-NHG	33.59	13.84	31.13
4-NHG	**35.03**	**14.97**	**32.87**

The evaluation results on Gigaword and DUC-2004 test sets are presented in Table 2. The baseline MOSES+ generates headline based on MOSES [16], which is a phrase-based machine translation system. ABS and ABS+ are an attention-based neural headline generation system of [5], and ABS+ is an enhanced version of ABS. First note that the baseline ABS+ performs better than ABS and

MOSES+ on both test sets except for the F1-score of ROUGE-2 in Gigaword. Both RAS-Elman and RAS-LSTM [8] which utilize a convolutional encoder and an attention-based decoder achieve statistically significant improvements from ABS+ for all three variants of ROUGE on Gigaword. The state-of-the-art baseline BWL [18], namely words-lvt5k-lsent, outperforms other baselines on both test sets.

Table 2. Results of our 4-NHG and CNHG models against other baselines on DUC-2004 and Gigaword English test sets.

Model	DUC-2004			Gigaword		
	ROUGE-1	ROUGE-2	ROUGE-L	ROUGE-1	ROUGE-2	ROUGE-L
MOSES+	26.50	8.13	22.85	28.77	12.10	26.44
ABS	26.55	7.06	22.05	29.55	11.32	26.42
ABS+	28.18	8.49	23.81	29.76	11.88	26.96
RAS-Elman	**28.97**	8.26	24.06	33.78	15.97	31.15
RAS-LSTM	27.41	7.69	23.06	32.55	14.70	30.03
BWL	28.61	9.42	25.24	35.30	**16.64**	32.62
4-NHG	27.31	8.68	24.74	35.03	14.97	32.87
CNHG	28.10	**9.56**	**25.71**	**35.51**	15.54	**33.38**

The results of our models is exciting and inspiring. For Gigaword corpus, we reported the F1-score of ROUGE-1, ROUGE-2, and ROUGE-L. AS we can see, our CNHG model outperforms 4-NHG model on all variants of ROUGE and improves the ROUGE scores up 0.5 points compared with 4-NHG model. Besides, our CNHG model outperforms the start-of-the-art baseline BWL on two of three variants of ROUGE on Gigaword test set, while being competitive on ROUGE-2. For DUC-2004 corpus, we computed the recall score of ROUGE-1, ROUGE-2, and ROUGE-L. The results show that our CNHG model improves the ROUGE scores up 1 points compared with 4-NHG model and outperforms BWL on ROUGE-2, ROUGE-L. In general, our CNHG model significantly and consistently improves the performance of 4-NHG, and outperforms the state-of-art system on both test sets, which also support our hypothesis 2.

Figure 4 shows a soft alignment between the input text and the generated headline. From this we see which words in input text were considered more important when generating the target word. For example, the word “fms” in headline depends on the phrase “foreign ministers” in input text.

Finally, in Table 3 we present several anecdotal examples of headlines by our models on Gigaword test set for discussion. We can observe that our CNHG model is capable of capturing the semantically important words of the input. For instance in Article 1, CNHG can successful use “human rights” to summarize “arbitrary arrests, torture, prisoners dying” while 4-NHG only use “torture”, and in Article 2 it generates headline with important information “religious unrest”. Compared to the true headline, CNHG can use some of words that

Table 3. Examples of original articles, reference headlines and generated headlines by our models on Gigaword test set.

Article(1):	arbitrary arrests, torture, prisoners dying in detention and the death penalty are current practices in guinea, human rights organization amnesty international said thursday in a report published here
Reference:	amnesty deplores human rights violations in guinea
4-NHG:	amnesty international condemns torture in guinea
CNHG:	amnesty slams human rights abuses in guinea
Article(2):	burma has put five cities on a security alert after religious unrest involving buddhists and moslems in the northern city of mandalay, an informed source said wednesday
Reference:	burma puts five cities on security alert after religious unrest
4-NHG:	burma puts five cities on security alert
CNHG:	burma puts five cities on alert after religious unrest
Article(3):	secretary of state warren christopher widened consultations on an israeli-lebanese ceasefire wednesday by including egypt and saudi arabia in the effort, an official said
Reference:	christopher widens consultations over israel-lebanon crisis
4-NHG:	christopher widens mideast talks with saudi arabia
CNHG:	christopher widens consultations on israel-lebanon ceasefire
Article(4):	the leader of germany 's jews, ignatz bubis, urged the government on friday to at least symbolically back an industry initiative to establish a fund for nazi slave laborers
Reference:	jewish leader calls on government to establish fund for nazi slave
4-NHG:	jewish leader urges government to fund nazi slave fund
CNHG:	jewish leader urges government to open fund for slave laborers
Article(5):	up to ## afghans have been killed and hundreds injured by a massive explosion at an ammunition depot in the eastern provincial capital jalalabad, kabul red cross officials said thursday
Reference:	up to ## killed in afghan blast accident suspected by terence white
4-NHG:	explosion at ammunition depot kills up to ## afghans
CNHG:	at least ## dead and hundreds injured in afghan blast
Article(6):	the eighth asia-pacific traditional arts festival opened saturday at the center for traditional arts in eastern yilan county saturday, featuring folk music, dance and theater groups from the mekong river region of indochina
Reference:	traditional arts center in yilan presents mekong art
4-NHG:	#th asia-pacific arts festival opens in eastern china
CNHG:	#th asia-pacific traditional arts festival opens

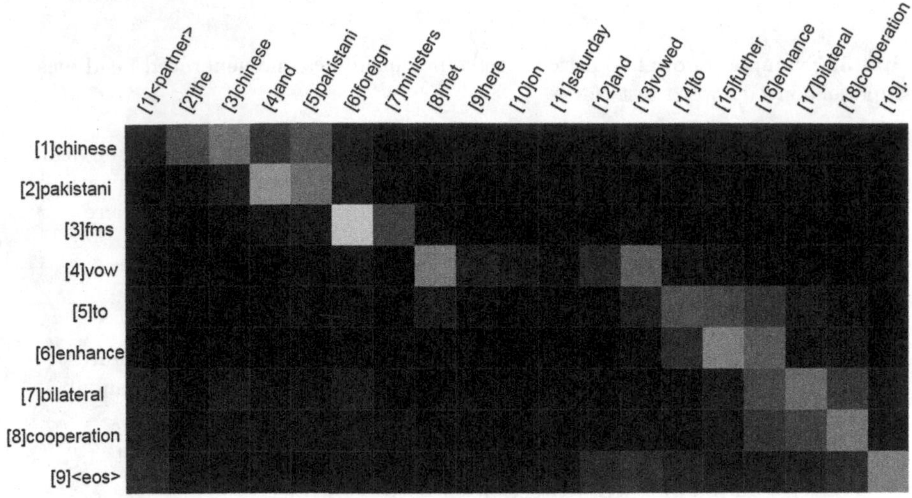

Fig. 4. A sample alignment generated by CNHG. The x-axis and y-axis of each plot correspond to the words in the input and the generated headline, respectively. The rows represent the distribution over the input for each generated word.

are different from reference to form a headline without changing the original meaning. For Article 3, CNHG uses word "ceasefire" while reference uses "crisis", and in Article 4 it uses word "open" not "establish". Despite our models capture a coherent and meaningful headline but differs from the true headline, however, the score of ROUGH is low. As shown in Article 5, two models capture the main information to generate headlines but the score of ROUGE is not high. On the other hand, our models sometimes pay attention to the wrong area in the article and generate an inferior headline as shown in Article 6.

6 Conclusion

In this paper, we proposed a concept sensitive NHG model for headline generation. In the model, we used a multi-layer Bi-LSTM encoder with attention mechanism to automatically generate coherent headlines. To enable the generated headlines fulfill the core concept from a document, the proposed model fed the extracted concepts into the encoder, which can be treated as a guidance to generate focused and salient headlines. The experimental results of headline generation on both Gigaword and DUC-2004 dataset show that our CNHG model outperforms the start-of-the-art models.

Acknowledgments. The work was supported by National Basic Research Program of China (973 Program, Grant No. 2013CB329303), National Nature Science Foundation of China (Grant No. 61602036), Beijing Advanced Innovation Center for Imaging Technology (BAICIT-2016007).

References

1. Dorr, B., Zajic, D., Schwartz, R.: Hedge trimmer: a parse-and-trim approach to headline generation. In: Proceedings of the HLT-NAACL 2003 on Text Summarization Workshop, vol. 5. Association for Computational Linguistics (2003)
2. Sutskever, I., Vinyals, O., Le, Q.V.: Sequence to sequence learning with neural networks. In: Advances in Neural Information Processing Systems (2014)
3. Cho, K., Merrienboer, B.V., Gulcehre, C., Bahdanau, D., Bougares, F., Schwenk, H., et al.: Learning phrase representations using RNN encoder-decoder for statistical machine translation. Computer Science (2014)
4. Bahdanau, D., Cho, K., Bengio, Y.: Neural machine translation by jointly learning to align and translate. Computer Science (2014)
5. Rush, A.M., Chopra, S., Weston, J.: A neural attention model for abstractive sentence summarization. Computer Science (2015)
6. Hochreiter, S., Schmidhuber, J.: Long short-term memory. Neural Comput. **9**(8), 1735 (1997)
7. Parker, R., Graff, D., Kong, J., Chen, K., Maeda, K.: English Gigaword, 5th edn. (2011)
8. Chopra, S., Auli, M., Rush, A.M.: Abstractive sentence summarization with attentive recurrent neural networks. In: Conference of the North American Chapter of the Association for Computational Linguistics: Human Language Technologies, pp. 93–98 (2016)
9. Flick, C.: ROUGE: a package for automatic evaluation of summaries. In: The Workshop on Text Summarization Branches Out, p. 10 (2004)
10. Over, P., Dang, H., Harman, D.: Duc in context. Inf. Process. Manag. **43**(6), 1506–1520 (2007)
11. Zajic, D., Dorr, B., Schwartz, R.: BBN/UMD at DUC-2004: Topiary. In: Document Understanding Conference at NLT/NAACL, pp. 112–119 (2004)
12. Cohn, T., Lapata, M.: Sentence compression beyond word deletion. In: Proceedings of the International Conference on Computational Linguistics, COLING 2008, Manchester, UK, vol. 163, pp. 137–144, 18–22 August 2008
13. Woodsend, K., Feng, Y., Lapata, M.: Title generation with quasi-synchronous grammar. In: Conference on Empirical Methods in Natural Language Processing, EMNLP 2010, Mit Stata Center, Massachusetts, USA, A Meeting of Sigdat, A Special Interest Group of the ACL, pp. 513–523, 9–11 October 2010
14. Takase, S., Suzuki, J., Okazaki, N., Hirao, T., Nagata, M.: Neural headline generation on abstract meaning representation. In: Conference on Empirical Methods in Natural Language Processing, pp. 1054–1059 (2016)
15. Gulcehre, C., Ahn, S., Nallapati, R., Zhou, B., Bengio, Y.: Pointing the unknown words. In: Meeting of the Association for Computational Linguistics, pp. 140–149 (2016)
16. Koehn, P., Hoang, H., Alexandra, B., Callison-Burch, C., et al.: Moses: open source toolkit for statistical machine translation. In: Proceedings of the Association for Computational Linguistics ACL 2007, vol. 9(1), pp. 177–180 (2007)
17. Ayana, S.S., Liu, Z., Sun, M.: Neural headline generation with minimum risk training (2016)
18. Nallapati, R., Zhou, B., Santos, C.N.D., Gulcehre, C., Xiang, B.: Abstractive text summarization using sequence-to-sequence RNNs and beyond (2016)

References

Social Computing and Sentiment Analysis

Local Community Detection Using Social Relations and Topic Features in Social Networks

Chengcheng Xu(✉), Huaping Zhang, Bingbing Lu, and Songze Wu

School of Computer Science, Beijing Institute of Technology, Beijing, China
{xuchengcheng2015, lubingbing2015, wusongze2015}@nlpir.org, kevinzhang@bit.edu.cn

Abstract. Local community detection is an important research focus in social network analysis. Most existing methods share the intrinsic limitation of utilizing undirected and unweighted networks. In this paper, we propose a novel local community detection algorithm that fuses social relations and topic features in social networks. By defining a new social similarity, the proposed algorithm can effectively reveal the dynamic characteristics in social networks. In addition, the topic similarity is measured by Jensen–Shannon divergence, in which the topics are extracted from the user-generated content by topic models. Extensive experiments conducted on a real social network dataset demonstrate that our proposed algorithm outperforms methods based on social relations or topic features alone.

Keywords: Social networks · Local community detection · Topic model

1 Introduction

Community detection has become an important research focus in the area of social network analysis, with the aim of exploring multiple subgraphs to closely connect nodes in the same subgraph and reduce the links between different subgraphs for applications, such as data mining, behavior analysis, and knowledge discovery [1, 2]. More specifically, global community detection, in which structural information about the entire network is required to divide it into a number of "internal" and "external" communities, has attracted substantial attention due to the promising empirical results that could be obtained. However, these approaches have some limitations: (1) from the perspective of network partitioning, it is difficult to obtain the needed structural information of the entire network for large and dynamic networks [3]; and (2) the computational complexity of a community detection algorithm is very high, even if the structure of a large-scale dynamic network can be obtained.

This work is sponsored by National Basic Research Program of China (973 Program, Grant No.: 2013CB32960601).

M. Sun et al. (Eds.): CCL 2017 and NLP-NABD 2017, LNAI 10565, pp. 371–383, 2017.
https://doi.org/10.1007/978-3-319-69005-6_31

Compared with global community detection methods, local community detection methods can effectively mine community structures without prior network information. These methods can usually be understood as exploring community structures from given seed nodes. Therefore, for large-scale dynamic social networks, local community detection methods have obvious advantages in terms of computational complexity and local characteristics. In practice, these local community detection methods are beneficial for public opinion monitoring, social network marketing, and personal friend recommendation.

However, most popular social networks are typical user-generated content (UGC) platforms, in which users often have both social relations and topic features. Social relations refer to the real interactions between users, including commenting, quoting (@), and retweeting. These are directed, weighted and dynamic link relationships. In addition, users in the same community often share common interests (i.e., topics), which can be extracted from UGC by topic models. Currently, the main research studies have explored the local community structure according to the undirected and unweighted relationships between different users. However, no mature algorithms to explore the local community structure by applying the above two features are available.

In this paper, we propose a new local community detection algorithm for social networks that is based on users' social relations and topic features. We define the social similarity between users and communities by utilizing their directed and weighted relationships. Then, the classical Jensen–Shannon divergence is used to calculate the topic similarity extracted from UGC with topic models. Finally, a novel algorithm based on the fusion of social relations and topic features is proposed for local community detection. We conduct extensive experiments on real social networks. The experimental results prove that our method performs effectively. In addition, comparative experiments involving different algorithm parameters also provide empirical guidance for practical applications.

The main contributions of this paper are as follows:

- This paper proposes a novel local community detection algorithm based on social relations and topic features in social networks.
- This paper defines the social similarity between the user and the community, taking advantage of directed and weighted information.
- The experimental results prove that our method performs effectively in a real social network dataset.

This paper is organized as follows. Section 2 reviews related works on local community detection and the topic model. Section 3 describes in detail the local community detection algorithm based on social relations and topic features. Section 4 presents the experimental results obtained from the real social network dataset. The entire paper is summarized in Sect. 5.

2 Related Work

The algorithm proposed in this paper is based on two user attributes in social networks: social relations and topic features. Thus, there are two lines of research related to our work, namely, local community detection and the topic model.

2.1 Local Community Detection Method

The purpose of local community detection is to explore the community network structure from a given seed node in a social network. In recent years, many researchers have proposed local methods for community detection. Some local community metrics have also been proposed, such as R [4], M [5], L [6] and LS [8]. Combining these methods can help us find correct community structures. However, the most serious drawback is that most algorithms are sensitive to the initial node, and as a result, a large number of outliers are introduced into the target community. Some papers attempt to set the initial node to the nearest core node for community detection [9, 10], but some limitations remain to be overcome. For example, when the core user belongs to several communities, substantial noise (i.e., nodes that do not belong to the target community) will appear. [11] proposed a local optimization method using random seed nodes (i.e.,

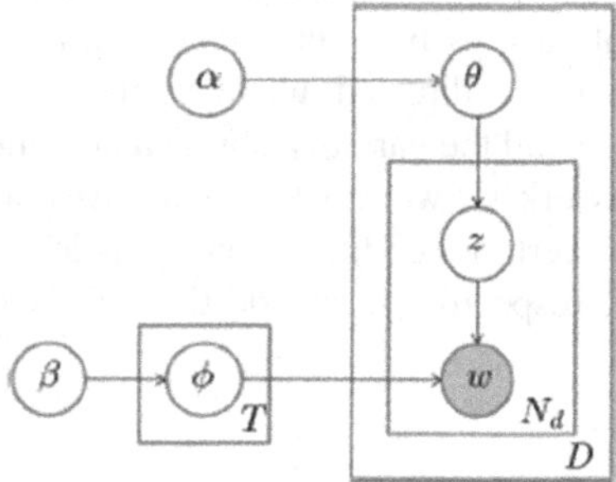

Fig. 1. Latent Dirichlet Allocation (LDA) Bayesian network

the Local Fitness Method [*LFM*] algorithm) to solve the problem that some methods cannot find the hierarchy and overlap community structures. [12–14] used edge clustering for local community detection.

The similarity of these methods is that they use social relationships alone as edges to aggregate nodes. The difference of our approach is that it combines both social relations and topic features for local community detection, making the experimental results more accurate and useful.

2.2 Topic Model

LDA, a three-layer Bayesian generative probability topic model, assumes that documents are composed of a series of potential topics [15]. The topic is the abstract of all the words in the vocabulary. The main difference between documents is that they have different topic distributions. *LDA* treats documents as word frequency vectors using the bag-of-words model, which converts the text information into a digital representation. The process of document generation by the *LDA* model is shown in Fig. 1.

$$p(\omega, z|\alpha, \beta) = p(\omega|\alpha, \beta)p(z|\alpha) = \int p(z|\theta)p(\theta|\alpha)d\theta \int p(\omega|z, \varphi)p(\varphi|\beta)d\varphi \quad (1)$$

Equation (1) is the joint probability distribution for all words and topics in a document. The random variable θ is the topic vector distribution of the documents, which plays an important role in the calculation of topic similarity in Sect. 3.2. When the correspondence between the user and the document is established, the topic similarity between users can be measured by Jensen–Shannon divergence. For dataset D, *LDA*'s topic extraction process is to maximize $p(D|\alpha, \beta)$ using *Gibbs Sampling*, *Variational Bayes* and *Expectation Propagation* [15–17].

3 Local Community Detection Using Social Relations and Topic Features

Let $G = (V, E)$ be the graphical representation of a directed social network, where $\leftarrow$ V corresponds to the node set representing the users, and E corresponds to the edge set representing the social relationships between users. Unlike the traditional social network structure, each edge in E is directed and weighted. We define the known local community of the graph as D and the partially observable neighbor set of nodes in D as B. To obtain the entire network G, we must visit the neighbor $b(b \in B)$ of the node $v(v \in D)$ constantly. When certain conditions are satisfied, we set b and b's neighboring nodes to D and B, respectively. In addition, D is usually divided into two

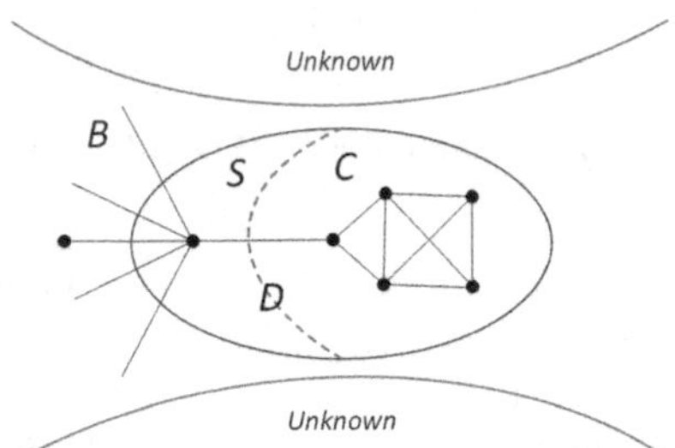

Fig. 2. Definition of the local community

subsets:

- The core node set C: any node $c \in C$ has no outward connections; that is to say, all the neighbors of c belong to D.
- The boundary set S: each node $s \in S$ has at least one neighbor in B.

The process of local community detection can now be formalized as follows. Given an initial node v, a node is added to D at each step to discover the target community. Figure 2 shows the sets of nodes D, B, C, and S in the social network.

Based on observations of the real social network, we find that social networks have two important features: information sharing and interest diversity. Information sharing means that users tend to share the same content topics in the same community. Interest diversity shows that users often focus on different topics and have social contacts with members in different communities. Traditional methods that always treat C as a target community are susceptible to outliers because of the above features. We propose a novel local community detection method setting D as the target community using both social relations and topic features.

The following parts of this section present specific interpretations of the proposed algorithm.

3.1 Social Similarity

Social similarity refers to the similarity between a user and a community based on social relations, such as commenting, quoting (@), and retweeting. The higher the social similarity, the higher the probability that the user belongs to the target community. We propose a method for measuring social similarity between user $v(v \in B)$ and community D:

$$\begin{aligned} SS_D(v) &= SW_D(v) * SP_D(v) \\ SW_D(v) &= \frac{1}{2|D|}\sum_{u \in D} \frac{T_{uv}}{K_u} + \frac{T_{vu}}{K_v} \\ SP_D(v) &= \frac{|\Gamma(v) \cap D|}{|D|} \end{aligned} \tag{2}$$

In Eq. (2), $SS_D(v)$ consists of two parts: the social weight $SW_D(v)$ and the social proportion $SP_D(v)$. $SW_D(v)$ represents the sum of social weights between node v and all nodes in community D. T_{uv} is the number of social interactions from user u to user v, and K_u is the total number of social interactions of user u. T_{vu} and K_v are similar to T_{uv} and K_u, respectively. $SW_D(v)$ takes into account the direction of social connections between users and normalizes the social weights. $SP_D(v)$ is the proportion of the node v's neighbors in community D, where $\Gamma(v)$ is the out neighbor set of v. The definition of $SS_D(v)$ is similar to term frequency-inverse document frequency (*TF-IDF*) [18] in the field of information retrieval and text mining. Therefore, social similarity has a positive correlation with social weight and social proportion. A user with greater social similarity is more likely to be a member in D.

The follower-ship/followee-ship are widely used as social relations in traditional methods, but they have some disadvantages. (1) Excavating the local community from popular users who are followed by many users will likely cause substantial noise. (2) The relationship of following is relatively static and easy to operate in general. To find a stable local community structure, we adopt relative dynamic social relations in the social networks (e.g., quoting, retweeting and commenting) to calculate the social similarity.

3.2 Topic Similarity

"Community Homophily" is when users have the same or similar natures in the same community, such as the same topics in generated content [19]. Inspired by "Community Homophily," we can judge whether an outside user belongs to a particular community by calculating the topic similarity between the user and the community. In general, each piece of generated content is too short to extract topics from; therefore, we aggregate all content from the same user into a document representing that user. The community document is generated by aggregating all users' documents in the community. Then, we calculate the similarity between users and communities using topic distributions, which are extracted from user and community documents by the *LDA* algorithm. In fact, the more similar the topics, the greater the similarity. Typically, Kullback-Leibler divergence is used to calculate the similarity of two distributions. However, we adopt Jensen–Shannon divergence to calculate the topic similarity because the symmetry and triangle inequality cannot be satisfied by Kullback-Leibler divergence. We modify the topic similarity, which is defined in [20], to calculate the topic similarity between user $v(v \in B)$ and community D as follows:

$$TS_D(v) = 1 - \sqrt{D_{JS}(v, D)} \tag{3}$$

$D_{JS}(v, D)$ is the Jensen–Shannon divergence between two probability distributions and is specifically defined as:

$$D_{JS}(v, D) = \frac{1}{2}(D_{KL}(\theta_v || M) + D_{KL}(\theta_D || M)) \tag{4}$$

θ_v refers to the topic probability distribution of user v, and θ_D is community D's topic probability distribution. M is the average of two probability distributions:

$$M = \frac{1}{2}(\theta_v + \theta_D) \tag{5}$$

D_{KL} is used to calculate the Kullback-Leibler divergence of probability distributions Q and P:

$$D_{KL}(P || Q) = \sum\nolimits_i P(i) \log \frac{P(i)}{Q(i)} \tag{6}$$

To reduce the computational complexity caused by the dynamic increase of community D, we adopt an alternative definition of $TS_D(v)$, as follows:

$$TS_D(v) = \frac{1}{|D|} \sum\nolimits_{u \in D} TS_u(v) \tag{7}$$

$TS_D(v)$ measures the average topic similarity between user v and all users in community D. In Eq. (7), u is a node in D, and $TS_u(v)$ is the topic similarity of user u and user v.

3.3 Algorithm to Detect Local Communities

In the first two parts of this section, the social similarity and topic similarity between users and communities are defined. Both can play important roles in the aggregation of community, and thus, the fusion similarity is proposed as follows:

$$FS_D(v) = \gamma SS_D(v) + (1 - \gamma)TS_D(v) \tag{8}$$

In Eq. (8), γ is the fusion coefficient that balances the proportions of social similarity and topic similarity. In the local community detection algorithm, the node v with the highest $FS_D(v)$ will be selected to be aggregated into D after each update. Usually, researchers are more concerned with the community network composed of the top N nodes sorted by fusion similarity to obtain fewer outliers and high precision.

By adding one node to set D at each step, our algorithm can explore a target community from an initial node. In each step, the algorithm calculates the social similarity and topic similarity simultaneously. Moreover, the algorithm can also be applied to explore more complete community structures using multiple initial nodes identified from the same community.

4 Experiment and Evaluation

To evaluate the performance of the proposed local community detection method, we employ the real Micro-Blog datasets. As a platform for information acquisition and sharing, Weibo (a micro-blog platform similar to Twitter) has become one of the most popular social networks in China and has significant community characteristics. Users in the same community are closely connected and share common interests, whereas connections between different communities are relatively loose, and their interests are often very different. The above characteristics are consistent with Newman and Girvan's formal definition of community [1].

4.1 Dataset Preparation

The data is crawled using the public API[1] of Weibo, and the preprocessing steps are as follows:

Remove the users with fewer than 10 micro-blogs: This step was performed because these users have a small number of micro-blogs and social relationships to be extracted.

Extract social relationships: For all the micro-blogs of each user, we found social relations, such as "@" and "//@:", using regular expressions and extracted the root

[1] http://open.weibo.com/wiki/.

users from forwarding or comment micro-blogs. A social relation matrix was formed after screening and statistics.

Preprocess the micro-blog text content: We put all of a user's aggregated micro-blogs into a document (i.e., forming a one-to-one relationship between the user and the document). We first removed the "@" and "//@:" behaviors from the texts and then used the Institute of Computing Technology, Chinese Lexical Analysis System (ICTCLAS)/Natural Language Processing Information Retrieval (NLPIR) [21] to cut documents into words and remove any nonsense words, symbols, and expressions. Finally, all of the documents were aggregated into one, and the mapping relationships between users and documents were saved.

Table 1 tabulates the statistics of the final experimental dataset. The users in the experimental dataset covered technology, politics, the economy and other fields, thus providing our method with broader applications.

According to [15, 16], the *LDA* parameters were set as follows: topic number

Table 1. Statistics of the dataset used for evaluation

Category	Amount
Number of total users	1206
Number of micro-blogs	1248071
Number of non-repeating items in micro-blog texts	293837
Number of social relations	157685
Average social interactions of users	130

$T = 50$, $\alpha = 50/T$, $\beta = 0.1$, and iteration number = 1000. These are empirical parameters used to produce better results after many tests.

4.2 Evaluation Criterion

Weibo provides a function that shows similar users on the homepage. For a user, we name his/her similar users as first-order-similarity users, and his/her first-order-similarity users' similar users are called second-order-similarity users. We crawled the seed user's first-order-similarity and second-order-similarity users as the candidates. We invited three experts to screen the candidate users manually. By considering the candidates' basic information, social rules, interest topics and other attributes, *M* users were selected as members of the local community of the seed user.

The evaluation metrics we used—precision (*P*), recall (*R*) and *F1-Score*—are quite simple and are quite frequently used in many areas, such as information retrieval and machine learning. Other papers focusing on the community detection problem have also adopted these metrics [6, 8, 10]. The size of the detected local community is *N*, and *A* is the correct number of users in the community. These metrics were calculated using Eq. (9):

$$P = \frac{A}{N}, R = \frac{A}{M}, F1 = \frac{2P * R}{P + R} \quad (9)$$

4.3 Experimental Results

In our experiments, we compared the results of different local community detection methods. Descriptions of the labels we used to denote each of these algorithms are presented below:

- **Clauset.** This is a basic algorithm defining the local modularity R [4].
- **LWP.** This is an improved two-phase algorithm that defines a new local modularity M [5].
- **Chen.** Chen proposed another method for local community detection that defines the metric L to evaluate the local community structure [6].
- **LS-M.** This method is a version that uses link similarity with local modularity M [8]
- **LS-R.** This method is another version that uses link similarity with local modularity R [8]
- **S-LCD.** This is a method that we proposed for local community detection based only on social relations.
- **T-LCD.** Similar to the above, this performs local community detection based only on topic features.
- **F-LCD.** Similar to the above, this performs local community detection based on both social relations and topic features.

A user was randomly selected as the seed in the data set; that user's ID was #130. The user is a researcher in the field of artificial intelligence through the observation of profiles.

Comparing the Precision with Traditional Local Detection Methods

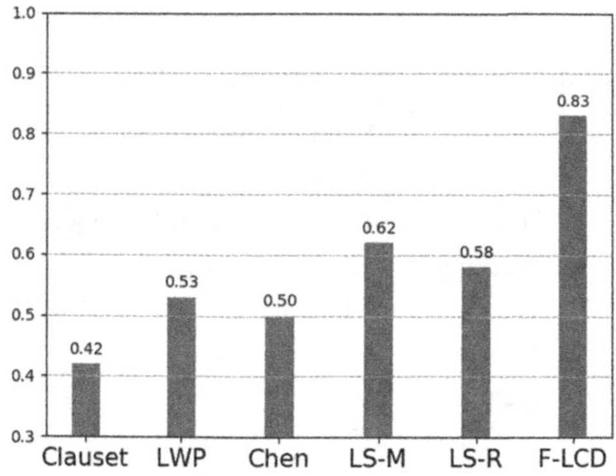

Fig. 3. Precision of different methods

We first compared the precision with those of traditional local detection methods. Figure 3 shows the results of different algorithms in terms of their precision. Our algorithm, which is based on both social relations and topic features, performs the best.

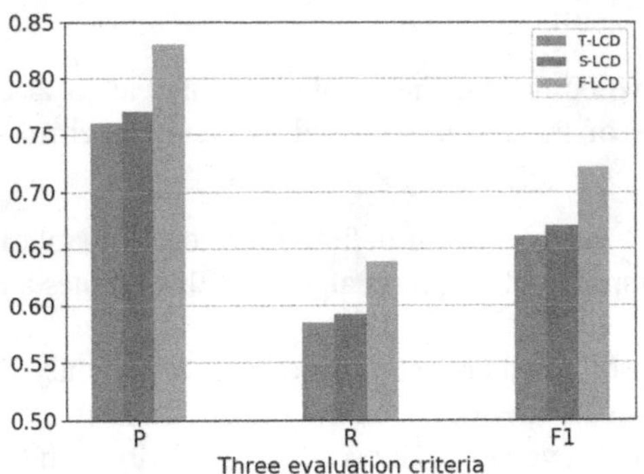

Fig. 4. Precision, recall, and F1-Score of different methods

In this experiment, the community size N was 100, and the fusion coefficient γ was set to 0.8. In the following experiments, we compare the influence of different effects of N and γ.

Comparing the Precision, Recall, and F1-Score of our Proposed Methods
The community size N was set to 100 and γ was set to 0.8. Figure 4 shows the specific experimental results.

As shown in Fig. 4, the local community detection method based on the fusion of social relations and topic features performs better than the other two methods in terms of their precision, recall and F1-Score. Local community detection based on social relations alone focuses on closely connected users within the community, but according to interactive topics, many users may not belong to the local community. In contrast, the approach that relies on topic features alone selects the most similar users based on

Table 2. Words with the highest topic probability in the distribution

Index	Word	Index	Word
1	Learning	11	System
2	Data	12	Artificial Intelligence
3	Machine	13	Microsoft
4	Thesis	14	Field
5	Research	15	Work
6	Deep	16	Model
7	Technology	17	Algorithm
8	Problem	18	Recommendation
9	Paper	19	Compute
10	Professor	20	Schoolmate

content topics as local community members, and the internal links within the community are usually very sparse and do not conform to the formal definition of a community.

Table 2 shows the top 20 words from the highest probability topic in the distribution θ of the target community. Translating the Chinese words in the micro-blogs

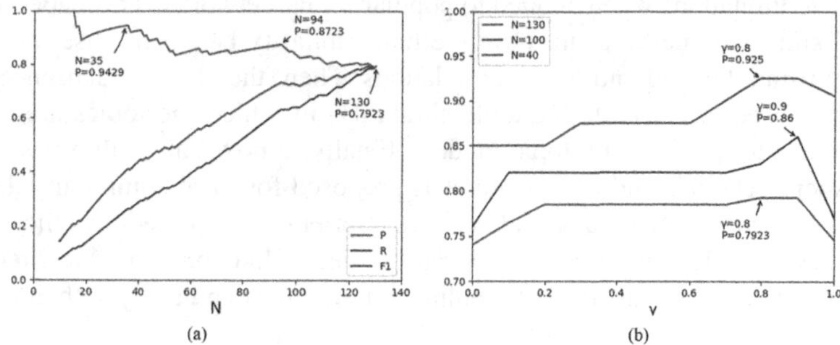

Fig. 5. (a) Comparison of precision, recall, and F1-Score for different community sizes; (b) Comparison of the precision for different fusion coefficients γ

into English reveals that the users in the target community are similar to the seed user in terms of their topic words.

Effects of Community Size N and Fusion Coefficients γ on Precision, Recall, and F1-Score

Community size N and fusion coefficients γ are important parameters, and different values of them will affect the final results. In this part, the experimental results obtained using different values of parameters are presented.

Figure 5 (a) compares the precision, recall, and F1-Score for different community sizes. The *F-LCD* algorithm is adopted in this part, and the fusion coefficient γ is set to 0.8. As N increases, the precision curve shows a decreasing trend. However, when N equals 35 or 94, the precision reaches a local optimal value. In fact, when N is equal to approximately 100, the *F-LCD* algorithm can achieve a precision of more than 83% after many tests, which is an acceptable result in practice. In addition, the recall and F1-score increase as N increases.

Figure 5 (b) shows the effects of different fusion coefficients γ on the precision. We use different values of N to implement the experiment to obtain the general rule. When γ is set to 0 or 1, the *F-LCD* method is equivalent to the *T-LCD* or *S-LCD* method. The precision is the highest when γ is between 0.8 and 0.9 for different values of N.

The community size N and fusion coefficient γ are important parameters in the local community detection algorithm. The last experiment compared the results obtained by using different N and γ in the *F-LCD* algorithm. People always want to get the maximum benefit with some prior knowledge. Therefore, the experimental results have significance for the practical application of this method.

5 Conclusions

Community detection is an important research focus in social network analysis. Currently, local community structures can only be detected from a given seed node because of the incomplete network structure and high computational complexity. Traditional local methods are mainly based on undirected and unweighted networks, and thus, such methods have limitations when applied to popular social networks. This paper defines a new social similarity metric to measure the link similarity between a user and a local community using directed and weighted relations. Then, the classical Jensen–Shannon divergence is used to calculate the topic similarity, in which the topics are extracted from the user's text content by topic models. Finally, a novel algorithm based on the fusion of social relations and topic features is proposed for local community detection. Extensive experiments on a real social network dataset demonstrated the efficacy of the proposed algorithm. Because the networks are studied offline, one possible direction for future work is to discover the dynamic online communities and analyze their evolution processes.

References

1. Newman, M.E., Girvan, M.: Finding and evaluating community structure in networks. Phys. Rev. E Stat. Nonlinear Soft Matter Phys. **69**(2 Pt 2), 026113 (2004)
2. Mislove, A., Marcon, M., Gummadi, K.P., et al.: Measurement and analysis of online social networks (2015)
3. Newman, M.E.J.: Detecting community structure in networks. Europ. Phys. J. B-Condens. Matter Complex Syst. **38**(2), 321–330 (2004)
4. Clauset, A.: Finding local community structure in networks. Phys. Rev. E **72**(2), 026132 (2005)
5. Luo, F., Wang, J.Z., Promislow, E.: Exploring local community structures in large networks. Web Intell. Agent Syst. Int. J. **6**(4), 387–400 (2008)
6. Chen, J., Zaïane, O., Goebel, R.: Local community identification in social networks. In: 2009 International Conference on Advances in Social Network Analysis and Mining, ASONAM 2009, pp. 237–242. IEEE (2009)
7. Bagrow, J.P., Bollt, E.M.: Local method for detecting communities. Phys. Rev. E **72**(4), 046108 (2005)
8. Wu, Y.J., Huang, H., Hao, Z.F., et al.: Local community detection using link similarity. J. Comput. Sci. Technol. **27**(6), 1261–1268 (2012)
9. Zhang, T., Wu, B.: A method for local community detection by finding core nodes. In: Proceedings of the 2012 International Conference on Advances in Social Networks Analysis and Mining (ASONAM 2012), pp. 1171–1176. IEEE Computer Society (2012)
10. Chen, Q., Wu, T.T., Fang, M.: Detecting local community structures in complex networks based on local degree central nodes. Physica A **392**(3), 529–537 (2013)
11. Lancichinetti, A., Fortunato, S., Kertész, J.: Detecting the overlapping and hierarchical community structure of complex networks. New J. Phys. **11**(3), 19–44 (2008)
12. Radicchi, F., Castellano, C., Cecconi, F., et al.: Defining and identifying communities in networks. Proc. Natl. Acad. Sci. U.S.A. **101**(9), 2658–2663 (2003)
13. Papadopoulos, S., Skusa, A., Vakali, A., et al.: Bridge bounding: a local approach for efficient community discovery in complex networks. Physics **1**(1–12), 174 (2009)

14. Ahn, Y.Y., Bagrow, J.P., Lehmann, S.: Link communities reveal multiscale complexity in networks. Nature **466**(7307), 761–764 (2010)
15. Blei, D.M., Ng, A.Y., Jordan, M.I.: Latent dirichlet allocation. J. Mach. Learn. Res. **3**, 993–1022 (2003)
16. Griffiths, T.L., Steyvers, M.: Finding scientific topics. Proc. Natl. Acad. Sci. U.S.A. **101** (Suppl 1), 5228–5235 (2004)
17. Minka, T., Lafferty, J.: Expectation-propagation for the generative aspect model. J. Comput. Appl. Math. **235**(11), 3257–3269 (2002)
18. Salton, G., Buckley, C.: Term-weighting approaches in automatic text retrieval. Inf. Process. Manage. Int. J. **24**(5), 513–523 (1988)
19. Bisgin, H., Agarwal, N., Xu, X.: Investigating homophily in online social networks. In: IEEE/WIC/ACM International Conference on Web Intelligence, Wi 2010, Toronto, Canada, 31 August–3 September 2010, Main Conference Proceedings, pp. 533–536 (2010)
20. Weng, J., Lim, E.P., Jiang, J., et al.: TwitterRank: finding topic-sensitive influential Twitterers. In: International Conference on Web Search and Web Data Mining, WSDM 2010, New York, NY, USA, pp. 261–270, February 2010
21. Zhang, H.P., Yu, H.K., Xiong, D.Y., et al.: HHMM-based Chinese lexical analyzer ICTCLAS. In: Sighan Workshop on Chinese Language Processing, pp. 758–759. Association for Computational Linguistics (2003)

NLP Applications

DIM Reader: Dual Interaction Model for Machine Comprehension

Zhuang Liu(✉), Degen Huang, Kaiyu Huang, and Jing Zhang

School of Computer Science and Technology, Dalian University of Technology, Dalian, China
{zhuangliu,zhangjingqf}@mail.dlut.edu.cn, huangdg@dlut.edu.cn, huangkaiyucs@foxmail.com

Abstract. Enabling a computer to understand a document so that it can answer comprehension questions is a central, yet unsolved goal of Natural Language Processing, so reading comprehension of text is an important problem in NLP research. In this paper, we propose a novel dual interaction model (called DIM Reader) (Our code is available at https://github.com/dlt/mrc-dim), which constructs dual iterative alternating attention mechanism over multiple hops. The proposed DIM Reader continually refines its view of the query and document while aggregating the information required to answer a query, aiming to compute the attentions not only for the document but also the query side, which will benefit from the mutual information. DIM Reader makes use of multiple turns to effectively exploit and perform deeper inference among queries, documents. We conduct extensive experiments on CNN/DailyMail News datasets, and our model achieves the best results on both machine comprehension datasets among almost published results.

Keywords: Machine comprehension · Bi-directional attention · Dual interaction model · Cloze-style

1 Introduction

Reading comprehension is the ability to read text, process it, and understand its meaning. How to endow computers with this capacity has been an elusive challenge and a long-standing goal of Artificial Intelligence, so machine comprehension of text is one of the ultimate goals of natural language processing. While the ability of a machine to understand text can be assessed in many different ways, in recent years, several benchmark datasets have been created to focus on Cloze-style questions as a way to evaluate machine reading comprehension [3,6,8,11,12,16,26]. Cloze-style queries are representative problems in machine reading comprehension. To teach the machine to do Cloze-style reading comprehensions, large-scale training data is necessary for learning relationships between the given document and query. Here we mainly focus on the related work in cloze-style datasets [11,12]. In the past few years, several large-scale datasets

M. Sun et al. (Eds.): CCL 2017 and NLP-NABD 2017, LNAI 10565, pp. 387–397, 2017.
https://doi.org/10.1007/978-3-319-69005-6_32

of Cloze-style questions over a context document have been introduced which allow the training of supervised machine learning systems [6,11,12]. Two large-scale machine comprehension datasets have been released: the CNN/DailyMail corpus, consisting of news articles from those outlets [11], and the Childrens Book Test (CBTest), consisting of short excerpts from books available through Project Gutenberg [12]. The size of these datasets makes them amenable to data-intensive deep learning techniques. Both corpora use Cloze-style questions [28], which are formulated by replacing a word or phrase in a given sentence with a placeholder token. The task is then to find the answer that "fills in the blank".

Over the past year, the tasks of machine comprehension have gained significant popularity within the natural language processing, and we have seen much progress that is utilizing neural network approach to solve Cloze-style questions. In tandem with these corpora (CNN/DailyMail and CBTest), a host of neural machine comprehension models has been developed [3,6,11,12,16]. All previous works are focusing on automatically generating large-scale training data for neural network training, which demonstrate its importance. The availability of relatively large training datasets has made it more feasible to train and estimate rather complex models in an end-to-end fashion for these problems, in which a whole model is fit directly with given question-answer tuples and the resulting model has shown to be rather effective.

In this paper, we propose the Dual Interaction Model (DIM), a novel attention-based neural network model called DIM Reader for machine comprehension tasks, designed to study machine comprehension of text, which constructs dual iterative alternating attention mechanism over multiple hops. The model first constructs the representations of the context paragraph at different levels of granularity. DIM Reader includes word-level and character-level embeddings, and uses bi-directional attention for query-aware context representation. Then, DIM Reader's core module, dual inference attention module, begins by deploying a dual multi-hop inference mechanism that alternates between attending query encodings and document encodings, to uncover the inferential links that exist between the document, the missing query word and the query. The results of the alternating attention is gated and fed back into the inference LSTM. After a number of steps, the weights of the document attention are used to estimate the probability of the answer.

To sum up, our contributions can be summarized as follows:

- We propose a novel end-to-end neural network models for machine reading comprehension, which combine a dual inference attention mechanism to handle the Cloze-style reading comprehension task.
- Also, we have achieved the state-of-the-art performance in public reading comprehension datasets such as CNN/DailyMail, and our experimental evaluations also show that our model performs well on machine comprehension datasets.
- Our further analyses with the models reveal some useful insights for further improving the method.

2 Problem Notation, Datasets

2.1 Definition and Notation

The task of the DIM Reader is to answer a Cloze-style question by reading and comprehending a supporting passage of text. Cloze-style questions are formulated by replacing a word or phrase in a given sentence with a placeholder token. The task is then to find the answer that "fills in the blank". The Cloze-style reading comprehension problem [28] aims to comprehend the given context or document, and then answer the questions based on the nature of the document, while the answer is a single word or phrase in the document. Thus, the Cloze-style reading comprehension can be described as a triple:

$$(\mathcal{Q},\ \mathcal{D},\ \mathcal{A})$$

where $\mathcal{Q}$ is the query (represented as a sequence of words), $\mathcal{D}$ is the document, $\mathcal{A}$ is the set of possible answers to the query.

2.2 Reading Comprehension Datasets

Recent advance on reading comprehension has been closely associated with the availability of various datasets. In the past few years, several institutes have released large-scale machine reading comprehension datasets of Cloze-style questions, and these have greatly accelerated the research of machine reading comprehension.

We begin with a brief introduction of the existing Cloze-style reading comprehension datasets. Richardson *et al.* [24] released the MCTest data consisting of 500 short, fictional open-domain stories and 2000 questions. MCTest is challenging because it is both complicated and small. But its size limits the number of parameters that can be trained, and prevents learning any complex language modeling simultaneously with the capacity to answer questions. Typically, there are two main genres of the English Cloze-style datasets publicly available, CNN/Daily Mail[1] [11] and Children's Book Test (CBTest)[2] [12], which all stem from the English reading materials. The CNN/DailyMail corpus [11], consisting of news articles from those outlets for close style machine comprehension, in which only entities are removed and tested for comprehension, and the Childrens Book Test (CBTest) [12], consisting of short excerpts from books available through Project Gutenberg, which leverages named entities, common nouns, verbs, and prepositions to test reading comprehension. The size of these datasets makes them amenable to data-intensive deep learning techniques. Table 1 provides some statistics on the two English datasets: CNN/Daily Mail and Children's Book Test (CBTest).

[1] CNN and Daily Mail datasets are available at http://cs.nyu.edu/%7ekcho/DMQA.

[2] CBTest datasets is available at http://www.thespermwhale.com/jaseweston/babi/CBTest.tgz.

Table 1. Data statistics of the CNN datasets and Children's Book Test datasets (CBTest). CBTest CN stands for CBTest Common Nouns and CBTest NE stands for CBTest Named Entites. CBTest had a fixed number of 10 options for answering each question. Statistics provided with the CBTest data set.

	CNN			CBTest CN			CBTest NE		
	Train	Valid	Test	Train	Valid	Test	Train	Valid	Test
# queries	380,298	3,924	3,198	879,450	2,000	2,500	108,719	2,000	2,500
Max# options	527	187	396	10	10	10	10	10	10
Avg# options	26.4	26.5	24.5	10	10	10	10	10	10
Avg# tokens	762	763	716	470	448	461	433	412	424
Vocab. size		118,497			53,185			53,063	

3 Proposed Approach

In this section, we will introduce our Dual Interaction Model (DIM Reader) for Cloze-style reading comprehension task. The proposed DIM Reader is shown in Fig. 1.

In encoder layer, we first convert the words to their respective word-level embeddings and character-level embeddings. The word embedding is a fixed vector for each individual word, which is pre-trained with word2vec [21]. We also embeds each word by encoding their character sequences with a convolutional neural network followed by max-pooling over time [17], resulting in a character-level embedding.

In DIM's core layer, dual inference attention module, our model is primarily motivated by Chen *et al.* [3], Kadlec *et al.* [16] and Sukhbaatar *et al.* [27], which aim to directly estimate the answer from the document, instead of making a prediction over the full vocabularies. But we have noticed that by just concatenating the final representations of the query RNN states are not enough for representing the whole information of query. So we propose to utilize the repeated, tight integration between query attention and document attention, which allows the model to explore dynamically which parts of the query are most important to predict the answer, and then to focus on the parts of the document that are most salient to the currently attended query components.

The top layer, the answer prediction layer, aims to predict the probability of the answer given the document and the query. We aggregate the probabilities for tokens which appear multiple times in a document before selecting the maximum as the predicted answer.

3.1 Document and the Query Encoder Layer

In machine reading comprehension task, the document and query are both word sequences. The goal of this layer is to represent each word in the document and query with a vector. We construct the d-dimensional vector with two components: word embeddings and character embeddings. This layer first maps each

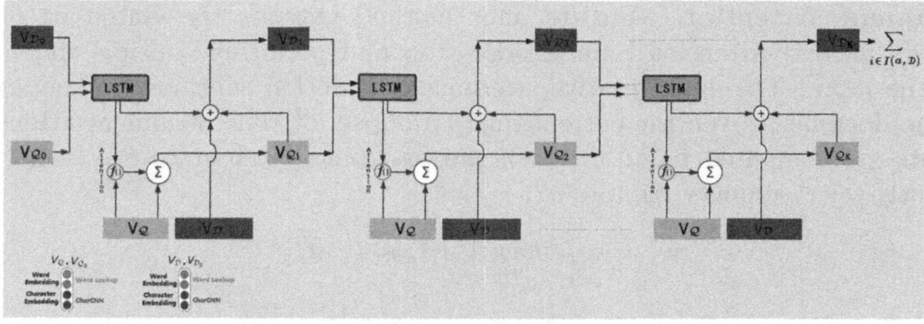

Fig. 1. Architecture of the proposed Dual Interaction Model (DIM Reader).

word to its corresponding word embedding $\{w_t^{\mathcal{D}}\}_{t=1}^m$ and $\{w_t^{\mathcal{Q}}\}_{t=1}^n$ (Consider a document $\mathcal{D} = \{x_t^{\mathcal{D}}\}_{t=1}^m$ and a query $\mathcal{Q} = \{x_t^{\mathcal{Q}}\}_{t=1}^n$, where m and n denote the length of document and query respectively), which is typically done by using pre-trained word vectors, which is pre-trained with word2vec [21], to obtain the fixed word embedding of each word. At a more low-level granularity, we also embeds each word by encoding their character sequences with a convolutional neural network followed by max-pooling over time [17]. Characters are embedded into vectors, which can be considered as 1D inputs to the convolutional neural network, and whose size is the input channel size of the convolutional neural network. The outputs of the convolutional neural network are max-pooled over the entire width to obtain a fixed-size vector for each word ($\{x_t^{\mathcal{D}}\}_{t=1}^m$ and $\{x_t^{\mathcal{Q}}\}_{t=1}^n$), resulting in a character-level embedding $\{c_t^{\mathcal{D}}\}_{t=1}^m$ and $\{c_t^{\mathcal{Q}}\}_{t=1}^n$. Each word embedding u_t ($\{u_t^{\mathcal{D}}\}_{t=1}^m$ and $\{u_t^{\mathcal{Q}}\}_{t=1}^n$) is then represented as the concatenation of word-level embedding and character-level embedding, denoted as $u_t = [w_t, c_t] \in R^d$, where d is the total dimensionality of word-level embedding and character-level embedding.

3.2 Dual Inference Interaction Layer

As shown in the previous section, we generates vector representations for the document encodings and query encodings separately. This layer aims to uncover a dual iterative inference chain that starts at the document and the query, and leads to the answer. Figure 1 illustrates dual inference attention module.

Query Attention Module. We use a bilinear attention to compute the importance of each query term (such as query vector $V_{\mathcal{Q}_0}$) in the current time step t. This bilinear term has been successfully used in [20]. It performs an attentive read on the query encodings, resulting in a query glimpse $\mathbf{q}_t$, and makes the model combine the information in the query with the new information digested from previous iterations. Here $\mathbf{q}_i$ are the query encodings, and we formulate a query glimpse $u_t^{\mathbf{q}}$ at time step t by:

$$u_t^{\mathbf{q}} = \sum_{i=1}^{|\mathcal{Q}|} softmax\, \mathbf{q}_i^T \mathbf{M}_q \mathbf{s}_{t-1} \mathbf{q}_i \tag{1}$$

Document Attention Module. Our method extends the Gated-attention Readers [8] and Attention Sum Reader [16], and performs multiple time-step over the input. The dual iterative alternating attention continues by aggregating the document given the current query glimpse $u_t^{\mathbf{q}}$. The document attention weights are computed based on both the previous search state $t-1$ and the currently selected query glimpse $u_t^{\mathbf{q}}$:

$$\mathbf{w}_i = \underset{i=1,\ldots,|\mathcal{D}|}{softmax}\, \mathbf{d}_i^T \mathbf{M}_d [\mathbf{s}_{t-1}, u_t^{\mathbf{q}}] \quad (2)$$

$$\mathbf{d}_t = \sum_{i=1}^{|\mathcal{D}|} \mathbf{w}_i \mathbf{d}_i \quad (3)$$

where $\mathbf{w}_i$ are the attention weights for each word in the document, $\mathbf{d}_i$ are the document encodings, and the document attention is conditioned on $\mathbf{s}_{t-1}$, so it reads documents and enriching the query in an iterative fashion, and makes the model perform transitive reasoning on the document side.

Inference Attention Module. The inference is modeled by an additional LSTM [13]. The recurrent network iteratively performs an alternating search step to probe information that may be useful to predict the answer. The module performs an attentive read on the query encodings, resulting in a query glimpse $u_t^{\mathbf{q}}$ at each time step, then gives the current query glimpse $u_t^{\mathbf{q}}$, it extracts a conditional document glimpse $\mathbf{d}_t$, representing the parts of the document that are relevant to the current query glimpse. It produces a new query glimpse and document glimpse in each iteration and utilizes them alternatively in the next iteration, then combines the information in the query with the new information digested from previous iterations. Both attentive reads are conditioned on the previous hidden state of the inference LSTM $\mathbf{s}_{t-1}$, summarizing the information that has been gathered from the query and the document up to time t, making it easier to determine the degree of matching between them. The inference LSTM uses both glimpses to update its recurrent state and thus decides which information needs to be gathered to complete the inference process. It explores the idea of using both attention-sum to aggregate candidate attention scores and multiple turns to attain a better reasoning capability.

3.3 Answer Prediction Layer

The top layer, the answer prediction layer, aims to predict the probability of the answer given the document and the query. After a maximum number of hops K, the document attention weights obtained in the last search step $d_{i,K}$ are used to predict the probability of the answer. We aggregate the probabilities for tokens which appear multiple times in a document before selecting the maximum as the predicted answer:

$$P(a|\mathcal{Q},\, \mathcal{D}) = \sum_{i \in I(a,\mathcal{D})} d_{i,K} \quad (4)$$

where $I(a, \mathcal{D})$ is the set of positions where token a appears in the document $\mathcal{D}$, the model is trained by minimizing the cross-entropy loss using the softmax-weights of candidate scores as the predicted probabilities.

4 Experiments

4.1 Experimental Setups

The general settings of our neural network model are detailed below.

- Embedding Layer: The embedding weights are randomly initialized with the uniformed distribution in the interval [−0.05, 0.05].
- Hidden Layer: We initialized the LSTM units with random orthogonal matrices [25].
- Vocabulary: For training efficiency and generalization, we truncate the full vocabulary (about 200 K) and set a shortlist of 100 K. During training we randomly shuffled all examples in each epoch. To speedup training, we always pre-fetched 10 batches worth of examples and sorted them according to the length of the document. This way each batch contained documents of roughly the same length.
- Optimization: In order to minimize the hyper-parameter tuning, we used stochastic gradient descent with the ADAM update rule [18] and learning rate of 0.001 or 0.0005, with an initial learning rate of 0.001.

Due to the time limitations, we only tested a few combinations of hyper-parameters, while we expect to have a full parameter tuning in the future. The results are reported with the best model, which is selected by the performance of validation set. Our model is implemented with Tensorflow [1] and Keras [4], and all models are trained on GTX Titan x GPU.

4.2 Results

We compared the proposed model with several baselines as summarized below. To verify the effectiveness of our proposed model, we tested our model on public english reading comprehension datasets. Our evaluation is carried out on CNN news datasets [11] and CBTest NE/CN datasets [12], and the statistics of these datasets are given in Table 2. As we can see that, the proposed DIM Reader achieves the state-of-the-art results in all types of test set, among almost published results.

In CNN news datasets, our model is on par with the AoA Reader [5], with 0.1% improvements in validation set. But we failed to outperform EpiReader [29]. In CBTest NE, though there is a drop in the validation set with 0.7% declines, there is a boost in the test set with an absolute improvements over other models, which suggest our model is effective. In CBTest CN dataset, our model outperforms all the state-of-the-art systems, where a 0.3% and 0.6% absolute accuracy improvements over the most recent state-of-the-art AoA Reader [5] in

Table 2. Results on the CNN news, CBTest NE (named entity) and CN (common noun) datasets. The result that performs best is depicted in bold face.

	CNN News		CBTest NE		CBTest CN	
	Valid	Test	Valid	Test	Valid	Test
Deep LSTM Reader (Hermann *et al.* [11])	55.0	57.0	-	-	-	-
Attentive Reader (Hermann *et al.* [11])	61.6	63.0	-	-	-	-
Impatient Reader (Hermann *et al.* [11])	61.8	63.8	-	-	-	-
LSTMs (context + query) (Hill *et al.* [12])	-	-	51.2	41.8	62.6	56.0
MemNN (window + self-sup.) (Hill *et al.* [12])	63.4	66.8	70.4	66.6	64.2	63.0
AS Reader (Kadlec *et al.* [16])	68.6	69.5	73.8	68.6	68.8	63.4
Stanford AR (Chen *et al.* [3])	72.4	72.4	-	-	-	-
Iterative Attention (Sordoni *et al.* [26])	72.6	73.3	75.2	68.6	72.1	69.2
GA Reader (Dhingra *et al.* [8])	73.0	73.8	74.9	69.0	69.0	63.9
EpiReader (Trischler *et al.* [29])	**73.4**	74.0	75.3	69.7	71.5	67.4
CAS Reader (avg mode) (Cui *et al.* [6])	68.2	70.0	74.2	69.2	68.2	65.7
AoA Reader (Cui *et al.* [5])	73.1	**74.4**	**77.8**	72.0	72.2	69.4
DIM Reader (our)	73.2	**74.4**	77.1	**72.2**	**72.5**	**70.0**

the validation and test set respectively. We have also noticed that, our model has an absolute improvement over EpiReader [29]. When compared with AoA Reader [5], GA Reader [8], EpiReader [29], our model shows a similar result, with improvements on validation and test set, experimental results demonstrate that our model is more general and powerful than previous works. This demonstrates that our model is powerful enough to compete with english reading comprehension, to tackle the Cloze-style reading comprehension task.

So far, we have good results in machine reading comprehension, all higher than most baselines above, verifying that dual interaction model is useful, suggesting that our DIM Reader performed better on relatively difficult reasoning questions.

5 Related Work

Neural attention models have been applied recently to machine learning and natural language processing problems. Cloze-style reading comprehension tasks have been widely investigated in recent studies. We will take a brief revisit to the previous works.

Hermann *et al.* [11] have proposed a methodology for obtaining large quantities of ($\mathcal{Q}$, $\mathcal{D}$, $\mathcal{A}$) triples through news articles and its summary. Along with the release of Cloze-style reading comprehension dataset, they also proposed an attention-based neural network to tackle the issues above. Experimental results showed that the proposed neural network is effective than traditional baselines. Hill *et al.* [12] released another dataset, which stems from the children's books.

Different from Hermann *et al.* [11]'s work, the document and query are all generated from the raw story without any summary, which is much more general than previous work. To handle the reading comprehension task, they proposed a window-based memory network, and self-supervision heuristics is also applied to learn hard-attention. Kadlec *et al.* [16] proposed a simple model that directly pick the answer from the document, which is motivated by the Pointer Network [30]. A restriction of this model is that, the answer should be a single word and appear in the document. Results on various public datasets showed that the proposed model is effective than previous works. Liu *et al.* [19] proposed to exploit these reading comprehension models into specific task. They first applied the reading comprehension model into Chinese zero pronoun resolution task with automatically generated large-scale pseudo training data. Trischler *et al.* [29] adopted a re-ranking strategy into the neural networks and used a joint-training method to optimize the neural network. Sordoni *et al.* [26] have proposed an iterative alternating attention mechanism and gating strategies to accumulatively optimize the attention after several hops, where the number of hops is defined heuristically. Seo *et al.* [22] proposed the BiDAF model, which computes both the context-to-query attention and the query-to-context attention by using second-order attention, and Cui *et al.* [5] computed a query-level average attention based on the alignment matrix, which is then used to further compute a weighted sum of context-level attention. Document Reader [7] and Dynamic Coattention Networks [2] utilized a multi-hop pointing decoder to indicate the answer span iteratively, and Answer Pointer [31] and Ruminating Reader [10] focused on the query-aware context representation and use query-independent pointer vector to select the answer boundary. Weissenborn *et al.* [9] and Zhang *et al.* [15] used one-hop reasoning models to emphasis relevant parts between the context and the query, and the architecture of these models is quite shallow, usually containing only one interaction layer.

6 Conclusions

In this paper we presented the novel dual interaction model (called DIM Reader), and showed it offered improved performance for machine comprehension tasks. Among the large, public english machine comprehension datasets, our model could give significant improvements over various state-of-the-art baselines.

As future work, we need to consider how we can utilize new corpora (such as SQuAD [23] and TriviaQA [14]) to solve more complex machine reading comprehension tasks, and we are going to investigate hybrid reading comprehension models to tackle the problems that rely on comprehensive induction of several sentences. We also plan to augment our framework with a more powerful model for question answering.

Acknowledgments. We would like to thank the reviewers for their helpful comments and suggestions to improve the quality of the paper. This research is supported by National Natural Science Foundation of China (No. 61672127).

References

1. Abadi, M., Agarwal, A., Barham, P., Brevdo, E., Chen, Z., Citro, C., Corrado, G.S., Davis, A., Dean, J., Devin, M., et al.: Tensorflow: large-scale machine learning on heterogeneous distributed systems. arXiv preprint arXiv:1603.04467 (2016)
2. Caiming Xiong, V.Z., Socher, R.: Dynamic coattention networks for question answering. In: Proceedings of ICLR (2017)
3. Chen, D., Bolton, J., Manning, C.D.: A thorough examination of the CNN/daily mail reading comprehension task. arXiv preprint arXiv:1606.02858 (2016)
4. Chollet, F.: Keras (2015)
5. Cui, Y., Chen, Z., Wei, S., Wang, S., Liu, T., Hu, G.: Attention-over-attention neural networks for reading comprehension. arXiv preprint arXiv:1607.04423 (2016)
6. Cui, Y., Liu, T., Chen, Z., Wang, S., Hu, G.: Consensus attention-based neural networks for Chinese reading comprehension. arXiv preprint arXiv:1607.02250 (2016)
7. Chen, D., Adam Fisch, J.W., Bordes, A.: Reading wikipedia to answer open-domain questions. arXiv preprint arXiv:1704.00051 (2017)
8. Dhingra, B., Liu, H., Cohen, W.W., Salakhutdinov, R.: Gated-attention readers for text comprehension. arXiv preprint arXiv:1606.01549 (2016)
9. Dirk Weissenborn, G.W., Seiffe, L.: FastQA: a simple and efficient neural architecture for question answering. arXiv preprint arXiv:1703.04816 (2017)
10. Gong, Y., Bowman, S.R.: Ruminating reader: reasoning with gated multi-hop attention. arXiv preprint arXiv:1704.07415 (2017)
11. Hermann, K.M., Kocisky, T., Grefenstette, E., Espeholt, L., Kay, W., Suleyman, M., Blunsom, P.: Teaching machines to read and comprehend. In: Advances in Neural Information Processing Systems, pp. 1693–1701 (2015)
12. Hill, F., Bordes, A., Chopra, S., Weston, J.: The Goldilocks principle: reading children's books with explicit memory representations. arXiv preprint arXiv:1511.02301 (2015)
13. Hochreiter, S., Schmidhuber, J.: Long short-term memory. Neural Comput. **9**(8), 1735–1780 (1997)
14. Joshi, M., Choi, E., Weld, D.S., Zettlemoyer, L.: TriviaQA: a large scale distantly supervised challenge dataset for reading comprehension. arXiv preprint arXiv:1705.03551 (2017)
15. Zhang, J., Xiaodan Zhu, Q., Jiang, H.: Exploring question understanding and adaptation in neural-network-based question answering. arXiv preprint arXiv:1703.04617 (2017)
16. Kadlec, R., Schmid, M., Bajgar, O., Kleindienst, J.: Text understanding with the attention sum reader network. arXiv preprint arXiv:1603.01547 (2016)
17. Kim, Y.: Convolutional neural networks for sentence classification. arXiv preprint arXiv:1408.5882 (2014)
18. Kinga, D., Adam, J.B.: A method for stochastic optimization. In: International Conference on Learning Representations (ICLR) (2015)
19. Liu, T., Cui, Y., Yin, Q., Wang, S., Zhang, W., Hu, G.: Generating and exploiting large-scale pseudo training data for zero pronoun resolution. arXiv preprint arXiv:1606.01603 (2016)
20. Luong, M.T., Pham, H., Manning, C.D.: Effective approaches to attention-based neural machine translation. arXiv preprint arXiv:1508.04025 (2015)
21. Mikolov, T., Sutskever, I., Chen, K., Corrado, G.S., Dean, J.: Distributed representations of words and phrases and their compositionality. In: Advances in Neural Information Processing Systems, pp. 3111–3119 (2013)

22. Seo, M., Aniruddha Kembhavi, A.F., Hajishirzi, H.: Bidirectional attention flow for machine comprehension. In: Proceedings of ICLR (2017)
23. Rajpurkar, P., Zhang, J., Lopyrev, K., Liang, P.: Squad: 100,000+ questions for machine comprehension of text. arXiv preprint arXiv:1606.05250 (2016)
24. Richardson, M., Burges, C.J., Renshaw, E.: MCTest: a challenge dataset for the open-domain machine comprehension of text. In: EMNLP, vol. 3, p. 4 (2013)
25. Saxe, A.M., McClelland, J.L., Ganguli, S.: Exact solutions to the nonlinear dynamics of learning in deep linear neural networks. arXiv preprint arXiv:1312.6120 (2013)
26. Sordoni, A., Bachman, P., Trischler, A., Bengio, Y.: Iterative alternating neural attention for machine reading. arXiv preprint arXiv:1606.02245 (2016)
27. Sukhbaatar, S., Weston, J., Fergus, R., et al.: End-to-end memory networks. In: Advances in Neural Information Processing Systems, pp. 2440–2448 (2015)
28. Taylor, W.L.: Cloze procedure: a new tool for measuring readability. Journalism Bull. **30**(4), 415–433 (1953)
29. Trischler, A., Ye, Z., Yuan, X., Suleman, K.: Natural language comprehension with the EpiReader. arXiv preprint arXiv:1606.02270 (2016)
30. Vinyals, O., Fortunato, M., Jaitly, N.: Pointer networks. In: Advances in Neural Information Processing Systems, pp. 2692–2700 (2015)
31. Wang, S., Jiang, J.: Machine comprehension using match-LSTM and answer pointer. In: Proceedings of ICLR (2017)

Multi-view LSTM Language Model with Word-Synchronized Auxiliary Feature for LVCSR

Yue Wu(✉), Tianxing He, Zhehuai Chen, Yanmin Qian, and Kai Yu

Key Laboratory of Shanghai Education Commission for Intelligent Interaction and Cognitive Engineering, SpeechLab, Department of Computer Science and Engineering Brain Science and Technology Research Center, Shanghai Jiao Tong University, Shanghai, China
{yuewu619,cloudygoose,chenzhehuai,yanminqian,kai.yu}@sjtu.edu.cn

Abstract. Recently long short-term memory language model (LSTM LM) has received tremendous interests from both language and speech communities, due to its superiorty on modelling long-term dependency. Moreover, integrating auxiliary information, such as context feature, into the LSTM LM has shown improved performance in perplexity (PPL). However, improper feed of auxiliary information won't give consistent gain on word error rate (WER) in a large vocabulary continuous speech recognition (LVCSR) task. To solve this problem, a multi-view LSTM LM architecture combining a tagging model is proposed in this paper. Firstly an on-line unidirectional LSTM-RNN is built as a tagging model, which can generate word-synchronized auxiliary feature. Then the auxiliary feature from the tagging model is combined with the word sequence to train a multi-view unidirectional LSTM LM. Different training modes for the tagging model and language model are explored and compared. The new architecture is evaluated on PTB, Fisher English and SMS Chinese data sets, and the results show that not only LM PPL promotion is observed, but also the improvements can be well transferred to WER reduction in ASR-rescore task.

Keywords: LSTM language model · Speech recognition · Multi-view · Auxiliary feature · Tagging model

1 Introduction

A language model judges the fluency and reasonability of a sentence. It is widely used in natural language processing, machine translation, automatic speech recognition (ASR) and other tasks. Statistical language models were developed in 1987, aiming to model the probability of the next word in a sentence given the preceding words [1].

The smoothed n-gram model has been the dominating model in the field for a long time. Nevertheless, it has been shown that recurrent neural network

M. Sun et al. (Eds.): CCL 2017 and NLP-NABD 2017, LNAI 10565, pp. 398–410, 2017.
https://doi.org/10.1007/978-3-319-69005-6_33

language models (RNN LM) can significantly outperform traditional n-gram models [2,3], because of its ability to memorize previous history. After that, the Long Short-Term Memory (LSTM) [4] RNN was proposed, being able to connect long time lags between the relevant input and target output, thereby incorporating long-range contexts. Nowadays, this structure has been widely applied to language modeling, achieving promising results [5].

In order to further promote the capability of a LSTM based language model, many works have been focused on adding additional word and sentence level information in the language model [6]. The additional information includes part of speech (POS), named entity recognition (NER), chunking [7], environment of a sentence, grammatical parser, etc. This auxiliary information is combined into traditional multi-view models as well as joint frameworks [8]. Although works have been proven to be effective regarding their perplexity performance, they fail to show corresponding WER and SER reduction in LVCSR task.

We argue that the key reason behind this performance inconsistency is that standard auxiliary features inference mechanisms (such as maximum entropy and BLSTM tagging model) utilize not only history words but also future word sequence, which should not be fed into a LM for next word prediction. It's like cheating, future information is given when predicting future words, which will easily decrease PPL, but won't help reduce WER and SER in n-best rescoring [6,8].

To address this problem, we propose to use word-synchronized features, by which we mean that the feature extraction process will only use history words and information. More details about are given below.

In our work, an unidirectional LSTM tagging model which differs from those traditional feature extractor, is utilized to produce auxiliary feature. Next, the tagging model is connected with a LSTM LM, forming a multi-view structure. For training our model, five methods are experimented to determine the most suitable training process. Finally, we compare our new multi-view LSTM LM with not only basic LSTM LM baseline but also models of related works on both PPL and ASR-rescoring.

The rest of the paper is organized as follows: Sect. 2 gives the detail of the related work of language model. We show how to connect the tagging model with the language model in Sect. 3. Section 4 shows the experimental setup and results. Finally, the conclusions can be found in Sect. 5.

2 Related Work

As LSTM RNN model has been proven to be a promising structure, many researches have been focusing on applying it in tasks like LM, tagging etc. In order to achieve further improvement, more useful and complex structures based on LSTM RNN model have been explored. Figure 1 shows three extensions of the basic LSTM language model, and all these models are reproduced and compared to proposed model. Concrete results and analysis are shown in Sect. 4.

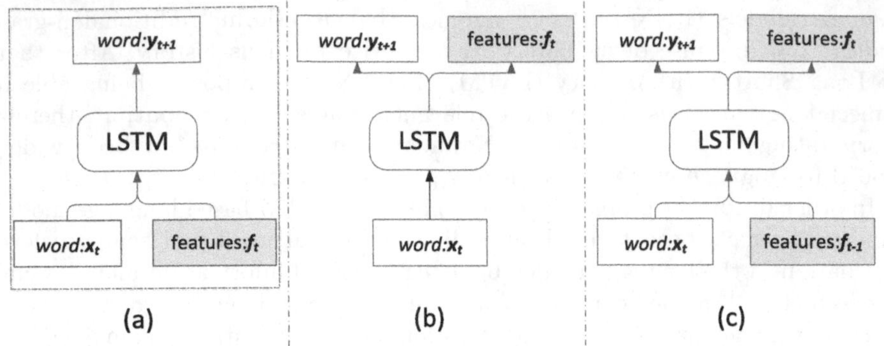

Fig. 1. (a) Multi-view LSTM language model. (b) Multi-task LSTM model. (c) Multi-view combine with multi-task LSTM joint model.

2.1 Multi-view Model

Considering that some extra linguistic features might contribute to language modeling, word and sentence level features were introduced in LM [6]. This model have multi inputs, which contains different views of information. So it is called multi-view model (see Fig. 1(a)).

As argued in Sect. 1, research on this kind of model shows improvements on perplexity and word prediction accuracy (WPA), but integrating this model with ASR did not lead to commensurate improvements [8]. That is to say, the straightforward combination of words and features as the inputs of a language model do not contribute to speech recognition.

Our proposed model is based on the multi-view structure, but is specially tailored for ASR task by using word-synchronized auxiliary feature.

2.2 Multi-task Model

As shown in Fig. 1(b), in a multi-task structure, a language model was designed to train with other tasks jointly [9], they share the same inputs and hidden layers. However most researches on multi-task structure show that usually performance gain is achieved in the cooperating task, instead of LM task itself.

2.3 Multi-task and Multi-view Joint Model

Other works combined the multi-task structure with multi-view structure, which is shown in Fig. 1(c). Not only multiple tasks were trained together, but also the inputs of this model were multi-view. LM was jointed with other spoken language understanding (SLU) or natural language process (NLP) task, some models of improved version are researched. Better than multi-task models, these works show slight improvement in PPL and ASR-rescoring, but more promotion is gained in the cooperating task [10].

3 Method

Our model is composed of two parts: The first one is a tagging model which produces word-synchronized auxiliary features, the other is a multi-view language model with auxiliary features propagated from the tagging model. For both of them, single layer unidirectional LSTMs are used. We connect the two LSTM in series on word-level. The structure and mathematical details are given below.

3.1 Uni-LSTM Tagging Model

Tagging is a classification task, where a tagging model is trained to determine the category of every element within the input sequence. Neural network tagging model utilizes the neural network to accomplish tagging task [11]. Much work has been proposed to improve the accuracy of the tagging model. Recently, unidirectional and bidirectional LSTM RNN with word embedding showed a significant improvement [12] compared to previous models.

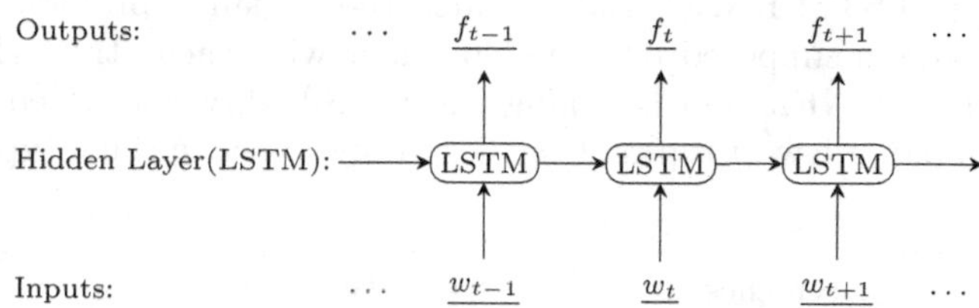

Fig. 2. Uni-directional LSTM tagging model

As illustrated in Fig. 2, in order to produce word-synchronized features, an unidirectional LSTM rather than bidirectional LSTM is utilized to build the tagging model. Moreover, in our preliminary experiments, bidirectional LSTM only give slight tagging accuracy gain over unidirectional ones.

An LSTM network is formed like the standard RNN except that the self-connected hidden units are replaced by specially designed units called memory blocks. In this paper, LSTM memory block is denoted as $\mathcal{L}$. To avoid confusion, the LSTM memory block of tagging model and language model are denoted as $\mathcal{L}_{\texttt{tag}}$ and $\mathcal{L}_{\text{LM}}$ severally.

The vector $\boldsymbol{w}_t$ uses one hot coding to represent the current word in the time step t, which is the input of both $\mathcal{L}_{\texttt{tag}}$ and $\mathcal{L}_{\text{LM}}$.

And then the word embedding can be obtained as $\boldsymbol{x}_t$:

$$\boldsymbol{x}_t = E_{tag}\boldsymbol{w}_t \tag{1}$$

here E_{tag} is the word embedding matrix of tagging model,

The output of the LSTM hidden layer $\boldsymbol{h}_t$ in unidirectional tagging model is calculated as:

$$\boldsymbol{h}_t = \mathcal{L}_{\texttt{tag}}(\boldsymbol{x}_t, \boldsymbol{h}_{t-1}) \tag{2}$$

The computational details in a LSTM memory block $\mathcal{L}$ is formulated as the following composite function:

$$\begin{aligned} i_t &= \sigma(W_{xi}x_t + W_{hi}h_{t-1} + W_{ci}c_{t-1} + b_i) \\ f_t &= \sigma(W_{xf}x_t + W_{hf}h_{t-1} + W_{cf}c_{t-1} + b_f) \\ c_t &= f_t c_{t-1} + i_t \tanh(W_{xc}x_t + W_{hc}h_{t-1} + b_c) \\ o_t &= \sigma(W_{xo}x_t + W_{ho}h_{t-1} + W_{co}c_t + b_o) \\ h_t &= o_t \tanh(c_t) \end{aligned} \tag{3}$$

where σ is the logistic (sigmoid) function, and i, f, o and c are respectively the *input gate*, *forget gate*, *output gate* and *cell* activation vectors.

$\boldsymbol{f}_t$ is the output of the tagging model, which is a probability distribution, and can be calculated from the LSTM memory block as:

$$\boldsymbol{f}_t = softmax(W_{ho}\boldsymbol{h}_t + \boldsymbol{b}_y) \tag{4}$$

where softmax is a normalizing separator.

According to LSTM-RNN tagging model, the obtained probability distribution of each step is supposed to be independent with each other. However, in some tasks such as NER and chunking, tags are highly correlated with each other, for example, a few of types of tags can only follow specific types of tags.

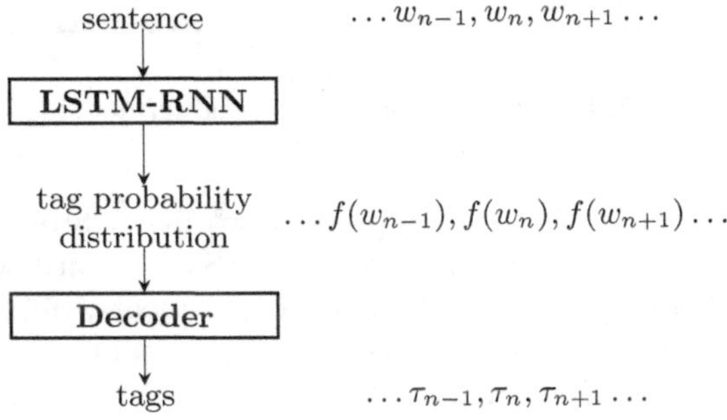

Fig. 3. LSTM tagging system with decoding

Adding these constrained relationships in prediction of tags can help a lot. As Fig. 3 shows, to make use of this kind of labeling constraints, a transition matrix between each step's output is utilized. This matrix is incorporated with probability distribution to generate a decoding process [12]. Which is a typical dynamic programming problem and can be solved with Viterbi algorithm [13].

In this paper, decoding process is denoted as $\mathcal{D}(\cdot)$, the output of decoder τ_t is a series of the final predicted tags, and they are also expressed as one hot vector:

$$\boldsymbol{\tau}_t = \mathcal{D}(\boldsymbol{f}_t) \tag{5}$$

3.2 Multi-view LSTM Language Model with Word-Synchronized Auxiliary Feature

Figure 4 shows the structure of the proposed multi-view LSTM language model with word-synchronized auxiliary feature.

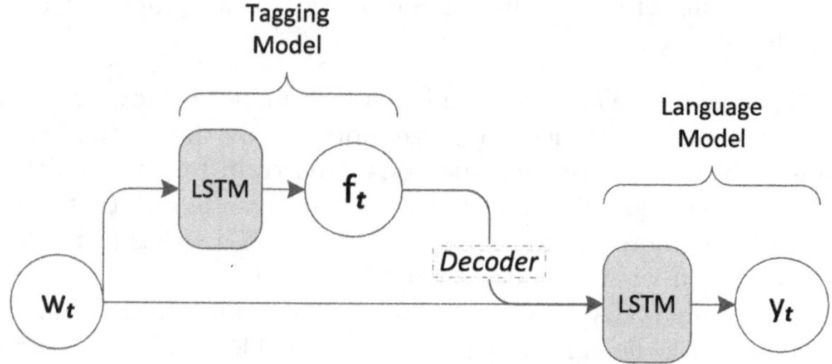

Fig. 4. Multi-view LSTM language model with word-synchronized auxiliary feature

Our proposed model is a multi-view language model connected with a uni-directional tagging model. The first input of language model $\boldsymbol{w}_t$ is a one hot vector representing the current word, which is also feed into tagging model. The second input can be the output of the tagging model or decoder. Whether the decoding process is used or not, experimentation and comparison of them have been accomplished in Sect. 4.

The difference of formula between them is reflected in the input part. If using the decoder, the input of multi-view language model is:

$$\zeta_t = W_{tag}\boldsymbol{\tau}_t + E_{word}\boldsymbol{w}_t \tag{6}$$

$\boldsymbol{\tau}_t$ is the output of decoder as one hot vector. Otherwise, the input of multi-view language model is:

$$\zeta_t = W_{tag}\boldsymbol{f}_t + E_{word}\boldsymbol{w}_t \tag{7}$$

$\boldsymbol{f}_t$ is the output of tagging model as probability distribution. E_{word} is the Word embedding matrix, and W_{tag} is the parameter matrix connecting output of tagging model and hidden layer of language model. They are added together as the final input for LM at each time-step.

The output of the LSTM hidden layer of language model $\boldsymbol{h}_t$ is calculated as:

$$\boldsymbol{h}_t = \mathcal{L}_{\text{LM}}(\zeta_t, \boldsymbol{h}_{t-1}) \tag{8}$$

The computational details in a LSTM memory block $\mathcal{L}$ is introduced in Eq. 3. $\boldsymbol{y}_t$ is the output of the language model, which is the probability distribution of the next word $P(\boldsymbol{x}_{t+1}|\boldsymbol{x}_1{:}\boldsymbol{x}_t)$, and can be calculated from output of the LSTM memory block as:

$$\boldsymbol{y}_t = softmax(W_{ho}\boldsymbol{h}_t + \boldsymbol{b}_y) \tag{9}$$

3.3 Training Method

The proposed model consists of two parts: language model and tagging model. The language model training process follows standard convention, calculates the cross entropy of each word and then conducts back-propagation. We use mini-batch based stochastic gradient descent (SGD) as optimization method.

Since the training of tagging model can be varied, we propose five different training methods:

(1) Train the tagging LSTM as an independent model in advance and fix it when training the multi-view language model. Only this method can utilize decoding process, because next methods need train tagging model but the decoding process doesn't support this. The advantage is that decoder is beneficial to promote the tagging model, but it has a disadvantage that it can't be updated when language model is training.
(2) Train the tagging LSTM in advance, which will also be jointly trained during LM training, with the same learning rate of LM. The trouble is that the well-trained tagging model might be destroyed when the language model has just started training with a relatively big learning rate.
(3) Randomize the parameters of the tagging part of our model and train the language model and tagging model jointly, with a same learning rate.
(4) Because the choke point of the second and third methods is learning rates, Utilize stabilizer [14,15] in the training process based on the second method, in order to adjust learning rates in different parts of proposed model dynamically.
(5) Similar to the forth method, this method adds beta stabilizer to the third method.

Since that which one is the best training method for our proposed model is unknown, these five methods are all tested and evaluated in experiments. The results are shown in Sect. 4.

4 Experiments

4.1 Setting

We test our models on both English and Chinese data sets, including PTB, Swb-Fisher and Chinese SMS.

The first data set is the Penn Treebank Corpus (PTB) [16], which is a widely used data set to evaluate the effectiveness of a language model. It contains about 40 K sentences of training, 3 K validation sentences and 4 K testing sentences.

Swb-Fisher data set is an English data set which contains ten millions words in training data. In the test stage, the switchboard subset of the NIST 2000 Hub5e set is used (referred to as hub5e, 1831 utterances). For the corresponding ASR-rescore task, the acoustic models are trained on English Switchboard task with 7-layer CD-DNN-HMM and 2048 neurons in each layer. Fourier transform based log filter-banks with 40 coefficients are used as feature. An English interpolated trigram language model trained on Swb-fisher data set is used in 1-pass decoding to generate N-best lists for ASR-rescore task.

SMS is a Chinese data set with two million words collected from the short message service (SMS). A mandarin spontaneous conversation test-set (about 25 h) is taken for the decoding stage. A 5000 h Mandarin corpus is used to train the DNN-HMM acoustic model. Lastly, a tri-gram language model trained on the SMS data set with forty thousand words is used in 1-pass decoding.

At first, we wanted to investigate which kind of linguistic features contribute the most to our model. As the two LSTM structures of our model are combined on word-level, we only considered word-level information such as part of speech (POS), name entity recognition (NER) and chunking (CHUNK). The chunking label is produced by a method described in [7], which can transform a syntax parser tree into chunking on word-level. As we don't have real tagging label on all our training data, we used the popular Stanford Core-NLP tools[1] to generate labels on the data, and treat them as ground truth in our experiment.

Regarding the training of our proposed tagging model, we try the five methods that mentioned in Sect. 3 on Chinese SMS. Then apply the best one to our following experiments with large scale.

Our general target is to compare our proposed multi-view LM with LSTM LM baseline and other LMs in Sect. 2. The multi-task model is a original single hidden layer LSTM model with two task. Multi-task and multi-view model is refer to the joint model in [10].

The hidden layers in all LSTM used in our experiments are of size 300, and the dropout rate is set to 0.5. SRILM [17] is used to produce n-gram LM.

4.2 Evaluation of the Tagging Model

POS, NER and CHUNK are the three different tag types used in our model. Table 1 shows the accuracy of unidirectional LSTM tagging model in proposed LM on all data sets. As we don't have real tagging label on all data sets, the training data sets are labeled by Standford tool and regarded as ground truth. So the accuracy is relative to Stanford label. The accuracy of these data-sets with POS are relatively high, with CHUNK and NER are not bad too. So it means we won't lose much information even if a unidirectional model is used.

4.3 Evaluation of Training Methods

Table 2 shows the perplexity comparison on five training methods of our proposed model, which are described in Sect. 3.2. The data set is Chinese SMS.

The result (Table 2) shows that the first method is superior for training a tagging model. The second and third methods are obviously worse than the first one, because language model and tagging model are relatively independent as two difference task. Connecting two models in series and training them with identical

[1] http://nlp.stanford.edu/software/.

Table 1. Accuracy of word-level features on all data-sets we used

Data	Accuracy(decoding/no decoding)		
	POS	NER	CHUNK
ptb	96.36/96.32	80.32/82.06	84.23/81.77
fisher	94.24/94.24	79.93/81.97	85.72/83.47
sms	94.87/94.84	80.44/82.12	85.55/82.98

Table 2. Perplexity comparison of different methods for training proposed model

Model	Training Method	PPL
LSTM LM	-	102.11
Multi-view LM	1	98.02
	2	135.72
	3	148.65
	4	105.47
	5	107.21

learning rate will fail to adjust an appropriate learning rate for both, so can not lead to a win-win result. This conclusion is supported by the result of forth and fifth methods. When utilizing the beta stabilizer which can adjust learning rates in different LSTM dynamically, the PPL will be much less than second and third methods. However the last two methods did not exceed the first one as expected, because the beta stabilizer can only compensate the shortage of the imperfect learning rate, worse than training them respectively with their own appropriate learning rate. Moreover, the tagging LSTM in the first method is well trained enough. Therefore, the first method is used to train the proposed model. For all the following experiments, the tagging model will be trained independently and combined with language LSTM after training.

4.4 Evaluation of Our Multi-view Language Model

In this section, the data sets introduced above are used to evaluate the effectiveness of our multi-view language model. First we tried a wide range of models on the PTB data set and compared them over their respective perplexity, but note that PTB set cannot be tested for ASR-rescore task.

As we can see at Table 3, either POS by Stanford tool or our unidirectional LSTM tagging model, can significantly boost the performance.

Table 4 shows the perplexity, WER and SER on different added tags. The result shows a large improvement from POS feature, while improvement from NER and CHUNK are negligible. The reason might be that not only the tagging accuracy of these two types of feature are not very high, but also NER feature

Table 3. Perplexity comparison of different LMs on PTB data set

Model	Tagging	PPL
4-gram	-	141.46
LSTM LM	-	98.73
Multi-task+POS	-	100.88
Multi-view+Multi-task+POS	-	93.47
Multi-view+POS	Standford	91.69
	LSTM	**93.82**
Multi-view+NER	Standford	97.63
	LSTM	**97.92**
Multi-view+CHUNK	Standford	94.34
	LSTM	**95.63**

is sparse and CHUNK feature is less precise. Based on this result, we only use the POS feature for the large scale Fisher data experiments.

Table 5 shows the perplexity, WER and CER on Swb-Fisher set using the POS feature. The observations from this data set are similar as those from Chinese SMS.

Table 4. Perplexity, WER (%) and SER (%) comparison on Chinese SMS task

Model	Tagging	PPL	WER	SER
4-gram	-	124.23	13.41	42.16
LSTM	-	102.11	11.30	41.59
Multi-task+POS	-	103.42	11.32	41.63
Multi-task+Multi-view+POS	-	98.24	10.91	40.89
Multi-view+POS	Standford	94.41	11.19	41.92
	LSTM	**98.02**	**10.83**	**40.71**
Multi-view+NER	Standford	101.88	11.28	41.59
	LSTM	**102.08**	**11.32**	**41.72**
Multi-view+CHUNK	Standford	96.71	11.25	41.63
	LSTM	**100.30**	**11.02**	**41.23**

When comparing our model with baseline, which is a ordinary LSTM LM, the perplexity, WER and SER are reduced with 4.0%, 4.0%, 2.0% relatively in both English and Chinese data set. Moreover, our proposed multi-view LSTM LM decreases the WER and SER with 4.4%, 2.2% and 3.2%, 2.8% than multi-view LSTM LM with Stanford POS. It needs to be emphasized that, our model doesn't perform better than multi-view LM with Stanford POS on PPL, because

Table 5. Perplexity, WER (%) and SER (%) comparison on English Fisher task

Model	Tagging	PPL	WER	SER
4-gram	-	79.12	16.3	53.75
LSTM	-	65.42	15.62	53.42
Multi-task+POS	-	65.93	15.60	53.65
Multi-task+Multi-view+POS	-	92.77	15.20	52.23
Multi-view+POS	Standford	60.24	15.73	53.40
	LSTM	**62.71**	**15.01**	**52.19**

the multi-view LM with Stanford POS feature uses future information which shouldn't be fed to LM, As we argued in Sect. 1.

For all data sets, the multi-view LSTM language model with POS feature by Stanford as well as LSTM tagging model is significantly improving with regards to perplexity, by comparing to the original LSTM RNN language model. The multi-view LSTM language model with Stanford POS works better in terms of perplexity, which is widely proved by previous works, but failed to show a commensurate increase in ASR-rescore task [8]. The stanford CoreNLP POS tagger model uses a maximum entropy algorithm [18] that utiliz future information, the future information only contributes to PPL task rather than the ASR-rescore task. A maximum entropy model uses contextual future information to calculate the posterior probability of the text. That is to say, adding this POS feature in language model training is equal to adding the future information in additional to the present word. This leads to a perplexity improvement, but no gain for WER and SER in the rescoring task is observed.

In addition, we want to confirm whether the POS tagging part contributed to the PPL or not, and thus add another contrasting experiment to validate our conclusion. In order to compare the influence of the tag information between the proposed and traditional model, we conduct experiments by removing and adding tag features to the model the input.

Table 6. Perplexity on different test-data

Data-set	Tagging	PPL	
		without-tag	with-tag
PTB	Standford	98.77	91.69
	LSTM	98.64	93.82
Fisher	Standford	66.25	60.24
	LSTM	65.79	62.71
SMS	Standford	102.20	94.41
	LSTM	102.13	98.02

The comparison is shown in Table 6. "Without-tag" means that we deliberately remove the feature feed from the trained tagging part of proposed model. The results indicate that tests with tag feature are generally better than those without. And the latter even does not outperform an ordinary LSTM LM, which means tag feature plays an important role in the LM performance. Furthermore, the result confirms the contribution of our POS tagging model. Moreover, our model performs better than the original multi-view LM without tags, which confirms the contribution of our tagging model in the proposed multi-view structure.

The proposed LSTM LM with word-synchronized auxiliary feature, performs better not only on ASR-rescore task but also PPL task. For this result, we consider the following two aspects. On one hand, the tagging model change the contextual information to word-synchronized auxiliary information, which is rather useful in ASR-rescore task. On the other hand, the proposed LM with unidirectional tagging process permits the decoding of LVCSR to proceed in real time.

5 Conclusion

In this paper, we propose a multi-view LSTM LM with unidirectional tagging model, which produces word-synchronized auxiliary feature that only incorporate previous contextual information. This auxiliary feature is combined with the word sequence to train a multi-view LSTM LM. Five different training methods for this model are tested, and the best one is used in the large-scale ASR task. In the comparison experiments between our model and related works (N-gram LM, multi-task LM, multi-view LM with Stanford tagging and multi-task combined with multi-view LM), the used data sets are PTB, English Fisher and Chinese SMS and PPL, WER and SER are used as the evaluation criteria. Our proposed model shows significant improvements for all word-level features including POS, NER and chunking on WER and SER. Especially for the POS feature on English Fisher, our proposed model not only gives gian (4.0%) on PPL, but also shows significant WER and SER reduction (relative 4.0% and 2.0%) in ASR task, compared with the baseline (LSTM LM). Most importantly, comparing to the multi-view LM with POS feature produced by traditional model (Stanford tool), our model shows better result of WER and SER (4.4% and 2.2%) in ASR-rescore task. For more related models like multi-task and multi-task combined with multi-view models, our model all shows achievement in varying degrees.

References

1. Katz, S.: Estimation of probabilities from sparse data for the language model component of a speech recognizer. IEEE Trans. Acoust. Speech Signal Process. **35**(3), 400–401 (1987)
2. Mikolov, T., Karafiát, M., Burget, L., Černocký, J., Khudanpur, S.: Recurrent neural network based language model. In: INTERSPEECH, Conference of the International Speech Communication Association, Makuhari, Chiba, Japan, September, DBLP, pp. 1045–1048 (2010)

3. Mikolov, T., Kombrink, S., Burget, L., Černocký, J., Khudanpur, S.: Extensions of recurrent neural network language model. In: IEEE International Conference on Acoustics, Speech and Signal Processing (ICASSP), pp. 5528–5531. IEEE (2011)
4. Hochreiter, S., Schmidhuber, J.: Long short-term memory. Neural Comput. **9**(8), 1735–1780 (1997)
5. Sundermeyer, M., Schlüter, R., Ney, H.: LSTM neural networks for language modeling. In: INTERSPEECH, vol. 31, pp. 194–197 (2012)
6. Shi, Y., Wiggers, P., Jonker, C.M.: Towards recurrent neural networks language models with linguistic and contextual features. In: INTERSPEECH, vol. 48, pp. 1664–1667 (2012)
7. Sang, T.K., Erik, F., Buchholz, S.: Introduction to the CoNLL-2000 shared task: chunking. In: The Workshop on Learning Language in Logic and the Conference on Computational Natural Language Learning, pp. 127–132 (2000)
8. Shi, Y., Larson, M., Pelemans, J., Jonker, C.M., Wambacq, P., Wiggers, P., Demuynck, K.: Integrating meta-information into recurrent neural network language models. Speech Commun. **73**, 64–80 (2015)
9. Collobert, R., Weston, J.: A unified architecture for natural language processing: deep neural networks with multitask learning. In: International Conference on Machine Learning, ICML 2008, pp. 160–167 (2008)
10. Liu, B., Lane, I.: Joint online spoken language understanding and language modeling with recurrent neural networks. In: IEEE International Conference on Acoustics, Speech and Signal Processing (ICASSP), pp. 160–167 (2016)
11. Schmid, H.: Part-of-speech tagging with neural networks. In: Proceedings of the 15th Conference on Computational Linguistics, vol. 1, pp. 172–176. Association for Computational Linguistics (1994)
12. Wang, P., Qian, Y., Soong, F.K., He, L., Zhao, H.: A unified tagging solution: bidirectional LSTM recurrent neural network with word embedding. Comput. Sci. (2015)
13. Viterbi, A.J.: Error bounds for convolutional codes and an asymptotically optimum decoding algorithm. IEEE Trans. Inf. Theory **13**, 260–269 (1967)
14. Ghahremani, P., Droppo, J.: Self-stabilized deep neural network. In: IEEE International Conference on Acoustics, Speech and Signal Processing, pp. 5450–5454 (2016)
15. Qi, L., Tian, T., Kai, Y.: An investigation on deep learning with beta stabilizer. In: IEEE International Conference on Signal Processing, pp. 557–561 (2017)
16. Taylor, A., Marcus, M., Santorini, B.: The penn treebank: an overview. In: Abeillé, A. (ed.) Treebanks. Text, Speech and Language Technology, vol. 20, pp. 5–22. Springer, Netherlands (2003). doi:10.1007/978-94-010-0201-1_1
17. Stolcke, A., et al.: SRILM-an extensible language modeling toolkit. In: International Conference on Spoken Language Processing, pp. 901–904 (2002)
18. Toutanova, K., Manning, C.D.: Enriching the knowledge sources used in a maximum entropy part-of-speech tagger. In: Joint Sigdat Conference on Empirical Methods in Natural Language Processing and Very Large Corpora: Held in Conjunction with the Meeting of the Association for Computational Linguistics, pp. 63–70 (2000)

Memory Augmented Attention Model for Chinese Implicit Discourse Relation Recognition

Yang Liu, Jiajun Zhang, and Chengqing Zong(✉)

Institute of Automation, Chinese Academy of Sciences, Beijing, China
{yang.liu2013,jjzhang,cqzong}@nlpr.ia.ac.cn

Abstract. Recently, Chinese implicit discourse relation recognition has attracted more and more attention, since it is crucial to understand the Chinese discourse text. In this paper, we propose a novel memory augmented attention model which represents the arguments using an attention-based neural network and preserves the crucial information with an external memory network which captures each discourse relation clustering structure to support the relation inference. Extensive experiments demonstrate that our proposed model can achieve the new state-of-the-art results on Chinese Discourse Treebank. We further leverage network visualization to show why our attention and memory model are effective.

Keywords: Chinese implicit relation recognition · Memory agumented neural network · Attention neural model

1 Introduction

The Chinese implicit discourse relation recognition has drawn more and more attention, because it is crucial for Chinese discourse understanding. Recently, the Chinese Discourse Treebank (CDTB) was released [1]. Although Chinese Discourse corpora shares the similar annotation framework with Penn Discourse Treebank (PDTB) for English, the statistical differences are obvious and significant. First, the connectives in Chinese occur much less frequently than those in English [2]. Second, the relation distribution in Chinese is more unbalanced than that in English. Third, the relation annotation for Chinese implicit case is more semantic due to the language essential characteristic [3]. These evidences indicate that implicit discourse relation recognition task for Chinese would be different from English.

Unfortunately, there is existing few work on Chinese discourse relation problem [4,7], thus our work is mainly inspired by the studies of English. Conventional approaches on identifying English discourse relation rely on handcrafted features extracted from two arguments, including word-pairs [8], VerbNet classes [10], brown clustering [24], production rules [15] and dependency rules [9]. These features indeed capture the correlation with discourse relation to some

M. Sun et al. (Eds.): CCL 2017 and NLP-NABD 2017, LNAI 10565, pp. 411–423, 2017.
https://doi.org/10.1007/978-3-319-69005-6_34

extent and achieve considerable performance in explicit cases. However, implicit discourse relation recognition is much harder, due to the absence of connectives[1]. Moreover, these hand-crafted features usually suffer from data sparsity problem [19] and are weak to capture the deep semantic feature of discourse [22].

To tackle this problem, deep learning methods are introduced to this area. It can learn dense real-valued vector representations of the arguments, which can capture the semantics in some extent, and alleviate the data sparsity problem simultaneously. Recently, a variety of neural network architectures have been explored on this task, such as convolution neural network [32], recursive network [22], feed-forward network [26], recurrent network [25], attentional network [23] and hybrid feature model [5,6]. These studies show that deep learning technology can achieve comparable or even better performance than the conventional approach with complicated hand-crafted features.

More recently, there are growing interest in memory augmented neural architecture. The advantage of extra memory is to capture and preserve useful information for task, the core of this idea is to keep those information in independent memory slot, and trigger and retrieval the related memory slot to support the inference. This design has proven effective in many works, including neural turing machine [17], memory network [28], dynamic memory networks [21], matching networks [29], etc.

Therefore, in this paper, we propose a memory augmented attention model (MAAM) to handle Chinese implicit discourse relation recognition task. It can represent arguments with an attention-based neural network, and then retrieval the external memory for relation inference support information, after that it combines the representation and memory support information to complete the classification.

More specifically, the procedure of our model can be divided into five steps: (1) Our model use a general encoder module to transform the input arguments from word sequence into dense vectors. (2) An attention module is proposed to score the importance of each word based on the given contexts and the weighted sum of the words is used as the argument representation. (3) An external memory is employed to produce an output based on this arguments representation. (4) The memory gate combines the memory output together with the attention representation to generate a refined representation of the arguments. (5) Finally, we stack a feed-forward network as the classification layer to predict the discourse relation. Extensive experiments and analysis show that our proposed method achieves the new state-of-the-art results on Chinese Discourse Treebank (CDTB).

2 Memory Augmented Attention Model

In this section, we first give an overview of the modules that build up memory augmented attention model (MAAM). We then introduce each module in detail and give intuitions about its formulation. A high-level illustration of the MAAM is shown in Fig. 1.

[1] The connective has strong correlation with discourse relations.

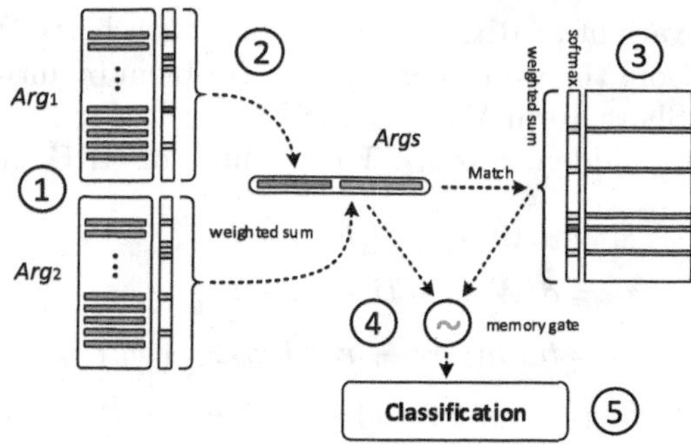

Fig. 1. The basic framework of our model, including (1) General Encoder Module, (2) Content-based Attention Module, (3) External Memory Module, (4) Memory Gate and (5) Classification Module.

As shown in Fig. 1, our framework consists of five modules: (1) general encoder module; (2) content-based attention module; (3) external memory module; (4) memory gate; (5) classification module.

The **General Encoder Module** encodes the word sequence of the two arguments into distributed vector representations. It is implemented by using the bidirectional recurrent neural network.

The **Attention Module** is proposed to capture the importance (attention) of each word in two arguments. We score the weight of each word in the argument based on its inner context and generates a weighted sum as the argument representation.

The **External Memory Module** consists of a fixed number of memory slots. The external memory computes the match score between the representation of arguments and yields a probability distribution. Then memory generates a weighted sum as memory output.

The **Memory Gate** is a learn-able controller component and it computes the convex combination of the original argument representation and the memory output to generate a refined representation.

The **Classification Module** stacks on the refined representation of the arguments and outputs the final discourse relation. We implement this module with a two-layer feed-forward network which can capture the interaction between two arguments implicitly.

2.1 General Encoder Module

In implicit discourse relation recognition, the input is the word sequence of two arguments Arg1 and Arg2. We choose recurrent neural network [16] to encode the arguments. Word embeddings are given as input to the recurrent network. At each time step t, the network updates its hidden state $h_t = RNN(x_t, h_{t-1})$, where x_t is the embedding vector of the t-th word of the input argument. In our model, we use a gated recurrent unit (GRU) to replace the normal RNN unit [12]. GRU is a variant of RNN, which works much better than the original one and suffers less from the vanishing gradient problem by introducing the gate structure like Long Short Term Memory (LSTM) [18]. Assume each time step t has an input x_t and a hidden state h_t. The formula of GRU shows as follows:

$$z_t = \sigma(W_z x_t + U_z h_{t-1} + b_z) \tag{1}$$

$$r_t = \sigma(W_r x_t + U_r h_{t-1} + b_r) \tag{2}$$

$$\tilde{h_t} = tanh(W x_t + r_t \circ U h_{t-1} + b_h) \tag{3}$$

$$h_t = z_t \circ h_{t-1} + (1 - z_t) \circ \tilde{h_t} \tag{4}$$

In brief, the simple version of GRU is $h_t = GRU(x_t; h_{t-1})$. RNN and its variant as described above read an input sequence x in order, starting from the first word to the last one. However, we expect the representation of each word to summarize not only the preceding words, but also the following words. Thus, we propose to use a bidirectional RNN [27]. A Bi-RNN consists of a forward and a backward RNN. The forward RNN reads the input sequence from left to right, while the backward RNN reads the sequence in the reverse order.

$$\overrightarrow{h_t} = \overrightarrow{GRU}(x_t, \overrightarrow{h_{t-1}}) \tag{5}$$

$$\overleftarrow{h_t} = \overleftarrow{GRU}(x_t, \overleftarrow{h_{t-1}}) \tag{6}$$

We obtain representation for each word by concatenating two hidden state sequences generated by the forward and backward RNNs.

$$h_t = [\overrightarrow{h_t}; \overleftarrow{h_t}] \tag{7}$$

In this way, the representation h_t of each word contains the summary of both the preceding words and the following words.

2.2 Attention Module

After obtaining the representation of the arguments by treating each word equally in general encoder module, we now apply the content-based attention module to score the importance of each word in the arguments. We evaluate the weight of each word only based on the its inner context. The motivation behind it is that since the connective is absent in implicit samples, we can utilize the context of the arguments to generate an appropriate representation. Obviously, the contribution of each word in the context is not same and it is natural to capture the correlation between the context dependent word feature and the discourse relation using attention mechanism. In our case, we use a multilayer perception to implement the attention module:

$$e_t = u_a^T tanh(W_a h_t + b_a) \tag{8}$$

Notice that h_t is generated by the general encoder module. The weight of each word h_t is computed using softmax:

$$a_t = \frac{exp(e_t)}{\sum_{j=1}^{T} exp(e_j)} \tag{9}$$

For instance, we consider the vector v_{Arg1} the weighted sum of the representations of Arg1:

$$v_{Arg1} = \sum_{j=1}^{T} a_t h_t \tag{10}$$

We generate the vector of Arg2 in the same way. Then we directly concatenate two vectors as the representation of arguments:

$$v_{Args} = [v_{Arg1}; v_{Arg2}] \tag{11}$$

2.3 External Memory Module

As long as we have the semantic representation of arguments, we can use it to interact with our augmented memory. Our external memory consists of the memory slots, which are activated by the particular pattern of the arguments and generate corresponding output as response. This memory output will be used in following step to refine the original argument representation. Concretely, we first compute the similarity score between v_{Args} and each memory slot m_i and produce a normalized weight w_i using similarity measure $K[\cdot, \cdot]$. Also, in order to improve the focus, a sharpen factor β is needed.

$$w_i \leftarrow \frac{exp(\beta K[v_{Args}, m_i])}{\sum_j exp(\beta K[v_{Args}, m_j]))} \tag{12}$$

In our case, we use the cosine similarity as our metric.

$$K[u, v] = \frac{u \cdot v}{||u|| \cdot ||v||} \tag{13}$$

Then, we generate the output from memory according to the weights.

$$m = \sum_i w_i m_i \tag{14}$$

The memory design is mainly inspired by Neural Turing Machine [17]. The memory will capture the common pattern of discourse relation distribution during training. For example, when an input relation sample accesses the external memory, the memory will response with an output vector which contains the information mostly related to the similar samples it has seen before. Intuitively, samples with similar representations usually belong to the same discourse relation. In summary, the memory actually implicitly holds the discourse relation clustering information for the following classification. The external memory component is randomly initialized and optimized during training.

2.4 Memory Gate

Once we can access the output information m from memory, we can use it to generate the refined representation $\widetilde{v}$ along with the original representation of arguments v_{Args}. We propose an interpolation strategy to combine these two vectors together and employ a sigmoid function called memory gate to control the final output.

$$\alpha = \sigma(W_g[v_{Args}; m] + b_g) \tag{15}$$

where σ is a sigmoid function. We then compute a convex combination of the memory output and the original argument representation:

$$\widetilde{v} = \alpha \cdot v_{Args} + (1 - \alpha) \cdot m \tag{16}$$

The memory gate is a learn-able neural layer. The idea behind it is that although memory can return the clustering structure information which is potentially useful. Also, we build a gate mechanism to control the output of memory and mix them with the original argument representations.

2.5 Classification Module

Given the refined representation vector $\widetilde{v}$ of the arguments, we implement the classification module using a two-layer feed-forward network which is followed by a standard softmax layer.

$$\tilde{y} = softmax(tanh(W_c\widetilde{v} + b_c)) \tag{17}$$

where $\tilde{y}$ is our output predicted label. During training, we optimize the network parameters by maximizing the cross-entropy loss function between the true and predicted labels.

3 Experiments

3.1 Corpora

We evaluate our model on Chinese Discourse Treebank (CDTB) [1–3,25], which has been published as standard corpora in CoNLL shared task 2016. In our work, we experiment on the ten relations in this corpus following the setup of suggestions given by the shared task. We directly adopt the standard training set, development set, test set and blind test set. We also use the word embeddings provided by the CoNLL 2016.

3.2 Training Details

To train our model, the objective function is defined as the cross-entropy loss between the outputs of the softmax layer and the ground-truth class labels. We use adadelta algorithm to optimize the whole neural networks. To avoid over-fitting, dropout operation is applied on the layer before softmax.

3.3 Experimental Results

To exhibit the effectiveness of our model, our experiment results consists of three parts: baselines, MAAM variants and MAAMs.

Baselines: We collect two baselines for our experiments, the one is "Conjunction" and another is "Focused RNN" which achieved the ***best*** result in CoNLL 2016 shared task.

We implement the first "Conjunction" system which directly annotates every test sample as "Conjunction". The reason behind is that due to the unbalanced problem of corpora (see Table 1), this baseline system is very strong according to the CoNLL report by Xue et al. [25] and many participated systems cannot beat this baseline.

The "Focused RNN" is proposed by Weiss and Bajec [31], which is implemented with a focused recurrent neural network which can selective react to different context. Its result is directly selected from the report of CoNLL 2016.

MAAM variants: Since there are few published results on CDTB, it is necessary to show variants of our model. These variants are helpful to understand the contribution of each module, since the variants we proposed is only sightly different from our final model. The detail of each MAAM variants is shown below.

MAAM+0memslot+no Encoder: It use no encoder module at all. In this variant, it directly uses word embedding sequence to encode arguments, and applies the same attention layer on them. This model explores the effectiveness of embedding features missing context dependent information.

MAAM+0memslot+GRU Encoder: This system only uses single GRU as the encoder of input module, it is used to understand the effectiveness of bidirectional encoder.

MAAM+0memslot+Mean(no Attention): Instead of using attention mechanism, this system directly represent argument as mean of all hidden states in Bi-GRU, treating each word in argument equally.

We can see from Table 2 that the proposed MAAM module is better than all the variants. It is obvious that both of the context and the attention are beneficial for distributed argument representation in discourse relation.

MAAMs: Now, we compare our memory augmented attention model (MAAM) with other approaches in the closed track. Our memory models (containing different numbers of slots $[1, 20, 50, 100, 150]$ can outperform the two baselines, and the one with 20 slots achieves the best result, which is the new state-of-the-art on CTDB. Specifically, we observe an interesting phenomenon in our memory models. Along with the number of memory slots grow, the performance is improved first (from 0 to 20 slots) but is gradually decreased (from 20 to 50, 100 and 150). We speculate that the under-fitting problem (no adequate training samples) is the main reason. When comparing to MAAM+0memslot, we can see that all the settings of memory model can obtain better results, demonstrating the effectiveness of proposed external memory component.

Table 1. The Experiment results on CoNLL 2016 Shared Task

System		Development	Test	Blind test
Baseline	Conjunction	61.96	63.59	68.14
	Focused RNN (2016, Best Result)	**66.67**	**64.07**	**70.68**
MAAM Variants	MAAM+0memslot+no Encoder	66.63	64.18	70.62
	MAAM+0memslot+GRU Encoder	66.67	65.01	71.62
	MAAM+0memslot+Mean(no Attention)	66.23	64.01	70.45
MAAMs	MAAM+0memslot	66.87	65.03	71.89
	MAAM+1memslot	67.00	65.02	72.10
	MAAM+20memslots	**67.54**	**66.02**	**73.16**
	MAAM+50memslots	68.43	65.92	72.77
	MAAM+100memslots	68.20	65.73	72.56
	MAAM+150memslots	67.44	65.08	72.38

3.4 Discussion and Analysis

The experimental results demonstrate the superiority of our memory augmented attention model. In this section, we discuss the behavior of the external memory and the attention module in the network.

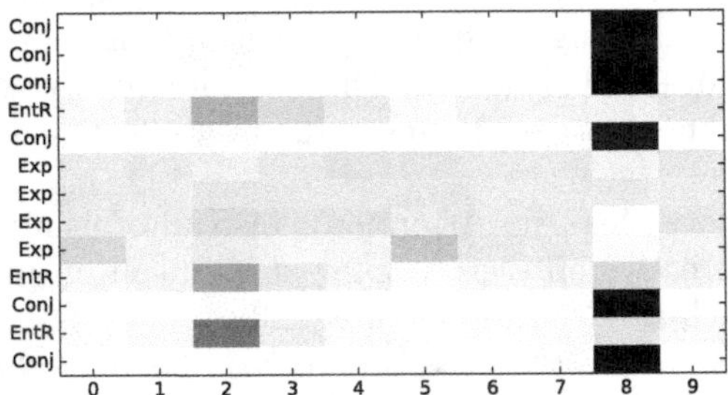

Fig. 2. Memory activation for different relation samples. Horizontal coordinate reflects the activation of 10 memory slots. Vertical coordinate reflects different discourse implicit relation samples. (Conjunction-Conj; Expansion-Exp; EntRel-EntR) Each row in figure represent the different activation of different memory slot for each input discourse relation sample. The deeper color indicate higher score.

Memory Analysis: The results show that the external memory component is significantly helpful for the performance. In order to understand how our memory component works, we show a memory component which contains 10 memory slots in Fig. 2. As we mentioned above, the memory slot will be triggered when the relevant input arguments retrial the memory component. The memory will compute scores for each memory slot based on input arguments, we call these scores as activation. We now feed 13 arguments belong to different discourse relation into memory component. The activations of each 10 memory slots triggered by different relation samples are shown in Fig. 2, the deeper color means this slot achieve higher activation, each row in Fig. 2 exhibits the different activation of memory slot for every input relation arguments. As we can see that, arguments belong to the same relation always trigger the same slots (location) in memory component. For instance, the "EntRel" samples always focus on the 2-nd slot (in horizontal) and the "Conjunction" samples trigger the 8-th slot.

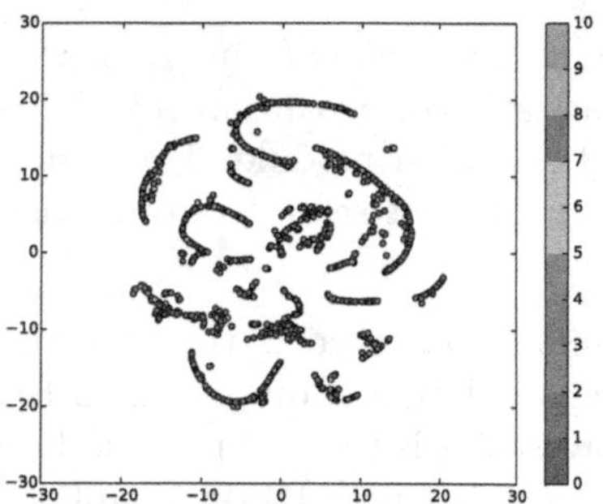

Fig. 3. t-SNE for Chinese discourse relation distribution. Notice that clustering for each relation in figure. The "Expansion" is in blue. Conjunction-0; Expansion-1; EntRel-2; AltLex-3; Causation-4; Contrast-5; Purpose-6; Conditional-7; Temporal-8; Progression-9. As we can see, the "Conjunction" relation plays as a background for the rest of relations.

Representation Analysis: In order to understand the discourse relation distribution (representation) in our model, we show the t-SNE visualization of Chinese implicit discourse relation samples in Fig. 3 (using feature space from classification module). As we can see, the "Conjunction" relation samples mostly play as a background for any other relation. This may be caused by the definition of "conjunction".[2] Meanwhile, other relation samples are hard to distinguish from "Conjunction" samples. This situation also indicates that the Chinese implicit relation recognition is a difficult task.

Attention Analysis: Our attention module scores each word relying on the inner content. It captures the correlation between content and discourse relation, different from independent word embedding information which can not access the surrounding context. In Fig. 4, the "Causation" relation example extracted from corpora shows our model pays more attention on the content words than the function words. We annotated the alignment relation between the Chinese relation sample and its English translation. The attention module focuses on the "*international;steady;expansion*" in Arg1 and "*for China's*

[2] Conjunction: relation between two equal-status statements serving a common communicative function, *from CoNLL 2016*. It is relative ambiguous.

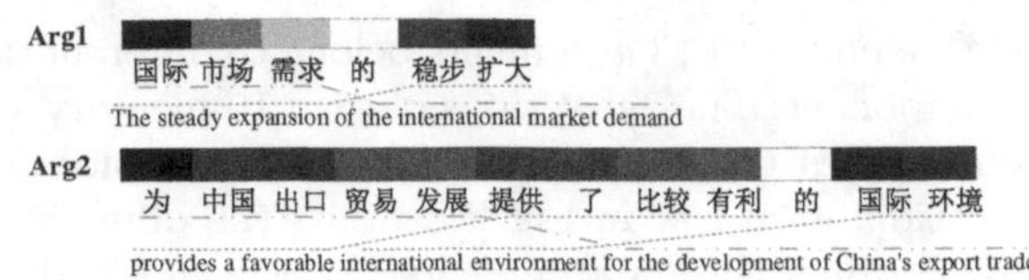

Fig. 4. Attention for *Causation* samples. The attention module focus on the "international, steady, expansion" in Arg1 and "for China's export,provides,international environment" in Arg2.

export;*provides*;*international environment*" in Arg2, which can be roughly considered as a simple summarization of two arguments. This example demonstrates the effect of the proposed attention module. The result of attention makes us to wonder if we should give different score to word when we deal with different relation.

Discussion: Another issue we observed is the ambiguity and data imbalance of Chinese implicit discourse relation. Comparing to English, Chinese contains more less explicit connectives, this is the main reason for Chinese implicit reason recognition problem. Therefore, many relation samples is hard distinguish from "Conjunction", unless it is pretty obvious for annotator. Our approach is actually based on a assumption that every relation has a *prototype* sample, thus we hope our memory component can capture each discourse relation prototype and identify it from unseen sample. However, we didn't observed positive result to support our assumption.

4 Related Work

Implicit discourse relation recognition has been a hot topic in recent years. However, most of the approaches focus on English. There are mainly two directions related to our study: (1) English implicit discourse relation recognition using neural networks, and (2) memory augmented networks.

Conventional implicit relation recognition approaches rely on kinds of handcrafted features [8,11,24], these surface features usually suffer from sparsity problem. Then, neural network based approaches are proposed. In order to alleviate feature sparsity problem, Ji and Eisenstein [19] first transform surface features of arguments into low dimension distributed representations to boost the performance. A discourse document usually covers different scale unit from word, sentence to paragraph. To model this kind of structures, Li [22] and Ji [20] both introduced the recursive network to represent arguments to facilitate the discourse parsing.Considering the discourse relation recognition as text classification problem, Liu et al. [23] propose a convolution neural network (CNN) to detect the sequence feature in arguments to predict relation. Rutherford et al. [25] conduct experiments to explore the effectiveness of feedforward neural network and recurrent neural network. Liu and Li [23] use attention mechanism to refine the representation of arguments by reweighing the importance of different parts of argument. Braud and Denis [13,14] utilize the word representation to improve implicit discourse relation classification. Their method investigates the correlation between word embedding and discourse relation.

The memory model is inspired by recently proposed memory augmented network. The Neural Turing Machine (NTM) [17] builds an external memory component to preserve kinds of subsequence pattern explicitly, and makes NTM more effective to learn from training samples. Another type of memory augmented network is memory network [28], which is different from NTM and works more like a cache for particular data. The memory network saves the sentences in memory to support multiple step question & answer inference. More recently, the matching network is proposed by Vinyals et al. [29], its memory component caches the common pattern of representation and corresponding label of training samples. It predicts label by matching input sample with memory caches then generate weighted sum label (with matching distribution) as final output. Since the memory network can capture particular pattern of samples and be optimized during training, we extend it in our framework to maintain crucial information for Chinese implicit relation recognition. The experimental results verify the efficacy of the proposed memory network and the memory augmented model achieves the best performance on CDTB.

5 Conclusion

In this paper, we have proposed a memory augmented attention model for Chinese implicit Discourse relation recognition. The attention network is employed to learn the semantic representation of the two arguments Arg1 and Arg2. The memory network is introduced to capture the underlying clustering structure of samples. The extensive experiments show that our proposed method achieves the new state-of-the-art results on CDTB.

Acknowledgments. The research work has been supported by the Natural Science Foundation of China under Grant No. 61333018 and No. 61403379.

References

1. Xue, N.: Annotating discourse connectives in the Chinese treebank. In: Proceedings of the Workshop on Frontiers in Corpus Annotations II: Pie in the Sky, pp. 84–91 (2005)
2. Zhou, Y., Xue, N.: PDTB-style discourse annotation of Chinese text. In: ACL 2012, pp. 69–77 (2012)
3. Zhou, Y., Xue, N.: The Chinese discourse treebank: a Chinese corpus annotated with discourse relations. Lang. Resour. Eval. **49**(2), 397–431 (2015)
4. Mei, T., Zhou, Y., Zong, C.: Automatically parsing Chinese discourse based on maximum entropy. Acta Scientiarum Naturalium Universitatis Pekinensis **50**(1), 125–132 (2014)

5. Li, H., Zhang, J., Zong, C.: Implicit discourse relation recognition for English and Chinese with multi-view modeling and effective representation learning. ACM Trans. Asian Low-Resour. Lang. Inf. Process. **16**(3), 19 (2017)
6. Li, H., Zhang, J., Zhou, Y., Zong, C.: Predicting implicit discourse relation with multi-view modeling and effective representation learning. In: Lin, C.-Y., Xue, N., Zhao, D., Huang, X., Feng, Y. (eds.) ICCPOL/NLPCC -2016. LNCS, vol. 10102, pp. 374–386. Springer, Cham (2016). doi:10.1007/978-3-319-50496-4_31
7. Li, Y., Feng, W., Sun, J., Kong, F., Zhou, G.: Building Chinese discourse corpus with connective-driven dependency tree structure. In: EMNLP, pp. 2105–2114 (2014)
8. Lin, Z., Kan, M.-Y., Ng, H.T.: Recognizing implicit discourse relations in the penn discourse treebank. In EMNLP, pp. 343–351 (2009)
9. Lin, Z., Ng, H.T., Kan, M.-Y.: A PDTB-styled end-to-end discourse parser. Nat. Lang. Eng. **20**(02), 151–184 (2014)
10. Kang, X., Li, H., Zhou, L., Zhang, J., Zong, C.: An end-to-end Chinese discourse parser with adaptation to explicit and nonexplicit relation recognition. In: ACL-CoNLL Shared Task, pp. 27–32 (2016)
11. Pitler, E., Nenkova, A.: Using syntax to disambiguate explicit discourse connectives in text. In: ACL-IJCNLP, pp. 13–16 (2009)
12. Bahdanau, D., Cho, K., Bengio, Y.: Neural machine translation by jointly learning to align and translate. arXiv preprint arXiv:1409.0473 (2014)
13. Braud, C., Denis, P.: Comparing word representations for implicit discourse relation classification. In: EMNLP (2015)
14. Braud, C., Denis, P.: Learning connective-based word representations for implicit discourse relation identification. In: EMNLP, pp. 203–213 (2016)
15. Chandrasekar, P., Zhang, X., Chakravarty, S., Ray, A., Krulick, J., Rozovskaya, A.: The Virginia Tech system at CoNLL-2016 shared task on shallow discourse parsing. In: CoNLL Shared Task 2016, pp. 115–121 (2016)
16. Elman, J.L.: Distributed representations simple recurrent networks, and grammatical structure. Mach. Learn. **7**(2–3), 195–225 (1991)
17. Graves, A., Wayne, G., Danihelka, I.: Neural turing machines. arXiv preprint arXiv:1410.5401 (2014)
18. Hochreiter, S., Schmidhuber, J.: Long short-term memory. Neural Comput. **9**(8), 1735–1780 (1997)
19. Ji, Y., Eisenstein, J.: Representation learning for text-level discourse parsing. In: ACL, pp. 13–24 (2014)
20. Ji, Y., Eisenstein, J.: One vector is not enough: entity-augmented distributed semantics for discourse relations. TACL **3**, 329–344 (2015)
21. Kumar, A., Irsoy, O., Jonathan, S., Bradbury, J., English, R., Pierce, B., Ondruska, P., Gulrajani, I., Socher, R.: Ask me anything: dynamic memory networks for natural language processing. CoRR, abs/1506.07285 (2015)
22. Li, J., Li, R., Hovy, E.H.: Recursive deep models for discourse parsing. In: EMNLP, pp. 2016–2069 (2014)
23. Liu, Y., Li, S.: Recognizing implicit discourse relations via repeated reading: neural networks with multi-level attention. In EMNLP, pp. 1224–1233 (2016)
24. Rutherford, A., Xue, N.: Discovering implicit discourse relations through brown cluster pair representation and coreference patterns. In: EACL, p. 645 (2014)
25. Rutherford, A.T., Demberg, V., Xue, N.: Neural network models for implicit discourse relation classification in English and Chinese without surface features. arXiv preprint arXiv:1606.01990 (2016)

26. Schenk, N., Chiarcos, C., Donandt, K., Ronnqvist, S., Stepanov, E.A., Riccardi, G.: Do we really need all those rich linguistic features? a neural network-based approach to implicit sense labeling. In: ACL, pp. 41–50 (2016)
27. Schuster, M., Paliwal, K.K.: Bidirectional recurrent neural networks. IEEE Trans. Signal Process. **45**(11), 2673–2681 (1997)
28. Sukhbaatar, S., Weston, J., Fergus, R., et al.: End-to-end memory networks. In: NIPS, pp. 2440–2448 (2015)
29. Vinyals, O., Blundell, C., Lillicrap, T., Kavukcuoglu, K., Wierstra, D.: Matching networks for one shot learning. In: NIPS 2016, pp. 3630–3638 (2016)
30. Wang, J., Lan, M.: Two end-to-end shallow discourse parsers for English and Chinese in CoNLL-2016 shared task. In: CoNLL-2016 Shared Task, pp. 33–40 (2016)
31. Weiss, G., Bajec, M.: Discourse sense classification from scratch using focused RNNs. In: ACL 2016 vol. 1(100), p. 50 (2016)
32. Xue, N., Ng, H.T., Rutherford, A., Webber, B., Wang, C., Wang, H.: CoNLL 2016 shared task on multilingual shallow discourse parsing. In: Proceedings of the CoNLL-16 Shared Task, pp. 1–19 (2016)

Natural Logic Inference for Emotion Detection

Han Ren[1], Yafeng Ren[2(✉)], Xia Li[1], Wenhe Feng[1], and Maofu Liu[3]

[1] Laboratory of Language Engineering and Computing, Guangdong University of Foreign Studies, Guangzhou 510420, China
hanren@gdufs.edu.cn, {200211025,201610128}@oamail.gdufs.edu.cn

[2] Collaborative Innovation Center for Language Research and Services, Guangdong University of Foreign Studies, Guangzhou 510420, China
201610151@oamail.gdufs.edu.cn

[3] College of Computer Science and Technology, Wuhan University of Science and Technology, Wuhan 430065, Hubei, China
liumaofu@wust.edu.cn

Abstract. Current research on emotion detection focuses on the recognizing explicit emotion expressions in text. In this paper, we propose an approach based on textual inference to detect implicit emotion expressions, that is, to capture emotion detection as an logical inference issue. The approach builds a natural logic system, in which emotional detection are decomposed into a series of logical inference process. The system also employ inference knowledge from textural inference resources for reasoning complex expressions in emotional texts. Experimental results show the efficiency in detecting implicit emotional expressions.

Keywords: Natural logic · Textual inference · Emotion detection · Implicit emotional expression

1 Introduction

Emotion detection refers to the identification of emotional expressions in texts, which are, although there is still no strict definition, generally categorized as happiness, sadness, anger, shame, and so on. As one of the most important research topics in natural language processing, emotion detection is widely used in opinion mining, product recommendation, dialog system, and so on [1].

Current research on emotion detection can be mainly classified as the feature-based and knowledge-based approaches. Feature-based approaches employ machine learning algorithms to classify emotion by building appropriate features [2–4], while knowledge-based approaches employ emotion lexicons [5], domain lexicons [6] or patterns extracted [7] to detect emotions. Many approaches show state-of-the-art performances in detecting explicit emotion expressions. However, it is hard to achieve acceptable performances of detecting implicit emotion expressions. For example,

M. Sun et al. (Eds.): CCL 2017 and NLP-NABD 2017, LNAI 10565, pp. 424–436, 2017.
https://doi.org/10.1007/978-3-319-69005-6_35

T: *The husband breaks his wife's head.*
Since there is no explicit emotion words in the sentence, it is difficult to identify the emotion of the agent *husband* by emotion lexicons or to define appropriate features to detect the emotion. In fact, *break* entails the action *hit*, while *hit* holds the emotion of *anger*[1]. Apparently, such inference process contributes to identifying the emotion and its holder.

Based on this idea, we propose an approach, that is, to treat emotion detection as an textual inference problem. Textual inference refers to that, given a text fragment, the goal of textual inference is to recognize a hypothesis that can be inferred from it or not. Textual inference is a notable field of research that are leveraged in many natural language processing areas, such as document summarization, information retrieval and question answering [8].

For emotion detection, a series of premises derived from the emotional sentence T can be generated, for example, a premise H can be *The husband is angry*. Then we judge if H can be inferred from T. If so, it means that the meaning of H is contained in T, in other words, H is true. Therefore, we can draw a conclusion that the emotion of the husband is angry. The idea has two advantages: (1) an implicit emotion detection problem can be formalized as an textual inference one, which can be handled by many state-of-the-art textual inference models for better performances; (2) the emotion holder in a sentence can be easily identified if a premise generated by such sentence is judged to be true.

In this paper, a natural logic-based approach is proposed to model the emotion detection process, and the aim is to capture emotional inference by appealing directly to the logical expressions. In this approach, inference relations between texts are viewed as logical containment ones [9], and emotional reasoning between semantic units in a same synset can be carried out like: *break* $\sqsubseteq$ *hit*, *hit* $\sqsubseteq$ *angry*, which shows a distinct cue of implicit emotions. Also, inferable relations without emotions are identified in this approach, like other textual inference systems, to benefit the emotional reasoning. Experiments show that the approach shows a higher efficiency on detecting implicit emotion expressions.

The rest of this paper is organized as follows. Section 2 gives a brief introduction of related work. Sections 3 and 4 gives a detailed description of the emotion detection approach based on natural logic. Section 5 shows experimental results as well as some discussions. Finally, the conclusion is drawn in Sect. 6.

2 Related Work

Knowledge-based Approaches for emotion detection focus on the construction of affective lexicons, and the assumption is that rich knowledge with emotion expressions will help to detect explicit emotion as well as implicit one. The most well-known emotion lexicon in English is WordNet-Affect, which annotates the words that represents emotional concepts in WordNet, then expands emotion word lists through synsets

[1] The mapping relation can be found in emotion lexicons, such as EmoLex.

that contains those words. Based on the idea, emotion lexicons of other languages such as Japanese [10] and Chinese [5] are built. However, such approaches may achieve low performances when facing complex emotion expressions, since the emotion of a single word can not determine the overall emotion type of expressions.

In order to handle emotion detection without complex knowledge machining, machine learning-based approaches are proposed, and feature engineering becomes a main strategy in order to profile emotional expressions in multiple aspects. Rao et al. [2] used spectral and prosodic features to recognize emotions, while Xu et al. [4] employed intra-sentences features as well as sentential contexts to classify emotions for sentential emotion expressions. In order to acquire features effectively and automatically, deep learning-based approaches are proposed, and researchers employ various deep models such as CNN [11], RNN [12] and LSTM [13] to identify sentiment in social texts. Although such approaches achieve better performances than lexicon-based or rule-based approaches in most cases, it is still difficult to detect implicit emotions in texts, since finding implicit emotions needs such systems having the ability of complex knowledge inference or deep semantic analysis.

3 Natural Logic for Emotion Detection

Logic-based approaches have been explored for textual inference, and the aim is to capture logical inferences by appealing directly to the structure of language. In comparison with other logic systems, natural logic is more appropriate to handle inference relations in natural language, since it has no need to define complex and strict production rules. It is also appropriate to handle commonplace phenomena such as negation, antonymy and downward-monotone quantifiers [14], which usually appear in emotional texts.

Based on the theoretical framework on natural logic and monotonicity calculus [15, 16], natural logic systems such as NatLog [17] and NaturalLI [18] are built for textual inference. Inspired by them, we construct a complete proof system in three parts: (1) define atomic relations; (2) define monotonicity over atomic relations and; (3) describe a proof system. Different from those systems, our system takes emotional relations into account, which provide efficiency for reasoning emotional expressions.

3.1 Atomic Relations

Atomic relations represent logical relations between fundamental units for logic deduction. In terms of textual inference, the uppermost relation is entailment, that is, one text entails another or not. In natural logic, entailment is viewed as a semantic containment relation, which can be analogous to containment relation in set relations. For example, the concept *car* entails the concept *vehicle* means the set *vechicle* contains the concept *car*. Following this idea, relations referring inference are easy to be defined using set relations.

Another important relation in the system is affection, which shows a relation between a state or action and an emotion reflected by it. Sometimes, affection can be roughly viewed as entailment, for example, the action *cry* reflects the emotion *sadness*, and it can be explained that *cry* entails *sadness*. In fact, however, affection expresses emotional reflection rather than containment relation in a fine view. For example, *celebrate* may indicates the emotion *joy*, whereas it is inappropriate to say that *celebration* belongs to the set *joy*. For a better understanding, a specialized relation should be defined to denote the relation between a state or action and an emotion reflected.

Table 1. Atomic relations in the system.

Relation	Description
$x \sqsubseteq y$	$x \rightarrow y,\ y \nrightarrow x$
$x \sqsupseteq y$	$x \nrightarrow y,\ y \rightarrow x$
$x \equiv y$	$x \rightarrow y,\ y \rightarrow x$
$x \wedge y$	x is the negation of y
$x \triangleright y$	x reflects y
$x \# y$	x and y are irrelative

Following the idea in [14], we define six relations shown in Table 1. In the table, relation represents logical relations, while description means semantic inference ones, in which $x \rightarrow y$ denotes x entails y and $x \nrightarrow y$ denotes x does not entail y.

Some examples for each atomic relation are shown as follows. Note that a denotation may be a lexiconsl entry, a phrase or an entailment rule, for example, *help X* $\sqsubseteq$ *give X a hand*.

$$
\begin{gathered}
car \sqsubseteq vehicle \\
plene \sqsupseteq jet\ plane \\
U.S. \equiv America \\
agree \curlywedge not\ agreee \\
celebrate \triangleright joy \\
car \# joy
\end{gathered}
$$

For the validity of emotional inference, some constraints are defined: in the first relation $\sqsubseteq$ in Table 1, if x is an emotional denotation, y must be an unemotional one; in the second relation $\sqsupseteq$, if y is an emotional denotation, x must be an unemotional one; in the third and the fourth relation, denotations of both side have the same category, namely they are both emotional denotations or unemotional ones; in the relation of affection $\triangleright$, x must be an unemotional denotation and y must be an emotional one. Such constraints ensure the monotonicity of emotional reasoning, namely each reasoning step referring emotions always proceeds from factive denotations to emotional ones.

3.2 Monotonicity

Monotonicity describes the containment relation between a meaning and its extension and intension of a denotation. More specifically, monotonicity shows if a meaning can be inferred from any premise set containing or contained by a set, i.e., subset or superset, which is the premise set that the meaning can be inferred from it. For textual inference, the aim of monotonicity calculus it to map semantic relations of text pieces (words, phrases, etc.) to semantic relations of sentences.

There are, generally, three monotonicity classes, that is, upward-monotone, downward-monotone and non-monotone. The upward-monotone indicates the extension of a meaning, while the downward-monotone indicates the intension of a meaning. In textual inference, many entailment phenomena can be cast as upward-monotone functions, such as *buy a car* $\sqsubseteq$ *buy a vehicle*, since *car* $\sqsubseteq$ *vehicle*. As to language expressions including negative words, downward-monotone may exists, such as *have not a vehicle* $\sqsubseteq$ *have not a car*, since *car* $\sqsubseteq$ *vehicle*. Table 2 shows the mapping relations for downward-monotone in the system.

Table 2. Downward-monotone mapping relations. *r* is the relation between two text pieces(e.g., words), and *f_* is the relation of the two sentences except the relation *r*.

r	$\sqsubseteq$	$\sqsupseteq$	$\equiv$	$\wedge$	$\triangleright$	#
f	$\sqsupseteq$	$\sqsubseteq$	$\equiv$	$\wedge$	#	#

As an example, a formal description of monotonicity over three classes for the relation entailment is shown as follows, along with MacCartney and Manning [17]: for all $x, y \in D$, the function f is upward-monotone iff $x \sqsubseteq y$ entails $f(x) \sqsubseteq f(y)$, f is downward-monotone iff $x \sqsubseteq y$ entails $f(y) \sqsubseteq f(x)$, and f is non-monotone iff $x \sqsubseteq y$ neither entails $f(x) \sqsubseteq f(y)$ nor $f(y) \sqsubseteq f(x)$.

There is still an issue when reasoning emotional expressions, that is, how to define monotonicity for the relation of affection. Since such relation can be roughly treated as the relation entailment, we may define it with an upward-monotone function, that is, for all $x \in D$, $y \in M$, the function f is upward-monotone iff $x \triangleright y$ entails $f(x) \triangleright f(y)$. Here D denotes an unemotional expression set and M an emotional expression set. However, such monotonicity calculus may lead to wrong inference. For example, according to the relation *beat* $\triangleright$ *angry*, we may obtain a correct relation that *The husband beat his wife* $\triangleright$ *The husband is angry* and a wrong relation that *The husband beat his wife* $\triangleright$ *His wife is angry*. The reason lies in that the relation *beat* $\triangleright$ *angry* holds only if the agent of the action beat is same with the holder of the emotion *angry*. More specifically, an action may lead to multiple emotions, thus yielding an appropriate emotional reasoning depends on judging if the agent or patient of such action and the holder of an emotion is same.

Therefore, it is necessary to make constraints for the monotonicity function of the relation affection. We re-define an upward-monotone function for the relation affection as follows: the function f is upward-monotone iff $x \triangleright y$ entails $f(x) \triangleright f(y)$, and the agent of x and the holder of the emotion y are same. Here we employ Stanford parser[2] to acquire agent of each sentence by shallow semantic analysis. If such agent is not found, the emotion holder labeled in the sentence will be the default agent.

[2] http://nlp.stanford.edu/software/lex-parser.shtml.

3.3 Proof System

The aim of the proof system is to join semantic relations, by which semantic relations between sentences can be inferred according to all atomic relations. Inferences iteratively join two relations together to get the final entailment relation. Such join relations are shown in Table 3.

Table 3. The join table of the proof system. Note that join relation is also subject to constraints mentioned in Sect. 3.1. For example, for $x \rhd y$, $y \sqsubseteq z$, if y is an emotional denotation and z is an unemotional denotation, then $\rhd \bowtie \sqsubseteq_{\ominus} = \#$.

$\bowtie$	$\sqsubseteq$	$\sqsupseteq$	$\equiv$	$\wedge$	$\rhd$	#
$\sqsubseteq$	$\sqsubseteq$	#	$\sqsubseteq$	$\sqsupseteq$	$\rhd$	#
$\sqsupseteq$	#	$\sqsupseteq$	$\sqsupseteq$	$\sqsubseteq$	#	#
$\equiv$	$\sqsubseteq$	$\sqsupseteq$	$\equiv$	$\wedge$	$\rhd$	#
$\wedge$	#	#	$\wedge$	$\equiv$	#	#
$\rhd$	$\rhd$	#	$\rhd$	#	#	#
#	#	#	#	#	#	#

The following example illustrates the proof process using the join table. Considering the text pair(T,H):

T: *The husband breaks his wife's head.*
H: *The husband is angry.*

Relations between T and H are listed as follows:

r_1: $\sqsubseteq$ *(break, hit)*
r_2: $\sqsubseteq$ *(his wife's head, his wife)*
r_3: $\rhd$ *(hit, angry)*

Assume $S = \{s_i\}$ is a transforming text set, let $s_0 = T$, an inference $T \rightarrow H$ proceeds by iteratively joining two relations like $s_{i+1} = s_i \bowtie r_i$ until the last output $s_n = H$. Note that if there is any downward-monotone expression, such as negative word, in T, we should use $f(r_i)$ instead of r_i to join with s_i.

4 Natural Logic Inference

Natural logic inference can be cast as a search problem, that is, given a query T, we search possible facts for a valid text H over the space. Angeli and Manning [18] introduced a natural logic based search approach by building a graph, in which nodes are text pieces derived from the query and the edges describe mutation of these text pieces. Transitions along the search denote inference steps in natural logic. Following the idea, we build a graph of transition candidates with a learning algorithm for emotional inference. Different with their approach, our graph builds nodes with emotional text pieces, that is, we builds transition candidates as nodes from T as well as emotional text pieces as nodes from H; we adopt multiple inference resources such as inference rules rather than only lexiconsl knowledge from WordNet for transition; we also introduce a method to estimate the contribution of each resource by parameter learning.

4.1 Inference Graph

The space of possible nodes in the search is the set of possible partial derivations. Each node constructed is a pair (*t*, *s*), in which *t* is a partial derivation from T and *s* is the state in the state set *valid*, *invalid*. Each edge expresses a mutation of a single text piece, such as a lexiconsl replacement or an entailment rule based transition.

Node. Considering that each T and automatic-generated H probably intuitively has a very different meaning, we generate nodes that approach the meaning of H as far as possible by using SentiSense[3]. a concept-based affective lexicon. The lexicon provides a mapping between emotional expressions and WordNet synsets, that is, assign a meaning of a word with a corresponding emotion that the word holds. The process of node generation is describes as follows: first, verbs, nouns and adjectives appeared in T are handled with NLTK[4], a natural language toolkit, for word sense disambiguation; then, find synsets or hypo-synsets of those words that having the same emotions with H. Finally, nodes are generated by using other words in the same synset to replace the original word in T and connect with the node of T. We also use synonyms of emotional word in H to generate nodes adjoining the node of H. All these nodes built are labeled valid without the need of logic proof. The advantage of generating adjoining nodes to T and H is to narrow the difference of both semantic gap and formal expression between T and H so that search can be proceeded smoothly.

Edge. An edge describes a transition of a text piece in one node to an entailment text in another. As illustrated in [18], a mapping is built to bridge type of edges(synonym, delete word, etc.) and atomic relations in Natural Logic. According to this idea, a graph search process can be cast as a logic proof one. We adopt such method to build the inference process in the our system.

To generate edges, the approach in [18] employ lexiconsl relations in WordNet and some edit changes to describe transitions. However, many entailment transitions are beyond lexiconsl relation. For example, *X help Y* $\rightarrow$ *X give Y a hand*. Such variation illustrates a paraphrase relation, which is a semantic combination of lexiconsl relations and syntactic variation. In the system, we employ multiple entailment knowledge resources to express transitions between nodes, in order to achieve a better transition performance. Since atomic relations in the system are also able to describe relations between text pieces such as phrases and entailment rules, as shown in Sect. 3.1, they can also illustrate the transition among nodes. Table 4 shows each type of edges and its corresponding atomic relation.

---

[3] http://nlp.uned.es/~jcalbornoz/SentiSense.html.

[4] http://www.nltk.org/.

Table 4. Types of edges and corresponding atomic relations. DIRT, binaryDIRT and MRPC are paraphrase collections, TEASE and FRED are entailment rule collections, WikiRules! is a collection of lexicons reference relation in Wikipedia, and Google Distance is an semantic similarity metric viewed as a synonym resource.

Resource	Type of edge	Relation
WordNet	Hypernym	$\sqsubset$
	Hyponym	$\sqsupset$
	Synonym	$\equiv$
	Antonym	$\wedge$
	Meronym	$\sqsubset$
DIRT	Paraphrase	$\equiv$
TEASE	Entailment	$\sqsubset$
FRED	Entailment	$\sqsubset$
WikiRules!	entailment	$\sqsubset$
binaryDIRT	Paraphrase	$\equiv$
MRPC	paraphrase	$\equiv$
Google Distance	co-occurrence	$\equiv$

After constructing an inference graph, textual inference is to find a nearest path from T to H over the graph leveraging on logic proof through inference resources.

4.2 Learning for Inference

Note that transitions derived from these knowledge bases are not always valid. A simple reason is that two parts of each paraphrase or entailment rule is not always semantically identical, and we cannot estimate semantic relation for each pair. Alternately, we can estimate the validity of each resource as an approximate performance for search (or inference). The proposed approach is described as follows: each resource has a feature f_i denoting all transitions using it, and a parameter θ_i is assigned to each f_i, denoting the validity degree of each resource. Then the transition validity for each inference process can be estimated through computing $\sum \theta_i f_i$. Given a score threshold α, we say that the inference is valid if

$$\sum \theta_i f_i + \alpha \geq 0 \tag{1}$$

Here f_i can be computed by:

$$f_i = p(t' \rightarrow h) - p(t \rightarrow h) \tag{2}$$

where $p(t \rightarrow h)$ denotes the probability of text t entails h, and $p(t' \rightarrow h)$ denotes the probability of transformed text t' entails h leveraging rules in the resource having feature f_i. Here we simply define p as the n-gram overlap. Intuitively, if the more the count of overlapped n-grams are, the more the transition is valid. Note that since auto-generated H is always an emotional expression and probably contain less words in T, it is necessary to generate h using affection lexicons so that the value of f_i is not trivial.

The learning process is a parameter estimation process of finding the optimal $(\hat{\theta}, \hat{\alpha})$. We apply averaged perceptron, a supervised linear learning model, to estimate parameters. For a new inference process, it is valid if the equation $\sum \hat{\theta} F + \hat{\alpha} \geq 0$ is satisfied.

5 Experiments

5.1 Data

Our evaluation data comes from International Survey of Emotion Antecedents and Reactions(ISEAR)[5], a affection corpus with 7 major emotions(joy, fear, anger, sadness, disgust, shame and guilt). Since ISEAR is a self-report emotion dataset, most emotion holders in texts are *I*, *my* or *me*. We delete data without the *I*, *my* or *me* from the corpus and get a total 5898 items. For each item we use a simple pattern *I feel Y* to generate hypothesis automatically. Here *Y* is replaced by an adjective word in the labeled emotion class of the item. A statistical result of the evaluation dataset is shown in Table 5.

Table 5. Statistical results of the evaluation dataset.

Emotion	#
Joy	873
Fear	859
Anger	842
Sadness	725
Disgust	776
Shame	891
Guilt	932
Total	5898

We choose 4000 items in the evaluation dataset as the training data and the rest 1898 items as the test data. For each item in the test data, six hypothesis texts such as "*I feel angry*", "*I feel happy*" are built automatically.

5.2 Results

Two experiments are settled. The first one is to evaluate the system in this paper against other emotion detection systems. In the experiment, four systems are set: the first

[5] http://emotion-research.net/toolbox/toolboxdatabase.2006-10-13.2581092615.

system(Lex) is a lexicon-based one, that is, we count the number of emotion words in a text for each emotion type, then the emotion label of the text is simply determined as the emotion type having most emotion words. The second system (SVM-word) is a feature-based one, that is, we employ word features to classify emotion using SVM. The second system (SVM-combined) is also a feature-based one, and the difference from the prior system is that, we employ word features as well as emotion lexicon features to build an SVM classifier; here each emotion lexicon feature is a count value of emotional words for each emotion type according to emotion lexicons. The fourth system (NaLogic) is the system proposed in this paper, that is, we use natural logic inference to detect emotions in texts. Evaluation metrics are precision, recall and F-1 score. Experimental results are shown in Table 6.

Table 6. Experiment results for emotion detection.

		Joy	Fear	Anger	Sadness	Disgust	Shame	Guilt
Lex	P	0.4204	0.3839	0.3342	0.3009	0.3823	0.1786	0.3241
	R	0.3596	0.3448	0.2970	0.2208	0.2509	0.1917	0.2587
	F1	0.3876	0.3633	0.3145	0.2599	0.3030	0.1849	0.2877
SVM-word	P	0.4825	0.4670	0.3801	0.3714	0.4677	0.2983	0.3602
	R	0.4029	0.4035	0.3516	0.2629	0.3128	0.2544	0.2954
	F1	0.4402	0.4329	0.3653	0.3079	0.3749	0.2746	0.3246
SVM-combined	P	0.5208	0.4793	0.3972	0.3908	0.4851	0.3106	0.3737
	R	0.4476	0.4656	0.3854	0.2711	0.3198	0.2793	0.3080
	F1	0.4814	0.4724	0.3912	0.3201	0.3855	0.2941	0.3377
NaLogic	P	0.5463	0.4970	0.4202	0.4184	0.5263	0.3503	0.3881
	R	0.4626	0.5002	0.3917	0.2740	0.3385	0.2767	0.3204
	F1	0.5010	0.4986	0.4054	0.3311	0.4120	0.3092	0.3510

The experiment results show that:

(1) The approach in this paper outperforms lexicon-based and feature-based approaches in this experiment. In comparison with the performance of the second best system (SVM-combined), the system of natural logic inference achieves an increasing 1.95% F1 performance of emotion joy, an increasing 2.62% of fear, an increasing 1.42% of anger, an increasing 1.1% of sadness, an increasing 2.65% of disgust, an increasing 1.51% of shame and an increasing 1.33% of guilt. It indicates that the inference-based approach helps to detect emotions in comparison with lexicon-based and feature-based approaches, especially for implicit emotions.

(2) It is better to adopt machine learning approaches rather than lexicon-based approaches to detect implicit emotions. In comparison with the lexicon-based system Lex, the system SVM-word achieves an increasing 5.26% F1 performance of emotion joy, an increasing 6.96% of fear, an increasing 5.08% of anger, an increasing 4.79% of sadness, an increasing 7.19% of disgust, an increasing 8.97% of shame and an increasing 3.69% of guilt, which occurs a distinguished

performance increase than those between the NaLogic system and the SVM-combined system.

(3) Knowledge from emotion lexicons helps to improve emotion detection performance. In comparison with the SVM-word system, the SVM-combined system achieves an increasing 4.12% F1 performance of emotion joy, an increasing 3.94% of fear, an increasing 2.59% of anger, an increasing 1.23% of sadness, an increasing 1.06% of disgust, an increasing 1.95% of shame and an increasing 1.31% of guilt. The reason is that, there are some implicit emotion expressions that cannot be detected by machine learning approaches are provided by emotion lexicons, thus using them will contribute to improving performance for detecting implicit emotions.

In addition, for detecting emotion joy, the NaLogic system achieves a best performance, while for shame, the system achieves a lower one. The reason probably lies in that there are more clue words for detecting the emotion joy than other emotions, such as *birthday* or *anniversary*, while there are less clue words for detecting the emotion shame than other emotions.

The second experiment investigates the contributions of knowledge resources listed in Table 4. The experiment is set as follows: every time only one resource is removed from the NaLogic system, and we use macro F1 score to evaluate the overall performance for detection of all emotion types. Experimental results are shown in Table 7.

Table 7. Knowledge resource evaluation results.

	Macro F1
NaLogic	0.4012
-WordNet	0.3635
-DIRT	0.3895
-TEASE	0.3907
-FRED	0.3919
-WikiRules!	0.3844
-binaryDIRT	0.3956
-MRPC	0.3917
-Google distance	0.3870

It can be seen from the evaluation results that, system achieves a lowest performance by removing WordNet. The reason lies in that, WordNet provides a good many of words and synsets, which may help to build the inference graph by bridging mappings between emotion expressions and common words in cooperation with SentiSence. It can be also seen that, the systems of removing WordNet, DIRT or WikiRules! achieve more decreasing performances in comparison with the performances of other system. Since such knowledge bases have a larger data scale than others in this experiment, it indicates that the scale of knowledge resources impact the construction of the inference graph, which will eventually influence the system performances.

6 Conclusion

In this paper, we propose a novel approach, that is, to detect implicit emotions by textual inference. Following this idea, an implicit emotion detection problem can be formalized as an textual inference one, which can be handled by many textual inference models for better performances, and the emotion holder in a sentence can be easily identified according to the premise generated. To this end, we build an emotional inference system that employs natural logic to handle emotional relations as well as non-emotional ones, and the experimental results show its efficiency of reasoning expressions with emotions.

Acknowledgements. This work is supported by National Natural Science Foundation of China (61402341, 61402119) and Bidding Project of GDUFS Laboratory of Language Engineering and Computing(LEC2016ZBKT001, LEC2016ZBKT002).

References

1. Das, D., Bandyopadhyay, S.: Emotion analysis on social media: natural language processing approaches and applications. In: Agarwal, N., Lim, M., Wigand, Rolf T. (eds.) Online Collective Action. LNSN, pp. 19–37. Springer, Vienna (2014). doi:10.1007/978-3-7091-1340-0_2
2. Rao, K.S., Koolagudi, S.G.: Robust Emotion Recognition Using Spectral and Prosodic Features. Springer, New York (2013)
3. Reisenzein, R., Hudlicka, E., Dastani, M., Gratch, J., Hindriks, K., Lorini, E., et al.: Computational modeling of emotion: toward improving the inter- and intradisciplinary exchange. IEEE Trans. Affect. Comput. **4**(3) (2013)
4. Xu, J., Xu, R., Lu, Q., Wang, X.: coarse-to-fine sentence-level emotion classification based on the intra-sentence features and sentential context. In: CIKM2012, Maui, USA (2012)
5. Xu, R., Gui, L., Xu, J., Lu, Q., Wong, K.F.: Cross lingual opinion holder extraction based on multiple kernel SVMs and transfer learning. Int. J. World Wide Web **18**(2) (2013)
6. Andreevskaia, A., Concordia, S.B.: Mining WordNet for a fuzzy sentiment: sentiment tag extraction from WordNet glosses. In: EACL 2006 (2006)
7. Xu, R., Wong, F.F.: Coarse-fine opinion mining - WIA in NTCIR-7 MOAT task. In: NTCIR-7 Workshop, Tokyo, Japan (2008)
8. Androutsopoulos, I., Malakasiotis, P.: A survey of paraphrasing and textul entailment methods. J. Artif. Intell. Res. **38**(1), 135–187 (2010)
9. MacCartney, B., Manning, C.D.: An extended model of natural logic. In: Proceedings of the 8th International Conference on Computational Semantics, Tilburg, Netherland (2009)
10. Torii, Y., Das, D., Bandyopadhyay, S., Okumura, M.: Developing Japanese WordNet affect for analyzing emotions. In: Proceedings of The 2nd Workshop on Computational Approaches to Subjectivity and Sentiment Analysis, Portland, Oregon (2011)
11. Santos, C.N.D., Gatti, M.: Deep convolutional neural networks for sentiment analysis of short texts. In: Proceedings of the COLING 2015, Dublin, Ireland (2014)
12. Wang, X., Jiang, W., Luo, Z.: Combination of convolutional and recurrent neural network for sentiment analysis of short texts. In: Proceedings of COLING 2016, Osaka, Japan (2016)

13. Wang, Y., Huang, M., Zhao, L., Zhu, X.: Attention-based LSTM for aspect-level sentiment classification. In: Proceedings of the 2016 Conference on Empirical Methods in Natural Language Processing, Austin, Texas (2016)
14. MacCartney, B., Manning, C.D.: An extended model of natural logic. In: Proceedings of the 8th International Conference on Computational Semantics (2009)
15. Benthem, J.V.: Essays in logical semantics. Studies in Linguistics and Philosophy, vol. 29. Springer, Dordrecht (1986)
16. Valencia, V.M.S.: Studies on natural logic and categorial grammar. Ph.D. Thesis, University of Amsterdam (1991)
17. MacCartney, B., Manning, C.D.: Natural logic for textual inference. In: ACL-PASCAL Workshop on Textual Entailment and Paraphrasing (2007)
18. Angeli, G., Manning, C.D.: NaturalLI: natural logic inference for common sense reasoning. In: Proceedings of the 2014 Conference on Empirical Methods in Natural Language Processing, Doha, Qatar (2014)

Minority Language Information Processing

Tibetan Syllable-Based Functional Chunk Boundary Identification

Shumin Shi[1,2(✉)], Yujian Liu[1], Tianhang Wang[1], Congjun Long[3], and Heyan Huang[1,2]

[1] School of Computer Science and Technology Beijing Institute of Technology, Beijing 100081, China
{bjssm,yjliu,hbcdwth,hy63}@bit.edu.cn

[2] Beijing Engineering Research Center of High Volume Language Information Processing and Cloud Computing Applications, Beijing 100081, China

[3] Institute of Ethnology and Anthropology Chinese Academy of Social Sciences, Beijing 100081, China
longcj@cass.org.cn

Abstract. Tibetan syntactic functional chunk parsing is aimed at identifying syntactic constituents of Tibetan sentences. In this paper, based on the Tibetan syntactic functional chunk description system, we propose a method which puts syllables in groups instead of word segmentation and tagging and use the Conditional Random Fields (CRFs) to identify the functional chunk boundary of a sentence. According to the actual characteristics of the Tibetan language, we firstly identify and extract the syntactic markers as identification characteristics of syntactic functional chunk boundary in the text preprocessing stage, while the syntactic markers are composed of the sticky written form and the non-sticky written form. Afterwards we identify the syntactic functional chunk boundary using CRF. Experiments have been performed on a Tibetan language corpus containing 46783 syllables and the precision, recall rate and F value respectively achieves 75.70%, 82.54% and 79.12%. The experiment results show that the proposed method is effective when applied to a small-scale unlabeled corpus and can provide foundational support for many natural language processing applications such as machine translation.

Keywords: Tibetan syntactic functional chunk · Chunk boundary recognition · Syllable · Syntactic marker · CRF

1 Introduction

Syntactic chunk parsing plays an important role in chunk parsing. It aims to annotate the essential syntactic constituents of a sentence through top-down splitting. Then it can obtain the basic structure information units of the sentence. In Machine Translation, syntactic parsing is able to reduce the difficulty of recombining the sentence of

M. Sun et al. (Eds.): CCL 2017 and NLP-NABD 2017, LNAI 10565, pp. 439–448, 2017.
https://doi.org/10.1007/978-3-319-69005-6_36

over segmentation and reduce the disorder in the target-language generation. And also the recognition of syntactic functional chunks on the basis of the sentence preprocessing plays a very important role in rule based Machine Translation.

There are rich research results in English and Chinese that can provide good references for the syntactic functional chunks parsing of Tibetan Language. However, in the past, the research in this area must be based on the word segmentation and part of speech (POS) tagging. On the one hand, the errors of word segmentation and POS tagging will directly affect the correctness of syntactic functional chunk parsing. On the other hand, it increases the time and space cost. From the point of view of the current study on Tibetan, the accuracy of word segmentation and tagging remains to be improved and there is hardly any related software as well. According to the characteristic that there are abundant formal syntax markers in Tibetan, we hope to explore a new way to resolve this problem without word segmentation and POS tagging.

In this paper, we try to use the CRFs model to identify the boundary by syllables without word segmentation and POS tagging based on the Tibetan syntactic functional chunk description system. In the experiment, we add the syntax markers as characters to the identification model. Through it, we have achieved satisfactory result on a small-scale unlabeled corpus.

2 Related Work

There are rich research results in English and Chinese about the chunk boundary identification and some related study. For example, English noun phrases identification using HMM (Hidden Markov Model) [1], tagging part of speech and chunk boundaries using a mixed model combined by finite state automaton and 2-gram model [2]. For the researches in Chinese, many scholars have tried to take advantage of the characteristics of Chinese and use methods based on rules including the identification of verb-object construction using rules [3], the identification of noun phrases consisting of noun phrases based on rules [4], the longest noun phrase identification using the method of tagging and phrase boundary co-occurrence probability [5]. Also, many scholars have applied machine learning methods such as Support Vector Machine (SVM), Hidden Markov Model (HMM), Maximum Entropy (ME) and Conditional Random Fields (CRFs) into this area. Huang and others carry out Chinese chunking parsing using CRFs and then use the error-driven learning method to correct the identification results [6]. Dai and others carry out the identification of longest noun phrases using CRFs then correct the results by the internal structure information [7]. In the aspect of functional chunk analysis, Zhou and others use a top-down approach to define the functional chunks of Chinese in order to describe the basic structure of a sentence [8]. Subsequently, they construct the Chinese chunk library ChunkBank on the basis of functional chunk system [9], and furthermore they consider the functional chunking as a process including the segmentation of a sentence and labeling chunks with different functional tags [10].

In Tibetan, the researchers carried out a great deal of basic research on Tibetan morphology and grammar. For instance, scholars have tried to deal with the stick-from writing in Tibetan [11], sort out the functions and meanings of synaptic markers in Tibetan [12] and then the Tibetan basic chunk description system was proposed [13]. To identify the chunk boundary, Wang tried to identify the Tibetan functional chunk boundary using an error-driven method [14]. Furthermore, Wang and his co-workers tried to take advantage of word segmentation and part of speech tagging using CRFs to identify the chunk boundary [15].

3 Tibetan Syntactic Markers

Tibetan uses an alphabetic writing system which has 30 consonants and 4 vowels. Through different collocation, we can get different syllables and then syllables make the word. In Tibetan, the punctuation mark "་" (tsheg) acting as delimiter between two syllables, similar to the informational value of a character in the orthography of Chinese. Syntactic markers in Tibetan especially in modern Tibetan are abundant. Generally speaking, syntactic markers here refer to form markers in sentence such as case marking and auxiliary marking, which can be used to divide the sentence into different functional chunks. For instance, there might be locative case marking after adverbial of place, agent case marking after subject and patient case marking after object. However, due to the habit of text writing, some case and auxiliary markings contract to one syllable which is called the sticky writing form [16]. In order to make full use of the case and auxiliary markings, not only do we need to take advantage of the case and the auxiliary makings that form to be independent syllable, but also to identify the sticky writing form and then separate them correctly.

3.1 Tibetan Abbreviated Syllable Mark

Tibetan has the following abbreviated syllables: (1) syllable+ས(-s) (agentive/instrumental markers), (2) syllable +འི (-vi) (genitive markers), (3) syllable +ར(-r) (dative and locative markers), (4) syllable +འང/འམ(vang/vam) (conjunction), (5) syllable +འོ(-vo) (sentence end markers). But for the purpose of syntactic functional chunk identification, different sticky writing forms are not of equal importance. Crudely put, (1) and (2) have a relatively high frequency and they play the most important role in chunking identification while (4) and (5) have a low frequency and they contribute a little to chunking even though they occur as the boundary of chunks at times. There are three approaches to identify the sticky writing form. The first is to implement the sticky writing identification simultaneously with the word segmentation [17]. The other one is to implement these two ways consecutively. Among them, one way is only recognize whether it is abbreviated syllables without distinguishing the type. The other one is to recognize both the form and the type. The other one is to identify both the form and type. This method is able to facilitate the identification of the chunk boundary and type. We adopt the last strategy in this paper. The labels we design for the experiment are as follows (Table 1):

Table 1. Types of abbreviated syllables.

Type	Example	Label
Syllable +ས(-s)(agentive/instrumental markers	ངས་ "I do"	S
Syllable +འི·(-vi)(genitive markers)	ངའི· "Mine"	V
Syllable +ར(-r)(dative and locative markers)	ངར་ "For me"	D
Syllable +འང/འམ(vang/vam)(conjunction)	ངའང་ "And me"	C

3.2 Tibetan Non-abbreviated Syllable Form Mark

Non-abbreviated syllable form in Tibetan language mainly refers to the case and the auxiliary markings which are independent syllables. The case makings include agentive marker, causative marker and instrumental marker such as གིས, གྱིས, ཡིས, ཀྱིས, time marker, locative marker, target marker, genitive marker, allative marker སུ, རུ, ལ, དུ, ཏུ, ན (variants of la don), comparative marker ལས, comitative marker དང་ and so on. The auxiliary word markers include analogical auxiliary word, pause auxiliary word, enumerative auxiliary word, manner auxiliary word, result auxiliary word, purpose auxiliary word markers and so on. Moreover, we can design different labels to annotate them according to their function and identify the chunk type at the same time. But in this paper, we only want to get the chunk boundary, so we annotate them with the same label "M".

4 Tibetan Functional Chunks

4.1 Tibetan Functional Chunk System

In this paper, we use the Tibetan functional chunk system which is defined following the descriptive definition in [18], and it includes subject chunking, predicate chunking, object chunking, adverbial chunking, completive chunking and syntactic markers chunking.

4.2 Tibetan Functional Chunk Annotation

We regard the identification of the boundary of each chunk as a problem of sequence labeling. We use the BIE tag set to mark chunks. That is, we tag the syllable with "B" when it is the start of a chunk, tag the syllable with "I" when it is inside of a chunk and tag it with "E" when it is the end of a chunk. Furthermore, we tag punctuation with "B".

Take the example of the sentence ཁོང་གིས་ང་ལ་དེབ་དེ་འཁྱེར་འདུག (They bring me a parcel, khong tshos nga la bskur ma zhig bskur shag.). Firstly, we identify the syntactic tag of it, we can get the intermediate results as follows: ཁོང་ཚོས་] [ང་ལ་] [བསྐུར་མ་ཞིག་] [བསྐུར་ཤག. Furthermore, we can get the final label results as Fig. 1.

Eg1: ཁོང་/Bཚོ/Mས་E ང་/Bལ་/E བསྐུར་/Bམ་/M ཞིག་/E བསྐུར་/Bཤག/E

Latin: khong/B tsho/M s/E nga/B la/E bskur/B ma/M zhig/E bskur/B shag/E.

En: They bring me a parcel.

Fig. 1. Tibetan functional chunk boundary identification mark examples.

5 Tibetan Functional Chunk Boundary Identification Based on CRFs

5.1 Conditional Random Fields Model

CRF model is a sequence labeling and disaggregated model which was put forward by John Lafferty in 2001. In this paper, we only give a simple introduction to CRF model, for details please see the reference. It is a conditional distribution model based on undirected graph. Given a certain observed sequence needs to be annotated, it calculates the joint probability of the whole sequence to find the optimal result of the labeling. CRF is able to express long distance dependence and overlapping features, which is conducive to the resolution of the problem of labeling (classification) bias, so as to get the optimal result. For the given observed sequence $x = x_1x_2 \ldots x_n$, with x_i denotes a word in the sequence. We define $y = y_1y_2 \ldots y_n$ is the sequence to output, which is the tag of each word. For a CRF which is given the parameter $\Lambda = \lambda_1\lambda_2 \ldots \lambda_k$, we will get the probability of the Y with the input of the sequence:

$$P_\Lambda(y|x) = \frac{1}{Z(x)} exp\left(\sum_{i=1}^{n}\sum_{k}\lambda_k f_k(y_{i-1}, y_i, x, t)\right)$$

Z(x) is the normalized functions and $f_k(y_{i-1}, y_i, x, t)$ denotes a feature function. The symbol f_k denotes the weight parameter which is relevant to λ_k. We will obtain it through training. And then the most possible labeling sequence $Y^* = arg_Y max P_\Lambda(Y|X)$ is the output.

In this paper, we use the CRF ++[1] which is developed by Taku Kudo as the CRFs model to accomplish the task of functional chunk parsing.

5.2 Text Preprocessing

Before identifying the chunk boundaries, we firstly do the text preprocessing to identify whether the Tibetan syntactic markers are sticky writing or not. We use the CRFs to solve the problem using the current syllable and the context feature as the template.

[1] http://taku910.github.io/crfpp/.

Table 2. Atomic feature template

ID	Template	ID	Template
1	CurSyllable	4	Syllable+1
2	Syllable-2	5	Syllable+2
3	Syllable-1		

In Table 2, the size of the context window is 5 and the ± indicate the syllables after/before the current syllable. Then we combine the atomic feature template to get the complex feature template as Table 3

Table 3. Complex feature template.

ID	Template
6	CurSyllable, Syllable-1
7	CurSyllable, Syllable+1
8	Syllable-1, Syllable+1

5.3 Tibetan Functional Chunk Boundary Identification Based on CRFs

After the identifying of syntactic markers, we label each syllable by the rule shown in 3.2. We define the atomic feature template in the process of functional chunk boundary identification, they are listed in Table 4.

Table 4. Atomic feature template

ID	Template	ID	Template
1	CurSyllable	6	CurCase
2	Syllable-2	7	Case-2
3	Syllable-1	8	Case-1
4	Syllable+1	9	Case + 1
5	Syllable 5	10	Case + 2

In Table 4, the symbol "Syllable" indicates the syllable. The symbol "case" indicates the result of text preprocessing. When the characteristic function takes a specific value, the template is instantiated (Fig. 2).

Eg3: [ཁོང་/][རྒྱལ་ནང་/ལ་/][ཕྱིར་ལོག་བྱས་/པ་/རེད་/]།

Latin: khong rgyal nang la phyir log byas ba red.

En3: He returns his home country.

Fig. 2. Atomic Template Feature Selection Sample.

In eg3, we select the syllable "གསར" as the CurSyllable, then we can get the features using templates in Table 4. For example, the Syllable + 2 will indicate the syllable "བཤད" and the Case + 1 will indicate "Non-abbreviated form".

We build on combinations of the atomic feature templates to get the complex feature template as Table 5.

Table 5. Complex feature template

ID	Template
11	CurSyllable, Syllable-1
12	CurSyllable, Syllable+1
13	Syllable-1, Syllable+1
14	CurCase, Case-1
15	CurCase, Case+1
16	Case-1, Case+1

6 Experiment and Analysis

6.1 Syntactic Marker Identification Result

In the experiment of identifying syntactic marker, we use the F-value as the evaluation criterion. The results are shown in Table 6.

Table 6. Syntactic marker identification result

	S	D	V	N	C	M	Total
F	0.95	0.85	0.93	1.00	0	0.93	0.98

From Table 6, we find that the overall effect is satisfying but for the identification effect of R is not very ideal. Through the analysis of the training corpus, the cause we find is the syllable ར(-r) can be suffixed to different syllables (some are abbreviated, but others not) and its frequency is very high. For example, "ངར", it is possibly a syllable, meaning "strength", and possibly an abbreviated form, meaning "ང+possessive ར". So we cannot train an effective model for it. It also occurs on abbreviated syllables, but the frequency is much lower than D type.

6.2 Syntactic Functional Chunk Identification Results

In order to verify the effect that syntactic markers have in the identification of Tibetan functional chunk boundary, we have conducted two experiments with treating the experiment 1 as the baseline. In experiment 1, we do not carry out the text preprocessing and identify the chunk boundary directly based on the "་" between different syllables. In experiment 2, we firstly identify the syntactic marker, then we split the

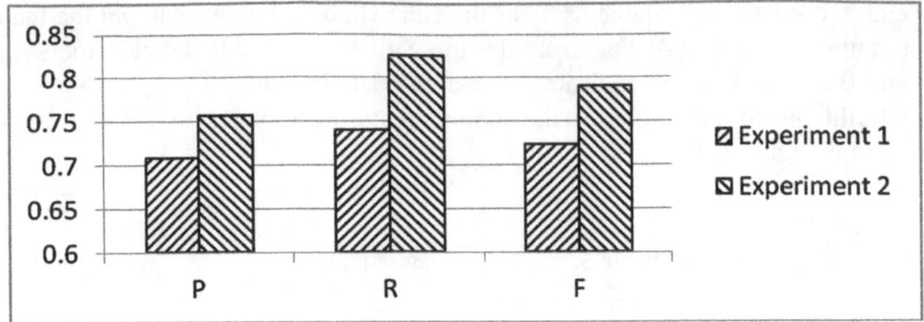

Fig. 3. Syntactic Functional Chunk Identification Result.

abbreviated syllables and finally we identify the chunk boundary. The results are shown as Fig. 3.

Comparison of experimental result in Fig. 3 shows that the identification of syntactic markers can improve the result significantly with the F value reaching 79.12% (6.71% higher than the baseline). From the result we can see that it does have a positive effect on the boundary identification through semantic information implied by syntactic markers.

6.3 Error Analysis

It is difficult to carry on the identification of syntactic markers on the original corpus or the corpus after preliminary processing. From our experimental results, although we have achieved certain effect, there are plenty of errors which can roughly sum up to several types as follows:

Boundary Identification Error of Non-predicate Verb Structure. Non-predicate verb structure is a syntactic chunk in a sentence, which is consist of phrases and clauses with nominal tag. They are typically long distance chunks, difficult to identify. For instance, ཤོག་ཕེ་རྩེ་རྒྱུ་ནི་སྤྲོ་སྣང་སྐྱེས་པའི་བྱ་བ་ཞིག་རེད(shog phe rtse rgyu ni spro snang skyes bavi bya ba zhig red. Playing cards is a great pleasure.) The result of boundary identification is [ཤོག་ཕེ་རྩེ] [རྒྱུ་] [ནི་] [སྤྲོ་སྣང་སྐྱེས་པའི་བྱ་བ་ཞིག] [རེད།]while the correct result should be [ཤོག་ཕེ་རྩེ་རྒྱུ་] [ནི་] [སྤྲོ་སྣང་སྐྱེས་པའི་བྱ་བ་ཞིག་] [རེད།]. The nominal tag རྒྱུ་ should be part of the previous chunk. This kind of errors contribute the most of all. It is the focus of following research.

Boundary Identification Error of Continuous Predicate Structure. For instance, ཁོ་མོ་མར་ལྷུང་སྟེར་མས།(kho mo mar lhung ster mas, she fell and hurt herself.) The result of boundary identification is [ཁོ་མོ་] [མར་ལྷུང་] [སྟེར་] [མས], while the correct result should be [ཁོ་མོ་][མར་ལྷུང་སྟེར་མས].

Boundary Identification Error of Appositive Structure and Structure of Modification Being Lack of Markers. The appositive structure and structure of modification consist of many syllables are short of dominant makers hence there are much errors. For instance, ཁྱོད་ཚང་ལ་མི་དུ་ཡོད།(khyod tshang la mi du yod, How many people are there in your family?) The word ཁྱོད་ཚང is lack of attributive marker so that the word was spilt into two parts in the experiment.

Boundary Identification Error of Core Predicate Chunk Lack of Tense Marker. In Tibetan language, the verbs and some adjectives serve as the predicate and appear at the end of the sentence. In a sentence directly ending with a verb or an adjective, there are few linguistic features after verbs, reducing the confidence of the training model and causing the identification errors. For instance, གཞུང་དྲང་པའི་མིས་གཏན་ནས་རྫུན་མི་བཤད། (gzhung drang pavi mis gtan nas rdzun mi bshad. Good people don't tell lies at all.) In this sentence, རྫུན་མི་བཤད is the predicate block errors. In spite of the errors above, we think if the identification features are further refined and the identification strategy is optimized, the results can be improved effectively.

7 Conclusions

Syntactic functional chunks represent different functional components of a sentence. Through the recognizing of syntactic functional chunks we can simplified the analysis of the structure in a sentence. In this paper, we propose a method that identifies the syntactic chunk boundary without word segmentation and POS tagging based on the Tibetan functional chunk system. Through the analysis of the Tibetan language and the experiment results, we add the Tibetan syntactic marker into the experiment and the precision, recall rate and F value respectively achieves 75.70%, 82.54% and 79.12%. In the next step, on one hand, we are ready to select better features to improve the identification effect of syntactic markers; on the other hand, we will expand the quantity of the training corpus and then provide basic support for the use of other nature language processing applications such as machine translation and so on.

Acknowledgement. This work is supported by the National Natural Science Foundation of China (61671064, 61201352, and 61132009), the National Key Basic Research Program of China (2013CB329303) and the Fundamental Research Fund of Beijing Institute of Technology (20130742010).

References

1. Church, K.W.: A stochastic parts program and noun phrase parser for unrestricted text. In: Proceedings of the second Conference on Applied Natural Language Processing, pp. 136–143. Association for Computational Linguistics (1988)
2. Pla, F., Molina, A., Prieto, N.: An integrated statistical model for tagging and chunking unrestricted text. In: The Third International Workshop on Text, Speech and Dialogue, Brno, Czech Republic, pp. 15–20 (2000)
3. Sun, H.L.: Induction of grammatical rules from an annotated corpus V+N sequence analysis. In: China National Conference on Computational Linguistics, pp. 157–163. Tsinghua University Press, Beijing(1997)
4. Liu, C.Z.: Research on binding of common noun sequences based on POS tagging corpus. In: Proceedings of the International Conference on Chinese Information Processing, Tsinghua University Press, Beijing (1998)

5. Li, W.J., Zhou, M., et al.: Automatic extraction of Chinese longest noun phrases based on corpus. In: Chen, L., Yuan, Q. (eds.) Progress and Application of Computational Linguistics, pp. 119–124. Tsinghua University Press, Beijing (1995)
6. Huang, D., Yu, J.: The combination of distributed strategy and CRFs to identify Chinese chunk. J. Chinese Inf. Proces. **23**(1), 16–22 (2009)
7. Dai, C., Zhou, Q.L., Cai, D.F., et al.: Automatic identification of Chinese maximum noun phrase based on statistics and rules. J. Chinese Inf. Proces. **22**(6), 110–115 (2008)
8. Drábek, E.F., Zhou, Q.: Experiments in learning models for functional chunking of Chinese text. In: IEEE International Conference on Systems, Man, and Cybernetics IEEE, vol. 2, pp. 859–864 (2001)
9. Chen, Y., Zhou, Q.: Analysis and construction of hierarchical chinese function block description library. J. Chinese Inf. Proces. **22**(3), 24–31 (2008)
10. Zhou, Q., Zhao, Y.Z.: Automatic parsing of chinese functional chunks. Chin. J. Inf. **21**(5), 18–24 (2007)
11. Jiang, D., Kang, C.J.: The methods of lemmatization of bound case makers in modern Tibetan. In: International Conference on Natural Language Processing and Knowledge Engineering, pp. 616–621(2003)
12. Jiang, D.: The method and process of block segmentation in modern Tibetan. Minor. Lang. China **2003**(4), 30–39 (2003)
13. Long, C.J., Kang, C.J., Jiang, D.: The comparative research on the segmentation strategies of tibetan bounded-variant forms. In: International Conference on Asian Language Processing 2013(30), pp. 243–246. IEEE Computer Society (2013)
14. Wang, T.H., Shi, S.H., Long, C.J., et al.: Syntactic boundary block identification of Tibetan syntactic functions based on error driven learning strategy. Chinese J. Inf. **28**(5), 170–175 (2014)
15. Wang, T.H.: Research on Tibetan functional block recognition for Machine Translation. Beijing Institute of Technology (2016)
16. Liu, H.D.: Research on Tibetan Word Segmentation and Text Resource Mining. University of the Chinese Academy of Sciences (2012)
17. Li, Y.C., Jia, Y.J., Zong, C.Q.: Research and implementation of tibetan automatic word segmentation based on conditional random field. J. Chinese Inf. Proces. **27**(4), 52–58 (2013)
18. Li, L., Long, C.J., Jiang, D.: Tibetan functional chunks boundary detection. J. Chinese Inf. Proces. **27**(6), 165–168 (2013)

Harvest Uyghur-Chinese Aligned-Sentences Bitexts from Multilingual Sites Based on Word Embedding

ShaoLin Zhu[1,2,3], Xiao Li[1,2], YaTing Yang[1,2(✉)], Lei Wang[1,2], and ChengGang Mi[1,2]

[1] The Xinjiang Technical Institute of Physics & Chemistry, Chinese Academy of Sciences, Urumqi, China
yangyt@ms.xjb.ac.cn

[2] Key Laboratory of Speech Language Information Processing of Xinjiang, Urumqi, China

[3] University of Chinese Academy of Sciences, Beijing, China

Abstract. Obtaining bilingual parallel data from the multilingual websites is a long-standing research problem, which is very benefit for resource-scarce languages. In this paper, we present an approach for obtaining parallel data based on word embedding, and our model only rely on a small scale of bilingual lexicon. Our approach benefit from the recent advances of continuous word representations, which can reveal more context information compared with traditional methods. Our experiments show that high-precision and sizable parallel Uyghur-Chinese data can be obtained for lacking bilingual lexicon.

Keywords: Bilingual parallel data · Word embedding · Resource-scarce languages

1 Introduction

Parallel data is one of the most important linguistic resources for cross-lingual natural language processing (Melamed et al. 2001), especially for statistical machine translation (SMT) and neural machine translation (NMT). Nowadays, the Internet may be seen as a large multilingual corpus as there a large number of websites in which different pages can be found containing the same content written in different languages. In our case, our approach is focused on using the web as a source of bitexts (parallel texts).

Many approaches have been presented for trying to exploit the multilingual sites as bitexts. There are several tools that can be used for automatically crawling parallel data from multilingual websites (Bitextor[1] 2013; PaCo 2012; ILSP-FC[2] 2012; WPDE 2006). However, all of them share the same limitations: (1) they require the user to provide the URLs of the multilingual websites to be crawled. The crawler downloads the all web pages texts, but the web pages contain a lot of noise such as advertising

[1] Bitextor: https://sourceforge.net/projects/bitextor.

[2] ILSP_FC: http://nlp.ilsp.gr/redmine/projects/ilsp-fc.

M. Sun et al. (Eds.): CCL 2017 and NLP-NABD 2017, LNAI 10565, pp. 449–460, 2017.
https://doi.org/10.1007/978-3-319-69005-6_37

links, hot recommended et al. To deal with the limitations, we implement the tool called Scrapy[3] to crawl the specific plain text part of web page. (2) those heavily depend on lexical information, past experiments indicate that the performance improves as the translation lexicon becomes larger. However, it is difficult to obtain a large translation lexicon for scarce resources language such as Uyghur-Chinese.

Unlike the other pair of languages, the Chinese sentences require word segmentation in order to word alignment. Most segmentation tools are based on semantics can give rise to the data sparse. For example, the same semantic word does not appear in the bilingual lexicon. We can illustrate the problem in Fig. 1.

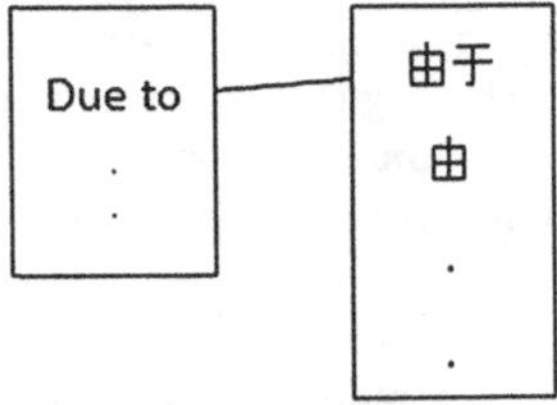

Fig. 1. One source word in the lexicon (left) is matched to a target word (right). However, we can find the other words also can be matched and they don't appear in the lexicon.

Thanks for the emerge of continuous vector representation of words, commonly known as Word Embedding (Mikolov et al. 2013b), which is supposed to carry semantic clues. The biggest contribution of the Word Embedding is to make the relevant or similar semantic words closer in the distance. For example, a Uyghur word can be translated more than one Chinese words, but only one of them in our lexicon. Others can be established connection by using the semantically related word embedding.

The same content of bilingual pages is a most important feature in identifying parallel pages, we encode our intuition into a novel computing term by combining the word embedding to identify the bilingual content. Somewhat surprisingly, even in a small bilingual lexicon (in our experiment, 12,000 bilingual entries), a sizable and high-precision parallel Uyghur-Chinese corpus can be obtained from the multilingual web sites.

The mainly contribution of this paper is as follows: (i) this paper combine word embedding to obtain aligning sentences, to deal with the limitation of the scarce resources. (ii) this approach allows to obtain parallel data in a totally automatic fashion, i.e. without having to provide a large seed lexicon.

[3] Scrapy: https://pypi.python.org/pypi/Scrapy/1.4.0.

2 Related Works

One of the most common strategies to crawl parallel data from the websites is to focus on multilingual web sites that make it straight-forward to detect parallel documents (Nie et al. 1999; Koehn 2005; Tiedemann 2012; Miquel 2013). Many approaches use content-based metrics (Jiang et al. 2009; Utiyama et al. 2009; Yan et al. 2009; Hong et al. 2010; Sridhar et al. 2011; Antonova and Misyurev 2011; Barbosa et al. 2012), such as bag-of-words co-occurrence. The method of content-based metrics is the most important feature in detecting the parallel texts. Although these metrics have proved to be useful for parallel data detection, their main limitation is that they require amount of linguistic resources (such as a bilingual lexicon or a basic machine translation system) which may not be available for some language pairs (such as Uyghur-Chinese). To avoid this problem, other works use the HTML tags of the web pages, which usually remains stable between different translations of the same document (Ma and Liberman 1999; Nie et al. 1999; Resnik and Smith 2003; Zhang et al. 2006; Espla-Gomis and Forcada 2010; San Vicente and Manterola 2012; Papavassiliou et al. 2013). Another useful strategy is to identify language markers in the URLs (Ma and Liberman 1999; Nie et al. 1999; Resnik and Smith 2003; Zhang et al. 2006; Desilets et al. 2008; Espla-Gomis and Forcada 2010; San Vicente and Manterola 2012) that help detect possible parallel documents. However, those methods only can be used in some specific sites and not be applicable to some news websites. The popularity of the dynamic website makes the application of this method gone away (see Fig. 2). We cannot learn any parallel information from the structure pages.

http://uy.ts.cn/homepage/content/2017-04/14/content_595263.htm
http://uy.ts.cn/homepage/content/2017-04/14/content_595234.htm
http://uy.ts.cn/homepage/content/2017-04/14/content_595262.htm
http://uy.ts.cn/homepage/content/2017-04/14/content_595237.htm
http://uy.ts.cn/homepage/content/2017-04/14/content_595240.htm

Fig. 2. URLs are very similar, but we cannot get any bilingual information.

Munteanu and Marcu (2005a) adopt a useful strategy to obtain bitexts, who compare the time of news published in news websites written in different languages by using a publication time stamp window. Zhang et al. (2006) present multiple features to identify English-Chinese bitexts via a k-nearest-neighbor classifier. To determine the parallelism between potential document pairs, they calculated the similarity of content translation feature by a large English-Chinese lexicon containing 250,000 entries. It indicates selecting alignment text sentences depending heavily on bilingual lexicon.

Even though these methods have proven to be useful for specific web sites, the real challenge is to find a large bilingual lexicon. For some language pairs (such as English-Spanish, English-French or English-Chinese et al.), it is easy to obtain. However, it is a challenge to obtain parallel corpora for some low resource language such as Uyghur-Chinese. On the other hand, those method use crawl the whole web pages to find potential parallel texts, but the current pages contains too many noise.

Such as the news web sites, it often contains advertising links, hot recommended or directory information et al.

In this paper we propose a novel strategy for building parallel corpora automatically only rely on a small scale of bilingual lexicon. This strategy mainly deal with the limitation of scarce bilingual lexicon, and the experiments indicate a sizable number of high-precision aligning Uyghur-Chinese sentences can be obtained, even in the a small bilingual lexicon (in our experiment, the entry is 12,000).

3 Methods

In this paper, we proposed a word embedding based parallel corpora extraction method, which can obtain a large scale of Uyghur-Chinese parallel corpus only rely on a small bilingual lexicon. In this section, we describe the details of our method, which include two main parts: (i) we firstly need to detect align-documents from the multilingual websites. (ii) Our objective is obtaining parallel sentences from the documents.

3.1 Detection of Alignment Document

Previous works extracted the alignment documents are based on multiple features such as the file length, the HTML tags, the co-occurrence of words et al. The co-occurrence is the most important feature to filter alignments. However, the features heavily depend on the bilingual lexicon (see Table 1).

Table 1. The number of words in our corpora is far more than the vocabulary

Language	#pages number	#tokens	Vocabulary size
Bitextor	295,303	323,102	7009
Ours	52,336	91,235	8528

In order to extract more candidate precise pair of documents, we urgently need a large bilingual lexicon to count the number of co-occurrence words in two language web pages. However, the actual situation deeply strike us, the lexicon is far away from us for scarce language resources. We only could obtain a small Uyghur-Chinese lexicon. Fortunately, we can reveal a lot new semantic information utilize word embedding, it convert words into vectors and the similar two vector in semantics is closer in distance (such as Cosine, Euclidean distance and others). For example, the words "提出" and "提议" are closer distance than "表明". We use Word2vec[4] (Mikolov et al. 2013a) to convert words into word embedding. We attempt to utilize word embedding to provide further bilingual information about whether the monolingual document should be aligned.

We calculate the similarity of bitexts content combining word embedding with k-nearest neighbor, the basic calculation is as the following measure:

[4] Word2vec: https://code.google.com/p/word2vec/.

$$F(d_1, d_2) = \frac{\sum Matching(s_i, t_j)}{\max len(d_1, d_2)} \quad (1)$$

where d_1 and d_2 are the source and target document, $s_i \in \{w_1, w_2 \ldots\ldots, w_n\}$ and w_i is the word of source document, the target side are similar. $Matching(s_i, t_j)$ is the matching mechanism which reveal the source word are translated into target word. The matching mechanism is calculated as following:

$$\mathrm{m}(s_i, t_j) = \begin{cases} 1 & \textit{if } s_i, t_j \textit{ in the bilingual lexicon and document} \\ c & \textit{if } s_i, t_j \textit{ in the bilingual lexicon but one of them in document} \\ 0 & \textit{others} \end{cases} \quad (2)$$

$$Matching(s_i, t_j) = \begin{cases} 1 & \textit{if } \mathrm{m}(s_i, t_j) = \mathrm{m}(t_i, s_j) \\ 0 & \textit{if } \mathrm{m}(s_i, t_j) \neq \mathrm{m}(t_i, s_j) \end{cases} \quad (3)$$

Specifically, to calculate the parameter c, we present combining word embedding with k-nearest neighbor. For $\mathrm{m}(s_i, t_j)$, we firstly retrieval source word s_i in lexicon, if the result w is not target word t_j and not null. We utilize the word embedding to calculate the k-nearest words z_i close to result w. $z_i \in \{W_1, W_2, \ldots, W_k\}$, which the set is k-nearest words from "w". The "k" explains the number of nearby the target side which can be retrieved. If the target document contains one of the "w", we will set the parameter c as $c = 1$ and other situation we set $c = 0$. The corresponding $\mathrm{m}(t_i, s_j)$ is generated analogously using this method. This method cannot conduct an explicit matching process in inference. To deal with the malpractice, we present two kinds of ways: (i) As our task is obtaining parallel corpora from the news websites, we consider it likely that articles with similar content have publication dates that are close to each other. Thus, each query is actually run only against documents published within a window of five days around the publication date of the other side query document. (ii) We detect the parallel documents by calculating alignment sentences model (we will explain in Sect. 4), which is a probability generative model based on Word Embedding.

3.2 Alignment Sentences Model

Like most approaches that obtain parallel sentences from websites, our learning objective is obtaining parallel sentences from the documents. However, unlike the previous works that need a large bilingual seed lexicon, ours additionally includes generative model that attempts to maximize translation probability from source side to target.

Our probability generative model is inspired by IBM model 1 (Brown et al. 1993). We begin by an exposition of source-to-target linking, at the same time the reverse direction follows by symmetry. We assume each source word in the source sentence s^s should have synonyms, namely can be formatted multivariate Gaussian (see Eq. 4); Then we use the Word2vec transform words into vector $w_i \in r^v$, which represent v-dimensional real number space vector. Then we can write out the basic source-to-target probability p_{s2t}:

$$w_i \sim \mathcal{N}(0, i_d) \tag{4}$$

$$P_{S2T} = \prod \log P(w^s|w^t) = \prod \log P(w^s|\{w^{s2t}\}_1^k) \tag{5}$$

w^{s2t} is a target word corresponding translation of the w^s and assuming that the vector w^{s2t} has k synonyms, which the set is $\{w^{s2t}\}_1^k$ and the set is k-nearest words from w^{s2t}. We leave the discussion on a practical choice to a later section. For the vector w^t in the target sentence, $w^t \in \{w^{s2t}\}_1^k$ specifies whether target word can be linked. The reverse direction follows by symmetry. We assume each vectors in the set is independent of each other, and it only depends on the premier word w^s. Therefore, we have:

$$P\left(w^s|\{w^{s2t}\}_1^k\right) = \mathrm{P}\left(w^s|w^t \in \{w^{s2t}\}_1^k\right) = P\left(w^s, w_i^{s2t}\right) \tag{6}$$

where $\{w^{s2t}\}_1^k$ can be computing by

$$\{w^{s2t}\}_1^k = \arg\min_k \left\| \{w_t^T\}_{t=1}^{V^t} - w^{s2t} \right\|^2 \tag{7}$$

where $\{w_t^T\}_{t=1}^{V^t}$ is a set that the target corpus contains the number of words are nearest distance from w^{s2t}. Finally, the parameterization of the probability can be expressed by the similarity distance, we can conclude:

$$P\left(w^s, w_i^{s2t}\right) = \begin{cases} 1 & if\ w_i^{s2t} = w^t \\ \dfrac{\max\left\| \{w_t^T\}_{t=1}^k - w^{s2t} \right\|^2 - \left\| w^{s2t} - w_i^{s2t} \right\|^2}{\max\left\| \{w_t^T\}_{t=1}^k - w^{s2t} \right\|^2} & otherwise \end{cases} \tag{8}$$

Next, we can further elaborate the documents alignment problem which is mentioned. Through calculating the number of alignment sentences, it is easy to decide whether the documents are aligned. For example:

$$\mathrm{m}(s_i, t_j) = \frac{\sum_1^k \prod \log P(w^s|\{w^{s2t}\}_1^k)}{\max len(d_s, d_t)} \tag{9}$$

It mainly explains the probability of alignment sentences how affect the parallel documents. If a pair of documents has many non-parallel sentences, we can mark them as non-parallel documents.

4 Experiment

In this section, we will explain the implementation details of our proposed system and verify the performance by experiment.

4.1 Data

In our experiments, the tested systems obtain parallel sentences form multilingual web sites on Uyghur-Chinese language pair by the crawler Scrapy[5]. For we couldn't obtain a large bilingual lexicon, we have a small lexicon about 12,000 entries. For the Chinese side, we first implement OpenCC[6] to normalize characters to be simplified, and perform Chinese word segmentation using Jieba.[7] The preprocessing of Uyghur side involves tokenization, POS tagging, lemmatization, which are carried out by a tool developed by our team. Then we use the Word2vec to convert the words into word embedding. The statistics of the preprocessed data is given in Table 1.

4.2 Baselines

We compare our approach to two existing system:

1. Bitextor (Espla-Gomis 2013).
2. INSP-FC (Vassilis 2012)

The first baseline (Bitextor) is a free/open-source tool for harvesting parallel data from multilingual websites; it is highly modular and is aimed at allowing users to easily obtain segment-aligned parallel corpora from the Internet. The core component of Bitextor to find document and sentence alignments is content-based and URL-based heuristics and algorithms applied to identify and align the parallel web pages in a website.

The second baseline (INSP-FC) is a modular system that includes components and methods for all the tasks required to acquire domain-specific corpora from the Web. The system is available as an open-source Java project and due to its modular architecture, each of its components can be easily substituted by alternatives with the same functionalities. Depending on user-defined configuration, the crawler employs processing workflows for the creation of either monolingual or bilingual collections.

4.3 Results and Discussion

In this section we examine how our system performance contrasting the baseline. Then we will discuss how the parameter "k" and the size of bilingual lexicon affect obtaining parallel data.

---

5 Scrapy: https://pypi.python.org/pypi/Scrapy/1.4.0.

6 OpenCC: https://pypi.python.org/pypi/opencc-python/.

7 Jieba: https://pypi.python.org/pypi/jieba/.

4.3.1 Overall Performance

Table 2 shows the performance of our system compare with two baselines. The bilingual lexicon size is 12,000 and the "k" is set as 3 in our experiment. As we downloaded the news data which can be marked release-time easily, the results of all system can be filtered by time. In our experiment, we only save the two documents which are published in three days.

Table 2. The number of obtained data for Uyghur-Chinese corpora

Methods	#documents	#sentences
Bitextor	71	828
INSP-FC	83	1047
Ours	316	5,628

Compared to the baseline, our system has a considerable promotion in obtaining parallel data. However, no matter what method the obtained data is too small to application. We analyze two factors affecting the obtaining: (i) the multilingual website contains a few of parallel pages so that we can't get a large data. For this problem, we can download more multilingual website to select bitexts which we need. (ii) another factor perhaps is the bilingual lexicon. In our experiment, Uyghur-Chinese is a resource-scarce language pair with limited parallel data. In fact, although it is very small, ours is still having a significant performance than the others.

Although ours outperform the others, we should analyze the precision of results and if the precision is too small, the system is not good. We use manual criteria to examine our system performance contrasting baseline. We first manually select 20 pairs of documents and 100 pairs of sentences randomly, then examine the accuracy of them. The precision of documents is defined as the number of correctly obtained over the total number of pairs documents obtained. The precision of sentences is defined similarly. The result is given in Table 3.

Table 3. Accuracies of random samples

Methods	Accuracy of document(%)	Accuracy of sentence(%)
Bitextor	83	93
INSP-FC	88	92
Ours	80	90

Table 3 shows the three system have an almost same precision. Combining Table 2 with Table 3, we can find that attain considerably better performance. We have more parallel data compared with the two baseline. The poor performance of the baseline should be attributed to the harsh condition they have to face, which only 12,000 entries can be used. It is too few for them to reveal bilingual signals and obtain parallel data. Table 1 shows that our monolingual corpus contains 323,102 and 91,235 words separately, but the bilingual lexicon only has 7009 and 8528 words each other. However, the success of our approach certificates that it is actually possible obtaining a considerable language pairs.

4.3.2 Effect of Bilingual Lexicon Size

In this section, we will investigate how the number of bilingual lexicon may affect the performance of obtaining parallel data. We change the bilingual lexicon size in {5,000; 8,000; 10,000; 1,2000}. Figure 3 shows the accuracies of the tested systems for Uyghur-Chinese. Figure 4 shows the results size varies as the bilingual lexicon size. We observe that although the result precision of ours is not performing out the baseline, the results size of ours far performance than the baseline. From the Fig. 3 we could find that obtaining parallel data form websites heavily depend on the bilingual lexicon. However, even in the more difficult cases, ours can obtain a sizable high-precision parallel data. We conjecture this is due to that our method provides a larger search-space to find bilingual signal, and then we can obtain more data.

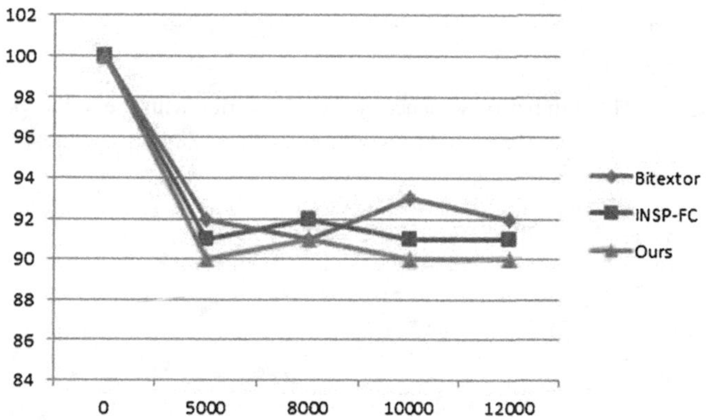

Fig. 3. Accuracies vary with the bilingual lexicon size

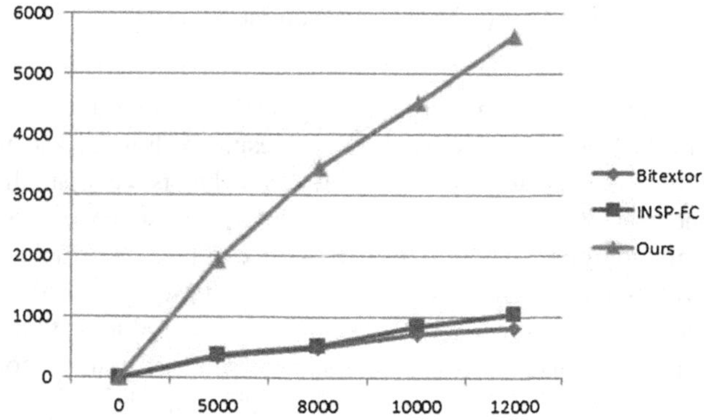

Fig. 4. The number of sentences in results varies with the bilingual lexicon size

4.3.3 Effect of the Value "K"

In this section, we discuss the value "k" proposed in Sect. 3. In order to investigate the effectiveness of the value "k", we run a version of our system with different value. We mainly discuss that the value "k" how affect the results size and accuracy. The bilingual lexicon size is 12,000 in our experiments.

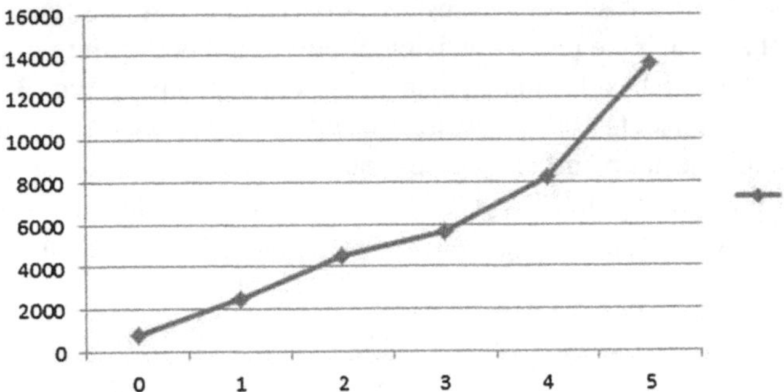

Fig. 5. The number of sentences in results varies with the value "k"

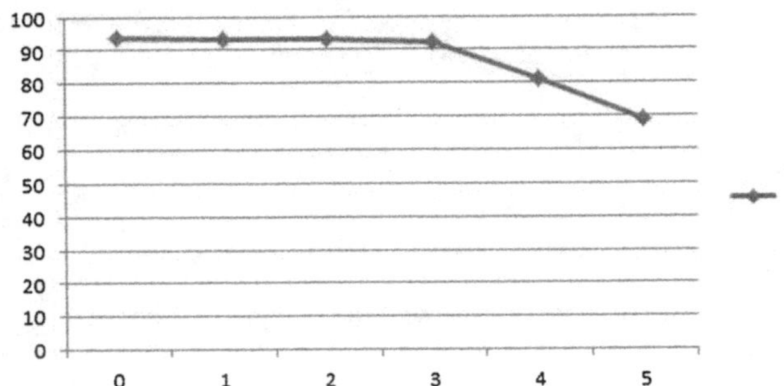

Fig. 6. Accuracies vary with the value "k"

From the two Figs. 5 and 6 we immediately see the important role the value "k" plays in our method. Varying the value "k" can result in dramatic accuracy and size gain. We conjecture this is due to that when the value is very small such as "1", although the 1-nearest words are very similar, the search-space is also too small to obtain more bilingual signal. It will cause that we can't get a sizable size. With the increase of the value, the accuracy will gradually decrease. We could find it is very obvious when the value is set as "5". We conjecture this is due to that increasing the value can bring a lot of noise, it arouses the system product many incorrect bilingual signals. Considering the size and accuracy, we set the value as "3".

5 Conclusions and Outlook

In this paper, we explore harvesting aligned-sentences parallel data from multilingual websites using currently popular Word Embedding. We mainly deal the limitation that the bilingual lexicon is heavily scarce in mining parallel data from the multilingual websites. We train monolingual word embedding in obtained monolingual corpora. In addition, we properly embed more signals cross-lingual by introducing the k-nearest words. We show our method dramatically improve the obtaining size, and allows that it has a high-precision.

Due to the training data used in our experiments is relatively small; therefore, we can't obtain a very large parallel data. We will increase the number of training data in our future work. In addition, we will further test our proposed approach in other language pairs.

Acknowledgments. This work is supported by the Xinjiang Fun under Grant (No. 2015KL031), the West Light Foundation of The Chinese Academy of Sciences (No. 2015-XBQN-B-10), the Xinjiang Science and Technology Major Project (No. 2016A03007-3) and Natural Science Foundation of Xinjiang (No. 2015211B034)

References

Espla-Gomis, M., Forcada, M.L.: Combining content-based and URL-based heuristics to harvest aligned bitexts from multilingual sites with bitextor. Prague Bull. Math. Linguist. **93**, 77–86 (2010)

Zhang, Y., Wu, K., Gao, J., Vines, P.: Automatic acquisition of Chinese–English parallel corpus from the web. In: Advances in Information Retrieval, vol. 3936, pp. 420–431 (2006)

San Vicente, I., Manterola, I.: PaCo2: a fully automated tool for gathering parallel corpora from the web. In: Proceedings of the 8th International Conference on Language Resources and Evaluation, pp. 1–6 (2012)

Resnik, P., Smith, N.A.: The Web as a parallel corpus. Comput. Linguist. **29**, 349–380 (2003)

Papavassiliou, V., Prokopidis, P., Thurmair, G.: A modular open-source focused crawler for mining monolingual and bilingual corpora from the web. In: Proceedings of the Sixth Workshop on Building and Using Comparable Corpora, pp. 43–51 (2013)

Munteanu, D.S., Marcu, D.: Improving machine translation performance by exploiting non-parallel corpora. Comput. Linguist. **31**, 477–504 (2005a)

Espla-Gomis, M.: Bitextor, a free/open-source software to harvest translation memories from multilingual websites. In: Beyond Translation Memories Workshop (MT Summit XII) (2009)

Espla-Gomis, M., Forcada, M.L.: Bitextor's participation in WMT'16: shared task on document alignment. In: Proceedings of the First Conference on Machine Translation, Volume 2: Shared Task Papers, pp. 685–691 (2016)

Ma, X., Liberman, M.Y.: BITS: a method for bilingual text search over the web. Linguist. Data Consort., 538–542 (1999)

Espla-Gomis, M., Klubicka, F., Ljube, N.: Comparing two acquisition systems for automatically building an English–Croatian parallel corpus from multilingual websites. In: LREC 2014 Proceedings, pp. 1252–1256 (2014)

Nie, J.-Y., Simard, M., Isabelle, P., Durand, R.: Cross-language information retrieval based on parallel texts and automatic mining of parallel texts from the Web. In: Proceedings of the 22nd Annual International ACM SIGIR Conference on Research and Development in Information Retrieval, pp. 74–81 (1999)

Ling, W., Marujo, L., Dyer, C., Black, A., Trancoso, I.: Crowdsourcing high-quality parallel data extraction from Twitter. In: Proceedings of the Ninth Workshop on Statistical Machine Translation, pp. 426–436 (2014)

Munteanu, D.S., Marcu, D.: Improving machine translation performance by exploiting non-parallel corpora. Comput. Linguist. **31**, 477–504 (2005b)

Mikolov, T., Chen, K., Corrado, G., Dean, J.: Efficient estimation of word representations in vector space. In: ICLR Workshop, pp. 1–12 (2013a)

Mikolov, T., Sutskever, I., Chen, K., Corrado, G.S., Dean, J.: Distributed representations of words and phrases and their compositionality. In: NIPS, pp. 3111–3119 (2013b)

Language Model for Mongolian Polyphone Proofreading

Min Lu, Feilong Bao(✉), and Guanglai Gao

College of Computer Science, Inner Mongolia University,
Hohhot 010021, China
csfeilong@imu.edu.cn

Abstract. Mongolian text proofreading is the particularly difficult task because of its unique polyphonic alphabet, morphological ambiguity and agglutinative feature, and coding errors are currently pervasive in the Mongolian corpus of electronic edition, which results in Mongolian statistic and retrieval research toughly difficult to carry out. Some conventional approaches have been proposed to solve this problem but with limitations by not considering proofreading of polyphone. In this paper, we address this problem by means of constructing the large-scale resource and conducting n-gram language model based approach. For ease of understanding, the entire proofreading system architecture is also introduced in this paper, since the polyphone proofreading is the important component of it. Experimental results show that our method performs pretty well. Polyphone correction accuracy is relatively improved by 62% and overall system accuracy is relatively promoted by 16.1%.

Keywords: Mongolian · Polyphone · Automatic proofreading system · Morphological ambiguity

1 Introduction

Coding errors are more seriously and universally presented in Mongolian corpus of electronic edition than other languages, which directly affects the development of Mongolian information technology such as Mongolian Named Entity Recognition (NER) [1], machine translation [2], Mongolian speech recognition [3], etc. From the objective perspective, the main reason is that Mongolian is an easily mistaken language due to its unique polyphonic alphabet, i.e. Mongolian letters and presentations are not corresponded one by one. Commonly, words written by different spellings can present one surface form if the intended word replaced by the letters with same shape. By the naked eye, we cannot judge from their appearances whether they are written in correct spelling or malapropism. Taking the Mongolian word "ᠦᠰᠦ" (meaning: hair) and "ᠳᠠᠯᠠᠢ" (meaning: ocean, waist belt) for example, the former one can be written in four different spellings. When presented in there national Latin transliteration (keyboard correspondence), they are spelled as "usu", "uso", "oso", "osu" respectively, among which only the first spelling "usu" (meaning: hair) is correct. The latter one "ᠳᠠᠯᠠᠢ" can be spelled in 8 different ways of "talai", "dalai", "telei", "delei", "talei", "delai", "dalei", "delei". Unlike the former instance, however, there are two correct spellings of "dalai"

M. Sun et al. (Eds.): CCL 2017 and NLP-NABD 2017, LNAI 10565, pp. 461–471, 2017.
https://doi.org/10.1007/978-3-319-69005-6_38

(meaning: ocean) and "telei" (meaning: waist belt) corresponded to the latter form "ᠳᠠᠯᠠᠢ". This kind of word is called polyphone. i.e. one form corresponds to multiple spellings, pronunciation and meanings as well. If the intended word "dalai" occurred in the phrase "ᠨᠣᠮᠣᠬᠠᠨ ᠳᠠᠯᠠᠢ" (meaning: Pacific Ocean) is replaced by the other correct spelling "telei", it is considered making misusing polyphone mistake. To sum up, Mongolian typo errors are frequently committed mainly because that typist usually just care about the correct shapes instead of the Mongolian orthographic (correct writing) rules and syntactic or semantic rules.

Misusing polyphone is contained in real-word error which refers to that the intended word is replaced by other correct spelling word with syntax or semantic error. Real-word error generally go unnoticed by most spellcheckers as they deal with words in isolation, accepting them as correct if they are found in the dictionary, and flagging them as errors if they are not [4]. So, as one kind of real-word error, polyphone proofreading is considered the more difficult task. Several approaches have been proposed in the literature. Su [5] adopted language model to correct the coding errors. Rule-based approaches to deal with the correction problem were discussed in [6, 7]. However, these approaches can only correct part of the coding errors and the real-word error did not be discussed systematically. Only in [6], human computer interaction approach is put forward which can be called half automatic operation implemented by manually selecting the proper one from the candidates generated from tools.

To solve this problem, we present a method for correcting polyphone mistakes using statistical language model based approach by building our own resource library. In this paper, we also introduce the MAPS (Mongolian automatic proofreading system), which applied the integration of rule-based approach and statistical language model approach as the polyphone proofreading module is the component of this system. Our intention is to improve the accuracy of polyphones and thus to improve the overall performance of the system. The system is built under the assumption that shapes in the text are correct, that is to say, the system doesn't correct the word form but their internal code assuming all the word form correct. Its implementation steps are as follow: Firstly, we use the approach of intermediate code [8] to unify the words with same presentation to one Latin letter lists. Secondly, according to dictionary and rule-based approach, the correct sets of the input tokens are obtained. Finally, polyphone correction module applies n-gram language model to select the proper spelling of polyphone, in which unigram, bigram and trigram model are conducted respectively. Experimental result shows that our proposed method performs very well.

The rest of the paper is organized as follows. Section 2 describes the Mongolian feature. Section 3 presents the whole system architecture. Our proposed method is described in Sect. 4. Experimental settings and results are discussed in Sect. 5. Section 6 draws the conclusion.

2 Mongolian Feature

Mongolian as language of great influence over the world, its main users are distributed in China, Mongolia and Russia. Currently, despite other approaches such as code transformation [9] (from Founder code, Menk code, etc. to National standard code),

ᠦᠨᠳᠦᠰᠦᠲᠡᠨ

correct spelling: **undusuten**

undusuden(36187)	**undusuten(24708)**	undvsvden(7902)	undvsvdan(5141)
ondosoden(2403)	undusudan(1989)	undusutan(1895)	undqsqden(1828)
undvsvten(1181)	ondvsvdan(976)	untusuten(915)	undusudee(869)
ondqsqden(860)	undvsvdaa(840)	ondvsvden(788)	untusutee(723)
uedvsvden(706)	undqsqdan(661)	untvsvtan(658)	ondosoten(650)
undvsuden(622)	undusvden(510)	uedvsvdee(474)	undusudaa(450)
uadvsvdan(406)	uadqsqden(363)	undvsudan(281)	undvsvtan(259)
uedqsqdan(256)	ondqsqdan(245)	uadusudee(240)	uedvsvdan(235)
uedusuden(230)	uadusudan(217)	oedvsvdan(199)	oetvsvten(193)
uadqsqdan(189)	untvsvten(187)	undusvdan(177)	ondosodan(160)
undqsuden(158)	undqsvden(136)	ondvsoden(132)	ondvsvten(128)
ondosotan(128)	undvsqden(128)	uetqsqtea(123)	undusoden(118)
oetvsvtan(115)	undvsuten(114)	undqsqtan(113)	undqsqten(106)
uadvsvden(106)	uadvsvdaa(100)		

Fig. 1. Different spelling and frequency about the same Mongolian word "ᠦᠨᠳᠦᠰᠦᠲᠡᠨ"

machine translation [2], speech recognition [3], etc., the Mongolian resource of electrical edition mainly comes from keyboard entry. The resource with serious typo errors is hardly utilized for the development of Mongolian information technology, which cause that, as one of the minority language in China, its informatization level is still lower than others like Tibetan and Uighur language. The following section presents detailed description of Mongolian character set and morphological ambiguity to illustrate the Mongolian unique feature. The intuitionistic interpretation of the reason why the typo errors are so seriously can be obtained in this section.

2.1 Mongolian Character Set

Mongolian characters contain two character types: nominal characters and presentation characters. According to Universal Coded Character Set (UCS) ISO/IEC 10646 and PRC GB 13000-2010, Mongolian character set only includes the nominal characters, and the units larger than one letter or less than one letter are not encoded. Generally, Mongolian letter set refers to the nominal characters (also known as nominal form). Each nominal character has several presentation forms according to its positions in words [10]. Table 1 shows Mongolian nominal characters and its corresponding presentation forms. Moreover, some characters have different nominal forms but same presentation forms. Mistakes are mainly committed by misusing those letters in the confusion set such as {a, e, n} (keyboard mapping) whose presentation forms are same. We use an example to illustrate this.

For the Mongolian word "ᠦᠨᠳᠦᠰᠦᠲᠡᠨ" (meaning: minority), its keyboard mapping is "undusuten". According to the analysis on a Mongolian corpus including 76 million Mongolian words, this word appears 102532 times, and only 24708 times of its codes are correctly. The other 78124 ones are typed as other words with the same presentation forms. Actually, there are 291 words that have the same presentation forms as the word "ᠦᠨᠳᠦᠰᠦᠲᠡᠨ" (meaning: minority). Figure 1 shows the Mongolian word "ᠦᠨᠳᠦᠰᠦᠲᠡᠨ" (meaning: minority) and its typos whose frequency is greater than 100 in the corpus.

Table 1. Example of the same presentation forms with distinct codes.

No.	Presentation from	Position in word	Nominal form	Keyboard mapping	Code
1	[illegible]	medial, final	ᠠ	a	0x1820
			ᠡ	e	0x1821
			ᠨ	n	0x1828
2	[illegible]	final	ᠠ	a	0x1820
			ᠡ	e	0x1821
3	[illegible]	medial, final	ᠣ	q	0x1823
			ᠤ	v	0x1824
			ᠥ	o	0x1825
			ᠦ	u	0x1826
			ᠸ	w	0x1838
4	[illegible]	initial, medial	ᠣ	q	0x1823
			ᠤ	v	0x1824
5	[illegible]	initial, medial, final	ᠥ	o	0x1825
			ᠦ	u	0x1826
6	[illegible]	medial, final	ᠢ	i	0x1822
			ᠶ	y	0x1836
7	[illegible]	initial, medial	ᠲ	t	0x1832
			ᠳ	d	0x1833
8	[illegible]	initial, medial	ᠬ	h	0x182c
			ᠭ	g	0x182d
9	[illegible]	medial	ᠵ	j	0x1835
			ᠢ	i	0x1832
			ᠶ	y	0x1836
10	[illegible]	medial, final	ᠸ	w	0x1838
			ᠧ	E	0x1827

2.2 Morphological Ambiguity

Morphological ambiguity is the possibility that a word is understood in multiple ways out of the context of their discourse. Words whose presentations look the same but spellings, pronunciations and meanings distinct according to the text called Polyphone. In Mongolian, polyphones are one of the most problematic objects in morphological analysis because they prevail all around frequent lexical items. Table 2 arranges polyphonic words with their corresponding pronunciations, meanings and part of speeches.

Table 2. Example of some Polyphone words.

No	Word from	Latin transliteration	Meaning	Font size and style
1	ᠣᠳᠣ	qdq	right now, stars	adverb, noun
2	ᠣᠳᠣ	qtq	omen	verb
3	ᠣᠳᠣ	vtv	smoke	verb
4	ᠣᠳᠣ	vdv	estrus	noun
5	ᠶᠢᠨ	jin	jin(loan word)	noun
6	ᠶᠢᠨ	-yin	's, of	noun

As for the upward 4 tokens, word form "ᠣᠳᠣ" has four kinds of pronunciation and obviously four kinds of coding. It can be represented by its corresponding Latin-transliteration (keyboard mapping) "qdq", "qtq", "vtv" and "vdv". The first word "qdq" is homonym which has multiple meanings of "now, right now" with part of speech adverb and "stars" with part of speech noun. The correct pronunciation or coding of them depends on the context of their discourse. The situation is same to the downward two tokens whose word form "ᠶᠢᠨ" maps to two distinct words of "jin" and "-yin". "jin" is the loanword whose pronunciation is about /dʒɪn/, commonly used in person name and geographic name. Phrase "ᠶᠢᠨ ᠤᠯᠤᠰ" (meaning: state) means *jin dynasty*. "-yin", being a genitive suffix (meaning: 's, of), is concatenated to stem by Mongolian space (0x202f) which is 2/3 length of common space to form one word. The phrase "ᠪᠠᠭᠰᠢ (meaning: teacher) ᠶᠢᠨ" means the teacher's. Although there is space between two tokens, "ᠪᠠᠭᠰᠢ ᠶᠢᠨ" is one word comprised of stem "ᠪᠠᠭᠰᠢ" and suffix "ᠶᠢᠨ". If "-yin" was mistakenly replaced by "jin", that is thought taking the misusing polyphone error by both changing its original meaning and even token quantity (from one to two).

The amount of polyphone in Mongolian corpus is comparatively larger than other languages which enjoyed the monophonic alphabet, and polyphone errors are badly serious in Mongolian corpus. Typists are always puzzled by the selection of the correct pronunciation of it or input the non-word which is out of correct spelling sets by just caring about correct shape instead of the correct coding for their laziness. Polyphone error detection and correction is one of the important tasks in Mongolian proofreading technology.

3 System Architecture

The polyphone proofreading module is one of the important tasks of the MAPS (Mongolian automatic proofreading system). It cannot run independently separated from the whole system. In this section, we give whole framework of the system as illustrated in Fig. 2. Polyphone proofreading is framed by rough line.

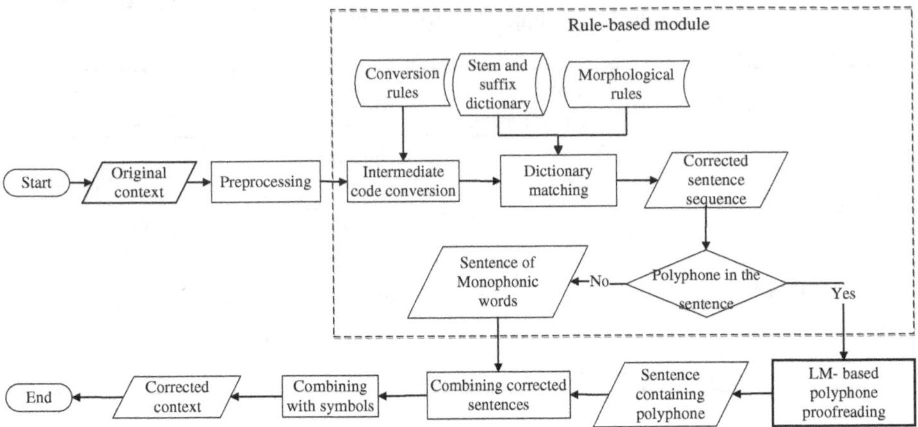

Fig. 2. System architecture

For considering that words with correct form but incorrect coding are far more than ones with incorrect form, the system dedicates to correct the words with correct form excluding those with formal error. The system takes the input text written by National Standard code in its original format, which undergoes preprocessing, rule-based module and LM-based process sequentially. In addition, it is worth noting that because of Mongolian agglutinative nature, the dictionary resource which is collated according to [11] applied in the system is comprised of the stem and suffix tokens instead of the whole word tokens.

Errors to be dealt with can be summed up as following three categories: (1) misspelled monophonic words, whose shapes and correct spellings are corresponded one by one, (2) misspelled plural case suffixes which are punctuated from the stem by Mongolian space and (3) misspelled polyphones, whose shape maps to multiple correct coding. The rule-based process, which is framed by dotted block, tackles the monophonic words and suffixes. The polyphones are processed in the LM-based component. The implementation steps are as follows:

Preprocessing: Sentence segmentation and special symbol processing are executed in this step.

Intermediate code transaction: This step is dedicated to convert each Mongolian input one by one into intermediate codes form utilizing the intermediate code transaction rules [8]. As the Fig. 3 is shown below, despite the variety of writings, the conversion approach makes one shape uniquely mapped to one intermediate code list.

Dictionary matching: Taking intermediate codes received from the previous step as finding entry, correct spelling sets of words are acquired based on morphological rules and dictionaries. As shown in Fig. 4, firstly, the intermediate code is segmented to stem and suffix according to morphological rules [12]. Then, Latin-transliteration form of the correct stem sets and suffix sets are obtained respectively by matching from the dictionaries. Finally, suffixes are concatenated to the stems based on morphological rule.

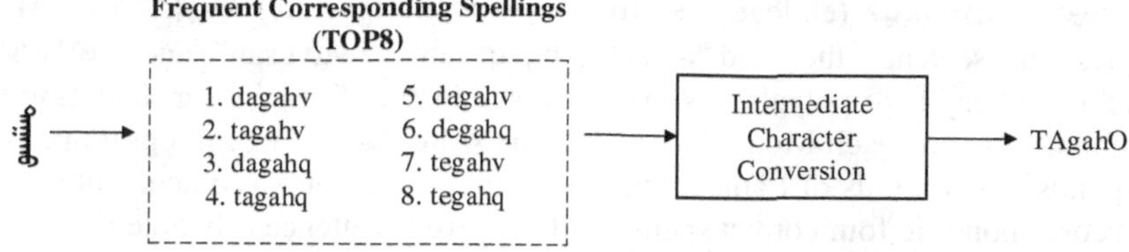

Fig. 3. Intermediate character conversion example

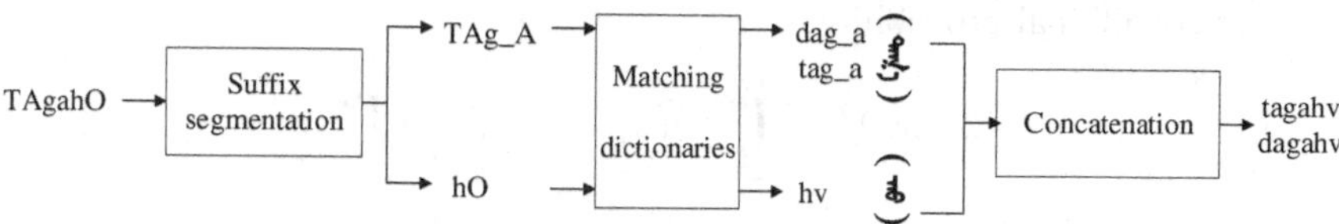

Fig. 4. Process of the matching from dictionary

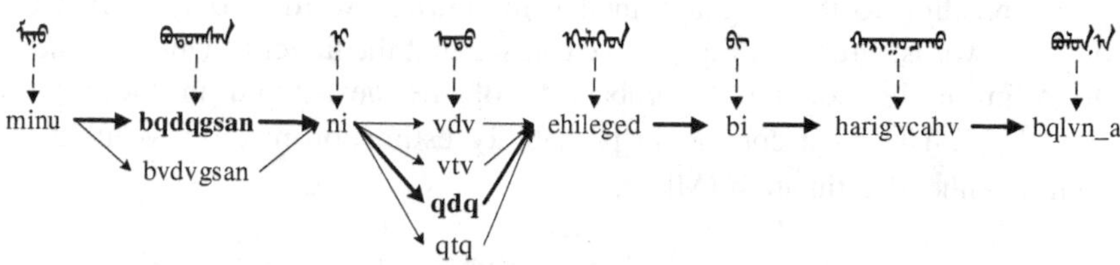

Fig. 5. Lexical chains of sentence

The output of this process is list of sentences, each of which is presented as chain of nodes (correct spelling sets of the word) as in the Fig. 5.

Polyphone proofreading: Each sentence produced from the *Dictionary matching step* can be thought as node chains. Nothing will be done to an atom-chain, i.e. the quantity of each node of the chain is only one. In the other word, the sentence is composed of monophonic words. ML-based process is carried out on those sentences which contain polyphones.

4 Language Model Establishment

This study aims at improving the performance of the polyphone proofreading. With the observation that words a writer intends are semantically related to their surrounding words, the polyphone proofreading can be dealt by performing a word-level N-gram model analysis which specifies a priori probability of a particular word sequence. In this section, we introduce our statistical language model methodology for processing polyphone. Polyphone has high occurrence frequency in Mongolian documents. In statistic, more than 46,000 sentences contained the polyphonic words in the corpus of 50,000 sentences. Take the polyphone contained sentence "ᠮᠢᠨᠤ (minu) ᠪᠣᠳᠣᠭᠰᠠᠨ (bqdqgsan)

ᠨᠢ (ni) ᠣᠳᠣ (qdq) ᠡᠬᠢᠯᠡᠭᠡᠳ (ehileged) ᠪᠢ (bi) ᠬᠠᠷᠢᠭᠤᠴᠠᠬᠤ (harigvcahv) ᠪᠣᠯᠤᠨ᠎ᠠ (bqlvn_a)" for example, in the sentence, the word "ᠪᠣᠳᠣᠭᠰᠠᠨ" ("bqdqgsan", "bvdvgsan") and "ᠣᠳᠣ" ("vdv", "vtv", "qdq", "qtq") are polyphones. As illustrated in Fig. 5, Latin-transliteration form was annotated below each Mongolian word. The word "ᠪᠣᠳᠣᠭᠰᠠᠨ" (meaning: think, paint) corresponds to two kinds of Latin form, the word "ᠣᠳᠣ" (meaning: omen, smoke, now, estrus) corresponds to four correct spellings; The correct sentence is denoted by the path with the line in bolder, i.e. "minu bqdqgsan ni qdq ehileged bi harigvcahv bqlvn_a."

N-gram language model [13] has been widely used in statistical language model. The probability of a Mongolian word sequence $w = w_1 w_2 \ldots\ldots w_m$ can be written in the form of conditional probability:

$$p(w) = p(w_1 w_2 \ldots\ldots w_m) = \prod_{i=1}^{m} p\left(w_i \vee w_1^{i-1}\right) \approx \prod_{i=1}^{m} p\left(w_i | w_{i-n+1}^{i-1}\right) \quad (1)$$

The probability of the m-th words w_m depends on all the words $w_1 w_2 \ldots\ldots w_{m-1}$. We can now use this model to estimate the probability of seeing sentences in the corpus by providing a simple independence assumption based on the Markov assumption [14]. Corresponding to the language model, the current word is only related to the previous n−1 words. From the Eq. (1), we can see that the target of language model is how to estimate the conditional probability of the next word in the list using $p\left(w_i \vee w_{i-n+1}^{i-1}\right)$. The most commonly probability estimation method we used is the maximum likelihood estimation (MLE).

$$p\left(w_i | w_{i-n+1}^{i-1}\right) = \frac{c\left(w_{i-n+1}^{i}\right)}{c\left(w_{i-n+1}^{i-1}\right)} \quad (2)$$

$c\left(w_{i-n+1}^{i-1}\right)$ means the total count of the N-gram in the corpus. However, a drawback of the MLE is that the N-tuple corpus which does not appear in the training set will be given zero-Probability. Smoothing algorithm can be used to solve this kind of zero-Probabilities problem. In this paper, we use the Kneser-Ney smoothing algorithm [15].

5 Experiment

The principle contribution in this paper is twofold: (1) we built our own resource library including dictionaries containing all polyphones, and dataset used in training corpus and test corpus; (2) We conduct the language model based method to deal with polyphone errors. In this section, we describe how the resource is created and show the experimental evaluation and analysis.

5.1 Data Resource

In general, there is a limitation in the number of Mongolian linguistic resources that are publicly available free for the research purpose. Therefore, we have to spend tangible efforts to acquire/annotate and verify our own linguistic resources in order to properly develop the proofreading system.

The proposed statistical approach rely on pre-defined confusion sets, which are comprised of commonly confounded words, such as polyphone sets of {"qdq", "qtq", "vtv", "vdv"} illustrated in Table 2 and the good-quality dataset used as training and testing dataset. After a period of collecting and collating, finally we finished creating the confusion sets by 252 verbal stems all put into the verbal stem dictionary and 998 whole words injected in nominal stem dictionary. Concatenated by verbal suffixes and case suffixes, the verbal stems can derive about 22,971 tokens and 998 whole words can derive about 19,407 tokens when concatenated by case suffixes. Since the textual resource in the Internet is full of coding errors, dataset used for creating training set and test data is constructed by following three steps: (1) Original Mongolian texts of about 50,000 sentences written in national standard code are obtained from the Mongolian news web. (2) The texts are corrected preliminarily by automatic proofreading system without polyphone correction module. For the polyphone, randomly select one candidate. Then, sentences which contain polyphone are picked out. (3) The manual annotation task carries out on those selected sentences under the open source platform BRAT [16]. The annotation takes about one and a half months with four Mongolian native persons. The collated Mongolian corpus, each of which contained the polyphones, consists of 41,416 sentences and 2,822,337 words. That was split into training data of 38,416 sentences and test data of 3,000 sentences.

5.2 N-gram Language Model Based Approach

We take the Correction Accurate Rate (CAR) as the evaluate metric, which is defined as

$$CAR = \frac{N_{correct}}{N_{total}} \tag{3}$$

$N_{correct}$ denotes the number of all polyphone that are correctly proofread. And N_{total} is the total number of all the polyphone needed to be corrected. We conduct the n-gram language model by SRILM toolkit [15] with Kneser-Ney discounting.

The calibration progress can be divided into two steps: Firstly, correct all Mongolian words one by one according to the rule based approach; Then, we check whether polyphone is contained or not in those sentences. If polyphone is contained, taking sentence as the basic unit, we further determine the best one according to the Language Model. To improve the performance of *CAR*, we respectively conduct unigram, bigram and trigram model to evaluate the experiment. As the result shown in Fig. 6, trigram model performs best by accuracy rate 95.36%, which is 62% higher than that of polyphones in original text without correction. Both bigram and trigram model outperformed the unigram model. The result shows that polyphone proofreading performance is effectively improved when contextual information is utilized in the process. Because of data sparseness, performance of trigram model did not show significant improvement with slight promotion of 0.06% compared to bigram model. Experiment will lead to better results if the experimental dataset become more adequate.

We also test the overall performance as the result illustrated in the Fig. 7. We can see that the overall system performance, when applied to the trigram model in polyphone proofreading, has the improvement by 16.1%.

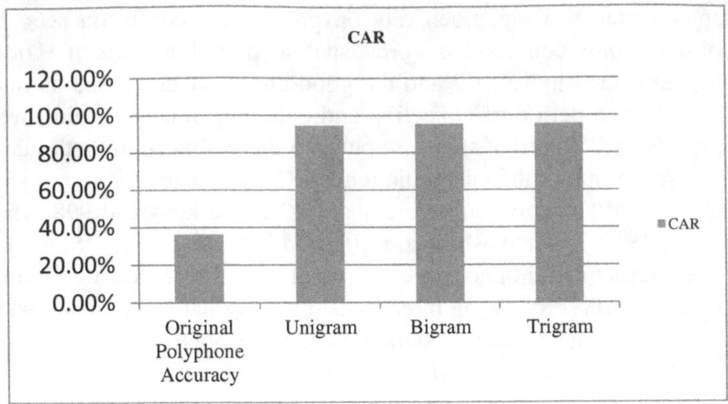

Fig. 6. Performance comparison between the Rule-based and LM based approaches

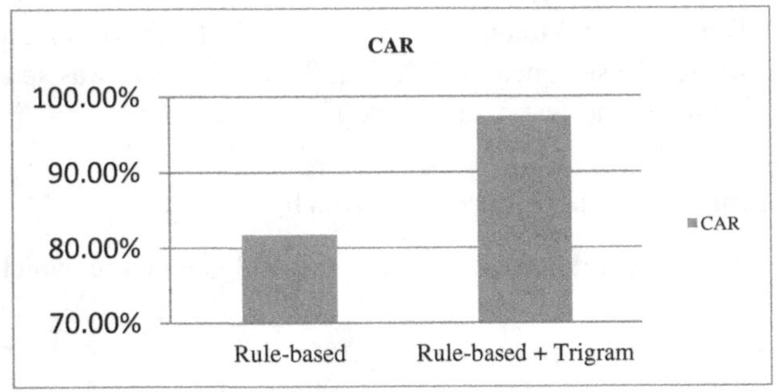

Fig. 7. Overall system performance comparison

6 Conclusion

In this paper, we present the statistical language model based approach after the description of the MAPS framework, and introduce in detail the construction of the resource library. Our purpose is the development of a high-quality correction module for polyphonic words which is one of the real-word correction problems. From the experiment result, N-gram language model was proved to be an effective approach to polyphone correction with the overall performance of the automatic proofreading system improved by 16.1%. In future work, we plan to expand our training sets and try to use other methods to detect and correct polyphones. Moreover, we will extend our method to allow for other kinds of real-word errors such as semantic errors, malapropisms structural errors and pragmatic errors.

Acknowledgements. This paper is supported by The National Natural Science Foundation of China (No. 61563040), Inner Mongolia Natural Science Foundation of major projects (No. 2016ZD06) and Inner Mongolia Natural Science Fund Project (No. 2017BS0601).

References

1. Wang, W., Bao, F., Gao, G.: Mongolian named entity recognition system with rich features. In: COLING, pp. 505–512 (2016)
2. Bao, F., Gao, G., Wang, H., et al.: Cyril Mongolian to traditional Mongolian conversion based on rules and statistics method. J. Chin. Inf. Process. **31**(3), 156–162 (2013)
3. Bao, F., Gao, G., Yan, X., et al.: Segmentation-based Mongolian LVCSR approach. In: 2013 IEEE International Conference on Acoustics, Speech and Signal Processing (ICASSP), pp. 8136–8139. IEEE (2013)
4. Islam, A., Inkpen, D.: Real-word spelling correction using Google web 1T n-gram data set. In: International Conference on Natural Language Processing and Knowledge Engineering, Nlp-Ke, pp. 1689–1692. IEEE (2009)
5. Su, C., Hou, H., Yang, P., Yuan, H.: Based on the statistical translation framework of the Mongolian automatic spelling correction method. J. Chin. Inf. Process. 175–179 (2013)
6. Si, L.: Mongolian proofreading algorithm based on nondeterministic finite automata. Chin. J. Inf. **23**(6), 110–115 (2009)
7. Jiang, B.: Research on Rule-Based the Method of Mongolian Automatic Correction. Inner Mongolia University, Hohhot (2014)
8. Yan, X., Bao, F., Wei, H., Su, X.: A novel approach to improve the Mongolian language model using intermediate characters. In: Sun, M., Huang, X., Lin, H., Liu, Z., Liu, Y. (eds.) CCL/NLP-NABD -2016. LNCS, vol. 10035, pp. 103–113. Springer, Cham (2016). doi:10.1007/978-3-319-47674-2_9
9. Gong, Z.: Research on Mongolian code conversion. Inner Mongolia University (2008)
10. GB 25914-2010: Information technology of traditional Mongolian nominal characters, presentation characters and control characters using the rules (2011)
11. Surgereltu, : Mongolia Orthography Dictionary, 5th edn. Inner Mongolia People's Publisher, Hohhot (2011)
12. Inner Mongolia University: Modern Mongolian. 2nd edn. Inner Mongolia People's Publisher, Hohhot (2005)
13. Zong, C.: Statistical Natural Language Processing, 2nd edn. Tsinghua University Press, Beijing (2008)
14. Jurafsky, D., Martin, J.: Speech and Language Processing, 2nd edn. Prentice Hall, Upper Saddle River (2009)
15. Stolcke, A.: SRILM - an extensible language modeling toolkit. In: Proceedings of International Conference on Spoken Language Processing, Denver, Colorado (2002)
16. Pontus, S., Sampo, P., Goran T.: Brat: a web-based tool for NLP-assisted text annotation. In: Proceedings of the Demonstrations at the 13th Conference of the European Chapter of the Association for Computational Linguistics, pp. 102–107

End-to-End Neural Text Classification for Tibetan

Nuo Qun[1,2], Xing Li[1], Xipeng Qiu[1(✉)], and Xuanjing Huang[1]

[1] School of Information Science and Technology, Tibet University, No. 10 Zangda, Tibet, China
xpqiu@fudan.edu.cn

[2] School of Computer Science, Fudan University, 825 Zhangheng Road, Shanghai, China

Abstract. As a minority language, Tibetan has received relatively little attention in the field of natural language processing (NLP), especially in current various neural network models. In this paper, we investigate three end-to-end neural models for Tibetan text classification. The experimental results show that the end-to-end models outperform the traditional Tibetan text classification methods. The dataset and codes are available on https://github.com/FudanNLP/Tibetan-Classification.

1 Introduction

Although some efforts have been made for Tibetan natural language processing (NLP), it still lags behind research on the other resource-rich and widely-used languages. Since Tibetan is a resource-poor language and is lack of large scale corpus, it is hard to build state-of-the-art machine learning based NLP systems. For example, Tibetan word segmentation technology is not well developed even until now.

Recently, deep learning approaches have achieved great successes in many natural language processing (NLP) tasks, which adopt various neural networks to model natural language, such as neural bag-of-words (NBOW), recurrent neural networks (RNNs) [2,17], recursive neural networks (RecNNs) [16], convolutional neural networks (CNN) [3,11]. Different from the traditional NLP methods, neural models take distributed representations (dense vectors) of words in a text as input, and generate a fixed-length vector as the representation of the whole text. A good representation of the variable-length text should fully capture the semantics of natural language.

These neural models can alleviate the burden of handcrafted feature engineering and allow researchers to build end-to-end NLP systems without the need for external NLP tools, such as word segmenter and parser. Therefore, deep learning provides a great opportunity to Tibetan NLP as well as other low-resource languages.

In this paper, we investigate several end-to-end neural models for Tibetan NLP. Specifically, we choose Tibetan text classification due to its popularity and

M. Sun et al. (Eds.): CCL 2017 and NLP-NABD 2017, LNAI 10565, pp. 472–480, 2017.
https://doi.org/10.1007/978-3-319-69005-6_39

wide applications. Since there is no explicit segmentation between Tibetan words and the word vocabulary is also very large, we directly model Tibetan text in syllable and letter (character) levels without any explicit word segmentation. In detail, we investigate three popular neural models: NBOW, RNN and CNN.

Our contributions can be summarized as follows.

- This is the first time to use end-to-end neural network method for Tibetan text classification. Experiments shown our proposed models are effective which do not rely on external NLP tools.
- We also construct a corpus for Tibetan text classification and make it available to anyone who need it.

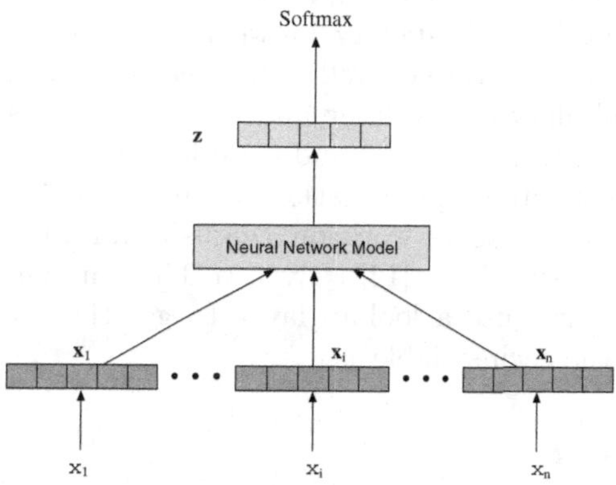

Fig. 1. Each syllable is converted to a multi-dimensional vector $\mathbf{x}_i$. All these vectors are feed into a neural network model and product $\mathbf{z}$ representing the text. Then the linear classifier with a softmax function would compute the probabilities of each class

2 The Proposed Framework

As shown in Fig. 1, our proposed framework consists of three layers: (1) the embedding layer maps each syllable or letter in text to a dense vector; (2) the encoding layer represents the text with a fixed-length vector and (3) the output layer predicts the class label.

2.1 Embedding Layer

In the Tibetan script, many Tibetan words are monosyllabic, consisting of several syllables. Syllables are separated by a tsheg, which often functions almost as a space and is not used to divide words. The Tibetan alphabet has 30 basic letters for consonants and 4 letters for vowels. Each consonant letter assumes an inherent vowel, in the Tibetan script it's ཨ /a/. The vowels ཨི /i/, ཨེ /e/, and ཨོ /o/ are placed above consonants as diacritics, while the vowel ཨུ /u/ is placed underneath consonants. Figure 2 shows an example of Tibetan word structure.

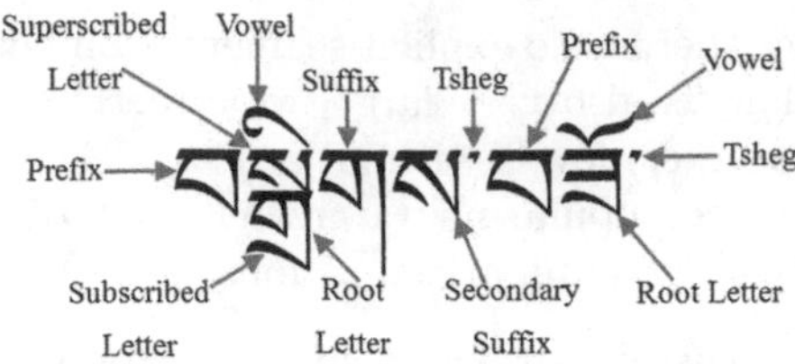

Fig. 2. Structure of a Tibetan word བསྒྲིགས་བཟོ་ (programming).

The neural NLP models usually take distributed representations of words as input, however it is difficult for Tibetan for two major reasons: one is that there is no delimiter to mark the boundary between two words and Tibetan word segmentation technology is still not well developed even until now; and another is that Tibetan vocabulary is very large and usually contains millions of words. Therefore, the representations of rare and complex words are poorly estimated.

Here, we gain distributed representations for each syllable by using a lookup table. Similarly, there are some work on English and Chinese to model text on character or morpheme level [13]. Given a Tibetan syllable sequence $x = \{x_1, x_2, \cdots, x_T\}$, we first use a lookup layer to get the vector representation (embeddings) $\mathbf{x}_i$ of the each syllable x_i.

2.2 Encoding Layer

The encoding layer converts an embeddings sequence of syllables into a vectorial representation $\mathbf{z}$ with different neural models, and then feed the representation to an output layer. A good representation should fully capture the semantics of natural language. The role of this layer is to capture the interaction among the syllables in text.

Neural Bag-of-Words. A simple and intuitive method is the Neural Bag-of-Words (NBOW) model, in which the representation of text can be generated by averaging its constituent word representations. However, the main drawback of NBOW is that the word order is lost. Although NBOW is effective for general document classification, it is not suitable for short sentences. Here, we adopt a simplified edition of Deep Averaging Networks (DAN) [7]. The difference is that all non-linear hidden layers are removed here.

Recurrent Neural Network. Sequence models construct the representation of sentences based on the recurrent neural network (RNN) [15] or the gated versions of RNN [2,17]. Sequence models are sensitive to word order, but they have a bias towards the latest input words.

Here, we adopt Long short-term memory network (LSTM) [5] to model text, which specifically address this issue of learning long-term dependencies of RNN. The LSTM maintains a separate memory cell inside it that updates and exposes its content only when deemed necessary.

Table 1. Dataset statistics.

Classes	Documents	Titles
Politics	2117	2132
Economics	983	986
Education	1359	1370
Tourism	510	512
Environment	945	953
Language	244	255
Literature	258	259
Religion	665	670
Arts	492	502
Medicine	519	520
Customs	272	275
Instruments	840	842
Total	9204	9276

Convolutional Models. Convolutional neural network (CNN) is also used to model sentences [3,6,10]. It takes as input the embeddings of words in the sentence aligned sequentially, and summarizes the meaning of a sentence through layers of convolution and pooling, until reaching a fixed-length vectorial representation in the final layer. CNN can maintain the word order information and learn more abstract characteristics. Here, we also adopt the CNN model used in [11].

2.3 Output Layer

After obtaining the text encoding $\mathbf{z}$, we feed it to a fully connected layer followed by a softmax non-linear layer that predicts the probability distribution over classes.

$$\hat{\mathbf{y}} = \text{softmax}(W\mathbf{z} + \mathbf{b}) \tag{1}$$

where $\hat{\mathbf{y}}$ is prediction probabilities, W is the weight which needs to be learned, $\mathbf{b}$ is a bias term.

Given a corpus with N training samples (x_i, y_i), the parameters of the network are trained to minimise the cross-entropy of the predicted and true distributions.

$$\mathcal{L}(\hat{y}, y) = -\sum_{i=1}^{N}\sum_{j=1}^{C} y_i^j \log(\hat{y}_i^j), \tag{2}$$

where y_i^j is the ground-truth label of x_i; $\hat{y}_i^j$ is the predicted probability, and C is the number of classes.

3 Experiments

In this section, we present our experiment results and perform some analyses to better understand our models.

3.1 Dataset

Although several pioneer papers [9,12] talk about Tibetan in many nature language tasks, there is no public available dataset for Tibetan text classification[1]. Hence we create the Tibetan News Classification Corpus (**TNCC**). This dataset is collected from China Tibet Online website[2]. It has the most abundant and official Tibetan articles and they are classified manually under twenty classes. We

Table 2. Performances on title classification.

Model	Acc.	Prec.	Rec.	F1
word2vec + GaussianNB	28.88	27.33	25.78	22.77
word2vec + SVM	46.84	45.70	32.00	32.19
CNN (syllable)	54.42	49.22	48.34	48.64
CNN (letter)	47.97	39.57	38.63	38.03
LSTM (syllable)	62.65	58.33	56.43	56.65
LSTM (letter)	59.74	59.57	56.06	57.44
NBOW (syllable)	61.56	60.35	55.52	56.99
NBOW (letter)	43.02	42.20	33.18	33.96

Table 3. Detailed results of LSTM model on title classification.

Class	Prec.	Rec.	F1
Politics	65.63	68.61	67.09
Economics	66.97	41.95	51.59
Education	57.87	70.47	63.55
Tourism	55.45	65.59	60.10
Environment	60.78	72.09	65.95
Language	70.37	54.29	61.29
Literature	27.78	15.15	19.61
Religion	70.51	56.12	62.50
Arts	56.72	49.35	52.78
Medicine	66.23	73.91	69.86
Customs	23.68	25.71	24.65
Instruments	78.01	83.97	80.88

[1] Although [12] built a large scale Tibetan text corpus, but they did not release it.
[2] http://tb.tibet.cn.

pick out the largest and most discriminative twelve classes where some articles still have ambiguity inherently.

To evaluate the ability of dealing with short and long Tibetan text, we construct two text classification datasets: one is news title classification; another is news document classification. The detailed statistics is shown in Table 1. There are 52,131 distinct syllable in the dataset. Each document contains 689 syllables and each title contains 16 syllables in average.

The corpus is split into training set, development set and test set. The training set makes up 80% of the dataset and both development set and test set take 10% of it.

Table 4. Performances on document classification.

Model	Acc.	Prec.	Rec.	F1
Onehot + MultinomialNB	59.72	67.18	53.65	55.17
word2vec + GaussianNB	52.77	54.24	54.97	52.22
Onehot + SVM	63.52	61.83	60.85	61.17
word2vec + SVM	69.71	67.75	67.59	67.45
CNN (syllable)	61.51	59.39	56.65	57.34
LSTM (syllable)	54.79	52.63	48.62	49.59
NBOW (syllable)	74.02	75.56	71.38	72.40
NBOW (letter)	57.93	49.34	45.45	46.08

3.2 Experimental Setup

In all models, syllable embedding size, text encoding size, learning rate and decaying rate are the same. We choose 500-dimensional vectors to represent both syllables and text. Other parameters are initialised randomly. In CNN model, we use three convolutional layers in the encoding layer. Adagrad optimizer [4] is used with decaying rate 0.93 and initial learning rates $0.5, 1.0, 1.5, 2.0$ to match different models respectively. To improve the performance, we use word2vec [14] to pre-train embeddings of Tibetan syllables on Tibetan Wikipedia corpus[3].

3.3 Results

We conduct two experiments on our corpus. One is news title classification, and another is news document classification.

Compared Models. To evaluate its effectiveness, we compare it with several baseline models, such as naive Bayesian classifier (NB) and support vector machine (SVM). Their inputs are embeddings trained by word2vec.

Besides syllables, we also investigate the performance of using Tibetan letters as input of neural models.

[3] https://bo.wikipedia.org.

News Title Classification. The results of news title classification are shown in Table 2. We can see that the end-to-end models consistently outperform the other methods. LSTM achieves better performance than CNN and NBOW. The detailed results are shown in Table 3.

News Document Classification. The results of news document classification are shown in Table 4. The end-to-end models consistently outperform the other methods. NBOW achieves better performance than CNN and LSTM, whose detailed results are shown in Table 5. The reason is that the length of document is large and CNN and LSTM suffer from its efficiency.

Table 5. Detailed results of NBoW model on document classification.

Class	Prec.	Rec.	F1
Politics	73.16	78.09	75.54
Economics	64.29	72.00	67.93
Education	75.00	69.44	72.11
Tourism	77.08	69.81	73.27
Environment	75.00	68.00	71.33
Language	72.73	50.00	59.26
Literature	100.00	53.85	70.00
Religion	62.34	84.21	71.64
Arts	58.54	57.14	57.83
Medicine	89.36	77.78	83.17
Customs	59.26	76.19	66.67
Instruments	100.00	100.00	100.00

4 Related Work

Recently, Tibetan text classification has become popular because of its wide applications. In the past years, several rule-based or machine learning based methods are adopted to improve the performance of Tibetan text classification [1,8,9]. These methods used word-based features, such as vector space model (VSM), to represent texts. [9] used distributed representations of Tibetan words as features to improve the performance of Tibetan text classification.

However, these methods are based on Tibetan words. Since the fundamental NLP tools, such as Tibetan word segmentation and part-of-speech tagging, are still undeveloped for Tibetan information processing, these methods are limited.

5 Conclusion

In this paper, we investigate several end-to-end neural models for Tibetan NLP. Specifically, we choose Tibetan text classification due to its popularity and wide applications. Since there is no explicit segmentation between Tibetan words and the word vocabulary is also very large, we directly model Tibetan text in syllable and letter (character) levels without any explicit word segmentation.

Acknowledgments. We would like to thank the anonymous reviewers for their valuable comments. This work was partially funded by "Everest Scholars" project of Tibet University, National Natural Science Foundation of China (No. 61262086), Autonomous Science and Technology Major Project of the Tibet Autonomous Region Science and Technology.

References

1. Cao, H., Jia, H.: Tibetan text classification based on the feature of position weight. In: International Conference on Asian Language Processing (IALP), pp. 220–223. IEEE (2013)
2. Chung, J., Gulcehre, C., Cho, K., Bengio, Y.: Empirical evaluation of gated recurrent neural networks on sequence modeling. arXiv preprint arXiv:1412.3555 (2014)
3. Collobert, R., Weston, J., Bottou, L., Karlen, M., Kavukcuoglu, K., Kuksa, P.: Natural language processing (almost) from scratch. J. Mach. Learn. Res. **12**, 2493–2537 (2011)
4. Duchi, J., Hazan, E., Singer, Y.: Adaptive subgradient methods for online learning and stochastic optimization. J. Mach. Learn. Res. **12**, 2121–2159 (2011)
5. Hochreiter, S., Schmidhuber, J.: Long short-term memory. Neural Comput. **9**(8), 1735–1780 (1997)
6. Hu, B., Lu, Z., Li, H., Chen, Q.: Convolutional neural network architectures for matching natural language sentences. In: Advances in Neural Information Processing Systems (2014)
7. Iyyer, M., Manjunatha, V., Boyd-Graber, J., Iii, H.D.: Deep unordered composition rivals syntactic methods for text classification. In: Meeting of the Association for Computational Linguistics and the International Joint Conference on Natural Language Processing, pp. 1681–1691 (2015)
8. Jiang, T., Yu, H.: A novel feature selection based on Tibetan grammar for Tibetan text classification. In: 2015 6th IEEE International Conference on Software Engineering and Service Science (ICSESS), pp. 445–448. IEEE (2015)
9. Jiang, T., Yu, H., Zhang, B.: Tibetan text classification using distributed representations of words. In: International Conference on Asian Language Processing (IALP), pp. 123–126. IEEE (2015)
10. Kalchbrenner, N., Grefenstette, E., Blunsom, P.: A convolutional neural network for modelling sentences. In: Proceedings of ACL (2014)
11. Kim, Y.: Convolutional neural networks for sentence classification. arXiv preprint arXiv:1408.5882 (2014)
12. Liu, H., Nuo, M., Wu, J., He, Y.: Building large scale text corpus for Tibetan natural language processing by extracting text from web. In: 24th International Conference on Computational Linguistics, p. 11. Citeseer (2012)
13. Luong, M.T., Socher, R., Manning, C.: Better word representations with recursive neural networks for morphology. In: CoNLL-2013, vol. 104 (2013)
14. Mikolov, T., Chen, K., Corrado, G., Dean, J.: Efficient estimation of word representations in vector space. Computer Science (2013)

15. Mikolov, T., Karafiát, M., Burget, L., Cernockỳ, J., Khudanpur, S.: Recurrent neural network based language model. In: INTERSPEECH (2010)
16. Socher, R., Perelygin, A., Wu, J.Y., Chuang, J., Manning, C.D., Ng, A.Y., Potts, C.: Recursive deep models for semantic compositionality over a sentiment treebank. In: Proceedings of EMNLP (2013)
17. Sutskever, I., Vinyals, O., Le, Q.V.: Sequence to sequence learning with neural networks. In: Advances in Neural Information Processing Systems, pp. 3104–3112 (2014)

Author Index